Captain Charles Johnson, Daniel Defoe

HISTORY OF PIRATES – True Story of the Most Notorious Pirates

e-artnow 2018

Daniel Defoe, Captain Charles Johnson

HISTORY OF PIRATES – True Story of the Most Notorious Pirates

Charles Vane, Mary Read, Captain Avery, Captain Blackbeard, Captain Phillips, John Rackam, Anne Bonny, Edward Low, Major Bonnet...

e-artnow, 2018
Contact: info@e-artnow.org
ISBN 978-80-273-3171-0

Contents

The Preface	13
Introduction	17
Chap. I. Of Captain Avery, And his Crew	30
Chap. II. Of Captain Martel, And his Crew	38
Chap. III. Of Captain Teach, alias Black-beard	41
Chap. IV. Of Major Stede Bonnet, And his Crew	51
Chap. V. Of Capt. Edward England, And his Crew	60
Chap. VI. Of Captain Charles Vane, And his Crew	72
Chap. VII. Of Captain John Rackam, And his Crew	76
Chap. VIII. The Life of Mary Read, And Anne Bonny	79
Chap. IX. Of Captain Howel Davis, And his Crew	86
Chap. X. Of Captain Bartho. Roberts, And his Crew	92
Chap. XI. Of Captain Anstis, And his Crew	146
Chap. XII. Of Captain Worley, And his Crew	151
Chap. XIII. Of Capt. George Lowther, And his Crew	153
Chap. XIV. Of Captain Edward Low, And his Crew	161
Chap. XV. Of Capt. John Evans, And his Crew	172
Chap. XVI. Of Captain John Phillips, And his Crew	174
Chap. XVII. Of Captain Spriggs, And his Crew	181
Chap. XVIII. An Account of the Pyracies and Murders committed by Philip Roche, &c.	185
Chap. XIX. An Abstract of the Civil Law and Statute Law now in Force, in Relation to Pyracy	188
Chap. XX. Of Captain Misson	190
Chap. XXI. Of Capt. JOHN Bowen	209
Chap. XXII. Of Capt. WILLIAM KID	216
Chap. XXIII. Of Captain Tew, And his Crew	223
Chap. XXIV. Of Capt. Halsey, And his Crew	234
Chap. XXV. Of Captain Thomas White, And his Crew	238
Chap. XXVI. Of Captain Condent, And his Crew	246
Chap. XXVII. A Description of Magadoxa	248
Chap. XXVIII. Of Capt. Bellamy	270
Chap. XXIX. Of Captain William Fly, And his Crew	275
Chap. XXX. Of Capt. Thomas Howard, And his Crew	280
Chap. XXXI. Of Captain Lewis. And his Crew	285
Chap. XXXII. Of Captain Cornelius, And his Crew	288

Chap. XXXIII. Of Capt. David Williams, And his Crew	292
Chap. XXXIV. Of Capt. Samuel Burgess, And his Crew	297
Appendix	301
I. Of Capt. Nathaniel North, And his Crew	302
II. Of Captain Teach	318
III. Of Major Bonnet	322
IV. Of Captain Worley	324
V. Of Captain Martel	327
VI. The Trial of the Pyrates at Providence	330
VII. Of Captain Vane	340
VIII. Of Captain Bowen	344
Footnotes	345

The Preface

Having taken more than ordinary Pains in collecting the Materials which compose the following History, we could not be satisfied with our selves, if any Thing were wanting to it, which might render it entirely satisfactory to the Public: It is for this Reason we have subjoined to the Work, a short Abstract of the Laws now in Force against Pyrates, and made Choice of some particular Cases, (the most curious we could meet with) which have been heretofore tried, by which it will appear what Actions have, and what have not been adjudged Pyracy.

It is possible this Book may fall into the Hands of some Masters of Ships, and other honest Mariners, who frequently, by contrary Winds or Tempests, or other Accidents incident to long Voyages, find themselves reduced to great Distresses, either through Scarcity of Provisions, or Want of Stores. I say, it may be a Direction to such as those, what Lengths they may venture to go, without violating the Law of Nations, in Case they should meet other Ships at Sea, or be cast on some inhospitable Shore, which should refuse to trade with them for such Things as are absolutely necessary for the Preservation of their Lives, or the Safety of the Ship and Cargo.

We have given a few Instances in the Course of this History of the Inducements Men have to engage themselves headlong in a Life of so much Peril to themselves, and so destructive to the Navigation of the trading World; to remedy which Evil there seems to be but two Ways, either to find Employment for the great Numbers of Seamen turn'd adrift at the Conclusion of a War, and thereby prevent their running into such Undertakings, or to guard sufficiently the Coast of *Africa,* the *West-Indies,* and other Places whereto Pyrates resort.

I cannot but take Notice in this Place, that during this long Peace, I have not so much as heard of a *Dutch* Pyrate: It is not that I take them to be honester than their Neighbours; but when we account for it, it will, perhaps, be a Reproach to our selves for our want of Industry: The Reason I take to be, that after a War, when the *Dutch* Ships are laid up, they have a Fishery, where their Seamen find immediate Business, and as comfortable Bread as they had before. Had ours the same Recourse in their Necessities, I'm certain we should find the same Effect from it; for a Fishery is a Trade that cannot be overstock'd; the Sea is wide enough for us all, we need not quarrel for Elbow-room: Its Stores are infinite, and will ever reward the Labourer. Besides, our own Coast, for the most Part, supply the *Dutch,* who employ several hundred Sail constantly in the Trade, and so sell to us our own Fish. I call it our own, for the Sovereignty of the *British Seas,* are to this Day acknowledged us by the *Dutch,* and all the neighbouring Nations; wherefore, if there was a public Spirit among us, it would be well worth our while to establish a National Fishery, which would be the best Means in the World to prevent Pyracy, employ a Number of the Poor, and ease the Nation of a great Burthen, by lowering the Price of Provision in general, as well as of several other Commodities.

I need not bring any Proofs of what I advance, *viz.* that there are Multitudes of Seamen at this Day unemploy'd; it is but too evident by their straggling, and begging all over the Kingdom. Nor is it so much their Inclination to Idleness, as their own hard Fate, in being cast off after their Work is done, to starve or steal. I have not known a Man of War commission'd for several Years past, but three times her Compliment of Men have offer'd themselves in 24 Hours; the Merchants take their Advantage of this, lessen their Wages, and those few who are in Business are poorly paid, and but poorly fed; such Usage breeds Discontents amongst them, and makes them eager for any Change.

I shall not repeat what I have said in the History concerning the Privateers of the *West-Indies,* where I have taken Notice they live upon Spoil; and as Custom is a second Nature, it is no Wonder that, when an honest Livlyhood is not easily had, they run into one so like their own; so that it may be said, that Privateers in Time of War are a Nursery for Pyrates against a Peace.

Now we have accounted for their Rise and Beginning, it will be natural to enquire why they are not taken and destroy'd, before they come to any Head, seeing that they are seldom less than twelve Men of War stationed in our *American* Plantations, even in Time of Peace; a Force sufficient to contend with a powerful Enemy. This Enquiry, perhaps, will not turn much to the Honour of those concerned in that Service; however, I hope I may be excus'd, if what I hint is with a Design of serving the Public.

I say, 'tis strange that a few Pyrates should ravage the Seas for Years, without ever being light upon, by any of our Ships of War; when in the mean Time, they (the Pyrates) shall take Fleets of Ships; it looks as if one was much more diligent in their Affairs, than the other. *Roberts* and his Crew, alone, took *400* Sail, before he was destroy'd.

This Matter, I may probably set right another Time, and only observe for the present, that the Pyrates at Sea, have the same Sagacity with Robbers at Land; as the latter understand what Roads are most frequented, and where it is most likely to meet with Booty, so the former know what Latitude to lie in, in order to intercept Ships; and as the Pyrates happen to be in want of Provisions, Stores, or any particular Lading, they cruise accordingly for such Ships, and are morally certain of meeting with them; and by the same Reason, if the Men of War cruise in those Latitudes, they might be as sure of finding the Pyrates, as the Pyrates are to find the Merchant Ships; and if the Pyrates are not to be met with by the Men of War in such a Latitude, then surely down the same Latitude may the Merchant Ships arrive safely to their Port.

To make this a little plainer to my Country Readers, I must observe that all our outward bound Ships, sometime after they leave the Land, steer into the Latitude of the Place they are bound to; if to the *West-India* Islands, or any Part of the Main of *America*, as *New-York, New-England, Virginia, &c.* because the Latitude is the only Certainty in those Voyages to be found, and then they sail due West, till they come to their Port, without altering their Course. In this West Way lie the Pyrates, whether it be to *Virginia, &c.* or *Nevis, St. Christophers, Montserat, Jamaica, &c.* so that if the Merchant Ships bound thither, do not fall a Prey to them one Day, they must another: Therefore I say, if the Men of War take the same Track, the Pyrates must unavoidably fall into their Mouths, or be frighted away, for where the Game is, there will the Vermin be; if the latter should be the Case, the trading Ships, as I said before, will pass unmolested and safe, and the Pyrates be reduced to take Refuge in some of their lurking Holes about the uninhabited Islands, where their Fate would be like that of the Fox in his Den, if they should venture out, they would be hunted and taken, and if they stay within they must starve.

I must observe another Thing, that the Pyrates generally shift their Rovings, according to the Season of the Year; in the Summer they cruise mostly along the Coast of the Continent of *America*, but the Winters there, being a little too cold for them, they follow the Sun, and go towards the Islands, at the approach of cold Weather. Every Man who has used the *West-India* Trade, knows this to be true; therefore, since we are so well acquainted with all their Motions, I cannot see why our Men of War under a proper Regulation, may not go to the Southward, instead of lying up all the Winter useless: But I shall proceed too far in this Enquiry, I shall therefore quit it, and say something of the following Sheets, which the Author may venture to assure the Reader that they have one Thing to recommend them, which is Truth; those Facts which he himself was not an Eye-Witness of, he had from the authentic Relations of the Persons concerned in taking the Pyrates, as well as from the Mouths of the Pyrates themselves, after they were taken, and he conceives no Man can produce better Testimonies to support the Credit of any History.

It will be observed, that the Account of the Actions of *Roberts* runs into a greater Length, than that of any other Pyrate, for which we can assign two Reasons, first, because he ravaged the Seas longer than the rest, and of Consequence there must be a greater Scene of Business in his Life: Secondly, being resolved not to weary the Reader, with tiresome Repetitions: When we found the Circumstances in *Roberts*'s Life, and other Pyrates, either as to piratical Articles, or any Thing else, to be the same, we thought it best to give them but once, and chose *Roberts*'s Life for that Purpose, he having made more Noise in the World, than some others.

As to the Lives of our two female Pyrates, we must confess they may appear a little Extravagant, yet they are never the less true for seeming so, but as they were publicly try'd for their Pyracies, there are living Witnesses enough to justify what we have laid down concerning them;

it is certain, we have produced some Particulars which were not so publicly known, the Reason is, we were more inquisitive into the Circumstances of their past Lives, than other People, who had no other Design, than that of gratifying their own private Curiosity: If there are some Incidents and Turns in their Stories, which may give them a little the Air of a *Novel,* they are not invented or contrived for that Purpose, it is a Kind of Reading this Author is but little acquainted with, but as he himself was exceedingly diverted with them, when they were related to him, he thought they might have the same Effect upon the Reader.

I presume we need make no Apology for giving the Name of a History to the following Sheets, though they contain nothing but the Actions of a Parcel of Robbers. It is Bravery and Stratagem in War which make Actions worthy of Record; in which Sense the Adventures here related will be thought deserving that Name. *Plutarch* is very circumstantial in relating the Actions of *Spartacus,* the Slave, and makes the Conquest of him, one of the greatest Glories of *Marcus Crassus;* and it is probable, if this Slave had liv'd a little longer, *Plutarch* would have given us his Life at large. *Rome,* the Mistress of the World, was no more at first than a Refuge for Thieves and Outlaws; and if the Progress of our Pyrates had been equal to their Beginning; had they all united, and settled in some of those Islands, they might, by this Time, have been honoured with the Name of a Commonwealth, and no Power in those Parts of the World could have been able to dispute it with them.

If we have seem'd to glance, with some Freedom, at the Behaviour of some Governors of Provinces abroad, it has been with Caution; and, perhaps, we have, not declar'd as much as we knew: However, we hope those Gentlemen in the same Station, who have never given Occasion for the like Censure, will take no Offence, tho' the Word Governor is sometimes made use of.

P. S. It will be necessary to add a Word or two to this Preface, in order to inform the Reader, that there are several material Additions made to this second Impression, which swelling the Book in Bulk, must of Consequence add a small Matter to its Price.

The first Impression having been received with so much Success by the Public, occasioned a very earnest Demand for a second: In the mean Time, several Persons who had been taken by the Pyrates, as well as others who had been concerned in taking of them, have been so kind to communicate several Facts and Circumstances to us, which had escaped us in the first Impression. This occasioned some Delay, therefore if we have not brought it out, as soon as wish'd, it was to render it the more complete.

We shall not enter into a Detail of all the new Matter inserted here, but the Description of the Islands *St. Thome, &c.* and that of *Brasil* are not to be passed by, without a little Notice. It must be observed, that our speculative Mathematicians and Geographers, who are, no doubt, Men of the greatest Learning, seldom travel farther than their Closets for their Knowledge, *&c.* are therefore unqualified to give us a good Description of Countries: It is for this Reason that all our Maps and Atlasses are so monstrously faulty, for these Gentlemen are obliged to take their Accounts from the Reports of illiterate Men.

It must be noted also, that when the Masters of Ships make Discoveries this Way, they are not fond of communicating them; a Man's knowing this or that Coast, better than others, recommends him in his Business, and makes him more useful, and he'll no more discover it than a Tradesman will the Mystery of his Trade.

The Gentleman who has taken the Pains to make these Observations, is *Mr. Atkins,* a Surgeon, an ingenious Man in his own Profession, and one who is not ty'd down by any narrow Considerations from doing a Service to the Public, and has been pleased generously to communicate them for the good of others. I don't doubt, but his Observations will be found curious and very serviceable to such as Trade to those Parts, besides a Method of Trade is here laid down with the *Portuguese,* which may prove of great Profit to some of our Countrymen, if followed according to his Plan.

It is hoped these Things will satisfy the Public, that the Author of the following Sheets considered nothing so much as making the Book useful; — tho' he has been informed, that some Gentlemen have rais'd an Objection against the Truth of its Contents, *viz.* that it seems calculated to entertain and divert. — If the Facts are related with some Agreeableness and Life, we hope it will not be imputed as a Fault; but as to its Credit, we can assure them that the Sea-faring Men, that is all that know the Nature of these Things, have not been able to make the least Objection to its Credit: — And he will be bold to affirm, that there is not a Fact or Circumstance in the whole Book, but he is able to prove by credible Witnesses.

There have been some other Pyrates, besides those whose History are here related, such as are hereafter named, and their Adventures are as extravagant and full of Mischief, as those who are the Subject of this Book. —— The Author has already begun to digest them into Method, and as soon as he receives some Materials to make them complete, (which he shortly expects from the *West-Indies)* If the Public gives him Encouragement he intends to venture upon a second Volume.

Introduction

> The Danger of Commonwealths from an Increase of Pyrates. Pyrates in the Times of Marius and Sylla. Takes Julius Cæsar. The Barbarity of those Pyrates. They spare Cæsar, and why. His Behaviour amongst them. Cæsar obtains his Liberty for a Ransom. Attacks and takes the Pyrates. Hangs them at Troy. They increase again to a prodigious Strength. Plunder at the Gates of Rome. The mock Homage they paid the Romans. Pompey the Great, appointed General against them. A prodigious Fleet and Army assign'd him. His Conduct and good Fortune. The Gallantry of those Pyrates. Receive an Overthrow. Barbarouse, a Pyrate, his Beginning. His great Strength. Selim Eutemi, King of Algiers, courts his Friendship. Makes himself King, and how. The King of Tunis overthrown by him. Leaves the Inheritance to his Brother. The West-Indies commodious for Pyrates, and why. The Explanation of the Word Keys. The Pyrates conceal their Booty on them. The Pyrates Security in those Parts. The Rise of Pyrates since the Peace of Utrecht accounted for. An Expedition from Jamaica, to plunder the Spaniards. The Spaniards sue for Justice to the Government of Jamaica. The Plunderers turn Pyrates. The Spaniards make Reprisals. The Names of Ships taken by them. The plunder'd Seamen join the Pyrates. Providence fixed on as a Place of Retreat by them. That Island described. The Lords Address to her late Majesty for securing Providence. An Order of Council in this Reign to the same Purpose. A List of Men of War employ'd for the Defence of the Plantations. Captain Woods Rogers made Governor of Providence. The King's Proclamation for suppressing Pyrates. How the Pyrates used the Proclamation. Great Divisions amongst them. How made quiet. Several of the Pyrates surrender to the Governor of Bermudas. The Fate of the rest. Woods Rogers his Arrival at Providence. Vane's Behavtour. Woods Rogers employs the pardon'd Pyrates, ib. Their Conduct. Some of them hang'd for new Pyracies. Their strange Behaviour at the Place of Execution. Some Proceedings betwixt the English and Spaniards. The Spaniards surprise the Greyhound Man of War, and how. Quit her. The Crew of a Spanish Guarda del Costa hang'd at Jamaica, and why. Sir Nicholas Laws his Letter to the Alcaldes of Trinidado. Mr. Joseph Laws, Lieutenant of the Happy Snow his Letter to the Alcaldes of Trinidado. The Alcaldes Answer to the Lieutenant's Letter. The Lieutenant's Reply to the Alcaldes Answer. The Alcaldes Answer again. Some Account of Richard Holland. Prizes taken by him.

As the Pyrates in the *West-Indies* have been so formidable and numerous, that they have interrupted the Trade of *Europe* into those Parts; and our *English* Merchants, in particular, have suffered more by their Depredations, than by the united Force of *France* and *Spain*, in the late War: We do not doubt but the World will be curious to know the Original and Progress of these Desperadoes, who were the Terror of the trading Part of the World.

But before we enter upon their particular History, it will not be amiss, by way of Introduction, to shew, by some Examples drawn from History, the great Mischief and Danger which threaten Kingdoms and Commonwealths, from the Increase of these sort of Robbers; when either by the Troubles of particular Times, or the Neglect of Governments, they are not crush'd before they gather Strength.

It has been the Case heretofore, that when a single Pyrate has been suffered to range the Seas, as not being worth the Notice of a Government, he has by Degrees grown so powerful, as to put them to the Expence of a great deal of Blood and Treasure, before he was suppress'd. We shall not examine how it came to pass, that our Pyrates in the *West-Indies* have continually increased till of late; this is an Enquiry which belongs to the Legislature, or Representatives of the People in Parliament, and to them we shall leave it.

Our Business shall be briefly to shew, what from Beginnings, as inconsiderable as these, other Nations have suffered.

In the Times of *Marius* and *Sylla, Rome* was in her greatest Strength, yet she was so torn in Pieces by the Factions of those two great Men, that every Thing which concerned the public Good was altogether neglected, when certain Pyrates broke out from *Cicilia*, a Country of *Asia Minor*, situate on the Coast of the *Mediteranean*, betwixt *Syria* on the East, from whence it is divided by Mount *Tauris*, and *Armenia Minor* on the West. This Beginning was mean and inconsiderable, having but two or three Ships, and a few Men, with which they cruised about the *Greek* Islands, taking such Ships as were very ill arm'd or weakly defended; however, by the taking of many Prizes, they soon increased in Wealth and Power: The first Action of their's which made a Noise, was the taking of *Julius Cæsar*, who was as yet a Youth, and who being obliged to fly from the Cruelties of *Sylla*, who sought his Life, went into *Bithinia*, and sojourned a while with *Nicomedes*, King of that Country; in his Return back by Sea, he was met with, and taken, by some of these Pyrates, near the Island of *Pharmacusa*: These Pyrates had a barbarous Custom of tying their Prisoners Back to Back and throwing them into the Sea; but, supposing *Cæsar* to be some Person of a high Rank, because of his purple Robes, and the Number of his Attendants, they thought it would be more for their Profit to preserve him, in hopes of receiving a great Sum for his Ransom; therefore they told him he should have his Liberty, provided he would pay them twenty Talents, which they judg'd to be a very high Demand, in our Money, about three thousand six hundred Pounds Sterling; he smiled, and of his own Accord promised them fifty Talents; they were both pleased, and surpriz'd at his Answer, and consented that several of his Attendants should go by his Direction and raise the Money; and he was left among these Ruffians with no more than 3 Attendants. He pass'd eight and thirty Days, and seemed so little concerned or afraid, that often when he went to sleep, he used to charge them not to make a Noise, threatening, if they disturbed him, to hang them all; he also play'd at Dice with them, and sometimes wrote Verses and Dialogues, which he used to repeat, and also cause them to repeat, and if they did not praise and admire them, he would call them Beasts and Barbarians, telling them he would crucify them. They took all these as the Sallies of a juvenile Humour, and were rather diverted, than displeased at them.

At length his Attendants return'd with his Ransom, which he paid, and was discharged; he sail'd for the Port of *Miletum*, where, as soon as he was arriv'd, he used all his Art and Industry in fitting out a Squadron of Ships, which he equipp'd and arm'd at his own Charges; and sailing in Quest of the Pyrates, he surpriz'd them as they lay at Anchor among the Islands, and took those who had taken him before, with some others; the Money he found upon them he made Prize of, to reimburse his Charges, and he carry'd the Men to *Pergamus* or *Troy*, and there secured them in Prison: In the mean Time, he apply'd himself to *Junius*, then Governor of *Asia*, to whom it belonged to judge and determine of the Punishment of these Men; but *Junius* finding there was no Money to be had, answered *Cæsar*, that he would think at his Leisure, what was to be done with those Prisoners; *Cæsar* took his Leave of him, returned back to *Pergamus*, and commanded that the Prisoners should be brought out and executed, according to Law in that Case provided; which is taken Notice of, in a Chapter at the End of this Book, concerning the Laws in Cases of Pyracy: And thus he gave them that Punishment in Earnest, which he had often threatned them with in Jest.

Cæsar went strait to *Rome*, where, being engaged in the Designs of his own private Ambition, as were almost all the leading Men in *Rome*, the Pyrates who were left, had Time to increase to a prodigious Strength; for while the civil Wars lasted, the Seas were left unguarded, so that *Plutarch* tells us, that they erected diverse Arsenals full of all manner of warlike Stores, made commodious Harbours, set up Watch-Towers and Beacons all along the Coasts of *Cilicia*; that they had a mighty Fleet, well equipp'd and furnish'd, with Galliots of Oars, mann'd, not only with Men of desperate Courage, but also with expert Pilots and Mariners; they had their Ships of Force, and light Pinnaces for cruising and making Discoveries, in all no less than a thousand Sail; so gloriously set out, that they were as much to be envied for their gallant Shew, as fear'd for their Force; having the Stern and Quarters all gilded with Gold and their Oars plated with Silver, as well as purple Sails; as if their greatest Delight had been to glory in their Iniquity. Nor were they content with committing Pyracies and Insolencies by Sea, they committed as great Depredations by Land, or rather made Conquests; for they took and sack'd no less than four hundred Cities, laid several others under Contributions, plundered the Temples of the Gods, and inriched themselves with the Offerings deposited in them; they often landed Bodies of Men, who not only plundered the Villages along the Sea Coast, but ransacked the fine Houses of the Noblemen along the *Tiber*. A Body of them once took *Sextillius* and *Bellinus*, two *Roman* Prætors, in their purple Robes, going from *Rome* to their Governments, and carried them away with all their Sergeants, Officers and Vergers; they also took the Daughter of *Antonius* a consular Person, and one who had obtained the Honour of a Triumph, as she was going to the Country House of her Father.

But what was most barbarous, was a Custom they had when they took any Ship, of enquiring of the Person on Board, concerning their Names and Country; if any of them said he was a *Roman*, they fell down upon their Knees, as if in a Fright at the Greatness of that Name, and begg'd Pardon for what they had done, and imploring his Mercy, they used to perform the Offices of Servants about his Person, and when they found they had deceived him into a Belief of their being sincere, they hung out the Ladder of the Ship, and coming with a shew of Courtesy, told him, he had his Liberty, desiring him to walk out the Ship, and this in the Middle of the Sea, and when they observed him in Surprize, as was natural, they used to throw him overboard with mighty shouts of Laughter; so wanton they were in their Cruelty.

Thus, while *Rome* was Mistress of the World, she suffered Insults and Affronts, almost at her Gates, from these powerful Robbers; but what for a while made Faction cease, and roused the Genius of that People, never used to suffer Wrongs from a fair Enemy, was an excessive Scarcity of Provisions in *Rome*, occasioned by all the Ships loaden with Corn and Provisions from *Sicily, Corsica*, and other Places, being intercepted and taken by these Pyrates, insomuch that they were almost reduced to a Famine: Upon this, *Pompey* the *Great* was immediately appointed General to manage this War; five hundred Ships were immediately fitted out, he had fourteen Senators, Men of Experience in the War, for his Vice-Admirals; and so considerable an Enemy, were these Ruffians become, that no less than an Army of a hundred thousand Foot, and five thousand Horse was appointed to invade them by Land; but it happened very luckily for *Rome*, that *Pompey* sail'd out before the Pyrate had Intelligence of a Design against them, so that their Ships were scattered all over the *Mediterranean*, like Bees gone out from a Hive, some one Way, some another, to bring Home their Lading; *Pompey* divided his Fleet into thirteen Squadrons, to whom he appointed their several Stations, so that great Numbers of the Pyrates fell into their Hands, Ship by Ship, without any Loss; forty Days he passed in scouring the *Mediterranean*, some of the Fleet cruising along the Coast of *Africa*, some about the Islands, and some upon the *Italian* Coasts, so that often those Pyrates who were flying from one Squadron, fell in with another; however, some of them escaped, and these making directly to *Cilicia*, and acquainting their Confederates on Shore with what had happened, they appointed a Rendezvous of all the Ships that had escaped at the Port of *Coracesium*, in the same Country. *Pompey* finding the *Mediterranean* quite clear, appointed a Meeting of all his Fleet at the Haven of *Brundusium*, and from thence sailing round into the *Adriatick*, he went directly to attack these Pyrates in their Hives; as soon as he came near the *Corecesium* in *Cilicia*, where the Remainder of the Pyrates now lay, they had the Hardiness to come and give him Battle, but the Genius of old *Rome* prevailed, and the Pyrates received an entire Overthrow, being all either taken or destroyed; but as they made many strong Fortresses upon the Sea Coast, and built Castles and strong Holds up the Country, about the Foot of Mount *Taurus*, he was obliged to besiege them with his Army; some Places he took by Storm, others surrendered to his Mercy, to whom he gave their Lives, and at length he made an entire Conquest.

But it is probable, that had these Pyrates receiv'd sufficient Notice of the *Roman* Preparation against them, so as they might have had Time to draw their scattered Strength into a Body, to have met *Pompey* by Sea, the Advantage appeared greatly on their Side, in Numbers of Shipping, and of Men; nor did they want Courage, as may be seen by their coming out of the Port of

Coracesium, to give the *Romans* Battle, with a Force much inferior to theirs; I say, had they overthrown *Pompey*, it is likely they would have made greater Attempts, and *Rome*, which had conquer'd the whole World, might have been subdued by a Parcel of Pyrates.

This is a Proof how dangerous it is to Governments to be negligent, and not take an early Care in suppressing these Sea Banditti, before they gather Strength.

The Truth of this Maxim may be better exemplified in the History of *Barbarouse*, a Native in the City of *Mitylene*, in the Island of *Lesbos*, in the *Egean* Sea; a Fellow of ordinary Birth, who being bred to the Sea, first set out from thence upon the pirating Account with only one small Vessel, but by the Prizes he took, he gain'd immense Riches, so that getting a great Number of large Ships, all the bold and dissolute Fellows of those Islands flock'd to him, and listed in his Service, for the Hopes of Booty; so that his Strength was increased to a formidable Fleet: With these he perform'd such bold and adventurous Actions, that he became the Terror of the Seas. About this Time it happened that *Selim Eutemi*, King of *Algiers*, having refused to pay the accustomed Tribute to the *Spaniards*, was apprehensive of an Invasion from thence; wherefore he treated with *Barbarouse*, upon the Foot of an Ally, to come and assist him, and deliver him from paying this Tribute; *Barbarouse* readily came into it, and sailing to *Algiers* with a great Fleet, he put part of his Men on Shore, and having laid a Plot to surprize the City, he effected it with great Success, and murder'd *Selim* in a Bath; soon after which, he was himself crowned King of *Algiers*; after this he made War upon *Abdilabde*, King of *Tunis*, and overthrew him in Battle; he extended his Conquests on all Sides; and thus from a Thief became a mighty King: and tho' he was at last kill'd in Battle, yet he had so well established himself upon that Throne, that, dying without Issue, he left the Inheritance of the Kingdom to his Brother, another Pyrate.

I come now to speak of the Pyrates infesting the *West-Indies*, where they are more numerous than in any other Parts of the World, on several Reasons:

First, Because there are so many uninhabited little Islands and Keys, with Harbours convenient and secure for cleaning their Vessels, and abounding with what they often want, Provision; I mean Water, Sea-Fowl, Turtle, Shell, and other Fish; where, if they carry in but strong Liquor, they indulge a Time, and become ready for new Expeditions before any Intelligence can reach to hurt them.

It may here perhaps be no unnecessary Digression, to explain upon what they call Keys in the *West-Indies*: These are small sandy Islands, appearing a little above the Surf of the Water, with only a few Bushes or Weeds upon them, but abound (those most at any Distance from the Main) with Turtle, amphibious Animals, that always chuse the quietest and most unfrequented Place, for laying their Eggs, which are to a vast Number in the Seasons, and would seldom be seen, but for this, (except by Pyrates:) Then Vessels from *Jamaica* and the other Governments make Voyages, called Turtling, for supplying the People, a common and approved Food with them. I am apt to think these *Keys*, especially those night Islands, to have been once contiguous with them, and separated by Earth-quakes (frequently there) or Inundations, because some of them that have been within continual View, as those nigh *Jamaica*, are observed within our Time, to be entirely wasted away and lost, and others daily wasting. There are not only of the Use above taken Notice of to Pyrates; but it is commonly believed were always in buccaneering piratical Times, the hiding Places for their Riches, and often Times a Shelter for themselves, till their Friends on the Main, had found Means to obtain Indemnity for their Crimes; for you must understand, when Acts of Grace were more frequent, and the Laws less severe, these Men continually found Favours and Incouragers at *Jamaica*, and perhaps they are not all dead yet; I have been told many of them them still living have been of the same Trade, and left it off only because they can live as well honestly, and gain now at the hazard of others Necks.

Secondly, another Reason why these Seas are chose by Pyrates, is the great Commerce thither by *French, Spaniards, Dutch*, and especially *English* Ships: They are sure in the Latitude of these trading Islands, to meet with Prizes, Booties of Provision, Cloathing, and Naval-Stores, and sometimes Money; there being great Sums remitted this Way to *England*; (the Returns of the

Assiento, and private Slave-Trade, to the *Spanish West-Indies*:) And in short, by some one or other, all the Riches of *Potost*.

A third Reason, is the Inconveniency and Difficulty of being pursued by the Men of War, the many small Inlets, Lagoons and Harbours, on these solitary Islands and Keys, is a natural Security.

'Tis generally here that the Pyrates begin their Enterprizes, setting out at first with a very small Force; and by infesting these Seas, and those of the Continent of *North-America*, in a Year's Time, if they have good luck on their Sides, they accumulate such Strength, as enables them to make foreign Expeditions: The first, is usually to *Guiney*, taking the *Azores* and *Cape de Verd* Islands in their Way, and then to *Brazil* and the *East-Indies*, where if they meet with prosperous Voyages, they set down at *Madagascar*, or the neighbouring Islands, and enjoy their ill gotten Wealth, among their elder Brethren, with Impunity. But that I may not give too much Encouragement to the Profession, I must inform my maritime Readers, that the far greater Part of these Rovers are cut short in the Pursuit, by a sudden Precipitation into the other World.

The Rise of these Rovers, since the Peace of *Utrecht*, or at least, the great Encrease of them, may justly be computed to the *Spanish* Settlements in the *West-Indies*; the Governors of which, being often some hungry Courtiers, sent thither to repair or make a Fortune, generally Countenance all Proceedings that bring in Profit: They grant Commissions to great Numbers of Vessels of War, on Pretence of preventing an interloping Trade, with Orders to seize all Ships or Vessels whatsoever, within five Leagues of their Coasts, which our *English* Ships cannot well avoid coming, in their Voyage to *Jamaica*. But if the *Spanish* Captains chance to exceed this Commission, and rob and plunder at Discretion, the Sufferers are allowed to complain, and exhibit a Process in their Court, and after great Expence of Suit, Delay of Time, and other Inconveniencies, obtain a Decree in their Favour, but then when the Ship and Cargo comes to be claim'd, with Costs of Suit, they find, to their Sorrow, that it has been previously condemn'd, and the Plunder divided among the Crew; the Commander that made the Capture, who alone is responsible, is found to be a poor raskally Fellow, not worth a Groat, and, no doubt, is plac'd in that Station for the like Purposes.

The frequent Losses sustain'd by our Merchants abroad, by these Pyrates, was Provocation enough to attempt something by way of Reprisal; and a fair Opportunity offering it self in the Year 1716, the Traders of the *West-Indies*, took Care not to slip it over, but made the best Use of it their Circumstances would permit.

It was about two Years before, that the *Spanish* Galleons, or Plate Fleet, had been cast away in the Gulf of *Florida*; and several Vessels from the *Havana*, were at work, with diving Engines, to fish up the Silver that was on board the Galleons.

The *Spaniards* had recovered some Millions of Pieces of Eight, and had carried it all to the *Havana*; but they had at present about 350000 Pieces of Eight in Silver, then upon the Spot, and were daily taking up more. In the mean time, two Ships, and three Sloops, fitted out from *Jamaica, Barbadoes, &c.* under Captain *Henry Jennings*, sail'd to the Gulf, and found the *Spaniards* there upon the Wreck; the Money before spoken of, was left on Shore, deposited in a Store-House, under the Government of two Commissaries, and a Guard of about 60 Soldiers.

The Rovers came directly upon the Place, bringing their little Fleet to an Anchor, and, in a Word, landing 300 Men, they attack'd the Guard, who immediately ran away; and thus they seized the Treasure, which they carried off, making the best of their Way to *Jamaica*.

In their Way they unhappily met with a *Spanish* Ship, bound from *Porto Bello* to the *Havana*, with a great many rich Goods, *viz*. Bales of Cochineal, Casks of Indico, and 60000 Pieces of Eight more, which their Hands being in, they took, and having rifled the Vessel, let her go.

They went away to *Jamaica* with their Booty, and were followed in View of the Port, by the *Spaniards*, who having seen them thither, went back to the Governor of the *Havana*, with the Account of it, who immediately sent a Vessel to the Governor of *Jamaica* to complain of this Robbery, and to reclaim the Goods.

As it was in full Peace, and contrary to all Justice and Right, that this Fact was committed, they were soon made sensible that the Government at *Jamaica* would not suffer them to go unpunished, much less protect them. Therefore they saw a Necessity of shifting for themselves; so, to make bad worse, they went to Sea again, tho' not without disposing of their Cargo to good Advantage, and furnishing themselves with Ammunition, Provisions, *&c.* and being thus made desperate, they turn'd Pyrates, robbing not the *Spaniards* only, but their own Countrymen, and any Nation they could lay their Hands on.

It happened about this Time, that the *Spaniards*, with three or four small Men of War, fell upon our Logwood Cutters, in the Bay of *Campeachy*, and Bay of *Honduras*; and after they had made Prizes of the following Ships and Vessels, they gave the Men belonging to them, three Sloops to carry them home, but these Men being made desperate by their Misfortunes, and meeting with the Pyrates, they took on with them, and so encreas'd their Number.

The *LIST of Ships and Vessels taken by the* Spanish *Men of War in the Year* 1716.

The *Stafford*, Captain *Knocks*, from *New-England*, bound for *London.*

   Anne, — — Gernish, for *London.*
   Dove — — Grimstone, for *New-England.*
   A Sloop, *— — Alden,* for *New-England.*
   A Brigantine, *— — Mosson,* for *New-England.*
   A Brigantine, *— — Turfield,* for *New-England.*
   A Brigantine, *— — Tennis,* for *New-England.*
   A Ship, *— — — — Porter,* for *New-England.*
   Indian Emperor, Wentworth, for *New-England.*
   A Ship, *— — Rich,* Master.
   A Ship, *— — Bay.*
   A Ship, *— — Smith.*
   A Ship, *— — Stockum.*
   A Ship, *— — Satlely.*
   A Sloop, *— — — — Richards,* belonging to *New-England.*
   Two Sloops, *— — — —* belonging to *Jamaica.*
   One Sloop *— — — —* of *Barbadoes.*
   Two Ships *— — — —* from *Scotland.*
   Two Ships *— — — —* from *Holland.*

The Rovers being now pretty strong, they consulted together about getting some Place of Retreat, where they might lodge their Wealth, clean and repair their Ships, and make themselves a kind of Abode. They were not long in resolving, but fixed upon the Island of *Providence*, the most considerable of the *Bahama* Islands, lying in the Latitude of about 24 Degrees North, and to the Eastward of the *Spanish Florida*.

This Island is about 28 Miles long, and eleven where broadest, and has a Harbour big enough to hold 500 Sail of Ships; before which lies a small Island, which makes two Inlets to the Harbour; at either Way there is a Bar, over which no Ship of 500 Tun can pass. The *Bahama* Islands were possess'd by the *English* till the Year 1700, when the *French* and *Spaniards* from *Petit Guavus*, invaded them, took the Fort and Governor in the Island of *Providence*, plunder'd and destroy'd the Settlements, *&c.* carried off half the Blacks, and the rest of the People, who fled to the Woods, retired afterwards to *Carolina*.

In *March* 1705-6, the House of Lords did in an Address to her late Majesty, set forth, 'That the *French* and *Spaniards* had twice, during the Time of the War, over run and plundered the *Bahama* Islands, that there was no Form of Government there: That the Harbour of the Isle of *Providence*, might be easily put in a Posture of Defence, and that it would be of dangerous Consequence, should those Islands fall into the Hands of the Enemy; wherefore the Lords humbly besought her Majesty to use such Methods as she should think proper for taking the said Island into her Hands, in order to secure the same to the Crown of this Kingdom, and to the Security and Advantage of the Trade thereof.

But, however it happened, no Means were used in compliance to that Address, for securing the *Bahama* Islands, till the *English* Pyrates had made *Providence* their Retreat and general Recepticle; then 'twas found absolutely necessary, in order to dislodge that troublesome Colony; and Information being made by the Merchants to the Government, of the Mischief they did, and were likely to do, his Majesty was pleased to grant the following Order.

Whitehall September 15, 1716.

'Complaint having been made to his Majesty, by great Number of Merchants, Masters of Sh ps and others, as well as by several Governors of his Majesty's Islands and Plantations in the *West-Indies*; that the Pyrates are grown so numerous, that they infest not only the Seas near *Jamaica*, but even those of the Northern Continent of *America*; and that, unless some effectual Means be used, the whole Trade from *Great Britain* to those Parts, will not be only obstructed, but in imminent Danger of being lost: His Majesty has, upon mature Deliberation in Council, been pleased, in the first Place, to order a proper Force to be employ'd for the suppressing the said Pyrates, which Force so to be employed, is as follows.

'A List of his Majesty's Ships and Vessels employed, and to be employed, at the *British* Governments and Plantations in the *West-Indies*.

Place where.	Rates,	Ships,	Guns.	
Jamaica,	5	*Adventure*,	40	Now there.
Jamaica,		*Diamond*,	40	Sail'd from hence thither 5th of last Month.
Jamaica,		*Ludlow Castle*,	40	To carry the Governor.
Jamaica,		*Swift* Sloop,		Now there.
Jamaica,	6	*Winchelsea*,	20	Surveying the Coast of the West-Indies, and then to return Home; but, during her being at Jamaica, is to join the others, for Security of the Trade, and intercepting Pyrates.
Barbadoes,	5	*Scarborough*,	30	Now there.
Leeward Islands,	6	Seaford,		Now there.
		Tryal Sloop,	6	
Virginia,	6	*Lime*,	20	Now there.
Virginia,	5	*Shoreham*,	30	Order'd Home.
Virginia,		*Pearl*,	40	Sailed thither from Home the 7th of last Month, and is to cruise about the Capes.

23

New-York,	6	*Phœnix,*	30	Now there.
New-England,		*Squirrel,*	20	
New-England,		*Rose,*	20	Order'd Home.

'Those at *Jamaica, Barbadoes* and the Leeward Islands, are to join upon Occasion, for annoying the Pyrates, and the Security of the Trade: And those at *New-England, Virginia* and *New-York*, are to do the like.

Besides these Frigots, two Men of War were ordered to attend Captain *Rogers*, late Commander of the two *Bristol* Ships, called the *Duke* and *Dutchess*, that took the rich *Acapulca* Ship, and made a Tour round the Globe. This Gentleman received a Commission from his Majesty, to be Governor of the Island of *Providence*, and was vested with Power to make Use of all possible Methods for reducing the Pyrates; and that nothing might be wanting, he carried with him, the King's Proclamation of Pardon, to those who should return to their Duty by a certain Time; the Proclamation is as follows;

By the KING,
A PROCLAMATION, for suppressing of Pyrates.
GEORGE R.

W*Hereas we have received Information, that several Persons, Subjects of* Great Britain, *have since the 24th Day of* June, *in the Year of our Lord* 1715, *committed divers Pyracies and Robberies upon the High-Seas, in the* West-Indies, *or adjoyning to our Plantations, which hath and may Occasion great Damage to the Merchants of* Great Britain, *and others trading into those Parts; and tho' we have appointed such a Force as we judge sufficient for suppressing the said Pyrates, yet the more effectually to put an End to the same, we have thought fit, by and with the Advice of our Privy Council, to Issue this our Royal Proclamation; and we do hereby promise, and declare, that in Case any of the said Pyrates, shall on or before the 5th of* September, *in the Year of our Lord* 1718, *surrender him or themselves, to one of our Principal Secretaries of State in* Great Britain *or* Ireland, *or to any Governor or Deputy Governor of any of our Plantations beyond the Seas; every such Pyrate and Pyrates so surrendering him, or themselves, as aforesaid, shall have our gracious Pardon, of and for such, his or their Pyracy, or Pyracies, by him or them committed before the fifth of* January *next ensuing. And we do hereby strictly charge and command all our Admirals, Captains, and other Officers at Sea, and all our Governors and Commanders of any Forts, Castles, or other Places in our Plantations, and all other our Officers Civil and Military, to seize and take such of the Pyrates, who shall refuse or neglect to surrender themselves accordingly. And we do hereby further declare, that in Case any Person or Persons, on, or after, the 6th Day of* September 1718, *shall discover or seize, or cause or procure to be discovered or seized, any one or more of the said Pyrates, so refusing or neglecting to surrender themselves as aforesaid, so as they may be brought to Justice, and convicted of the said Offence, such Person or Persons, so making such Discovery or Seizure, or causing or procuring such Discovery or Seizure to be made, shall have and receive as a Reward for the same, viz. for every Commander of any private Ship or Vessel, the Sum of* 100 l. *for every Lieutenant, Master, Boatswain, Carpenter, and Gunner, the Sum of* 40 l; *for every inferior Officer, the Sum of* 30 l. *and for every private Man, the Sum of* 20 l. *And if any Person or Persons, belonging to and being Part of the Crew of any such Pyrate Ship or Vessel, shall on or after the said sixth Day of* September 1718, *seize and deliver, or cause to be seized or delivered, any Commander or Commanders, of such Pyrate Ship or Vessel, so as that he or they be brought to Justice, and convicted of the said Offence, such Person or Persons, as a Reward for the same, shall receive for every such Commander, the Sum of* 200 l. *which said Sums, the Lord Treasurer, or the Commissioners of our Treasury for the Time being, are hereby required, and desired to pay accordingly.*

Given at our Court, at *Hampton-Court*, the fifth Day of *September*, 1717, in the fourth Year of our Reign.

God save the KING.

Before Governor *Rogers* went over, the Proclamation was sent to them, which they took as *Teague* took the Covenant, that is, they made Prize of the Ship and Proclamation too; however, they sent for those who were out a Cruising, and called a general Council, but there was so much Noise and Clamour, that nothing could be agreed on; some were for fortifying the Island, to stand upon their own Terms, and Treating with the Government upon the Foot of a Commonwealth; others were also for strengthening the Island for their own Security, but were not strenuous for these Punctillios, so that they might have a general Pardon, without being obliged to make any Restitution, and to retire, with all their Effects, to the neighbouring *British* Plantations.

But Captain *Jennings*, who was their Commadore, and who always bore a great Sway among them, being a Man of good Understanding, and a good Estate, before this Whim took him of going a Pirating, resolved upon surrendering, without more ado, to the Terms of the Proclamation, which so disconcerted all their Measures, that the *Congress* broke up very abruptly without doing any Thing; and presently *Jennings*, and by his Example, about 150 more, came in to the Governor of *Bermudas*, and had their Certificates, tho' the greatest Part of them returned again, like the Dog to the Vomit. The Commanders who were then in the Island, besides Captain *Jennings* abovementioned, I think were these, *Benjamin Hornigold Edward Teach, John Martel, James Fife, Christopher Winter, Nicholas Brown, Paul Williams, Charles Bellamy, Oliver la Bouche,* Major *Penner, Ed. England, T. Burgess Tho. Cocklyn, R. Sample, Charles Vane,* and two or three others: *Hornigold, Williams Burgess* and *la Bouche* were afterwards cast away; *Teach* and *Penner* killed, and their Crews taken; *James Fife* killed by his own Men; *Martel*'s Crew destroyed, and he forced on an uninhabited Island; *Cocklyn, Sample* and *Vane* hanged; *Winter* and *Brown* surrendered to the *Spaniards* at *Cuba*, and *England* lives now at *Madagascar*.

In the Month of *May* or *June* 1718, Captain *Rogers* arrived at his Government, with two of his Majesty's Ships, and found several of the abovesaid Pyrates there, who upon the coming of the Men of War, all surrendered to the Pardon, except *Charles Vane* and his Crew, which happened after this Manner.

I have before described the Harbour to have two Inlets, by Means of a small Island lying at the Mouth of it; at one of which, both the Men of War entered, and left the other open, so that *Vane* slip'd his Cable, set Fire to a large Prize they had there, and resolutely put out, firing at the Man of War as he went off.

As soon as Captain *Rogers* had settled himself in his Government, he built a Fort for his Defence, and garrisoned it with the People he found upon the Island; the *quondam*Pyrates, to the Number of 400, he formed into Companies, appointed Officers of those whom he most confided in, and then set about to settle a Trade with the *Spaniards*, in the Gulf of *Mexico*; in one of which Voyages, Captain *Burgess* abovementioned, died, and Captain *Hornigold*, another of the famous Pyrates, was cast away upon Rocks, a great Way from Land, and perished, but five of his Men got into a Canoe and were saved.

Captain *Rogers* sent out a Sloop to get Provisions, and gave the Command to one *John Augur*, one of the Pyrates, who had accepted of the Act of Grace; in their Voyage they met with two Sloops, and *John* and his Comrades not yet forgetting their former Business, made Use of their old Freedom, and took out of them in Money and Goods, to the Value of about 500 l. after this they steered away for *Hispaniola*, not being satisfy'd whether the Governor would admit them to carry on two Trades at once, and so thought to have bidden Farewel to the *Bahama* Islands; but as ill Luck would have it, they met with a violent Turnado, wherein they lost their Mast, and were drove back to one of the uninhabited *Bahama*'s, and lost their Sloop; the Men got all ashore, and lived up and down in the Wood, for a little Time, till Governor *Rogers* happening to hear of their Expedition, and where they had got to, sent out an armed Sloop to the aforesaid Island; the Master of which, with good Words and fair Promises, got them on Board, and brought them all to *Providence*, being a eleven Persons, ten of which were try'd at a Court of Admiralty, convicted, and hanged by the other's Evidence, in the Sight of all their former Companions and fellow Thieves. The Criminals would fain have spirited up the pardoned Pyrates, to rescue them out of the Hands of the Officers of Justice, telling them from the Gallows, that, *They never thought to have seen the Time, when ten such Men as they should be ty'd up and hanged like Dogs, and four hundred of their sworn Friends and Companions quietly standing by to behold the Spectacle.* One *Humphrey Morrice* urged the Matter further than the rest, taxing them with Pusilanimity and Cowardice, as if it were a Breach of Honour in them not to rise and save them from the ignominious Death they were going to suffer. But 'twas all in vain, they were now told, it was their Business to turn their Minds to another World, and sincerely to repent of what Wickedness they had done in this. Yes, answered one of them, *I do heartily repent; I repent I had not done more Mischief, and that we did not cut the Throats of them that took us, and I am extremely sorry that you an't all hang'd as well as we.* So do I, says another: And I, says a third; and then they were all turned off, without making any other dying Speeches, except one *Dennis Macarty*, who told the People, *That some Friends of his had often said he should die in his Shoes, but that he would make them Lyars*, and so kicked them off. And thus ended the Lives, with their Adventures, of those miserable Wretches, who may serve as sad Examples of the little Effect Mercy has upon Men once abandoned to an evil Course of Life.

Least I be thought severe in my Animadversions upon the *Span sh* Proceedings in the *West-Indies*, in respect to their Dealings with us; I shall mention an Instance or two, wherein I'll be as concise as possible, and then transcribe some original Letters from the Governor of *Jamaica*, and an Officer of a Man of War, to the *Alcaldees* of *Trinidado*, on the Island of *Cuba*, with their Answers, translated into *English*, and then proceed to the particular Histories of the Pyrates and their Crews, that have made most Noise in the World in *our own Times*.

About *March* 1722, one of our Men of War trading upon the Coast, *viz.* the *Greyhound Galley*, Captain *Walron*, the said Captain invited some of the Merchants to Dinner, who with their Attendants and Friends came on Board to the Number of 16 or 18 in all; and having concerted Measures, about six or eight dined in the Cabin, and the rest were waiting on the Deck. While the Captain and his Guests were at Dinner, the Boatswain Pipes for the Ship's Company to dine; accordingly the Men take their Platters, receive their Provisions, and down they go between Decks, leaving only 4 or 5 Hands besides the *Spaniards*, above, who were immediately dispatched by them, and the Hatches laid on the rest; those in the Cabin were as ready as their Companions, for they pulled out their Pistols and shot the Captain, Surgeon and another dead, and grievously wounded the Lieutenant; but he geting out of the Window upon a Side-Ladder, thereby saved his Life, and so they made themselves Masters of the Ship in an Instant: But by accidental good Fortune, she was recovered before she was carry'd off; for Captain *Walron* having mann'd a Sloop with 30 Hands out of his Ship's Company, had sent her to Windward some Days before, also for Trade, which the *Spaniards* knew very well; and just as the Action was over they saw this Sloop coming down, before the Wind, towards their Ship; upon which the *Spaniards* took about 10000 *l.* in Specie, as I am informed, quitted the Ship, and went off in their Launch unmolested.

About the same Time, a *Guard le Coast*, of *Porto Rico*, commanded by one *Matthew Luke*, an *Italian*, took four *English* Vessels, and murthered all the Crews: He was taken by the *Lanceston* Man of War, in *May* 1722, and brought to *Jamaica*, were they were all but seven deservedly hanged. It is likely the Man of War might not have meddled with her, but that she blindly laid the *Lanceston* on Board, thinking she had been a Merchant Ship, who thereupon catched a Tartar. Afterwards in rummaging there was found a Cartridge of Powder ma e up with a Piece of an *English* Journal, belonging, I believe, to the *Crean* Snow; and upon Examination, at last, it was discovered that they had taken this Vessel and murthered the Crew; and one of the *Spaniards*, when he came to die, confessed that he had killed twenty *English* Men with his own Hands.

S. Jago de la Vega, Febr 20.
A Letter from his Excellency Sir Nicolas Laws, *our Governor, to the Alcaldes of* Trinidado *on* Cuba, *dated the 26th of* Jan. 1721-2.

Gentlemen,

'THE frequent Depredations, Robberies, and other Acts of Hostility, which have been committed on the King my Royal Master's Subjects, by a Parcel of Banditti, who pretend to have Commissions from you, and in Reality are sheltered under your Government, is the Occasion of my sending the Bearer Captain *Chamberlain*, Commander of his Majesty's Snow *Happy*, to demand Satisfaction of you for so many notorious Robberies which your People have lately committed on the King's Subjects of this Island; particularly by those Traytors, *Nicolas Brown* and *Christopher Winter*, to whom you have given Protection. Such Proceedings as these are not only a Breach of the Law of Nations, but must appear to the World of a very extraordinary Nature, when considered that the Subjects of a Prince in Amity and Friendship with another, should give Countenance and encourage such vile Practices. I confess I have had long Patience, and declined using any violent Measures to obtain Satisfaction, hoping the Cessation of Arms, so happily concluded upon between our respective Sovereigns, would have put an effectual Stop to those Disorders; but on the contrary, I now find the Port of *Trinidado* a Receptacle to Villains of all Nations. I do therefore think fit to acquaint you, and assure you in the King my Master's Name, that if I do meet with any of your Rogues for the future upon the Coast of this Island, I will order them to be hanged directly without Mercy; and I expect and demand of you to make ample Restitution to Captain *Chamberlain* of all the Negroes which the said *Brown* and *Winter* have lately taken off from the North-Side of this Island, and also of such Sloops and other Effects as they have been taken and robbed of, since the Cessation of Arms, and that you will deliver up to the Bearer such *English* Men as are now detained, or otherwise remain at *Trinidado*; and also expect you will hereafter forbear granting any Commissions, or suffer any such notorious Villains to be equipp'd and fitted out from your Port: otherwise you may depend upon it, those that I can meet with, shall be esteemed Pyrates, and treated as such; of which I thought proper to give you Notice, and am, *&c*.

A Letter from Mr. Joseph Laws, *Lieutenant of his Majesty's Ship*, Happy *Snow, to the Alcaldes of* Trinidado.

Genlemen,

'I Am sent by Commadore *Vernon*, Commander in Chief of all his Majesty's Ships in the *West-Indies*, to demand in the King our Master's Name, all the Vessels, with their Effects, *&c.* and also the Negroes taken from *Jamaica* since the Cessation of Arms; likewise all *Englishmen* now detained, or otherwise remaining in your Port of *Trinidado*, particularly *Nicholas Brown* and *Christopher Winter*, both of them being Traytors, Pyrates and common Enemies to all Nations: And the said Commadore hath ordered me to acquaint you, that he is surprized that the Subjects of a Prince in Amity and Friendship with another, should give Countenance to such notorious Villains. In Expectation of your immediate Compliance, I am, Gentlemen,

Off the River *Trinidado, Feb.* 8. 1720.

Your humble Servant, *Joseph Laws.*

The Answer of the Alcaldes of Trinidado, to Mr. Laws's Letter

Capt. *Laws*,

'IN Answer to yours, this serves to acquaint you, that neither in this City, nor Port, are there any Negroes or Vessels which have been taken at your Island of *Jamaica*, nor

Chap. I
Of Captain *Avery*, And his Crew

> Romantic Reports of his Greatness. His Birth. Is Mate of a Bristol Man. For what Voyage design'd. Tampers with the Seamen. Forms a Plot for carrying off the Ship. Executes it, and how. The Pyrates take a rich Ship belonging to the Great Mogul. The Great Mogul threaten the English Settlements. The Pyrates steer their Course back for Madagascar. Call a Council. Put all the Treasure on Board of Avery's Ship. Avery and his Crew treacherously leaves his Confederates; go to the Isle of Providence in the West-Indies. Sell the Ship, go to North-America in a Sloop. They disperse, Avery goes to New-England. From thence to Ireland. Avery afraid to expose his Diamonds to sale. Goes over to England. Puts his Wealth into Merchants Hands, of Bristol. Changes his Name. Lives at Biddiford. The Merchants send him no Supplies. Importunes them. Goes privately to Bristol, they threaten to discover him. Goes over to Ireland, sollicites them from thence. Is very poor, works his Passage over to Plymouth, walks to Biddiford. Dies a Beggar. An Account of Avery's Confederates. Their Settlement at Madagascar. They meet other Pyrates; an Account of them, ib. The Pyrates arrive to great Power. The Inhabitants described. Their Policy, Government, &c. Places describ'd. The Arrival of Captain Woods Rogers at that Part of the Island. Their Design of surprizing his Ship. One of these Princes formerly a Waterman on the Thames. Their Secretaries, Men of no Learning. Could neither write nor read.

None of these bold Adventurers were ever so much talked of, for a while, as *Avery*; he made as great a Noise in the World as *Meriveis* does now, and was looked upon to be a Person of as great Consequence; he was represented in *Europe*, as one that had raised himself to the Dignity of a King, and was likely to be the Founder of a new Monarchy; having, as it was said, taken immense Riches, and married the *Great Mogul*'s Daughter, who was taken in an *Indian* Ship, which fell into his Hands; and that he had by her many Children, living in great Royalty and State; that he had built Forts, erected Magazines, and was Master of a stout Squadron of Ships, mann'd with able and desperate Fellows of all Nations; that he gave Commissions out in his own Name to the Captains of his Ships, and to the Commanders of his Forts, and was acknowledged by them as their Prince. A Play was writ upon him, called, the *Successful Pyrate*; and, these Accounts obtained such Belief, that several Schemes were offered to the Council for fitting out a Squadron to take him; while others were for offering him and his Companions an Act of Grace, and inviting them to *England*, with all their Treasure, least his growing Greatness might hinder the Trade of *Europe* to the *East-Indies*.

Yet all these were no more than false Rumours, improved by the Credulity of some, and the Humour of others who love to tell strange Things; for, while it was said, he was aspiring at a Crown, he wanted a Shilling; and at the same Time it was given out he was in Possession of such prodigious Wealth in *Madagascar*, he was starving in *England*.

No doubt, but the Reader will have a Curiosity of knowing what became of this Man, and what were the true Grounds of so many false Reports concerning him; therefore, I shall, in as brief a Manner as I can, give his History.

He was born in the West of *England* near *Plymouth* in *Devonshire*, being bred to the Sea, he served as a Mate of a Merchant-Man, in several trading Voyages: It happened before the Peace of *Ryswick*, when there was an Alliance betwixt *Spain, England, Holland, &c.* against *France*, that the *French* in *Martinico*, carried on a smugling Trade with the *Spaniards* on the Continent of *Peru*, which by the Laws of *Spain*, is not allowed to Friends in Time of Peace, for none but native *Spaniards* are permitted to Traffick in those Parts, or set their Feet on Shore, unless at any Time they are brought as Prisoners; wherefore they constantly keep certain Ships cruising along the Coast, whom they call *Guarda del Costa*, who have the Orders to make Prizes of all Ships they can light of within five Leagues of Land. Now the *French* growing very bold in Trade, and the *Spaniards* being poorly provided with Ships, and those they had being of no Force, it often fell out, that when they light of the *French* Smuglers, they were not strong enough to attack them, therefore it was resolv'd in *Spain*, to hire two or three stout foreign Ships for their Service, which being known at *Bristol*, some Merchants of that City, fitted out two Ships of thirty odd Guns, and 120 Hands each, well furnished with Provision and Ammunition, and all other Stores; and the Hire being agreed for, by some Agents for *Spain*, they were commanded to sail for *Corunna* or the *Groine*, there to receive their Orders, and to take on Board some *Spanish* Gentlemen, who were to go Passengers to *New-Spain*.

Of one of these Ships, which I take to be call'd the *Duke*, Capt. *Gibson* Commander, *Avery* was first Mate, and being a Fellow of more Cunning than Courage, he insinuated himself into the good Will of several of the boldest Fellows on Board the other Ship, as well as that which he was on Board of; having sounded their Inclinations before he opened himself, and finding them ripe for his Design, he, at length, proposed to them, to run away with the Ship, telling them what great Wealth was to be had upon the Coasts of *India*: It was no sooner said than agreed to, and they resolved to execute their Plot at Ten a Clock the Night following.

It must be observ'd, the Captain was one of those who are mightily addicted to Punch, so that he passed most of his Time on Shore, in some little drinking Ordinary; but this Day he did not go on Shore as usual; however, this did not spoil the Design, for he took his usual Dose on Board, and so got to Bed before the Hour appointed for the Business: The Men also who were not privy to the Design, turn'd into their Hammocks, leaving none upon Deck but the Conspirators, who, indeed, were the greatest Part of the Ship's Crew. At the Time agreed on, the *Dutchess*'s Long-Boat appear'd, which *Avery* hailing in the usual Manner, was answered by the Men in her, *Is your drunken Boatswain on Board?* Which was the Watch-Word agreed between them, and *Avery* replying in the Affirmative, the Boat came aboard with sixteen stout Fellows, and joined the Company.

When our Gentry saw that all was clear, they secured the Hatches, so went to work; they did not slip the Anchor, but weigh'd it leisurely, and so put to Sea without any Disorder or Confusion, tho' there were several Ships then lying in the Bay, and among them a *Dutch* Frigate of forty Guns, the Captain of which was offered a great Reward to go out after her; but *Mynheer*, who perhaps would not have been willing to have been served so himself, could not be prevail'd upon to give such Usage to another, and so let Mr. *Avery* pursue his Voyage, whither he had a Mind to.

The Captain, who by this Time, was awaked, either by the Motion of the Ship, or the Noise of working the Tackles, rung the Bell; *Avery* and two others went into the Cabin; the Captain, half asleep, and in a kind of Fright, ask'd, *What was the Matter? Avery* answered cooly, *Nothing*; the Captain replied, *something's the Matter with the Ship, Does she drive? What Weather is it?* Thinking nothing less then that it had been a Storm, and that the Ship was driven from her Anchors: *No, no,* answered *Avery, we're at Sea, with a fair Wind and good Weather. At Sea!* says the Captain, *How can that be? Come,* says *Avery, don't be in a Fright, but put on your Cloaths, and I'll let you into a Secret: —— You must know, that I am Captain of this Ship now, and this is my Cabin, therefore you must walk out; I am bound to* Madagascar, *with a Design of making my own Fortune, and that of all the brave Fellows joined with me.*

The Captain having a little recovered his Senses, began to apprehend the meaning; however, his Fright was as great as before, which *Avery* perceiving, bad him fear nothing, for, says he, if you have a Mind to make one of us, we will receive you, and if you'll turn sober, and mind your Business, perhaps in Time I may make you one of my Lieutenants, if not, here's a Boat a-long-side, and you shall be set ashore.

The Captain was glad to hear this, and therefore accepted of his Offer, and the whole Crew being called up, to know who was willing to go on Shore with the Captain, and who to seek their Fortunes with the rest; there were not above five or six who were willing to quit this Enterprize; wherefore they were put into the Boat with the Captain that Minute, and made their Way to the Shore as well as they could.

They proceeded on their Voyage to *Madagascar*, but I do not find they took any Ships in their Way; when they arrived at the N. E. Part of that Island, they found two Sloops at Anchor, who, upon seeing them, slip'd their Cables and run themselves ashore, the Men all landing, and running into the Woods; these were two Sloops which the Men had run away with from the *West-Indies*, and seeing *Avery*, they supposed him to be some Frigate sent to take them, and therefore not being of Force to engage him, they did what they could to save themselves.

He guessed where they were, and sent some of his Men on Shore to let them know they were Friends, and to offer they might join together for their common Safety; the Sloops Men were well arm'd, and had posted themselves in a Wood, with Centinels just on the out-side, to observe whether the Ship landed her Men to pursue them, and they observing only two or three Men to come towards them without Arms, did not oppose them, but having challenged them, and they answering they were Friends, they lead them to their Body, where they delivered their Message; at first, they apprehended it was a Stratagem to decoy them on Board, but when the Ambassadors offered that the Captain himself, and as many of the Crew as they should name, would meet them on Shore without Arms, they believed them to be in Earnest, and they soon entered into a Confidence with one another; those on Board going on Shore, and some of those on Shore going on Board.

The Sloops Men were rejoiced at the new Ally, for their Vessels were so small, that they could not attack a Ship of any Force, so that hitherto they had not taken any considerable Prize, but now they hop'd to fly at high Game; and *Avery* was as well pleased at this Reinforcement, to strengthen them for any brave Enterprize, and tho' the Booty must be lessened to each, by being divided into so many Shares, yet he found out an Expedient not to suffer by it himself, as shall be shewn in its Place.

Having consulted what was to be done, they resolved to sail out together upon a Cruize, the Galley and two Sloops; they therefore fell to work to get the Sloops off, which they soon effected, and steered towards the *Arabian* Coast; near the River *Indus*, the Man at the Mast-Head spied a Sail, upon which they gave Chace, and as they came nearer to her, they perceived her to be a tall Ship, and fancied she might be a *Dutch East-India* Man homeward bound; but she proved a better Prize; when they fired at her to bring too, she hoisted *Mogul's* Colours, and seemed to stand upon her Defence; *Avery* only canonaded at a Distance, and some of his Men began to suspect that he was not the Hero they took him for: However, the Sloops made Use of their Time, and coming one on the Bow, and the other on the Quarter, of the Ship, clapt her on Board, and enter'd her, upon which she immediately struck her Colours and yielded; she was one of the *Great Mogul's* own Ships, and there were in her several of the greatest Persons of his Court, among whom it was said was one of his Daughters, who were going on a Pilgrimage to *Mecca*, the *Mahometans* thinking themselves obliged once in their Lives to visit that Place, and they were carrying with them rich Offerings to present at the Shrine of *Mahomet*. It is known that the Eastern People travel with the utmost Magnificence, so that they had with them all their Slaves and Attendants, their rich Habits and Jewels, with Vessels of Gold and Silver, and great Sums of Money to defray the Charges of their Journey by Land; wherefore the Plunder got by this Prize, is not easily computed.

Having taken all the Treasure on Board their own Ships, and plundered their Prize of every Thing else they either wanted or liked, they let her go; she not being able to continue her Voyage, returned back: As soon as the News came to the *Mogul*, and he knew that they were *English* who had robbed them, he threatened loud, and talked of sending a mighty Army with Fire and Sword, to extirpate the *English* from all their Settlements on the *Indian* Coast. The *East-India* Company in *England*, were very much alarmed at it; however, by Degrees, they found Means to pacify him, by promising to do their Endeavours to take the Robbers, and deliver them into his Hands; however, the great Noise this Thing made in *Europe*, as well as *India*, was the Occasion of all these romantic Stories which were formed of *Avery's* Greatness.

In the mean Time our successful Plunderers agreed to make the best of their Way back to *Madagascar*, intending to make that Place their Magazine or Repository for all their Treasure, and to build a small Fortification there, and leave a few Hands always ashore to look after it, and defend it from any Attempts of the Natives; but *Avery* put an End of this Project, and made it altogether unnecessary.

As they were Steering their Course, as has been said, he sends a Boat on Board of each of the Sloops, desiring the Chief of them to come on Board of him, in order to hold a Council; they did so, and he told them he had something to propose to them for the common Good, which was to provide against Accidents; he bad them consider the Treasure they were possess'd of, would be sufficient for them all if they could secure it in some Place on Shore; therefore all they had to fear, was some Misfortune in the Voyage; he bad them consider the Consequences of being separated by bad Weather, in which Case, the Sloops, if either of them should fall in with any Ships of Force, must be either taken or sunk, and the Treasure on Board her lost to the rest, besides the common Accidents of the Sea; as for his Part he was so strong, he was able to make his Party good with any Ship they were like to meet in those Seas; that if he met with any Ship of such Strength, that he could not take her, he was safe from being taken, being so well mann'd; besides his Ship was a quick Sailor, and could carry Sail, when the Sloops could not, wherefore, he proposed to them, to put the Treasure on Board his Ship, to seal up each Chest with 3 Seals, whereof each was to keep one, and to appoint a Rendezvous, in Case of Separation.

Upon considering this Proposal, it appeared so seasonable to them, that they readily came into it, for they argued to themselves, that an Accident might happen to one of the Sloops and the other escape, wherefore it was for the common Good. The Thing was done as agreed to, the Treasure put on Board of *Avery*, and the Chests seal'd; they kept Company that Day and the next, the Weather being fair, in which Time *Avery* tampered with his Men, telling them they now had sufficient to make them all easy, and what should hinder them from going to some Country, where they were not known, and living on Shore all the rest of their Days in Plenty; they understood what he meant: And in short, they all agreed to bilk their new Allies, the Sloop's Men, nor do I find that any of them felt any Qualms of Honour rising in his Stomach, to hinder them from consenting to this Piece of Treachery. In fine, they took Advantage of the Darkness that Night, steer'd another Course, and, by Morning, lost Sight of them.

I leave the Reader to judge, what Swearing and Confusion there was among the Sloop's Men, in the Morning, when they saw that *Avery* had given them the Slip; for they knew by the Fairness of the Weather, and the Course they had agreed to steer, that it must have been done on purpose: But we leave them at present to follow Mr. *Avery*.

Avery, and his Men, having consulted what to do with themselves, came to a Resolution, to make the best of their Way towards *America*; and none of them being known in those Parts, they intended to divide the Treasure, to change their Names, to go ashore, some in one Place, some in other, to purchase some Settlements, and live at Ease. The first Land they made, was the Island of *Providence*, then newly settled; here they staid some Time, and having considered that when they should go to *New-England*, the Greatness of their Ship, would cause much Enquiry about them; and possibly some People from *England*, who had heard the Story of a Ship's being run away with from the *Groine*, might suspect them to be the People; they therefore took a Resolution of disposing of their Ship at *Providence*: Upon which, *Avery* pretending that the Ship being fitted out upon the privateering Account, and having had no Success, he had received Orders from the Owners, to dispose of her to the best Advantage, he soon met with a Purchaser, and immediately bought a Sloop.

In this Sloop, he and his Companions embarq'd, they touch'd at several Parts of *America*, where no Person suspected them; and some of them went on Shore, and dispersed themselves about the Country, having received such Dividends as *Avery* would give them; for he concealed the greatest Part of the Diamonds from them, which in the first Hurry of plundering the Ship, they did not much regard, as not knowing their Value.

At length he came to *Boston*, in *New-England*, and seem'd to have a Desire of settling in those Parts, and some of his Companions went on Shore there also, but he changed his Resolution, and proposed to the few of his Companions who were left, to sail for *Ireland*, which they consented to: He found out that *New-England* was not a proper Place for him, because a great deal of his Wealth lay in Diamonds; and should he have produced them there, he would have certainly been seiz'd on Suspicion of Pyracy.

In their Voyage to *Ireland*, they avoided St. *George*'s Channel, and sailing North about, they put into one of the Northern Ports of that Kingdom; there they disposed of their Sloop, and coming on Shore they separated themselves, some going to *Cork*, and some to *Dublin*, 18 of whom obtain'd their Pardons afterwards of K. *William*. When *Avery* had remain'd some Time in this Kingdom, he was afraid to offer his Diamonds to sale, least an Enquiry into his Manner of coming by them should occasion a Discovery; therefore considering with himself what was best to be done, he fancied there were some Persons at *Bristol*, whom he might venture to trust; upon which, he resolved to pass over into *England*; he did so, and going into *Devonshire*, he sent to one of these Friends to meet him at a Town called *Biddiford*; when he had communicated himself to his Friends, and consulted with him about the Means of his Effects, they agreed, that the safest Method would be, to put them in the Hands of some Merchants, who being Men of Wealth and Credit in the World, no Enquiry would be made how they came by them; this Friend telling him he was very intimate with some who were very fit for the Purpose, and if he would but allow them a good Commission would do the Business very faithfully.

Avery liked the Proposal, for he found no other Way of managing his Affairs, since he could not appear in them himself; therefore his Friend going back to *Bristol*, and opening the Matter to the Merchants, they made *Avery* a Visit at *Biddiford*, where, after some Protestations of Honour and Integrity, he delivered them his Effects, consisting of Diamonds and some Vessels of Gold; they gave him a little Money for his present Subsistance, and so they parted.

He changed his Name and lived at *Biddiford*, without making any Figure, and therefore there was no great Notice taken of him; yet let one or two of his Relations know where he was, who came to see him. In some Time his little Money was spent, yet he heard nothing from his Merchants; he writ to them often, and after much Importunity they sent him a small Supply, but scarce sufficient to pay his Debts: In fine, the Supplies they sent him from Time to Time, were so small, that they were not sufficient to give him Bread, nor could he get that little, without a great deal of Trouble and Importunity, wherefore being weary of his Life, he went privately to *Bristol*, to speak to the Merchants himself, where instead of Money he met a most shocking Repulse, for when he desired them to come to an Account with him, they silenced him by threatening to discover him, so that our Merchants were as good Pyrates at Land as he was at Sea.

Whether he was frightened by these Menaces, or had seen some Body else he thought knew him, is not known; but he went immediately over to *Ireland*, and from thence sollicited his Merchants very hard for a Supply, but to no Purpose, for he was even reduced to beggary: In this Extremity he was resolved to return and cast himself upon them, let the Consequence be what it would. He put himself on Board a trading Vessel, and work'd his Passage over to *Plymouth*, from whence he travelled on Foot to *Biddiford*, where he had been but a few Days before he fell sick and died; not being worth as much as would buy him a Coffin.

Thus have I given all that could be collected of any Certainty concerning this Man; rejecting the idle Stories which were made of his fantastic Greatness, by which it appears, that his Actions were more inconsiderable than those of other Pyrates, since him, though he made more Noise in the World.

Now we shall turn back and give our Readers some Account of what became of the two Sloops.

We took Notice of the Rage and Confusion, which must have seized them, upon their missing of *Avery*; however, they continued their Course, some of them still flattering themselves that he had only out failed them in the Night, and that they should find him at the Place of Rendezvous: But when they came there, and could hear no Tydings of him, there was an End of Hope. It was Time to consider what they should do with themselves, their Stock of Sea Provision was almost spent, and tho' there was Rice and Fish, and Fowl to be had ashore, yet these would not keep for Sea, without being properly cured with Salt, which they had no Conveniency of doing; therefore, since they could not go a Cruizing any more, it was Time to think of establishing themselves at Land; to which Purpose they took all Things out of the Sloops, made Tents of the Sails, and encamped themselves, having a large Quantity of Ammunition, and abundance of small Arms.

Here they met with several of their Countrymen, the Crew of a Privateer Sloop which was commanded by Captain *Thomas Tew*; and since it will be but a short Digression, we will give an Account how they came here.

Captain *George Dew* and Captain *Thomas Tew*, having received Commissions from the then Governor of *Bermudas*, to sail directly for the River *Gambia* in *Africa*; there, with the Advice and Assistance of the Agents of the Royal *African* Company, to attempt the taking the *French* Factory at *Goorie*, lying upon that Coast. In a few Days after they sailed out, *Dew* in a violent Storm, not only sprung his Mast, but lost Sight of his Consort; *Dew* therefore returned back to refit, and *Tew* instead of proceeding on his Voyage, made for the *Cape of Good Hope*, and doubling the said Cape, shaped his Course for the Straits of *Babel Mandel*, being the Entrance into the *Red Sea*. Here he came up with a large Ship, richly laden, bound from the *Indies* to *Arabia*, with three hundred Soldiers on Board, besides Seamen; yet *Tew* had the Hardiness to board her, and soon carried her; and, 'tis said, by this Prize, his Men shared near three thousand Pounds a Piece: They had Intelligence from the Prisoners, of five other rich Ships to pass that Way, which *Tew* would have attacked, tho' they were very strong, if he had not been over-ruled by the Quarter-Master and others. — This differing in Opinion created some ill Blood amongst them, so that they resolved to break up pirating, and no Place was so fit to receive them as *Madagascar*; hither they steered, resolving to live on Shore and enjoy what they got.

As for *Tew* himself, he with a few others in a short Time went off to *Rhode Island*, from whence he made his Peace.

Thus have we accounted for the Company our Pyrates met with here.

It must be observed that the Natives of *Madagascar* are a kind of Negroes, they differ from those of *Guiney* in their Hair, which is long, and their Complexion is not so good a Jet; they have innumerable little Princes among them, who are continually making War upon one another; their Prisoners are their Slaves, and they either sell them, or put them to death, as they please: When our Pyrates first settled amongst them, their Alliance was much courted by these Princes, so they sometimes joined one, sometimes another, but wheresoever they sided, they were sure to be Victorious; for the Negroes here had no Fire-Arms, nor did they understand their Use; so that at length these Pyrates became so terrible to the Negroes, that if two or or three of them were only seen on one Side, when they were going to engage, the opposite Side would fly without striking a Blow.

By these Means they not only became feared, but powerful; all the Prisoners of War, they took to be their Slaves; they married the most beautiful of the Negroe Women, not one or two, but as many as they liked; so that every one of them had as great a Seraglio as the Grand Seignior at *Constantinople*: Their Slaves they employed in planting Rice, in Fishing Hunting, &c. besides which, they had abundance of others, who lived, as it were, under their Protection, and to be secure from the Disturbances or Attacks of their powerful Neighbours; these seemed to pay them a willing Homage. Now they began to divide from one another, each living with his own Wives, Slaves and Dependants, like a separate Prince; and as Power and Plenty naturally beget Contention, they sometimes quarrelled with one another, and attacked each other at the Head of their several Armies; and in these civil Wars, many of them were killed; but an Accident happened, which obliged them to unite again for their common Safety.

It must be observed that these sudden great Men, had used their Power like Tyrants, for they grew wanton in Cruelty, and nothing was more common, than upon the slightest Displeasure, to cause one of their Dependants to be tied to a Tree and shot thro' the Heart, let the Crime be what it would, whether little or great, this was always the Punishment; wherefore the Negroes conspired together, to rid themselves of these Destroyers, all in one Night; and as they now lived separate, the Thing might easily have been done, had not a Woman, who had been Wife or Concubine to one of them, run near twenty Miles in three Hours, to discover the Matter to them: Immediately upon the Alarm they ran together as fast as they could, so that when the Negroes approached them, they found them all up in Arms; wherefore they retired without making any Attempt.

This Escape made them very cautious from that Time, and it will be worth while to describe the Policy of these brutish Fellows, and to shew what Measures they took to secure themselves.

They found that the Fear of their Power could not secure them against a Surprize, and the bravest Man may be kill'd when he is asleep, by one much his inferior in Courage and Strength, therefore, as their first Security, they did all they could to foment War betwixt the neighbouring Negroes, remaining Neuter themselves, by which Means, those who were overcome constantly fled to them for Protection, otherwise they must be either killed or made Slaves. They strengthened their Party, and tied some to them by Interest; when there was no War, they contrived to spirit up private Quarrels among them, and upon every little Dispute or Misunderstanding, push on one Side or other to Revenge; Instruct them how to attack or surprize their Adversaries, and lend them loaded Pistols or Firelocks to dispatch them with; the Consequence of which was, that the Murderer was forced to fly to them for the safety of his Life, with his Wives, Children and Kindred.

Such as these were fast Friends, as their Lives depended upon the safety of his Protectors; for as we observed before, our Pyrates were grown so terrible, that none of their Neighbours had Resolution enough to attack them in an open War.

By such Arts as these, in the Space of a few Years, their Body was greatly increased, they then began to separate themselves, and remove at a greater Distance from one another, for the Convenience of more Ground, and were divided like Jews, into Tribes, each carrying with him his Wives and Children, (of which, by this Time they had a large Family,) as also their Quota of Dependants and Followers; and if Power and Command be the Thing which distinguish a Prince, these Ruffians had all the Marks of Royalty about them, nay more, they had the very Fears which commonly disturb Tyrants, as may be seen by the extreme Caution they took in fortifying the Places where they dwelt.

In this Plan of Fortification they imitated one another, their Dwellings were rather Citadels than Houses; they made Choice of a Place overgrown with Wood, and situate near a Water; they raised a Rampart or high Ditch round it, so strait and high, that it was impossible to climb it, and especially by those who had not the Use of scaling Ladders: Over this Ditch there was one Passage into the Wood; the Dwelling, which was a Hut, was built in that Part of the Wood which the Prince, who inhabited it, thought fit, but so covered that it could not be seen till you came at it; but the greatest Cunning lay in the Passage which lead to the Hut, which was so narrow, that no more than one Person could go a Breast, and contrived in so intricate a Manner, that it was a perfect Maze or Labyrinth, it being round and round, with several little cross Ways, so that a Person that was not well acquainted with the Way, might walk several Hours round and cross these Ways without being able to find the Hut; moreover all along the Sides of these narrow Paths, certain large Thorns which grew upon a Tree in that Country, were struck into the Ground with their Points uppermost, and the Path it self being made crooked and serpentine, if a Man should attempt to come near the Hut at Night, he would certainly have struck upon these Thorns, tho' he had been provided with that Clue which *Ariadne* gave to *Theseus* when he entered the Cave of the *Minataur*.

Thus Tyrant like they lived, fearing and feared by all; and in this Scituation they were found by Captain *Woods Rogers*, when he went to *Madagascar*, in the *Delicia*, a Ship of forty Guns, with a Design of buying Slaves in order to sell to the *Dutch* at *Batavia* or *New-Holland*: He happened to touch upon a Part of the Island, where no Ship had been seen for seven or eight Years before, where he met with some of the Pyrates, at which Time, they had been upon the Island above 25 Years, having a large motly Generation of Children and Grand-Children descended from them, there being about that Time, eleven of them remaining alive.

Upon their first seeing a Ship of this Force and Burthen, they supposed it to be a Man of War sent to take them; they therefore lurked within their Fastnesses, but when some from the Ship came on Shore, without any shew of Hostility, and offering to trade with the Negroes, they ventured to come out of their Holes, attended like Princes; and since they actually are Kings *De Facto*, which is a kind of a Right, we ought to speak of them as such.

Having been so many Years upon this Island, it may be imagined, their Cloaths had long been worn out, so that their Majesties were extremely out at the Elbows; I cannot say they were ragged, since they had no Cloaths, they had nothing to cover them but the Skins of Beasts without any tanning, but with all the Hair on, nor a Shoe nor Stocking, so they looked like the Pictures of *Hercules* in the Lion's Skin; and being overgrown with Beard, and Hair upon their Bodies, they appeared the most savage Figures that a Man's Imagination can frame.

However, they soon got rigg'd, for they sold great Numbers of those poor People under them, for Cloaths, Knives, Saws, Powder and Ball, and many other Things, and became so familiar that they went aboard the *Delicia*, and were observed to be very curious, examining the inside of the Ship, and very familiar with the Men, inviting them ashore. Their Design in doing this, as they afterwards confessed, was to try if it was not practicable to surprize the Ship in the Night, which they judged very easy, in case there was but a slender Watch kept on Board, they having Boats and Men enough at Command, but it seems the Captain was aware of them, and kept so strong a Watch upon Deck, that they found it was in vain to make any Attempt; wherefore, when some of the Men went ashore, they were for inveigling them, and drawing them into a Plot, for feizing the Captain and securing the rest of the Men under Hatches, when they should have the Night-Watch, promising a Signal to come on Board to join them; proposing, if they succeeded, to go a Pirating together, not doubting but with that Ship they should be able to take any Thing they met on the Sea: But the Captain observing an Intimacy growing betwixt them and some of his Men, thought it could be for no good, he therefore broke it off in Time, not suffering them so much as to talk together; and when he sent a Boat on Shore with an Officer to treat with them about the Sale of Slaves, the Crew remained on Board the Boat, and no Man was suffered to talk with them, but the Person deputed by him for that Purpose.

Before he sailed away, and they found that nothing was to be done, they confessed all the Designs they had formed against him. Thus he left them as he found them, in a great deal of dirty State and Royalty, but with fewer Subjects than they had, having, as we observed, sold many of them; and if Ambition be the darling Passion of Men, no doubt they were happy. One of these great Princes had formerly been a Waterman upon the *Thames*, where having committed a Murder, he fled to the *West-Indies*, and was of the Number of those who run away with the Sloops; the rest had been all foremast Men, nor was there a Man amongst them, who could either read or write, and yet their Secretaries of State had no more Learning than themselves. This is all the Account we can give of these Kings of *Madagascar*, some of whom it is probable are reigning to this Day.

Chap. II
Of Captain *Martel*, And his Crew

>Way to suppress Pyrates. The Increase of Pyrates accounted for. Where Martel learned his Trade. The Names of several Prizes taken, by him. His Strength at Sancta Cruz. His Manner of fortifying himself there. Is attack'd by the Scarborough Man of War. His defence by land and Sea. His desperate Escape. His miserable End, ib.

I come now to the Pyrates that have rose since the Peace of *Vtrecht*; in War Time there is no room for any, because all those of a roving advent'rous Disposition find Employment in Privateers, so there is no Opportunity for Pyrates; like our Mobs in *London*, when they come to any Height, our Superiors order out the Train Bands, and when once they are raised, the others are suppressed of Course; I take the Reason of it to be, that the Mob go into the tame Army, and immediately from notorious Breakers of the Peace, become, by being put into order, solemn Preservers of it. And should our Legislators put some of the Pyrates into Authority, it would not only lessen their Number, but, I imagine, set them upon the rest, and they would be the likeliest People to find them out, according to the Proverb, *set a Thief to catch a Thief*.

To bring this about, there needs no other Encouragement, but to give all the Effects taken aboard a Pyrate Vessel to the Captors; for in Case of Plunder and Gain, they like it as well from Friends, as Enemies, but are not fond, as Things are carry'd, *of ruining poor Fellowes*, say the *Creoleans, with no Advantage to themselves*.

The Multitude of Men and Vessels, employ'd this Way, in Time of War, in the *West-Indies*, is another Reason, for the Number of Pyrates in a Time of Peace: This cannot be supposed to be a Reflection on any of our *American* Governments, much less on the King himself, by whose Authority such Commissions are granted, because of the Reasona-bleness, and absolute Necessity, there is for the doing of it; yet the Observation is just, for so many idle People employing themselves in Privateers, for the sake of Plunder and Riches, which they always spend as fast as they get, that when the War is over, and they can have no farther Business in the Way of Life they have been used to, they too readily engage in Acts of Pyracy, which being but the same Practice without a Commission, they make very little Distinction betwixt the Lawfulness of one, and the Unlawfulness of the other.

I have not enquired so far back, as to know the Original of this Rover, but I believe he and his Gang, were some Privateer's Men belonging to the Island of *Jamaica*, in the preceding War; his Story is but short, for his Reign was so; an End having been put to his Adventures in good Time, when he was growing strong and formidable. We find him Commander of a Pyrate Sloop of eight Guns, and 80 Men, in the Month of *September*, 1716, cruising off *Jamaica, Cuba, &c.* about which Time he took the *Berkley* Galley, Captain *Saunders*, and plundered him of 1000 l. in Money, and afterwards met with a Sloop call'd the *King Solomon*, from whom he took some Money, and Provisions, besides Goods, to a good Value.

They proceeded after this to the Port of *Cavena*, at the Island of *Cuba*, and in their Way took two Sloops, which they plundered, and let go; and off the Port fell in with a fine Galley, with 20 Guns, call'd the *John* and *Martha*, Captain *Wilson*, which they attacked under the piratical Black-Flag, and made themselves Masters of her. They put some of the Men ashore, and others they detain'd, as they had done several Times, to encrease their Company; but Captain *Martel*, charged Captain *Wilson*, to advise his Owners, that their Ship would answer his Purpose exactly, by taking one Deck down, and as for the Cargo, which consisted chiefly of Logwood and Sugar, he would take Care it should be carry'd to a good Market.

Having fitted up the aforesaid Ship, as they design'd, they mounted her with 22 Guns, 100 Men, and left 25 Hands in the Sloop, and so proceeded to Cruize off the Leeward Islands, where they met with but too much Success. After the taking of a Sloop and a Brigantine, they gave Chase to a stout Ship, which they came up with, and, at Sight of the Pyrate's Flag, she struck to the Robbers, being a Ship of 20 Guns, call'd the *Dolphin*, bound for *Newfoundland*. Captain *Martel* made the Men Prisoners, and carry'd the Ship with him.

The middle of *December* the Pyrates took another Galley in her Voyage home from *Jamaica*, call'd the *Kent*, Captain *Lawton*, and shifted her Provisions aboard their own Ship, and let her go, which obliged her to Sail back to *Jamaica* for a Supply for her Voyage. After this they met with a small Ship and a Sloop, belonging to *Barbadoes*, out of both they took Provisions, and then parted with them, having first taken out some of their Hands, who were willing to be forced to go along with them. The *Greyhound* Galley of *London*, Captain *Evans*, from *Guiney* to *Jamaica*, was the next that had the Misfortune to fall in their Way, which they did not detain long, for as soon as they could get out all her Gold Dust, Elephant's Teeth, and 40 Slaves, they sent her onwards upon her Voyage.

They concluded now, that 'twas high Time to get into Harbour and refit, as well as to get Refreshments themselves, and wait an Opportunity to dispose of their Cargo; therefore 'twas resolved to make the best of their Way to *Santa Crux*, a small Island in the Lattitude of 18, 30, N. ten Mile long, and two broad, lying South-East of *Porto Rico*, belonging to the *French* Settlements. Here they thought they might lye privately enough for some Time, and fit themselves for further Mischief. They met with a Sloop by the Way, which they took along with them, and in the Beginning of the Year 1716-17, they arrived at their Port, having a Ship of 20 Guns, a Sloop of eight, and three Prizes, *viz.* another Ship of 20 Guns, a Sloop of four Guns, and another Sloop last taken; with this little Fleet, they got into a small Harbour, or Road, the N. W. Part of the Island, and warp'd up two Creeks, which were made by a little Island lying within the Bay; (I am the more particular now, because I shall take Leave of the Gentlemen, at this Place.) They had here bare 16 Foot Water, at the deepest, and but 13 or 14, at the shallowest, and nothing but Rocks and Sands without, which secured them from Wind and Sea, and likewise from any considerable Force coming against them.

When they had all got in, the first Thing they had to do, was to Guard themselves in the best Manner they could; they made a Battery of four Guns upon the Island, and another Battery of two Guns on the North Point of the Road, and warp'd in one of the Sloops with eight Guns, at the Mouth of the Channel, to hinder any Vessels from coming in; when this was done they went to Work on their Ship, unrigging, and unloading, in order to Clean, where I shall leave them a while, till I bring other Company to 'em.

In the Month of *November*, 1716, General *Hamilton*, Commander in chief of all the *Leeward Carribee Islands*, sent a Sloop Express to Captain *Hume*, at *Barbadoes*, Commander of his Majesty's Ship, *Scarborough*, of 30 Guns, and 140 Men, to acquaint him, that two Pyrate Sloops of 12 Guns each, molested the Colonies, having plun ered several Vessels. The *Scarborough* had bury'd twenty Men, and had near forty Sick, and therefore was but in ill State to go to Sea: However, Captain *Hume* left his sick Men behind, and sailed to the other Islands, for a supply of Men, taking 20 Soldiers from *Antegoa*; at *Nevis*, he took 10, and 10 at St. *Christophers*, and then sailed to the Island of *Anguilla*, where he learned, that some Time before, 2 such Sloops had been at *Spanish-Town*, otherwise called, one of the *Virgin* Islands: Accordingly, the next Day, the *Scarborough* came to *Spanish-Town*, but could hear no News of the Sloops, only, that they had been there about *Christmas*, (it being then the 15th of *January*.)

Captain *Hume*, finding no Account could be had of these Pyrates, designed to go back, the next Day, to *Barbadoes*; but, it happened, that Night, that a Boat anchor'd there from *Santa Crux*, and informed him, that he saw a Pyrate Ship of 22 or 24 Guns, with other Vessels, going in to the North West Part of the Island aforesaid. The *Scarborough* weigh'd immediately, and the next Morning came in Sight of the Rovers, and their Prizes, and stood to them, but the Pilot refused to venture in with the Ship; all the while the Pyrates fir'd red hot Bullets from the Shore. At length, the Ship came to an Anchor, along Side the Reef, near the Channel, and cannonaded for several Hours, both the Vessels and Batteries: About four in the Afternoon, the Sloop that guarded the Channel, was sunk by the Shot of the Man of War; then she cannonaded the Pyrate Ship of 22 Guns, that lay behind the Island. The next Night, *viz.* the 18th, it falling Calm, Captain *Hume* weigh'd, fearing he might fall on the Reef, and so stood off and on for a Day or two, to block them up. On the 20th, in the Evening, they observed the Man of War to stand off to Sea, and took the Opportunity to warp out, in order to slip away from the Island; but at Twelve o'Clock they run a-ground, and then seeing the *Scarborough* about, standing in again, as their Case was desperate, so they were put into the utmost Confusion; they quitted their Ship, and set her on Fire, with 20 Negroes in her, who were all burnt; 19 of the Pyrates made their Escape in a small Sloop, but the Captain and the rest, with 20 Negroes, betook to the Woods, where 'twas probable they might starve, for we never heard what became of 'em afterwards: Captain *Hume* released the Prisoners, with the Ship and Sloop that remained, and then went after the two Pyrate Sloops first mentioned.

Chap. III
Of Captain *Teach*, alias Black-beard

His Beginning. His Confederacy with Hornygold. The Confederacy broke. Takes a large Guiney Man. Engages the Scarborough Man of War. His Alliance with Major Stede Bonnet. Deposes his new Ally. His Advice to the Major. His Progress and Success. Takes Prizes in Sight of Charles-Town. Sends Ambassadors to the Governor of Carolina, upon an impudent Demand. Runs his Ship aground designedly. His Cruelty to some of his own Companions. Surrenders to the King's Proclamation. The Governor of North-Carolina's exceeding Generosity to him. He marries. The Number of his Wives then living. His conjugal Virtues. Makes a second Excursion in the Way of pirating. Some State Legerdemain betwixt him and the Governor. His modest Behaviour in the River. His Frolicks on Shore. The Merchants apply for a Force against him, and where. A Proclamation with a Reward for taking or killing of Pyrates. Lieutenant Maynard sent in pursuit of him. Black-beard's good Intelligence. The Lieutenant engages Black-beard. A most execrable Health drank by Black-beard. The Fight bloody; the Particulars of it. Black-beard kill'd. His Sloop taken. The Lieutenant's Conduct. A Reflection on the Humours of Seamen. Black-beard's Correspondents discover'd by his Papers. Black-beard's desperate Resolution before the Fight. The Lieutenant and Governor no very good Friends. The Prisoners hang'd. Samuel Odel saved, and why. The good Luck of Israel Hands. Black-beard's mischievous Frolicks. His Beard described. Several Instances if his Wickedness. Some Memorandums taken from his Journal. The Names of the Pyrates kill'd in the Engagement. Of those executed. The Value of the Prize.

Edward Teach was a *Bristol* Man born, but had sailed some Time out of *Jamaica* in Privateers, in the late *French* War; yet tho' he had often distinguished himself for his uncommon Boldness and personal Courage, he was never raised to any Command, till he went a-pirating, which I think was at the latter End of the Year 1716, when Captain *Benjamin Hornigold* put him into a Sloop that he had made Prize of, and with whom he continued in Consortship till a little while before *Hornigold* surrendered.

In the Spring of the Year 1717, *Teach* and *Hornigold* sailed from *Providence*, for the Main of *America*, and took in their Way a Billop from the *Havana*, with 120 Barrels of Flower, as also a Sloop from *Bermuda, Thurbar* Master, from whom they took only some Gallons of Wine, and then let him go; and a Ship from *Madera* to *South-Carolina*, out of which they got Plunder to a considerable Value.

After cleaning on the Coast of *Virginia*, they returned to the *West-Indies*, and in the Latitude of 24, made Prize of a large *French Guiney* Man, bound to *Martinico*, which by *Hornigold*'s Consent, *Teach* went aboard of as Captain, and took a Cruize in her; *Hornigold* returned with his Sloop to *Providence*, where, at the Arrival of Captain *Rogers*, the Governor, he surrendered to Mercy, pursuant to the King's Proclamation.

Blackbeard the Pirate.

    Aboard of this *Guiney* Man *Teach* mounted 40 Guns, and named her the *Queen Ann's Revenge*; and cruising near the Island of St. *Vincent*, took a large Ship, called the *Great Allen*, *Christopher Taylor* Commander; the Pyrates plundered her of what they though fit, put all the Men ashore upon the Island above mentioned, and then set Fire to the Ship.

    A few Days after, *Teach* fell in with the *Scarborough* Man of War, of 30 Guns, who engaged him for some Hours; but she finding the Pyrate well mann'd, and having tried her strength, gave over the Engagement, and returned to *Barbadoes*, the Place of her Station; and *Teach* sailed towards the *Spanish America*.

    In his Way he met with a Pyrate Sloop of ten Guns, commanded by one Major *Bonnet*, lately a Gentleman of good Reputation and Estate in the Island of *Barbadoes*, whom he joyned; but in a few Days after, *Teach*, finding that *Bonnet* knew nothing of a maritime Life, with the Consent of his own Men, put in another Captain, one *Richards*, to Command *Bonnet*'s Sloop, and took the Major on aboard his own Ship, telling him, *that as he had not been used to the Fatigues and Care of such a Post, it would be better for him to decline it, and live easy and at his Pleasure, in such a Ship as his, where he should not be obliged to perform Duty, but follow his own Inclinations.*

At *Turniff*, ten Leagues short of the Bay of *Honduras*, the Pyrates took in fresh Water; and while they were at an Anchor there, they saw a Sloop coming in, whereupon, *Richards* in the Sloop called the *Revenge*, slipped his Cable, and run out to meet her; who upon seeing the black Flag hoisted, struck his Sail and came to, under the Stern of *Teach* the Commadore. She was called the *Adventure*, from *Jamaica, David Harriot* Master. They took him and his Men aboard the great Ship, and sent a Number of other Hands with *Israel Hands*, Master of *Teach*'s Ship, to Man the Sloop for the piratical Account.

The 9th of *April*, they weighed from *Turniff*, having lain there about a Week, and sailed to the Bay, where they found a Ship and four Sloops, three of the latter belonged to *Jonathan Bernard*, of *Jamaica*, and the other to Captain *James*; the Ship was of *Boston*, called the *Protestant Cæsar*, Captain *Wyar* Commander. *Teach* hoisted his Black Colours, and fired a Gun, upon which Captain *Wyar* and all his Men, left their Ship, and got ashore in their Boat. *Teach*'s Quarter-Master, and eight of his Crew, took Possession of *Wyar*'s Ship, and *Richards* secured all the Sloops, one of which they burnt out of spight to the Owner; the *Protestant Cæsar* they also burnt, after they had plundered her, because she belonged to *Boston*, where some Men had been hanged for Pyracy; and the three Sloops belonging to *Bernard* they let go.

From hence the Rovers sailed to *Turkill*, and then to the *Grand Caimanes*, a small Island about thirty Leagues to the Westward of *Jamaica*, where they took a small Turtler, and so to the *Havana*, and from thence to the *Bahama* Wrecks, and from the *Bahama* Wrecks, they sailed to *Carolina*, taking a Brigantine and two Sloops in their Way, where they lay off the Bar of *Charles-Town* for five or six Days. They took here a Ship as she was coming out, bound for *London*, commanded by *Robert Clark*, with some Passengers on Board for *England*; the next Day they took another Vessel coming out of *Charles-Town*, and also two Pinks coming into *Charles-Town*; likewise a Brigantine with 14 Negroes aboard; all which being done in the Face of the Town, struck a great Terror to the whole Province of *Carolina*, having just before been visited by *Vane*, another notorious Pyrate, that they abandoned themselves to Dispair, being in no Condition to resist their Force. They were eight Sail in the Harbour, ready for the Sea, but none dared to venture out, it being almost impossible to escape their Hands. The inward bound Vessels were under the same unhappy Dilemma, so that the Trade of this Place was totally interrupted: What made these Misfortunes heavier to them, was a long expensive War, the Colony had had with the Natives, which was but just ended when these Robbers infested them.

Teach detained all the Ships and Prisoners, and, being in want of Medicines, resolves to demand a Chest from the Government of the Province; accordingly *Richards*, the Captain of the *Revenge* Sloop, with two or three more Pyrates, were sent up along with Mr. *Marks*, one of the Prisoners, whom they had taken in *Clark*'s Ship, and very insolently made their Demands, threatning, that if they did not send immediately the Chest of Medicines, and let the Pyrate-Ambassadors return, without offering any Violence to their Persons, they would murder all their Prisoners, send up their Heads to the Governor, and set the Ships they had taken on Fire.

Whilst Mr. *Marks* was making Application to the Council, *Richards*, and the rest of the Pyrates, walk'd the Streets publicly, in the Sight of all People, who were fired with the utmost Indignation, looking upon them as Robbers and Murtherers, and particularly the Authors of their Wrongs and Oppressions, but durst not so much as think of executing their Revenge, for fear of bringing more Calamities upon themselves, and so they were forced to let the Villains pass with Impunity. The Government were not long in deliberating upon the Message, tho' 'twas the greatest Affront that could have been put upon them; yet for the saving so many Mens Lives, (among them, Mr. *Samuel Wragg*, one of the Council;) they comply'd with the Necessity, and sent aboard a Chest, valued at between 3 and 400 *l.* and the Pyrates went back safe to their Ships.

Blackbeard, (for so *Teach* was generally called, as we shall hereafter show) as soon as he had received the Medicines and his Brother Rogues, let go the Ships and the Prisoners; having first taken out of them in Gold and Silver, about 1500 *l.* Sterling, besides Provisions and other Matters.

From the Bar of *Charles-Town*, they sailed to *North-Carolina*; Captain *Teach* in the Ship, which they called the Man of War, Captain *Richards* and Captain *Hands* in the Sloops, which they termed Privateers, and another Sloop serving them as a Tender. *Teach* began now to think of breaking up the Company, and securing the Money and the best of the Effects for himself, and some others of his Companions he had most Friendship for, and to cheat the rest: Accordingly, on Pretence of running into *Topsail* Inlet to clean, he grounded his Ship, and then, as if it had been done undesignedly, and by Accident; he orders *Hands*'s Sloop to come to his Assistance, and get him off again, which he endeavouring to do, ran the Sloop on Shore near the other, and so were both lost. This done, *Teach* goes into the Tender Sloop, with forty Hands, and leaves the *Revenge* there; then takes seventeen others and Marroons them upon a small sandy Island, about a League from the Main, where there was neither Bird, Beast or Herb for their Subsistance, and where they must have perished if Major *Bonnet* had not two Days after taken them off.

Teach goes up to the Governor of *North-Carolina*, with about twenty of his Men, surrender to his Majesty's Proclamation, and receive Certificates thereof, from his Excellency; but it did not appear that their submitting to this Pardon was from any Reformation of Manners, but only to wait a more favourable Opportunity to play the same Game over again; which he soon after effected, with greater Security to himself, and with much better Prospect of Success, having in this Time cultivated a very good understanding with *Charles Eden*, Esq; the Governor above mentioned.

The first Piece of Service this kind Governor did to *Black-Beard*, was, to give him a Right to the Vessel which he had taken, when he was a pirating in the great Ship called the *Queen Ann's Revenge*; for which purpose, a Court of Vice-Admiralty was held at *Bath-Town*; and, tho' *Teach* had never any Commission in his Life, and the Sloop belonging to the *English* Merchants, and taken in Time of Peace; yet was she condemned as a Prize taken from the *Spaniards*, by the said *Teach*. These Proceedings shew that Governors are but Men.

Before he sailed upon his Adventures, he marry'd a young Creature of about sixteen Years of Age, the Governor performing the Ceremony. As it is a Custom to marry here by a Priest, so it is there by a Magistrate; and this, I have been informed, made *Teach*'s fourteenth Wife, whereof, about a dozen might be still living. His Behaviour in this State, was something extraordinary; for while his Sloop lay in *Okerecock* Inlet, and he ashore at a Plantation, where his Wife lived, with whom after he had lain all Night, it was his Custom to invite five or six of his brutal Companions to come ashore, and he would force her to prostitute her self to them all, one after another, before his Face.

In *June* 1718, he went to Sea, upon another Expedition, and steered his Course towards *Bermudas*; he met with two or three *English* Vessels in his Way, but robbed them only of Provisions, Stores and other Necessaries, for his present Expence; but near the Island aforementioned, he fell in with two *French* Ships, one of them was loaded with Sugar and Cocoa, and the other light, both bound to *Martinico*; the Ship that had no Lading he let go, and putting all the Men of the loaded Ship aboard her, he brought home the other with her Cargo to *North-Carolina*, where the Governor and the Pyrates shared the Plunder.

When *Teach* and his Prize arrived, he and four of his Crew went to his Excellency, and made Affidavit, that they found the *French* Ship at Sea, without a Soul on Board her; and then a Court was called, and the Ship condemned: The Governor had sixty Hogsheads of Sugar for his Dividend, and one Mr. *Knight*, who was his Secretary, and Collector for the Province, twenty, and the rest was shared among the other Pyrates.

The Business was not yet done, the Ship remained, and it was possible one or other might come into the River, that might be acquainted with her, and so discover the Roguery; but *Teach* thought of a Contrivance to prevent this, for, upon a Pretence that she was leaky, and that she might sink, and so stop up the Mouth of the Inlet or Cove where she lay, he obtained an Order from the Governor, to bring her out into the River, and set her on Fire, which was accordingly executed, and she was burnt down to the Water's Edge, her Bottom sunk, and with it, their Fears of her ever rising in Judgment against them.

Captain *Teach*, alias *Black-beard*, passed three or four Months in the River, sometimes lying at Anchor in the Coves, at other Times failing from one Inlet to another, trading with such Sloops as he met, for the Plunder he had taken, and would often give them Presents for Stores and Provisions took from them; that is, when he happened to be in a giving Humour; at other Times he made bold with them, and took what he liked, without saying, *by your Leave*, knowing well, they dared not send him a Bill for the Payment. He often diverted himself with going ashore among the Planters, where he revelled Night and Day: By these he was well received, but whether out of Love or Fear, I cannot say; sometimes he used them courteously enough, and made them Presents of Rum and Sugar, in Recompence of what he took from them; but, as for Liberties (which 'tis said) he and his Companions often took with the Wives and Daughters of the Planters, I cannot take upon me to say, whether he paid them *ad Valorem*, or no. At other Times he carried it in a lordly Manner towards them, and would lay some of them under Contribution; nay, he often proceeded to bully the Governor, not, that I can discover the least Cause of Quarrel betwixt them, but it seemed only to be done, to show he dared do it.

The Sloops trading up and down this River, being so frequently pillaged by *Black-beard*, consulted with the Traders, and some of the best of the Planters, what Course to take; they saw plainly it would be in vain to make any Application to the Governor of *North-Carolina*, to whom it properly belonged to find some Redress; so that if they could not be relieved from some other Quarter *Black-beard* would be like to reign with Impunity, therefore, with as much Secrecy as possible, they sent a Deputation to *Virginia*, to lay the Affair before the Governor of that Colony, and to solicit an armed Force from the Men of War lying there, to take or destroy this Pyrate.

This Governor consulted with the Captains of the two Men of War, *viz.* the *Pearl* and *Lime*, who had lain in St. *James*'s River, about ten Months. It was agreed that the Governor should hire a couple of small Sloops, and the Men of War should Man them; this was accordingly done, and the Command of them given to Mr. *Robert Maynard*, first Lieutenant of the *Pearl*, an experienced Officer, and a Gentleman of great Bravery and Resolution, as will appear by his gallant Behaviour in this Expedition. The Sloops were well mann'd and furnished with Ammunition and small Arms, but had no Guns mounted.

About the Time of their going out, the Governor called an Assembly, in which it was resolved to publish a Proclamation, offering certain Rewards to any Person or Persons, who, within a Year after that Time, should take or destroy any Pyrate: The original Proclamation being in our Hands, is as follows.

> By his Majesty's Lieutenant Governor, and Commander in Chief, of the Colony and Dominion of *Virginia*,
>
> A PROCLAMATION,
>
> Publishing the Rewards given for apprehending, or killing, Pyrates.
>
> W*Hereas, by an Act of Assembly, made at a Session of Assembly, begun at the Capital in* Williamsburgh, *the eleventh Day of* November, *in the fifth Year of his Majesty's Reign, entituled,* An Act to encourage the apprehending and destroying of Pyrates: *It is, amongst other Things enacted, that all and every Person, or Persons, who, from and after the fourteenth Day of* November, *in the Year of our Lord one thousand seven hundred and eighteen, and before the fourteenth Day of* November, *which shall be in the Year of our Lord one thousand seven hundred and nineteen, shall take any Pyrate, or Pyrates, on the Sea or Land, or in Case of Resistance, shall kill any such Pyrate, or Pyrates, between the Degrees of thirty four, and thirty nine, of Northern Latitude, and within one hundred Leagues of the Continent of* Virginia, *or within the Provinces of* Virginia, *or* North Carolina, *upon the Conviction, or making due Proof of the killing of all, and every such Pyrate, and Pyrates, before the Governor and Council, shall be entitled to have, and receive out of*

the public Money, in the Hands of the Treasurer of this Colony, the several Rewards following; that is to say, for Edward Teach, commonly call'd Captain Teach, or Black-Beard, one hundred Pounds, for every other Commander of a Pyrate Ship, Sloop, or Vessel, forty Pounds; for every Lieutenant, Master, or Quarter-Master, Boatswain, or Carpenter, twenty Pounds; for every other inferior Officer, fifteen Pounds, and for every private Man taken on Board such Ship, Sloop, or Vessel, ten Pounds; and, that for every Pyrate, which shall be taken by any Ship, Sloop or Vessel, belonging to this Colony, or North-Carolina, within the Time aforesaid, in any Place whatsoever, the like Rewards shall be paid according to the Quality and Condition of such Pyrates. Wherefore, for the Encouragement of all such Persons as shall be willing to serve his Majesty, and their Country, in so just and honourable an Undertaking, as the suppressing a Sort of People, who may be truly called Enemies to Mankind: I have thought fit, with the Advice and Consent of his Majesty's Council, to issue this Proclamation, hereby declaring, the said Rewards shall be punctually and justly paid, in current Money of Virginia, according to the Directions of the said Act. And, I do order and appoint this Proclamation, to be published by the Sheriffs, at their respective County-Houses, and by all Ministers and Readers, in the several Churches and Chappels, throughout this Colony.

Given at our Council-Chamber at *Williamsburgh*, this 24th Day of *November*, 1718, in the fifth Year of his Majesty's Reign.
GOD SAVE THE KING.
A. SPOTSWOOD.

The 17th of *November*, 1718, the Lieutenant sail'd from *Kicquetan*, in *James* River in *Virginia*, and, the 21st in the Evening, came to the Mouth of *Okerecock* Inlet, where he got Sight of the Pyrate. This Expedition was made with all imaginable Secrecy, and the Officer manag'd with all the Prudence that was necessary, stopping all Boats and Vessels he met with, in the River, from going up, and thereby preventing any Intelligence from reaching *Black-Beard*, and receiving at the same time an Account from them all, of the Place where the Pyrate was lurking; but notwithstanding this Caution, *Black-beard* had Information of the Design, from his Excellency of the Province; and his Secretary, Mr. *Knight*, wrote him a Letter, particularly concerning it, intimating, *That he had sent him four of his Men, which were all he could meet with, in or about Town, and so bid him be upon his Guard.* These Men belonged to *Black-beard*, and were sent from *Bath-Town* to *Okerecock* Inlet, where the Sloop lay, which is about 20 Leagues.

Black-beard had heard several Reports, which happened not to be true, and so gave the less Credit to this, nor was he convinced till he saw the Sloops: Whereupon he put his Vessel in a Posture of Defence; he had no more than twenty five Men on Board, tho' he gave out to all the Vessels he spoke with, that he had 40. When he had prepared for Battle, he set down and spent the Night in drinking with the Master of a trading Sloop, who, 'twas thought, had more Business with *Teach*, than he should have had.

Lieutenant *Maynard* came to an Anchor, for the Place being shoal, and the Channel intricate, there was no getting in, where *Teach* lay, that Night; but in the Morning he weighed, and sent his Boat a-head of the Sloops to sound; and coming within Gun-Shot of the Pyrate, received his Fire; whereupon *Maynard* hoisted the King's Colours, and stood directly towards him, with the best Way that his Sails and Oars could made. *Black-beard* cut his Cable, and endeavoured to make a running Fight, keeping a continual Fire at his Enemies, with his Guns; Mr. *Maynard* not having any, kept a constant Fire with small Arms, while some of his Men laboured at their Oars. In a little Time *Teach*'s Sloop ran a-ground, and Mr. *Maynard*'s drawing more Water than that of the Pyrate, he could not come near him; so he anchored within half Gun-Shot of the Enemy, and, in order to lighten his Vessel, that he might run him aboard, the Lieutenant ordered all his Ballast to be thrown over-board, and all the Water to be staved, and then weigh'd and stood for him; upon which *Black-beard* hail'd him in this rude Manner : *Damn you for Villains, who are you? And, from whence came you?* The Lieutenant made him Answer, *You may see by our Colours we are no Pyrates.* *Black-beard* bid him send his Boat on Board, that he might see who he was; but Mr. *Maynard* reply'd thus; *I cannot spare my Boat, but I will come aboard of you as soon as I can, with my Sloop.* Upon this, *Black-beard* took a Glass of Liquor, and drank to him with these Words: *Damnation seize my Soul if I give you Quarters, or take any from you.* In Answer to which, Mr. *Maynard* told him, *That he expected no Quarters from him, nor should he give him any.*

By this time *Black-beard*'s Sloop fleeted, as Mr. *Maynard*'s Sloops were rowing towards him, which being not above a Foot high in the Waste, and consequently the Men all exposed, as they came near together, (there being hitherto little or no Execution done, on either Side,) the Pyrate fired a Broadside, charged with all Manner of small Shot. —— A fatal Stroke to them! The Sloop the Lieutenant was in, having twenty Men killed and wounded, and the other Sloop nine : This could not be help'd, for there being no Wind, they were oblig'd to keep to their Oars, otherwise the Pyrate would have got away from him, which, it seems, the Lieutenant was resolute to prevent.

After this unlucky Blow, *Black-beard*'s Sloop fell Broadside to the Shore; Mr. *Maynard*'s other Sloop, which was called the *Ranger*, fell a-stern, being, for the present, disabled; so the Lieutenant finding his own Sloop had Way, and would soon be on Board of *Teach*, he ordered all his Men down, for fear of another Broadside, which must have been their Destruction, and the loss of their Expedition. Mr. *Maynard* was the only Person that kept the Deck, except the Man at the Helm, whom he directed to lye down snug, and the Men in the Hold were ordered to get their Pistols and their Swords ready for close fighting, and to come up at his Command; in order to which, two Ladders were placed in the Hatch-Way for the more Expedition. When the Lieutenant's Sloop boarded the other, Captain *Teach*'s Men threw in several new fashioned sort of Grenadoes, *viz.* Case Bottles fill'd with Powder, and small Shot, Slugs, and Pieces of Lead or Iron, with a quick Match in the Mouth of it, which being lighted without Side, presently runs into the Bottle to the Powder, and as it is instantly thrown on Board, generally does great Execution, besides putting all the Crew into a Confusion; but by good Providence, they had not that Effect here; the Men being in the Hold, and *Black-beard* seeing few or no Hands aboard, told his Men, *That they were all knock'd on the Head, except three or four; and therefore*, says he, *let's jump on Board, and cut them to Pieces.*

Whereupon, under the Smoak of one of the Bottles just mentioned, *Black-beard* enters with fourteen Men, over the Bows of *Maynard*'s Sloop, and were not seen by him till the Air cleared; however, he just then gave a Signal to his Men, who all rose in an Instant, and attack'd the Pyrates with as much Bravery as ever was done upon such an Occasion: *Black-beard* and the Lieutenant fired the first Pistol at each other, by which the Pyrate received a Wound, and then engaged with Swords, till the Lieutenant's unluckily broke, and stepping back to cock a Pistol, *Black-beard*, with his Cutlash, was striking at that instant, that one of *Maynard*'s Men gave him a terrible Wound in the Neck and Throat, by which the Lieutenant came off with a small Cut over his Fingers.

They were now closely and warmly engaged, the Lieutenant and twelve Men, against *Black-beard* and fourteen, till the Sea was tinctur'd with Blood round the Vessel; *Black-beard* received a Shot into his Body from the Pistol that Lieutenant *Maynard* discharg'd, yet he stood his Ground, and sought with great Fury, till he received five and twenty Wounds, and five of them by Shot. At length, as he was cocking another Pistol, having fired several before, he fell down dead; by which Time eight more out of the fourteen dropp'd, and all the rest, much wounded, jump'd over-board, and call'd out for Quarters, which was granted, tho' it was only prolonging their Lives for a few Days. The Sloop *Ranger* came up, and attack'd the Men that remain'd in *Black-beard*'s Sloop, with equal Bravery, till they likewise cry'd for Quarters.

Here was an End of that couragious Brute, who might have pass'd in the World for a Heroe, had he been employ'd in a good Cause; his Destruction, which was of such Consequence to the Plantations, was entirely owing to the Conduct and Bravery of Lieutenant *Maynard* and his Men, who might have destroy'd him with much less Loss, had they had a Vessel with great Guns; but they were obliged to use small Vessels, because the Holes and Places he lurk'd in, would not admit of others of greater Draught; and it was no small Difficulty for this Gentleman to get to him, having grounded his Vessel, at least, a hundred times, in getting up the River, besides other Discouragements, enough to have turn'd back any Gentleman without Dishonour, who was less resolute and bold than this Lieutenant. The Broadside that did so much Mischief before they boarded, in all Probability saved the rest from Destruction; for before that *Teach* had little or no Hopes of escaping, and therefore had posted a resolute Fellow, a Negroe, whom he had bred up, with a lighted Match, in the Powder-Room, with Commands to blow up, when he should give him Orders, which was as soon as the Lientenant and his Men could have entered, that so he might have destroy'd his Conquerors: and when the Negro found how it went with *Black-beard*, he could hardly be perswaded from the rash Action, by two Prisoners that were then in the Hold of the Sloop.

What seems a little odd, is, that some of these Men, who behaved so bravely against *Black-beard*, went afterwards a pirating themselves, and one of them was taken along with *Roberts*; but I do not find that any of them were provided for, except one that was hanged; but this is a Digression.

The Lieutenant caused *Black-beard*'s Head to be severed from his Body, and hung up at the Boltsprit End, then he failed to *Bath-Town*, to get Relief for his wounded Men.

It must be observed, that in rummaging the Pyrate's Sloop, they found several Letters and written Papers, which discovered the Correspondence betwixt Governor *Eden*, the Secretary and Collector, and also some Traders at *New-York*, and *Black-beard*. It is likely he had Regard enough for his Friends, to have destroyed these Papers before the Action, in order to hinder them from falling into such Hands, where the Discovery would be of no Use, either to the Interest or Reputation of these fine Gentlemen, if it had not been his fixed Resolution to have blown up together, when he found no possibility of escaping.

When the Lieutenant came to *Bath-Town*, he made bold to seize in the Governor's Store-House, the sixty Hogsheads of Sugar, and from honest Mr. *Knight*, twenty; which it seems was their Dividend of the Plunder taken in the *French* Ship; the latter did not long survive this shameful Discovery, for being apprehensive that he might be called to an Account for these Trifles, fell sick with the Fright, and died in a few Days.

After the wounded Men were pretty well recover'd, the Lieutenant sailed back to the Men of War in *James River*, in *Virginia*, with *Black-beard*'s Head still hanging at the Bolt-sprit End, and five-teen Prisoners, thirteen of whom were hanged. It appearing upon Tryal, that one of them, *viz. Samuel Odell*, was taken out of the trading Sloop, but the Night before the Engagement. This poor Fellow was a little unlucky at his first entering upon his new Trade, there appearing no less than 70 Wounds upon him after the Action, notwithstanding which, he lived, and was cured of them all. The other Person that escaped the Gallows, was one *Israel Hands*, the Master of *Black-beard*'s Sloop, and formerly Captain of the same, before the *Queen Ann's Revenge* was lost in *Topsail* Inlet.

The aforesaid *Hands* happened not to be in the Fight, but was taken afterwards ashore at *Bath-Town*, having been sometime before disabled by *Black-beard*, in one of his savage Humours, after the following Manner. — One Night drinking in his Cabin with *Hands*, the Pilot, and another Man; *Black-beard* without any Provocation privately draws out a small Pair of Pistols, and cocks them under the Table, which being perceived by the Man, he withdrew and went upon Deck, leaving *Hands*, the Pilot, and the Captain together. When the Pistols were ready, he blew out the Candle, and crossing his Hands, discharged them at his Company; *Hands*, the Master, was shot thro' the Knee, and lam'd for Life; the other Pistol did no Execution.

— Being asked the meaning of this, he only answered, by damning them, that *if he did not now and then kill one of them, they would forget who he was.*

Hands being taken, was try'd and condemned, but just as he was about to be executed, a Ship arrives at *Virginia* with a Proclamation for prolonging the Time of his Majesty's Pardon, to such of the Pyrates as should surrender by a limited Time therein expressed: Notwithstanding the Sentence, *Hands* pleaded the Pardon, and was allowed the Benefit of it, and is alive at this Time in *London*, begging his Bread.

Now that we have given some Account of *Teach*'s Life and Actions, it will not be amiss, that we speak of his Beard, since it did not a little contribute towards making his Name so terrible in those Parts.

Plutarch, and other grave Historians have taken Notice, that several great Men amongst the *Romans*, took their Sir-Names from certain odd Marks in their Countenances; as *Cicero*, from a Mark or Vetch on his Nose; so our Heroe, Captain *Teach*, assumed the Cognomen of *Black-beard*, from that large Quantity of Hair, which, like a frightful Meteor, covered his whole Face, and frightened *America* more than any Comet that has appeared there a long Time.

This Beard was black, which he suffered to grow of an extravagant Length; as to Breadth, it came up to his Eyes; he was accustomed to twist it with Ribbons, in small Tails, after the Manner of our Ramilies Wiggs, and turn them about his Ears: In Time of Action, he wore a Sling over his Shoulders, with three brace of Pistols, hanging in Holsters like Bandaliers; and stuck lighted Matches under his Hat, which appearing on each Side of his Face, his Eyes naturally looking fierce and wild, made him altogether such a Figure, that Imagination cannot form an Idea of a Fury, from Hell, to look more frightful.

If he had the look of a Fury, his Humours and Passions were suitable to it; we shall relate two or three more of his Extravagancies, which we omitted in the Body of his History, by which it will appear, to what a Pitch of Wickedness, human Nature may arrive, if it's Passions are not checked.

In the Common wealth of Pyrates, he who goes the greatest Length of Wickedness, is looked upon with a kind of Envy amongst them, as a Person of a more extraordinary Gallantry, and is thereby entitled to be distinguished by some Post, and if such a one has but Courage, he must certainly be a great Man. The Hero of whom we are writing, was thoroughly accomplished this Way, and some of his Frolicks of Wickedness, were so extravagant, as if he aimed at making his Men believe he was a Devil incarnate; for being one Day at Sea, and a little flushed with drink: — *Come*, says he, *let us make a Hell of our own, and try how long we can bear it*; accordingly he, with two or three others, went down into the Hold, and closing up all the Hatches, filled several Pots full of Brimstone, and other combustible Matter, and set it on Fire, and so continued till they were almost suffocated, when some of the Men cried out for Air; at length he opened the Hatches, not a little pleased that he held out the longest.

The Night before he was killed, he set up and drank till the Morning, with some of his own Men, and the Master of a Merchant-Man, and having had Intelligence of the two Sloops coming to attack him, as has been before observed; one of his Men asked him, in Case any thing should happen to him in the Engagement with the Sloops, whether his Wife knew where he had buried his Money? He answered, *That no Body but himself and the Devil, knew where it was, and the longest Liver should take all*.

Those of his Crew who were taken alive, told a Story which may appear a little incredible; however, we think it will not be fair to omit it, since we had it from their own Mouths. That once upon a Cruize, they found out that they had a Man on Board more than their Crew; such a one was seen several Days amongst them, sometimes below, and sometimes upon Deck, yet no Man in the Ship could give an Account who he was, or from whence he came; but that he disappeared a little before they were cast away in their great Ship, but, it seems, they verily believed it was the Devil.

One would think these Things should induce them to reform their Lives, but so many Reprobates together, encouraged and spirited one another up in their Wickedness, to which a continual Course of drinking did not a little contribute; for in *Black-beard*'s Journal, which was taken, there were several Memorandums of the following Nature, found writ with his own Hand. — *Such a Day, Rum all out: — Our Company somewhat sober: — A damn'd Confusion amongst us! — Rogues a plotting; — great Talk of Separation. — So I look'd sharp for a Prize; — such a Day took* one, with a great deal of Liquor on Board, so kept the Company hot, damned hot, then all Things went well again.

Thus it was these Wretches passed their Lives, with very little Pleasure or Satisfaction, in the Possession of what they violently take away from others, and sure to pay for it at last, by an ignominious Death.

The Names of the Pyrates killed in the Engagement, are as follow.

> *Edward Teach*, Commander.
> *Phillip Morton*, Gunner.
> *Garrat Gibbens*, Boatswain.
> *Owen Roberts*, Carpenter.
> *Thomas Miller*, Quarter-Master.
> *John Husk*,
> *Joseph Curtice*,
> *Joseph Brooks*, (1)
> *Nath. Jackson*.

All the rest, except the two last, were wounded and afterwards hanged in *Virginia*.

> *John Carnes*,
> *Joseph Brooks, (2)*
> *James Blake*,
> *John Gills*,
> *Thomas Gates*,
> *James White*,
> *Richard Stiles*,
> *Caesar*,
> *Joseph Philips*,
> *James Robbins*,
> *John Martin*,
> *Edward Salter*,
> *Stephen Daniel*,
> *Richard Greensail*.
> *Israel Hands*, pardoned.
> *Samuel Odel*, acquited.

There were in the Pyrate Sloops, and ashore in a Tent, near where the Sloops lay, 25 Hogsheads of Sugar, 11 Teirces, and 145 Bags of Cocoa, a Barrel of Indigo, and a Bale of Cotton; which, with what was taken from the Governor and Secretary, and the Sale of the Sloop, came to 2500 l. besides the Rewards paid by the Governor of *Virginia*, pursuant to his Proclamation; all which was divided among the Companies of the two Ships, *Lime* and *Pearl*, that lay in *James* River; the brave Fellows that took them coming in for no more than their Dividend amongst the rest, and was paid it within these three Months.

Chap. IV
Of Major *Stede Bonnet*, And his Crew

Bred a Gentleman. Supposed to be disorder'd in his Senses. His Beginning as a Pyrate, ib. Takes Prizes. Divisions in his Crew. Meets Black-beard. Is deposed from his Command. His melancholy Reflections. Surrenders to the King's Proclamation. His new Project. Saves some Pyrates marroon'd. Begins the old Trade again. An Account of Prizes taken by him. Colonel Rhet goes in Quest of Pyrates. Yates the Pyrate surrenders. An Engagement betwixt Colonel Rhet and Major Bonnet. An Account of the kill'd and wounded. The Prisoners carried to Charles-Town. The Major and the Master Escape, ib. Taken again by Colonel Rhet. A Court of Vice-Admiralty held. The Names of those arraign'd. The Form of their Indictment. Their Defence. The Names of those who received Sentence. An excelleot Speech made by the Lord Chief Justice on pronouncing Sentence on the Major.

The Major was a Gentleman of good Reputation in the Island of *Barbadoes*, was Master of a plentiful Fortune, and had the Advantage of a liberal Education. He had the least Temptation of any Man to follow such a Course of Life, from the Condition of his Circumstances. It was very surprizing to every one, to hear of the Major's Enterprize, in the Island were he liv'd; and as he was generally esteem'd and honoured, before he broke out into open Acts of Pyracy, so he was afterwards rather pitty'd than condemned, by those that were acquainted with him, believing that this Humour of going a pirating, proceeded from a Disorder in his Mind, which had been but too visible in him, some Time before this wicked Undertaking; and which is said to have been occasioned by some Discomforts he found in a married State; be that as it will, the Major was but ill qualify'd for the Business, as not understanding maritime Affairs.

However, he fitted out a Sloop with ten Guns and 70 Men, entirely at his own Expence, and in the Night-Time sailed from *Barbadoes*. He called his Sloop the *Revenge*; his first Cruize was off the Capes of *Virginia*, where he took several Ships, and plundered them of their Provisions, Cloaths, Money, Ammunition, *&c.* in particular the *Anne*, Captain *Montgomery*, from *Glascow*; the *Turbet* from *Barbadoes*, which for Country sake, after they had taken out the principal Part of the Lading, the Pyrate Crew set her on Fire; the *Endeavour*, Captain *Scot*, from *Bristol*, and the *Young* from *Leith*. From hence they went to *New-York*, and off the East End of *Long-Island*, took a Sloop bound for the *West-Indies*, after which they stood in and landed some Men at *Gardner's Island*, but in a peaceable Manner, and bought Provisions for the Company's Use, which they paid for, and so went off again without Molestation.

Some Time after, which was in *August* 1717, *Bonnet* came off the Bar of *South-Carolina*, and took a Sloop and a Brigantine bound in; the Sloop belonged to *Barbadoes, Joseph Palmer* Master, laden with Rum, Sugar and Negroes; and the Brigantine came from *New-England*, *Thomas Porter* Master, whom they plundered, and then dismiss'd; but they sailed away with the Sloop, and at an Inlet in *North-Carolina* careened by her, and then set her on Fire.

After the Sloop had cleaned, they put to Sea, but came to no Resolution what Course to take; the Crew were divided in their Opinions, some being for one Thing, and some another, so that nothing but Confusion seem'd to attend all their Schemes.

The Major was no Sailor as was said before, and therefore had been obliged to yield to many Things that were imposed on him, during their Undertaking, for want of a competent Knowledge in maritime Affairs; at length happening to fall in Company with another Pyrate, one *Edward Teach*, (who for his remarkable black ugly Beard, was more commonly called *Black-Beard*:) This Fellow was a good Sailor, but a most cruel hardened Villain, bold and daring to the last Degree, and would not stick at the perpetrating the most abominable Wickedness imaginable; for which he was made Chief of that execrable Gang, that it might be said that his Post was not unduly filled, *Black-beard* being truly the Superior in Roguery, of all the Company, as has been already related.

To him *Bonnet*'s Crew joined in Consortship, and *Bonnet* himself was laid aside, notwithstanding the Sloop was his own; he went aboard *Black-beard*'s Ship, not concerning himself with any of their Affairs, where he continued till she was lost in *Topsail* Inlet, and one *Richards* was appointed Captain in his Room. The Major now faw his Folly, but could not help himself, which made him Melancholy; he reflected upon his past Course of Life, and was confounded with Shame, when he thought upon what he had done: His Behaviour was taken Notice of by the other Pyrates, who liked him never the better for it; and he often declared to some of them, that he would gladly leave off that Way of Living, being fully tired of it; but he should be ashamed to see the Face of any *English* Man again; therefore if he could get to *Spain* or *Portugal*, where he might be undiscovered, he would spend the Remainder of his Days in either of those Countries, otherwise he must continue with them as long as he lived.

When *Black-beard* lost his Ship at *Topsail* Inlet, and surrendered to the King's Proclamation, *Bonnet* reassumed the Command of his own Sloop, *Revenge*, goes directly away to *Bath-Town* in *North-Carolina*, surrenders likewise to the King's Pardon, and receives a Certificate. The War was now broke out between the *Tripple* Allies and *Spain*; so Major *Bonnet* gets a Clearence for his Sloop at *North-Carlina*, to go to the Island of St. *Thomas*, with a Design (at least it was pretended so) to get the Emperor's Commission, to go a Privateering upon the *Spaniards*. When *Bonnet* came back to *Topsail* Inlet, he found that *Teach* and his Gang were gone, and that had taken all the Money, small Arms and Effects of Value out of the great Ship, and set ashore on a small sandy Island above a League from the Main, seventeen Men, no doubt with a Design they should perish, there being no Inhabitant, or Provisions to subsist withal, nor any Boat or Materials to build or make any kind of Launch or Vessel, to escape from that desolate Place: They remained there two Nights and one Day, without Subsistance, or the least Prospect of any, expecting nothing else but a lingering Death; when to their inexpressable Comfort, they saw Redemption at Hand; for Major *Bonnet* happening to get Intelligence of their being there, by two of the Pyrates who had escaped *Teach*'s Cruelty, and had got to a poor little Village at the upper End of the Harbour, sent his Boat to make Discovery of the Truth of the Matter, which the poor Wretches seeing, made a signal to them, and they were all brought on Board *Bonnet*'s Sloop.

Major *Bonnet* told all his Company, that he would take a Commission to go against the *Spaniards*, and to that End, was going to St. *Thomas*'s therefore if they would go with him, they should be welcome; whereupon they all consented, but as the Sloop was preparing to sail, a Bom-Boat, that brought Apples and Sider to sell to the Sloop's Men, informed them, that Captain *Teach* lay at *Ocricock* Inlet, with only 18 or 20 Hands. *Bonnet*, who bore him a mortal Hatred for some Insults offered him, went immediately in pursuit of *Black-beard*, but it happened too late, for he missed of him there, and after four Days Cruize, hearing no father News of him, they steered their Course towards *Virginia*.

In the Month of *July*, these Adventurers came off the Capes, and meeting with a Pink with a Stock of Provisions on Board, which they happened to be in Want of, they took out of her ten or twelve Barrels of Pork, and about 400 Weight of Bread; but because they would not have this set down to the Account of Pyracy, they gave them eight or ten Casks of Rice, and an old Cable, in lieu thereof.

Two Days afterwards they chased a Sloop of sixty Ton, and took her two Leagues off of Cape *Henry*; they were so happy here as to get a Supply of Liquor to their Victuals, for they brought from her two Hogsheads of Rum, and as many of Molosses, which, it seems, they had need of, tho' they had not ready Money to purchase them: What Security they intended to give, I can't tell, but *Bonnet* sent eight Men to take Care of the Prize Sloop, who, perhaps, not caring to make Use of those accustom'd Freedoms, took the first Opportunity to go off with her, and *Bonnet* (who was pleased to have himself called Captain *Thomas*,) saw them no more.

After this, the Major threw off all Restraint, and though he had just before received his Majesty's Mercy, in the Name of *Stede Bonnet*, he relaps'd in good Earnest into his old Vocation, by the Name of Captain *Thomas*, and recommenced a down-right Pyrate, by taking and plundering all the Vessels he met with: He took off Cape *Henry*, two Ships from *Virginia*, bound to *Glascow*, out of which they had very little besides an hundred Weight of Tobacco. The next Day they took a small Sloop bound from *Virginia* to *Bermudas*, which supply'd them with twenty Barrels of Pork, some Bacon, and they gave her in return, two Barrels of Rice, and a Hogshead of Molossus; out of this Sloop two Men enter'd voluntarily. The next they took was another *Virginia* Man, bound to *Glascow*, out of which they had nothing of Value, save only a few Combs, Pins and Needles, and gave her instead thereof, a Barrel of Pork, and two Barrels of Bread.

From *Virginia* they sailed to *Philadelphia*, and in the Latitude of 38 North, they took a Scooner, coming from *North-Carolina*, bound to *Boston*, they had out of her only two Dozen of Calf-Skins, to make Covers for Guns, and two of their Hands, and detained her some Days. All this was but small Game, and seem'd as if they design'd only to make Provision for their Sloop against they arrived at St. *Thomas*'s; for they hitherto had dealt favourably with all that were so unhappy as so fall into their Hands; but those that came after, fared not so well, for in the Latitude of 32, off of *Delaware* River, near *Philadelphia*, they took two Snows bound to *Bristol*, out of whom they got some Money, besides Goods, perhaps to the Value of 150 Pounds; at the same Time they took a Sloop of sixty Tons bound from *Philadelphia* to *Barbadoes*, which after taking some Goods out, they dismissed along with the Snows.

The 29th Day of *July*, Captain *Thomas* took a Sloop of 50 Tons, six or seven Leagues off *Delaware* Bay, bound from *Philadelphia* to *Barbadoes, Thomas Read* Master, loaden with Provisions, which they kept, and put four or five of their Hands on Board her. The last Day of *July*, they took another Sloop of 60 Tons, commanded by *Peter Manwaring*, bound from *Antegoa* to *Philadelphia*, which they likewise kept with all the Cargo, consisting chiefly of Rum, Molosses, Sugar, Cotton, Indigo, and about 25 Pound in Money, valued in all to 500 Pound.

The last Day of *July*, our Rovers with the Vessels last taken, left *Delaware* Bay, and sailed to Cape *Fear* River, where they staid too long for their Safety, for the Pyrate Sloop which they now new named the *Royal James*, proved very leaky, so that they were obliged to remain here almost two Months, to refit and repair their Vessel: They took in this River a small Shallop, which they ripped up to mend the Sloop, and retarded the further Prosecution of their Voyage, as before mentioned, till the News came to *Carolina*, of a Pyrate Sloop's being there to carreen with her Prizes.

Upon this Information, the Council of *South-Carolina* was alarmed, and apprehended they should receive another Visit from them speedily; to prevent which, Colonel *William Rhet*, of the same Province, waited on the Governor, and generously offered himself to go with two Sloops to attack this Pyrate; which the Governor readily accepted, and accordingly gave the Colonel a Commission and full Power, to fit such Vessels as he thought proper for the Design.

In a few Days two Sloops were equipped and manned: The *Henry* with 8 Guns and 70 Men, commanded by Captain *John Masters*, and the *Sea Nymph*, with 8 Guns and 60 Men, commanded by Captain *Fayrer Hall*, both under the entire Direction and Command of the aforesaid Colonel *Rhet*, who, on the 14th of *September*, went on Board the *Henry*, and, with the other Sloop, sailed from *Charles-Town* to *Swillivants* Island, to put themselves in order for the Cruize. Just then arrived a small Ship from *Antigoa*, one *Cock* Master, with an Account, that in Sight of the Bar he was taken and plundered by one *Charles Vane*, a Pyrate, in a Brigantine of 12 Guns and 90 Men; and who had also taken two other Vessels bound in there, one a small Sloop, Captain *Dill* Master, from *Barbadoes*; the other a Brigantine, Captain *Thompson* Master, from *Guiney*, with ninety odd Negroes, which they took out of the Vessel, and put on Board another Sloop then under the Command of one *Yeats*, his Consort, with 25 Men. This prov'd fortunate to the Owners of the *Guiney* Man, for *Yea's* having often attempted to quit this Course of Life, took an Opportunity in the Night, to leave *Vane* and to run into *North-Edisto* River, to the Southward of *Charles-Town*, and surrendered to his Majesty's Pardon. The Owners got their Negroes, and *Yeats* and his Men had Certificates given them from the Government.

George Rose, late of *Glascow*, Mariner.
George Dunkin, late of *Glascow*, Mariner.
*Thomas Nicholas, late of *London*, Mariner.
John Ridge, late of *London*, Mariner.
Matthew King, late of *Jamaica*, Mariner.
Daniel Perry, late of *Guernsey*, Mariner.
Henry Virgin, late of *Bristol*, Mariner.
James Robbins, alias *Rattle*, late of *London*, Mariner.
James Mullet, alias *Millet*, late of *London*, Mariner.
Thomas Price, late of *Bristol*, Mariner.
James Wilson, late of *Dublin*, Mariner.
John Lopez, late of *Oporto*, Mariner.
Zachariah Long, late of the Province of *Holland*, Mariner.
Job Bayly, late of *London*, Mariner.
John-William Smith, late of *Charles-Town, Carolina*, Mariner.
Thomas Carman, late of *Maidstone* in *Kent*, Mariner.
John Thomas, late of *Jamaica*, Mariner.
William Morrison, late of *Jamaica*, Mariner.
Samuel Booth, late of *Charles-Town*, Mariner.
William Hewet, late of *Jamaica*, Mariner.
John Levit, late of *North-Carolina*, Mariner.
William Livers, alias *Evis*.
John Brierly, alias *Timberhead*, late of *Bath-Town* in *North Carolina*, Mariner.
Robert Boyd, late of *Bath-Town* aforesaid, Mariner.
*Rowland Sharp, of *Bath-Town*, Mariner.
*Jonathan Clarke, late of *Charles-Town, South Carolina*, Mariner.
*Thomas Gerrard, late of *Antegoa*, Mariner.

And all, except the three last, and *Thomas Nicholas*, were found Guilty, and received Sentence of Death.

They were most of them try'd upon two Indictments, as follows.

T*HE Jurors for our Sovereign Lord the King, do upon their Oath present, that* Stede Bonnet, *late of* Barbadoes, *Mariner*, Robert Tucker, &c. &c. *The 2d Day of* August, *in the fifth Year of the Reign of our Sovereign Lord* George, &c. *By Force of Arms upon the High-Sea, in a certain Place called Cape* James, &c. *did piratically, and fellonionsly set upon, break, board, and enter, a certain Merchant Sloop, called the* Frances, Peter Manwaring *Commander, by Force*, &c. *upon the High-Sea, in a certain Place, called Cape* James, *alias Cape* Inlope, *about two Miles distant from the Shore, in the Lattitude of* 39, *or thereabouts; and within the Jurisdiction of the Court of Vice-Admiralty, of* South-Carolina, *being a Sloop of certain Persons, (to the Jurors, unknown) and then, and there, piratically, and fellonionsly did make an Assault, in, and upon the said* Peter Manwaring, *and others his Mariners, (whose Names to the Jurors aforesaid, are unknown,) in the same Sloop, against the Peace of God, and of our said now Sovereign Lord the King, then, and there being, piratically and fellonionsly, did put the aforesaid* Peter Manwaring, *and others, his Mariners, of the same Sloop, in the Sloop aforesaid, then being, in corporal Fear of their Lives, then and there, in the Sloop aforesaid, upon the* High-Sea, *in the Place aforesaid, called Cape* James, *alias Cape* Inlopen, *about two Miles from the Shore, in the Lattitude of* 39, *or thereabouts, as aforesaid, and within the Jurisdiction aforesaid; piratically, and fellonionsly, did steal, take, and carry away the said Merchant Sloop, called the* Frances, *and also twenty six Hogsheads*, &c. &c. &c. *being found in the aforesaid Sloop, in the Custody and Possession of the said* Peter Manwaring, *and others, his Mariners of the said Sloop, and from their Custody and Possession, then and there, upon the High-Sea aforesaid, called Cape* James, *alias Cape* Inlopen, *as aforesaid, and within the Jurisdiction aforesaid, against the Peace of our now Sovereign Lord the King, his Crown and Dignity.*

This was the Form of the Indictments they were arraigned upon, and tho' they might have proved several more Facts upon the major Part of the Crew, the Court thought fit to prosecute but two; the other was for seizing in a piratical and felonious Manner, the Sloop *Fortune, Thomas Read* Commander; which Indictment running in the same Form with the above-mentioned, it will be unnecessary to say more of it.

All the Prisoners arraigned, pleaded Not Guilty, and put themselves upon their Tryals, except *James Wilson*, and *John Levit*, who pleaded Guilty to both Indictments, and *Daniel Perry*, to one only. The Major would have gone through both the Indictments at once, which the Court not admitting, he pleaded Not Guilty to both Indictments, but being convicted of one, he retracted his former Plea to the second Indictment, and pleaded Guilty to it.

The Prisoners made little or no Defence, every one pretending only that they were taken off a Maroon Shore, and were shipped with Major *Bonnet* to go to St. *Thomas*'s; but being out at Sea, and wanting Provisions, they were obliged to do what they did by others; and so did Major *Bonnet* himself, pretend that 'twas Force, not Inclination, that occasioned what had happened. However, the Facts being plainly proved, and that they had all shared ten or eleven Pounds a Man, excepting the three last, and *Thomas Nichols*, they were all but they, found Guilty. The Judge made a very grave Speech to them, setting forth *the Enormity of their Crimes, the Condition they were now in, and the Nature and Necessity of an unseigned Repentance*; and then recommended them to the Ministers of the Province, for more ample Directions, to fit them for Eternity, *for* (concluded he) *the Priest's Lips shall keep Knowledge, and you shall seek the Law at their Mouths; for they are the Messengers of the Lord.* Mat. II. 57. *And the Ambassadors of Christ, and unto them is committed the* Word [or Doctrine] *of Reconciliation,* 2 Cor. V. 19. 20. And then pronounced Sentence of Death upon them.

On *Saturday November* the 8th, 1711. *Robert Tucker, Edward Robinson, Neal Paterson, William Scot, Job Bayley, John-William Smith, John Thomas, William Morrison, Samuel Booth, William Hewit, William Eddy,* alias *Neddy, Alexander Annand, George Ross, George Dunkin, Matthew King, Daniel Perry, Henry Virgin, James Robbins, James Mullet,* alias *Millet, Thomas Price, John Lopez,* and *Zachariah Long,* were executed at the *White-Point* near *Charles-Town,* pursuant to their Sentence.

As for the Captain, his Escape protracted his Fate, and spun out his Life a few Days longer, for he was try'd the 10th, and being found Guilty, received Sentence in like Manner as the former; before which Judge *Trot,* made a most excellent Speech to him, rather somewhat too long to be taken into our History, yet I could not tell how to pass by so good and useful a Piece of Instruction, not knowing whose Hands this Book may happen to fall into.

*The Lord Chief Justices's*Speech, *upon his pronouncing Sentence on Major*Stede Bonnet.

MAjor *Stede Bonnet*, you stand here convicted upon two Indictments of Pyracy; one by the Verdict of the Jury, and the other by your own Confession.

Altho' you were indicted but for *two* Facts, yet you know that at your Tryal it was fully proved even by an unwilling Witness, that you *piratically* took and rifled no less than *thirteen* Vessels, since you sail'd from *North-Carolina*.

So that you might have been indicted, and convicted of *eleven* more Acts of *Pyracy*, since you took the Benefit of the King's *Act of Grace*, and pretended to leave that wicked Course of Life.

Not to mention the many *Acts* of *Pyracy* you committed before; for which if your Pardon from *Man* was never so authentick, yet you must expect to answer for them before God.

You know that the Crimes you have committed are *evil* in themselves, and contrary to the *Light* and *Law* of *Nature,* as well as the *Law* of God, by which you are commanded that *you shall not steal,* Exod. 20. 15. And the Apostle St. *Paul* expresly affirms, That *Thieves shall not inherit the Kingdom of God,* 1 Cor. 6. 10.

But to *Theft* you have added a greater Sin, which is *Murder*. How many you may have *killed* of those that resisted you in the committing your former *Pyracies,* I know not: But this we all know, That besides the Wounded, you kill'd no less than *eighteen* Persons out of those that were sent by lawful Authority to suppress you, and put a Stop to those Rapines that you daily acted.

And however you may fancy that that was killing Men fairly in open *Fight*, yet this know, that the Power of the *Sword* not being committed into your Hands by any lawful Authority, you were not impowered to use any *Force*, or *fight* any one; and therefore those Persons that fell in that Action, in doing their Duty to their King and Country, were *murdered*, and their *Blood* now cries out for *Vengeance* and *Justice* against you: For it is the *Voice of Nature*, confirmed by the *Law* of God, That *whosoever sheddeth Man's Blood, by Man shall his Blood be shed*. Gen. 9. 6.

And consider that Death is not the only Punishment due to *Murderers*; for they are threatened to have *their Part in the Lake which burneth with Fire and Brimstone, which is the second Death*, Rev. 21. 8. See *Chap*. 22. 15. Words which carry that Terror with them, that considering your Circumstances and your Guilt, surely the Sound of them must make you tremble; *For who can dwell with everlasting Burnings?* Chap. 33. 14.

As the *Testimony* of your *Conscience* must convince you of the great and many Evils you have committed, by which you have highly offended God, and provoked most justly his Wrath and Indignation against you, so I suppose I need not tell you that the only Way of obtaining Pardon and Remission of your Sins from God, is by a true and unfeigned *Repentance* and *Faith* in Christ, by whose meritorious Death and Passion, you can only hope for Salvation.

You being a Gentleman that have had the Advantage of a *liberal Education*, and being generally esteemed a Man of *Letters*, I believe it will be needless for me to explain to you the Nature of *Repentance* and *Faith* in Christ, they being so fully and so often mentioned in the Scriptures, that you cannot but know them. And therefore, perhaps, for that Reason it might be thought by some improper for me to have said so much to you, as I have already upon this Occasion; neither should I have done it, but that considering the Course of your Life and Actions, I have just Reason to fear, that the Principles of Religion that had been instilled into you by your *Education*, have been at least corrupted, if not entirely defaced, by the *Scepticism* and *Infidelity* of this wicked Age; and that what Time you allowed for Study, was rather applied to the *Polite Literature*, and the vain *Philosophy* of the Times, than a serious Search after the *Law* and *Will* of God, as revealed unto us in the Holy *Scriptures*: For *had your Delight been in the Law of the Lord, and that you had meditated therein Day and Night*, Psal. 1. 2. you would then have found that God's *Word was a Lamp unto your Feet, and a Light to your Path*, Psal. 119. 105. and that you would account all other Knowledge but *Loss*, in Comparison of *the Excellency of the Knowledge of Christ Jesus*, Phil. 3. 8. *who to them that are called is the Power of God, and the Wisdom of God*, 1 Cor. 1. 24. *even the hidden Wisdom which God ordained before the World*, Chap. 2. 7.

You would then have esteemed the *Scriptures* as the *Great Charter* of Heaven, and which delivered to us not only the most perfect *Laws* and *Rules* of Life, but also discovered to us the Acts of *Pardon* from God, wherein they have offended those righteous Laws: For in them only is to be found the great *Mystery* of fallen Man's *Redemption, which the Angels desire to look into*, 1 Pet. 1. 12.

And they would have taught you that *Sin* is the debasing of *Human Nature*, as being a *Derivation* from that *Purity, Rectitude*, and *Holiness*, in which God created us, and that *Virtue* and *Religion*, and walking by the Laws of God, were altogether preferable to the Ways of *Sin* and *Satan*; for that the *Ways* of Virtue are *Ways of Pleasantness, and all their Paths are Peace*, Prov. 3. 17.

But what you could not learn from God's Word, by reason of your *carelesly*, or but *superficially* considering the same, I hope the Course of his *Providence*, and the present *Afflictions* that he hath laid upon you, hath now convinced you of the same: For however in your seeming Prosperity you might make a *Mock at your Sins* Prov. 3. 17. yet now that you see that God's Hand hath reached you, and brought you to public Justice, I hope your present unhappy Circumstances hath made you seriously reflect upon your past Actions and Course of Life; and that you are now sensible of the Greatness of your Sins, and that you find the Burden of them is intolerable.

And that therefore being thus *labouring, and heavy laden with Sin*, Mat. 11. 28. you will esteem that as the most valuable *Knowledge*, that can show you how you can be reconciled to that Supreme God that you have so highly offended; and that can reveal to you Him who is not only the powerful *Advocate with the Father for you*, 1 John 2. 1. but also who hath paid that

Debt that is due for your Sins by his own Death upon the Cross for you; and thereby made full Satisfaction for the Justice of God. And this is to be found no where but in God's Word, which discovers to us that *Lamb of God which takes away the Sins of the World*, John 1. 29. which is *Christ* the Son of God: For this know, and be assured, *that there is none other Name under Heaven given among Men, whereby we must be saved*, Acts 4. 12. but only by the Name of the Lord *Jesus*.

But then consider how he invites all Sinners to come unto him, and, *that he will give them rest*, Matt. 11. 28. for he assures us, *that he came to seek and to save that which was lost*, Luke 19. 10, Mat. 18. 11. and hath promised, *that he that cometh unto him, he will in no wise cast out*, John 6. 37.

So that if now you will sincerely turn to him, tho' late, even at the *eleventh Hour*, Mat. 20. 6, 9. he will receive you.

But surely I need not tell you, that the *Terms* of his *Mercy* is *Faith* and *Repentance*.

And do not mistake the *Nature* of Repentance to be only a bare Sorrow for your Sins, arising from the Consideration of the *Evil* and *Punishment* they have now brought upon you; but your Sorrow must arise from the Consideration of your having offended a gracious and merciful God.

But I shall not pretend to give you any particular Directions as to the Nature of Repentance: I consider that I speak to a Person, whose Offences have proceeded not so much from his not *knowing*, as his *slighting* and *neglecting* his *Duty*: Neither is it proper for me to give Advice out of the Way of my own Profession.

You may have that better delivered to you by those who have made Divinity their particular Study; and who, by their Knowledge, as well as their Office, as being the *Ambassadors of Christ*, 2 Cor. 5. 20. are best qualified to give you Instructions therein.

I only heartily wish, that what, in Compassion to your Soul, I have now said to you upon this sad and solemn Occasion, by exhorting you in general to *Faith* and *Repentance*, may have that due Effect upon you, that thereby you may become a true *Penitent*.

And therefore having now discharged my Duty to you as a *Christian*, by giving you the best Counsel I can, with respect to the Salvation of your Soul, I must now do my Office as a *Judge*.

The *Sentence* that the Law hath appointed to pass upon you for your Offences, and which this Court doth therefore award, is,

That you, the said Stede Bonnet, *shall go from hence to the Place from whence you came, and from thence to the Place of Execution, where you shall be hanged by the Neck till you are dead.*

And the God of infinite Mercy be merciful to your Soul.

Chap. V
Of Capt. *Edward England*, And his Crew

HIS Beginning and Character. A most barbarous Action of his Crew. The Names of Prizes taken by him. The Misfortunes of his Confederates. England's Progress half round the Globe. A short Description of the Coast of Malabar. What they did at Madagascar. Takes an East-India Man. The Particulars of the Action in Captain Mackra's Letter. Captain Mackra ventures on Board the Pyrate. Is in Danger of being murder'd. Preserv'd by a pleasant Incident. The Pyrates Generosity to him. Captain England deposed, and why. Maroon'd on the Island Mauritius. Some Account of that Island. The Adventures of the Company continued. Angria, an Indian Pyrate. his Strength by Land and Sea. The East-India Company's Wars with him. The Pyrates go to the Island of Melinda. Their barbarous Behaviour there. Hear of Captain Mackra's Designs against them. Their Reflections thereupon. Sail for Cochin, a Dutch Settlement. The Pyrates and the Dutch very good Friends. Mutual Presents made betwixt the Pyrates and the Governor. The Pyrates in a Fright. Almost starv'd. Take a Prize of an immense Value. Take an Ostend East-India Man. A short Description of Madagascar. A prodigious Dividend made by the Pyrates. A Fellow's Way of increasing his Diamonds. Some of the Pyrates quit, and join th Remains of Avery. The Proceedings of the Men of War in those Parts. Some Dutch Men petition to be among the Pyrates. The Pyrates divided in their Measures. Break up. What became of them.

Edward *England* went Mate of a Sloop that sail'd out of *Jamaica*, and was taken by Captain *Winter*, a Pyrate, just before their Settlement at *Providence*; from whence *England* had the Command of a Sloop in the same laudable Employment: It is surprizing that Men of good Understanding should engage in a Course of Life, that so much debases humane Nature, and sets them upon a Level with the wild Beasts of the Forest, who live and prey upon their weaker Fellow Creatures: A Crime so enormous! That it includes almost all others, as Murder, Rapine, Theft, Ingratitude, *&c.* and tho' they make these Vices familiar to them by their daily Practice, yet these Men are so inconsistent with themselves, that a Reflection made upon their Honour, their Justice, or their Courage, is look'd upon as an Offence that ought to be punished with the Life of him that commits it: *England* was one of these Men, who seem'd to have such a Share of Reason, as should have taught him better Things. He had a great deal of good Nature, and did not want for Courage; he was not avaritious, and always averse to the ill Usage Prisoners received: He would have been contented with moderate Plunder, and less mischievous Pranks, could his Companions have been brought to the same Temper, but he was generally over-rul'd, and as he was engaged in that abominable Society, he was obliged to be a Partner in all their vile Actions.

Captain *England* sail'd to the Coast of *Africa*, after the Island of *Providence* was settled by the *English* Government, and the Pyrates surrendered to his Majesty's Proclamation; and took several Ships and Vessels, particularly the *Cadogan* Snow belonging to *Bristol*, at *Sierraleone*, one *Skinner* Master, who was inhumanly murthered by some of the Crew, that had lately been his own Men, and served in the said Vessel. It seems some Quarrel had happened between them, so that *Skinner* thought fit to remove these Fellows on Board of a Man of War, and at the same Time refused them their Wages; not long after they found Means to desert that Service, and shipping themselves aboard a Sloop in the *West-Indies*, was taken by a Pyrate, and brought to *Providence*, and sailed upon the same Account along with Captain *England*.

Assoon as *Skinner* had struck to the Pyrate, he was ordered to come on Board in his Boat, which he did, and the Person that he first cast his Eye upon, proved to be his old Boatswain, who star'd him in the Face like his evil Genius, and accosted him in this Manner. — *Ah, Captain Skinner! Is it you? The only Man I wished to see; I am much in your Debt, and now I shall pay you all in your own Coin.*

The poor Man trembled every Joint, when he found into what Company he had fallen, and dreaded the Event, as he had Reason enough so to do; for the Boatswain immediately called to his Consorts, laid hold of the Captain, and made him fast to the Windless, and there pelted him with Glass Bottles, which cut him in a sad Manner; after which they whipp'd him about the Deck, till they were weary, being deaf to all his Prayers and Intreaties, and at last, because he had been a good Master to his Men, they said, he should have an easy Death, and so shot him thro' the Head. They took some few Things out of the Snow, but gave the Vessel and all her Cargo to *Howel Davis* the Mate; and the rest of the Crew, as will be hereafter mentioned in the Chapter of Captain *Davis*.

Captain *England* took a Ship called the *Pearl*, Captain *Tyzard* Commander, for which he exchanged his own Sloop, fitted her up for the piratical Account, and new christen'd her, the *Royal James*, with which he took several Ships and Vessels of different Nations at the *Azores* and *Cape de Verd Islands*.

In the Spring, 1719, the Rovers returned to *Africa*, and beginning at the River *Gambia*, sailed all down the Coast; and between that and *Cape Corso*, took the following Ships and Vessels.

The *Eagle* Pink, Captain *Rickets* Commander belonging to *Cork*, taken the 25th of *March*, having 6 Guns and 17 Men on Board, seven of which turned Pyrates.

The *Charlotte*, Captain *Oldson*, of *London*, taken *May* the 26th, having 8 Guns and 18 Men on Board, 13 of which turned Pyrates.

The *Sarah*, Captain *Stunt*, of *London*, taken the 27th of *May*, having 4 Guns and 18 Men on Board, 3 of which turned Pyrates.

The *Bentworth*, Captain *Gardener*, of *Bristol*, taken the 27th of *May*, having 12 Guns and 30 Men on Board, 12 of which turned Pyrates.

The *Buck* Sloop, Captain *Sylvester*, of *Gambia*, taken the 27th of *May*, having 2 Guns and 2 Men on Board, and both turned Pyrates.

The *Carteret*, Captain *Snow*, of *London*, taken the 28th of *May*, having 4 Guns and 18 Men on Board, 5 of which turned Pyrates.

The *Mercury*, Captain *Maggott*, of *London*, taken the 29th of *May*, having 4 Guns and 18 Men on Board, 5 of which turned Pyrates.

The *Coward* Galley, Captain *Creed*, of *London*, taken the 17th of *June*, having 2 Guns and 13 Men on Board, 4 of which turned Pyrates.

The *Elizabeth* and *Katherine*, Captain *Bridge* of *Barbadoes*, taken *June* the 27th, having 6 Guns and 14 Men on Board, 4 of which turned Pyrates.

The *Eagle* Pink being bound to *Jamaica*, the *Sarah* to *Virginia*, and the *Buck* to *Maryland*, they let them go, but the *Charlotte*, the *Bentworth*, the *Carteret*, and the *Coward* Galley, they burnt; and the *Mercury*, and the *Elizabeth* and *Katherine* were fitted up for Pyrate Ships, the former was new nam'd *Queen Ann's Revenge*, and commanded by one *Lane*, and the other was call'd the *Flying King*, of which *Robert Sample* was appointed Captain. These two left *England* upon the Coast, sail'd to the *West-Indies*, where they took some Prizes, clean'd, and sail'd to *Brasil* in *November*; they took several *Portuguese* Ships there, and did a great deal of Mischief, but in the height of their Undertakings, a *Portuguese* Man of War, which was an excellent Sailor, came a very unwelcome Guest to them, and gave them Chace; the Queen *Ann's Revenge* got off, but was lost a little while after upon that Coast; and the *Flying King*, giving herself over for lost, ran ashore: There were then 70 Men on Board, 12 of which were kill'd, and the rest taken Prisoners, of whom the *Portuguese* hang'd 38, of which 32 were *English*, three *Dutch*, two *French*, and one of their own Nation.

England, in going down the Coast, took the *Peterborough* Galley of *Bristol*, Captain *Owen*; and the *Victory*, Captain *Ridout*; the former they detained, but plundered the latter, and let her go. In *Cape Corso* Road, they saw two Sail at Anchor, but before they could reach them, they slipp'd their Cables and got close under *Cape Corso Castle*, these were the *Whydah*, Captain *Prince*, and the *John*, Captain *Rider*: The Pyrates upon this made a fire Ship of a Vessel they had lately taken, and attempted to burn them, as tho' they had been a common Enemy, which if effected, they could not have been one Farthing the better for it; but the Castle firing warmly upon them, they withdrew, and sail'd down to *Whydah* Road, where they found another Pyrate, one Captain *la Bouche*, who getting thither before *England* arrived, had forestall'd the Market, and greatly disappointed their Brethren.

Captain *England*, after this Baulk, went into a Harbour, clean'd his own Ship, and fitted up the *Peterborough*, which he call'd the *Victory*; they liv'd there very wantonly for several Weeks, making free with the Negroe Women, and committing such outragious Acts, that they came to an open Rupture with the Natives, several of whom they kill'd, and one of their Towns they set on Fire.

When the Pyrates came out to Sea, they put it to a Vote what Voyage to take, and the Majority carrying it for the *East-Indies*, they shap'd their Course accordingly, and arrived at *Madagascar*, the Beginning of the Year 1720. They staid not long there, but after taking in Water and Provisions, sail'd for the Coast of *Malabar*, which is a fine fruitful Country in the *East-Indies*, in the Empire of the *Mogul*, but immediately subject to its own Princes: It reaches from the Coast of *Canara* to *Cape Camorin*, which is between 7° 30, and 12° North Lattitude, and in about 75° East Longitude, counting from the Meridian of *London*. The old Natives are Pagans, but there are a great Number of *Mahometans* inhabiting among them, who are Merchants, and generally rich. On the same Coast, but in a Province to the Northward lies *Goa, Surat, Bombay*, where the *English, Dutch,* and *Portuguese* have Settlements.

Hither our Pyrates came, having made a Tour of half the Globe, as the Psalmist says of the Devils, *Going about like roaring Lions, seeking whom they might devour.* They took several Country Ships, that is, *Indian* Vessels, and one European, a *Dutch* Ship, which they exchanged for one of their own, and then came back to *Madagascar*.

They sent several of their Hands on Shore with Tents, Powder, and Shot, to kill Hogs, Venison, and such other fresh Provision as the Island afforded, and a Whim came into their Heads to seek out for the Remains of *Avery*'s Crew, whom they knew to be settled somewhere in the Island. —— Accordingly some of them travell'd several Days Journey, without hearing any Intelligence of them, and so were forc'd to return with the Loss of their Labour, for these Men were settled on the other Side of the Island, as has been taken Notice of under the Chapter of *Avery*.

They stay'd not long here, after they had clean'd their Ships, but sailing to *Juanna*; they met two *English*, and one *Ostend India* Men, coming out of that Harbour, one of which, after a desperate Resistance, they took; the Particulars of which Action is at length related in the following Letter, wrote by the Captain from *Bombay*.

A LETTER from Captain *Mackra*, dated at *Bombay, Nov.* 16, 1720.

*W*E *arrived the* 25th *of* July *last, in Company of the* Greenwich, *at* Juanna, (*an Island not far from* Madagascar) *putting in there to refresh our Men, we found fourteen Pyrates that came in their Canoes from the* Mayotta, *where the Pyrate Ship to which they belong'd, viz. the* Indian Queen, *two hundred and fifty Tons, twenty eight Guns, and ninety Men, commanded by Capt.* Oliver de la Bouche, *bound from the* Guinea *Coast to the* East-Indies, *had been bulged and lost. They said they left the Captain and* 40 *of their Men building a new Vessel to proceed on their wicked Design. Capt.* Kirby *and I concluding it might be of great Service to the* East-India *Company to destroy such a Nest of Rogues, were ready to sail for that Purpose the* 17th *of* August, *about Eight o'Clock in the Morning, when we discovered two Pyrate Ships standing into the Bay of* Juanna, *one of thirty four, and the other of thirty Guns. I immediately went on Board the* Greenwich, *where they seem'd very diligent in Preparations for an Engagement, and I left Capt.* Kirby *with mutual Promises of standing by each other. I then unmoor'd, got under Sail, and brought two Boats a-head to row me close to the* Greenwich; *but he being open to a Valley and a Breeze, made the best of his Way from me; which an* Ostender *in our Company, of* 22 *Guns, seeing, did the same, though the Captain had promised heartily to engage with us, and I believe would have been as good as his Word, if Capt.* Kirby *had kept his. About half an Hour after Twelve, I called several times to the* Greenwich *to bear down to our Assistance, and fir'd Shot at* him, but to no Purpose. For tho' we did not doubt but he would join us, because when he got about a League from us, he brought his Ship to, and look'd on, yet both he and the Ostender basely deserted us, and left us engaged with barbarous and inhuman Enemies, with their black and bloody Flags hanging over us, without the least Appearance of escaping being cut to Pieces. But God, in his good Providence, determin'd otherwise; for notwithstanding their Superiority, we engaged 'em both about three Hours, during which, the biggest received some Shot betwixt Wind and Water, which made her keep off a little to stop her Leaks. The other endeavoured all she could to board us, by rowing with her Oars, being within half a Ship's Length of us above an Hour; but by good Fortune we shot all her Oars to Pieces, which prevented them, and by consequence saved our Lives.

About Four o'Clock, most of the Officers and Men posted on the Quarter-Deck being killed and wounded, the largest Ship making up to us with all Diligence, being still within a Cable's Length of us, often giving us a Broadside, and no hopes of Capt. Kirby's coming to our Assistance, we endeavoured to run ashoar; and tho' we drew four Foot Water more than the Pyrate, it pleased God that he stuck fast on a higher Ground than we happily fell in with; so was disappointed a second time from boarding us. Here we had a more violent Engagement than before. All my Officers, and most of my Men, behaved with unexpected Courage; and as we had a considerable Advantage by having a Broadside to his Bow, we did him great Damage, so that had Capt. Kirby come in then, I believe we should have taken both, for we had one of them sure; but the other Pyrate (who was still firing at us) seeing the Greenwich did not offer to assist us, he supplied his Consort with three Boats full of fresh Men. About Five in the Evening the Greenwich stood clear away to Sea, leaving us struggling hard for Life in the very Jaws of Death; which the other Pyrate, that was afloat, seeing, got a-warp out, and was hauling under our Stern; by which time many of my Men being killed and wounded, and no Hopes left us from being all murdered by enraged barbarous Conquerors, I order'd all that could, to get into the Long-Boat under the Cover of the Smoak of our Guns; so that with what some did in Boats, and others by swimming, most of us that were able got ashoar, by Seven o' Clock. When the Pyrates came aboard, they cut three of our wounded Men to Pieces. I, with a few of my People, made what haste I could to the King's-Town, twenty five Miles from us, where I arrived next Day, almost dead with Fatigue and Loss of Blood, having been sorely wounded in the Head by a Musket Ball.

At this Town I heard that the Pyrates had offered ten thousand Dollars to the Country People to bring me in, which many of them would have accepted, only they knew the King and all his chief People were in my Interest. Mean time, I caused a Report to be spread, that I was dead of my Wounds, which much abated their Fury. About ten Days after, being pretty well recovered, and hoping the Malice of our Enemies was nigh over, I began to consider the dismal Condition we were reduced to, being in a Place where we had no Hopes of getting a Passage home, all of us in a manner naked, not having had Time to get another Shirt, or a Pair of Shoes.

Having obtained Leave to go on Board the Pyrates, and a Promise of Safety, several of the Chief of them knew me, and some of them had failed with me, which I found of great Advantage; because, notwithstanding their Promise, some of them would have cut me, and all that would not enter with them, to Pieces, had it not been for the chief Captain, Edward England, and some others I knew. They talked of burning one of their Ships, which we had so entirely disabled, as to be no farther useful to them, and to fit the Cassandra in her room; but in the End I managed my Tack so well, that they made me a Present of the said shattered Ship, which was Dutch built, called the Fancy, about three hundred Tons, and also a hundred and twenty nine Bales of the Company's Cloth, tho' they would not giveme a Rag of my Cloathes.

They failed the 3d of September; and with Jury-Masts, and such old Sails as they left me, I made shift to do the like on the 8th, together with forty three of my Ship's Crew, including two Passengers and twelve Soldiers, having but five Tons of Water aboard; and after a Passage of forty eight Days, I arrived here October 26, almost naked and starv'd, having been reduced to a Pint of Water a Day, and almost in despair of ever seeing Land, by Reason of the Calms we met with between the Coast of Arabia and Malabar. —— We had in all thirteen Men killed and twenty four wounded; and we were told, that we had destroyed about ninety or a hundred of the Pyrates. When they left us, they were about three hundred Whites and eighty Blacks in both Ships. I am persuaded, had our Confort the Greenwich done his Duty, we had destroyed both of them, and got two hundred thousand Pounds for our Owners and selves; whereas to his deserting us, the Loss of the Caffandra may justly be imputed. I have delivered all the Bales that were given me into the Company's Warehouse, for which the Governor and Council have ordered me a Reward. Our Governor, Mr. Boon, *who is extreme kind and civil to me, has ordered me home with this Pacquet; but Captain* Harvey, *who had a prior Promise, being come in with the Fleet, goes in my room. The Governor hath promis'd me a Country Voyage, to help make me up my Losses, and would have me stay to go home with him next Year.*

Captain *Mackra* certainly run a great Hazard, in going aboard the Pyrate, and began quickly to repent his Credulity; for though they had promised, that no Injury should be done to his Person, he found their Words were not to be trusted; and it may be supposed, that nothing but the desperate Circumstances Captain *Mackra* imagined himself to be in, could have prevailed upon him to fling himself and Company into their Hands, perhaps not knowing how firmly the Natives of that Island were attach'd to the *English* Nation; for about 20 Years ago, Captain *Cornwall*, Commadore of an *English* Squadrou, assisted them against another Island called *Mohilla*, for which they have ever since communicated all the grateful Offices in their Power, insomuch that it became a Proverb,

That an Englishman, *and a* Juanna *Man were all one.*

England was inclined to favour Captain *Mackra*; but he was so free to let him know, that his Interest was declining amongst them; and that the Pyrates were so provoked at the Resistance he made against them, that he was afraid he should hardly be able to protect him; he therefore advised him to sooth up and manage the Temper of Captain *Taylor*, a Fellow of a most barbarous Nature, who was become a great Favourite amongst them for no other Reason than because he was a greater Brute than the rest. *Mackra* did what he could to soften this Beast, and ply'd him with warm Punch; notwithstanding which, they were in a Tumult whether they should make an End of him, or no, when an Accident happen'd which turn'd to the Favour of the poor Captain; a Fellow with a terrible pair of Whiskers, and a wooden Leg, being stuck round with Pistols, like the Man in the Almanack with Darts, comes swearing and vapouring upon the Quarter-Deck, and asks, in a damning Manner, which was Captain *Mackra*: The Captain expected no less than that this Fellow would be his Executioner; —— but when he came near him, he took him by the Hand, swearing, *Damn him he was glad to see him; and shew me the Man,* says he, *that offers to hurt Captain* Mackra, *for I'll stand by him*; and so with many Oaths told him, *he was an honest Fellow, and that he had formerly sail'd with him.*

This put an End to the Dispute, and Captain *Taylor* was so mellow'd with the Punch, that he consented that the old Pyrate Ship, and so many Bales of Cloth should be given to Captain *Mackra*, and so he fell asleep. *England* advised Captain *Mackra* to get off with all Expedition, least when the Beast should awake, he might repent his Generosity: Which Advice was followed by the Captain.

Captain *England* having sided so much to Captain *Mackra*'s Interest, was a Means of making him many Enemies among the Crew; they thinking such good Usage inconsistent with their Polity, because it looked like procuring Favour at the Aggravation of their Crimes; therefore upon Imagination or Report, that Captain *Mackra* was fitting out against them, with the Company's Force, he was soon *abdicated* or pulled out of his Government, and marooned with three more on the Island of *Mauritius*: An Island indeed, not to be complained of, had they accumulated any Wealth by their Villanies that would have afforded some future comfortable Prospect, for it abounds with Fish, Deer, Hogs and other Flesh. Sir *Thomas Herbert*, says, the Shores with Coral and Ambergrease; but I believe the *Dutch* had not deserted it, had there been much of these Commodities to have been found. It was in 1722, resettled by the *French*, who have a Fort at another neighbouring Island, called *Don Mascarine*, and are touched at for Water, Wood, and Refreshments, by *French* Ships bound to, or for *India*; as St. *Helena* and *Cape Bon Esperance*, are by us and the *Dutch*. From this Place, Captain *England* and his Companions having made a little Boat of Staves and old Pieces of Deal left there, went over to *Madagascar*, where they subsist at present on the Charity of some of their Brethren, who had made better Provision for themselves, than they had done.

The Pyrates detained some Officers and Men belonging to Captain *Mackra*, and having repaired the Damages received in their Rigging, they sailed for *India*. The Day before they made Land, saw two Ships to the Eastward, who at first Sight, they took to be *English*, and ordered one of the Prisoners, who had been an Officer with Captain *Mackra*, to tell them the private Signals between the Company's Ships, the Captain swearing he would cut him in pound Pieces, if he did not do it immediately; but unable, was forced to bear their Scurility, till they came up with them, and found they were two *Moor* Ships from *Muscat*, with Horses; they brought the Captain of them, and Merchants, on Board, torturing them, and rifling the Ships, in order to discover Riches, as believing they came from *Mocha*; but being baulked in their Expectation, and next Morning seeing Land, and at the same Time a Fleet in Shore plying to Windward, they were puzzled how to dispose of them; to let them go, was to discover and ruin the Voyage, and it was cruel to sink the Men and Horses with the Ships, (as many of them were inclined to,) therefore, as a Medium, they brought them to an Anchor, threw all their Sails over-board, and cut one of the Ships Masts half through.

While they lay at an Anchor, and were all the next Day employed in taking out Water, one of the aforementioned Fleet bore towards them with *English* Colours, answered with a red Ensign from the Pyrates, but did not speak with one another. At Night they left the *Muscatt* Ships, weighed with the Sea Wind, and stood to the Northward after this Fleet: About four next Morning, just as they were getting under sail, with the Land Wind, the Pyrates came amongst them, made no stop, but fired their great and small Guns very briskly, till they got through; and as Day-Light cleared, were in a great Consternation in their Minds, having all along taken them for *Angria*'s Fleet; what to do was the Point, whether run or pursue? They were sensible of their Inferiority of Strength, having no more than 300 Men in both Ships, and 40 of them Negroes; besides, the *Victory* had then four Pumps at Work, and must inevitably been lost before, had it not been for some Hand-Pumps, and several pair of Standards brought out of the *Cassandra*, to relieve and strengthen her; but observing the Indifferency of the Fleet, chose rather to chase than run; and thought the best Way to save themselves, was to play at Bullbeggar with the Enemy: So they came up with the Sea Wind, about Gun-Shot to Leeward, the great Ships of the Fleet a-head, and some others a-stern; which latter they took for Fire-Vessels: And these a-head gaining from them by cutting away their Boats, they could do nothing more than continue their Course all Night, which they did, and found them next Morning out of Sight, excepting a Ketch and some few Gallivats, (*small sort of Vessels something like the Feluccas of the* Mediterranean, *and hoists, like them, triangular Sails.*) They bore down, which the Ketch perceiving, transported her People on Board a Gallivat, and set fire to her; the other proved too nimble and made off. The same Day they chased another Gallivat and took her, being come from *Gogo*, bound for *Callicut* with Cotton. Of these Men they enquired concerning the Fleet, supposing they must have been in it; and altho' they protested they had not seen a Ship or Boat since they left *Gogo*, and pleaded very earnestly for Favour; yet they threw all their Cargo over-board, and squezed their Joints in a Vice, to extort Confession: But they entirely ignorant of who or what this Fleet should be, were obliged not only to sustain this Torment, but next Day a fresh easterly Wind having split the Gallivats Sails, they put her Company into the Boat, with nothing but a Trysail, no Provisions, and only four Gallons of Water, (half of it Salt,) and then out of Sight of Land, to shift for themselves.

For the better elucidating of this Story, it may be convenient to inform the Reader, who *Angria* is, and what the Fleet were, that had so scurvily behaved themselves.

Angria is a famous *Indian*Pyrate, of considerable Strength and Territories, that gives continual Disturbance to the *European* (and especially the *English*) Trade: His chief Hold is *Callaba*, not many Leagues from *Bombay*, and has one Island in Sight of that Port, whereby he gains frequent Opportunities of annoying the Company. It would not be so insuperable a Difficulty to suppress him, if the Shallowness of the Water did not prevent Ships of War coming nigh:

And a better Art he has, of bribing the *Mogul*'s Ministers for Protection, when he finds an Enemy too powerful.

In the Year 1720, the *Bombay* Fleet consisting of four *Grabbs*, *(Ships built in* India *by the Company, and have three Masts, a Prow like a Row-Galley, instead of a Boltsprit, about* 150 *Tons; are officered and armed like a Man of War, for Defence and Protection of the Trade,)* the *London, Chandois,* and two other Ships with Gallivats, who besides their proper Compliments, carried down 1000 Men to bombard and batter *Gayra,* a Fort belonging to *Angria,* on the *Malabar* Coast, which they having performed ineffectually, were returning to *Bombay,* and, to make amends, fell in with the Pyrates, to the Purpose has been already related. Captain *Upon,* Commadore of that Fleet, prudently objecting to Mr. *Brown,* (who went General,) That the Ships were not to be hazarded, since they sailed without their Governor *Boon*'s Orders to engage; and besides, that they did not come out with such a Design. This favourable Opportunity of destroying the Pyrates, angered the Governor, and he transferred the Command of the Fleet to Captain *Mackra,* who had Orders immediately to pursue and engage, where ever he met them.

The Vice-Roy of *Goa,* assisted by the *English* Company's Fleet from *Bombay,* did attempt the Reduction of *Callaba,* his principal Place, landed 8 or 10000 Men the next Year, the *English* Squadron of Men of War being then in those Seas; but having viewed the Fortification well, and expended some of their Army by Sickness and the Fatigues of a Camp, carefully withdrew again.

I return to the Pyrates, who, after they had sent away the Gallivats People, resolved to cruise to the Southward; and the next Day, between *Goa* and *Carwar,* heard several Guns, which brought them to an Anchor, and they sent their Boat on the Scent, who returned about two in the Morning, and brought Word of two Grabs lying at Anchor in the Road. They weighed and ran towards the Bay, till Day-Light gave the Grabs Sight of them, and was but just Time enough to get under *India Diva* Castle, out of their reach; this displeased the Pyrates the more, in that they wanted Water; and some were for making a Descent that Night and taking the Island, but it not being approved of by the Majority, they proceeded to the Southward, and took next in their Way, a small Ship out of *Onnore* Road, with only a *Dutch* Man and two *Portuguese* on Board. They sent one of these on Shore to the Captain, to acquaint him, if he would supply them with some Water, and fresh Provisions, he should have his Ship again; and the Master returned for answer, by his Mate *Frank Harmless,* that if they would deliver him Possession over the Bar, he would comply with their Request; the Proposal the Mate thought was collusive, and they rather jump'd into *Harmless*'s Opinion, (who very honestly entered with them,) and resolved to seek Water at the *Laccadeva* Islands; so having sent the other Persons on Shore, with threats, that he should be the last Man they would give Quarter too, (by Reason of this uncivil Usage;) they put directly for the Islands, and arrived there in three Days: Where being informed by a Menchew they took (with the Governor of *Canwars* Pass,) of there being no Anchor-Ground among them, and *Melinda* being the next convenient Island, they sent their Boats on Shore, to see if there was any Water, and whether it was inhabited or not; who returned with an Answer to their Satisfaction, *viz.* that there was abundance of good Water, and many Houses, but deserted by the Men, who had fled to the neighbouring Islands on the Approach of Ships, and left only the Women and Children to guard one another. The Women they forced in a Barbarous Manner to their Lusts, and to require them, destroyed their Cocoa Trees, and fired several of their Houses and *Churches.* (I suppose built by the *Portuguese,* who formerly used there, in their Voyages to *India.*)

While they were at this Island, they lost three or four Anchors, by the Rockyness of the Ground, Freshness of Winds, and at last were forced thence by a harder Gale than ordinary, leaving 70 People, Blacks and Whites, and most of their Water Casks: In ten Days they regained the Island again, filled their Water, and took the People on Board.

Provisions were very scarce, and they now resolved to visit their good Friends the *Dutch,* at *Cochin,* who, if you will believe these Rogues, never fail of supplying Gentlemen of their Profession. After three Days sail, they arrived off *Tellechery,* and took a small Vessel belonging to Governor *Adams, John Tawke* Master, whom they brought on Board very drunk, and he giving an

Account of Captain *Mackra*'s fitting out, put them in a Tempest of Passion: *A Villain*, say they, *that we have treated so civilly, as to give him a Ship and other Presents, and now to be armed against us, he ought to be hanged*; *and since we cannot show our Resentment on him, let us hang the Dogs his People, who wish him well, and would do the same, if clear. If it be in my Power*, says the Quarter-Master, *both Masters and Officers of Ships shall be carried with us for the future, only to plague them.* — d — n England.

Thence they proceeded to *Calicut*, where they endeavoured to take a large *Moor* Ship out of the Road, but was prevented by some Guns mounted on Shore, and discharged at them: Mr. *Lasinby*, who was one of Captain *Mackra*'s Officers, and detained, was under the Deck at this Time, and commanded both by the Captain and QuarterMaster of the Pyrates, to tend the Braces on the Booms, in hopes, it was believed, a Shot would take him before they got clear, asking the Reason why he was not there before? And when he would have excused himself, threat'ned on the like Neglect to shoot him; at which the other beginning to expostulate farther, and claim their Promise of putting him ashore, got an unmerciful beating from the Quarter-Master. Captain *Taylor*, who was now Successor to *England*, and whose Priviledge it was to do so, being lame of his Hands, and unable.

The next Day in their Passage down, came up with a *Dutch* Galliot, bound for *Calicut* with Lime Stone, and aboard of her they put Captain *Tawke*, and sent him away, and several of the People interceeded for *Lasinby* in vain, *For*, says *Taylor* and his Party, *if we let this Dog go, who has heard our Designs and Resolutions, we overset all our well advised Projections, and partiularly this Supply we are now seeking for, at the Hands of the* Dutch.

It was but one Day more before they arrived off *Cochin*, where, by a Fishing-Canoe, they sent a Letter on Shore; and in the Afternoon, with the Sea-breeze, ran into the Road and anchored, saluting the Fort with 11 Guns each Ship, and received the Return, in an equal Number; a good Omen of the welcome Reception they found; for at Night there came on Board a large Boat, deeply laden with fresh Provisions and Liquors, and with it a Servant (of a favourite Inhabitant) called *John Trumpet*: He told them they must immediately weigh, and run farther to the Southward, where they should be supplied with all Things they wanted, naval Stores or Provisions.

They had not been long at Anchor again, before they had several Canoes on Board with both black and white Inhabitants, who continued, without Interruption, all good Offices, during their Stay; particularly *John Trumpet* brought a large Boat of Arrack, than which, nothing could be more pleasing (about 90 Legers,) as also 60 Bales of Sugar; an Offering, its presumed, from the Governor and his Daughter, who, in Return, had a fine Table-Clock sent him, (the Plunder of Captain *Mackra*'s Ship,) and she a large Gold Watch, Earnests of the Pay they designed to make.

When they had all on Board, they paid Mr. *Trumpet* to his Satisfaction, it was computed, 6 or 7000 *l.* gave him three Cheers, 11 Guns each Ship, and throw'd Ducatoons into his Boat by handfuls, for the Boat-Men to scramble for.

That Night being little Wind, did not weigh, and *Trumpet*, in the Morning, waked them to the Sight of more Arrack, Chests of Piece-Goods, and ready made Clothes, bringing the Fiscal of the Place also with him. At Noon, while those were on Board, saw a Sail to the Southward, which they weighed, and chaced after; but she having a good Offing, got to the Northward of them, and anchored a small Distance from *Cochin* Fort; the aforementioned Gentlemen assuring them, that they would not be molested in taking her from under the Castle, sollicited before hand for the buying her, and advised them to stand in, which they did boldly, to board her; but when they came within a Cable's length or two of the Chace, now near Shore, the Fort fired two small Guns, whose Shot falling nigh their Muzzels, they instantly bore out of the Road, made an easy Sail to the Southward, and anchored at Night in their former Birth, where *John Trumpet*, to engage their Stay a little longer, informed them, that in a few Days a very rich Ship was to pass by, commanded by the General of *Bombay*'s Brother.

This Governor is an Emblem of foreign Power. What Inconvenience and Injury must the Master's Subjects sustain under one who can truckle to such treacherous and base Means, as corresponding and trading with Pyrates to enrich himself? Certainly such a Man will stickle at no Injustice to repair or make a Fortune. He has the *Argumentum bacillum* always in his own Hands, and can convince, when he pleases, in half the Time of other Arguments, that Fraud and Oppression is Law. That he imploys Instruments in such dirty Work, expresses the Guilt and Shame, but no way mitigates the Crime. *John Trumpet* was the Tool; but, as the Dog said in the Fable, on another Occasion, *What is done by the Master's Orders, is the Master's Actions.*

I cannot but reflect, on this Occasion, what a vile Government *Sancho Pancho* had of it; he had not only such *Perquisites* rescinded, but was really almost starved; the Victuals taken from him almost every Day, and only under a Pretence of preserving his Excellency's Health: But Governments differ.

From *Cochin* some were for proceeding to *Madagascar* directly; others thought it proper to cruize till they got a Store-Ship, and these being the Majority, they ply'd to the Southward, and after some Days saw a Ship in Shore, which being to Windward of them, they could not get nigh, till the Sea Wind, and Night, favouring, they separated, one to the Northward, the other to the Southward, thinking to enclose her between: But to their Astonishment, and contrary to Expectation, when Day broke, instead of the Chace, found themselves very near five Sail of tall Ships, who immediately making a Signal for the Pyrates to bear down, put them in the utmost Confusion, particularly *Taylor*'s Ship, because their Consort was at a Distance from them, (at least three Leagues to the Southward) they stood to one another, and joined, and then together made the best of their Way from the Fleet, whom they judged to be commanded by Captain *Mackra*; of whose Courage having Experience, they were glad to shun any farther Taste of.

In three Hours Chace, none of the Fleet gaining upon them, excepting one Grab, their dejected Countenances cleared up again, the more, in that a Calm succeeded for the Remainder of that Day; and in the Night, with the Land Wind, they ran directly off Shore, and found next Day, to their great Consolation, that they had lost Sight of all the Fleet.

This Danger escaped, they proposed to spend *Christmas* (the *Christmas* of 1720) in Carowzing and Forgetfulness, and kept it for three Days in a wanton and riotous Way, not only eating, but wasting their fresh Provisions in so wretched and inconsiderable a Manner, that when they had agreed after this to proceed to *Mauritius*, they were in that Passage at an Allowance of a Bottle of Water *per Diem*, and not above two Pounds of Beef, and a small Quantity of Rice, for ten Men for a Day; so that had it not been for the leaky Ship, (which once they were about to have quitted, and had done, but for a Quantity of Arrack and Sugar She had on Board,) they must most of them have perished.

In this Condition they arrived at the Island of *Mauritius*, about the Middle of *February*, sheathed and refitted the *Victory*, and on the 5th of *April* sailed again, leaving this terrible Inscription on one of the Walls. *Left this Place the 5th of* April, *to go to* Madagascar *for Limes*, and this, least (like Lawyers and Men of Business) any Visits should be paid in their Absence: However, they did not sail directly for *Madagascar*, but the Island *Mascarine*, and luckily as Rogues could wish, they found at their Arrival on the 8th, a *Portuguese* Ship at Anchor, of 70 Guns, but most of them thrown overboard, her Masts lost, and so much disabled by a violent Storm they had met with in the Latitude of 13° South, that she became a Prize to the Pyrates, with very little or no Resistance, and a glorious one indeed, having the *Conde de Ericeira*, Viceroy of *Goa*, who made that fruitless Expedition against *Angria*, the *Indian*, and several other Passengers on Board; who, as they could not be ignorant of the Treasure she had in, did assert, that in the single Article of Diamonds, there was to the Value of between three and four Millions of Dollars.

The Vice-Roy, who came on Board that Morning, in Expectation of the Ships being *English*, was made a Prisoner, and obliged to ransome; but in Consideration of his great Loss, (the Prize being Part his own,) they agreed after some Demurrings, to accept of 2000 Dollars, and set him and the other Prisoners ashore, with Promises to leave a Ship that they might Transport themselves, because the Island was not thought in a Condition to maintain so great a Number; and tho' they had learned from them, the Account of an *Ostender* being to Leeward of the

Island, which they took on that Information, (being formerly the *Greyhound* Galley of *London*,) and could conveniently have comply'd with so reasonable a Request; yet they sent the *Ostender* with some of their People to *Madagascar*, with News of their Success, and to prepare Masts for the Prize; and followed themselves soon after, without regard to the Sufferers, carrying 200 *Mozambique* Negroes with them in the *Portuguese* Ship.

Madagascar is an Island larger than *Great-Britain*, most of it within the Tropick of *Capricorn*, and lays East from the Eastern Side of *Africa*: It abounds with Provisions of all Sorts, Oxen, Goats, Sheep, Poultry, Fish, Citrons, Oranges, Tamarinds, Dates, Coco-Nuts, Bananas, Wax, Honey, Rice; or in short, Cotton, Indigo, or any other Thing they will take Pains to plant, and have Understanding to manage: They have likewise Ebony, a hard Wood like Brasil, of which they make their Lances; and Gum of several Sorts, Benzin, Dragon's Blood, Aloes, *&c.* What is most incommodious, are the numerous Swarms of Locusts on the Land, and Crocodiles or Alligators in their Rivers. Hither, in St. *Augustin*'s Bay, the Ships sometimes touch for Water, when they take the inner Passage for *India*, and do not design to stop at *Johanna*; and we may observe from the sixth general Voyage set forth by the *East-India* Company, in Confirmation of what is hereafter said in Relation to Currents in general; that this inner Passage or Channel, has its Northern and Southern Currents strongest where the Channel is narrowest, and is less, and varies on different Points of the Compass, as the Sea comes to spread again, in the Passage cross the Line.

Since the Discovery of this Island by the *Portuguese, A. D.* 1506, the *Europeans*, and particularly Pyrates, have increased a dark Mulatto Race there, tho' still few in Comparison with the Natives, who are Negroes, with curled short Hair, Active, and formerly represented malicious and revengeful, now tractable and communicable, perhaps owing to the Favours and Generosity in Cloathing and Liquors, they from Time to Time have received from these Fellows, who live in all possible Friendship, and can, any single Man of them, command a Guard of 2 or 300 at a Minute's warning: This is farther the Native's Interest, to cultivate with them, because the Island being divided into petty Governments and Commands, the Pyrates, settled here, who are now a considerable Number, and have little Castles of their own, can preponderate where-ever they think fit to side.

When *Taylor* came with the *Portuguese* Prize here, they found the *Ostender* had played their Men a Trick, for they, took Advantage of their Drink, rise upon them, and (as they heard afterwards) carried the Ship to *Mozambique*, whence the Governor ordered her for *Goa*.

Here the Pyrates came, cleaned the *Cassandra*, and divided their Plunder, sharing 42 small Diamonds a Man, or in less Proportion according to their Magnitude. An ignorant, or a merry Fellow, who had only, one in this Division, as being judged equal, in Value to 42 small, muttered very much at the Lot, and went and broke it in a Morter, swearing afterwards, he had a better Share than any of them, for he had beat it, he said, into 43 Sparks.

Those who were not for running the Hazard of their Necks, with 42 Diamonds, besides other Treasure, in their Pockets, knocked off, and stay'd with their old Acquaintance at *Madagascar*, on mutual Agreements, the longer Livers to take all. The Residue having therefore no Occasion for two Ships, the *Victory* being leaky, she was burnt, the Men (as many as would) coming into the *Cassandra*, under the Command of *Taylor*, who we must leave a Time, projecting either for *Cochin*, to dispose of their Diamonds among their old Friends the *Dutch*, or else for the *Red* or *China* Seas, to avoid the Men of War, that continually clamoured in their Ears, a Noise of Danger, and give the *little* Account we are able, of that Squadron, who arrived in *India*, early in the Year 1721.

At *Cape Good Hope*, in *June*, the Commadore met with a Letter, which was left for him by the Governor of *Madras*, to whom it was wrote by the Governor of *Pandicherry*, a *French* Factory, on the *Coromondel* Coast, signifying, the Pyrates at the Writing of it, were then strong in the *Indian* Seas, having 11 Sail and 1500 Men, but that many of them went away about that Time, for the Coast of *Brazil* and *Guinea*; others settled and fortified themselves at *Madagascar, Mauritius, Johanna* and *Mohilla*: And that others under *Conden*, in a Ship called the *Dragon*, took a large *Moor*'s Vessel, coming from *Iudda* and *Mocho*, with thirteen Lackies of Rupees on Board, (*i. e.* 1300000 half Crowns,) who having divided the Plunder, burnt their Ship and Prize, and sat down quietly with their other Friends at *Madagascar*.

The Account contain'd several other Things which we have before related. — Commadore *Matthews*, upon receiving this Intelligence, and being fond of the Service he came out for, hastened to those Islands, as the most hopeful Places of Success; at St. *Mary*'s would have engaged *England* with Promises of Favour, if he would communicate what he knew, concerning the *Cassandra*, and the rest of the Pyrates, and assist in the Pilotage; but *England* was wary, and thought this was to *surrender at Discretion*, so they took up the *Judda* Ship's Guns that was burnt, and the Men of War dispersed themselves on several Voyages and Cruises afterwards, as was thought likeliest to succeed, tho' to no Purpose: Then the Squadron went down to *Bombay*, were saluted by the Fort, and came home.

The Pyrates, I mean those of the *Cassandra*, now Captain *Taylor*, fitted the *Portuguese* Man of War, and resolved upon another Voyage to the *Indies*, notwithstanding the Riches they had heaped up; but as they were preparing to sail, they heard of the four Men of War coming after them to those Seas, therefore they altered their Minds, sail'd for the Main of *Africa*, and put in at a little Place called *Delagoa*, near the River *de Spiritu Sancto*, on the Coast of *Monomotapa*, in 268 South Latitude. They believed this to be a Place of Security, in regard that the Squadron could not possibly get Intelligence of them, there being no Correspondence over Land, nor any Trade carried on by Sea, between that and the Cape, where the Men of War were then supposed to be. The Pyrates came to in the Evening, and were surprized with a few Shot from the Shore, not knowing of any Fortification or *European* Settlement in that Part of the World; so they anchored at a Distance that Night, and perceiving, in the Morning, a small Fort of six Guns, they run up to it, and battered it down.

This Fort was built and settled by the *Dutch East-India* Company, a few Months before, for what Purpose, I know not, and having left 150 Men upon the Place, they were then dwindled to a third Part by Sickness and Casualties, and never after received any Relief or Necessaries; so that Sixteen of those that were left, upon their humble Petition, were admitted on Board the Pyrates, and all the rest would have had the same Favour (they said) had they been any other than *Dutch*. I mention this, as an Instance of their Ingratitude, who had been so much obliged to their Countrymen for Support.

Here they staid above four Months, carreened both their Ships, and took their Diversions with Security, till they had expended all their Provisions, and then put to Sea, leaving considerable Quantities of Muslins, Chintzes, and such Goods behind, to the half starved *Dutch* Men, which enabled them to make good Pennyworths to the next that came, to whom they bartered for Provisions, at the Rate of three Farthings an *English* Yard.

They left *Delagoa* the latter End of *December* 1722, but not agreeing where, or how to proceed, they concluded to part, so those who were for continuing that sort of Life, went on Board the *Portuguese* Prize, and steered for *Madagascar* to their Friends, with whom I hear they are now settled; and the rest took the *Cassandra* and sailed for the *Spanish West-Indies*. The *Mermaid* Man of War happening then to be down on the Main with a Convoy, about 30 Leagues from these Pyrates, would have gone and attacked them; but on a Consultation of the Masters, whose Safety he was particularly to regard, they agreed their own Protection was of more Service than destroying the Pyrate, and so the Commander was unwillingly withheld. He dispatched a Sloop to *Jamaica*, with the News, which brought down the *Lanceston*, only a Day, or two, too late, they having just before he came, surrendered with all their Riches, to the Governor of *Porto Bello*.

Here they sate down to spend the Fruits of their dishonest Industry, dividing the Spoil and Plunder of Nations among themselves, without the least Remorse or Compunction, satisfying their Conscience with this Salvo, that other People would have done as much, had they the like Opportunitiess. I can't say, but that if they had known what was doing in *England*, at the same Time by the *South-Sea* Directors, and their Directors, they would certainly have had this

Reflection for their Consolation, *viz. That what ever Robberies they had committed, they might be pretty sure they were not the greatest Villains then living in the World.*

It is a difficult Matter to make a Computation of the Mischief that was done by this Crew, in about five Years Time, which is much more than the Plunder they gained, for they often sunk or burnt the Vessel they took, as it suited their Humour or Circumstances, sometimes to prevent giving Intelligence, sometimes because they did not leave Men to navigate them, and at other Times out of Wantonness, or because they were displeased at the Master's Behaviour; for any of these, it was but to give the Word, and down went Ships and Cargoes to the Bottom of the Sea.

Since their Surrender to the *Spaniards*, I am informed several of them have left the Place, and dispersed themselves elsewhere; eight of them were shipp'd about *November* last, in one of the *South-Sea* Company's Assiento Sloops, and passed for Ship-wreck'd Men, came to *Jamaica*, and there sailed in other Vessels; and I know one of them that came to *England* this Spring from that Island. 'Tis said that Captain *Taylor* has taken a Commission in the *Spanish* Service, and commanded the Man of War that lately attack'd the *English* Log-Wood Cutters, in the Bay of *Honduras*.

Chap. VI
Of Captain *Charles Vane*, And his Crew

>Vane's Behaviour at Providence. The Names of Prizes taken by him. Is deserted by his Consort Yates. Yates surrenders at Charles-Town. A Stratagem of Vane's. Blackbeard and Vane meet. They salute after the Pyrates Manner. Vane deposed from his Command, and why. 15 Hands degraded, and turned out with him. A Sloop given them. They sail in Quest of Adventures, and take Prizes. Vane cast away upon an uninhabited Island. Meets with an old Acquaintance. Vane seiz'd with a Qualm of Honour. Ships himself on Board a Vessel, passing for another Man. Is discover'd, with the Manner how. Carried to Jamaica, and hang'd.

Charles *Vane* was one of those who stole away the Silver which the *Spaniards* had fished up from the Wrecks of the Galleons, in the Gulph of *Florida*, and was at *Providence* (as has been before hinted) when Governor *Rogers* arrived there with two Men of War.

All the Pyrates who were found at this Colony of Rogues, submitted, and received Certificates of their Pardon, except Captain *Vane* and his Crew; who, as soon as they saw the Men of War enter, slipp'd their Cable, set Fire to a Prize they had in the Harbour, and sailed out with their piratical Colours flying, firing at one of the Men of War as they went off.

Two Days after they went out, they met with a Sloop belonging to *Barbadoes*, which they made Prize of, and kept the Vessel for their own Use, putting aboard five and twenty Hands, with one *Years* to command them. A Day or two afterwards they fell in with a small interloping Trader, with a Quantity of *Spanish* Pieces of Eight aboard, bound into *Providence*, called the *John and Elizabeth*, which they also took along with them. With these two Sloops *Vane* went to a small Island and cleaned; where they shared their Booty, and spent some Time in a riotous Manner of Living, as is the Custom of Pyrates.

The latter End of *May* 1718, they sail'd, and being in want of Provisions, they beat up for the Windward Islands, and met with a *Spanish* Sloop bound from *Porto Rico* to the *Havana*, which they burnt, and stowed the *Spaniards* in a Boat, and left them to get to the Island, by the Light of their Vessel. But steering between St. *Christopher*'s and *Anguilla*, they fell in with a Brigantine and a Sloop, with the Cargo they wanted; from whom they got Provisions for Sea-Store.

Sometime after this, standing to the Northward, in the Track the *Old-England* Ships take, in their Voyage to the *American* Colonies, they took several Ships and Vessels, which they plundered of what they thought fit, and let them pass.

The latter End of *August, Vane*, with his Consort *Yeats*, came off *South-Carolina*, and took a Ship belonging to *Ipswich*, one *Coggershall* Commander, laden with Logwood, which was thought convenient enough for their own Business, and therefore ordered their Prisoners to work, and throw all the Lading over-board; but when they had more than half cleared the Ship, the Whim changed, and then they would not have her; so *Coggershall* had his Ship again, and he was suffered to pursue his Voyage home. In this Cruize the Rover took several other Ships and Vessels, particularly a Sloop from *Barbadoes, Dill* Master; a small Ship from *Antegoa, Cock* Master; a Sloop belonging to *Curacco, Richards* Master; and a large Brigantine, Captain *Thompson*, from *Guiney*, with ninety odd Negroes aboard. The Pyrates plundered them all and let them go, putting the Negroes out of the Brigantine aboard of *Yeat*'s Vessel, by which Means they came back again to the right Owners.

For Captain *Vane*, having always treated his Consort with very little Respect, assuming a Superiority over *Yeats* and his small Crew, and regarding the Vessel but as a Tender to his own; gave them a Disgust, who thought themselves as good Pyrates, and as great Rogues as the best of them; so they caball'd together, and resolved to take the first Opportunity to leave the Company; and accept of his Majesty's Pardon, or set up for themselves, either of which they thought more honourable than to be Servants to the former; and the putting aboard so many

Negroes, where they found so few Hands to take Care of them, still aggravated the Matter, though they thought fit to conceal or stifle their Resentments at that Time.

A Day or two afterwards, the Pyrates lying off at Anchor, *Yeats* in the Evening flipp'd his Cable, and put his Vessel under Sail, standing into the Shore; which, when *Vane* saw, he was highly provoked, and got his Sloop under Sail to chase his Consort, who, he plainly perceived, had a Mind to have no further Affairs with him: *Vane*'s Brigantine sailing best, he gained Ground of *Yeats*, and would certainly have come up with him, had he had a little longer Run for it; but just as he got over the Bar, when *Vane* came within Gun-shot of him, he fired a Broadside at his old Friend, (which did him no Damage,) and so took his Leave.

Yeats came into *North Edisto* River, about ten Leagues Southward of *Charles-Town*, and sent an Express to the Governor, to know if he and his Comrades might have the Benefit of his Majesty's Pardon, and they would surrender themselves to his Mercy, with the Sloops and Negroes; which being granted, they all came up and received Certificates; and Captain *Thompson*, from whom the Negroes were taken, had them restored to him, for the Use of his Owners.

Vane cruised some Time off the Bar, in hopes to catch *Yeats* at his coming out again, but therein he was disappointed; however, he unfortunately for them, took two Ships from *Charles-Town*, bound home to *England*. It happen'd that just at this Time two Sloops well mann'd and arm'd, were equipp'd to go after a Pyrate, which the Governor of *South-Carolina* was informed, lay then in Cape *Fear* River, a cleaning: But Colonel *Rhet*, who commanded the Sloops, meeting with one of the Ships that *Vane* had plundered, going back over the Bar, for such Necessaries as had been taken from her, and she giving the Colonel an Account of her being taken by the Pyrate *Vane*, and also, that some of her Men, while they were Prisoners on Board of him, had heard the Pyrates say, they should clean in one of the Rivers to the Southward; he altered his first Design, and instead of standing to the Northward, in pursuit of the Pyrate in Cape *Fear* River, he turns to the Southward after *Vane*; who had ordered such Reports to be given out, on purpose to send any Force that should come after him, upon a wrong Scent; for in Reality he stood away to the Northward, so that the Pursuit proved to be the contrary Way.

Colonel *Rhet*'s speaking with this Ship, was the most unlucky Thing that could have happened, because it turned him out of the Road, which in all Probability, would have brought him into the Company of *Vane*, as well as of the Pyrate he went after; and so they might have been both destroy'd; whereas, by the Colonel's going a different Way, he not only lost the Opportunity of meeting with one, but if the other had not been infatuated, to lye six Weeks together at Cape *Fear*, he would have missed of him likewise: However, the Collonel having searched the Rivers and Inlets, as directed, for several Days, without Success, at length failed in Prosecution of his first Design, and met with the Pyrate accordingly, whom he fought and took, as has been before spoken of, in the History of Major *Bonnet*.

Captain *Vane* went into an Inlet to the Northward, where he met with Captain *Thatch*, or *Teach*, otherwise call'd *Black-beard*, whom he saluted (when he found who he was) with his great Guns, loaded with Shot, (as is the Custom among Pyrates when they meet) which are fired wide, or up into the Air: *Black-beard* answered the Salute in the same Manner, and mutual Civilities passed for some Days; when about the Beginning of *October*, *Vane* took Leave, and sailed further to the Northward.

On the 23d of *October*, off of *Long Island*, he took a small Brigantine, bound from *Jamaica* to *Salem* in *New-England, John Shattock* Master, and a little Sloop; they rifled the Brigantine, and sent her away. From hence they resolved on a Cruize between Cape *Meise* and Cape *Nicholas*, where they spent some Time, without seeing or speaking with any Vessel, till the latter End of *November*; then they fell upon a Ship, which 'twas expected would have struck as soon as their black Colours were hoisted; but instead of that, she discharged a Broadside upon the Pyrate, and hoisted Colours, which showed her to be a *French* Man of War. *Vane* desired to have nothing further to say to her, but trimm'd his Sails, and stood away from the *French* Man; but *Monsieur* having a Mind to be better informed who he was, set all his Sails, and crowded after him. During this Chace, the Pyrates were divided in their Resolutions what to do: *Vane*, the Captain, was for making off as fast as he could, alledging the Man of War was too strong to cope with; but one *John Rackam*, who was an Officer, that had a kind of a Check upon the Captain, rose up in Defence of a contrary Opinion, saying, *That tho' she had more Guns, and a greater Weight of Mettal, they might board her, and then the best Boys would carry the Day.* Rackam was well seconded, and the Majority was for boarding; but *Vane* urged, *That it was too rash and desperate an Enterprize, the Man of War appearing to be twice their Force; and that their Brigantine might be sunk by her before they could reach on board.* The Mate, one *Robert Deal*, was of *Vane*'s Opinion, as were about fifteen more, and all the rest joined with *Rackam*, the Quarter-Master. At length the Captain made use of his Power to determine this Dispute, which, in these Cases, is absolute and uncontroulable, by their own Laws, *viz.* in *fighting, chasing*, or *being chased*; in all other Matters whatsoever, he is governed by a Majority; so the Brigantine having the Heels, as they term it, of the *French* Man, she came clear off.

But the next Day, the Captain's Behaviour was obliged to stand the Test of a Vote, and a Resolution passed against his Honour and Dignity, branding him with the Name of Coward, deposing him from the Command, and turning him out of the Company, with Marks of Infamy; and, with him, went all those who did not Vote for boarding the *French* Man of War. They had with them a small Sloop that had been taken by them some Time before, which they gave to *Vane*, and the discarded Members; and, that they might be in a Condition to provide for themselves, by their own honest Endeavours, they let them have a sufficient Quantity of Provisions and Ammunition along with them.

John Rackam was voted Captain of the Brigantine, in *Vane*'s Room, and proceeded towards the *Caribbee Islands*, where we must leave him, till we have finished our Story of *Charles Vane*.

The Sloop failed for the Bay of *Honduras*, and *Vane* and his Crew put her into as good a Condition as they could by the Way, to follow the old Trade. They cruised two or three Days off the North-West Part of *Jamaica*, and took a Sloop and two Pettiagas, and all the Men entered with them; the Sloop they kept, and *Robert Deal* went Captain of her.

On the 16th of *December* the two Sloops came into the Bay, where they found only one at an Anchor, call'd the *Pearl*, of *Jamaica*, Captain *Charles Rowling* Master, who got under Sail at the Sight of them; but the Pyrate Sloops coming near *Rowling*, and showing no Colours, he gave them a Gun or two; whereupon they hoisted the black Flag, and fired three Guns each, at the *Pearl*; she struck, and the Pyrates took Possession, and carried her away to a small Island called *Barnacko*, and there they cleaned, meeting in the Way with a Sloop from *Jamaica*, Captain *Wallden* Commander, going down to the Bay, which they also made Prize of.

In *February, Vane* sailed from *Barnacko*, in order for a Cruize; but some Days after he was out, a violent Turnado overtook him, which separated him from his Consort, and after two Days Distress, threw his Sloop upon a small uninhabited Island, near the Bay of *Honduras*, where she was staved to Pieces, and most of her Men drowned: *Vane* himself was saved, but reduced to great Streights, for want of Necessaries, having no Opportunity to get any Thing from the Wreck. He lived here some Weeks, and was subsisted chiefly by Fishermen, who frequented the Island with small Craft, from the Main, to catch Tuttles, *&c.*

While *Vane* was upon this Island, a Ship put in from *Jamaica* for Water, the Captain of which, one *Holford*, an old Buccaneer, happened to be *Vane*'s Acquaintance; he thought this a good Opportunity to get off, and accordingly applied to his old Friend; but he absolutely refused him, saying to him, Charles, *I shan't trust you aboard my Ship, unless I carry you a Prisoner; for I shall have you caballing with my Men, knock me on the Head, and run away with my Ship a pirating.* *Vane* made all the Protestations of Honour in the World to him; but, it seems, Captain *Holford* was too intimately acquainted with him, to repose any Confidence at all in his Words or Oaths. He told him, *He might easily find a Way to get off, if he had a Mind to it: I am now going down the Bay,* says he, *and shall return hither, in about a Month; and if I find you upon the Island when I come back, I'll carry you to* Jamaica, *and hang you. Which Way can I get away?* Answers *Vane. Are there not Fishermen's Dories upon the Beach? Can't you take one of them?* Replies *Holford. What*, says *Vane, would you have me steal a Dory then? Do you make it a Matter of Conscience?* Said *Holford*, *to steal a Dory, when you have been a common Robber and Pyrate, stealing Ships and Cargoes, and plundering all Mankind that fell in your Way? Stay there, and be d — n'd, if you are so Squeamish*: And so left him.

After Captain *Holford*'s Departure, another Ship put in to the same Island in her Way home for Water; none of whose Company knowing *Vane*, he easily passed upon them for another Man, and so was shipp'd or the Voyage. One would be apt to think that *Vane* was now pretty safe, and likely to escape the Fate which his Crimes had merited; but here a cross Accident happen'd that ruin'd all: *Holford*, returning from the Bay, was met with by this Ship; the Captains being very well acquainted together, *Holford* was invited to dine aboard of him, which he did; and as he passed along to the Cabin, he chanced to cast his Eye down the Hold, and there saw *Charles Vane* at work; he immediately spoke to the Captain, saying, *Do you know who you have got aboard here?* Why, says he, *I have shipp'd a Man at such an Island, who was cast away in a trading Sloop, he seems to be a brisk Hand. I tell you*, says Captain *Holford, it is* Vane *the notorious Pyrate. If it be him*, replies the other, *I won't keep him: Why then*, says *Holford, I'll send and take him aboard, and surrender him at* Jamaica. Which being agreed to, Captain *Holford*, as soon as he returned to his Ship, sent his Boat with his Mate armed, who coming to *Vane*, showed him a Pistol, and told him, *He was his Prisoner*; which none opposing, he was brought aboard, and put in Irons; and when Captain *Holford* arrived at *Jamaica*, he delivered his old Acquaintance into the Hands of Justice; at which Place he was try'd, convicted, and executed, as was, some Time before, *Vane*'s Consort, *Robert Deal*, brought thither by one of the Men of War.

Chap. VII
Of Captain *John Rackam*, And his Crew

Rackam's beginning as a Pyrate. An Account of Prizes taken by him. Is attack'd by a Spanish Guard Ship. His Stratagem to escape. More Prizes taken by him. Is taken, and how. Tried, condemned, and executed at Jamaica. The Names of his Crew condemn'd with him. An extraordinary Case of nine taken with him. Some Account of the Proceedings against them.

This *John Rackam*, as has been mentioned in the last Chapter, was Quarter-Master to *Vane*'s Company, till they were divided, and *Vane* turned out for refusing to board and fight the *French* Man of War; then *Rackam* was voted Captain of that Division that remained in the Brigantine. The 24th of *November* 1718, was the first Day of his Command, and his first Cruize was among the *Caribbee Islands*, where he took and plunder'd several Vessels.

We have already taken Notice, that when Captain *Woodes Rogers* went to the Island of *Providence*, with the King's Pardon to such as should surrender, this Brigantine, which *Rackam* now commanded, made its Escape, thro' another Passage, bidding Defiance to Mercy.

To Windward of *Jamaica*, a *Madera* Man fell into the Pyrates Way, which they detained two or three Days, till they had made their Market out of her, and then gave her back to the Master, and permitted one *Hosea Tisdell*, a Tavern-Keeper at *Jamaica*, who had been pick'd up in one of their Prizes, to depart in her, she being then bound for that Island.

After this Cruize, they went into a small Island and cleaned, and spent their *Christmas* ashore, drinking and carousing as long as they had any Liquor left, and then went to Sea again for more, where they succeeded but too well, though they took no extraordinary Prize, for above two Months, except a Ship laden with Thieves from *Newgate*, bound for the Plantations, which, in a few Days, was retaken with all her Cargo, by an *English* Man of War.

Rackam stood off towards the Island of *Burmudas*, and took a Ship bound to *England* from *Carolina*, and a small Pink from *New-England*, and brought them to the *Bahama* Islands, where with the Pitch, Tar, and Stores, they clean'd again, and refitted their own Vessel; but staying too long in that Neighbourhood, Captain *Rogers*, who was Governor of *Providence*, hearing of these Ships being taken, sent out a Sloop well mann'd and arm'd, which retook both the Prizes, and in the mean while the Pyrate had the good Fortune to escape.

From hence they sailed to the Back of *Cuba*, where *Rackam* kept a little kind of a Family, at which Place, they staid a considerable Time, living ashore with their Dalilahs, till their Money and Provision were expended, and then they concluded it Time to look out: They repaired to their Vessel, and was making ready to put Sea, when a *Guarda del Costa* came in with a small *English* Sloop, which she had taken as an Interloper on the Coast. The *Spanish* Guardship attack'd the Pyrate, but *Rackam* being close in behind a little Island, she could do but little Execution where she lay, therefore the *Spaniard* warps into the Channel that Evening, in order to make sure of her the next Morning.

Rackam finding his Case desperate, and hardly any Possibility of escaping, resolved to attempt the following Enterprize: The *Spanish* Prize lying for better Security close into the Land, between the little Island and the Main; *Rackam* takes his Crew into the Boat, with their Pistols and Cutlashes, rounds the little Island, and falls aboard their Prize silently in the dead of the Night, without being discovered, telling the *Spaniards* that were aboard of her, that if they spoke a Word, or made the least Noise, they were dead Men, and so became Master of her; when this was done, he slipt her Cable, and drove out to Sea: The *Spanish* Man of War, was so intent upon their expected Prize, that they minded nothing else, and assoon as Day broke, made a furious Fire upon the empty Sloop, but it was not long before they were rightly apprized of the Matter, and cursed themselves for Fools, to be bit out of a good rich Prize, as she prov'd to be, and to have nothing but an old crazy Hull in the room of her.

Rackam and his Crew had no Occasion to be displeased at the Exchange, that enabled them to continue some Time longer in a Way of Life that suited their depraved Tempers: In *August*

1720, we find him at Sea again, scouring the Harbours and Inlets of the North and West Parts of *Jamaica*, where he took several small Crast, which proved no great Booty to the Rovers, but they had but few Men, and therefore they were obliged to run at low Game, till they could encrease their Company.

In the Beginning of *September*, they took seven or eight Fishing-Boats in *Harbour Island*, stole their Nets and other Tackle, and then went off the *French* Part of *Hispaniola*, and landed, and took Cattle away, with two or three *French* Men they found near the Water-Side, hunting of wild Hogs in the Evening: The *French* Men came on Board, whether by Consent or Compulsion, I can't say. They afterwards plundered two Sloops, and returned to *Jamaica*, on the North Coast of which Island, near *Porto Maria* Bay, they took a Scooner, *Thomas Spenlow* Master; it was then the 19th of *October*. The next Day, *Rackam* seeing a Sloop in *Dry Harbour* Bay, he stood in and fired a Gun; the Men all run ashore, and he took the Sloop and Lading, but when those ashore found them to be Pyrates, they hailed the Sloop, and let them know they were all willing to come aboard of them.

Rackam's coasting the Island in this Manner, proved fatal to him, for Intelligence came to the Governor, of his Expedition, by a Canoa which he had surprized ashore, in *Ocho* Bay; upon which a Sloop was immediately fitted out, and sent round the Island in quest of him, commanded by Captain *Barnet*, with a good Number of Hands. *Rackam* rounding the Island, and drawing near the Westermost Point, called Point *Negril*, saw a small Pettiauger, which at sight of the Sloop, run ashore and landed her Men; when one of them hailed her, Answer was made, *They were* English *Men*, and desired the Pettiauger's Men to come on Board, and drink a Bowl of Punch, which they were prevailed upon to do; accordingly the Company came all aboard of the Pyrate, consisting of nine Persons, in an ill Hour; they were armed with Muskets and Cutlashes, but, what was their real Design by so doing, I shall not take upon me to say; but they had no sooner laid down their Arms, and taken up their Pipes, but *Barnet*'s Sloop, which was in Pursuit of *Rackam*'s, came in Sight.

The Pyrates finding she stood directly towards her, fear'd the Event, and weighed their Anchor, which they but lately let go, and stood off: Captain *Barnet* gave them Chace, and having the Advantage of little Breezes of Wind, which blew off the Land, came up with her, and, after a very small Dispute, took her, and brought her into *Port Royal*, in *Jamaica*.

In about a Fortnight after the Prisoners were brought ashore, *viz. November* 16, 1720, a Court of Admiralty was held at St. *Jago de la Vega*, before which the following Persons were convicted, and Sentence of Death passed upon them, by the President, Sir *Nicholas Laws, viz. John Rackam* Captain, *George Fetherston* Master, *Richard Corner* Quarter-Master, *John Davis, John Howell, Patrick Carty, Thomas Earl, James Dobbin* and *Noah Harwood*. The five first were executed the next Day at *Gallows Point*, at the Town of *Port Royal*, and the rest, the Day after, at *Kingston*; *Rackam, Feverston* and *Corner*, were afterwards taken down and hang'd up in Chains, one at *Plumb Point*, one at *Bush Key*, and the other at *Gun Key*.

But what was very surprizing, was, the Conviction of the nine Men that came aboard the Sloop the same Day she was taken. They were try'd at an Adjournment of the Court, on the 24th of *January*, waiting all that Time, it is supposed, for Evidence, to prove the piratical Intention of going aboard the said Sloop; for it seems there was no Act of Pyracy committed by them, after their coming on Board, as appeared by the Witnesses against them, who were two *French* Men taken by *Rackam*, off from the Island of *Hispaniola*, and deposed in the following Manner.

'That the Prisoners at the Bar, *viz. John Eaton, Edward Warner, Thomas Baker, Thomas Quick, John Cole, Benjamin Palmer, Walter Rouse, John Hanson,* and *John Howard*, came aboard the Pyrate's Sloop at *Negril Point, Rackam* sending his Canoe ashore for that Purpose: That they brought Guns and Cutlashes on Board with them: That when Captain *Barnet* chased them, some were drinking, and others walking the Deck: That there was a great Gun and a small Arm fired by the Pyrate Sloop, at Captain *Barnet*'s Sloop, when he chased her; and that when Captain *Barnet*'s Sloop fired at *Rackam*'s Sloop, the Prisoners at the Bar went down under Deck. That during the Time Captain *Barnet* chased them, some of the Prisoners at the Bar (but which of them he could not tell) helped to row the Sloop, in order to escape from *Barnet*: That they all seemed to be consorted together.

This was the Substance of all that was evidenced against them, the Prisoners answered in their Defence, 'That they had no Witnesses: That they had bought a Pettiauger in order to go a Turtleing; and being at *Negril Point*, and just got ashore, they saw a Sloop with a white Pendant coming towards them, upon which they took their Arms, and hid themselves in the Bushes: That one of them hail'd the Sloop, who answer'd, *They were* English *Men*, and desired them to come aboard and drink a Bowl of Punch; which they at first refused, but afterwards with much perswasion, they went on Board, in the Sloop's Canoe, and left their own Pettiauger at Anchor: That they had been but a short Time on Board, when Captain *Barnet*'s Sloop heaved in Sight: That *Rackam* ordered them to help to weigh the Sloop's Anchor immediately, which they all refused: That *Rackam* used violent Means to oblige them; and that when Captain *Barnet* came up with them, they all readily and willingly submitted.

When the Prisoners were taken from the Bar, and the Persons present being withdrawn, the Court considered the Prisoners Cases, and the Majority of the Commissioners being of Opinion, that they were all Guilty of the Pyracy and Felonly they were charged with, which was, *the going over with a piratical and felonious Intent to* John Rackam, &c. *then notorious Pyrates, and by them known to be so,* they all received Sentence of Death; which every Body must allow proved somewhat unlucky to the poor Fellows.

On the 17th of *February, John Eaton, Thomas Quick* and *Thomas Baker*, were executed at *Gallows Point*, at *Port Royal*, and the next Day *John Cole, John Howard* and *Benjamin Palmer*, were executed at *Kingston*; whether the other three were executed afterwards, or not, I never heard.

Two other Pyrates were try'd that belonged to *Rackam*'s Crew, and being convicted, were brought up, and asked if either of them had any Thing to say why Sentence of Death should not pass upon them, in like Manner as had been done to all the rest; and both of them pleaded their Bellies, being quick with Child, and pray'd that Execution might be stay'd, whereupon the Court passed Sentence, as in Cases of Pyracy, but ordered them back, till a proper Jury should be appointed to enquire into the Matter.

Chap. VIII
The Life of Mary Read, And Anne Bonny

The Life of Mary Read

> Mary Read's Birth. Reasons for dressing her in Breeches. Waits upon a Lady; goes into the Army. Her Behaviour in several Engagements. She falls in Love with her Comrade. Her Sex discovered; the two Troopers married. Settles at Breda. Her Husband dies, she reassumes the Breeches. Goes to Holland. To the West-Indies. Turns Pyrate. Anne Bonny, another Pyrate, falls in Love with her. Her Adventures.

Now we are to begin a History full of surprizing Turns and Adventures; I mean, that of *Mary Read* and *Anne Bonny*, alias *Bonn*, which were the true Names of these two Pyrates; the odd Incidents of their rambling Lives are such, that some may be tempted to think the whole Story no better than a Novel or Romance; but since it is supported by many thousand Witnesses, I mean the People of *Jamaica*, who were present at their Tryals, and heard the Story of their Lives, upon the first discovery of their Sex; the Truth of it can be no more contested, than that there were such Men in the World, as *Roberts* and *Black-beard*, who were Pyrates.

Mary Read was born in *England*, her Mother was married young, to a Man who used the Sea, who going a Voyage soon after their Marriage, left her with Child, which Child proved to be a Boy. As to the Husband, whether he was cast away, or died in the Voyage, *Mary Read* could not tell; but however, he never returned more; nevertheless, the Mother, who was young and airy, met with an Accident, which has often happened to Women who are young, and do not take a great deal of Care; which was, she soon proved with Child again, without a Husband to Father it, but how, or by whom, none but her self could tell, for she carried a pretty good Reputation among her Neighbours. Finding her Burthen grow, in order to conceal her Shame, she takes a formal Leave of her Husband's Relations, giving out, that she went to live with some Friends of her own, in the Country: Accordingly she went away, and carried with her her young Son, at this Time, not a Year old: Soon after her Departure her Son died, but Providence in Return, was pleased to give her a Girl in his Room, of which she was safely delivered, in her Retreat, and this was our *Mary Read*.

Here the Mother liv'd three or four Years, till what Money she had was almost gone; then she thought of returning to *London*, and considering that her Husband's Mother was in some Circumstances, she did not doubt but to prevail upon her, to provide for the Child, if she could but pass it upon her for the same, but the changing a Girl into a Boy, seem'd a difficult Piece of Work, and how to deceive an experienced old Woman, in such a Point, was altogether as impossible; however, she ventured to dress it up as a Boy, brought it to Town, and presented it to her Mother in Law, as her Husband's Son; the old Woman would have taken it, to have bred it up, but the Mother pretended it would break her Heart, to part with it; so it was agreed betwixt them, that the Child should live with the Mother, and the supposed Grandmother should allow a Crown a Week for it's Maintainance.

Thus the Mother gained her Point, she bred up her Daughter as a Boy, and when she grew up to some Sense, she thought proper to let her into the Secret of her Birth, to induce her to conceal her Sex. It happen'd that the Grandmother died, by which Means the Subsistance that came from that Quarter, ceased, and they were more and more reduced in their Circumstances; wherefore she was obliged to put her Daughter out, to wait on a *French* Lady, as a Foot-boy, being now thirteen Years of Age: Here she did not live long, for growing bold and strong, and having also a roving Mind, she entered her self on Board a Man of War, where she served some Time, then quitted it, went over into *Flanders*, and carried Arms in a Regiment of Foot, as a *Cadet*; and tho' upon all Actions, she behaved herself with a great deal of Bravery, yet she could not get a Commission, they being generally bought and sold; therefore she quitted the Service, and took on in a Regiment of Horse; she behaved so well in several Engagements, that she got the Esteem of all her Officers; but her Comrade who was a *Fleming*, happening to be a handsome young Fellow, she falls in Love with him, and from that Time, grew a little more negligent in her Duty, so that, it seems, *Mars* and *Venus* could not be served at the same Time; her Arms and Accoutrements which were always kept in the best Order, were quite neglected: 'tis true, when her Comrade was ordered out upon a Party, she used to go without being commanded, and frequently run herself into Danger, where she had no Business, only to be near him; the rest of the Troopers little suspecting the secret Cause which moved her to this Behaviour, fancied her to be mad, and her Comrade himself could not account for this strange Alteration in her, but Love is ingenious, and as they lay in the same Tent, and were constantly together, she found a Way of letting him discover her Sex, without appearing that it was done with Design.

He was much surprized at what he found out, and not a little pleased, taking it for granted, that he should have a Mistress solely to himself, which is an unusual Thing in a Camp, since there is scarce one of those Campaign Ladies, that is ever true to a Troop or Company; so that he thought of nothing but gratifying his Passions with very little Ceremony; but he found himself strangely mistaken, for she proved very reserved and modest, and resisted all his Temptations, and at the same Time was so obliging and insinuating in her Carriage, that she quite changed his Purpose, so far from thinking of making her his Mistress, he now courted her for a Wife.

This was the utmost Wish of her Heart, in short, they exchanged Promises, and when the Campaign was over, and the Regiment marched into Winter Quarters, they bought Woman's Apparel for her, with such Money as they could make up betwixt them, and were publicly married.

The Story of two Troopers marrying each other, made a great Noise, so that several Officers were drawn by Curiosity to assist at the Ceremony, and they agreed among themselves that every one of them should make a small Present to the Bride, towards House-keeping, in Consideration of her having been their fellow Soldier. Thus being set up, they seemed to have a Desire of quitting the Service, and settling in the World; the Adventure of their Love and Marriage had gained them so much Favour, that they easily obtained their Discharge, and they immediately set up an Eating House or Ordinary, which was the Sign of the *Three Horse-Shoes*, near the Castle of *Breda*, where they soon run into a good Trade, a great many Officers eating with them constantly.

But this Happiness lasted not long, for the Husband soon died, and the Peace of *Reswick* being concluded, there was no Resort of Officers to *Breda*, as usual; so that the Widow having little or no Trade, was forced to give up House-keeping, and her Substance being by Degrees quite spent, she again assumes her Man's Apparel, and going into *Holland*, there takes on in a Regiment of Foot, quarter'd in one of the Frontier Towns: Here she did not remain long, there was no likelihood of Preferment in Time of Peace, therefore she took a Resolution of seeking her Fortune another Way; and withdrawing from the Regiment, ships herself on Board of a Vessel bound for the *West-Indies*.

It happen'd this Ship was taken by *English*Pyrates, and *Mary Read* was the only *English* Person on Board, they kept her amongst them, and having plundered the Ship, let it go again; after following this Trade for some Time, the King's Proclamation came out, and was publish'd in all Parts of the *West-Indies*, for pardoning such Pyrates, who should voluntarily surrender themselves by a certain Day therein mentioned. The Crew of *Mary Read* took the Benefit of this Proclamation, and having surrender'd, liv'd quietly on Shore; but Money beginning to grow short, and hearing that Captain *Woods Rogers*, Governor of the Island of *Providence*, was fitting out some Privateers to cruise against the *Spaniards*, she with several others embark'd for that Island, in order to go upon the privateering Account, being resolved to make her Fortune one way or other.

These Privateers were no sooner sail'd out, but the Crews of some of them, who had been pardoned, rose against their Commanders, and turned themselves to their old Trade: In this Number was *Mary Read*. It is true, she often declared, that the Life of a Pyrate was what she always abhor'd, and went into it only upon Compulsion, both this Time, and before, intending to quit it, whenever a fair Opportunity should offer it self; yet some of the Evidence against her, upon her Tryal, who were forced Men, and had sailed with her, deposed upon Oath, that in Times of Action, no Person amongst them were more resolute, or ready to Board or undertake any Thing that was hazardous, as she and *Anne Bonny*; and particularly at the Time they were attack'd and taken, when they came to close Quarters, none kept the Deck except *Mary Read* and *Anne Bonny*, and one more; upon which, she, *Mary Read*, called to those under Deck, to come up and fight like Men, and finding they did not stir, fired her Arms down the Hold amongst them, killing one, and wounding others.

This was part of the Evidence against her, which she denied; which, whether true or no, thus much is certain, that she did not want Bravery, nor indeed was she less remarkable for her Modesty, according to her Notions of Virtue: Her Sex was not so much as suspected by any Person on Board, till *Anne Bonny*, who was not altogether so reserved in point of Chastity, took a particular liking to her; in short, *Anne Bonny* took her for a handsome young Fellow, and for some Reasons best known to herself, first discovered her Sex to *Mary Read; Mary Read* knowing what she would be at, and being very sensible of her own Incapacity that Way, was forced to come to a right Understanding with her, and so to the great Disappointment of *Anne Bonny*, she let her know she was a Woman also; but this Intimacy so disturb'd Captain *Rackam*, who was the Lover and Gallant of *Anne Bonny*, that he grew furiously jealous, so that he told *Anne Bonny*, he would cut her new Lover's Throat, therefore, to quiet him, she let him into the Secret also.

Captain *Rackam*, (as he was enjoined,) kept the Thing a Secret from all the Ship's Company, yet, notwithstanding all her Cunning and Reserve, Love found her out in this Disguise, and hinder'd her from forgetting her Sex. In their Cruize they took a great Number of Ships belonging to *Jamaica*, and other Parts of the *West-Indies*, bound to and from *England*; and when ever they meet any good Artist, or other Person that might be of any great Use to their Company, if he was not willing to enter, it was their Custom to keep him by Force. Among these was a young Fellow of a most engaging Behaviour, or, at least, he was so in the Eyes of *Mary Read*, who became so smitten with his Person and Address, that she could neither rest, Night or Day; but as there is nothing more ingenious than Love, it was no hard Matter for her, who had before been practiced in these Wiles, to find a Way to let him discover her Sex: She first insinuated her self into his liking, by talking against the Life of a Pyrate, which he was altogether averse to, so they became Mess-Mates and strict Companions: When she found he had a Friendship for her, as a Man, she suffered the Discovery to be made, by carelesly showing her Breasts, which were very White.

The young Fellow, who was made of Flesh and Blood, had his Curiosity and Desire so rais'd by this Sight, that he never ceased importuning her, till she confessed what she was. Now begins the Scene of Love; as he had a Liking and Esteem for her, under her supposed Character, it was now turn'd into Fondness and Desire; her Passion was no less violent than his, and perhaps she express'd it, by one of the most generous Actions that ever Love inspired. It happened this young Fellow had a Quarrel with one of the Pyrates, and their Ship then lying at an Anchor, near one of the Islands, they had appointed to go ashore and fight, according to the Custom of the Pyrates: *Mary Read*, was to the last Degree uneasy and anxious, for the Fate of her Lover; she would not have had him refuse the Challenge, because, she could not bear the Thoughts of his being branded with Cowardise; on the other Side, she dreaded the Event, and apprehended the Fellow might be too hard for him: When Love once enters into the Breast of one who has any Sparks of Generosity, it stirs the Heart up to the most noble Actions; in this Dilemma, she show'd, that she fear'd more for his Life than she did for her own; for she took a Resolution of quarreling with this Fellow her self, and having challenged him ashore, she appointed the Time two Hours sooner than that when he was to meet her Lover, where she fought him at Sword and Pistol, and killed him upon the Spot.

It is true, she had fought before, when she had been insulted by some of those Fellows, but now it was altogether in her Lover's Cause, she stood as it were betwixt him and Death, as if she could not live without him. If he had no regard for her before, this Action would have bound him to her for ever; but there was no Occasion for Ties or Obligations, his Inclination towards her was sufficient; in fine, they applied their Troth to each other, which *Mary Read* said, she look'd upon to be as good a Marriage, in Conscience, as if it had been done by a Minister in Church; and to this was owing her great Belly, which she pleaded to save her Life.

She declared she had never committed Adultery or Fornication with any Man, she commended the Justice of the Court, before which she was tried, for distinguishing the Nature of their Crimes; her Husband, as she call'd him, with several others, being acquitted; and being ask'd, who he was? she would not tell, but, said he was an honest Man, and had no Inclination to such Practices, and that they had both resolved to leave the Pyrates the first Opportunity, and apply themselves to some honest Livelyhood.

It is no doubt, but many had Compassion for her, yet the Court could not avoid finding her Guilty; for among other Things, one of the Evidences against her, deposed, that being taken by *Rackam*, and detain'd some Time on Board, he fell accidentally into Discourse with *Mary Read*, whom he taking for a young Man, ask'd her, what Pleasure she could have in being concerned in such Enterprizes, where her Life was continually in Danger, by Fire or Sword; and not only so, but she must be sure of dying an ignominious Death, if she should be taken alive? —— She answer'd, that as to hanging, she thought it no great Hardship, for, were it not for that, every cowardly Fellow would turn Pyrate, and so infest the Seas, that Men of Courage must starve: — That if it was put to the Choice of the Pyrates, they would not have the punishment less than Death, the Fear of which, kept some dastardly Rogues honest; that many of those who are now cheating the Widows and Orphans, and oppressing their poor Neighbours, who have no Money to obtain Justice, would then rob at Sea, and the Ocean would be crowded with Rogues, like the Land, and no Merchant would venture out; so that the Trade, in a little Time, would not be worth following.

Being found quick with Child, as has been observed, her Execution was respited, and it is possible she would have found Favour, but she was seiz'd with a violent Fever, soon after her Tryal, of which she died in Prison.

The Life of Anne Bonny

>ANNE Bonny born a Bastard. Her Mother's Intrigues strangely discover'd. Her Father lies with his own Wife, by mistake. She proves with Child; the Husband jealous. He separates from his Wife; lives with Anne Bonny's Mother. Anne Bonny put into Breeches for a Disguise, how discovered. The Father becomes poor. Goes to Carolina. Improves his Fortune. Anne Bonny marries against his Consent. Her fierce Temper. Goes to Providence with her Husband. Enticed to Sea in Men's Cloaths, by Rackam the Pyrate. Reproaches Rackam with Cowardice at his Execution.

AS we have been more particular in the Lives of these two Women, than those of other Pyrates, it is incumbent on us, as a faithful Historian, to begin with their Birth. *Anne Bonny* was born at a Town near *Cork*, in the Kingdom of *Ireland*, her Father an Attorney at Law, but *Anne* was not one of his legitimate Issue, which seems to cross an old Proverb, which says, *that Bastards have the best Luck.* Her Father was a Married Man, and his Wife having been brought to Bed, contracted an Illness in her lying in, and in order to recover her Health, she was advised to remove for Change of Air; the Place she chose, was a few Miles distance from her Dwelling, where her Husband's Mother liv'd. Here she sojourn'd some Time, her Husband staying at Home, to follow his Affairs. The Servant-Maid, whom she left to look after the House, and attend the Family, being a handsome young Woman, was courted by a young Man of the same Town, who was a *Tanner*; this *Tanner* used to take his Opportunities, when the Family was out of the Way, of coming to pursue his Courtship; and being with the Maid one Day as she was employ'd in the Houshold Business, not having the Fear of God before his Eyes, he takes his Opportunity, when her Back was turned, of whipping three Silver Spoons into his Pocket. The Maid soon miss'd the Spoons, and knowing that no Body had been in the Room, but herself and the young Man, since she saw them last, she charged him with taking them; he very stifly denied it, upon which she grew outragious, and threatned to go to a Constable, in order to carry him before a Justice of Peace: These Menaces frighten'd him out of his Wits, well knowing he could not stand Search; wherefore he endeavoured to pacify her, by desiring her to examine the Drawers and other Places, and perhaps she might find them; in this Time he slips into another Room, where the Maid usually lay, and puts the Spoons betwixt the Sheets, and then makes his Escape by a back Door, concluding she must find them, when she went to Bed, and so next Day he might pretend he did it only to frighten her, and the Thing might be laugh'd off for a Jest.

As soon as she miss'd him, she gave over her Search, concluding he had carried them off, and went directly to the Constable, in order to have him apprehended: The young Man was informed, that a Constable had been in Search of him, but he regarded it but little, not doubting but all would be well next Day. Three or four Days passed, and still he was told, the Constable was upon the Hunt for him, this made him lye concealed, he could not comprehend the Meaning of it, he imagined no less, than that the Maid had a Mind to convert the Spoons to her own Use, and put the Robbery upon him.

It happened, at this Time, that the Mistress being perfectly recovered of her late Indisposition, was return'd Home, in Company with her Mother-in-Law; the first News she heard, was of the Loss of the Spoons, with the Manner how; the Maid telling her, at the same Time, that the young Man was run away. The young Fellow had Intelligence of the Mistress's Arrival, and considering with himself, that he could never appear again in his Business, unless this Matter was got over, and she being a good natured Woman, he took a Resolution of going directly to her, and of telling her the whole Story, only with this Difference, that he did it for a Jest.

The Mistress could scarce believe it, however, she went directly to the Maid's Room, and turning down the Bed Cloaths, there, to her great Surprize, found the three Spoons; upon this she desired the young Man to go Home and mind his Business, for he should have no Trouble about it.

The Mistress could not imagine the Meaning of this, she never had found the Maid guilty of any pilfering, and therefore it could not enter her Head, that she designed to steal the Spoons her self; upon the whole, she concluded the Maid had not been in her Bed, from the Time the Spoons were miss'd, she grew immediately jealous upon it, and suspected, that the Maid supplied her Place with her Husband, during her Absence, and this was the Reason why the Spoons were no sooner found.

She call'd to Mind several Actions of Kindness, her Husband had showed the Maid, Things that pass'd unheeded by, when they happened, but now she had got that Tormentor, Jealousy, in her Head, amounted to Proofs of their Intimacy; another Circumstance which strengthen'd the whole, was, that tho' her Husband knew she was to come Home that Day, and had had no Communication with her in four Months, which was before her last Lying in, yet he took an Opportunity of going out of Town that Morning, upon some slight Pretence: —— All these Things put together, confirm'd her in her Jealousy.

As Women seldom forgive Injuries of this Kind, she thought of discharging her Revenge upon the Maid: In order to this, she leaves the Spoons where she found them, and orders the Maid to put clean Sheets upon the Bed, telling her, she intended to lye there herself that Night, because her Mother in Law was to lye in her Bed, and that she (the Maid) must lye in another Part of the House; the Maid in making the Bed, was surprized with the Sight of the Spoons, but there were very good Reasons, why it was not proper for her to tell where she found them, therefore she takes them up, puts them in her Trunk, intending to leave them in some Place, where they might be found by chance.

The Mistress, that every Thing might look to be done without Design, lies that Night in the Maid's Bed, little dreaming of what an Adventure it would produce: After she had been a Bed some Time, thinking on what had pass'd, for Jealousy kept her awake, she heard some Body enter the Room; at first she apprehended it to be Thieves, and was so fright'ned, she had not Courage enough to call out; but when she heard these Words, Mary, *are you awake*? She knew it to be her Husband's Voice; then her Fright was over, yet she made no Answer, least he should find her out, if she spoke, therefore she resolved to counterfeit Sleep, and take what followed.

The Husband came to Bed, and that Night play'd the vigorous Lover; but one Thing spoil'd the Diversion on the Wife's Side, which was, the Reflection that it was not design'd for her; however she was very passive, and bore it like a Christian. Early before Day, she stole out of Bed, leaving him asleep, and went to her Mother in Law, telling her what had passed, not forgetting how he had used her, as taking her for the Maid; the Husband also stole out, not thinking it convenient to be catch'd in that Room; in the mean Time, the Revenge of the Mistress was strongly against the Maid, and without considering, that to her she ow'd the Diversion of the Night before, and that one good *Turn* should deserve another; she sent for a Constable, and charged her with stealing the Spoons: The Maid's Trunk was broke open, and the Spoons found, upon which she was carried before a Justice of Peace, and by him committed to Goal.

The Husband loiter'd about till twelve a Clock at Noon, then comes Home, pretended he was just come to Town; as soon as he heard what had passed, in Relation to the Maid, he fell into a great Passion with his Wife; this set the Thing into a greater Flame, the Mother takes the Wife's Part against her own Son, insomuch that the Quarrel increasing, the Mother and Wife took Horse immediately, and went back to the Mother's House, and the Husband and Wife never bedded together after.

The Maid lay a long Time in the Prison, it being near half a Year to the Assizes; but before it happened, it was discovered she was with Child; when she was arraign'd at the Bar, she was discharged for want of Evidence; the Wife's Conscience touch'd her, and as she did not believe the Maid Guilty of any Theft, except that of Love, she did not appear against her; soon after her Acquittal, she was delivered of a Girl.

But what alarm'd the Husband most, was, that it was discovered the Wife was with Child also, he taking it for granted, he had had no Intimacy with her, since her last lying in, grew jealous of her, in his Turn, and made this a Handle to justify himself, for his Usage of her, pretending now he had suspected her long, but that here was Proof; she was delivered of Twins, a Boy and a Girl.

The Mother fell ill, sent to her Son to reconcile him to his Wife, but he would not hearken to it; therefore she made a Will, leaving all she had in the Hands of certain Trustees, for the Use of the Wife and two Children lately born, and died a few Days after.

This was an ugly Turn upon him, his greatest Dependence being upon his Mother; however, his Wife was kinder to him than he deserved, for she made him a yearly Allowance out of what was left, tho' they continued to live separate: It lasted near five Years; at this Time having a great Affection for the Girl he had by his Maid, he had a Mind to take it Home, to live with him; but as all the Town knew it to be a Girl, the better to disguise the Matter from them, as well as from his Wife, he had it put into Breeches, as a Boy, pretending it was a Relation's Child he was to breed up to be his Clerk.

The Wife heard he had a little Boy at Home he was very fond of, but as she did not know any Relation of his that had such a Child, she employ'd a Friend to enquire further into it; this Person by talking with the Child, found it to be a Girl, discovered that the Servant-Maid was its Mother, and that the Husband still kept up his Correspondence with her.

Upon this Intelligence, the Wife being unwilling that her Children's Money should go towards the Maintenance of Bastards, stopped the Allowance: The Husband enraged, in a kind of Revenge, takes the Maid home, and lives with her publicly, to the great Scandal of his Neighbours; but he soon found the bad Effect of it, for by Degrees lost his Practice, so that he saw plainly he could not live there, therefore he thought of removing, and turning what Effects he had into ready Money; he goes to *Cork*, and there with his Maid and Daughter embarques for *Carolina*.

At first he followed the Practice of the Law in that Province, but afterwards fell into Merchandize, which proved more successful to him, for he gained by it sufficient to purchase a considerable Plantation: His Maid, who passed for his Wife, happened to dye, after which his Daughter, our *Anne Bonny*, now grown up, kept his House.

She was of a fierce and couragious Temper, wherefore, when she lay under Condemnation, several Stories were reported of her, much to her Disadvantage, as that she had kill'd an *English* Servant-Maid once in her Passion with a Case-Knife, while she look'd after her Father's House; but upon further Enquiry, I found this Story to be groundless: It was certain she was so robust, that once, when a young Fellow would have lain with her, against her Will, she beat him so, that he lay ill of it a considerable Time.

While she lived with her Father, she was look'd upon as one that would be a good Fortune, wherefore it was thought her Father expected a good Match for her; but she spoilt all, for without his Consent, she marries a young Fellow, who belonged to the Sea, and was not worth a Groat; which provoked her Father to such a Degree, that he turned her out of Doors, upon which the young Fellow, who married her, finding himself disappointed in his Expectation, shipped himself and Wife, for the Island of *Providence*, expecting Employment there.

Here she became acquainted with *Rackam* the Pyrate, who making Courtship to her, soon found Means of withdrawing her Affections from her Husband, so that she consented to elope from him, and go to Sea with *Rackam* in Men's Cloaths: She was as good as her Word, and after she had been at Sea some Time, she proved with Child, and beginning to grow big, *Rackam* landed her on the Island of *Cuba*; and recommending her there to some Friends of his, they took Care of her, till she was brought to Bed: When she was up and well again, he sent for her to bear him Company.

The King's Proclamation being out, for pardoning of Pyrates, he took the Benefit of it, and surrendered; afterwards being sent upon the privateering Account, he returned to his old Trade, as has been already hinted in the Story of *Mary Read*. In all these Expeditions, *Anne Bonny* bore him Company, and when any Business was to be done in their Way, no Body was more forward or couragious than she, and particularly when they were taken; she and *Mary Read*, with one more, were all the Persons that durst keep the Deck, as has been before hinted.

Her Father was known to a great many Gentlemen, Planters of *Jamaica*, who had dealt with him, and among whom he had a good Reputation; and some of them, who had been in *Carolina*, remember'd to have seen her in his House; wherefore they were inclined to show her Favour, but the Action of leaving her Husband was an ugly Circumstance against her. The Day that *Rackam* was executed, by special Favour, he was admitted to see her; but all the Comfort she gave him, was, *that she was sorry to see him there, but if he had fought like a Man, he need not have been hang'd like a Dog.*

She was continued in Prison, to the Time of her lying in, and afterwards reprieved from Time to Time; but what is become of her since, we cannot tell; only this we know, that she was not executed.

Chap. IX
Of Captain *Howel Davis*, And his Crew

The Original of Davis. Is taken by the Pyrate England. England's Generosity to him. Is cast into Prison at Barbadoes, and why. Goes to Providence. Employ'd in a trading Vessel, seizes the Ship. An Instance of his great Courage and good Conduct. Goes to Cape de Verd Islands. Take several Prizes. Take the Fort of St. Jago by Storm. A Council call'd. Sail for Gambia. Takes Gambia Castle by Stratagem. Meets La Bouche, a French Pyrate. His Adventures with Cocklyn the Pyrate, at Sierraleone. The Fort attack d and taken, by theee Consederate Pyrates. The Pyrates quarrel and part. The laconic Speech of Davis to them. His fierce Engagement with a large Dutch Ship. An Account of several Prizes taken by him. A Description of the Island of St. Thome, Del Principe, and Annobono. The Dutch Governor of Acra taken by Davis. Davis well received by the Governor of Princes. His Stratagem to come at the Wealth of the Island. Is counterplotted and kill'd, by an Ambuscade.

Captain *Howel Davis* was born at *Milford*, in *Monmouthshire*, and was from a Boy brought up to the Sea. The last Voyage he made from *England*, was in the *Cadogan* Snow of *Bristol*, Captain *Skinner* Commander, bound for the Coast of *Guiney*, of which Snow *Davis* was chief Mate: They were no sooner arrived at *Sierraleon* on the aforesaid Coast, but they were taken by the Pyrate*England*, who plunder'd them, and *Skinner* was barbarously murdered, as has been related before in the Story of Captain *England*.

After the Death of Captain *Skinner*, *Davis* pretended that he was mightily sollicited by *England* to engage with him; but that he resolutely answered, he would sooner be shot to Death than sign the Pyrates Articles. Upon which, *England*, pleased with his Bravery, sent him and the rest of the Men again on Board the Snow, appointing him Captain of her, in the Room of *Skinner*, commanding him to pursue his Voyage. He also gave him a written Paper sealed up, with Orders to open it when he should come into a certain Latitude, and at the Peril of his Life follow the Orders therein set down. This was an Air of Grandeur like what Princes practice to their Admirals and Generals. — It was punctually complied with by *Davis*, who read it to the Ship's Company; it contained no less than a generous Deed of Gift of the Ship and Cargoe, to *Davis* and the Crew, ordering him to go to *Brasil* and dispose of the Lading to the best Advantage, and to make a fair and equal Dividend with the rest.

Davis proposed to the Crew, whether they were willing to follow their Directions, but to his great Surprize, found the Majority of them altogether averse to it, wherefore in a Rage, he bad them be damn'd, and go where they would. They knew that Part of their Cargoe was consigned to certain Merchants at *Barbadoes*, wherefore they steered for that Island. When they arrived, they related to these Merchants the unfortunate Death of *Skinner*, and the Proposal which had been made to them by *Davis*; upon which *Davis* was seized and committed to Prison, where he was kept three Months; however, as he had been in no Act of Pyracy, he was discharged without being brought to any Tryal, yet he could not expect any Employment there; wherefore knowing that the Island of *Providence* was a kind of Rendevouz of Pyrates, he was resolved to make one amongst them, if possible, and to that Purpose, found Means of shipping himself for that Island; but he was again disappointed, for when he arrived there, the Pyrates had newly surrendered to Captain *Woods Rogers*, and accepted of the Act of Grace, which he had just brought from *England*.

However, *Davis* was not long out of Business, for Captain *Rogers* having fitted out two Sloops for Trade, one called the *Buck*, the other the *Mumvil Trader;* *Davis* found an Employment on Board of one of them; the Lading of these Sloops was of considerable Value, consisting of *European* Goods, in order to be exchanged with the *French* and *Spaniards*; and many of the Hands on Board of them, were the Pyrates lately come in upon the late Act of Grace. The first Place they touched at, was the Island of *Martinico*, belonging to the *French*, where *Davis* having conspired with some others, rise in the Night, secured the Master and seized the Sloop; as soon as this was done, they called to the other Sloop, which lay a little Way from them, among whom they knew there were a great many Hands ripe for Rebellion, and ordered them to come on Board of them; they did so, and the greatest Part of them agreed to join with *Davis*; those who were otherwise inclined, were sent back on Board the *Mumvil* Sloop, to go where they pleased, *Davis* having first taken out of her, every Thing which he thought might be of Use.

After this, a Counsel of War was called over a large Bowl of Punch, at which it was proposed to chuse a Commander; the Election was soon over, for it fell upon *Davis* by a great Majority of *legal Pollers*, there was no Scrutiny demanded, for all acquiesced in the Choice: As soon as he was possess'd of his Command, he drew up Articles, which were signed and sworn to by himself and the rest, then he made a short Speech, the sum of which, was, a Declaration of War against the whole World.

After this they consulted about a proper Place where they might clean their Sloop, a light Pair of Heels being of great Use either to take, or escape being taken; for this purpose they made Choice of *Coxon*'s *Hole*, at the East End of the Island of *Cuba*, a Place where they might secure themselves from Surprize, the Entrance being so narrow, that one Ship might keep out a hundred.

Here they cleaned with much Difficulty, for they had no Carpenter in their Company, a Person of great Use upon such Exigencies; from hence they put to Sea, making to the North-Side of the Island of *Hispaniola*. The first Sail which fell in their Way, was a *French* Ship of twelve Guns; it must be observed, that *Davis* had but thirty five Hands, yet Provisions began to grow short with him; wherefore he attacked this Ship, the soon struck, and he sent twelve of his Hands on Board of her, in order to plunder: This was no sooner done, but a Sail was spied a great Way to Windward of them; they enquired of the *French* Man what she might be, he answered, that he had spoke with a Ship, the Day before, of 24 Guns and 60 Men, and he took this to be the same.

Davis then proposed to his Men to attack her, telling them, she would be a rare Ship for their Use, but they looked upon it to be an extravagant Attempt, and discovered no Fondness for it, but he assured them he had a Stratagem in his Head would make all safe; wherefore he gave Chace, and ordered his Prize to do the same. The Prize being a slow Sailor, *Davis* first came up with the Enemy, and standing along Side of them, showed his piratical Colours: They, much surpriz'd, called to *Davis*, telling him, they wondered at his Impudence in venturing to come so near them, and ordered him to strike; but he answered, that he intended to keep them in Play, till his Consort came up, who was able to deal with them, and that if they did not strike to him, they should have but bad Quarters; whereupon he gave them a Broad-Side, which they returned.

In the mean Time the Prize drew near, who obliged all the Prisoners to come upon Deck in white Shirts, to make a Show of Force, as they had been directed by *Davis*; they also hoisted a dirty Tarpawlin, by Way of black Flag, they having no other, and fir'd a Gun: The *French* Men were so intimidated by this Appearance of Force, that they struck. *Davis* called out to the Captain to come on Board of him, with twenty of his Hands; he did so, and they were all for the greater Security clapt into Irons, the Captain excepted: Then he sent four of his own Men on Board the first Prize, and in order still to carry on the Cheat, spoke aloud, that they should give his Service to the Captain, and desire him to send some Hands on Board the Prize, to see what they had got; but at the same Time gave them a written Paper, with Instructions what to do. Here he ordered them to nail up the Guns in the little Prize, to take out all the small Arms and Powder, and to go every Man of them on Board the second Prize; when this was done, he ordered that more of the Prisoners should be removed out of the great Prize, into the little one, by which he secured himself from any Attempt which might be feared from their Numbers; for those on Board of him were fast in Irons, and those in the little Prize had neither Arms nor Ammunition.

Thus the three Ships kept Company for 2 Days, when finding the great Prize to be a very dull Sailor, he thought she would not be fit for his Purpose, wherefore he resolved to restore her to the Captain, with all his Hands; but first, he took Care to take out all her Ammunition, and every Thing else which he might possibly want. The *French* Captain was in such a Rage, at being so outwitted, that when he got on Board his own Ship, he was going to throw himself over-board, but was prevented by his Men.

Having let go both his Prizes, he steered Northward, in which Course he took a small *Spanish* Sloop; after this, he made towards the *Western* Islands, but met with no Booty thereabouts; then he steered for the *Cape de Verde* Islands, they cast Anchor at St. *Nicholas*, hoisting *English* Colours; the *Portuguese* inhabiting there, took him for an *English* Privateer, and *Davis* going ashore, they both treated him very civilly, and also traded with him. Here he remained five Weeks, in which Time, he and half his Crew, for their Pleasure, took a Journey to the chief Town of the Island, which was 19 Miles up the Country: *Davis* making a good Appearance, was caressed by the Governor and the Inhabitants, and no Diversion was wanting which the *Portuguese* could show, or Money could purchase; after about a Week's Stay, he came back to the Ship, and the rest of the Crew went to take their Pleasure up to the Town, in their Turn.

At their Return they clean'd their Ship, and put to Sea, but not with their whole Company; for five of them, like *Hannibal*'s Men, were so charm'd with the Luxuries of the Place, and the free Conversation of some Women, that they staid behind; and one of them, whose Name was *Charles Franklin*, a *Monmouthshire* Man, married and settled himself, and lives there to this Day.

From hence they sailed to *Bonevista*, and looked into that Harbour, but finding nothing, they steer'd for the Isle of *May*: When they arrived here, they met with a great many Ships and Vessels in the Road, all which they plundered, taking out of them whatever they wanted; and also strengthen'd themselves with a great many fresh Hands, who most of them enter'd voluntarily. One of the Ships they took to their own Use, mounted her with twenty six Guns, and call'd her the *King James*. There being no fresh Water hereabouts, they made towards St. *Jago*, belonging to the *Portuguese*, in order to lay in a Store; *Davis*, with a few Hands, going ashore to find the most commodious Place to water at, the Governor, with some Attendants, came himself and examined who they were, and whence they came? And not liking *Davis*'s Account of himself, the Governor was so plain to tell them, he suspected them to be Pyrates. *Davis* seemed mightily affronted, standing much upon his Honour, replying to the Governor, he scorn'd his Words; however, as soon as his Back was turn'd, for fear of Accidents, he got on Board again as fast as he could. *Davis* related what had happened, and his Men seemed to resent the Affront which had been offered him. *Davis*, upon this, told them, he was confident he could sur prize the Fort in the Night; they agreed with him to attempt it, and accordingly, when it grew late, they went ashore well arm'd; and the Guard which was kept, was so negligent, that they got within the Fort before any Alarm was given: When it was too late there was some little Resistance made, and three Men killed on *Davis*'s Side. Those in the Fort, in their Hurry, run into the Governor's House to save themselves, which they barricadoed so strongly, that *Davis*'s Party could not enter it; however, they threw in Granadoe-Shells, which not only ruin'd all the Furniture, but kill'd several Men within.

When it was Day the whole Country was alarm'd, and came to attack the Pyrates; wherefore it not being their Business to stand a Siege, they made the best of their Way on Board their Ship again, after having dismounted the Guns of the Fort. By this Enterprize they did a great Deal of Mischief to the *Portuguese*, and but very little Good to themselves.

Having put to Sea they muster'd their Hands, and found themselves near seventy strong; then it was proposed what Course they should steer, and differing in their Opinions, they divided, and by a Majority it was carried for *Gambia* on the Coast of *Guiney;* of this Opinion was *Davis*, he having been employ'd in that Trade, was acquainted with the Coast: He told them, that there was a great deal of Money always kept in *Gambia* Castle, and that it would be worth their while to make an Attempt upon it. They ask'd him how it was possible, since it was garrisoned? He desired they would leave the Management of it to him, and he would undertake to make them Masters of it. They began now to conceive so high an Opinion of his Conduct, as well as Courage, that they thought nothing impossible to him, therefore they agreed to obey him, without enquiring further into his Design.

Having come within Sight of the Place, he ordered all his Men under Deck, except as many as were absolutely necessary for working the Ship, that those from the Fort seeing a Ship with so few Hands, might have no Suspicion of her being any other than a trading Vessel; then he ran close under the Fort, and there cast Anchor; and having ordered out the Boat, he commanded six Men in her, in old ordinary Jackets, while he himself, with the Master and Doctor, dressed themselves like Gentlemen; his Design being, that the Men should look like common Sailors, and they like Merchants. In rowing ashore he gave his Men Instructions what to say in Case any Questions should be asked them.

Being come to the landing Place, he was received by a File of Musqueteers, and conducted into the Fort, where the Governor accosting them civilly, ask'd them who they were, and whence they came? They answered they were of *Liverpool*, bound for the River of *Sinnegal*, to trade for Gum and Elephants Teeth, but that they were chaced on that Coast by two *French* Men of War, and narrowly escaped being taken, having a little the Heels of them; but now they were resolved to make the best of a bad Market, and would Trade here for Slaves; then the Governor ask'd them, what was the chief of their Cargo? They answered, Iron and Plate, which were good Things there; the Governor told them he would Slave them to the full Value of their Cargoe, and asked them, if they had any *European* Liquor on Board? they answered, a little for their own Use; however, a Hamper should be at his Service. The Governor then very civilly invited them all to stay and dine with him; *Davis* told him, that being Commander of the Ship, he must go on Board to see her well moored, and give some other Orders, but those two Gentlemen might stay, and that he himself would also return before Dinner, and bring the Hamper of Liquor with him.

While he was in the Fort, his Eyes were very busy in observing how Things lay; he took Notice there was a Centry at the Entrance, and a Guard-House just by it, where the Soldiers upon Duty commonly waited, their Arms standing in a Corner, in a Heap; he saw also a great many small Arms in the Governor's Hall; now when he came on Board, he assured his Men of Success, defiring them not to get drunk, and that as soon as they saw the Flag upon the Castle struck, they might conclude he was Master, and send twenty Hands immediately ashore; in the mean Time, there being a Sloop at Anchor near them, he sent some Hands in a Boat, to secure the Master and all the Men, and bring them on Board of him, least they observing any Bustle or arming in his Ship, might send ashore and give Intelligence.

These Precautions being taken, he ordered his Men, who were to go in the Boat with him, to put two Pair of Pistols each under their Cloaths, he doing the like himself, and gave them Directions to go into the Guard-Room, and to enter into Conversation with the Soldiers, and observe when he should fire a Pistol thro' the Governor's Window, to start up at once and secure the Arms in the Guard-Room.

When *Davis* arrived, Dinner not being ready, the Governor proposed that they should pass their Time in making a Bowl of Punch till Dinner-Time: It must be observed, that *Davis*'s Coxen waited upon them, who had an Opportunity of going about all Parts of the House, to see what Strength they had, he whispered *Davis*, there being no Person then in the Room, but he, (*Davis*) the Master, the Doctor, the Coxen and Governor; *Davis* on a sudden drew out a Pistol, clapt it to the Governor's Breast, telling him, he must surrender the Fort and all the Riches in it, or he was a dead Man. The Governor being no Ways prepared for such an Attack, promised to be very Passive, and do all they desired, therefore they shut the Door, took down all the Arms that hung in the Hall, and loaded them. *Davis* fires his Pistol thro' the Window, upon which his Men, without, executed their Part of the Scheme, like Heroes, in an Instant; getting betwixt the Soldiers and their Arms, all with their Pistols cock'd in their Hands, while one of them carried the Arms out. When this was done, they locked the Soldiers into the Guard-Room, and kept Guard without.

In the mean Time one of them struck the Union Flag on the Top of the Castle, at which Signal those on Board sent on Shore a Reinforcement of Hands, and they got Possession of the Fort without the least Hurry or Confusion, or so much as a Man lost of either Side.

Davis harangued the Soldiers, upon which a great many of them took on with him, those who refused, he sent on Board the little Sloop, and because he would not be at the Trouble of a Guard for them, he ordered all the Sails and Cables out of her, which might hinder them from attempting to get away.

This Day was spent in a kind of Rejoycing, the Castle firing her Guns to salute the Ship, and the Ship the Castle; but the next Day they minded their Business, that is, they fell to plundering, but they sound Things fall vastly short of their Expectation; for they discovered, that a great deal of Money had been lately sent away; however, they met with the Value of about two thousand Pounds Sterling in Bar Gold, and a great many other rich Effects: Every Thing they liked, which was portable, they brought aboard their Ship; some Things which they had no Use for, they were so generous to make a Present of, to the Master and Crew of the little Sloop, to whom they also returned his Vessel again, and then they fell to work in dismounting the Guns, and demolishing the Fortifications.

After they had done as much Mischief as they could, and were weighing Anchor to be gone, they spy'd a Ship bearing down upon them in full Sail; they soon got their Anchor's up, and were in a Readiness to receive her. This Ship prov'd to be a *French* Pyrate of fourteen Guns and sixty four Hands, half *French*, half Negroes; the Captain's Name was *La Bouse*; he expected no less than a rich Prize, which made him so eager in the Chace; but when he came near enough to see their Guns, and the Number of their Hands upon Deck, he began to think he should catch a *Tartar*, and supposed her to be a small *English* Man of War; however, since there was no escaping, he resolved to do a bold and desperate Action, which was to board *Davis*. As he was making towards her, for this Purpose, he fired a Gun, and hoisted his black Colours; *Davis* returned the Salute, and hoisted his black Colours also. The *French* Man was not a little pleased at this happy Mistake; they both hoisted out their Boats, and the Captains went to meet and congratulate one another with a Flag of Truce in their Sterns; a great many Civilities passed between them, and *La Bouse* desired *Davis*, that they might sail down the Coast together, that he *(La Bouse)* might get a better Ship: *Davis* agreed to it, and very courteously promised him the first Ship he took, fit for his Use, he would give him, as being willing to encourage a willing Brother.

The first Place they touch'd at, was *Sierraleon*, where at first going in, they spied a tall Ship at Anchor; *Davis* being the best Sailor first came up with her, and wondering that she did not try to make off, suspected her to be a Ship of Force. As soon as he came along Side of her, she brought a Spring upon her Cable, and fired a whole Broadside upon *Davis*, at the same Time hoisted a black Flag; *Davis* hoisted his black Flag in like Manner, and fired one Gun to Leeward.

In fine, she proved to be a Pyrate Ship of twenty four Guns, commanded by one *Cocklyn*, who expecting these two would prove Prizes, let them come in, least his getting under Sail might frighten them away.

This Satisfaction was great on all Sides, at this Junction of Confederates and Brethren in Iniquity; two Days they spent in improving their Acquaintance and Friendship, the third Day *Davis* and *Cocklyn*, agreed to go in *La Bouse*'s Brigantine and attack the Fort; they contrived it so, as to get up thither by high Water; those in the Fort suspected them to be what they really were, and therefore stood upon their Defence; when the Brigantine came within Musket-Shot, the Fort fired all their Guns upon her, the Brigantine did the like upon the Fort, and so held each other in Play for several Hours, when the two confederate Ships were come up to the Assistance of the Brigantine; those who defended the Fort, seeing such a Number of Hands on Board these Ships, had not the Courage to stand it any longer, but abandoning the Fort, left it to the Mercy of the Pyrates.

They took Possession of it, and continued there near seven Weeks, in which Time they all cleaned their Ships. We should have observed, that a Galley came into the Road while they were there, which *Davis* insisted should be yielded to *La Bouse*, according to his Word of Honour before given; *Cocklyn* did not oppose it, so *La Bouse* went into her, with his Crew, and cutting away her half Deck, mounted her with twenty four Guns.

Having called a Counsel of War, they agreed to sail down the Coast together, and for the greater Grandeur, appointed a Commadore, which was *Davis*; but they had not kept Company long, when drinking together on Board of *Davis*, they had like to have fallen together by the Ears, the strong Liquor stirring up a Spirit of Discord among them, and they quarrelled, but *Davis* put an End to it, by this short Speech: —— *Heark ye, you* Cocklin *and* La Bouse, *I find by strengthening you, I have put a Rod into your Hands to whip my self, but I'm still able to deal with you both; but since we met in Love, let us part in Love, for I find, that three of a Trade can never agree.* —— Upon which the other two went on Board their respective Ships, and immediately parted, each steering a different Course.

Davis held on his Way down the Coast, and making Cape *Appollonia*, he met with two *Scotch* and one *English* Vessel, which he plundered, and then let go. About five Days after he fell in with a *Dutch* Interloper of thirty Guns and ninety Men, (half being *English*,) off Cape *Three Points* Bay; *Davis* coming up along Side of her, the *Dutch* Man gave the first Fire, and pouring in a broad-Side upon *Davis*, killed nine of his Men, *Davis* returned it, and a very hot Engagement followed, which lasted from one a Clock at Noon, till nine next Morning, when the *Dutch* Man struck, and yielded her self their Prize.

Davis fitted up the *Dutch* Ship for his own Use, and called her the *Rover*, aboard of which he mounted thirty two Guns, and twenty seven Swivels, and proceeded with her and the *King James*, to *Anamaboe*; he entered the Bay betwixt the Hours of twelve and one at Noon, and found there three Ships lying at Anchor, who were trading for Negroes, Gold and Teeth: The Names of these Ships were the *Hink* Pink, Captain *Hall* Commander, the *Princess*, Captain *Plumb*, of which *Roberts*, who will make a considerable Figure in the sequel of this History, was second Mate, and the *Morrice* Sloop, Captain *Fin*; he takes these Ships without any Resistance, and having plundered them, he makes a Present of one of them, *viz.* the *Morrice* Sloop, to the *Dutch* Men, on Board of which alone were found a hundred and forty Negroes, besides dry Goods, and a considerable Quantity of Gold-Dust.

It happened there were several Canoes along Side of this last, when *Davis* came in, who saved themselves and got ashore; these gave Notice at the Fort, that these Ships were Pyrates, upon which the Fort fired upon them, but without any Execution, for their Mettle was not of Weight enough to reach them; *Davis* therefore, by Way of Defiance, hoisted his black Flag and returned their Compliment.

The same Day he sail'd with his three Ships, making his Way down the Coast towards *Princes*, a *Portuguese* Colony: But, before we proceed any farther in *Davis*'s Story, we shall give our Reader an Account of the *Portuguese* Settlements on this Coast, with other curious Remarks, as they were communicated to me by an ingenious Gentleman, lately arved from those Parts.

Chap. X
Of Captain *Bartho. Roberts*, And his Crew

HIS Beginning. Elected Captain in the Room of Davis. The Speech of Lord Dennis at the Election. Lord Sympson objects against a Papist. The Death of Davis reveng'd. Roberts sails Southward, in Quest of Adventures. The Names of the Prizes taken by them. Brasil describ'd. Roberts falls into a Fleet of Portuguese. Boards and takes the richest Ship amongst them. Make the Devil's Islands. An unfortunate Adventure of Roberts. Kennedy's Treachery. Irishmen excluded by Roberts and his Crew. Articles sworn to by them. A Copy of them. Some Account of the Laws and Customs of the Pyrates. An Instance of Roberts his Cunning. He proceeds again upon Business, and takes Prizes. Narrowly escapes being taken. Sails for the Island Dominico. Another Escape. Sails for Newfoundland. Plunders, sinks and burns 22 Sail in the Harbour of Trepassi. Plunders ten Sail of French Men. The mad Behaviour of the Crew. A Correspondence hinted at. The Pyrates caress'd at the Island of St. Bartholomew. In extream Distress. Sail for Martinico. A Stratagem of Roberts. The insolent Device in his Colours. And odd Compliment paid to Roberts. Three Men desert the Pyrates, and are taken by them. Their Tryal. Two executed, and one saved. The Brigantine deserts them. Great Divisions in the Company. A Description of Serraleone River. The Names of English settled there, and Way of Life. The Onflow, belonging to the African Company taken. The Pyrates Contempt of Soldiers. They are for entertaining a Chaplain. Their Skirmish with the Calabar Negroes. The King Solomon, belonging to the African Company, taken. The Frolicks of the Pyrates. Take eleven Sail in Whydah Road. A comical Receipt given by the Pyrates. A cruel Action of Roberts. Sails for Anna Bona. The Progress of the Swallow Man of War, in Pursuit of Roberts. Roberts his Consort taken. The Bravery of Skyrme, a Welch Pyrate. The surly Humour of some of the Prisoners. The Swallow comes up with Roberts. Roberts his Dress described. Is kill'd. His Character. His Ship taken. The Behaviour of the Pyrates, when Prisoners. A Conspyracy of theirs discovered. Reflections on the Manner of trying them. The Form of the Commission for trying the Pyrates. The Oath taken by the Commissioners. The Names of those arraign'd taken in the Ship Ranger. The Form of the Indictment. The Sum of the Evidence against them. Their Defence. The Names of the Prisoners of the Royal Fortune. Proceedings against them. Harry Glasby acquitted. The particular Tryal of Captain James Skyrme. Of John Walden. Of Peter Soudamore. Of Robert Johnson. Of George Wilson. Of Benjamin Jeffries. Of John Mansfield. Of William Davis. The Names of those executed at Cape Corso. The Petition of some condemn'd. The Courts Resolution. The Form of an Indenture of a pardon'd Pyrate. The Names of those pardon'd upon Indenture to serve seven Tears. The Pyrates how disposed of. The dying Behaviour of those executed.

B*Artholomew Roberts* sailed in an honest Employ, from *London* aboard of the *Princess*, Captain *Plumb* Commander, of which Ship he was second Mate: He left *England, November* 1719, and arrived at *Guiney* about *February* following, and being at *Anamaboe*, taking in Slaves for the *West-Indies*, was taken in the said Ship by Captain *Howel Davis*, as mentioned in the preceeding Chapter. In the beginning he was very averse to this sort of Life, and would certainly have escaped from them, had a fair Opportunity presented it self; yet afterwards he changed his Principles, as many besides him have done upon another Element, and perhaps for the same Reason too, *viz.* Preferment, — — and what he did not like as a private Man he could reconcile to his Conscience as a Commander.

Davis being cut off in the manner beforementioned, the Company found themselves under a Necessity of filling up his Post, for which there appear'd two or three Candidates among the select Part of them, that were distinguish'd by the Title of Lords, such were *Sympson, Ashplant,*

Anstis, &c. and on canvassing this Matter, how shatter'd and weak a Condition their Government must be without a Head, since *Davis* had been remov'd, in the manner beforemention'd, my Lord *Dennis* propos'd, its said, over a Bowl to this Purpose.

That it was not of any great Signification who was dignify'd with Title; for really and in Truth, all good Governments had (like theirs) the supream Power lodged with the Community, who might doubtless depute and revoke as suited Interest or Humour. We are the Original of this Claim (says he) *and should a Captain be so sawcy as to exceed Prescription at any time,* why down with Him! *it will be a Caution after he is dead to his Successors, of what fatal Consequence any sort of assuming may be. However, it is my Advice, that, while we are sober, we pitch upon a Man of Courage, and skill'd in Navigation, one, who by his Council and Bravery seems best able to defend this Commonwealth, and ward us from the Dangers and Tempests of an instable Element, and the fatal Consequences of Anarchy; and such a one I take* Roberts *to be. A Fellow! I think, in all Respects, worthy your Esteem and Favour.*

This Speech was loudly applauded by all but Lord *Sympson*, who had secret Expectations himself, but on this Disappointment, grew sullen, and left them, swearing, *he did not care who they chose Captain, so it was not a Papist, for against them he had conceiv'd an irreconcileable Hatred, for that his Father had been a Sufferer in* Monmouth's *Rebellion.*

Roberts was accordingly elected, tho' he had not been above six Weeks among them, the Choice was confirm'd both by the Lords and Commoners, and he accepted of the Honour, saying, *That since he had dipp'd his Hands in muddy Water, and must be a Pyrate, it was better being a Commander than a common Man.*

As soon as the Government was settled, by promotion other Officers in the room of those that were kill'd by the *Portugueze*, the Company resolv'd to revenge Captain *Davis*'s Death, he being more than ordinarily respected by the Crew for his Affability and good Nature, as well as his Conduct and Bravery upon all Occasions; and pursuant to this Resolution, about 30 Men were landed in order to make an Attack upon the Fort, which must be ascended to by a steep Hill against the Mouth of the Caunon. These Men were headed by one *Kennedy*, a bold daring Fellow, but very wicked and profligate; they march'd directly up under the Fire of their Ship Guns, and as soon as they were discover'd, the *Portugueze* quitted their Post and fled to the Town, and the Pyrates march'd in without Opposition, set Fire to the Fort, and threw all the Guns off the Hill into the Sea, which after they had done, they retreated quietly to their Ship.

But this was not look'd upon as a sufficient Satisfaction for the Injury they received, therefore most of the Company were for burning the Town, which *Roberts* said he would yield to, if any Means could be proposed of doing it without their own Destruction, for the Town had a securer Scituation than the Fort, a thick Wood coming almost close to it, affording Cover to the Defendants, who under such an Advantage, he told them, it was to be fear'd, would fire and stand better to their Arms; besides, that bare Houses would be but a slender Reward for their Trouble and Loss. This prudent Advice prevailed; however, they mounted the *French* Ship, they seiz'd at this Place, with 12 Guns, and light'ned her, in order to come up to the Town, the Water being shoal, and battered down several Houses; after which they all returned on Board, gave back the *French* Ship to those that had most Right to her, and sailed out of the Harbour by the light of two *Portuguese* Ships, which they were pleased to set on Fire there.

Roberts stood away to the Southward, and met with a *Dutch Guiney* Man, which he made Prize of, but after having plundered her, the Skipper had his Ship again: Two Days after, he took an *English* Ship, called the *Experiment*, Captain *Cornet*, at *Cape Lopez*, the Men went all into the Pyrate Service, and having no Occasion for the Ship, they burnt her, and then steered for St. *Thome*, but meeting with nothing in their Way, they failed for *Annabona*, and there water'd, took in Provisions, and put it to a Vote of the Company, whether their next Voyage should be, to the *East-Indies*, or to *Brasil*; the latter being resolved on, they sailed accordingly, and in 28 Days arrived at *Ferdinando*, an uninhabited Island, on that Coast: Here they water'd, boot-top'd their Ship, and made ready for the designed Cruise.

Now that we are upon this Coast, I think it will be the proper Place to present our Readers with a Description of this Country, and some ingenious Remarks of a Friend, how beneficial a Trade might be carried on here by our *West-India* Merchants, at a little Hazard.

A Description of Brasil, &c

B*RASIL (*a Name signifying the holy Cross*)* was discovered for the King of *Portugal*, by *Alvarez Cabral, Ann. Dom.* 1501. extending almost from the *Æquinoctial* to 28° South. The Air is temperate and cool, in comparison of the *West-Indies*, from stronger Breezes and an opener Country, which gives less Interruption to the Winds.

The northernmost Part of it stretching about 180 Leagues, (a fine fertile Country,) was taken from the *Portuguese* by the *Dutch West-India* Company, *Anno.* 1637 or thereabouts; but the Conquerors, as is natural where there is little or no Religion subsisting, made such heavy Exactions on the *Portuguese*, and extended such Cruelty to the Natives, that prepared them both easily to unite for a Revolt, facilitated by the *Dutch* Mismanagement: For the States being at this Time very intent on their *India* Settlements, not only recalled Count *Morrice* their Governor, but neglected Supplies to their Garrisons; however, tho' the others were countenanced with a Fleet from *Portugal*, and had the Affection of the Natives, yet they found Means to withstand and struggle with this superior Power, from 1643 to 1660, and then was wholly abandoned by them, on Articles dishonourable to the *Portuguese*, viz.

That the *Dutch*, on Relinquishing, should keep all the Places they had conquered in *India* from *Portugal*. That they should pay the States 800000 *l.* and permit them still the Liberty of Trade to *Africa* and *Brasil*, on the same Custom and Duties with the King of *Portugal*'s Subjects. But since that Time, new Stipulations and Treaties have been made; wherein the *Dutch*, who have been totally excluded the *Brasil* Trade, have, in lieu thereof, a Composition of 10 *per Cent.* for the Liberty of trading to *Africa*; and this is always left by every *Portuguese* Ship (before she begins her Slaving) with the *Dutch* General of the *Gold-Coast*, at *Des Minas.*

There are only three principal Towns of Trade on the *Brasil* Coast, St. *Salvadore*, St. *Sebastian*, and *Pernambuca.*

St. *Salvadore* in the *Bahia los todos Santos*, is an Archbishoprick and Seat of the Viceroy, the chief Port of Trade for Importation, where most of the Gold from the Mines is lodged, and whence the Fleets for *Europe* generally depart. The Seas about it abound with Whale-Fish, which in the Season they catch in great Numbers; the Flesh is salted up generally to be the Victualling of their Slave-Ships, and the Train reserved for Exportation, at 30 and 35 Millrays a Pipe.

*Rio Janeiro (*the Town St. *Sebastian)* is the Southernmost of the *Portuguese*, the worst provided of Necessaries, but commodious for a Settlement, because nigh the Mine, and convenient to supervise the Slaves, who, as I have been told, do usually allow their Master a Dollar *per Diem*, and have the Overplus of their Work (if any) to themselves.

The Gold from hence is esteemed the best, (for being of a copperish Colour,) and they have a Mint to run it into Coin, both here and at *Bahia*; the Moidors of either having the initial Letters of each Place upon them.

Pernambuca (tho' mention'd last) is the second in Dignity, a large and populous Town, and hasits rise from the Ruins of *Olinda*, (or the handsome,) a City of a far pleasanter Situation, six Miles up the River, but not so commodious for Traffick and Commerce. Just above the Town the River divides it self into two Branches, not running directly into the Sea, but to the Southward; and in the Nook of the Island made by that Division, stands the Governor's House, a square plain Building of Prince *Maurice*'s, with two Towers, on which are only this Date inscribed, *Anno* 1641. The Avenues to it are every way pleasant, thro' Visto's of tall CocoNut Trees.

Over each Branch of the River is a Bridge; that leading to the Country is all of Timber, but the other to the Town (of twenty six or twenty eight Arches) is half of Stone, made by the *Dutch*, who in their Time had little Shops and gaming Houses on each Side for Recreation.

The Pavements also of the Town are in some Places of broad Tiles, the remaining Fragments of their Conquest. The Town has the outer Branch of the River behind it, and the Harbour before it, jetting into which latter are close Keys for the weighing and receiving of Customage on Merchandize, and for the meeting and conferring of Merchants and Traders. The Houses are strong built, but homely, letticed like those of *Lisbon*, for the Admission of Air, without Closets, and what is worse, Hearths; which makes their Cookery consist all in frying and stewing upon Stoves; and that they do till the Flesh become tender enough to shake it to Pieces, and one Knife is then thought sufficient to serve a Table of half a Score.

The greatest Inconvenience of *Pernambuca* is, that there is not one Public-House in it; so that Strangers are obliged to hire any ordinary one they can get, at a Guinea a Month: And others who come to transact Affairs of Importance, must come recommended, if it were only for the sake of Privacy.

The Market is stocked well enough, Beef being at five Farthings *per l.* a Sheep or Goat at nine Shillings, a Turkey four Shillings, and Fowls two Shillings, the largest I ever saw, and may be procured much Cheaper, by hiring a Man to fetch them out of the Country. The dearest in its kind is Water, which being setch'd in Vessels from *Olinda*, will not be put on Board in the Road under two Crusado's a Pipe.

The *Portuguese* here are darker than those of *Europe*, not only from a warmer Climate, but their many Intermarriages with the Negroes, who are numerous there, and some of them of good Credit and Circumstances. The Women (not unlike the Mulatto Generation every where else) are fond of Strangers; not only the Courtezans, whose Interest may be supposed to wind up their Affections, but also the married Women who think themselves obliged, when you favour them with the Secrecy of an Appointment; but the Unhappiness of pursuing Amours, is, that the generallity of both Sexes are touched with veneral Taints, without so much as one Surgeon among them, or any Body skilled in Physic, to cure or palliate the progressive Mischief: The only Person pretending that Way, is an *Irish* Father, whose Knowledge is all comprehended in the Virtues of two or three Simples, and those, with the Salubrity of the Air and Temperance, is what they depend on, for subduing the worst of Malignity; and it may not be unworthy Notice, that tho' few are exempted from the Misfortune of a Running, Eruptions, or the like, yet I could hear of none precipitated into those deplorable Circumstances we see common in unskillful mercurial Processes.

There are three Monasteries, and about six Churches, none of them Rich or Magnificent, unless one dedicated to St. *Antonio*, the Patron of their Kingdom, which shines all over with exquisite Pieces of Paint and Gold.

The Export of *Brasil* (besides Gold) is chiefly Sugars and Tobacco; the latter are sent off in Rowls of a Quintal Weight, kept continually moistened with Mulossus, which, with the Soil it springs from, imparts a strong and peculiar Scent, more sensible in the Snuff made from it, which tho' under Prohibition of importing to *Lisbon*, sells here at 2 *s. per l.* as the Tobacco does at about 6 Millraies a Rowl. The finest of their Sugars sells at 8 *s.* per Roove, and a small ill tasted Rum drawn from the Dregs and Mulossus, at two Testunes a Gallon.

Besides these, they send off great Quantities of Brasil Wood, and Whale Oyl, some Gums and Parrots, the latter are different from the *African* in Colour and Bigness, for as they are blue and larger, these are green and smaller; and the Females of them ever retain the wild Note, and cannot be brought to talk.

In lieu of this Produce, the *Portugueze*, once every Year by their Fleet from *Lisbon*, import all manner of European Commodities; and whoever is unable or negligent of supplying himself at that Season, buys at a very advanced Rate, before the Return of another.

To transport Passengers, Slaves, or Merchandize from one Settlement to another, or in Fishing; they make use of Bark-Logs, by the *Brasilians* called *fingadahs*: They are made of four

Pieces of Timber (the two outermost longest) pinned and fastened together, and sharpened at the Ends: Towards each Extremity a Stool is fixed to sit on for paddling, or holding by, when the Agitation is more than ordinary; with these odd sort of Engines, continually washed over by the Water, do these People, with a little triangular Sail spreeted about the Middle of it, venture out of Sight of Land, and along the Coasts for many Leagues, in any sort of Weather; and if they overset with a Squall (which is not uncommon) they swim and presently turn it up right again.

The Natives are of the darkest Copper Colour, with thin Hair, of a square strong make, and muscular; but not so well looking as the Wooley Generation: They acquiesce patiently to the *Portugueze* Government, who use them much more humanly and Christian-like than the *Dutch* did, and by that Means have extended Quietness and Peace, as well as their Possessions, three or four hundred Miles into the Country. A Country abounding with fine Pastures and numerous Herds of Cattle, and yields a vast Increase from every thing that is sown: Hence they bring down to us Parrots, small Monkies, Armadillos and Sanguins, and I have been assured, they have, (far In-land,) a Serpent of a vast Magnitude, called *Siboya*, able, they say, to swallow a whole Sheep; I have seen my self here the Skin of another Specie full six Yards long, and therefore think the Story not improbable.

The Harbour of *Pernambuca* is, perhaps, singular, it is made of a Ledge of Rocks, half a Cables length from the Main, and but little above the Surface of the Water, running at that equal Distance and Heighth several Leagues, towards Cape *Augustine*, a Harbour running between them capable of receiving Ships of the greatest Burthen: The Northermost End of this Wall of Rock, is higher than any Part of the contiguous Line, on which a little Fort is built, commanding the Passage either of Boat or Ship, as they come over the Bar into the Harbour: On the Starboard Side, (*i. e.* the Main) after you have entered a little way, stands another Fort (a *Pentagon*) that would prove of small Account, I imagine, against a few disciplined Men; and yet in these consists all their Strength and Security, either for the Harbour or Town: They have begun indeed a Wall, since their removing from *Olinda*, designed to surround the latter; but the slow Progress they make in raising it, leaves Room to suspect 'twill be a long time in finishing.

The Road without, is used by the *Portugueze*, when they are nigh sailing for *Europe*, and wait for the Convoy, or are bound to *Bahia* to them, and by Strangers only when Necessity compels; the best of it is in ten Fathom Water, near three Miles W. N. W. from the Town; nigher in, is foul with the many Anchors lost there by the *Portugueze* Ships; and farther out (in 14 Fathom) corally and Rocky. *July* is the worst and Winter Season of this Coast, the Trade Winds being then very strong and dead, bringing in a prodigious and unsafe Swell into the Road, intermixed every Day with Squalls, Rain, and a hazey Horizon, but at other times serener Skies and Sunshine.

In these Southern Latitudes is a Constellation, which from some Resemblance it bears to a *Jerusalem* Cross, has the Name of *Crosiers*, the brightest of this Hemisphere, and are observed by, as the North Star is in Northern Latitudes; but what I mention this for, is, to introduce the admirable Phænomenon in these Seas of the Megellanick Clouds, whose Risings and Sittings are so regular, that I have been assured, the same Nocturnal Observations are made by them as by the Stars; They are two Clouds, small and whitish, no larger in Appearance than a Man's Hat, and are seen here in *July* in the Latitude of 88 S. about four of the Clock in the Morning; if their Appearance should be said to be the Reflection of Light, from some Stellary Bodies above them, yet the Dissiculty is not easily answered, how these, beyond others, become so durable and regular in their Motions.

From these casual Observations on the Country, the Towns, Coast, and Seas of *Brasil*, it would be an Omission to leave the Subject, without some Essay on an inter loping Slave Trade here, which none of our Countrymen are adventrous enough to pursue, though it very probably, under a prudent Manager, would be attended with Safety and very great Profit; and I admire the more it is not struck at, because Ships from the Southern Coast of *Africa*, don't lengthen the Voyage to the *West-Indies* a great deal, by taking a Part of *Brasil* in their Way.

The Disadvantages the *Portugueze* are under for purchasing Slaves, are these, that they have very few proper Commodities for *Guiney*, and the Gold, which was their chiefest, by an Edict in *July* 1722, stands now prohibited from being carried thither, so that the Ships employed therein are few, and insufficient for the great Mortality and Call of their Mines; besides, should they venture at breaking so destructive a Law, as the abovementioned (as no doubt they do, or they could make little or no Purchace) yet Gold does not raise its Value like Merchandize in travelling (especially to *Africa*) and when the Composition with the *Dutch* is also paid, they may be said to buy their Negroes at almost double the Price the *English, Dutch*, or *French* do, which necessarily raises their Value extravagantly at *Brasil*; (those who can purchase one, buying a certainer Annuity than *South-Sea* Stock.)

Thus far of the Call for Slaves at *Brasil*; I shall now consider and obviate some Difficulties objected against any Foreigners (suppose *English*) interposing in such a Trade, and they are some on theirs, and some on our Side.

On their Side it is prohibited under Pain of Death, a Law less effectual to the Prevention of it than pecuniary Muicts would be, because a Penalty so inadequate and disproportioned, is only *In terrorem*, and makes it merciful in the Governor, or his Instruments, to take a Composition of eight or ten Moidors, when any Subject is catched, and is the common Custom so to do as often as they are found out.

On our Side it is Confiscation of what they can get, which considering, they have no Men of Was to guard the Coast, need be very little, without supine Neglect and Carelessness.

I am a Man of War, or Privateer, and being in Want of Provisions, or in Search of Pyrates, put in to *Pernambuca* for Intelligence, to enable me for the Pursuit: The Dread of Pyrates keeps every one off, till you have first sent an Officer, with the proper Compliments to the Governor, who immediately gives Leave for your buying every Necessary you are in want of, provided it be with Money, and not an Exchange of Merchandize, which is against the Laws of the Country.

On this first time of going on Shore, depends the success of the whole Affair, and requires a cautious and discreet Management in the Person entrusted: He will be immediately surrounded at landing with the great and the small Rabble, to enquire who? and whence he comes? and whether bound? *&c.* and the Men are taught to answer, from *Guiney*, denying any thing of a Slave on Board, which are under Hatches, and make no Show; nor need they, for those who have Money to lay out will conclude on that themselves.

By that time the Compliment is paid to the Governor, the News has spread all round the Town, and some Merchant addresses you, as a Stranger, to the Civility of his House, but privately desires to know what Negroes he can have, and what Price. A Governor may possibly use an Instrument in sifting this, but the Appearance of the Gentleman, and the Circumstance of being so soon engaged after leaving the other, will go a great way in forming a Man's Judgment, and leaves him no room for the Suspicion of such a Snare; however, to have a due Guard, Intimations will suffice, and bring him, and Friends enough to carry off the best Part of a Cargo in two Nights time, from 20 to 30 Moidors a Boy, and from 30 to 40 a Man Slave. The Hazard is less at *Rio Janeiro*.

There has been another Method attempted, of settling a Correspondence with some *Portugueze* Merchant or two, who, as they may be certain within a Fortnight of any Vessels arriving on their Coast with Slaves, might settle Signals for the debarquing them at an unfrequented Part of the Coast, but whether any Exceptions were made to the Price, or that the *Portuguese* dread Discovery, and the severest Prosecution on so notorious a Breach of the Law, I cannot tell but it has hither to proved abortive.

However, Stratagems laudable, and attended with Profit, at no other Hazard (as I can perceive) then loss of Time, are worth attempting; it is what is every Day practised with the *Spaniards* from *Jamaica*.

Upon this Coast our Rovers cruiz'd for about nine Weeks, keeping generally out of Sight of Land, but without seeing a Sail, which discourag'd them so, that they determined to leave the Station, and steer for the *West-Indies*, and in order thereto, stood in to make the Land for the taking of their Departure, and thereby they fell in, unexpectedly, with a Fleet of 42 Sail of *Portuguese* Ships, off the Bay of *los todos Santos*, with all their Lading in for *Lisbon*, several of them of good Force, who lay too waiting for two Men of War of 70 Guns each, their Convoy. However, *Roberts* thought it should go hard with him, but he would make up his Market among them, and thereupon mix'd with the Fleet, and kept his Men hid till proper Resolutions could be form'd; that done, they came close up to one of the deepest, and ordered her to send the Master on Board quietly, threat'ning to give them no Quarters, if any Resistance, or Signal of Distress was made. The *Portuguese* being surprized at these Threats, and the sudden flourish of Cutlashes from the Pyrates, submitted without a Word, and the Captain came on Board; *Roberts* saluted him after a friendly manner, telling him, that they were Gentlemen of Fortune, but that their Business with him, was only to be informed which was the richest Ship in that Fleet; and if he directed them right, he should be restored to his Ship without Molestation, otherwise, he must expect immediate Death.

Whereupon this *Portuguese* Master pointed to one of 40 Guns, and 150 Men, a Ship of greater Force than the *Rover*, but this no Ways dismayed them, *they mere* Portuguese, they said, and so immediately steered away for him. When they came within Hail, the Master whom they had Prisoner, was ordered to ask, *how Seignior Capitain did*? And to invite him on Board, *for that he had a Matter of Consequence to impart to him*, which being done, he returned for Answer, *That he would wait upon him presently*: But by the Bustle that immediately followed, the Pyrates perceived, they were discovered, and that this was only a deceitful Answer to gain Time to put their Ship in a Posture of Defence; so without further Delay, they poured in a Broad-Side, boarded and grapled her; the Dispute was short and warm, wherein many of the *Portuguese* fell, and two only of the Pyrates. By this Time the Fleet was alarmed, Signals of Top-gallant Sheets flying, and Guns fired, to give Notice to the Men of War, who rid still at an Anchor, and made but scurvy hast out to their Assistance; and if what the Pyrates themselves related, be true, the Commanders of those Ships were blameable to the highest Degree, and unworthy the Title, or so much as the Name of Men: For *Roberts* finding the Prize to sail heavy, and yet resolving not to loose her, lay by for the headmost of them (which much out sailed the other) and prepared for Battle, which was ignominiously declined, tho' of such superior Force; for not daring to venture on the Pyrate alone, he tarried so long for his Consort as gave them both time leisurely to make off.

They found this Ship exceeding rich, being laden chiefly with Sugar, Skins, and Tobacco, and in Gold 40000 Moidors, besides Chains and Trinckets, of considerable Value; particularly a Cross set with Diamonds, designed for the King of *Portugal*; which they afterwards presented to the Governor of *Caiana*, by whom they were obliged.

Elated with this Booty, they had nothing now to think of but some safe Retreat, where they might give themselves up to all the Pleasures that Luxury and Wantonness could bestow, and for the present pitch'd upon a Place called the *Devil's Islands*, in the River of *Surinam*, on the Coast of *Caiana*, where they arrived, and found the civilest Reception imaginable, not only from the Governor and Factory, but their Wives, who exchanged Wares and drove a considerable Trade with them.

They seiz'd in this River a Sloop, and by her gained Intelligence, that a Brigantine had also sailed in Company with her, from *Rhode-Island*, laden with Provisions for the Coast. A Welcome Cargo! They growing short in the Sea Store, and as *Sancho* says, *No Adventures to be made without Belly-Timber*. One Evening as they were rumaging (their Mine of Treasure) the *Portuguese* Prize, this expected Vessel was descry'd at Mast-Head, and *Roberts*, imagining no Body could do the Business so well as himself, takes 40 Men in the Sloop, and goes in pursuit of her; but a fatal Accident followed this rash, tho' inconsiderable Adventure, for *Roberts* thinking of nothing less than bringing in the Brigantine that Afternoon, never troubled his Head about the Sloop's Provision, nor inquired what there was on Board to subsist such a Number of Men; but out he sails after his expected Prize, which he not only lost further Sight of, but after eight Days contending with contrary Winds and Currents, found themselves thirty Leagues to Leeward.

The Current still opposing their Endeavours, and perceiving no Hopes of beating up to their Ship, they came to an Anchor, and inconsiderately sent away the Boat to give the rest of the Company Notice of their Condition, and to order the Ship to them; but too soon, even the next Day, their Wants made them sensible of their Infatuation, for their Water was all expended, and they had taken no thought how they should be supply'd, till either the Ship came, or the Boat returned, which was not likely to be under five or six Days. Here like *Tantalus*, they almost famished in Sight of the fresh Streams and Lakes; being drove to such Extremity at last, that they were forc'd to tare up the Floor of the Cabin, and patch up a sort of Tub or Tray with Rope Yarns, to paddle ashore, and fetch off immediate Supplies of Water to preserve Life.

After some Days, the long-wish'd-for Boat came back, but with the most unwelcome News in the World, for *Kennedy*, who was Lieutenant, and left in Absence of *Roberts*, to Command the Privateer and Prize, was gone off with both. This was Mortification with a Vengeance, and you may imagine, they did not depart without some hard Speeches from those that were left, and had suffered by their Treachery: And that there need be no further mention of this *Kennedy*, I shall leave Captain *Roberts*, for a Page or two, with the Remains of his Crew, to vent their Wrath in a few Oaths and Execrations, and follow the other, whom we may reckon from that Time, as steering his Course towards *Execution Dock*.

Kennedy was now chosen Captain of the revolted Crew, but could not bring his Company to any determined Resolution; some of them were for pursuing the old Game, but the greater Part of them seem'd to have Inclinations to turn from those evil Courses, and get home privately, (for there was no Act of Pardon in Force,) therefore they agreed to break up, and every Man to shift for himself, as he should see Occasion. The first Thing they did, was to part with the great *Portugueze* Prize, and having the Master of the Sloop (whose Name I think was *Cane*) aboard, who they said was a very honest Fellow, (for he had humoured them upon every Occasion,) told them of the Brigantine that *Roberts* went after; and when the Pyrates first took him, he complemented them at an odd Rate, telling them they were welcome to his Sloop and Cargo, and wish'd that the Vessel had been larger, and the Loading richer for their Sakes: To this good natured Man they gave the *Portugueze* Ship, (which was then above half loaded,) three or four Negroes, and all his own Men, who returned Thanks to his kind Benefactors, and departed.

Captain *Kennedy* in the *Rover*, sailed to *Barbadoes*, near which Island, they took a very peaceable Ship belonging to *Virginia*; the Commander was a Quaker, whose Name was *Knot*; he had neither Pistol, Sword, nor Cutlash on Board; and Mr. *Knot* appearing so very passive to all they said to him, some of them thought this a good Opportunity to go off; and accordingly eight of the Pyrates went aboard, and he carried them safe to *Virginia*; They made the Quaker a Present of 10 Chests of Sugar, 10 Rolls of *Brasil* Tobacco, 30 Moidors, and some Gold-Dust, in all to the value of about 250 *l.* They also made Presents to the Sailors, some more, some less, and lived a jovial Life all the while they were upon their Voyage, Captain *Knot* giving them their Way; nor indeed could he help himself, unless he had taken an Opportunity to surprize them, when they were either drunk or asleep; for awake they wore Arms aboard the Ship, and put him in a continual Terror; it not being his Principle (or the Sect's) to fight, unless with Art and Collusion; he managed these Weapons well till he arrived at the Capes, and afterwards four of the Pyrates went off in a Boat, which they had taken with them, for the more easily making their Escapes, and made up the Bay towards *Maryland*, but were forced back by a Storm into an obscure Place of the Country, where meeting with good Entertainment among the Planters, they continued several Days without being discovered to be Pyrates. In the mean Time Captain *Knot* leaving four others on Board his Ship, (who intended to go to *North-Carolina*,) made what hast he could to discover to Mr. *Spotswood* the Governor, what sort of Passengers he had been forced to bring with him, who by good Fortune got them seized; and Search being made after the others, who were revelling about the Country, they were also taken, and all try'd, convicted and hang'd, two *Portuguese* Jews who were taken on the Coast of *Brasil*, and whom they brought with them to *Virginia*, being the principal Evidences. The latter had found Means to lodge Part of their Wealth with the Planters, who never brought it to Account: But Captain

Knot surrendered up every Thing that belonged to them, that were taken aboard, even what they presented to him, in lieu of such Things as they had plundered him of in their Passage, and obliged his Men to do the like.

Some Days after the taking of the *Virginia* Man last mentioned, in cruising in the Latitude of *Jamaica*, *Kennedy* took a Sloop bound thither from *Boston*, loaded with Bread and Flower; aboard of this Sloop went all the Hands who were for breaking the Gang, and left those behind that had a Mind to pursue further Adventures. Among the former were *Kennedy*, their Captain, of whole Honour they had such a dispicable Notion, that they were about to throw him overboard, when they found him in the Sloop, as fearing he might betray them all, at their return to *England*; he having in his Childhood been bred a Pick-pocket, and before he became a Pyrate, a House-breaker; both Professions that these Gentlemen have a very mean Opinion of. However, Captain *Kennedy*, by taking solemn Oaths of Fidelity to his Companions, was suffered to proceed with them.

In this Company there was but one that pretended to any skill in Navigation, (for *Kennedy* could neither write nor read, he being preferred to the Command merely for his Courage, which indeed he had often signaliz'd, particularly in taking the *Portuguese* Ship,) and he proved to be a Pretender only; for shaping their Course to *Ireland*, where they agreed to land, they ran away to the North-West Coast of *Scotland*, and there were tost about by hard Storms of Wind for several Days, without knowing where they were, and in great Danger of perishing: At length they pushed the Vessel into a little Creek, and went all ashore, leaving the Sloop at an Anchor for the next Comers.

The whole Company refresh'd themselves at a little Village about five Miles from the Place where they left the Sloop, and passed there for Ship-wreck'd Sailors, and no doubt might have travelled on without Suspicion; but the mad and riotous Manner of their Living on the Road, occasion'd their Journey to be cut short, as we shall observe presently.

Kennedy and another left them here, and travelling to one of the Sea-Ports, ship'd themselves for *Ireland*, and arrived there in Safety. Six or seven wisely withdrew from the rest, travelled at their leasure, and got to their much desired Port of *London*, without being disturbed or suspected; but the main Gang alarm'd the Country where-ever they came, drinking and roaring at such a Rate, that the People shut themselves up in their Houses, in some Places, not daring to venture out among so many mad Fellows: In other Villages, they treated the whole Town, squandering their Money away, as if, like *Æsop*, they wanted to lighten their Burthens: This expensive manner of Living procured two of their drunken Straglers to be knocked on the Head, they being found murdered in the Road, and their Money taken from them: All the rest, to the Number of seventeen as they drew nigh to *Edinburgh*, were arrested and thrown into Goal, upon Suspicion, of they knew not what; However, the Magistrates were not long at a Loss for proper Accusations, for two of the Gang offering themselves for Evidences were accepted of; and the others were brought to a speedy Tryal, whereof nine were convicted and executed.

Kennedy having spent all his Money, came over from *Ireland*, and kept a common B — —y- House on *Deptford* Road, and now and then, 'twas thought, made an Excursion abroad in the Way of his former Profession, till one of his Houshold W — —s gave Information against him for a Robbery, for which he was committed to *Bridewell*; but because she would not do the Business by halves, she found out a Mate of a Ship that *Kennedy* had committed Pvracy upon, as he foolishly confess'd to her. This Mate, whose Name was *Grant*, paid *Kennedy* a Visit in *Bridewell*, and knowing him to be the Man, procured a Warrant, and had him committed to the *Marshalsea* Prison.

The Game that *Kennedy* had now to play was to turn Evidence himself; accordingly he gave a List of eight or ten of his Comrades; but not being acquainted with their Habitations, one only was taken, who, tho' condemn'd, appeared to be a Man of a fair Character, was forc'd into their Service, and took the first Opportunity to get from them, and therefore receiv'd a Pardon; but *Walter Kennedy* being a notorious Offender, was executed the 19th of *July*, 1721, at *Execution Dock*.

The rest of the Pyrates who were left in the Ship *Rover*, staid not long behind, for they went ashore to one of the *West-India* Islands; what became of them afterwards, I can't tell, but the Ship was found at Sea by a Sloop belonging to St. *Christophers*, and carried into that Island with only nine Negroes aboard.

Thus we see what a disastrous Fate ever attends the Wicked, and how rarely they escape the Punishment due to their Crimes, who, abandon'd to such a profligate Life, rob, spoil, and prey upon Mankind, contrary to the Light and Law of Nature, as well as the Law of God. It might have been hoped, that the Examples of these Deaths, would have been as Marks to the Remainder of this Gang, how to shun the Rocks their Companions had split on; that they would have surrendered to Mercy, or divided themselves, for ever from such Pursuits, as in the End they might be sure would subject them to the same Law and Punishment, which they must be conscious they now equally deserved; *impending Law*, which never let them sleep well, unless when drunk. But all the Use that was made of it here, was to commend the Justice of the Court, that condemn'd *Kennedy, for he was a sad Dog* (they said) *and deserved the Fate he met with.*

But to go back to *Roberts*, whom we left on the Coast of *Caiana*, in a grievous Passion at what *Kennedy* and the Crew had done; and who was now projecting new Adventures with his small Company in the Sloop; but finding hitherto they had been but as a Rope of Sand, they formed a Set of Articles, to be signed and sworn to, for the better Conservation of their Society, and doing Justice to one another; excluding all *Irish* Men from the Benefit of it, to whom they had an implacable Aversion upon the Account of *Kennedy*. How indeed *Roberts* could think that an Oath would be obligatory, where Defiance had been given to the Laws of God and Man, I can't tell, but he thought their greatest Security lay in this, *That it was every one's Interest to observe them if they were minded to keep up so abominable a Combination.*

The following, is the Substance of the Articles, as taken from the Pyrates own Informations.

1. E*Very Man has a Vote in Affairs of Moment; has equal Title to the fresh Provisions, or strong Liquors, at any Time seized, and use them at pleasure, unless a Scarcity* (no uncommon Thing among them) *make it necessary, for the good of all, to vote a Retrenchment.*
2. *Every Man to be called fairly in turn, by List, on Board of Prizes, because,* (over and above their proper Share,) *they were on these Occasions allowed a Shift of Cloaths: But if they defrauded the Company to the Vaue of a Dollar, in Plate, Jewels, or Money*, Marooning*was their Punishment.* This was a Barbarous Custom of putting the Offender on Shore, on some desolate or uninhabited Cape or Island, with a Gun, a few Shot, a Bottle of Water, and a Bottle of Powder, to subsist with, or starve. *If the Robbery was only between one another, they contented themselves with slitting the Ears and Nose of him that was Guilty, and set him on Shore, not in an uninhabited Place, but somewhere, where he was sure to encounter Hardships.*
3. *No Person to Game at Cards or Dice for Money.*
4. *The Lights and Candles to be put out at eight o'Clock at Night: If any of the Crew, after that Hour, still remained inclined for Drinking, they were to do it on the open Deck*; which *Roberts* believed would give a Check to their Debauches, for he was a sober Man himself, but found at length, that all his Endeavours to put an End to this Debauch, proved ineffectual.
5. *To keep their Piece, Pistols, and Cutlash clean, and fit for Service*: In this they were extravagantly nice, endeavouring to outdo one another, in the Beauty and Richness of their Arms, giving sometimes at an Auction (at the Mast,) 30 or 40 *l.* a Pair, for Pistols. These were slung in Time of Service, with different coloured Ribbands, over their Shoulders, in a Way peculiar to these Fellows, in which they took great Delight.
6. *No Boy or Woman to be allowed amongst them. If any Man were sound seducing anny of the latter Sex, and carried her to Sea, disguised, he was to suffer Death*; so that when any fell into their Hands, as it chanced in the *Onslow*, they put a Centinel immediately over her to prevent ill Consequences from so dangerous an Instrument of Division and Quarrel; but then here lies the Roguery; they contend who shall be Centinel, which happens generally to one of the greatest Bullies, who, to secure the Lady's Virtue, will let none lye with her but himself.

7. *To Desert the Ship, or their Quarters in Battle, was punished with Death, or Marooning.*

8. *No striking one another on Board, but every Man's Quarrels to be ended on Shore, at Sword and Pistol, Thus;* The Quarter-Master of the Ship, when the Parties will not come to any Reconciliation, accompanies them on Shore with what Assistance he thinks proper, and turns the Disputants Back to Back, at so many Paces Distance: At the Word of Command, they turn and fire immediately, (or else the Piece is knocked out of their Hands:) If both miss, they come to their Cutlashes, and then he is declared Victor who draws the first Blood.

9. *No Man to talk of breaking up their Way of Living, till each had shared a* 1000 *l. If in order to this, any Man should lose a Limb, or become a Cripple in their Service, he was to have* 800 *Dollars, out of the public Stock, and for lesser Hurts, proportionably.*

10. *The Captain and Quarter-Master to receive two Shares of a Prize; the Master, Boatswain, and Gunner, one Share and a half, and other Officers, one and a Quarter.*

11. *The Musicians to have Rest on the Sabbath Day, but the other six Days and Nights, none without special Favour.*

These, we are assured, were some of *Roberts*'s Articles, but as they had taken Care to throw over-board the Original they had sign'd and sworn to, there is a great deal of Room to suspect, the remainder contained something too horrid to be disclosed to any, except such as were willing to be Sharers in the Iniquity of them; let them be what they will, they were together the Test of all new Comers, who were initiated by an Oath taken on a Bible, reserv'd for that Purpose only, and were subscrib'd to in Presence of the worshipful Mr. *Roberts*. And in Case any Doubt should arise concerning the Construction of these Laws, and it should remain a Dispute whether the Party had infring'd them or no, a Jury is appointed to explain them, and bring in a Verdict upon the Case in Doubt.

Since we are now speaking of the Laws of this Company, I shall go on, and, in as brief a Manner as I can, relate the principal Customs, and Government, of this roguish Common-Wealth; which are pretty near the same with all Pyrates.

For the Punishment of small Offences, which are not provided for by the Articles, and which are not of Consequence enough to be left to a Jury, there is a principal Officer among the Pyrates, called the Quarter-Master, of the Mens own chusing, who claims all Authority this Way, (excepting in Time of Battle:) If they disobey his Command, are quarrelsome and mutinous with one another, misuse Prisoners, plunder beyond his Order, and in particular, if they be negligent of their Arms, which he musters at Discretion, he punishes at his own Arbitrement, with drubbing or whipping, which no one else dare do without incurring the Lash from all the Ships Company: In short, this Officer is Trustee for the whole, is the first on Board any Prize, separating for the Company's Use, what he pleases, and returning what he thinks fit to the Owners, excepting Gold and Silver, which they have voted not returnable.

After a Description of the Quarter-Master, and his Duty, who acts as a sort of a civil Magistrate on Board a Pyrate Ship; I shall consider their military Officer, the Captain; what Privileges he exerts in such anarchy and unrulyness of the Members: Why truly very little, they only permit him to be Captain, on Condition, that they may be Captain over him; they separate to his Use the great Cabin, and sometimes vote him small Parcels of Plate and China, (for it may be noted that *Roberts* drank his Tea constantly) but then every Man, as the Humour takes him, will use the Plate and China, intrude into his Apartment, swear at him, seize a Part of his Victuals and Drink, if they like it, without his offering to find Fault or contest it: Yet *Roberts*, by a better Management than usual, became the chief Director in every Thing of Moment, and it happened thus:—The Rank of Captain being obtained by the Suffrage of the Majority, it falls on one superior for Knowledge and Boldness, *Pistol Proof* (as they call it,) and can make those fear, who do not love him; *Roberts* is said to have exceeded his Fellows in these Respects, and when advanced, enlarged the Respect that followed it, by making a sort of Privy-Council of half a Dozen of the greatest Bullies; such as were his Competitors, and had Interest enough to make his Government easy; yet even those, in the latter Part of his Reign, he had run counter to in every Project that opposed his own Opinion; for which, and because he grew reserved, and would not drink and roar at their Rate, a Cabal was formed to take away his Captainship, which Death did more effectually.

The Captain's Power is uncontroulable in Chace, or in Battle, drubbing, cutting, or even shooting any one who dares deny his Command. The same Privilege he takes over Prisoners, who receive good or ill Usage, mostly as he approves of their Behaviour, for tho' the meanest would take upon them to misuse a Master of a Ship, yet he would controul herein, when he see it, and merrily over a Bottle, give his Prisoners this double Reason for it. First, That it preserved his Precedence; and secondly, That it took the Punishment out of the Hands of a much more rash and mad Sett of Fellows than himself. When he found that Rigour was not expected from his People, (for he often practised it to appease them,) then he would give Strangers to understand, that it was pure Inclination that induced him to a good Treatment of them, and not any Love or Partiality to their Persons; for, says he, *there is none of you but will hang me, I know, whenever you can clinch me within your Power.*

And now seeing the Disadvantages they were under for pursuing the Account, *viz.* a small Vessel ill repaired, and without Provisions, or Stores; they resolved one and all, with the little Supplies they could get, to proceed for the *West-Indies,* not doubting to find a Remedy for all these Evils, and to retreive their Loss.

In the Latitude of *Deseada,* one of the Islands, they took two Sloops, which supply'd them with Provisions and other Necessaries; and a few Days afterwards, took a Brigantine belonging to *Rhode Island,* and then proceeded to *Barbadoes,* off of which Island, they fell in with a *Bristol* Ship of 10 Guns, in her Voyage out, from whom they took abundance of Cloaths, some Money, twenty five Bales of Goods, five Barrels of Powder, a Cable, Hawser, 10 Casks of Oatmeal, six Casks of Beef, and several other Goods, besides five of their Men; and after they had detained her three Days, let her go; who being bound for the abovesaid Island, she acquainted the Governor with what had happened, as soon as she arrived.

Whereupon a *Bristol* Galley that lay in the Harbour, was ordered to be fitted out with all imaginable Expedition, of 20 Guns, and 80 Men, there being then no Man of War upon that Station, and also a Sloop with 10 Guns, and 40 Men: The Galley was commanded by one Captain *Rogers,* of *Bristol,* and the Sloop by Captain *Graves,* of that Island, and Captain *Rogers* by a Commission from the Governor, was appointed Commadore.

The second Day after *Rogers* sailed out of the Harbour, he was discovered by *Roberts,* who knowing nothing of their Design, gave them Chase: The *Barbadoes* Ships kept an easy sail till the Pyrates came up with them, and then *Roberts* gave them a Gun, expecting they would have immediately struck to his piratical Flag, but instead thereof, he was forced to receive the Fire of a Broadside, with three Huzzas at the same Time; so that an Engagement ensued, but *Roberts* being hardly put to it, was obliged to crowd all the Sail the Sloop would bear, to get off: The Galley sailing pretty well, kept Company for a long while, keeping a constant Fire, which gail'd the Pyrate; however, at length by throwing over their Guns, and other heavy Goods, and thereby light'ning the Vessel, they, with much ado, got clear; but *Roberts* could never endure a *Barbadoes* Man afterwards, and when any Ships belonging to that Island fell in his Way, he was more particularly severe to them than others.

Captain *Roberts* sailed in the Sloop to the Island of *Dominico,* where he watered, and got Provisions of the Inhabitants, to whom he gave Goods in Exchange. At this Place he met with 13 *Englishmen,* who had been set ashore by a *French Guard de la Coste,* belonging to *Martinico,* taken out of two *New-England* Ships, that had been seiz'd, as Prize, by the said *French* Sloop: The Men willingly entered with the Pyrates, and it proved a seasonable Recruit.

They staid not long here, tho' they had immediate Occasion for cleaning their Sloop, but did not think this a proper Place, and herein they judg'd right; for the touching at this Island, had like to have been their Destruction, because they having resolved to go away to the *Granada Islands*, for the aforesaid Purpose, by some Accident it came to be known to the *French* Colony, who sending Word to the Governor of *Martinico*, he equipped and manned two Sloops to go in Quest of them. The Pyrates sailed directly for the *Granadilloes*, and hall'd into a Lagoon, at *Corvocoo*, where they cleaned with unusual Dispatch, staying but a little above a Week, by which Expedition they missed of the *Martinico* Sloops, only a few Hours; *Roberts* sailing over Night, that the *French* arrived the next Morning. This was a fortunate Escape, especially considering, that it was not from any Fears of their being discovered, that they made so much hast from the Island; but, as they had the Impudence themselves to own, for the want of Wine and Women.

Thus narrowly escaped, they sailed for *Newfoundland*, and arrived upon the Banks the latter end of *June*, 1720. They entered the Harbour of *Trepassi*, with their black Colours flying, Drums beating, and Trumpets sounding. There were two and twenty Vessels in the Harbour, which the Men all quitted upon the Sight of the Pyrate, and fled ashore. It is impossible particularly to recount the Destruction and Havock they made here, burning and sinking all the shipping, except a *Bristol* Galley, and destroying the Fisheries, and Stages of the poor Planters, without Remorse or Compunction; for nothing is so deplorable as Power in mean and ignorant Hands, it makes Men wanton and giddy, unconcerned at the Misfortunes they are imposing on their Fellow Creatures, and keeps them smiling at the Mischiefs, that bring themselves no Advantage. *They are like mad Men, that cast Fire-Brands, Arrows, and Death, and say, are not we in Sport?*

Roberts mann'd the *Bristol* Galley he took in the Harbour, and mounted 16 Guns on Board her, and cruising out upon the Banks, he met with mine or ten Sail of *French* Ships, all which he destroyed except one of 26 Guns, which they seiz'd, and carried off for their own Use. This Ship they christ'ned *the Fortune,* and leaving the *Bristol* Galley to the *French* Men, they sailed away in Company with the Sloop, on another Cruise, and took several Prizes, viz. the *Richard* of *Biddiford, Jonathan Whitfield* Master; the *Willing Mind* of *Pool;* the *Expectation* of *Topsham;* and the *Samuel,* Captain *Cary,* of *London;* out of these Ships they encreased their Company, by entring all the Men they could well spare, in their own Service. The *Samuel* was a rich Ship, and had several Passengers on Board, who were used very roughly, in order to make them discover their Money, threatning them every Moment with Death, if they did not resign every Thing up to them. They tore up the Hatches and entered the Hold like a parcel of Furies, and with Axes and Cutlashes, cut and broke open all the Bales, Cases, and Boxes, they could lay their Hands on; and when any Goods came upon Deck, that they did not like to carry aboard, instead of tossing them into the Hold again, threw them over-board into the Sea; all this was done with incessant cursing and swearing, more like Fiends than Men. They carried with them, Sails, Guns, Powder, Cordage, and 8 or 9000 l. worth of the choicest Goods; and told Captain *Cary, That they should accept of no Act of Grace; that the K — and P — t might be damned with their Acts of G — for them; neither would they go to* Hope-Point, *to be hang'd up a Sun drying, as* Kidd's, *and* Braddish's *Company were; but that if they should ever be overpower'd, they would set Fire to the Powder, with a Pistol, and go all merrily to Hell together.*

After they had brought all the Booty aboard, a Consultation was held whether they should sink or burn the Ship, but whilst they were debating the Matter, they spyed a Sail, and so left the *Samuel,* to give her Chace; at Midnight they came up with the same, which proved to be a Snow from *Bristol,* bound for *Boston,* Captain *Bowles* Master: They us'd him barbarously, because of his Country, Captain *Rogers,* who attack'd them off *Barbadoes,* being of the City of *Bristol.*

July the 16th, which was two Days afterwards, they took a *Virginia* Man called the *Little York, James Philips* Master, and the *Love,* of *Leverpool,* which they plundered and let go; the next Day a Snow from *Bristol,* call'd the *Phœnix, John Richards* Master, met with the same Fate from them; as also a Brigantine, Captain *Thomas,* and a Sloop called the *Sadbury;* they took all the Men out of the Brigantine, and sunk the Vessel.

When they left the Banks of *Newfoundland,* they sailed for the *West-Indies,* and the Provisions growing short, they went for the Latitude of the Island *Deseada,* to cruise, it being esteemed the likeliest Place to meet with such Ships as (they used in their Mirth to say) were consigned to them, with Supplies. And it has been very much suspected that Ships have loaded with Provisions at the *English* Colonies, on pretence of Trading on the Coast of *Africa,* when they have in reality been consigned to them; and tho' a show of Violence is offered to them when they meet, yet they are pretty sure of bringing their Cargo to a good Market.

However, at this Time they missed with their usual Luck, and Provisions and Necessaries becoming more scarce every Day, they retired towards St. *Christophers,* where being deny'd all Succour or Assistance from the Government, they fir'd in Revenge on the Town, and burnt two Ships in the Road, one of them commanded by Captain *Cox,* of *Bristol;* and then retreated farther to the Island of St. *Bartholomew,* where they met with much handsomer Treatment. The Governor not only supplying them with Refreshments, but he and the Chiefs carressing them in the most friendly Manner: And the Women, from so good an Example, endeavoured to outvie each other in Dress, and Behaviour, to attract the good Graces of such generous Lovers, that paid well for their Favours.

Sated at length with these Pleasures, and having taken on Board a good supply of fresh Provisions, they voted unanimously for the Coast of *Guiney,* and in the Latitude of 22 N. in their Voyage thither, met with a *French* Ship from *Martinico,* richly laden, and, which was unlucky for the Master, had a property of being fitter for their Purpose, than the Banker. *Exchange was no Robbery* they said, and so after a little mock Complaisance to *Monsieur,* for the Favour he had done them, they shifted their Men, and took leave: This was their first *Royal Fortune.*

In this Ship *Roberts* proceeded on his designed Voyage; but before they reached *Guiney,* he proposed to touch at *Brava,* the Southermost of *Cape*

Verd Islands and clean. But here again by an intolerable Stupidity and want of Judgment, they got so far to Leeward of their Port, that despairing to regain it, or any of the Windward Parts of *Africa,* they were obliged to go back again with the Trade-Wind, for the *West-Indies;* which had very near been the Destruction of them all. *Surinam* was the Place now designed for, which was at no less than 700 Leagues Distance, and they had but one Hogshead of Water left to supply 124 Souls for that Passage; a sad Circumstance that eminently exposes the Folly and Madness among Pyrates, and he must be an inconsiderate Wretch indeed, who, if he could separate the Wickedness and Punishment from the Fact, would yet hazard his Life amidst such Dangers, as their want of Skill and Forecast made them liable to.

Their Sins, we may presume were never so troublesome to their Memories, as now, that inevitable Destruction seem'd to threaten them, without the least Glympse of Comfort or Alleviation to their Misery; for, with what Face could Wretches who had ravaged and made so many Necessitous, look up for Relief; they had to that Moment lived in Defiance of the Power that now alone they must trust for their Preservation, and indeed without the miraculous Intervention of Providence, there appeared only this miserable Choice, viz. a present Death by their own Hands, or a ling'ring one by Famine.

They continued their Course, and came to an Allowance of one single Mouthful of Water for 24 Hours; many of them drank their Urine, or Sea Water, which, instead of allaying, gave them an inextinguishable Thirst, that killed them: Others pined and wasted a little more Time in Fluxes and Apyrexies, so that they dropped away daily. Those that sustain'd the Misery best, were such as almost starved themselves, forbearing all sorts of Food, unless a Mouthful or two of Bread the whole Day, so that those who survived were as weak as it was possible for Men to be and alive.

But if the dismal Prospect they set out with, gave them Anxiety, Trouble, or Pain, what must their Fears and Apprehensions be, when they had not one Drop of Water left, or any other Liquor to moisten or animate. This was their Case, when (by the working of Divine Providence, no doubt,) they were brought into Soundings, and at Night anchored in seven Fathom Water: This was an inexpressible Joy to them, and, as it were, fed the expiring Lamp of Life with fresh Spirits; but this could not hold long. When the Morning came, they saw Land from the Mast-Head, but it was at so great a Distance, that it afforded but an indifferent Prospect to Men who had drank nothing for the two last Days; however, they dispatch'd their Boat away, and late the same Night it return'd, to their no small Comfort, with a load of Water, informing them, that they had got off the Mouth of *Meriwinga* River on the Coast of *Surinam.*

One would have thought so miraculous an Escape should have wrought some Reformation, but alass, they had no sooner quenched their Thirst, but they had forgot the Miracle, till Scarcity of Provisions awakened their Senses, and bid them guard against starving; their allowance was very small, and yet they would profanely say, *That Providence which had gave them Drink, would, no doubt, bring them Meat also, if they would use but an honest Endeavour.*

In pursuance of these honest Endeavours, they were steering for the Latitude of *Barbadoes,* with what little they had left, to look out for more, or Starve; and, in their Way, met a Ship that answered their Necessities, and after that a Brigantine; the former was called the *Greyhound,* belonging to St. *Christophers,* and bound to *Philadelphia,* the Mate of which signed the Pyrate's Articles, and was afterwards Captain of the *Ranger,* Consort to the *Royal Fortune.*

Out of the Ship and Brigantine, the Pyrates got a good supply of Provisions and Liquor, so that they gave over the designed Cruise, and watered at *Tobago,* and hearing of the two Sloops that had been fitted out and sent after them at *Corvocoo,* they sailed to the Island of *Martinico,* to make the Governor some sort of an Equivalent, for the Care and Expedition he had shown in that Affair.

It is the Custom at *Martinico,* for the *Dutch* Interlopers that have a Mind to Trade with the People of the Island, to hoist their Jacks when they come before the Town: *Roberts* knew the Signal, and being an utter Enemy to them, he bent his Thoughts upon Mischief; and accordingly came in with his Jack flying, which, as he expected, they mistook for a good Market, and thought themselves happiest that could soonest dispatch off their Sloops and Vessels for Trade. When *Roberts* had got them within his Power, (one after another,) he told them, he would not have it said that they came off for nothing, and therefore ordered them to leave their Money behind, for that they were a Parcel of Rogues, and hoped they would always meet with such a *Dutch* Trade as this was; he reserved one Vessel to set the Passengers on Shore again, and fired the rest, to the Number of twenty.

Roberts was so enraged at the Attempts that had been made for taking of him, by the Governors of *Barbados* and *Martinico,* that he ordered a new Jack to be made, which they ever after hoisted, with his own Figure pourtray'd, standing upon two Skulls, and under them the Letters *A B H* and *A M H,* signifying a *Barbadian*'s and a *Martinican*'s Head, as may be seen in the Plate of Captain *Roberts.*

At *Dominico,* the next Island they touched at, they took a *Dutch* Interloper of 22 Guns and 75 Men, and a Brigantine belonging to *Rhode-Island,* one *Norton* Master. The former made some Defence, till some of his Men being killed, the rest were discouraged and struck their Colours. With these two Prizes they went down to *Guadalupe,* and brought out a Sloop, and a *French* Fly-Boat laden with Sugar; the Sloop they burnt, and went on to *Moonay,* another Island, thinking to clean, but finding the Sea ran too high there to undertake it with Safety, they bent their Course for the North Part of *Hispaniola,* where, at Bennet's Key, in the Gulf of *Saminah,* they cleaned both the Ship and the Brigantine. For tho' *Hispaniola* be settled by the *Spaniards* and *French,* and is the Residence of a President from *Spain,* who receives, and finally determines Appeals from all the other *Spanish West-India* Islands; yet is its People by no Means proportioned to its Magnitude, so that there are many Harbours in it, to which Pyrates may securely resort without Fear of Discovery from the Inhabitants.

Whilst they were here, two Sloops came in, as they pretended, to pay *Roberts* a Visit, the Masters, whose Names were *Porter* and *Tuckerman,* addressed the Pyrate, as the Queen of Skeba did *Solomon,* to wit, *That having heard of his Fame and Atchievements,* they had put in there to learn his Art and Wisdom in the Business of pirating, being Vessels on the same honourable Design with himself; and hoped with the Communication of his Knowledge, they should also receive his Charity, being in want of Necessaries for such Adventures. *Roberts* was won upon by the Peculiarity and Bluntness of these two Men, and gave them Powder, Arms, and what ever else they had Occasion for, spent two or three merry Nights with them, and at parting, said, *he hoped the L — would Prosper their handy Works.*

They passed some Time here, after they had got their Vessel ready, in their usual Debaucheries; they had taken a considerable Quanty of Rum and Sugar, so that Liquor was as plenty as Water, and few there were, who denied themselves the immoderate Use of it; nay, Sobriety brought a Man under a Suspicion of being in a Plot against the Commonwealth, and in their Sense, he was looked upon to be a Villain that would not be drunk. This was evident in the Affair of *Harry Glasby,* chosen Master of the *Royal Fortune,* who, with two others, laid hold of the Opportunity at the last Island they were at, to move off without bidding Farewel to his Friends. *Glasby* was a reserved sober Man, and therefore gave Occasion to be suspected, so that he was soon missed after he went away; and a Detachment being sent in quest of the Deserters, they were all three brought back again the next Day. This was a capital Offence, and for which they were ordered to be brought to an immediate Tryal.

Here was the Form of Justice kept up, which is as much as can be said of several other Courts, that have more lawful Commissions for what they do. — Here was no feeing of Council, and bribing of Witnesses was a Custom not known among them; no packing of Juries, no torturing and wresting the Sense of the Law, for bye Ends and Purposes, no puzzling or perplexing the Cause with unintelligible canting Terms, and useless Distinctions; nor was their Sessions burthened with numberless Officers, the Ministers of Rapine and Extortion, with ill boding Aspects, enough to fright Aftraa from the Court.

The Place appointed for their Tryals, was the Steerage of the Ship; in order to which, a large Bowl of Rum Punch was made, and placed upon the Table, the Pipes and Tobacco being ready, the judicial Proceedings began; the Prisoners were brought forth, and Articles of Indictment against them read; they were arraigned upon a Statute of their own making, and the Letter of the Law being strong against them, and the Fact plainly proved, they were about to pronounce Sentence, when one of the Judges mov'd, that they should first Smoak t'other Pipe; which was accordingly done.

All the Prisoners pleaded for Arrest of Judgment very movingly, but the Court had such an Abhorrence of their Crime, that they could not be prevailed upon to show Mercy, till one of the Judges, whose Name was *Valentine Ashplant,* stood up, and taking his Pipe out of his Mouth, said, he had something to offer to the Court in behalf of one of the Prisoners; and spoke to this Effect. — *By G* — Glasby *shall not dye; d — n me if he shall.* After this learned Speech, he sat down in his Place, and resumed his Pipe. This Motion was loudly opposed by all the rest of the Judges, in equivalent Terms; but *Ashplant,* who was resolute in his Opinion, made another pathetical Speech in the following Manner. *G — d — n ye Gentlemen, I am as good a Man as the best of you; d — m my S — l if ever I turned my Back to any Man in my Life, or ever will, by G —;* Glasby *is an honest Fellow, notwithstanding this Misfortune, and I love him, D — l d — n me if I don't: I hope he'll live and repent of what he has done; but d — n me if he must dye, I will dye along with him.* And thereupon, he pulled out a pair of Pistols, and presented them to some of the learned Judges upon the Bench; who, perceiving his Argument so well supported, thought it reasonable that *Glasby* should be acquitted; and so they all came over to his Opinion, and allowed it to be Law.

But all the Mitigation that could be obtained for the other Prisoners, was, that they should have the Liberty of choosing any four of the whole Company to be their Executioners. The poor Wretches were ty'd immediately to the Mast, and there shot dead, pursuant to their villainous Sentence.

When they put to Sea again, the Prizes which had been detained only for fear of spreading any Rumour concerning them, which had like to have been so fatal at *Corvocoo,* were thus disposed of: They burnt their own Sloop, and mann'd *Norton's* Brigantine, sending the Master away in the *Dutch* Interloper, not dissatisfied.

With the *Royal Fortune,* and the Brigantine, which they christened the *Good Fortune,* they pushed towards the Latitude of *Deseada,* to look out for Provisions, being very short again, and just to their Wish, Captain *Hingstone*'s ill Fortune brought him in their Way, richly laden for *Jamaica*; him they carried to *Berbudas* and plundered; and stretching back again to the *West-Indies,* they continually met with some Consignment or other, (chiefly *French,*) which stored them with Plenty of Provisions, and recruited their starving Condition; so that stocked with this sort of Ammunition, they began to think of something worthier their Aim, for these Robberies that only supplied what was in constant Expenditure, by no Means answered their Intentions; and accordingly they proceeded again for the Coast of *Guiney,* where they thought to buy Gold-Dust very cheap. In their Passage thither, they took Numbers of Ships of all Nations, some of which they burnt or sunk, as the Carriage or Characters of the Masters displeased them.

Notwithstanding the successful Adventures of this Crew, yet it was with great Difficulty they could be kept together, under any kind of Regulation; for being almost always mad or drunk, their Behaviour produced infinite Disorders, every Man being in his own Imagination a Captain, a Prince, or a King. When *Roberts* saw there was no managing of such a Company of wild ungovernable Brutes, by gentle means, nor to keep them from drinking to excess, the Cause of all their Disturbances, he put on a rougher Deportment, and a more magesterial Carriage towards them, correcting whom he thought fit; and if any seemed to resent his Usage, he told them, *they might go ashore and take Satisfaction of him, if they thought fit, at Sword and Pistol, for he neither valu'd or fear'd any of them.*

About 400 Leagues from the Coast of *Africa,* the Brigantine who had hitherto lived with them, in all amicable Correspondence, thought fit to take the Opportunity of a dark Night, and leave the Commadore, which leads me back to the Relation of an Accident that happened at one of the Islands of the *West-Indies,* where they water'd before they undertook this Voyage, which had like to have thrown their Government (such as it was) off the Hinges, and was partly the Occasion of the Separation: The Story is as follows.

Captain *Roberts* having been insulted by one of the drunken Crew, (whose Name I have forgot,) he, in the Heat of his Passion killed the Fellow on the Spot, which was resented by a great many others, put particularly one *Jones,* a brisk active young Man, who died lately in the *Marshalsea,* and was his Mess-Mate. This *Jones* was at that Time ashore a watering the Ship, but as soon as he came on Board, was told that Captain *Roberts* had killed his Comrade; upon which he cursed *Roberts,* and said, he ought to be served so himself. *Roberts* hearing *Jones*'s Invective, ran to him with a Sword, and ran him into the Body; who, notwithstanding his Wound, seized the Captain, threw him over a Gun, and beat him handsomely. This Adventure put the whole Company in an Uproar, and some taking Part with the Captain, and others against him, there had like to have ensued a general Battle with one another, like my Lord *Thomont*'s Cocks; however, the Tumult was at length appeas'd by the Mediation of the Quarter-Master; and as the Majority of the Company were of Opinion that the Dignity of the Captain, ought to be supported on Board; that it was a Post of Honour, and therefore the Person whom they thought fit to confer it on, should not be violated by any single Member; wherefore they sentenced *Jones* to undergo two Lashes from every one of the Company, for his Misdemeanour, which was executed upon him as soon as he was well of his Wound.

This severe Punishment did not at all convince *Jones* that he was in the wrong, but rather animated him to some sort of a Revenge; but not being able to do it upon *Roberts*'s Person, on Board the Ship, he and several of his Comrades, correspond with *Anstis,* Capt in of the Brigantine, and conspire with him and some of the principal Pyrates on Board that Vessel, to go off from the Company. What made *Anstis* a Malecontent, was, the Inferiority he stood in, with Respect to *Roberts,* who carried himself with a haughty and magisterial Air, to him and his Crew, he regarding the Brigantine only as a Tender, and, as such, left them no more than the Refuse of their Plunder. In short, *Jones* and his Consort go on Board of Captain *Anstis,* on Pretence of a Visit, and there consulting with their Brethren, they find a Majority for leaving of *Roberts,* and so came to a Resolution to bid a soft Farewel, as they call it, that Night, and to throw over-board whosoever should stick out; but they proved to be unanimous, and effected their Design as above-mentioned.

I shall have no more to say of Captain *Anstis,* till the Story of *Roberts* is concluded, therefore I return to him, in the pursuit of his Voyage to *Guiney.* The loss of the Brigantine was a sensible Shock to the Crew, she being an excellent Sailor, and had 70 Hands aboard; however, *Roberts* who was the Occasion of it, put on a Face of Unconcern at this his ill Conduct and Mismanagement, and resolved not to alter his Purposes upon that Account.

Roberts fell in to Windward nigh the *Senegal,* a River of great Trade for Gum, on this Part of the Coast, monopolized by the *French,* who constantly keep Cruisers, to hinder the interloping Trade: At this Time they had two small Ships on that Service, one of 10 Guns and 65 Men, and the other of 16 Guns and 75 Men; who having got a Sight of Mr. *Roberts,* and supposing him to be one of these prohibited Traders, chased with all the Sail they could make, to come up with him; but their Hopes which had brought them very nigh, too late deceived them, for on the hoisting of *Jolly Roger,* (the Name they give their black Flag,) their *French* Hearts failed, and they both surrendred without any, or at least very little Resistance. With these Prizes they went into *Sierraleon,* and made one of them their Consort, by the Name of the *Ranger,* and the other a Store-Ship, to clean by.

Sierraleon River disgorges with a large Mouth, the Starboard-Side of which, draughts into little Bays, safe and convenient for cleaning and watering; what still made it preferable to the Pyrates, is, that the Traders settled here, are naturally their Friends. There are about 30 *English* Men in all, Men who in some Part of their Lives, have been either privateering, buccaneering, or pirating, and still retain and love the Riots, and Humours, common to that sort of Life. They live very friendly with the Natives, and have many of them of both Sexes, to be their *Grometta*'s, or Servants: The Men are faithful, and the Women so obedient, that they are very ready to prostitute themselves to whomsoever their Masters shall command them. The Royal *African* Company has a Fort on a small Island call'd *Bence* Island, but 'tis of little Use, besides keeping their Slaves; the Distance making it incapable of giving any Molestation to their Starboard Shore. Here lives at this Place an old Fellow, who goes by the Name of *Crackers,* who was formerly a noted Buccaneer, and while he followed the Calling, robb'd and plundered many a Man; he keeps the best House in the Place, has two or three Guns before his Door, with which he Salutes his Friends, (the Pyrates, when they put in) and lives a jovial Life with him, all the while they are there.

Here follows a List, of the rest of those lawless Merchants, and their Servants, who carry on a private Trade with the Interlopers, to the great Prejudice of the Royal *African* Company, who with extraordinary Industry and Expence, have made, and maintain, Settlements without any Consideration from those, who, without such Settlements and Forts, would soon be under an Incapacity of pursuing any such private Trade. Wherefore, 'tis to be hop'd, proper Means will be taken, to root out a pernicious set of People, who have all their Lives, supported themselves by the Labours of other Men.

Two of these Fellows enter'd with *Robert*'s Crew, and continued with them, till the Destruction of the Company.

A List of the White-Men, now living on the high Land of Sierraleon, *and the Craft they occupy.*

JOHN *Leadstone,* three Boats and Periagoe.
His Man *Tom,*
His Man *John Brown.*
Alexander Middleton, one Long-Boat,
His Man *Charles Hawkins.*
John Pierce, Partners, one Long-Boat.
William Mead, Partners, one Long-Boat.
Their Man *John Vernon.*
David Chatmers, one Long-Boat.
John Chatmers, one Long-Boat.
Richard Richardson, one Long-Boat.
Norton, Partners, two Long-Boats, and two small Boats.

Richard Warren, Partners, two Long-Boats, and two small Boats.
Roberts Glynn, Partners, two Long-Boats, and two small Boats.
His Man *John Franks.*
William Waits, and one young Man.
John Bonnerman.John England, one Long-Boat.
Robert Samples, one Long-Boat.
William Presgrove, one Sloop, two Long-Boats, a small Boat, and Periagoe.
Harry, one Sloop, two Long-Boats, a small Boat, and Periagoe.
Davis, one Sloop, two Long-Boats, a small Boat, and Periagoe.
Mitchel, one Sloop, two Long-Boats, a small Boat, and Periagoe.
Richard Lamb,
With *Roquis Rodrigus,* a *Portuguese.*
George Bishop.Peter Brown.John Jones, one Long-Boat,
His *Irish* young Man.
At *Rio Pungo, Benjamen Gun.*
At *Kidham, George Yeats.*
At *Gallyneas, Richard Lemmons.*

The Harbour is so convenient for Wooding and Watering, that it occasions many of our trading Ships, especially those of *Bristol,* to call in there, with large Cargoes of Beer, Syder, and strong Liquors, which they Exchange with these private Traders, for Slaves and Teeth, purchased by them at the *Rio Nune*'s, and other Places to the Northward, so that here was what they call good Living.

Hither *Roberts* came the End of *June,* 1721, and had Intelligence that the *Swallow,* and *Weymouth,* two Men of War, of 50 Guns each, had left that River about a Month before, and designed to return about *Christmas;* so that the Pyrates could indulge themselves with all the Satisfaction in the World, in that they knew they were not only secure whilst there, but that in going down the Coast, after the Men of War, they should always be able to get such Intelligence of their Rendezvous, as would serve to make their Expedition safe. So after six Weeks stay, the Ships being cleaned and fitted, and the Men weary of whoring and drinking, they bethought themselves of Business, and went to Sea the Beginning of *August,* taking their Progress down the whole Coast, as low as *Jaquin,* plundering every Ship they met, of what was valuable in her, and sometimes to be more mischievously wicked, would throw what they did not want, overboard, accumulating Cruelty to Theft.

In this Range, they exchanged their old *French* Ship, for a fine Frigate built Ship, call'd the *Onslow,* belonging to the Royal *African* Company, Captain *Gee* Commander, which happened to lye at *Sestos,* to get Water and Necessaries for the Company. A great many of Captain *Gee*'s Men were ashore, when *Robert*'s bore down, and so the Ship consequently surpriz'd into his Hands, tho' had they been all on Board, it was not likely the Case would have been otherwise, the Sailors, most of them, voluntarily joyning the Pyrates, and encouraging the same Disposition in the Soldiers, (who were going Passengers with them to *Cape-Corso-Castle*) whose Ears being constantly tickled with the Feats and Gallantry of those Fellows, made them fancy, that *to go,* was only being bound on a Voyage of Knight Errantry (to relieve the Distress'd, and gather up Fame) and so they likewise offer'd themselves; but here the Pyrates were at a Stand, they entertain'd so contemptible a Notion of Landmen, that they put 'em off with Refusals for some time, till at length, being weary'd with Solicitations, and pittying a Parcel of stout Fellows, which they said, were going to starve upon a little Canky and Plantane, they accepted of them, and allow'd them ¼ Share, as it was then term'd out of Charity.

There was a Clergyman on Board the *Onslow,* sent from *England,* to be Chaplain of *Cape-Corso-Castle,* some of the Pyrates were for keeping him, alledging merrily, that their Ship wanted a Chaplain; accordingly they offered him a Share, to take on with them, promising, he should do nothing for his Money, but make Punch, and say Prayers; yet, however brutish they might be in other Things, they bore so great a Respect to his Order, that they resolved not to force him against his Inclinations; and the Parson having no Relish for this sort of Life, excused himself from accepting the Honour they designed him; they were satisfied, and generous enough to deliver him back every Thing he owned to be his: The Parson laid hold of this favourable Disposition of the Pyrates, and laid Claim to several Things belonging to others, which were also given up, to his great Satisfaction; in fine, they kept nothing which belonged to the Church, except three Prayer-Books, and a Bottle-Screw.

The Pyrates kept the *Onslow* for their own Use, and gave Captain *Gee* the *French* Ship, and then fell to making such Alterations as might fit her for a Sea-Rover, pulling down her Bulk-Heads, and making her flush, so that she became, in all Respects, as complete a Ship for their Purpose, as any they could have found; they continued to her the Name of the *Royal Fortune,* and mounted her with 40 Guns.

She and the *Ranger* proceeded (as I said before,) to *Jaquin,* and from thence to *Old Calabar,* where they arrived about *October,* in order to clean their Ships, a Place the most suitable along the whole Coast, for there is a Bar with not above 15 Foot Water upon it, and the Channel intricate, so that had the Men of War been sure of their being harbour'd here, they might still have bid Defiance to their Strength, for the Depth of Water at the Bar, as well as the want of a Pilot, was a sufficient Security to the Rovers, and invincible Impediments to them. Here therefore they sat easy, and divided the Fruits of their dishonest Instustry, *and drank and drove Care away.* The Pilot who brought them into this Harbour, was Captain *L — e,* who for this, and other Services, was extreamly well paid, according to the Journal of their own Accounts, which do not run in the ordinary and common way, of *Debtor, contra Creditor,* but much more concise, lumping it to their Friends, and so carrying the Debt in their Heads, against the next honest Trader they meet.

They took at *Calabar,* Captain *Loane,* and two or three *Bristol* Ships, the Particulars of all which would be an unnecessary Prolixity, therefore I come now to give an Account of the Usage they received from the Natives of this Place. The *Calabar* Negroes did not prove so civil as they expected, for they refused to have any Commerce or Trade with them, when they understood they were Pyrates: An Indication that these poor Creatures, in the narrow Circumstances they were in, and without the Light of the Gospel, or the Advantage of an Education, have, notwithstanding, such a moral innate Honesty, as would upbraid and shame the most knowing Christian: But this did but exasperate these lawless Fellows, and so a Party of 40 Men were detach'd to force a Correspondence, or drive the Negroes to Extremities; and they accordingly landed under the Fire of their own Cannon. The Negroes drew up in a Body of 2000 Men, as if they intended to dispute the Matter with them, and staid till the Pyrates advanced within Pistol-shot; but finding the Loss of two or three, made no Impression on the rest, the Negroes thought fit to retreat, which they did, with some Loss: The Pyrates set Fire to the Town, and then return'd to their Ships. This terrified the Natives, and put an entire stop to all the Intercourse between them; so that they could get no Supplies, which obliged them, as soon as they had finished the cleaning and triming of their Ships, to lose no Time, but went for Cape *Lopez,* and watered, and at *Anna-Bona* took aboard a Stock of fresh Provisions, and then sailed for the Coast again.

This was their last and fatal Expedition, which we shall be more particular in, because, it cannot be imagined that they could have had Assurance to have undertaken it, but upon a Presumption, that the Men of War, (whom they knew were upon the Coast,) were unable to attack them, or else pursuant to the Rumour that had indiscretionally obtained at *Sierraleon,* were gone thither again.

It is impossible at this Time, to think they could know of the weak and fickly Condition they were in, and therefore founded the Success of this second Attempt upon the Coast, on the latter Presumption, and this seems to be confirmed by their falling in with the Coast as low as Cape *Lahou,* (and even that was higher than they designed,) in the beginning of *January,* and took the Ship called the *King Solomon,* with 20 Men in their Boat, and a trading Vessel, both belonging to the Company. The Pyrate Ship happened to fall about a League to Leeward of the *King Solomon,* at Cape *Appollonia,* and the Current and Wind opposing their working up with the Ship, they agreed to send the Long-Boat, with a sufficient Number of Men to take her: The Pyrates are all Volunteers on these Occasions, the Word being always given, *who will go!* And presently the stanch and firm Men offer themselves; because, by such Readiness, they recommend their Courage, and have an Allowance also of a Shift of Cloaths, from Head to Foot, out of the Prize.

They rowed towards the *King Solomon* with a great deal of Alacrity, and being hailed by the Commander of her, answered, *Defiance;* Captain *Trahern,* before this, observing a great Number of Men in the Boat, began not to like his Visitors, and prepared to receive them, firing a Musket as they come under his Stern, which they returned with a Volley, and made greater Speed to get on Board: Upon this, he applied to his Men, and ask'd them, whether they would stand by him, to defend the Ship, it being a Shame they should be taken by half their Number, without any Repulse? But his Boatswain, *Philips,* took upon him to be the Mouth of the People, and put an End to the Dispute; he said plainly, he would not, laid down his Arms in the King's Name, as he was pleased to term it, and called out to the Boat for Quarters, so that the rest, by his Example, were mislead to the losing of the Ship.

When they came on Board, they brought her under Sail, by an expeditious Method, of cutting the Cable; *Walden,* one of the Pyrates, telling the Master, this *yo hope* of heaving up the Anchor was a needless trouble, when they designed to burn the Ship. They brought her under Commadore *Roberts*'s Stern, and not only rifled her of what Sails, Cordage, *&c.* they wanted for themselves, but wantonly throw'd the Goods of the Company overboard, like Spend-thrifts, that neither expected or designed any Account.

On the same Day also, they took the *Flushing,* a *Dutch* Ship, robbed her of Masts, Yards and Stores, and then cut down her Fore-Mast; but what sat as heavily as any thing with the *Skipper,* was, their taking some fine Sausages he had on Board, of his Wife's making, and stringing them in a ludicrous Manner, round their Necks, till they had sufficiently shew'd their Contempt of them, and then threw them into the Sea. Others chopp'd the Heads of his Fowls off, to be dressed for their Supper, and courteously invited the Landlord, provided he would find Liquor. It was a melancholly Request to the Man, but it must be comply'd with, and he was obliged, as they grew drunk, to sit quietly, and hear them sing *French* and *Spanish* Songs out of his *Dutch* Prayer-Books, with other Prophaness, that he (tho' a *Dutch* Man) stood amazed at.

In chasing too near in, they alarmed the Coast, and Expresses were sent to the *English* and *Dutch* Factories, giving an Account of it: They were sensible of this Error immediately, and because they would make the best of a bad Market, resolved to keep out of sight of Land, and lose the Prizes they might expect between that and *Whydah,* to make the more sure of that Port, where commonly is the best Booty; all Nations trading thither, especially *Portuguese,* who purchase chiefly with Gold, the Idol their Hearts were bent upon. And notwithstanding this unlikely Course, they met and took several Ships between *Axim* and that Place; the circumstantial Stories of which, and the pannick Terrors they struck into his Majesty's Subjects, being tedious and unnecessary to relate, I shall pass by, and come to their Arrival in that Road.

They came to *Whydah* with a St. *George*'s Ensign, a black Silk Flag flying at their Mizen-Peek, and a Jack and Pendant of the same: The Flag had a Death in it, with an Hour-Glass in one Hand, and cross Bones in the other, a Dart by it, and underneath a Heart dropping three Drops of Blood. — The Jack had a Man pourtray'd in it, with a flaming Sword in his Hand, and standing on two Skulls, subscribed *A B H* and *A M H i. e.* a *Barbadian*'s and a *Martinican*'s Head, as has been before taken Notice of. Here they found eleven Sail in the Road, *English, French* and *Portuguese;* the *French* were three stout Ships of 30 Guns, and upwards of 100 Men each, yet when *Roberts* came to Fire, they, with the other Ships, immediately struck their Colours and surrendred to his Mercy. One Reason, it must be confess'd, of his easy Victory, was, the Commanders and a good Part of the Men being ashore, according to the Custom of the Place, to receive the Cargoes, and return the Slaves, they being obliged to watch the Seasons for it, which otherwise, in so dangerous a Sea as here, would be impracticable. These all, except the *Porcupine,* ransomed with him for eight Pound of Gold-Dust, a Ship, not without the trouble of some Letters passing and repassing from the Shore, before they could settle it; and notwithstanding the Agreement and Payment, they took away one of the *French* Ships, tho' with a Promise to return her, if they found she did not sail well, taking with them several of her Men for that End.

Some of the Foreigners, who never had Dealing this Way before, desired for Satisfaction to their Owners, that they might have Receipts for their Money, which were accordingly given, a Copy of one of them, I have here subjoined, *viz.*

THIS is to certify whom it may or doth concern, that we GENTLEMEN OF FORTUNE, *have received eight Pounds of Gold-Dust, for the Ransom of the* Hardey, *Captain* Dittwitt *Commander, so that we Discharge the said Ship,*
Witness our Hands, this

13*th of* Jan. 1721-2.
Batt. Roberts,
Harry Glasby.

Others were given to the *Portuguese* Captains, which were in the same Form, but being sign'd by two waggish Fellows, *viz. Sutton,* and *Sympson,* they subscribed by the Names of,
Aaron Whifflingpin,

Sin. Tugmuttou.

But there was something so singularly cruel and barbarous done here to the *Porcupine,* Captain *Fletcher,* as must not be passed over without special Remark.

This Ship lay in the Road, almost slaved, when the Pyrates came in, and the Commander being on Shore, settling his Accounts, was sent to for the Ransom, but he excused it, as having no Orders from the Owners; though the true Reason might be, that he thought it dishonourable to treat with Robbers; and that the Ship, separate from the Slaves, towards whom he could mistrust no Cruelty, was not worth the Sum demanded; hereupon, *Roberts* sends the Boat to transport the Negroes, in order to set her on Fire; but being in hast, and finding that unshackling them cost much Time and Labour, they actually set her on Fire, with eighty of those poor Wretches on Board, chained two and two together, under the miserable Choice of perishing by Fire or Water: Those who jumped overboard from the Flames, were seized by Sharks, a voracious Fish, in Plenty in this Road, and, in their Sight, tore Limb from Limb alive. A Cruelty unparalell'd! And for which had every Individual been hanged, few I imagine would think that Justice had been rigorous.

The Pyrates, indeed, were obliged to dispatch their Business here in hast, because they had intercepted a Letter from General *Phips* to Mr. *Baldwin,* the Royal *African* Company's Agent at *Whydah,* (giving an Account, that *Roberts* had been seen to Windward of Cape *Three Points,*) that he might the better guard against the Damages to the Company's Ships, if he should arrive at that Road before the *Swallow* Man of War, which he assured him, (at the Time of that Letter,) was pursuing them to that Place. *Roberts* call'd up his Company, and desired they would hear *Phip*'s Speech, (for so he was pleased to call the Letter,) and notwithstanding their vapouring, perswaded them of the Necessity of moving; for, says he, such brave Fellows cannot be supposed to be frightned at this News, yet that it were better to avoid dry Blows, which is the best that can be expected, if overtaken.

This Advice weigh'd with them, and they got under Sail, having stay'd only from *Thursday* to *Saturday* Night, and at Sea voted for the Island of *Anna Bona;* but the Winds hanging out of the Way, crossed their Purpose, and brought them to Cape *Lopez,* where I shall leave them for their approaching Fate, and relate some further Particulars of his Majesty's Ship the *Swallow, viz.* where it was she had spent her Time, during the Mischief that was done, and by what Means unable to prevent it; what also was the Intelligence she received, and the Measures thereon formed, that at last brought two such Strangers as Mr *Roberts* and Capt. *Ogle,* to meet in so remote a Corner of the World.

The *Swallow* and *Weymouth* left *Sierraleon, May* 28, where, I have already taken Notice, *Roberts* arrived about a Month after, and doubtless learn'd the Intent of their Voyage, and cleaning on the Coast; which made him set down with more Security to his Diversion, and furnish him with such Intimations, as made his first Range down the Coast in *August* following, more prosperous; the *Swallow* and *Weymouth* being then at the Port of *Princes* a cleaning.

Their Stay at *Princes* was from *July* 28 to *Sept.* 20, 1721, where, by a Fatality, common to the Irregularities of Seamen, (who cannot in such Cases be kept under due Restraints,) they buried 100 Men in three Weeks time, and reduced the Remainder of the Ships Companies into so sickly a State, that it was with Difficulty they brought them to sail; and this Misfortune was probably the Ruin of *Roberts,* for it prevented the Men of War's going back to *Sierraleon,* as it was intended, there being a Necessity of leaving his Majesty's Ship *Weymouth* (in much the worse Condition of the two) under the Guns of Cape *Corso,* to impress Men, being unable at this Time, either to hand the Sails, or weigh her Anchor; and *Roberts* being ignorant of the Occasion or Alteration of the first Design, fell into the Mouth of Danger, when he thought himself the farthest from it; for the Men of War not endeavouring to attain further to Windward (when they came from *Princes*) then to secure Cape *Corso* Road under their Lee, they luckily hovered in the Track he had took.

The *Swallow* and *Weymouth* fell in with the Continent at Cape *Appollonia, Octo.* 20th, and there received the ungrateful News from one Captain *Bird;* a Notice that awaken'd and put them on their Guard; but they were far from expecting any Temerity should ever bring him a second Time on the Coast, while they were there; therefore the *Swallow* having seen the *Weymouth* into Cape *Corso* Road *Nov.* 10th, she ply'd to Windward as far as *Bassam,* rather as an Airing to recover a sickly Ship's Company, and show herself to the Trade, which was found every where undisturb'd, and were, for that Reason, returning to her Consort, when accidently meeting a *Portuguese* Ship, she told her, that the Day before she saw two Ships Chace into *Junk,* an *English* Vessel, which she believed must have fallen into their Hands. On this Story, the *Swallow* clung her Wind, and endeavoured to gain that Place, but receiving soon after (*Octo.* the 14th) a contrary Report from Captain *Plummer,* an intelligent Man, in the *Jason* of *Bristol,* who had come further to Windward, and neither saw or heard any Thing of this; she turned her Head down the second Time, anchored at Cape *Appollonia* the 23d, at Cape *Tres Puntas* the 27th, and in *Corso* Road *January* the 7th, 1721-2.

They learned that their Consort the *Weymouth,* was, by the Assistance of some Soldiers from the Castle, gone to Windward, to demand Restistution of some Goods or Men belonging to the *African* Company, that were illegally detained by the *Dutch* at *Des Minas;* and while they were regretting so long a Separation, an Express came to General *Phips,* from *Axim,* the 9th, and followed by another from *Dixcove,* (an *English* Factory,) with Information that three Ships had chased and taken a Galley nigh *Axim* Castle, and a trading Boat belonging to the Company: No doubt was made, concerning what they were, it being taken for granted they were Pyrates, and supposed to be the same that had the *August* before infested the Coast. The natural Result therefore, from these two Advices, was, to hasten for *Whydah;* for it was conclued the Prizes they had taken, had informed them how nigh the *Swallow* was, and withal, how much better in Health than she had been for some Months past; so that unless they were very mad indeed, they would (after being discovered) make the best of their Way for *Whydah,* and secure the Booty there, without which, their Time and Industry had been entirely lost; most of the Gold lying in that Corner.

The *Swallow* weighed from *Cape-Corso, January* the 10th, but was retarded by waiting some Hours on the *Margaret,* a Company's Ship, at *Accra,* again on the *Portugal,* and a whole Day at *Apong,* on a Person they used to stile *Miss Betty:* A Conduct that Mr. *Phips* blamed, when he heard the Pyrates were miss'd at *Whydah,* altho' he had given it as his Opinion, they could not be passed by, and intimated, that to stay a few Hours would prove no Prejudice.

This, however, hinder'd the *Swallow*'s catching them at *Whydah,* for the Pyrates came into that Road, with a fresh Gale of Wind, the same Day the *Swallow* was at *Apong,* and sail'd the 13th of *January* from thence, that she arrived the 17th. She gained Notice of them by a *French* Shallop from *Grand Papa,* the 14th at Night, and from *Little Papa* next Morning by a *Dutch* Ship; so that the Man of War was on all Sides, as she thought, sure of her Purchase, particularly when she made the Ships, and discovered three of them to get under Sail immediately at Sight of her, making Signals to one another, as tho' they designed a Defence; but they were found to be three *French* Ships; and those at Anchor, *Portuguese* and *English,* all honest Traders, who had been ransack'd and ransom'd.

This Disappointment chagreen'd the Ship's Company, who were very intent upon their Market; which was reported to be an Arm-Chest full of Gold, and kept with three Keys; tho' in all liklyhood, had they met with them in that open Road, one or both would have made their Escapes; or if they had thought sit to have fought, an Emulation in their Defence would probably have made it desperate.

While they were contemplating on the Matter, a Letter was received from Mr. *Baldwin,* (Governor here for the Company,) signifying, that the Pyrates were at *Jaquin,* seven Leagues lower. The *Swallow* weighed at two next Morning, *January* the 16th, and got to *Jaquin* by Day-Light, but to no other End, than frightening the Crews of two *Portuguese* Ships on Shore, who took her for the Pyrate that had struck such Terror at *Whydah:* She returned therefore that Night, and having been strengthened with thirty Volunteers, *English* and *French,* the discarded Crews of the *Porcupine,* and the *French* Ship they had carried from hence, she put to Sea again *January* the 19th, conjecturing, that either *Calabar, Princes,* the River *Gabone,* Cape *Lopez,* or *Annabona,* must be touched at for Water and Refreshment, tho' they should resolve to leave the Coast. As to the former of those Places, I have before observed, it was hazardous to think of, or rather impracticable; *Princes* had been a sower Grape to them, but being the first in the Way, she came before the Harbour the 29th, where learning no News, without loosing Time, steered for the River *Gabone,* and anchored at the Mouth of it *February* the 1st.

This River is navigable by two Channels, and has an Island about five Leagues up, called *Popaguays* or *Parrots,* where the *Dutch* Cruisers, for this Coast, generally Clean, and where sometimes Pyrates come in to look for Prey, or to Refit, it being very convenient, by Reason of a soft Mud about it, that admits a Ship's lying on Shore, with all her Guns and Stores in, without Damage. Hither Captain *Ogle* sent his Boat and a Lieutenant, who spoke with a *Dutch* Ship, above the Island, from whom he had this Account, *viz.* That he had been four Days from Cape *Lopez,* and had left no Ship there. However, they beat up for the Cape, without regard to this Story, and on the 5th, at Dawning, was surprized with the Noise of a Gun, which, as the Day brightened, they found was from Cape *Lopez* Bay, where they discovered three Ships at Anchor, the largest with the King's Colours and Pendant flying, which was soon after concluded to be Mr. *Roberts* and his Consorts; but the *Swallow* being to Windward, and unexpectedly deep in the Bay, was obliged to Steer off, for avoiding a Sand, called the *French Man's Bank,* which the Pyrates observed for some Time, and rashly interpreting it to be Fear in her, righted the *French Ranger,* which was then on the Heel, and ordered her to chase out in all hast, bending several of their Sails in the Pursuit. The Man of War finding they had foolishly mistaken her Design, humoured the Deceit, and kept off to Sea, as if she had been really afraid, and managed her Steerage so, under the Direction of Lieutenant *Sun,* an experienced Officer, as to let the *Ranger* come up with her, when they thought they had got so far as not to have their Guns heard by her Consort at the Cape. The Pyrates had such an Opinion of their own Courage, that they could never dream any Body would use a Stratagem to speak with them, and so was the more easily drawn into the Snare.

The Pyrates now drew nigh enough to fire their Chase Guns; they hoisted the black Flag that was worn in *Whydah* Road, and got their Spritsail Yard along-ships, with Intent to board; no one having ever asked, all this while, what Country Ship they took the Chase to be; they would have her to be a *Portuguese,* (Sugar being then a Commodity among them,) and were swearing every Minute at the Wind or Sails to expedite so sweet a Chase; but, alass, all turned sour in an Instant: It was with the utmost Consternation they saw her suddenly bring to, and hawl up her lower Ports, now within Pistol-shot, and struck their black Flag upon it directly. After the first Surprize was over, they kept firing at a Distance, hoisted it again, and vapoured with their Cutlashes on the Poop; tho' wisely endeavouring at the same Time to get away. Being now at their Wits end, boarding was proposed by the Heads of them, and so to make one desperate Push; but the Motion not being well seconded, and their Main-Top-Mast coming down by a Shot, after two Hours firing, it was declin'd; they grew Sick, struck their Colours, and called out for Quarters; having had 10 Men killed out right, and 20 wounded, without the loss or hurt of one of the King's Men. She had 32 Guns, mann'd with 16 *French* Men, 20 Negroes, and 77 *English*. The Colours were thrown over board, that they might not rise in Judgment, nor be display'd in Tryumph over them.

While the *Swallow* was sending their Boat to fetch the Prisoners, a Blast and Smoak was seen to pour out of the great Cabin, and they thought they were blowing up; but upon enquiry afterwards, found that half a dozen of the most Desperate, when they saw all Hopes fled, had drawn themselves round what Powder they had left in the Steerage, and fired a Pistol into it, but it was too small a Quantity to effect any Thing more, than burning them in a frightful Manner.

This Ship was commanded by one *Skyrmé,* a *Welch* Man, who, tho' he had lost his Leg in the Action, would not suffer himself to be dressed, or carried off the Deck; but, like *Widrington,* fought upon his Stump. The rest appeared gay and brisk, most of them with white Shirts, Watches, and a deal of Silk Vests, but the Gold-Dust belonging to them, was most of it left in the *Little Ranger* in the Bay, (this Company's proper Ship,) with the *Royal Fortune.*

I cannot but take Notice of two among the Crowd, of those disfigured from the Blast of Powder just before mentioned, *viz. William Main* and *Roger Ball*. An Officer of the Ship seeing a Silver Call hang at the Wast of the former, said to him, *I presume you are Boatswain of this Ship. Then you presume wrong,* answered he, *for I am Boatswain of the* Royal Fortune, *Captain* Roberts *Commander. Then Mr.* Boatswain *you will be hanged I believe,* replies the Officer. *That is as your Honour pleases,* answered he again, and was for turning away: But the Officer desired to know of him, how the Powder, which had made them in that Condition, came to take Fire. — *By G —* says he, *they are all mad and bewitch'd, for I have lost a good Hat by it.* (the Hat and he being both blown out of the Cabin Gallery, into the Sea.) *But what signifies a Hat Friend,* says the Officer. — *Not much* answer'd he, the Men being busy in stripping him of his Shoes and Stockings. — The Officer then enquired of him, whether *Roberts*'s Company were as likely Fellows as these. — *There are 120 of them,* (answered he) *as clever Fellows as ever trod Shoe Leather: Would I were with them!* — *No doubt on't,* says the Officer. — *By G — it is naked Truth,* answered he, looking down and seeing himself, by this Time, quite striped.

The Officer then approached *Roger Ball,* who was seated in a private Corner, with a Look as sullen as Winter, and asked him, how he came blown up in that frightful Manner. — *Why,* says he, John Morris *fired a Pistol into the Powder, and if he had not done it, I would,* (bearing his Pain without the least Complaint.) The Officer gave him to understand he was Surgeon, and if he desired it, he would dress him; but he swore it should not be done, and that if any Thing was applied to him, he would tear it off. — Nevertheless the Surgeon had good Nature enough to dress him, tho' with much trouble: At Night he was in a kind of *Delirium,* and raved on the Bravery of *Roberts,* saying, he should shortly be released, as soon as they should meet him, which procured him a lashing down upon the Forecastle, which he resisting with all his Force, caused him to be used with the more Violence, so that he was tied down with so much Severity, that his Flesh being sore and tender with the blowing up, he died next Day of a Mortification.

They secured the Prisoners with Pinions, and Shackles, but the Ship was so much disabled in the Engagement, that they had once Thoughts to set her on Fire; but this would have given them the Trouble of taking the Pyrates wounded Men on Board themselves, and that they were certain the *Royal Fortune* would wait for their Consort's Return, they lay by her two Days, repaired her Rigging and other Damages, and sent her into *Princes,* with the *French* Men, and four of their own Hands.

On the 9th in the Evening, the *Swallow* gained the Cape again, and saw the *Royal Fortune* standing into the Bay with the *Neptune,* Captain *Hill,* of *London:* A good Presage of the next Day's Success, for they did not doubt but the Temptation of Liquor, and Plunder, they might find in this their new Prize, would make the Pyrates very confused; and so it happened.

On the 10th, in the Morning, the Man of War bore away to round the Cape. *Roberts*'s Crew discerning their Masts over the Land, went down into the Cabin, to acquaint him of it, he being then at Breakfast with his new Guest, Captain *Hill,* on a savory Dish of Solomongundy, and some of his own Beer. He took no Notice of it, and his Men almost as little, some saying she was a *Portuguese* Ship, others a *French* Slave Ship, but the major Part swore it was the *French Ranger* returning, and were merrily debating for some Time, on the Manner of Reception, whether they should salute, or not; but as the *Swallow* approached nigher, Things appeared plainer, and though they were stigmatiz'd with the Name of Cowards, who showed any Apprehension of Danger, yet some of them, now undeceived, declared it to *Roberts,* especially one *Armstrong,* who had deserted from that Ship, and knew her well: Those *Roberts* swore at as Cowards, who meant to dishearten the Men, asking them if it were so, whether they were afraid to fight, or no? And hardly refrained from Blows. What his own Apprehensions were, till she hawled up her Ports, and hoisted their proper Colours, is uncertain; but then being perfectly convinced, he slipped his Cable, got under Sail, and ordered his Men to Arms, without any show of Timidity, dropping a first Rate Oath, *that it was a Bite,* but, at the same Time, resolved, like a gallant Rogue, to get clear, or die.

There was one *Armstrong,* as I just mention'd, a Deserter from the *Swallow,* whom they enquired of concerning the Trim and Sailing of that Ship; he told them she sail'd best upon a Wind, and therefore, if they designed to leave her, they should go before it.

The Danger was imminent, and Time very short, to consult of Means to extricate himself; his Resolution in this Streight, was as follows: To pass close to the *Swallow,* with all their Sails, and receive her Broadside, before they returned a Shot; if disabled by this, or that they could not depend on sailing, then to run on Shore at the Point, (which is steep to) and every one to shift for himself among the Negroes; or sailing in these, to board, and blow up together, for he saw that the greatest Part of his Men were drunk, passively Couragious, unfit for Service.

Roberts himself made a gallant Figure, at the Time of the Engagement, being dressed in a rich crimson Damask Wastcoat and Breeches, a red Feather in his Hat, a Gold Chain round his Neck, with a Diamond Cross hanging to it, a Sword in his Hand, and two Pair of Pistols hanging at the End of a Silk Sling, flung over his Shoulders (according to the Fashion of the Pyrates;) and is said to have given his Orders with Boldness, and Spirit; coming, according to what he had purposed, close to the Man of War, received her Fire, and then hoisted his Black Flag, and returned it, shooting away from her, with all the Sail he could pack; and had he took *Armstrong*'s Advice, to have gone before the Wind, he had probably escaped; but keeping his Tacks down, either by the Winds shifting, or ill Steerage, or both, he was taken a-back with his Sails, and the *Swallow* came a second Time very nigh to him: He had now perhaps finished the Fight very desperately, if Death, who took a swift Passage in a Grape-Shot, had not interposed, and struck him directly on the Throat. He settled himself on the Tackles of a Gun, which one *Stephenson,* from the Helm, observing, ran to his Assistance, and not perceiving him wounded, swore at him, and bid him stand up, and fight like a Man; but when he found his Mistake, and that his Captain was certainly dead, he gushed into Tears, and wished the next Shot might be his Lot. They presently threw him over-board, with his Arms and Ornaments on, according to the repea ed Request he made in his Life-time.

Roberts was a tall black Man, near forty Years of Age, born at *Newey-bagh,* nigh *Haverford-West,* in *Pembrokshire,* of good natural Parts, and personal Bravery, tho' he applied them to such wicked Purposes, as made them of no Commendation, frequently drinking *D — n to him who ever lived to wear a Halter.* He was forc'd himself at first among this Company out of the *Prince,* Captain Plamb at *Anamaboe,* about three Years before, where he served as second Mate, and shed, as he us'd to tell the *fresh Men,* as many Crocodile Tears then as they did now, but Time and good Company had wore it off. He could not plead Want of Employment, nor Incapacity of getting his Bread in an honest way, to favour so vile a Change, nor was he so much a Coward as to pretend it; but frankly own'd, it was to get rid of the disagreeable Superiority of some Masters he was acquainted with, and the Love of Novelty and Change, Maritime Peregrinations had accustom'd him to. *In an honest Service,* says he, *there is thin Commons, low Wages, and hard Labour; in this, Plenty and Satiety, Pleasure and Ease, Liberty and Power; and who would not ballance Creditor on this Side, when all the Hazard that is run for it, at worst, is only a*

soür Look or two at choaking. No, A merry Life and a short one, *shall be my Motto.* Thus he preach'd himself into an Approbation of what he at first abhorr'd; and being daily regal'd with Musick, Drinking, and the Gaiety and Diversions of his Companions, these deprav'd Propensities were quickly edg'd and strengthen'd, to the extinguishing of Fear and Conscience. Yet among all the vile and ignominious Acts he had perpetrated, he is said to have had an Aversion towards forcing Men into that Service, and had procured some their Discharge, notwithstanding so many made it their Plea.

When *Roberts* was gone, as tho' he had been the Life and Soul of the Gang, their Spirits sunk; many deserted their Quarters, and all stupidly neglected any Means for Defence, or Escape; and their Main-mast soon after being shot by the Board, they had no Way left, but to surrender and call for Quarters. The *Swallow* kept aloof, while her Boat passed, and repassed for the Prisoners; because they understood they were under an Oath to blow up; and some of the Desperadoes showed a Willingness that Way, Matches being lighted, and Scuffles happening between those who would, and those who opposed it: But I cannot easily account for this Humour, which can be term'd no more than a false Courage, since any of them had Power to destroy his own Life, either by Pistol, or Drowning, without involving others in the same Fate, who are in no Temper of Mind for it: And at best, it had been only dying, for fear of Death.

She had 40 Guns, and 157 Men, 45 whereof were Negroes; three only were killed in the Action, without any Loss to the *Swallow.* There was found upwards of 2000 *l.* in Gold-Dust in her. The Flag could not be got easily from under the fallen Mast, and was therefore recover'd by the *Swallow;* it had the Figure of a Skeleton in it, and a Man pourtray'd with a flaming Sword in his Hand, intimating a Defyance of Death it self.

The *Swallow* returned back into Cape *Lopez* Bay, and found the little *Ranger,* whom the Pyrates had deserted in hast, for the better Defence of the Ship: She had been plunder'd, according to what I could learn, of 2000 l. in Gold-Dust, (the Shares of those Pyrates who belonged to her;) and Captain *Hill,* in the *Neptune,* not unjustly suspected, for he would not wait the Man of War's returning into the Bay again, but sail'd away immediately, making no Scruple afterwards to own the Seizure of other Goods out of her, and surrender'd, as a Confirmation of all, 50 Ounces at *Barbadoes,* for which, see the Article at the End of this Book.

All Persons who after the 29th of Septem. 1690, &c.

To sum up the whole, if it be considered, first, that the sickly State of the Men of War, when they sail'd from *Princes,* was the Misfortune that hindered their being as far as *Sierraleon,* and consequently out of the Track the Pyrates then took. That those Pyrates, directly contrary to their Design, in the second Expedition, should get above Cape *Corso,* and that nigh *Axim,* a Chace should offer, that inevitably must discover them, and be soon communicated to the Men of War. That the satiating their evil and malicious Tempers at *Whydah,* in burning the *Porcupine,* and running off with the *French* Ship, had strengthened the *Swallow* with 30 Men. That the *Swallow* should miss them in that Road, where probably she had not, or at least so effectually obtained her End. That they should be so far infatuated at Cape *Lopez,* as to divide their Strength, which when collected, might have been so formidable. And lastly, that the Conquest should be without Bloodshed: I say, considering all these Circumstances, it shows that the Hand of Providence was concerned in their Destruction.

As to their Behaviour after they were taken, it was found that they had great Inclinations to rebel, if they could have laid hold of any Opportunity. For they were very uneasy under Restraint, having been lately all Commanders themselves; nor could they brook their Diet, or Quarters, without cursing and swearing, and upbraiding each other, with the Folly that had brought them to it.

So that to secure themselves against any mad desperate Undertaking of theirs, they strongly barricado'd the Gun-Room, and made another Prison before it; an Officer, with Pistols and Cutlashes, doing Duty, Night and Day, and the Prisoners within, manacled and shackled.

They would yet in these Circumstances be impudently merry, saying, when they viewed their Nakedness, *that they had not left them a halspenny, to give old* Charon, *to ferry them over* Stix: And at their thin Commons, they would observe, that they fell away so fast, that they should not have Weight left to hang them. *Sutton* used to be very prophane; he happening to be in the same Irons with another Prisoner, who was more serious than ordinary, and read and pray'd often, as became his Condition; this Man *Sutton* used to swear at, and ask him, *what he proposed by so much Noise and Devotion? Heaven,* says the other, *I hope, Heaven, you Fool,* says Sutton, *did you ever hear of any Pyrates going thither? Give me H — ll, it's a merrier Place; I'll give* Roberts *a Salute of* 13 *Guns at Entrance.* And when he found such ludicrous Expressions had no Effect on him, he made a formal Complaint, and requested that the Officer would either remove this Man, or take his Prayer-Book away, as a common Disturber.

A Combination and Conspyracy was formed, betwixt *Moody, Ashplant, Magnes, Mare,* and others, to rise, and kill the Officers, and run away with the Ship. This they had carried on by Means of a Mulatto Boy, who was allow'd to attend them, and proved very trusty in his Messages, between the Principals; but the Evening of that Night they were to have made this Struggle, two of the Prisoners that sat next to *Ashplant,* heard the Boy whisper them upon the Project, and naming to him the Hour they should be ready, presently gave Notice of it to the Captain, which put the Ship in an Alarm, for a little Time; and, on Examination, several of them had made shift to break off, or lose, their Shackles, (no doubt for such Purpose;) but it tended only to procure to themselves worse Usage and Confinement.

In the same Passage to Cape *Corso,* the Prize, *Royal Fortune,* was in the same Danger. She was left at the Island of St. *Thomas*'s, in the Possession of an Officer, and a few Men, to take in some fresh Provisions, (which were scarce at Cape *Corso*) with Orders to follow the Ship. There were only some of the Pyrates Negroes, three or four wounded Prisoners, and *Scudamore,* their Surgeon; from whom they seemed to be under no Apprehension, especially from the last, who might have hoped for Favour, on Account of his Employ; and had stood so much indebted for his Liberty, eating and drinking constantly with the Officer; yet this Fellow, regardless of the Favour, and lost to all Sense of Reformation, endeavoured to bring over the Negroes to his Design of murdering the People, and running away with the Ship. He easily prevailed with the Negroes to come into the Design; but when he came to communicate it to his Fellow Prisoners, and would have drawn them into the same Measures, by telling them, he understood Navigation, that the Negroes were stout Fellows, and by a Smattering he had in the *Angolan* Language, he had found willing to undertake such an Enterprize; and that it was better venturing to do this, run down the Coast, and raise a new Company, than to proceed to Cape *Corso,* and be hanged like a Dog, and Sun dry'd. One of them abhorring the Cruelty, or fearing the Success, discovered it to the Officer, who made him immediately a Prisoner, and brought the Ship safe.

When they came to be lodg'd in Cape *Corso-Castle,* their Hopes of this kind all cut off, and that they were assured they must there soon receive a final Sentence; the Note was changed among most of them, and from vain insolent jesting, they became serious and devout, begging for good Books, and joyning in public Prayers, and singing of Psalms, twice at least every Day.

As to their Tryals, if we should give them at length, it may appear tedious to the Reader, for which Reason, I have, for the avoiding Tautology and Repetition, put as many of them together as were try'd for the same Fact, reserving the Circumstances which are most material, with Observations on the dying Behaviour of such of them, as came to my Knowledge.

And first, it may be observed from the List, that a great Part of these Pyrate Ships Crews, were Men entered on the Coast of *Africa,* not many Months before they were taken; from whence, it may be concluded, that the pretended Constraint of *Roberts,* on them, was very often a Complotment between Parties equally willing: And this *Roberts* several Times openly declared, particularly to the *Onslow*'s People, whom he called aft, and ask'd of them, *who was willing to go, for he would force no Body?* As was deposed, by some of his best Hands, after Acquittal; nor is it reasonable to think, he should reject *Irish* Volunteers, only from a Pique against *Kennedy,* and force others, that might hazard, and, in Time, destroy his Government: But their Behaviour soon put him out of this Fear, and convinc'd him, that the Plea of Force was only the best Artifice they had to shelter themselves under, in Case they should be taken; and that they were less Rogues than others, only in Point of Time.

It may likewise be taken Notice of, that the Country, wherein they happened to be tried, is among other Happinesses, exempted from Lawyers, and Law-Books, so that the Office of Register, of necessity fell on one, not versed in those Affairs, which might justify the Court in want of Form, more essentially supply'd with Integrity and Impartiality.

But, perhaps, if there was less Law, there might be more Justice, than in some other Courts; for, if the civil Law be a Law of universal Reason, judging of the Rectitude, or Obliquity of Mens Actions, every Man of common Sense is endued with a Portion of it, at least sufficient to make him distinguish Right from Wrong, or what the Civilians call, *Malum in se.*

Therefore, here, if two Persons were equally Guilty of the same Fact, there was no convicting one, and bringing the other off, by any Quirk, or turn of Law; for they form'd their Judgments upon the Constraint, or Willingness, the Aim, and Intention of the Parties, and all other Circumstances, which make a material Difference. Besides, in Crimes of this Nature, Men bred up to the Sea, must be more knowing, and much abler, than others more learned in the Law; for, before a Man can have a right Idea of a Thing, he must know the Terns standing for that Thing: The Sea-Terms being a Language by it self, which no Lawyer can be supposed to understand, he must of Consequence want that discriminating Faculty, which should direct him to judge right of the Facts meant by those Terms.

The Court well knew, it was not possible to get the Evidence of every Sufferer by this Crew, and therefore, first of all, considered how that Deficiency should be supplied; whether, or no, they could pardon one *Jo. Dennis,* who had early offered himself, as King's Evidence, and was the best read in their Lives and Conversations: Here indeed, they were at a Loss for Law, and concluded in the Negative, because it look'd like compounding with a Man to swear falsly, losing by it, those great Helps he could have afforded.

Another great Difficulty in their Proceedings, was, how to understand those Words in the Act of Parliament, of, *particularly specifying in the Charge, the Circumstances of Time, Place,* &c. *i. e.* so to understand them, as to be able to hold a Court; for if they had been indicted on particular Robberies, the Evidence had happened mostly from the Royal *African* Company's Ships, on which these Gentlemen of *Cape-Corso-Castle,* were not qualify'd to sit, their Oath running, *That they have no Interest directly, or indirectly, in the Ship, or Goods, for the Robbery of which, the Party stands accused:* And this they thought they had, Commissions being paid them, on such Goods: And on the other Side, if they were incapacitated, no Court could be formed, the Commission absolutely requiring three of them by Name.

To reconcile all Things, therefore, the Court resolved, to bottom the whole of their Proceedings on the *Swallow*'s Depositions, which were clear and plain, and had the Circumstance of Time when, Place where, Manner how, and the like, particularly specified according to the Statute in that Case made, and provided. But this admitted only a general Intimation of Robbery in the Indictment, therefore *to approve their Clemency,* it looking Arbitrary on the Lives of Men, to lump them to the Gallows, in such a summary Way as must have been done, had they solely adhered to the *Swallow*'s Charge, they resolved to come to particular Tryals.

Secondly, *That the Prisoners might not be ignorant whereon to answer,* and so have all fair Advantages, to excuse and defend themselves; the Court farther agreed with Justice and Equanimity, to hear any Evidence that could be brought, to weaken or corroborate the three Circumstances that complete a Pyrate; first, being a Volunteer amongst them at the Beginning; secondly, being a Volunteer at the taking or robbing of any Ship; or lastly, voluntarily accepting a Share in the Booty of those that did; for by a Parity of Reason, where these Actions were of their own disposing, and yet committed by them, it must be believed their Hearts and Hands joyned together, in what they acted against his Majesty's Ship the *Swallow*.

The Tryals of the Pyrates,

Taken by his Majesty's Ship the Swallow, *begun at Cape* Corso-Castle, *on the Coast of* Africa, March *the* 28th, 1722.

THE Commission impowered any three named therein, to call to their Assistance, such a Number of qualified Persons as might make the Court always consist of seven: And accordingly Summons were signed to Lieut. *Jo. Barnsley,* Lieut. *Ch. Fanshaw,* Capt. *Samuel Hartsease,* and Capt. *William Menzies, viz.*

'BY Virtue of a Power and Authority, to us given, by a Commission from the King, under the Seal of Admiralty, You are hereby required to attend, and make one of the Court, for the trying and adjudging of the Pyrates, lately taken on this Coast, by his Majesty's Ship the *Swallow*.

Given under our Hands this 28th of *March,* 1722, at Cape *Carso-Castle.*

Mungo Heardman,

James Phips,

Henry Dodson,

Francis Boy,

Edward Hide.

The Commissioners being met in the Hall of the Castle, the Commission was first read, after which, the President, and then the other Members, took the Oath, prescribed in the Act of Parliament, and having directed the Form of that for Witnesses, as follows, the Court was opened.

I, A. B. *solemnly promise and swear on the Holy Evangelists, to bear true and faithful Witness between the King and Prisoner, or Prisoners, in Relation to the Fact, or Facts, of Pyracy and Robbery, he or they do now stand accused of.* So help me God.

The Court consisted of Captain *Mungo Heardman,* President.
James Phips, *Esq; General of the Coast,*
Mr. H. Dodson, *Mer.*
Mr. F. Boye, *Mer.*
Mr. Edward Hyde, *Secretary to the Company.*
Lieut. John Barnsley,
Lieut. Ch. Fanshaw.

The following Prisoners, out of the Pyrate Ship *Ranger,* having been commanded before them, the Charge, or Indictment, was exhibited.

Prisoners taken in the Ranger.

Mens Names.	Ships from	Time when.
*James Skyrm	*Greyhound* Sloop	Oct. 1720
*Rich. Hardy	Pyrate with *Davis*	1718
*Wm. Main	Brigantine Capt. *Peet*	June 1720
*Henry Dennis	Pyrates with Capt. *Davis*	1718
*Val. Ashplant	Pyrates with Capt. *Davis*	1719
*Rob. Birdson	Pyrates with Capt. *Davis*	1719
*Rich. Harris	*Phœnix* of *Bristol*, Capt. *Richards*	June 1720
*D. Littlejohn	*Phœnix* of *Bristol*, Capt. *Richards*	June 1720
*Thomas How	at *Newfoundland*	June 1720
†Her. Hunkins	*Success* Sloop	
*Hugh Harris	Willing Mind	July 1720
*W. Mackintosh		July 1720
Thomas Wills	*Richard* of *Biddiford*	July 1720
†John Wilden	*Mary* and *Martha*	July 1720
*Ja. Greenham	Little York, *Phillips* Mr.	July 1720
*John Jaynson	*Love* of *Lancaster*	July 1720
†Chri. Lang	*Thomas* Brigantine	Sept. 1720
*John Mitchel	*Norman* Galley	Oct. 1720
T. Withstandenot	*Norman* Galley	Oct. 1720
Peter la Fever	*Jeremiah* and *Ann*	Ap. 1720
*Wm. Shurin	*Jeremiah* and *Ann*	Ap. 1720
*Wm. Wats	*Sierraleon* of Mr. *Glin*	July 1721
*Wm. Davis	*Sierraleon* of Seig. *Josseé*	July 1721
†James Barrow	*Martha* Snow Capt *Lady*	
*Joshua Lee	*Martha* Snow Capt *Lady*	
Rob. Hartley (1)	*Robinson* of *Leverpole* Capt. *Kanning*	Aug. 1721
†James Crane	*Robinson* of *Leverpole* Capt. *Kanning*	Aug. 1721
George Smithson	*Stanwich* Galley Captain *Tarlton*	Aug. 1721
Roger Pye	*Stanwich* Galley Captain *Tarlton*	Aug. 1721
†Rob. Fletcher	*Stanwich* Galley Captain *Tarlton*	Aug. 1721

*Ro. Hartley (2)	*Stanwich*Galley Captain *Tarlton*	Aug.1721
†Andrew Rance	A *Dutch* Ship	Aug.1721
*Cuthbert Goss	*Mercy*Galley of *Bristol* at *Callibar*	Oct.1721
*Tho. Giles	*Mercy*Galley of *Bristol* at *Callibar*	Oct.1721
*Israel Hynde	*Mercy*Galley of *Bristol* at *Callibar*	Oct.1721
William Church	*Gertruycht* of *Holland*	Jan.1721½
Philip Haak	*Flushingham* of *Holland*	Jan.1721½
William Smith	*Elizabeth*Capt.*Sharp*	Jan.1721½
Adam Comry	*Elizabeth*Capt.*Sharp*	Jan.1721½
William Graves	*King Solomon*Capt.*Trehern* off Cape*Appollonia*	Jan.1721½
*Peter de Vine	*King Solomon*Capt.*Trehern* off Cape*Appollonia*	Jan.1721½
John Johnson	*King Solomon*Capt.*Trehern* off Cape*Appollonia*	Jan.1721½
John Stodgill	*King Solomon*Capt.*Trehern* off Cape*Appollonia*	Jan.1721½
Henry Dawson	*Whydah*Sloop at *Jaquin*	Jan.1721½
William Glass	*Whydah*Sloop at *Jaquin*	Jan.1721½
Josiah Robinson	*Tarlton*Capt.*Tho. Tarlton*,	Jan.1721½
John Arnaught	*Tarlton*Capt.*Tho. Tarlton*,	Jan.1721½
John Davis	*Tarlton*Capt.*Tho. Tarlton*,	Jan.1721½
†Henry Graves	*Tarlton*Capt.*Tho. Tarlton*,	Jan.1721½
Tho. Howard	*Tarlton*Capt.*Tho. Tarlton*,	Jan.1721½
†John Rimer	*Tarlton*Capt.*Tho. Tarlton*,	Jan.1721½
Thomas Clephen	*Tarlton*Capt.*Tho. Tarlton*,	Jan.1721½
Wm. Guineys	*Porcupine*Capt.*Fletcher*	Jan.1721½
†James Cosins		Jan.1721½
Tho. Stretton	*Onslow*Capt.*Gee* at *Cestos*	Jan.1721½
*William Petty	*Onslow*Capt.*Gee* at *Cestos*	Jan.1721½
Mic. Lemmon	*Onslow*Capt.*Gee* at *Cestos*	Jan.1721½
*Wm. Wood	*Onslow*Capt.*Gee* at *Cestos*	Jan.1721½
*Ed. Watts	*Onslow*Capt.*Gee* at *Cestos*	Jan.1721½
*John Horn	*Onslow*Capt.*Gee* at *Cestos*	Jan.1721½
Pierre Ravon	Peter Grossey	From the *French* ship in *Whydah* Road Feb.1721-2.
John Dugan	Rence Frogier	From the *French* ship in *Whydah* Road Feb.1721-2.

James Ardeon	Lewis Arnaut	From the *French* ship in *Whydah* Road Feb. 1721-2.
Ettrien Gilliot	Rence Thoby	From the *French* ship in *Whydah* Road Feb. 1721-2.
Ren. Marraud	Meth Roulac	From the *French* ship in *Whydah* Road Feb. 1721-2.
John Gittin	John Gumar	From the *French* ship in *Whydah* Road Feb. 1721-2.
Jo. Richardeau	John Paquete	From the *French* ship in *Whydah* Road Feb. 1721-2.
John Lavogue	Allan Pigan	
John Duplaissey	Pierce Shillot	From the *French* ship in *Whydah* Road Feb. 1721-2.

You, *James Skyrm, Michael Lemmon, Robert Hartley,* &c.

YE, *and every one of you, are in the Name, and by the Authority, of our dread Sovereign Lord,* George, *King of* Great Britain, *indicted as follows;*

Forasmuch as in open Contempt of the Laws of your Country, ye have all of you been wickedly united, and articled together, for the Annoyance and Disturbance of his Majesty's trading Subjects by Sea. And have in Conformity to the most evil and mischievous Intentions, been twice down the Coast of Africa, *with two Ships; once in the Beginning of* August, *and a second Time, in* January *last, sinking, burning, or robbing such Ships, and Vessels, as then happened in your Way.*

Particularly, ye stand charged at the Instance, and Information of Captain Chaloner Ogle, *as Traitors and Pyrates, for the unlawful Opposition ye made to his Majesty's Ship, the* Swallow, *under his Command.*

For that on the 5th of February *last past, upon Sight of the aforesaid King's Ship, ye did immediately weigh Anchor from under Cape* Lopez, *on the Southern Coast of* Africa, *in a* French *built Ship of 32 Guns, called the*

Ranger, *and did pursue and chase the aforesaid King's Ship, with such Dispatch and Precipitancy, as declared ye common Robbers and Pyrates.*

That about Ten of the Clock the same Morning, drawing within Gun-shot of his Majesty's aforesaid Ship the Swallow, *ye hoisted a piratical black Flag, and fired several chace Guns, to deter, as much as ye were able, his Majesty's Servants from their Duty.*

That an Hour after this, being very nigh to the aforesaid King's Ship, ye did audaciously continue in a hostile Defence and Assault, for about two Hours more, in open Violation of the Laws, and in Defiance to the King's Colours and Commission.

And lastly, that in the acting, and compassing of all this, ye were all, and every one of you, in a wicked Combination, voluntarily to exert, and actually did, in your several Stations, use your utmost Endeavours to distress the said King's Ship, and murder his Majesty's good Subjects.

To which they severally pleaded, *Not Guilty.*

Then the Court called for the Officers of the *Swallow,* Mr. *Isaac Sun,* Lieutenant, *Ralph Baldrick,* Boatswain, *Daniel Maclauglin,* Mate, desiring them to view the Prisoners, whether they knew them? And to give an Account in what Manner they had attack'd and fought the King's Ship; and they agreed as follows.

That they had viewed all the Prisoners, as they stood now before the Court, and were assured they were the same taken out of one, or other, of the Pyrate Ships, *Royal Fortune,* or *Ranger;* but verily believe them to be taken out of the *Ranger.*

That they did in the King's Ship, at break of Day, on *Monday,* the 5th of *February,* 1721-2, discover three Ships at Anchor, under Cape *Lopez,* on the Southern Coast of *Africa;* the Cape bearing then W. S. W. about three Leagues, and perceiving one of them to have a Pendant flying, and having heard their Morning-Gun before, they immediately suspected them to be *Roberts* the Pyrate, his consort, and a *French* Ship, they knew had been lately carried out of *Whydah* Road.

The King's Ship was obliged to hawl off N. W. and W. N. W. to avoid a Sand, called, the *French Man's Bank,* the Wind then at S. S. E. and found in half an Hour's time, one of the three had got under Sail from the Careen, and was bending her Sails, in a Chace towards them. To encourage this Rashness and Precipitancy, they kept away before the Wind, (as though afraid,) but with their Tacks on Board, their Main-Yard braced, and making, at the same Time, very bad Steerage.

About half an Hour after Ten, in the Morning, the Pyrate Ship came within Gun-shot, and fired four Chace Guns, hoisted a black Flag at the Mizen-Peek, and got their Sprit-sail Yard under their Bowsprit, for boarding. In half an Hour more, approaching still nigher, they Starboarded their Helm, and gave her a Broadside, the Pyrate bringing to, and returning the same.

After this, the Deponents say, their Fire grew slack for some Time, because the Pyrate was shot so far a Head on the Weather-Bow, that few of their Guns could Point to her; yet in this Interval their black Flag was either Shot away, or hawled down a little Space, and hoisted again.

At length, by their ill Steerage, and Favour of the Wind, they came near, a second Time; and about Two in the Afternoon shot away their Maintopmast.

The Colours they fought under, besides a black Flag, were a red *English* Ensign, a King's Jack, and a *Dutch* Pendant, which they struck at, or about, Three in the Afternoon, and called for Quarters; it proving to be a *French* built Ship of 32 Guns, called the *Ranger.*

Isaac Sun,

Ralph Baldrick,

Daniel Maclauglin.

When the Evidence had been heard, the Prisoners were called upon to answer, how they came on Board this Pyrate Ship; and their Reason for so audacious a Resistance, as had been made against the King's Ship.

To this, each, in his Reply, owned himself to be one of those taken out of the *Ranger;* that he had signed their piratical Articles, and shared in their Plunder, some few only accepted, who had been there too short a Time. But that neither in this signing, or sharing, nor in the Resistance had been made against his Majesty's Ship, had they been Volunteers, but had acted in these several Parts, from a Terror of Death; which a Law amongst them, was to be the Portion of those who refused. The Court then ask'd, who made those Laws? How those Guns came to be fired? Or why they had not deserted their Stations, and mutinied, when so fair a Prospect of Redemption offered? They replied still, with the same Answers, and could extenuate their Crimes, with no other Plea, than being forced Men. Wherefore the Court were of Opinion, that the Indictment, as it charged them with an unlawful Attack and Resistance of the King's Ship, was sufficiently proved; but then it being undeniably evident, that many of these Prisoners had been forced, and some of them of very short standing, they did, on mature Deliberation, come to this merciful Resolution;

That they would hear further Evidence for, or against, each Person singly, in Relation to those Parts of the Indictment, which declared them Volunteers, or charged them with aiding and assisting, at the burning, sinking, or robbing of other Ships; for if they acted, or assisted, in any Robberies or Devastations, it would be a Conviction they were Volunteers; here such Evidence, though it might want the Form, still carried the Reason of the Law with it.

The Charge was exhibited also against the following Pyrates taken out of the *Royal Fortune.*

*Mich. Mare	in the *Rover* 5 Years ago	
*Chris. Moody	under *Davis*	1718.
*Mar. Johnson	a *Dutch* Ship	18.
*James Philips	the *Revenge* Pyrate Sloop	17.
*David Symson	Pyrates with *Davis*	
*Tho. Sutton	Pyrates with *Davis*	
*Hag. Jacobson	a *Dutch* Ship	1719
*W. Williams 1	*Sadbury* Captain *Thomas Newfoundland*	1719
*Wm. Fernon	*Sadbury* Captain *Thomas Newfoundland*	*June* 1720.
*W. Willams 2	*Sadbury* Captain *Thomas Newfoundland*	*June* 1720.
*Roger Scot	*Sadbury* Captain *Thomas Newfoundland*	
*Tho. Owen	*York* of *Bristol*	*May* 1720.
*Wm. Taylor	*York* of *Bristol*	*May* 1720.
*Joseph Nositer	*Expedition* of *Topsham*	*May* 1720.
*John Parker	*Willing Mind* of *Pool*	*July* 1720.
*Robert Crow	*Happy Return* Sloop	*July* 1720.
*George Smith	*Mary* and *Martha*	*July* 1720.
*Ja. Clements	*Success* Sloop	*July* 1720.
*John Walden	*Blessing* of *Lymington*	*July* 1720.
*Jo. Mansfield	from *Martinico*	
†James Harris	*Richard* Pink	
*John Philips	a fishing Boat	
Harry Glasby	*Samuel* Capt. *Cary*.	*July* 1720.
Hugh Menzies	*Samuel* Capt. *Cary*.	*July* 1720.
*Wm. Magnus		
*Joseph Moor	*May Flower* Sloop	Feb. 1720.
†John du Frock	*Loyd* Gally Capt. *Hyngston*	*May* 1721.
Wm. Champnies	*Loyd* Gally Capt. *Hyngston*	*May* 1721.
George Danson	*Loyd* Gally Capt. *Hyngston*	*May* 1721.
†Isaac Russel	*Loyd* Gally Capt. *Hyngston*	
Robert Lilbourn	*Jeremiah* and *Ann*, Capt. *Turner*	Ap. 1721.
*Robert Johnson	*Jeremiah* and *Ann*, Capt. *Turner*	Ap. 1721.
Wm. Darling	*Jeremiah* and *Ann*, Capt. *Turner*	Ap. 1721.

†Wm. Mead	*Jeremiah* and *Ann*, Capt. *Turner*	
Thomas Diggles	*Christopher* Snow	*Ap.* 1721.
*Ben. Jeffreys	*Norman* Galley	*Ap.* 1721.
John Francia	a Sloop at St. *Nicholas*	*Ap.* 1721.
*D. Harding	a *Dutch* Ship	*Ap.* 1721.
*John Coleman	*Adventure* Sloop	*Ap.* 1721.
*Charles Bunce	a *Dutch* Galley	*Ap.* 1721.
*R. Armstrong	a *Dutch* run from the *Swallow*	*Ap.* 1721.
*Abra. Harper	*Onslow* Capt. *Gee* at *Sestos*,	May 1721.
*Peter Lesley	*Onslow* Capt. *Gee* at *Sestos*,	May 1721.
*John Jessup 1	*Onslow* Capt. *Gee* at *Sestos*,	May 1721.
Thomas Watkins	*Onslow* Capt. *Gee* at *Sestos*,	May 1721.
*Philip Bill	*Onslow* Capt. *Gee* at *Sestos*,	May 1721.
*Jo. Stephenson	*Onslow* Capt. *Gee* at *Sestos*,	May 1721.
*James Cromby	*Onslow* Capt. *Gee* at *Sestos*,	May 1721.
Thomas Garrat	*Onslow* Capt. *Gee* at *Sestos*,	May 1721.
†George Ogle	*Onslow* Capt. *Gee* at *Sestos*,	May 1721.
Roger Gorsuch	*Martha* Snow	*Au.* 1721.
John Watson	*Martha* Snow	*Au.* 1721.
William Child	*Mercy* Gally at *Callabar*	*Oct.* 1721.
*John Griffin	*Mercy* Gally at *Callabar*	*Oct.* 1721.
*Pet. Scudamore	*Mercy* Gally at *Callabar*	
Christ. Granger	*Cornwall* Galley at *Callabar*	
Nicho. Brattle	*Cornwall* Galley at *Callabar*	
James White	*Cornwall* Galley at *Callabar*	*Oct.* 1721.
Tho. Davis	*Cornwall* Galley at *Callabar*	*Oct.* 1721.
Tho. Sever	*Cornwall* Galley at *Callabar*	*Oct.* 1721.
*Rob. Bevins	*Cornwall* Galley at *Callabar*	
*T. Oughterlaney	*Cornwall* Galley at *Callabar*	
*David Rice	*Cornwall* Galley at *Callabar*	
*Rob. Haws	*Joceline* Capt. *Loane*	*Oct.* 1721.
Hugh Riddle	*Diligence* Boat	*Ja.* 1721.
Stephen Thomas	*Diligence* Boat	*Ja.* 1721.
*John Lane	King Solomon	*Ja.* 1721.
*Sam. Fletcher	King Solomon	*Ja.* 1721.
*Wm. Philips	King Solomon	*Ja.* 1721.
Jacob Johnson	King Solomon	*Ja.* 1721.

*John King	King Solomon	Ja.1721.
Benjamin Par	*Robinson*Capt.*Kanning*	Ja.1721.
William May	*Elizabeth*Capt.*Sharp*	Ja.1721.
Ed. Thornden	*Elizabeth*Capt.*Sharp*	Ja.1721.
*George Wilson	*Tarlton*of*Leverpool*at Cape*la Hou*	Ja.1721.
Edward Tarlton	*Tarlton*of*Leverpool*at Cape*la Hou*	Ja.1721.
*Robert Hays	*Tarlton*of*Leverpool*at Cape*la Hou*	
Thomas Roberts	*Charlton*Capt.*Allwright*	Feb.1721.
John Richards	*Charlton*Capt.*Allwright*	Feb.1721.
John Cane	*Charlton*Capt.*Allwright*	Feb.1721.
Richard Wood	*Porcupine*Capt.*Fletcher Whydah*Road	
Richard Scot	*Porcupine*Capt.*Fletcher Whydah*Road	Feb.1721.
Wm. Davison	*Porcupine*Capt.*Fletcher Whydah*Road	Feb.1721.
Sam. Morwell	*Porcupine*Capt.*Fletcher Whydah*Road	Feb.1721.
Edward Evans	*Porcupine*Capt.*Fletcher Whydah*Road	
*John Jessup2	surrender'd up at*Princes*	

You, *Harry Glasby, William Davison, William Champnies, Samuel Morwell,* &c.

YE, and every one of you, are, in the Name, and by the Authority of our most dread Sovereign Lord George, *King of* Great Britain, *indicted as follows.*

Forasmuch as in open Contempt and Violation of the Laws of your Country, to which ye ought to have been subject,) ye have all of you been wickedly united and articled together, for the Annoyance and Destruction of his Majesty's trading Subjects by Sea; and in Conformity to so wicked an Agreement and Association, ye have been twice lately down this Coast of Africa, *once in* August, *and a second Time in* January *last, spoiling and destroying many Goods and Vessels of his Majesty's Subjects, and other trading Nations.*

Particularly ye stand indicted at the Information and Instance of Captain Chaloner Ogle, *as Traytors, Robbers, Pyrates, and common Enemies to Mankind.*

For that on the 10*th of* February *last, in a Ship ye were possess'd of called the* Royal Fortune, *of* 40 *Guns, ye did maintain a hostile Defence and Resistance for some Hours, against his Majesty's Ship the* Swallow, *nigh Cape* Lopez *Bay, on the Southern Coast of* Africa.

That this Fight and insolent Resistance against the King's Ship, was made, not only without any Pretence of Authority, more than that of your own private depraved Wills, but was done also under a black Flag, flagrantly by that, denoting your selves common Robbers and Traitors, Opposers and Violators of the Laws.

And lastly, that in this Resistance, ye were all of you Volunteers, and did, as such, contribute your utmost Efforts, for disabling and distressing the aforesaid King's Ship, and deterring his Majesty's Servants therein, from their Duty.

To which they severally pleaded, *Not Guilty.*

Whereupon the Officers of his Majesty's Ship, the *Swallow,* were called again, and testified as follows.

That they had seen all the Prisoners now before the Court, and knew them to be the same which were taken out of one or other of the Pyrate Ships, *Royal Fortune* or *Ranger,* and verily believe them to be those taken out of the *Royal Fortune.*

That the Prisoners were possess'd of a Ship of 40 Guns, called the *Royal Fortune,* and were at an Anchor under Cape *Lopez,* on the Coast of *Africa,* with two others: When his Majesty's Ship the *Swallow,* (to which the Deponents belong'd, and were Officers,) stood in for the Place, on *Saturday* the 10th of *February* 1721-2: The largest had a Jack, Ensign and Pendant flying, (being this *Royal Fortune,*) who on Sight of them, had their Boats passing and repassing, from the other two, which they supposed to be with Men: The Wind not favouring the aforesaid King's Ship, she was obliged to make two Trips to gain nigh enough the Wind, to setch in with the Pyrates; and being at length little more than random Shot from them, they found she slipped her Cable, and got under Sail.

At Eleven, the Pyrate was within Pistol-Shot, a Breast of them, with a black Flag, and Pendant hoisted at their Main-topmast Head. The Deponents say, they then struck the *French* Ensign that had continued hoisted at their Staff all the Morning till then; and display'd the King's Colours, giving her, at the same Time, their Broadside, which was immediately returned.

The Pyrate's Mizen-topmast fell, and some of her Rigging was torn, yet she still out sailed the Man of War, and slid half Gun-Shot from them, while they continued to fire without Intermission, and the other to return such Guns as could be brought to bear, till by favour of the Winds, they were advanced very nigh again; and after exchanging a few more Shot, about half an Hour past one, his Main-Mast came down, having received a Shot a little below the Parrel.

At Two she struck her Colours, and called for Quarters, proving to be a Ship, formerly call'd the *Onslow,* but by them, the *Royal Fortune;* and the Prisoners from her, assured them, that the smallest Ship of the two, then remaining in the Road, belong'd to them, by the Name of the *Little Ranger,* which they had deserted on this Occasion.

Isaac Sun,

Ralph Baldrick,

Daniel Maclaughlin.

The Prisoners were asked by the Court, to the same Purpose the others had been in the Morning; what Exception they had to make against what had been sworn? And what they had to say in their Defence? And their Reply were much the same with the other Prisoners; that they were forc'd Men, had not fired a Gun in this Resistance against the *Swallow,* and that what little Assistance they did give on this Occasion, was to the Sails and Rigging, to comply with the arbitrary Commands of *Roberts,* who had threaten'd, and they were perswaded would, have Shot them on Refusal.

The Court, to dispense equal Justice, mercifully resolved for these, as they had done for the other Pyrate Crew; that further Evidence should be heard against each Man singly, to the two Points, of being a Volunteer at first, and to their particular Acts of Pyracy and Robbery since: That so Men, who had been lately received amongst them, and as yet, had not been at the taking, or plundering, of any Ship, might have the Opportunity, and Benefit, of clearing their Innocence, and not fall promiscuously with the Guilty.

By Order of the Court,

John Atkins, *Register.*

Wm. Magnes, Tho. Oughterlauney, Wm. Main, Wm. Mackintosh, Val. Ashplant, John Walden, Israel Hind, Marcus Johnson, Wm. Petty, Wm. Fernon, Abraham Harper, Wm. Wood, Tho. How, John Stephenson, Ch. Bunce, and *John Griffin*

Against these it was deposed by Captain *Joseph Trahern,* and *George Fenn,* his Mate, that they were all of them, either at the attacking and taking of the Ship King *Solomon,* or afterwards at the robbing and plundering of her, and in this Manner;

That on the 6th of *January* last their Ship riding at Anchor near Cape *Appollonia* in *Africa,* discovered a Boat rowing towards them, against Wind and Stream, from a Ship that lay about three Miles to Leeward. They judged from the Number of Men in her, as she nearer advanced, to be a Pyrate, and made some Preparation for receiving her, believing, on a nigher View, they would think fit to withdraw from an Attack that must be on their Side with great Disadvantage in an open Boat, and against double the Number of Men; yet by the Rashness, and the Pusillanimity of his own People (who laid down their Arms, and immediately called for Quarter) the Ship was taken, and afterwards robbed by them.

President. Can you charge your Memory with any Particulars in the Seizure and Robbery?

Evidence. We know that *Magnes,* Quarter-Master of the Pyrate Ship, commanded the Men in this Boat that took us, and assumed the Authority of ordering her Provisions and Stores out, which being of different Kinds, we soon found, were seized and sent away under more particular Directions; for *Main,* as Boatswain of the Pyrate Ship, carried away two Cables, and several Coils of Rope, as what belonged to his Province, beating some of our own Men for not being brisk enough at working in the Robbery. *Petty,* as Sail-maker, saw to the Sails and Canvas; *Harper,* as Cooper to the Cask and Tools; *Griffin,* to the Carpenter's Stores, and *Oughterlauney,* as Pilot, having shifted himself with a Suit of my Clothes, a new tye Wig, and called for a Bottle of Wine, ordered the Ship, very arrogantly, to be steered under Commadore *Robert*'s Stern, (I suppose to know what Orders there were concerning her.) So far particularly. In the general, Sir, they were very outragious and emulous in Mischief.

President. Mr. *Castel,* acquaint the Court of what you know in Relation to this Robbery of the King *Solomon;* after what Manner the Pyrate-Boat was dispatch'd for this Attempt.

Tho. Castel. I was a Prisoner, Sir, with the Pyrates when their Boat was ordered upon that Service, and found, upon a Resolution of going, Word was passed through the Company, Who would go? And I saw all that did, did it voluntarily; no Compulsion, but rather pressing who should be foremost.

The Prisoners yielded to what had been sworn about the Attack and Robbery, but denied the latter Evidence, saying, *Roberts* hector'd, and upbraided them of Cowardice on this very Occasion; and told some, they were very ready to step on Board of a Prize when within Command of the Ship, but now there seem'd to be a Tryal of their Valour, backward and fearful.

President. So that *Roberts* forc'd ye upon this Attack.

Prisoners. Roberts commanded us into the Boat, and the Quarter-Master to rob the Ship; neither of whose Commands we dared to have refused.

President. And granting it so, those are still your own Acts, since done by Orders from Officers of your own Election. Why would Men, honestly disposed, give their Votes for such a Captain and such a Quarter-Master as were every Day commanding them on distastful Services?

Here succeeded a Silence among the Prisoners, but at length *Fernon* very honestly own'd, that he did not give his Vote to *Magnes,* but to *David Sympson* (the old Quarter-Master,) *for in Truth,* says he, *I took* Magnes *for too honest a Man, and unfit for the Business.*

The Evidence was plain and home, and the Court, without any Hesitation, brought them in *Guilty.*

WILLIAM *Church, Phil. Haak, James White, Nich. Brattle, Hugh Riddle, William Thomas, Tho. Roberts, Jo. Richards, Jo. Cane, R. Wood, R. Scot, Wm. Davison, Sam. Morwell, Edward Evans, Wm. Guineys,* and 18 *French* Men.

The four first of these Prisoners, it was evident to the Court, served as Musick on Board the Pyrate, were forced lately from the several Merchant Ships they belonged to; and that they had, during this Confinement, an uneasy Life of it, having sometimes their Fiddles, and often their Heads broke, only for excusing themselves, or saying they were tired, when any Fellow took it in his Head to demand a Tune.

The other *English* had been a very few Days on Board the Pyrate, only from *Whydah* to Cape *Lopez,* and no Capture or Robbery done by them in that Time. And the *French* Men were brought with a Design to reconduct their own Ship (or the *Little Ranger* in Exchange) to *Whydah* Road again, and were used like Prisoners; neither quarter'd nor suffered to carry Arms. So that the Court immediately acquiesced in, *Acquitting them.*

THO. Sutton, David Sympson, Christopher Moody, Phil. Bill, R. Hardy, Hen. Dennis, David Rice, Wm. Williams, R. Harris, Geo. Smith, Ed. Watts, Jo. Mitchell and *James Barrow.*

The Evidence against these Prisoners, were *Geret de Haen,* Master of the *Flushingham,* taken nigh *Axim,* the Beginning of *January* last.

Benj. Krest Master, and *James Groet* Mate of the *Gertruycht,* taken nigh *Gabone* in *December* last, and Mr. *Castel, Wingfield* and others, that had been Prisoners with the Pyrates.

The former deposed, that all these Prisoners (excepting *Hardy*) were on Board at the Robbery and Plunder of their Ships, behaving in a vile outragious Manner, putting them in bodily Fears, sometimes for the Ship, and sometimes for themselves; and in particular, *Kreft* charged it on *Sutton,* that he had ordered all their Gunner's Stores out; on which that Prisoner presently interrupted, and said, he was perjured, *That he had not taken half.* A Reply, I believe, not designed as any sawcy Way of jesting, but to give their Behaviour an Appearance of more Humanity than the *Dutch* would allow.

From Mr. *Castel, Wingfield* and others, they were proved to be distinguished Men, Men who were consulted as Chiefs in all Enterprizes; belonged most of them to the House of Lords, (as they call'd it,) and could carry an Authority over others. The former said, particularly of *Hardy,* (Quarter-Master of the *Ranger,*) that when the *Diligence* Sloop was taken, (whereto he belonged,) none was busier in the Plunder, and was the very Man who scuttled and sunk that Vessel.

From some of the Prisoners acquitted, it was farther demanded, whether the Acceptance or Refusal of any Office was not in their own Option? And it was declared, that every Officer was chose by a Majority of Votes, and might refuse, if he pleased, since others gladly embraced what brought with it an additional Share of Prize. *Guilty*

The Court on the 31st of *March,* remanded the following six before them, for Sentence, *viz. Dav. Sympson, Wm. Magnes, R. Hardy, Thomas Sutton, Christopher Moody,* and *Valen. Ashplant.*

To whom the President spoke to the following Purpose; *The Crime of Pyracy, of which all of ye have been justly convicted, is of all other Robberies the most aggravating and inhumane, in that being removed from the Fears of Surprize, in remote and distant Parts, ye do in Wantonness of Power often add Cruelty to Theft.*

Pyrates unmoved at Distress or Poverty, not only spoil and rob, but do it from Men needy, and who are purchasing their Livlihoods thro' Hazards and Difficulties, which ought rather to move Compassion; and what is still worse, do often, by Perswasion or Force, engage the inconsiderate Part of them, to their own and Families Ruin, removing them from their Wives and Children, and by that, from the Means that should support them from Misery and Want.

To a trading Nation, nothing can be so Destructive as Pyracy, or call for more exemplary Punishment; besides, the national Reflection it infers: It cuts off the Returns of Industry, and those plentiful Importations that alone can make an Island flourishing; and it is your Aggravation, that ye have been the Chiefs and Rulers in these licentious and lawless Practices.

However, contrary to the Measures ye have dealt, ye have been heard with Patience, and tho' little has, or possibly could, have been said in Excuse or Extenuation of your Crimes, yet Charity makes us hope that a true and sincere Repentance (which we heartily recommend) may entitle ye to Mercy and Forgiveness, after the Sentence of the Law has taken Place, which now remains upon me to pronounce.

YOU Dav. Simpson, William Magnes, R. Hardy, Tho. Sutton, Christopher Moody, *and* Val. Ashplant.

Ye, and each of you, are adjudged and sentenced, to be carried back to the Place from whence ye came, from thence to the Place of Execution, without the Gates of this Castle, and there within the Flood-Marks, to be hanged by the Neck till ye are dead.

After this, ye, and each of you shall be taken down, and your Bodies hanged in Chains.

Warrant for Execution

PURSUANT to the Sentence given on Saturday, *by the Court of Admiralty, at* Cape-Corso-Castle, *against* Dav. Simpson, Wm. Magnes, R. Hardy, Tho. Sutton, Christopher Moody, *and* Valentine Ashplant.

You are hereby directed to carry the aforesaid Malefactors to the Place of Execution, without the Gates of this Castle, to Morrow Morning at Nine of the Clock, and there within the Flood-Marks, cause them to be hanged by the Neck till they are dead, for which, this shall be your Warrant. Given under my Hand, this 2d Day of April 1722.

To Joseph Gordyn, *Provost-Marshal.*
Mungo Heardman.
The Bodies remove in Chains, to the Gibbets already erected on the adjacent Hillocks.

M. H.

William Phillips.

IT appeared by the Evidence of Captain *Jo. Trahern,* and *George Fenn,* Mate of the King *Solomon,* that this Prisoner was Boatswain of the same Ship, when she was attacked and taken off Cape *Appollonia,* the 6th of *January* last, by the Pyrate's Boat.

When the Boat drew nigh, (they say,) it was judged from the Number of Men in her, that they were Pyrates, and being hailed, answered, *Defiance;* at which the Commander snatched a Musquet from one of his Men, and fired, asking them at the same Time, whether they would stand by him, to defend the Ship? But the Pyrates returning a Volley, and crying out, they would give no Quarters if any Resistance was made; this Prisoner took upon him to call out for Quarters, without the Master's Consent, and mislead the rest to the laying down their Arms, and giving up the Ship, to half the Number of Men, and in an open Boat. It was further evident he became, after this, a Volunteer amongst them. First, because he was presently very forward and brisk, in robbing the Ship *King Solomon,* of her Provisions and Stores. Secondly, because he endeavoured to have his Captain ill used; and lastly, because he had confessed to *Fenn,* that he had been obliged to sign their Articles that Night, (a Pistol being laid on the Table, to signify he must do it, or be shot,) when the whole appeared to be an Untruth from other Evidence, who also asserted his being armed in the Action against the *Swallow.*

In answer to this, he first observed upon the Unhappiness of being friendless in this Part of the World, which, elsewhere, by witnessing to the Honesty of his former Life, would, he believed, in a great Measure, have invalidated the wrong Evidence had been given of his being a Volunteer with the Pyrates. He owns indeed, he made no Application to his Captain, to intercede for a Discharge, but excuses it with saying, he had a dislike to him, and therefore was sure that such Application would have avail'd him nothing.

The Court observed the Pretences of this, and other of the Pyrates, of a Pistol and their Articles being served up in a Dish together, or of their being misused and forced from an honest Service, was often a Complotment of the Parties, to render them less suspected of those they came from, and was to answer the End of being put in a News-Paper or Affidavit: and the

Pyrates were so generous as not to refuse a Compliment to a Brother that cost them nothing, and, at the same Time, secured them the best Hands; the best I call them, because such a Dependance made them act more boldly. *Guilty.*

Harry Glasby, Master

There appearing several Persons in Court, who had been taken by *Roberts*'s Ship, whereof the Prisoner was Master, their Evidence was accepted as follows.

Jo. Trahern, Commander of the *King Solomon,* deposed, the Prisoner, indeed, to act as Master of the Pyrate Ship (while he was under Restraint there) but was observed like no Master, every one obeying at Discretion, of which he had taken Notice, and complained to him, how hard a Condition it was, to be a Chief among Brutes; and that he was weary of his Life, and such other Expressions, (now out of his Memory,) as shew'd in him a great Disinclination to that Course of Living.

Jo. Wingfield, a Prisoner with them at *Calabar,* says the same, as to the Quality he acted in, but that he was Civil beyond any of them, and verily believes, that when the Brigantine he served on Board of, as a Factor for the *African* Company, was voted to be burnt, this Man was the Instrument of preventing it, expressing himself with a great deal of Sorrow, for this and the like malicious Rogueries of the Company he was in; that to him showed, he had acted with Reluctancy, as one who could not avoid what he did. He adds further, that when one *Hamilton,* a Surgeon, was taken by them, and the Articles about to be imposed on him, he opposed, and prevented it. And that *Hunter,* another Surgeon, among them, was cleared at the Prisoner's Instance and Perswasion; from which last, this Deponent had it assured to him, that *Glasby* had once been under Sentence of Death, on Board of them, with two more, for endeavouring an Escape in the *West-Indies,* and that the other two were really shot for it.

Elizabeth Trengrove, who was taken a Passenger in the *African* Company's Ship *Onslow,* strengthen'd the Evidence of the last Witness; for having heard a good Character of this *Glasby,* she enquired of the Quarter-Master, who was then on Board a robbing, whether or no she could see him? And he told her, *No;* they never ventured him from the Ship, for he had once endeavoured his Escape, and they had ever since continued jealous of him.

Edward Crisp, Captain *Trengrove,* and Captain *Sharp,* who had all been taken in their Turns, acknowledge for themselves and others, who had unluckily fallen into those Pyrates Hands, that the good Usage they had met with, was chiefly thro' the Prisoner's Means, who often interposed, for leaving sufficient Stores and Instruments on Board the Ships they had robbed, alledging, they were superfluous and unnecessary there.

James White, whose Business was Musick, and was on the Poop of the Pyrate Ship in Time of Action with the *Swallow,* deposed, that during the Engagement, and Defence she made, he never saw the Prisoner busied about the Guns, or giving Orders, either to the loading or firing of them; but that he wholly attended to the setting, or trimming, of the Sails, as *Roberts* commanded; and that in the Conclusion, he verily believed him to be the Man who prevented the Ship's being blown up, by setting trusty Centinels below, and opposing himself against such hot-headed Fellows as had procured lighted Matches, and were going down for that Purpose.

Isaac Sun, Lieutenant of the Man of War, deposed, that when he came to take Possession of the Prize, in the King's Boat, he found the Pyrates in a very distracted and divided Condition; some being for blowing up, and others (who perhaps supposed themselves least culpable) opposing it: That in this Confusion he enquired for the Prisoner, of whom he had before heard a good Character; and thinks he rendered all the Service in his Power, for preventing it; in particular, he understood by all Hands, that he had seized, and taken, from one *James Philips,* a lighted Match, at the Instant he was going down to the Magazine, swearing, that he should send them all to H———l together. He had heard also, that after *Roberts* was killed, the Prisoner ordered the Colours to be struck; and had since shown, how opposite his Practice and Principles had been, by discovering who were the greatest Rogues among them.

The Prisoner, in his own Defence, says, when he had the Misfortune of falling into the Pyrates Hands, he was chief Mate of the *Samuel,* of *London,* Captain *Cary;* and when he had hid himself, to prevent the Design of carrying him away, they found him, and beat and threw him over-board. Seven Days afterwards, upon his objecting against, and refusing to sign their Articles, he was cut and abus'd again: That tho' after this he ingratiated himself, by a more humble Carriage, it was only to make Life easy; the Shares they had given him, having been from Time to Time returned again to such Prisoners as fell in his Way; till of late, indeed, he had made a small Reservation, and had desired Captain *Loan* to take two or three Moidores from him, to carry to his Wife. He was once taken, he says, at making his Escape, in the *West-Indies,* and, with two more, sentenced to be shot for it, by a drunken Jury; the latter actually suffered, and he was preserved only by one of the chief Pyrates taking a sudden Liking to him, and bullying the others. A second time he ran away at *Hispaniola,* carrying a Pocket Compass, for conducting him through the Woods; but that being a most desolate and wild Part of the Island he fell upon, and he ignorant how to direct his Course, was obliged, after two or three Days wandering, to return towards the Ship again, denying with egregious Oaths, the Design he was charg'd with, for Fear they should shoot him. From this Time he hopes it will be some Extenuation of his Fault, that most of the acquitted Prisoners can witness, they entertained Jealousies of him, and *Roberts* would not admit him into his Secrets; and withal, that Captain *Cary,* (and four other Passengers with him) had made Affidavit of his having been forced from his Employ, which tho' he could not produce, yet he humbly hoped the Court would think highly probable from the Circumstances offered.

On the whole, the Court was of Opinion Artists had the best Pretension to the Plea of Force, from the Necessity Pyrates are sometimes under of engaging such, and that many Parts of his own Defence had been confirmed by the Evidence, who had asserted he acted with Reluctance, and had expressed a Concern and Trouble for the little Hopes remained to him, of extricating himself. That he had used all Prisoners (as they were called) well, at the hazard of ill Usage to himself. That he had not in any military Capacity assisted their Robberies. That he had twice endeavoured his Escape, with the utmost Danger. *Acquitted him.*

Captain James Skyrm.

It appeared from the Evidence of several Prisoners acquitted, that this *Skyrm* commanded the *Ranger,* in that Defence she made against the King's Ship; that he ordered the Men to their Quarters, and the Guns to be loaded and fired, having a Sword in his Hand, to enforce those Commands; and beat such to their Duty whom he espied any way negligent or backward. That altho' he had lost a Leg in the Action, his Temper was so warm, as to refuse going off the Deck, till he found all was lost.

In his Defence, he says, he was forced from a Mate's Employ on Board a Sloop call'd the *Greyhound,* of St. *Christophers, Oct.* 1720. The Pyrate having drubbed him, and broke his Head, only for offering to go away when that Sloop was dismissed. Custom and Success had since indeed blunted, and, in some Measure, worn out the Sense of Shame; but that he had really for several Months past been sick, and disqualified for any Duty, and though *Roberts* had forced him on this Expedition much against his Will, yet the Evidence must be sensible, the Title of Captain gave him no Pre-eminence, for he could not be obeyed, though he had often called to them, to leave off their Fire, when he perceived it to be the King's Ship.

The Sickness he alledged, but more especially the Circumstance of losing his Leg, were Aggravations of his Fault, showing him more alert on such Occasions, than he was now willing to be thought: As to the Name of Captain, if it were allowed to give him no Precedence out of Battle, yet here it was proved a Title of Authority; such an Authority as could direct an Engagement against the King's Colours, and therefore he was in the highest Degree, *Guilty.*

John Walden.

Captain *John Trahern,* and *George Fenn,* deposed, the Prisoner to be one of the Number, who, in an open Boat, piratically assailed, and took their Ship, and was remarkably busy at Mischief, having a Pole-Ax in his Hand, which served him instead of a Key, to all the lock'd Doors and Boxes he come nigh: Also in particular, he cut the Cable of our Ship, when the other Pyrates were willing, and busied at heaving up the Anchor, saying, Captain, what signifies this Trouble of *Yo Hope* and straining in hot Weather; there are more Anchors at *London,* and besides, your Ship is to be burnt.

William Smith, (a Prisoner acquitted,) says *Walden* was known among the Pyrates mostly, by the Nick-Name of *Miss Nanney* (ironically its presumed from the Hardness of his Temper) that he was one of the twenty who voluntarily came on Board the *Ranger,* in the Chace she made out after the *Swallow,* and by a Shot from that Ship, lost his Leg; his Behaviour in the Fight, till then, being bold and daring.

The *President,* called for *Harry Glasby,* and bid him relate a Character of the Prisoner, and what Custom was among them, in Relation to these voluntary Expeditions, out of their proper Ship; and this of going on Board the *Ranger,* in particular.

And he gave in for Evidence, that the Prisoner was looked on as a brisk Hand, (*i. e.* as he farther explained it, a stanch Pyrate, a great Rogue) that when the *Swallow* first appeared in Sight, every one was willing to believe her a *Portuguese,* because Sugar was very much in Demand, and had made some Jarring and Dissention between the two Companies, (the *Fortune*'s People drinking Punch, when the *Ranger*'s could not) that *Roberts,* on Sight of the *Swallow,* hailed the new *Ranger,* and bid them right Ship, and get under Sail; there is, says he, Sugar in the Offing, bring it in, that we may have no more Mumbling; ordering at the same Time the Word to be pass'd among the Crew, who would go to their Assistance, and immediately the Boat was full of Men, to transport themselves.

President. Then every one that goes on Board of any Prize, does it voluntarily? Or were there here any other Reasons for it?

H. Glasby. Every Man is commonly called by List, and insists, in his Turn, to go on Board of a Prize, because they then are allowed a Shift of Cloaths, (the best they can find) over and above the Dividend from the Robbery, and this they are so far from being compelled to, that it often becomes the Occasion of Contest and Quarrel amongst them: But in the present, or such like Cases, where there appears a Prospect of Trouble, the Lazy and Timerous are often willing to decline this Turn, and yield to their Betters, who thereby establish a greater Credit.

The Prisoner, and the rest of those Men who went from the *Fortune* on Board the *Ranger,* to assist in this Expedition, were Volunteers, and the trustiest Men among us.

President. Were there no Jealousies of the *Ranger*'s leaving you in this Chace, or at any other Time, in order to surrender?

H. Glasby. Most of the *Ranger*'s Crew were fresh Men, Men who had been enter'd only since their being on the Coast of *Guiney,* and therefore had not so liberal a Share in fresh Provisions, or Wine, as the *Fortune*'s People, who thought they had born the Burthen and Heat of the Day, which had given Occasion indeed to some Grumblings and Whispers, as tho' they would take an Opportunity to leave us, but we never supposed (if they did) it would be with any other Design then setting up for themselves, they having (many of them) behaved with greater Severity than the old Standers.

The Prisoner appeared undaunted, and rather solicitous, about resting his Stump, than giving any Answer to the Court, or making any Defence for himself, till called upon; then he related in a careless, or rather hopeless Manner, the Circumstances of his first Entrance, being forced, he said, out of the *Blessing* of *Lemmington,* at *Newfoundland,* about 12 Months past; this, he is sure, most of the old Pyrates knew, and that he was for some Time as sick of the Change as any Man; but Custom and ill Company had altered him, owning very frankly, that he was at the Attack, and taking of the *King Solomon,* that he did cut her Cable, and that none were forced on those Occasions.

As to the last Expedition in the *Ranger,* he confesses he went on Board of her, but that it was by *Robert's* Order; and in the Chace loaded one Gun, to bring her to, but when he saw it was a Bite, he declared to his Comrades, that it was not worth while to resist, sorbore firing, and assisted to reeve the Braces, in order, if they could, to get away, in which sort of Service he was busied, when a Shot from the Man of War took off his Leg: And being asked, that supposing the Chace had proved a *Portuguese?* Why then, says he, I dont know what I might have done, intimating withal, that every Body then would have been ready enough at plundering. *Guilty.*

Peter Scudamore.

Harry Glasby, Jo. Wingfield, and *Nicholas Brattle,* depose thus much, as to his being a Volunteer with the Pyrates, from Capt. *Rolls,* at *Calabar.* First, That he quarrelled with *Moody,* (one of the Heads of the Gang) and fought with him, because he opposed his going, asking *Rolls,* in a leering manner, whether he would not be so kind, as to put him into the *Gazette,* when he came Home. And, at another Time, when he was going from the Pyrate Ship, in his Boat, a Turnado arose, *I wish,* says he, *the Rascal may be drowned, for he is a great Rogue, and has endeavoured to do me all the ill Offices he could among these Gentlemen,* (i. e.Pyrates.)

And secondly, That he had signed the Pyrate's Articles with a great deal of Alacrity, and gloried in having been the first Surgeon that had done so, (for before this, it was their Custom to change their Surgeons, when they desired it, after having served a Time, and never obliged them to sign, but he was resolved to break thro' this, for the good of those who were to follow,) swearing immediately upon it, he was now, he hoped, as great a Rogue as any of them.

Captain *Jo. Trahern,* and *George Fenn,* his Mate, deposed, the Prisoner to have taken out of the *King Solomon,* their Surgeon's capital Instruments, some Medicines, and a Back-Gammon Table; which latter became the Means of a Quarrel between one *Wincon,* and he, whose Property they should be, and were yielded to the Prisoner.

Jo. Sharp, Master of the *Elizabeth,* heard the Prisoner ask *Roberts* leave to force *Comry,* his Surgeon, from him, which was accordingly done, and with him, carried also some of the Ship's Medicines: But what gave a fuller Proof of the dishonesty of his Principles, was, the treacherous Design he had formed of running away with the Prize, in her Passage to Cape *Corso,* though he had been treated with all Humanity, and very unlike a Prisoner, on Account of his Employ and better Education, which had rendred him less to be suspected.

Mr. *Child,* (acquitted) depos'd, that in their Passage from the Island of St. *Thomas,* in the *Fortune* Prize, this Prisoner was several Times tempting him, into Measures of rising with the Negroes, and killing the *Swallow's* People, showing him, how easily the white Men might be demolished, and a new Company raised at *Angola,* and that Part of the Coast, *for,* says he, *I understand how to navigate a Ship, and can soon teach you to steer; and is it not better to do this, than to go back to* Cape-Corso, *and be hanged and Sun-dryed?* To which the Deponent replying, he was not afraid of being hanged, *Scudamore* bid him be still, and no Harm should come to him; but before the next Day-Evening, which was the designed Time of executing this Project, the Deponent discovered it to the Officer, and assured him, *Scudamore* had been talking all the preceeding Night to the Negroes, in *Angolan* Language.

Isaac Burnet heard the Prisoner ask *James Harris,* a Pyrate, (left with the wounded in the Prize,) whether he was willing to come into the Project of running away with the Ship, and endeavour the raising of a new Company, but turned the Discourse to Horse-Racing, as the Deponent crept nigher; he acquainted the Officer with what he had heard, who kept the People under Arms all Night, their Apprehensions of the Negroes not being groundless; for many of them having lived a long Time in this piratical Way, were, by the thin Commons they were now reduced to, as ripe for Mischief as any.

The Prisoner in his Defence said, he was a forced Man from Captain *Rolls,* in *October* last, and if he had not shown such a Concern as became him, at the Alteration, he must remark the Occasion to be, the Disagreement and Enmity between them; but that both *Roberts,* and *Val. Ashplant,* threat'ned him into signing their Articles, and that he did it in Terror.

The *King Solomon,* and *Elizabeth* Medicine-Chest, he owns he plundered, by Order of *Hunter,* the then chief Surgeon, who, by the Pyrates Laws, always directs in this Province, and Mr. *Child,* (tho' acquitted) had by the same Orders taken out a whole *French* Medicine-Chest, which he must be sensible for me, as well as for himself, we neither of us dared to have denied; it was their being the proper Judges, made so ungrateful an Office imposed. If after this he was elected chief Surgeon himself, both *Comry* and *Wilson* were set up also, and it might have been their Chance to have carried it, and as much out of their Power to have refused.

As to the Attempt of rising and running away with the Prize, he denies it altogether as untrue; a few foolish Words, but only by Way of Supposition, that if the Negroes should take it in their Heads (considering the Weakness, and ill look-out that was kept;) it would have been an easy Matter, in his Opinion for them to have done it; but that he encouraged such a Thing, was false, his talking to them in the *Angolan* Language, was only a Way of spending his Time, and trying his Skill to tell twenty, he being incapable of further Talk. As to his understanding Navigation, he had frequently acknowledg'd it to the Deponent *Child,* and wonders he should now so circumstantiate this Skill against him. *Guilty.*

Robert Johnson.

It appeared to the Court, that the Prisoner was one of the twenty Men, in that Boat of the Pyrates, which afterwards robb'd the *King Solomon,* at an Anchor near Cape *Appollonia:* That all Pyrates on this, and the like Service, were Volunteers, and he, in particular, had contested his going on Board a second Time, tho' out of his Turn.

The Prisoner in his Defence, called for *Harry Glasby,* who witnessed to his being so very drunk, when he first came among their Crew, that they were forced to hoist him out of one Ship into the other, with a Tackle, and therefore without his Consent; but had since been a trusty Man, and was placed to the Helm, in that running Battle they made with the *Swallow.*

He insisted for himself likewise, on Captain *Turner*'s Affidavit of his being forced, on which others (his Ship-mates) had been cleared.

The Court considering the Partiality that might be objected in acquitting one, and condemning another of the same standing, thought sit to remark it as a clear Testimony of their Integrity, that their Care and Indulgence to each Man, in allowing his particular Defence, was to exempt from the Rigour of the Law, such, who it must be allowed, would have stood too promiscuously condemned, if they had not been heard upon any other Fact than that of the *Swallow;* and herein what could better direct them, than a Character and Behaviour from their own Associates; for tho' a voluntary Entry with the Pyrates may be doubtful, yet his consequent Actions are not, and it is not so material how a Man comes among Pyrates, as how he acts when he is there. *Guilty.*

George Wilson.

John Sharp, Master of the *Elizabeth,* in which Ship the Prisoner was Passenger, and fell a second Time into the Pyrates Hands, deposes, that he took the said *Wilson* off from *Sestos,* on this Coast, paying to the Negroes for his Ransom, the Value of three Pound five Shillings in Goods, for which he had taken a Note, that he thought he had done a charitable Act in this, till meeting with one Captain *Canning,* he was ask'd, why he would release such a Rogue as *Wilson* was? For that he had been a Volunteer with the Pyrates, out of *John Tarlton.* And when the Deponent came to be a Prisoner himself, he found *Thomas,* the Brother of this *John Tarlton,* a Prisoner with the Pyrates also, who was immediately on *Wilson*'s Instigation, in a most sad manner misused and beat, and had been shot, through the Fury and Rage of some of those Fellows, if the Town-side, (*i. e. Liverpool*) Men, had not hid him in a Stay-Sail, under the Bowsprit; for *Moody* and *Harper,* with their Pistols cock'd, searched every Corner of the Ship to find him, and came to this Deponent's Hammock, whom they had like fatally to have mistaken for *Tarlton,* but on his calling out, they found their Error, and left him with this comfortable Anodyne, That he was the honest Fellow who brought the Doctor. At coming away, the Prisoner asked about his Note, whether the Pyrates had it or no? Who not being able readily to tell, he reply'd, it's no Matter Mr. *Sharp,* I believe I shall hardly ever come to *England* to pay it.

Adam Comry, Surgeon of the *Elizabeth,* says, that altho' the Prisoner had, on Account of his Indisposition and Want, received many Civilities from him, before meeting with the Pyrates, he yet understood it was thro' his and *Scudamore*'s Means, that he had been compelled among them: The Prisoner was very alert and chearful, he says, at meeting with *Roberts,* hailed him, told him he was glad to see him, and would come on Board presently, borrowing of the Deponent a clean Shirt and Drawers, for his better Appearance and Reception; he signed their Articles willingly, and used Arguments with him to do the same, saying, they should make their Voyage in eight Months, to *Brasil,* Share 6 or 700 *l.* a Man, and then break up. Again, when the Crew came to an Election of a chief Surgeon, and this Deponent was set up with the others, *Wilson* told him, he hoped he should carry it from *Scudamore,* for that a quarter Share (which they had more than others) would be worth looking after; but the Deponent missed the Preserment, by the good Will of the *Ranger*'s People, who, in general, voted for *Scudamore,* to get rid of him, (the chief Surgeon being always to remain with the Commadore.)

It appeared likewise by the Evidence of Captain *Jo. Trahern, Tho. Castel,* and others, who had been taken by the Pyrates, and thence had Opportunities of observing the Prisoners Conduct, that he seem'd thoroughly satisfy'd with that Way of Life, and was particularly intimate with *Roberts;* they often scoffing at the Mention of a Man of War, and saying, if they should meet with any of the Turnip-Man's Ships, they would blow up, and go to H — ll together. Yet setting aside these silly Freaks, to recommend himself, his Laziness had got him many Enemies, even *Roberts* told him, (on the Complaint of a wounded Man, whom he had refused to dress) that he was a double Rogue, to be there a second Time, and threat'ned to cut his Ears off.

The Evidence further assured the Court, from Captain *Thomas Tarlton,* that the Prisoner was taken out of his Brother's Ship, some Months before, a first Time, and being forward to oblige his new Company, had presently ask'd for the Pyrates Boat, to fetch the Medicine Chest away; when the Wind and Current proving too hard to contend with, they were drove on Shore at Cape *Montzerado.*

The Prisoner called for *William Darling,* and *Samuel Morwel,* (acquitted) and *Nicholas Butler.*

William Darling deposed, the first Time the Prisoner fell into their Hands, *Roberts* mistook him for *Jo. Tarlton* the Master, and being informed it was the Surgeon who came to represent him, (then indisposed,) he presently swore he should be his Mess-Mate, to which *Wilson* reply'd, he hop'd not, he had a Wife and Child, which the other laughed at; and that he had been two Days on Board, before he went in that Boat, which was drove on Shore at Cape *Montzerado.* And at his second coming, in the *Elizabeth,* he heard *Roberts* order he should be brought on Board in the first Boat.

Samuel Morwel says, that he has heard him bewail his Condition, while on Board the Pyrate, and desired one *Thomas,* to use his Interest with *Roberts,* for a Discharge, saying, his Employ, and the little Fortune he had left at Home, would, he hop'd, exempt him the further Trouble of seeking his Bread at Sea.

Nicholas Butler, who had remained with the Pyrates about 48 Hours, when they took the *French* Ships at *Whydah,* deposes, that in this Space the Prisoner addressed him in the *French* Language, several Times, deploring the Wretchedness and ill Fortune of being confined in such Company.

The Prisoner desiring Liberty of two or three Questions, ask'd, whether or no he had not expostulated with *Roberts,* for a Reason of his obliging Surgeons to sign their Articles, when heretofore they did not; Whether he had not expressed himself glad of having formerly escaped from them? Whether he had not said, at taking the Ships in *Whydah* Road, that he could like the Sport, were it lawful? And whether if he had not told him, should the Company discharge any Surgeon, that he would insist on it as his Turn? The Deponent answered, Yes, to every Question separately; and farther, that he believes *Scudamore* had not seen *Wilson* when he first came and found him out of the *Elizabeth*.

He added, in his own Defence, that being Surgeon with one *John Tarlton,* of *Leverpool,* he was met a first Time on this Coast of *Guiney,* by *Roberts* the Pyrate; who, after a Day or two, told him, to his Sorrow, that he was to stay there, and ordered him to fetch his Chest, (not Medicines, as asserted,) which Opportunity he took to make his Escape; for the Boat's Crew happening to consist of five *French* and one *English* Man, all as willing as himself, they agreed to push the Boat on Shore, and trust themselves with the Negroes of Cape *Montzerado:* Hazardous, not only in Respect of the dangerous Seas that run there, but the Inhumanity of the Natives, who sometimes take a liking to humane Carcasses. Here he remained five Months, till *Thomas Tarlton,* Brother to his Captain chanced to put in the Road for Trade, to whom he represented his Hardships and starving Condition; but was, in an unchristian Manner, both refused a Release of this Captivity, or so much as a small Supply of Biscuit and salt Meat, because, as he said, he had been among the Pyrates. A little Time after this, the Master of a *French* Ship paid a Ransom for him, and took him off; but, by Reason of a nasty leperous Indisposition he had contracted by hard and bad living, was, to his great Misfortune set ashore at *Sestos* again, when Captain *Sharp* met him, and generously procured his Release in the Manner himself has related, and for which he stands infinitely obliged. — That ill Luck threw him a second Time into the Pyrate's Hands, in this Ship *Elizabeth,* where he met *Thomas Tarlton,* and thoughtlesly used some Reproaches of him, for his severe Treatment at *Montzerado;* but protests without Design his Words should have had so bad a Consequence; for *Roberts* took upon him, as a Dispenser of Justice, the Correction of Mr. *Tarlton,* beating him unmercifully; and he hopes it will be belived, contrary to any Intention of his it should so happen, because as a Stranger he might be supposed to have no Influence, and believes there were some other Motives for it. — He cannot remember he expressed himself glad to see *Roberts* this second Time, or that he dropped those Expressions about *Comry,* as are sworn; but if immaturity of Judgment had occasioned him to slip rash and inadvertent Words, or that he had paid any undue Compliments to *Roberts,* it was to ingratiate himself, as every Prisoner did, for a more civil Treatment, and in particular to procure his Discharge, which he had been promised, and was afraid would have been revoked, if such a Person as *Comry* did not remain there to supply his Room; and of this, he said, all the Gentlemen (meaning the Pyrates) could witness for him.

He urged also his Youth in Excuse for his Rashness. — The first time he had been with them (only a Month in all,) and that in no military Employ; but in particular, the Service he had done in discovering the Design the Pyrates had to rise in their Passage on Board the *Swallow. Guilty.*

But Execution respited till the King's Pleasure be known, because the Commander of the *Swallow* had declared, the first Notice he received of this Design of the Pyrates to rise, was from him.

Benjamin Jefferys

By the Depositions of *Glasby* and *Lillburn* (acquitted) against this Prisoner, it appeared, that his Drunkenness was what at first detained him from going away in his proper Ship, the *Norman* Galley; and next Morning, for having been abusive in his Drink, saying to the Pyrates, there was not a Man amongst them, he received for a Welcome, six Lashes from every Person in the Ship, which disordered him for some Weeks, but on Recovery was made Boatswain's Mate; the serving of which, or any Office on Board a Pyrate, is at their own Option, (tho' elected,) because others are glad to accept what brings an additional Share in Prize.

The Deponents further say, that at *Sierraleon* every Man had more especially the Means of escaping; and that this Prisoner, in particular, neglected it, and came off from that Place after their Ship was under Sail, and going out of the River.

The Prisoner, in his Defence, protests, he was at first forc'd; and that the Office of Boatswain's Mate was imposed on him, and what he would have been glad to have relinquish'd. That the barbarous Whipping he had received from the Pyrates at first, was for telling them, that none who could get their Bread in an honest Way, would be on such an Account. And he had certainly taken the Opportunity which presented at *Sierraleon,* of ridding himself from so distastful a Life, if there had not been three or four of the old Pyrates on Shore at the same Time, who, he imagined, must know of him, and would doubtless have served him the same, if not worse, than they since had done *William Williams;* who, for such a Design, being delivered up by the treacherous Natives, had received two Lashes thro' the whole Ship's Company.

The Court observed, the Excuses of these Pyrates, about want of Means to escape, was oftentimes as poor and evasive as their Pleas of being forced at first; for here, at *Sierraleon,* every Man had his Liberty on Shore, and it was evident, might have kept it, if he, or they, had so pleased. And such are further culpable, who having been introduced into the Society, by such uncivil Methods, as whipping, or beating, neglect less likely Means of regaining Liberty; it shows strong Inclinations to Dishonesty, and they stand inexcusably, *Guilty.*

Jo. Mansfield.

It was proved against this Prisoner, by Captain *Trahern* and *George Fenn,* that he was one of those Volunteers who was at the Attack and Robbery of the Company's Ship, called the *King Solomon:* That he bully'd well among them who dar'd not make any Reply, but was very easy with his Friends, who knew him; for *Moody,* on this Occasion, took a large Glass from him, and threatned to blow his Brains out, (a favourite Phrase with these Pyrates) if he muttered at it.

From others acquitted, it likewise appeared, that he was at first a Volunteer among them, from an Island call'd *Dominico,* in the *West-Indies,* and had to recommend himself, told them, he was a Deserter from the *Rose* Man of War, and before that, had been on the High-Way; he was always drunk, they said, and so bad at the Time they met with the *Swallow,* that he knew nothing of the Action, but came up vapouring with his Cutlash, after the *Fortune* had struck her Colours, to know who would go on Board the Prize; and it was some Time before they could perswade him into the Truth of their Condition.

He could say little in Defence of himself, acknowledg'd this latter Part of Drunkenness; a Vice, he says, that had too great a Share in insnaring him into this Course of Life, and had been a greater Motive with him than Gold. *Guilty.*

William Davis.

William Allen deposed, he knew this Prisoner at *Sierraleon,* belonging to the *Ann* Galley; that he had a Quarrel with, and beat the Mate of that Ship, for which (as he said) being afraid to return to his Duty, he consorted to the idle Customs and Ways of living among the Negroes, from whom he received a Wife, and ungratefully sold her, one Evening, for some Punch to quench his Thirst. After this, having put himself under the Protection of Mr. *Plunket,* Governor there for the Royal *African* Company: The Relations and Friends of the Woman, apply'd to him for Redress, who immediately surrendered the Prisoner, and told them, he did not care if they took his Head off; but the Negroes wisely judging it would not fetch so good a Price, they sold him in his Turn again to Seignior *Jossee,* a Christian Black, and Native of that Place; who expected and agreed for two Years Service from him, on Consideration of what he had disbursed, for the Redemption of the Woman: But long before the Expiration of this Time, *Roberts* came into *Sierraleon* River, where the Prisoner, (as Seignior *Jossee* assured the Deponent,) entered a Volunteer with them.

The Deponent further corroborates this Part of the Evidence; in that he being obliged to call at Cape *Mount,* in his Passage down hither, met there with two Deserters from *Roberts*'s Ship, who assured him of the same; and that the Pyrates did design to turn *Davis* away the next Opportunity, as an idle good-for-nothing Fellow.

From *Glasby* and *Lilburn,* it was evident, that every Pyrate, while they stay'd at *Sierraleon,* went on Shore at Discretion. That *Roberts* had often assured Mr. *Glyn* and other Traders, at that Place, that he would force no Body; and in short, there was no Occasion for it; in particular, the Prisoner's Row-Mate went away, and thinks, he might have done the same, if he had pleased.

The Prisoner alledged his having been detained against his Will, and says, that returning with Elephants Teeth for *Sierraleon,* the Pyrate's Boat pursued and brought him on Board, where he was kept on Account of his understanding the Pilotage and Navigation of that River.

It was obvious to the Court, not only how frivolous Excuses of Constraint and Force were among these People, at their first commencing Pyrates, but also it was plain to them, from these two Deserters, met at Cape *Mount,* and the discretional Manner they lived in, at *Sierraleon;* thro' how little Difficulty several of them did, and others might, have escaped afterwards, if they could but have obtained their own Consents for it. *Guilty.*

This is the Substance of the Tryals of *Roberts*'s Crew, which may suffice for others, that occur in this Book. The foregoing Lists, shows, by a * before the Names, who were condemn'd; those Names with a † were referred for Tryal to the *Marshalsea,* and all the rest were acquitted.

The following Pyrates were executed, according to their Sentence, without the Gates of Cape *Corso-Castle,* within the Flood-Marks, *viz.*

Mens Names	Years of Age	Habitations.
William Magnes	35	Minehead.
Richard Hardy	25	Wales.
David Sympson	36	North-Berwick.
Christopher Moody	28	
Thomas Sutton	23	Berwick.
Valentine Ashplant	32	Minories.
Peter de Vine	42	Stepney.
William Philips	29	Lower-Shadwell.
Philip Bill	27	St. *Thomas*'s.
William Main	28	
William Mackintosh	21	Canterbury.
William Williams	40	nigh*Plymouth.*
Robert Haws	31	Yarmouth.
William Petty	30	Deptford.
John Jaynson	22	nigh*Lancaster.*
Marcus Johnson	21	Smyrna.
Robert Crow	44	Isle of Man.
Michael Maer	41	Ghent.
Daniel Harding	26	*Croomsbury*in*Somersetshire.*
William Fernon	22	Somersetshire.
Jo. More	19	*Meer*in*Wiltshire.*
Abraham Harper	23	Bristol.

Jo. Parker	22	*Winfred* in *Dorsetshire*.
Jo. Philips	28	*Alloway* in *Scotland*.
James Clement	20	Jersey.
Peter Scvdamore	35	Bristol.
James Skyrm	44	Wales.
John Walden	24	Somersetshire.
Jo. Stephenson	40	Whitby.
Jo. Mansfield	30	Orkneys.
Israel Hynde	30	Bristol.
Peter Lesley	21	Aberdeen.
Charles Bunce	26	Excter
Robert Birtson	30	*Other* St. *Maries Devonshire*.
Richard Harris	45	Cornwall.
Joseph Nosuter	26	*Sadbury* in *Devonshire*.
William Williams	30	Speechless at Execution.
Agge Jacobson	30	Holland.
Benjamin Jefferys	21	Bristol.
Cuthbert Goss	21	Topsham.
John Jessup	20	Plymouth.
Edward Watts	22	Dunmore.
Thomas Giles	26	Mine-head.
William Wood	27	York.
Thomas Armstrong	34	*London*, executed on board the *Weymouth*.
Robert Johnson	32	at *Whydah*.
George Smith	25	Wales.
William Watts	23	Ireland.
James Philips	35	Antegoa.
John Coleman	24	Wales.
Robert Hays	20	Liverpool.
William Davis	23	Wales.

 The Remainder of the Pyrates, whose Names are under mentioned, upon their humble Petition to the Court, had their Sentence changed from Death, to seven Years Servitude, conformable to our Sentence of Transportation; the Petition is as follows.

 To the Honourable the President and Judges of the Court of Admiralty, for trying of Pyrates, sitting at Cape Corso-Castle. *the* 20*th Day of* April, 1722.

 The humble Petition of *Thomas How, Samuel Fletcher,* &c.

 Humbly sheweth,

 THAT *your Petitioners being unhappily, and unwarily drawn into that wretched and detestable Crime of Pyracy, for which they now stand justly condemned, they most humbly pray the Clemency of the Court, in the Mitigation of their Sentence, that they may be permitted to serve the Royal* African

Company of England, *in this Country for seven Years, in such a Manner as the Court shall think proper; that by their just Punishment, being made sensible of the Error of their former Ways, they will for the future become faithful Subjects, good Servants, and useful in their Stations, if it please the Almighty to prolong their Lives.*

And your Petitioners, as in Duty, *&c.*

The Resolution of the Court was,

THAT the Petitioners have Leave by this Court of Admiralty, to interchange Indentures with the Captain General of the Gold Coast, for the Royal African Company, for seven Years Servitude, at any of the Royal African Company's Settlements in Africa, in such Manner as he the said Captain General shall think proper.

On Thursday *the 26th Day of* April, *the Indentures being all drawn out, according to the Grant made to the Petitioners, by the Court held on* Friday *the 20th of this Instant; each Prisoner was sent for up, signed, sealed and exchanged them in the Presence of*

Captain Mungo Herdman, *President,*
James Phipps, *Esq;*
Mr. Edward Hyde,
Mr. Charles Fanshaw,
And Mr. John Atkins, *Register.*

A Copy of the Indenture.

The Indenture of a Person condemned to serve abroad for Pyracy, which, upon the humble Petition of the Pyrates therein mentioned, was most mercifully granted by his Imperial Majesty's Commissioners and Judges appointed to hold a Court of Admiralty, for the Tryal of Pyrates at Cape *Corso-Castle,* in *Africa,* upon Condition of serving seven Years, and other Conditions, are as follows, *viz.*

THIS Indenture made the twenty sixth Day of April, Anno Regni Regis Georgii magnæ Britanniæ, *&c.* Septimo, Domini, Millessimo, Sepcentessimo viginti duo, *between* Roger Scot, *late of the City of* Bristol *Mariner, of the one Part, and the Royal* African *Company of* England, *their Captain General and Commander in Chief, for the Time being, on the other Part,* Witnesseth, *that the said* Roger Scot, *doth hereby covenant, and agree to, and with, the said Royal* African *Company, their Captain General, and Commander in chief for the Time being, to serve him, or his lawful Successors, in any of the Royal* African *Company's Settlements on the Coast of* Africa, *from the Day of the Date of these Presents, to the full Term of seven Years, from hence next ensuing, fully to be complete and ended; there to serve in such Employment, as the said Captain General, or his Successors shall employ him; according to the Custom of the Country in like Kind.*

In Consideration whereof, the said Captain General, and Commander in chief doth covenant and agree, to, and with, the said Roger Scot, *to find and allow him Meat, Drink, Apparel and Lodging, according to the Custom of the Country.*

In witness whereof, the Parties aforesaid, to these Presents, have interchangably put their Hands and Seals, the Day and Year first above written.

Signed, sealed and delivered, in the Presence of us, at Cape Corso-Castle, *in* Africa, *where no stamp'd Paper was to be had.*

Mungo Heardman, *President,* Witnesses.
John Atkins, *Register,* Witnesses.
In like Manner was drawn out and exchanged the Indentures of
THomas How of *Barnstable,* in the County of *Devon.*
Samuel Fletcher of *East-Smithfield, London.*
John Lane of *Lombard-Street, London.*
David Littlejohn of *Bristol.*
John King of *Shadwell* Parish, *London.*

Henry Dennis of *Bidiford.*
Hugh Harris of *Corf-Castle, Devonshire.*
William Taylor of *Bristol.*
Thomas Owen of *Bristol.*
John Mitchel of *Shadwell* Parish, *London.*
Joshua Lee of *Leverpool.*
William Shuren of *Wapping* Parish, *London.*
Robert Hartley of *Leverpool.*
John Griffin of *Blackwall, Middlesex.*
James Cromby of *London, Wapping.*
James Greenham of *Marshfield, Gloucestershire.*
John Horn of St. *James's* Parish, *London.*
John Jessop of *Wisbich, Cambridgshire.*
David Rice of *Bristol.*

None of which, I hear, are now living, two others, *viz. George Wilson* and *Thomas Oughterlaney*, were respited from Execution, till his Majesty's Pleasure should be known; the former dy'd abroad, and the latter came Home, and received his Majesty's Pardon; the Account of the whole stands thus,

Acquitted,	74
Executed,	52
Respited,	2
To Servitude,	20
To the *Marshalsea,*	17
Kill'd in the *Ranger,*	10
Kill'd in the *Fortune,*	3
Dy'd in the Passage to Cape *Corso,*	15
Dy'd afterwards in the Castle,	4
Negroes in both Ships,	70
Total,	276

I am not ignorant how acceptable the Behaviour and dying Words of Malefactors are to the generallity of our Countrymen, and therefore shall deliver what occurr'd, worthy of Notice, in the Behahaviour of these Criminals.

The first fix that were called to Execution, were *Magnes, Moody, Sympson, Sutton, Ashplant,* and *Hardy;* all of them old Standers and notorious Offenders: When they were brought out of the Hold, on the Parade, in order to break off their Fetters, and fit the Halters; none of them, it was observed, appeared the least dejected, unless *Sutton,* who spoke faint, but it was rather imputed to a Flux that had seiz'd him two or three Days before, than Fear. A Gentleman, who was Surgeon of the Ship, was so charitable at this Time, to offer himself in the room of an Ordinary, and represented to them, as well as he was able, the Heinousness of their Sin, and Necessity which lay on them of Repentance; one particular Part of which ought to be, acknowledging the Justice they had met with. They seem'd heedless for the present, some calling for Water to drink, and others applying to the Soldiers for Caps, but when this Gentleman press'd them for an Answer, they all exclaim'd against the Severity of the Court, and were so harden'd, as to curse, and wish the same Justice might overtake all the Members of it, as had been dealt to them. *They were poor Rogues,* they said, *and so hang'd, while others, no less guilty in another Way, escaped.*

When he endeavoured to compose their Minds, exhorting them to dye in Charity with all the World, and would have diverted them from such vain Discourse, by asking them their Country, Age, and the like; some of them answered, 'What was that to him, they suffered the Law, and should give no Account but to God;' walking to the Gallows without a Tear, in Token of Sorrow for their past Offences, or showing as much Concern as a Man would express at travelling a bad Road; nay, *Sympson,* at seeing a Woman that he knew, said, 'he had lain with that B — h three times, and now she was come to see him hang'd.' And *Hardy,* when his Hands were ty'd behind him, (which happened from their not being acquainted with the Way of bringing Malefactors to Execution,) observed, 'that he had seen many a Man hang'd, but this Way of the Hands being ty'd behind them, he was a Stranger to, and never saw before in his Life.' I mention these two little Instances, to show how stupid and thoughtless they were of their End, and that the same abandoned and reprobate Temper that had carried them thro' their Rogueries, abided with them to the last.

Samuel Fletcher, another of the Pyrates ordered for Execution, but reprieved, seem'd to have a quicker Sense of his Condition; for when he saw those he was allotted with gone to Execution, he sent a Message by the Provost-Marshal to the Court, to be 'inform'd of the Meaning of it, and humbly desir'd to know whether they design'd him Mercy, or not? If they did, he stood infinitely oblig'd to them, and thought the whole Service of his Life an incompetent Return for so great a Favour; but that if he was to suffer, the sooner the better, *he said,* that he might be out of his Pain.'

There were others of these Pyrates the reverse of this, and tho' destitute of Ministers, or fit Persons to represent their Sins, and assist them with spiritual Advice, were yet always imploying their Time to good Purposes, and behaved with a great deal of seeming Devotion and Penitence; among these may be reckon'd *Scudamore, Williams, Philips, Stephenson, Jefferys, Lesly, Harper, Armstrong, Bunce,* and others.

Scudamore too lately discerned the Folly and Wickedness of the Enterprize, that had chiefly brought him under Sentence of Death, from which, seeing there was no Hopes of escaping, he petitioned for two or three Days Reprieve, which was granted; and for that Time apply'd himself incessantly to Prayer, and reading the Scriptures, seem'd to have a deep Sense of his Sins, of this in particular, and desired, at the Gallows, they would have Patience with him, to sing the first Part of the thirty first Psalm; which he did by himself throughout.

Armstrong, having been a Deserter from his Majesty's Service, was executed on Board the *Weymouth,* (and the only one that was;) there was no Body to press him to an Acknowledgement of the Crime he died for, nor of sorrowing in particular for it, which would have been exemplary, and made suitable Impressions on Seamen; so that his last Hour was spent in lamenting and bewailing his Sins in general, exhorting the Spectators to an honest and good Life, in which alone they could find Satisfaction. In the End, he desir'd they would join with him in singing two or three latter Verses of the 140th Psalm; and that being concluded, he was, at the firing of a Gun, tric'd up at the Fore-Yard-Arm.

Bunce was a young Man, not above 26 Years old, but made the most pathetical Speech of any at the Gallows. He first declaim'd against the guilded Bates of Power, Liberty, and Wealth, that had ensnar'd him among the Pyrates, his unexperienc'd Years not being able to withstand the Temptation; but that the Briskness he had shown, which so fatally had procured him Favour amongst them, was not so much a Fault in Principle, as the Liveliness and Vivacity of his Nature. He was now extreamly afflicted for the Injuries he had done to all Men, and begg'd their's and God's Forgiveness, very earnestly exhorting the Spectators to remember their Creator in their Youth, and guard betimes, that their Minds took not a wrong Byass, concluding with this apt Similitude, *That he stood there as a Beacon upon a Rock,* (the Gallows standing on one) *to warn erring Marriners of Danger.*

Chap. XI
Of Captain *Anstis,* And his Crew

HIS Beginning as a Pyrate. A most brutish Action supposed to be committed by his Crew. Civil Discords amongst them. The Pyrates Term of Round Robin explain'd. They land on an uninhabited Island. A Petition for Pardon agreed on. The Form of that Petition. Their Diversions, and Manner of living on the Island. Their mock Tryal of one another. They put to Sea again. Their Petition not answer'd. The Morning Srar Wreck'd. Anstis narrowly esoapes being taken. A Plot discover'd. The Crew gathers Strength again. Surprised by the Winchelsea Man of War at Tobago. Fire one of their Ships. Anstis escapes. Is killed by a Conspyracy of his own Men. The Ship surrender'd at Curaco. Several hang'd there. Fen hanged at Antegoa. The good Luck of those who fled to the Woods.

Thomas Anstis ship'd himself at *Providence* in the Year 1718, aboard the *Buck* Sloop, and was one of six that conspired together to go off a pirating with the Vessel; the rest were, *Howel Davis, Roberts*'s Predecessor, killed at the Island of *Princes; Dennis Topping,* killed at the taking of the rich *Portuguese* Ship on the Coast of *Brasil; Walter Kennedy,* hanged at *Execution-Dock,* and two others, which I forbear to name, because, I understand they are at this Day employ'd in an honest Vocation in the City.

What followed concerning *Anstis*'s Pyracies, has been included in the two preceeding Chapters; I shall only observe that the Combination of these six Men abovementioned, was the Beginning of that Company, that afterwards proved so formidable under Captain *Roberts,* from whom *Anstis* separated the 18th of *April* 1721, in the *Good Fortune* Brigantine, leaving his Commadore to pursue his Adventures upon the Coast of *Guiney,* whilst he returned to the *West-Indies,* upon the like Design.

About the Middle of *June,* these Pyrates met with one Captain *Marston,* between *Hispaniola* and *Jamaica,* bound on a Voyage to *New-York;* from whom they took all the wearing Apparel they could find, as also his Liquors and Provision, and five of his Men, but did not touch his Cargo; two or three other Vessels were also plundered by them, in this Cruise, out of whom they stocked themselves with Provision and Men; among the rest, I think, was the *Irwin,* Captain *Ross,* from *Cork* in *Ireland;* but this I won't be positive of, because they denied it themselves. This Ship had 600 Barrels of Beef aboard, besides other Provisions, and was taken off *Martinico,* wherein Colonel *Doyly* of *Montserrat,* and his Family were Passengers. The Colonel was very much abused and wounded, for endeavouring to save a poor Woman, that was also a Passenger, from the Insults of that brutish Crew; and the Pyrates prevailing, twenty one of them forced the poor Creature successively, afterwards broke her Back and flung her into the Sea. I say, I will not be positive it was *Anstis*'s Crew that acted this unheard of Violence and Cruelty, tho' the Circumstances of the Place, the Time, the Force of the Vessel, and the Number of Men, do all concur, and I can place the Villany no where else; but that such a Fact was done, there is too much Evidence for it to be doubted of.

When they thought fit to put an End to this Cruize, they went into one of the Islands to clean, which they effected without any Disturbance, and came out again, and stretching away towards *Burmudas,* met with a stout Ship, called the *Morning Star,* bound from *Guiney* to *Carolina;* they made Prize of her, and kept her for their own Use. In a Day or two, a Ship from *Barbadoes* bound to *New-York,* fell into their Hands, and taking out her Guns and Tackle, mounted the *Morning Star* with 32 Pieces of Canron, mann'd her with a 100 Men, and appointed one *John Fenn* Captain; for the Brigantine being of far less Force, the *Morning Star* would have fallen to *Anstis,* as elder Officer, yet he was so in Love with his own Vessel, (she being an excellent Sailor,) that he made it his Choice to stay in her, and let *Fenn,* who was, before, his Gunner, Command the great Ship.

Now, that they had two good Ships well mann'd, it may be supposed they were in a Condition to undertake something bold: But their Government was disturbed by Malecontents, and a

Kingdom divided within it self cannot stand; they had such a Number of new Men amongst them, that seem'd not so violently enclined for the Game; that whatever the Captain proposed, it was certainly carried against him, so that they came to no fix'd Resolution for the undertaking any Enterprize; therefore there was nothing to be done, but to break up the Company, which seemed to be the Inclination of the Majority, but the Manner of doing so, concerned their common Safety; to which Purpose various Means were proposed, at length it was concluded to send home a Petition to his Majesty (there being then no Act of Indemnity in Force) for a Pardon, and wait the Issue; at the same Time one *Jones,* Boatswain of the *Good Fortune,* proposed a Place of safe Retreat, it being an uninhabited Island near *Cuba,* which he had been used to in the late War, when he went a privateering against the *Spaniards.*

This being approved of, it was unanimously resolved on, and the underwritten Petition drawn up and signed by the whole Company in the Manner of what they call a *Round Robin,* that is, the Names were writ in a Circle, to avoid all Appearance of Pre-eminence, and least any Person should be mark'd out by the Government, as a principal Rogue among them.

To his most sacred Majesty George, *by the Grace of God, of* Great-Britain, France *and* Ireland, *King, Defender of the Faith,* &c.

The humble PETITION of the Company, now belonging to the Ship *Morning Star,* and Brigantine *Good Fortune,* lying under the ignominious Name and Denomination of Pyrates.

Humbly sheweth,

THAT we your Majesty's most loyal Subjects, have, at sundry Times, been taken by Bartholomew Roberts, *the then Captain of the abovesaid Vessels and Company, together with another Ship, in which we left him; and have been forced by him and his wicked Accomplices, to enter into, and serve, in the said Company, as Pyrates, much contrary to our Wills and Inclinations: And we your loyal Subjects utterly abhoring and detesting that impious way of Living, did, with an unanimous Consent, and contrary to the Knowledge of the said* Roberts, *or his Accomplices, on, or about the* 18*th Day of* April 1721, *leave, and ran away with the aforesaid Ship* Morning Star, *and Brigantine* Good Fortune, *with no other Intent and Meaning than the Hopes of obtaining your Majesty's most gracious Pardon. And, that we your Majesty's most loyal Subjects, may with more Safery return to our native Country, and serve the Nation, unto which we belong, in our respective Capacities, without Fear of being prosecuted by the Injured, whose Estates have suffered by the said* Roberts *and his Accomplices, during our forcible Detainment, by the said Company: We most humbly implore your Majesty's most royal Assent, to this our humble Petition.*

And your Petitioners shall ever pray.

This Petition was sent home by a Merchant Ship bound to *England,* from *Jamaica,* who promised to speak with the Petitioners, in their Return, about 20 Leagues to Windward of that Island, and let them know what Success their Petition met with. When this was done, the Pyrates retires to the Island before proposed, with the Ship and Brigantine.

This Island (which I have no Name for) lies off the Southwest End of *Cuba,* uninhabited, and little frequented. On the East End is a Lagune, so narrow, that a Ship can but just go in, tho' there's from 15 to 22 Foot Water, for almost a League up: On both Sides of the Lagune grows red Mangrove Trees, very thick, that the Entrance of it, as well as the Vessels laying there, is hardly to be seen. In the Middle of the Island are here and there a small thick Wood of tall Pines, and other Trees scattered about in different Places.

Here they staid about nine Months, but not having Provision for above two, they were forced to take what the Island afforded, which was Fish of several Sorts, particularly Turtle, which latter was the chiefest Food they lived on, and was found in great Plenty on the Coasts of this Island; whether there might be any wild Hogs, Beef, or other Cattle, common to several Islands of the *West-Indies,* or that the Pyrates were too idle to hunt them, or whether they preferr'd other Provisions to that sort of Diet, I know not; but I was informed by them, that for the whole Time they eat not a Bit of any kind of Flesh-Meat, nor Bread; the latter was supply'd by Rice, of which they had a great Quantity aboard: This was boyl'd and squeez'd dry, and so eat with the Turtle.

There are three or four Sorts of these Creatures in the *West-Indies,* the largest of which will weight 150 or 200 Pound Weight or more, but those that were found upon this Island were of the smallest Kind, weighing 10 or 12 Pounds each, with a fine natural wrought Shell, and beautifully clouded; the Meat sweet and tender, some Part of it eating like Chicken, some like Veal, *&c.* so that it was no extraordinary Hardship for them to live upon this Provision alone, since it affords variety of Meats to the Taste, of it self. The manner of catching this Fish is very particular; you must understand, that in the Months of *May, June* and *July,* they lay their Eggs in order to hatch their Young, and this three times in a Season, which is always in the Sand of the Sea-shore, each laying 80 or 90 Eggs at a time. The Male accompanies the Female, and come ashore in the Night only, when they must be watch'd, without making any Noise, or having a Light; as soon as they land, the Men that watch for them, turn them on their Backs, then haul them above high Water Mark, and leave them till next Morning, where they are sure to find them, for they can't turn again, nor move from the Place. It is to be observ'd, that besides their laying time, they come ashore to feed, but then what's very remarkable in these Creatures, they always resort to different Places to breed, leaving their usual Haunts for two or three Months, and 'tis thought they eat nothing in all that Season.

They pass'd their Time here in Dancing, and other Diversions, agreeable to these sort of Folks; and among the rest, they appointed a Mock Court of Judicature to try one another for Pyracy, and he that was a Criminal one Day was made Judge another. — I had an Account given me of one of these merry Tryals, and as it appeared diverting, I shall give the Readers a short Account of it.

The Court and Criminals being both appointed, as also Council to plead, the Judge got up in a Tree, and had a dirty Taurpaulin hung over his Shoulders; this was done by Way of Robe, with a Thrum Cap on his Head, and a large Pair of Spectacles upon his Nose: Thus equipp'd, he settled himself in his Place, and abundance of Officers attending him below, with Crows, Handspikes, *&c.* instead of Wands, Tipstaves, and such like. — The Criminals were brought out, making a thousand four Faces; and one who acted as Attorney-General opened the Charge against them; their Speeches were very laconic, and their whole Proceedings concise. We shall give it by Way of Dialogue.

Attorn. Gen. An't please your Lordship, and you Gentlemen of the Jury, here is a Fellow before you that is a sad Dog, a sad sad Dog; and I humbly hope your Lordship will order him to be hang'd out of the Way immediately. — He has committed Pyracy upon the High Seas, and we shall prove, an't please your Lordship, that this Fellow, this sad Dog before you, has escap'd a thousand Storms, nay, has got safe ashore when the Ship has been cast away, which was a certain Sign he was not born to be drown'd; yet not having the Fear of hanging before his Eyes, he went on robbing and ravishing Man, Woman and Child, plundering Ships Cargoes fore and aft, burning and sinking Ship, Bark and Boat, as if the Devil had been in him. But this is not all, my Lord, he has committed worse Villanies than all these, for we shall prove, that he has been guilty of drinking Small-Beer; and your Lordship knows, there never was a sober Fellow but what was a Rogue. — My Lord, I should have spoke much finer than I do now, but that, as your Lordship knows our Rum is all out, and how should a Man speak good Law that has not drank a Dram. — However, I hope, your Lordship will order the Fellow to be hang'd.

Judge. — Hearkee me, Sirrah, — you lousy, pittiful, ill-look'd Dog; what have you to say why you should not be tuck'd up immediately, and set a Sun-drying like a Scare-crow? — Are you guilty, or not guilty?

Pris. Not guilty, an't please your Worship.

Judge. Not guilty! say so again, Sirrah, and I'll have you hang'd without any Tryal.

Pris. An't please your Worship's Honour, my Lord, I am as honest a poor Fellow as ever went between Stem and Stern of a Ship, and can hand, reef, steer, and clap two Ends of a Rope together, as well as e'er a He that ever cross'd salt Water; but I was taken by one *George Bradley* [the Name of him that sat as Judge,] a notorious Pyrate, a sad Rogue as ever was unhang'd, and he forc'd me, an't please your Honour.

Judge. Answer me, Sirrah, — How will you be try'd?

Pris. By G — and my Country.

Judge. The Devil you will. — Why then, Gentlemen of the Jury, I think we have nothing to do but to proceed to Judgment.

Attor. Gen. Right, my Lord; for if the Fellow should be suffer'd to speak, he may clear himself, and that's an Affront to the Court.

Pris. Pray, my Lord, I hope your Lordship will consider —

Judge. Consider! — How dare you talk of considering? — Sirrah, Sirrah, I never consider'd in all my Life. — I'll make it Treason to consider.

Pris. But, I hope, your Lordship will hear some Reason.

Judge. D'ye hear how the Scoundrel prates? — What have we to do with Reason? — I'd have you to know, Raskal, we don't sit here to hear Reason; — we go according to Law. — Is our Dinner ready?

Attor. Gen. Yes, my Lord.

Judge. Then heark'ee, you Raskal at the Bar; hear me, Sirrah, hear me. — You must suffer, for three Reasons; first, because it is not fit I should sit here as Judge, and no Body be hang'd. — Secondly, you must be hang'd, because you have a damn'd hanging Look: — And thirdly, you must be hang'd, because I am hungry; for know, Sirrah, that 'tis a Custom, that whenever the Judge's Dinner is ready before the Tryal is over, the Prisoner is to be hang'd of Course. — There's Law for you, ye Dog. — So take him away Goaler.

This is the Tryal just as it was related to me; the Design of my setting it down, is only to show how these Fellows can jest upon Things, the Fear and Dread of which, should make them tremble.

The beginning of *August* 1722, the Pyrates made ready the Brigantine, and came out to Sea, and beating up to Windward, lay in the Track for their Correspondant in her Voyage to *Jamaica,* and spoke with her; but finding nothing was done in *England* in their Favour, as 'twas expected, they return'd to their Consorts at the Island with the ill News, and found themselves under a Necessity, as they fancied, to continue that abominable Course of Life they had lately practis'd; in order thereto, they sail'd with the Ship and Brigantine to the Southward, and the next Night, by intolerable Neglect, they run the *Morning Star* upon the *Grand Caimanes,* and wreck'd her; the Brigantine seeing the Fate of her Consort, hall'd off in Time, and so weather'd the Island. The next Day Captain *Anstis* put in, and found that all, or the greatest part of the Crew, were safe ashore, whereupon she came to an Anchor, in order to fetch them off; and having brought *Fenn* the Captain, *Philips* the Carpenter, and a few others aboard, two Men of War came down upon them, *viz.* the *Hector* and *Adventure,* so that the Brigantine had but just Time to cut their Cable, and get to Sea, with one of the Men of War after her, keeping within Gun-shot for several Hours. *Anstis* and his Crew were now under the greatest Consternation imaginable, finding the Gale freshen, and the Man of War gaining Ground upon them, so that, in all Probability, they must have been Prisoners in two Hours more; but it pleased God to give them a little longer Time, the Wind dying away, the Pyrates got out their Oars, and row'd for their Lives, and thereby got clear of their Enemy.

The *Hector* landed her Men upon the Island, and took 40 of the *Morning Star*'s Crew, without any Resistance made by them; but on the contrary, alledging, they were forc'd Men, and that they were glad of this Opportunity to escape from the Pyrates; the rest hid themselves in the Woods, and could not be found. *George Bradley* the Master, and three more, surrender'd afterwards to a *Burmudas* Sloop, and were carried to that Island.

The Brigantine, after her Escape, sail'd to a small Island near the Bay of *Honduras,* to clean and refit, and, in her Way thither, took a *Rhode Island* Sloop, Captain *Durfey,* Commander, and two or three other Vessels, which they destroy'd, but brought all the Hands aboard their own.

While she was cleaning, a Scheme was concerted between Captain *Durfey,* some other Prisoners, and two or three of the Pyrates, for to seize some of the Chiefs, and carry off the Brigantine; but the same being discovered before she was fit for sailing, their Design was prevented:

However, Captain *Durfey,* and four or five more, got ashore with some Arms and Ammunition; and when the Pyrates Canoe came in for Water, he seiz'd the Boat with the Men; upon which *Anstis* ordered another Boat to be mann'd with 30 Hands and sent ashore, which was accordingly done; but Captain *Durfey,* and the Company he had by that Time got together, gave them such a warm Reception, that they were contented to betake themselves to their Vessel again.

About the beginning of *December,* 1722, *Anstis* left this Place and return'd to the Islands, designing to accumulate all the Power and Strength he could, since there was no looking back. He took in the Cruise a good Ship, commanded by Captain *Smith,* which he mounted with 24 Guns, and *Fenn,* a one handed Man, who commanded the *Morning-Star* when she was lost, went aboard to command her. They cruis'd together, and took a Vessel or two, and then went to the *Bahama Islands,* and there met with what they wanted, *viz.* a Sloop loaded with Provisions, from *Dublin,* called the *Antelope.*

It was time now to think of some Place to fit up and clean their Frigate lately taken, and put her in a Condition to do Business; accordingly they pitch'd upon the Island of *Tobago,* where they arrived the beginning of *April,* 1723, with the *Antelope* Sloop and her Cargo.

They fell to work immediately, got the Guns, Stores, and every Thing else out upon the Island, and put the Ship upon the Heel; and just then, as ill Luck would have it, came in the *Winchelsea* Man of War, by Way of Visit, which put the Marooners into such a Surprize, that they set Fire to the Ship and Sloop, and fled ashore to the Woods. *Anstis,* in the Brigantine, escap'd, by having a light Pair of Heels, but it put his Company into such a Disorder, that their Government could never be set to rights again; for some of the New-Comers, and those who had been tir'd with the Trade, put an End to the Reign, by shooting *Tho. Anstis* in his Hammock, and afterwards the Quarter-Master, and two or three others; the rest submitting, they put into Irons, and surrender'd them up, and the Vessel, at *Curacco,* a *Dutch* Settlement, where they were try'd and hang'd; and those concerned in delivering up the Vessel, acquitted.

But to return to Captain *Fenn,* he was taken stragling with his Gunner and three more, a Day or two after their Misfortune, by the Man of War's Men, and carry'd to *Antegoa,* where they were all executed, and *Fenn* hang'd in Chains. Those who remain'd, staid some Time in the Island, keeping up and down in the Woods, with a Hand to look out; at length Providence so order'd it, that a small Sloop came into the Harbour, which they all got aboard of, except two or three Negroes, and those they left behind. They did not think fit to pursue any further Adventures, and therefore unanimously resolved to steer for *England,* which they accordingly did, and in *October* last came into *Bristol* Channel, sunk the Sloop, and getting ashore in the Boat, dispersed themselves to their Abodes.

Chap. XII
Of Captain *Worley,* And his Crew

> HIS mad Beginning. His Success. Bind themselves by Oath to take no Quarters. A false Alarm at James-Town. Worley catches a Tartar. The desperate Resolution of the Pyrates. Worley hanged.

His reign was but short, but his Beginning somewhat particular, setting out in a small open Boat, with eight others, from *New-York.* This was as resolute a Crew as ever went upon this Account: They took with them a few Biscuits, and a dry'd Tongue or two, a little Cag of Water, half a dozen old Muskets and Ammunition accordingly. Thus provided, they left *New-York* the latter End of *September* 1718, but it cannot be supposed that such a Man of War as this, could undertake any considerable Voyage, or attempt any extraordinary Enterprize; so they stood down the Coast, till they came to *Delaware* River, which is about 150 Miles distant, and not meeting with any Thing in their Way, they turn'd up the same River as high as *Newcastle,* near which Place they fell upon a Shallop belonging to *George Grant,* who was bringing Houshold Goods, Plate, *&c.* from *Oppoquenimi* to *Philadelphia;* they made Prize of the most valuable Part of them, and let the Shallop go. This Fact could not come under the Article of Pyracy, it not being committed *super altum Mare,* upon the High-Sea, therefore was a simple Robbery only; but they did not stand for a Point of Law in the Case, but easing the Shallop Man of his Lading, the bold Adventurers went down the River again.

The Shallop came straight to *Philadelphia,* and brought the ill News thither, which so alarm'd the Government, as if War had been declared against them; Expresses were sent to *New-York,* and other Places, and several Vessels fitted out against this powerful Rover, but to no manner of Purpose; for after several Days Cruize, they all return'd, without so much as hearing what became of the Robbers.

Worley and his Crew, in going down the River, met with a Sloop of *Philadelphia,* belonging to a Mulatto, whom they call'd *Black Robbin;* they quitted their Boat for this Sloop, taking one of *Black Robin*'s Men along with them, as they had also done from *George Grant,* besides two Negroes, which encreased the Company one Third. A Day or two after, they took another Sloop belonging to *Hull,* homeward bound, which was somewhat fitter for their Purpose; they found aboard her, Provisions and Necessaries, which they stood in need of, and enabled them to prosecute their Design, in a manner more suitable to their Wishes.

Upon the Success of these Rovers, the Governor issued out a Proclamation, for the apprehending and taking all Pyrates, who had refused or neglected to surrender themselves, by the Time limited in his Majesty's Proclamation of Pardon; and thereupon, ordered his Majesty's Ship *Phœnix,* of 20 Guns, which lay at *Sandy Hook,* to Sea, to cruize upon this Pyrate, and secure the Trade to that, and the adjoining Colonies.

In all probability, the taking this Sloop sav'd their Bacons, for this Time, tho' they fell into the Trap presently afterwards; for they finding themselves in tolerable good Condition, having a Vessel newly cleaned, with Provisions, *&c.* they stood off to Sea, and so missed the *Phœnix,* who expected them to be still on the Coast.

About six Weeks afterwards they returned, having taken both a Sloop and a Brigantine, among the *Bahama* Islands; the former they sunk, and the other they let go: The Sloop belonged to *New-York,* and they thought the sinking of her good Policy, to prevent her returning to tell Tales at Home.

Worley had by this Time encreased his Company to about five and twenty Men, had six Guns mounted, and small Arms as many as were necessary for them, and seem'd to be in a good thriving sort of a Way. He made a black Ensign, with a white Death's Head in the Middle of it, and other Colours suitable to it. They all signed Articles, and bound themselves under a solemn Oath, to take no Quarters, but to stand by one another to the last Man, which was rashly fulfill'd a little afterwards.

For going into an Inlet in *North-Carolina,* to clean, the Governor received Information of it, and sitted out two Sloops, one of eight Guns, and the other with six, and about seventy Men between them. *Worley* had clean'd his Sloop, and sail'd before the *Carolina* Sloops reached the Place, and steered to the Northward; but the Sloops just mentioned, pursuing the same Course, came in sight of *Worley,* as he was cruising off the Capes of *Virginia,* and being in the Offin, he stood in as soon as he saw the Sloops, intending thereby to have cut them off from *James* River; for he verily believed they had been bound thither, not imagining, in the least, they were in Pursuit of him.

The two Sloops standing towards the Capes at the same Time, and *Worley* hoisting of his black Flag, the Inhabitants of *James* Town were in the utmost Consternation, thinking that all three had been Pyrates, and that their Design had been upon them; so that all the Ships and Vessels that were in the Road, or in the Rivers up the Bay, had Orders immediately to hale in to the Shore, for their Security, or else to prepare for their Defence, if they thought themselves in a Condition to fight. Soon after two Boats, which were sent out to get Intelligence, came crowding in, and brought an Account, that one of the Pyrates was in the Bay, being a small Sloop of six Guns. The Governor expecting the rest would have followed, and altogether make some Attempt to land, for the sake of Plunder, beat to Arms, and collected all the Force that could be got together, to oppose them; he ordered all the Guns out of the Ships, to make a Platform, and, in short, put the whole Colony in a warlike Posture; but was very much surprised at last, to see all the supposed Pyrates fighting with one another.

The Truth of the Matter is, *Worley* gained the Bay, thinking to make sure of his two Prizes, by keeping them from coming in; but by the hoisting of the King's Colours, and firing a Gun, he quickly was sensible of his Mistake, and too soon perceived that the Tables were turned upon him; that instead of keeping them out, he found himself, by a superior Force kept in. When the Pyrates saw how Things went, they resolutely prepar'd themselves for a desperate Defence; and tho' three to one odds, *Worley* and his Crew determined to fight to the last Gasp, and receive no Quarters, agreeably to what they had before sworn; so that they must either Dye or Conquer upon the Spot.

The *Carolina* Men gave the Pyrate a Broadside, and then Boarded him, one Sloop getting upon his Quarter, and the other on his Bow; *Worley* and the Crew, drew up upon the Deck, and fought very obstinately, Hand to Hand, so that in a few Minutes, abundance of Men lay weltering in their Gore; the Pyrates proved as good as their Words, not a Man of them cry'd out for Quarter, nor would accept of such, when offered, but were all killed except the Captain and another Man, and those very much wounded, whom they reserved for the Gallows. They were brought ashore in Irons, and the next Day, which was the 17th of *February* 1718-19, they were both hanged up, for fear they should dye, and evade the Punishment as was thought due to their Crimes.

Chap. XIII
Of Capt. *George Lowther,* And his Crew

>His Beginning. Plots with Massey. Massey's Conduct. Lowther's Proposal. A Copy of Articles drawn up, and sworn to. The Pyrates going by the Ears. How Rogues are made Friends. Lowther and Massey part. A Digression concerning Massey's mad Conduct. Lowther and Low meet. An Alliance betwixt them. A List of Prizes taken by them. An unlucky Adventure at Cape Mayo. Lowther and Low break the Alliance, and part. The Bravery of Captain Gwatkins. The Pyrates much reduced. Winter in North-Carolina. Put to Sea again. Make for the Island of Blanco. The Island described. Ara surprised and taken. Lowther escapes. The Names of the Prisoners, and Fate. Lowther's Death.

George Lowther sailed out of the River of *Thames,* in one of the Royal *African* Company's Ships, call'd the *Gambia Castle,* of 16 Guns and 30 Men, *Charles Russel* Commander; of which Ship, the said *Lowther* was second Mate. Aboard of the same Ship, was a certain Number of Soldiers, commanded by one *John Massey,* who were to be carried to one of the Company's Settlements, on the River of *Gambia,* to Garrison a Fort, which was sometime ago taken and destroy'd by Captain *Davis* the Pyrate.

In *May* 1721, the *Gambia Castle* came safe to her Port in *Africa,* and landed Captain *Massey* and his Men on *James*'s Island, where he was to Command under the Governor, Colonel *Whitney,* who arrived there at the same Time, in another Ship: And here, by a fatal Misunderstanding, between the military Folks and the Trading People, the Fort and Garrison not only came to be lost again to the Company, but a fine Galley well provided, and worth 10000 *l.* turned against her Masters.

The Names of Governor and Captain sounded great, but when the Gentlemen found that the Power that generally goes along with those Titles, was oversway'd and born down by the Merchants and Factors, (mechanic Fellows as they thought them) they grew very impatient and disatisfy'd, especially *Massey,* who was very loud in his Complaints against them, particularly at the small Allowance of Provisions to him and his Men; for the Garrison and Governor too, were victualled by the Merchants, which was no small Grievance and Mortification to them. And as the want of eating was the only Thing that made the great *Sancho* quit his Government, so did it here rend and tare their's to Pieces: For *Massey* told them, *that he did not come there to be a* Guiney *Slave, and that he had promised his Men good Treatment, and Provisions fitting for Soldiers: That as he had the Care of so many of his Majesty's Subjects, if they would not provide for them in a handsome Manner, he should take suitable Measures for the Preservation of so many of his Countrymen and Companions.*

The Governor at this Time was very ill of a Fever, and, for the better Accomodation in his Sickness, was carried aboard the Ship *Gambia Castle,* where he continued for about three Weeks, and therefore could have little to say in this Dispute, tho' he resolved not to stay in a Place, where there was so little Occasion for him, and where his Power was so confin'd. The Merchants had certainly Orders from the Company, to issue the Provisions out to the Garrison, and the same is done along the whole Coast; but whether they had cut them short of the Allowance that was appointed them, I can't say, but if they did, then is the Loss of the Ship and Garrison owing principally to their ill Conduct.

However, an Accident that happened on Board the Ship, did not a little contribute to this Misfortune, which was a Pique that the Captain of her took against his second Mate, *George Lowther,* the Man who is the Subject of this short History; and who losing his Favour, found Means to ingratiate himself into the good liking of the common Sailors, insomuch that when Captain *Russel* ordered him to be punish'd, the Men took up Handspikes, and threat'ned to knock that Man down, that offered to lay hold of the Mate. This served but to widen the Differences between him and the Captain, and more firmly attach'd *Lowther* to the Ship's Company, the greatest Part of which, he found ripe for any Mischief in the World.

Captain *Massey* was no wit the better reconciled to the Place, by a longer Continuance, nor to the Usage he met with there, and having often Opportunities of conversing with *Lowther,* with whom he had contracted an Intimacy in the Voyage; they aggravated one another's Grievances to such a height, that they resolved upon Measures to curb the Power that controul'd them, and to provide for themselves after another Manner.

When the Governor recover'd of his Fever, he went ashore to the Island, but took no Notice of *Massey*'s Behaviour, tho' it was such as might give Suspicion of what he designed; and *Lowther,* and the common Sailors, who were in the Secret of Affairs, grew insolent and bold, even refusing to obey when commanded to their Duty by Captain *Russel* and the chief Mate. The Captain seeing how Things were carried, goes ashore early one Morning to the Governor and Factory, in order to hold a Council, which *Lowther* apprehending, was in order to prevent his Design, sent a Letter in the same Boat to *Massey,* intimating it to him, and *that he should repair on Board, for it was high Time to put their Project in Execution.*

As soon as *Massey* received this Letter, he went to the Soldiers at the *Barracks,* and said to them, and others, *You that have a Mind to go to* England, *now is your Time;* and they generally consenting, *Massey* went to the Store-Room, burst open the Door, set two Centinels upon it, and ordered that no Body should come near it; then he went to the Governor's Apartment, and took his Bed, Baggage, Plate and Furniture, (in Expectation that the Governor himself, as he had promised *Massey,* would have gone on Board, which he afterwards refused, by Reason, as he said, he believed they were going a-pirating; which at first, whatever *Lowther* designed, *Massey* certainly proposed only the going to *England;*) when this was done, he sent the Boat off to the chief Mate, with this Message, *That he should get the Guns ready, for that the King of* Barro (a Negro Kingdom near the Royal *African* Settlement) *would come aboard to Dinner.* But *Lowther* understanding best, the meaning of those Orders, he confined the chief Mate, shotted the Guns, and put the Ship in a Condition for sailing. In the Afternoon *Massey* came on Board with the Governor's Son, having sent off all the Provisions of the Island, and eleven Pipes of Wine, leaving only two half Pipes behind in the Store-House, and dismounted all the Guns of the Fort.

In the Afternoon they weigh'd one Anchor, but fearing to be too late to get out of the River, they slipp'd the other, and so fell down; in doing of which, they run the Ship a-ground. *Massey* shew'd himself a Soldier upon this Accident, for as soon as the Misfortune happen'd, he left the Ship with about sixteen Hands, and rows directly to the Fort, remounts the Guns, and keeps Garrison there all the Night, while the Ship was ashore; and obliged some of the Factory to assist in getting her clear. In the mean while, *Russel* came off, but not being suffered to come on Board, he call'd to *Lowther,* and offered him and the Company, whatever Terms they would be pleased to accept of, upon Condition of surrendering up the Ship, which had no Effect upon any of them. In the Morning they got her afloat, and *Massey* and his Men came aboard, after having nailed up and dismounted all the Cannon of the Fort: They put the Governor's Son, and two or three others ashore, who were not willing to go without the Governor, and sail'd out of the River, having exchanged several Shot with the *Martha, Otter, &c.* that lay there, without doing Execution on either Side.

When the Ship came out to Sea, *Lowther* called up all the Company, and told them, *it was the greatest Folly imaginable, to think of returning to* England, *for what they had already done, could not be justifyed upon any Pretence whatsoever, but would be look'd upon, in the Eye of the Law, a capital Offence, and that none of them were in a Condition to withstand the Attacks of such powerful Adversaries, as they would meet with at Home; for his Part he was determined not to run such a Hazard, and therefore if his Proposal was not agreed to, he desired to be set a Shore in some Place of Safety: That they had a good Ship under them, a parcel of brave Fellows in her, that it was not their Business to starve, or be made Slaves; and therefore, if they were all of his Mind, they should seek their Fortunes upon the Seas, as other Adventurers had done before them.* They one and all came into the Measures, knocked down the Cabins, made the Ship flush fore and aft, prepared black Colours, new named her, *the Delivery,* having about 50 Hands and 16 Guns, and the following short Articles were drawn up, signed and sworn to upon the Bible.

The Articles of Captain George Lowther, and his Company

1. *The Captain is to have two full Shares; the Master is to have one Share and a half; the Doctor, Mate, Gunner, and Boatswain, one Share and a quarter.*
2. *He that shall be found Guilty of taking up any unlawful Weapon on Board the Privateer, or any Prize, by us taken, so as to strike or abuse one another, in any regard, shall suffer what Punishment the Captain and Majority of the Company shall think fit.*
3. *He that shall be found Guilty of Cowardize, in the Time of Engagement, shall suffer what Punishment the Captain and Majority shall think fit.*
4. *If any Gold, Jewels, Silver, &c. be found on Board of any Prize or Prizes, to the Value of a Piece of Eight, and the Finder do not deliver it to the Quarter-Master, in the Space of 24 Hours, shall suffer what Punishment the Captain and Majority shall think fit.*
5. *He that is found Guilty of Gaming, or Defrauding another to the Value of a Shilling, shall suffer what Punishment the Captain and Majority of the Company shall think fit.*
6. *He that shall have the Misfortune to lose a Limb, in Time of Engagement, shall have the Sum of one hundred and fifty Pounds Sterling, and remain with the Company as long as he shall think fit.*
7. *Good Quarters to be given when call'd for.*
8. *He that sees a Sail first, shall have the best Pistol, or Small-Arm, on Board her.*

It was the 13th of *June,* that *Lowther* left the Settlement, and on the 20th, being then within twenty Leagues of *Barbadoes,* he came up with a Brigantine, belonging to *Boston,* called the *Charles, James Douglass* Master, which they plundered in a piratical Manner, and let the Vessel go; but least she should meet with any of the Station Ships, and so give Information of the Robbery, *in Terrorem,* to prevent a Pursuit, *Lowther* contrived a sort of a Certificate, which he directed the Master to show to their Consort, if they should meet with her; and upon Sight of it the Brigantine would pass unmolested: This Consort, he pretended, was a 40 Gun Ship, and cruising therabouts.

After this the *Delivery* proceeded to *Hispaniola;* near the West End of the Island she met with a *French* Sloop loaden with Wine and Brandy; aboard of this Vessel went Captain *Massey,* as a Merchant, and ask'd the Price of one Thing, and then another, bidding Money for the greatest Part of the Cargo; but after he had trifled a while, he whisper'd a Secret in the *French* Man's Ear, viz. *That they must have it all without Money.* Monsieur presently understood his Meaning, and unwillingly agreed to the Bargain. They took out of her thirty Casks of Brandy, five Hogsheads of Wine, several Pieces of Chintzes, and other valuable Goods, and about 70 *l. English,* in Money; of which *Lowther* generously return'd five Pounds back to the *French* Master for his Civilities.

But as all Constitutions grow old, and thereby shake and totter, so did our Commonwealth in about a Month of its Age, feel Commotions and intestine Disturbances, by the Divisions of its Members, which had near hand terminated in its Destruction; these civil Discords were owing to the following Occasion. Captain *Massey* had been a Soldier almost from his Infancy, but was but very indifferently acquainted with Maritime Affairs, and having an enterprizing Soul, nothing would satisfy him, but he must be doing Business in his own Way, therefore he required *Lowther* to let him have thirty Hands to land with, and he would attack the *French* Settlements, and bring aboard the Devil and all of Plunder.

Lowther did all that he could do, and said all that he could say, to disswade *Massey* from so rash and dangerous an Attempt; pointing out to him the Hazard the Company would run, and the Consequences to them all, if he should not succeed, and the little Likelihood there was to expect Success from the Undertaking: But 'twas all one for that, *Massey* would go and attack the *French* Settlements, for any thing *Lowther* could say against it; so that he was obliged to propose the Matter to the Company, among whom *Massey* found a few Fellows as resolute as himself; however, a great Majority being against it, the Affair was over-ruled in Opposition to Captain *Massey,* notwithstanding which, *Massey* grew fractious, quarrelled with *Lowther,* and the Men divided into Parties, some siding with the Land Pyrate, and some with the Sea Rover, and were all ready to fall together by the Ears, when the Man at the Mast-head cry'd out, A Sail! A Sail! then they gave over the Dispute, set all their Sails, and steered after the Chace. In a few Hours they came up with her, she being a small Ship from *Jamaica,* bound to *England;* they took what they thought fit out of her, and a Hand or two, and then *Lowther* was for sinking the Ship, with several Passengers that were in her, for what Reason I know not, but *Massey* so that he interposed, prevented their cruel Fate, and the Ship safely arrived afterwards in *England.*

The next Day they took a small Sloop, an interloping Trader, which they detain'd with her Cargo. All this while *Massey* was uneasy, and declar'd his Resolution to leave them, and *Lowther* finding him a very troublesome Man to deal with, consented that he should take the Sloop, last made Prize of, with what Hands had a Mind to go with him, and shift for himself. Whereupon *Massey,* with about ten more Malecontents, goes aboard the Sloop, and comes away in her directly for *Jamaica.*

Notwithstanding what had passed, Captain *Massey* puts a bold Face upon the Matter, and goes to Sir *Nicholas Laws,* the Governor, informs him of his leaving *Lowther* the Pyrate, owns, *That he assisted in going off with the Ship, at the River* Gambia; but said, *'twas to save so many of his Majesty's Subjects from perishing, and that his Design was to return to* England; *but* Lowther *conspiring with the greater Part of the Company, went a pirating with the Ship; and that he had taken this Opportunity to leave him, and surrender himself and Vessel to his Excellency.*

Massey was very well received by the Governor, and had his Liberty given him, with a Promise of his Favour, and so forth; and, at his own Request, he was sent on Board the *Happy* Sloop, Captain *Laws,* to cruise off *Hispaniola,* for *Lowther;* but not being so fortunate as to meet with him, Captain *Massey* returned back to *Jamaica* in the Sloop, and getting a Certificate, and a Supply of Money, from the Governor, he came home Passenger to *England.*

When *Massey* came to Town, he writes a long Letter to the Deputy Governor and Directors of the *African* Company, wherein he imprudently relates the whole Transactions of his Voyage, the going off with the Ship, and the Acts of Pyracy he had committed with *Lowther;* but excuses it as Rashness and Inadvertency in himself, occasioned by his being ill used, contrary to the Promises that had been made him, and the Expectations he had entertained; but own'd, that he deserved to dye for what he had done; yet, if they had Generosity enough to forgive him, as he was still capable to do them Service, as a Soldier, so he should be very ready to do it; but if they resolved to prosecute him, he begg'd only this Favour, that he might not be hang'd like a Dog, but to die like a Soldier, as he had been bred from his Childhood, that is, that he might be shot.

This was the Substance of the Letter, which, however, did not produce so favourable an Answer as he hoped for, Word being brought back to him, *That he should be fairly hang'd.* Whereupon, *Massey* resolved not to be out of the Way, when he found what important Occasion there was likely to be for him, but takes a Lodging in *Aldersgate-Street,* the next Day went to the Lord Chief Justice's Chambers, and enquired, if my Lord had granted a Warrant against Captain *John Massey,* for Pyracy: But being told by the Clerks, that they knew of no such Thing; he informed them, he was the Man, that my Lord would soon be apply'd to for that Purpose, and the Officer might come to him at such a Place, where he lodg'd: They took the Directions in Writing, and, in a few Days, a Warrant being issued, the Tipstaff went directly, by his own Information, and apprehended him, without any other Trouble, than walking to his Lodging.

There was then no Person in Town to charge him with any Fact, upon which he could be committed; nor could the Letter be proved to be of his Hand-Writing, so that they had been obliged to let him go again, if he had not helped his Accusers out at Pinch: The Magistrate was reduced to the putting of this Question to him, *Did you write this Letter?* He answered, *He did:* And not only that, but confessed all the Contents of it; upon which, he was committed to *Newgate,* but was afterwards admitted to a hundred Pounds Bail, or thereabouts.

On the 5th of *July* 1723, he was brought to his Tryal, at a Court of Admiralty held at the *Old-Baily,* when Captain *Russel,* Governor *Whitney*'s Son, and others, appeared as Evidences, by whom the Indictment was plainly proved against him; which, if it had not been done, the Captain was of such an heroic Spirit, that he would have deny'd nothing; for instead of making a Defence, he only entertained the Court with a long Narrative of his Expedition, from the first setting out, to his Return to *England,* mentioning two Acts of Pyracy committed by him, which he was not charged with, often challenging the Evidences to contradict him, if in any Thing he related the least Syllable of an Untruth; and instead of denying the Crimes set forth in the Indictment, he charged himself with various Circumstances, which fixed the Facts more home upon him. Upon the whole, the Captain was found Guilty, received Sentence of Death, and was executed three Weeks after, at *Execution-Dock.*

We return now to *Lowther,* whom we left cruising off *Hispaniola,* from whence he plyed to Windward, and, near *Porto Rico,* chased two Sail, and spoke with them; they proving to be a small *Bristol* Ship, commanded by Captain *Smith,* and a *Spanish*Pyrate, who had made Prize of the said Ship. *Lowther* examined into the *Spaniard*'s Authority for taking an *English* Vessel, and threat'ned to put every Man of them to death, for so doing; so that the *Spaniards* fancied themselves to be in a very pittiful Condition, till Matters cleared up, and they found their Masters as great Rogues as themselves, from whom some Mercy might be expected, in regard to the near Relation they stood with them, as to their Profession; in short, *Lowther* first rifled, and then burnt both the Ships, sending the *Spaniards* away in their Launch, and turning all the *English* Sailors into Pyrates.

After a few Days Cruise, *Lowther* took a small Sloop belonging to St. *Christophers,* which they mann'd and carried along with them to a small Island, where they cleaned, and stay'd some Time to take their Diversions, which consisted in unheard of Debaucheries, with drinking, swearing and rioting, in which there seemed to be a kind of Emulation among them, resembling rather Devils than Men, striving who should out do one another in new invented Oaths and Execrations.

They all got aboard about *Christmas,* observing neither Times nor Seasons, for perpetrating their villainous Actions, and sailed towards the Bay of *Honduras;* but stopping at the *Grand Caimanes* for Water, they met with a small Vessel with 13 Hands, in the same honourable Employment with themselves; the Captain of this Gang was one *Edward Lowe,* whom we shall particularly discourse of in a Chapter by it self: *Lowther* received them as Friends, and treated them with all imaginable Respect, inviting them, as they were few in Number, and in no Condition to pursue the Account, (as they called it) to join their Strength together, which on the Consideration aforesaid, was accepted of, *Lowther* still continuing Commander, and *Lowe* was made Lieutenant: The Vessel the new Pyrates came out of, they sunk, and the Confederates proceed on the Voyage as *Lowther* before intended.

The 10th of *January,* the Pyrates came into the Bay, and fell upon a Ship of 200 Tun, called the *Greyhound, Benjamin Edwards* Commander, belonging to *Boston. Lowther* hoisted his piratical Colours, and fired a Gun for the *Greyhound* to bring to, which she refusing, the *Happy Delivery* (the Name of the Pyrate) edg'd down, and gave her a Broadside, which was returned by Captain *Edwards* very bravely, and the Engagement held for an Hour; but Captain *Edwards,* finding the Pyrate too strong for him, and fearing the Consequence of too obstinate a Resistance against those lawless Fellows, ordered his Ensign to be struck. The Pyrates Boat came aboard, and not only rifled the Ship, but whipp'd, beat, and cut the Men in a cruel Manner, turned them aboard their own Ship, and then set Fire to theirs.

In cruising about the Bay, they met and took several other Vessels without any Resistance, *viz.* two Brigantines of *Boston* in *New-England,* one of which they burnt, and sunk the other; a Sloop belonging to *Connecticut,* Captain *Airs,* which they also burnt; a Sloop of *Jamaica,* Captain *Hamilton,* they took for their own Use; a Sloop of *Virginia* they unladed, and was so generous as to give her back to the Master that own'd her. They took a Sloop of 100 Ton, belonging to *Rhode Island,* which they were pleased to keep, and mount with eight Carriage, and ten Swivel Guns.

With this little Fleet, *viz.* Admiral *Lowther,* in the *Happy Delivery;* Captain *Low,* in the *Rhode Island* Sloop; Captain *Harris,* (who was second Mate in the *Greyhound* when taken,) in *Hamilton*'s Sloop, and the little Sloop formerly mentioned, serving as a Tender; I say, with this Fleet the Pyrates left the Bay, and came to *Port Mayo* in the Gulph of *Matique,* and there made Preparations to careen; they carried ashore all their Sails, and made Tents by the Water-Side, wherein they laid their Plunder, Stores, *&c.* and fell to work; and at the Time that the Ships were upon the Heel, and the good Folks employ'd in heaving down, scrubbing, tallowing, and so forth; of a sudden came down a considerable Body of the Natives, and attack'd the Pyrates unprepared. As they were in no Condition to defend themselves, they sled to their Sloops, leaving them Masters of the Field and the Spoil thereof, which was of great Value, and set Fire to the *Happy Delivery,* their capital Ship.

Lowther made the best Provision he could in the largest Sloop, which he called the *Ranger,* having ten Guns and eight Swivels, and she sailing best, the Company went all aboard of her, and left the other at Sea. Provisions was now very short, which, with the late Loss, put them in a confounded ill Humour, insomuch that they were every now and then going together by the Ears, laying the Blame of their ill Conduct sometimes upon one, then upon another.

The Beginning of *May* 1722, they got to the *West-Indies,* and near the Island of *Diseada,* took a Brigantine, one *Payne* Master, that afforded them what they stood in need of, which put them in better Temper, and Business seemed to go on well again. After they had pretty well plundered the Brigantine, they sent her to the Bottom. They went into the Island and watered, and then stood to the Northward, intending to visit the Main-Coast of *America.*

In the Latitude of 38, they took a Brigantine called the *Rebecca* of *Boston,* Captain *Smith,* bound thither from St. *Christophers.* At the taking of this Vessel, the Crews divided; for *Low,* whom *Lowther* joined at the *Grand Caimanes,* proving always a very unruly Member of the Commonwealth, always aspiring, and never satisfy'd with the Proceedings of the Commander; he thought it the safest Way to get rid of him, upon any Terms; and according to the Vote of the Company, they parted the Bear Skin between them: *Low* with 44 Hands went aboard the Brigantine, and *Lowther* with the same Number stay'd in the Sloop, and separated that very Night, being the 28th of *May* 1722.

Lowther proceeding on his Way to the Main-Coast, took three or four fishing Vessels off *New-York,* which was no great Booty to the Captors. The 3d of *June,* they met with a small *New-England* Ship, bound home from *Barbadoes,* which stood an Attack a small Time, but finding it to no Purpose, yielded herself a Prey to the Booters: The Pyrates took out of her fourteen Hogsheads of Rum, six Barrels of Sugar, a large Box of *English* Goods, several Casks of Loaf Sugar, a considerable Quantity of Pepper, six Negroes, besides a Sum of Money and Plate, and then let her go on her Voyage.

The next Adventure was not so fortunate for them, for coming pretty near the Coast of *South-Carolina,* they met with a Ship just come out, on her Voyage to *England; Lowther* gave her a Gun, and hoisted his piratical Colours; but this Ship, which was called the *Amy,* happening to have a brave gallant Man to command her, who was not any ways daunted with that terrible Ensign, the black Flag, he instead of striking immediately, as 'twas expected, let fly a Broadside at the Pyrate. *Lowther* (not at all pleased with the Compliment, tho' he put up with it for the present) was for taking Leave; but the *Amy* getting the Pyrate between her and the Shore, stood after him to clap him aboard; to prevent which, *Lowther* run the Sloop a-ground, and landed all the Men with their Arms. Captain *Gwatkins,* the Captain of the *Amy,* was obliged to stand off, for fear of running his own Ship ashore; but at the same Time thought fit for the public Good, to destroy the Enemy; and thereupon went into the Boat, and rowed towards the Sloop, in order to set her on Fire; but before he reached the Vessel, a fatal Shot from *Lowther*'s Company ashore, put an End to their Design and Captain *Gwatkin*'s Life. After this unfortunate Blow, the Mate returned aboard with the Boat, and not being enclined to pursue them any farther, took Charge of the Ship.

Lowther got off the Sloop after the Departure of the *Amy,* and brought all his Men aboard again, but was in a poor shattered Condition, having suffered much in the Engagement, and had a great many Men kill'd and wounded: He made Shift to get into an Inlet somewhere in *North-Carolina,* where he staid a long while before he was able to put to Sea again.

He and his Crew laid up all the Winter, and shifted as well as they could among the Woods, divided themselves into small Parties, and hunted generally in the Day Times, killing of black Cattle, Hogs, *&c.* for their Subsistance, and in the Night retired to their Tents and Huts, which they made for Lodging; and sometimes when the Weather grew very cold, they would stay aboard of their Sloop.

In the Spring of the Year 1723, they made Shift to get to Sea, and steered their Course for *Newfoundland,* and upon the Banks took a Scooner, call'd the *Swift, John Hood* Master; they found a good Quantity of Provisions aboard her, which they very much wanted at that Time, and after taking three of their Hands, and plundering her of what they thought fit, they let her depart. They took several other Vessels upon the Banks, and in the Harbour, but none of any great Account; and then steering for a warmer Climate, in *August* arrived at the *West-Indies.* In their Passage thither, they met with a Brigantine, called the *John* and *Elizabeth, Richard Stanny* Master, bound for *Boston,* which they plundered, took two of her Men, and discharged her.

Lowther cruised a pretty while among the Islands without any extraordinary Success, and was reduced to a very small Allowance of Provisions, till they had the luck to fall in with a *Martinico* Man, which proved a seasonable Relief to them; and after that, a *Guiney* Man had the ill Fortune to become a Prey to the *Rovers;* she was called the *Princess,* Captain *Wicksted* Commander.

It was now thought necessary to look out for a Place to clean their Sloop in, and prepare for new Adventures: Accordingly the Island of *Blanco* was pitched upon for that Purpose, which lies in the Latitude of 11° 50 m. N. about 30 Leagues from the Main of the *Spanish America,* between the Islands of *Margarita* and *Rocas,* and not far from *Tortuga.* It is a low even Island, but healthy and dry, uninhabited, and about two Leagues in Circumference, with Plenty of Lignum Vitæ Trees thereon, growing in Spots, with shrubby Bushes of other Wood about them. There are, besides Turtle, great Numbers of Guanoes, which is an amphibious Creature like a Lizard, but much larger, the Body of it being as big as a Man's Leg; they are very good to eat, and are much used by the Pyrates that come here: They are of divers Colours, but such as live upon dry Ground, as here at *Blanco,* are commonly yellow. On the N. W. End of this Island, there is a small Cove or sandy Bay, all round the rest of the Island is deep Water, and steep close to the Island. Here *Lowther* resorted to, the Beginning of *October* last, unrigged his Sloop, sent his Guns, Sails, Rigging, *&c.* ashore, and put his Vessel upon the Careen. The *Eagle* Sloop of *Barbadoes,* belonging to the *South-Sea* Company, with 35 Hands, commanded by *Walter Moore,* coming near this Island, in her Voyage to *Comena,* on the *Spanish* Continent, saw the said Sloop just careen'd, with her Guns out, and Sails unbent, which she supposed to be a Pyrate, because it was a Place where Traders did not commonly use, so took the Advantage of attacking her, as she was then unprepared; the *Eagle* having fired a Gun to oblige her to show her Colours, the Pyrate hoisted the St. *George*'s Flag at their Topmast-Head, as it were to bid Defiance to her; but when they found *Moore* and his Crew resolved to board them in good earnest, the Pyrates cut their Cable and hawled their Stern on Shore, which obliged the *Eagle* to come to an Anchor a-thwart their Hawse, where she engaged them till they called for Quarter and struck; at which Time *Lowther* and twelve of the Crew made their Escape out of the Cabin Window. The Master of the *Eagle* got the Pyrate Sloop off, secured her, and went ashore with 25 Hands, in Pursuit of *Lowther* and his Gang; but after five Day's search, they could find but five of them, which they brought aboard, and then proceeded with the Sloop and Pyrates to *Comena* aforesaid, where they soon arrived.

The *Spanish* Governor being informed of this brave Action, condemned the Sloop to the Captors, and sent a small Sloop with 23 Hands to scower the Bushes and other Places of the

Island of *Blanco,* for the Pyrates that remained there, and took four more, with seven small Arms, leaving behind them Captain *Lowther,* three Men, and a little Boy, which they could not take; the above four the *Spaniards* try'd and condemned to Slavery for Life; three to the Gallies, and the other to the Castle of *Arraria.*

The *Eagle* Sloop brought all their Prisoners afterwards to St. *Christopher's,* where the following were try'd by a Court of Vice Admiralty, there held *March* the 11th, 1722, *viz. John Churchill, Edward Mackdonald, Nicholas Lewis, Richard West, Sam. Levercott, Robert White, John Shaw, Andrew Hunter, Jonathan Delve, Matthew Freebarn, Henry Watson,*

Roger Grange, Ralph Candor, and *Robert Willis;* the three last were acquitted, the other thirteen were found Guilty, two of which were recommended to Mercy by the Court, and accordingly pardoned; and the rest executed at that Island, on the 20th of the same Month.

As for Captain *Lowther,* it is said that he afterwards shot himself upon that fatal Island, where his Pyracies ended, being found, by some Sloop's Men, dead, and a Pistol burst by his Side.

Chap. XIV
Of Captain *Edward Low,* And his Crew

    Low's Original. The Virtues of his Family. His bold Beginnings. Declares War against the whole World. His Success. Like to perish by a Storm. Sail for the Western Island. Treats with the Governor of St. Michael for Water. Several Instances of their wanton Cruelty. Low's Consort taken, and how. A horrid Massacre committed by Low. Takes a Multitude of Prizes. Another barharous Massacre. More Cruelties. Low and his Consort attack'd by the Greyhound Man of War. Low deserts his Consort. The Consort taken. Carried to Rhode Island. The Names, Age, and Places of Birth, of the Prisoners. A Compliment paid to Captain Solgard, by the Corporation of New-York. The Resolution of the Mayor and Common-Council. The Preamble of the Captain's Freedom. More Instances of Low's Cruelty. His Adventures.

Edward Low was born in *Westminster,* and had his Education there, such as it was, for he could neither write or read. Nature seem'd to have designed him for a Pyrate from his Childhood, for very early he began the Trade of plundering, and was wont to raise Contributions among all the Boys of *Westminster;* and if any were bold enough to refuse it, a Battle was the Consequence; but *Low* was so hardy, as well as bold, there was no getting the better of him, so that he robbed the Youths of their Farthings, with Impunity; when he grew bigger he took to Gaming in a low Way, for it was commonly among the Footmen in the *Lobby* of the House of Commons, where he used to play the whole Game, (as they term it,) that is, cheat all he could, and those who pretended to dispute it with him, must fight him.

    The Virtues of some of his Family were equal to his; one of his Brothers was a Youth of Genius, when he was but seven Years old, he used to be carried in a Basket, upon a Porter's Back, into a Crowd, and snatch Hats and Wigs: According to the exact Chronology of *Newgate,* he was the first who practised this ingenious Trick. After this, he applied himself to picking of Pockets; when he increased in Strength, he attempted greater Things, such as House-breaking, *&c.* But after he had run a short Race, he had the Misfortune of ending his Days at *Tyburn,* in Company with *Stephen Bunce,* and the celebrated *Jack Hall* the Chimney-Sweeper.

    But to return to *Ned,* when he came to Man's Estate, at his eldest Brother's Desire, he went to Sea with him, and so continued for three or four Years, and then parted; and *Ned* work'd in a Rigging-House in *Boston* in *New-England,* for a while. About six Years ago, he took a Trip home to *England,* to see his Mother, who is yet Living. His Stay was not long here; but taking Leave of his Friends and Acquaintance, for the last Time he should see them; for so he was pleased to say; he returned to *Boston,* and work'd a Year or two longer at the Rigging Business. But being too apt to disagree with his Masters, he left them, and shipp'd himself in a Sloop that was bound to the Bay of *Honduras.*

    When the Sloop arrived in the Bay, *Ned Low* was appointed Patron of the Boat, which was employ'd in cutting of Logwood, and bringing it aboard to lade the Ship; for that is the Commodity they make the Voyage for: In the Boat were twelve Men besides *Low,* who all go arm'd, because of the *Spaniards,* from whom this Logwood is but little better than stole. It happened that the Boat one Day came aboard just before Dinner was ready, and *Low* desired that they might stay and Dine; but the Captain, being in a Hurry for his Lading, ordered them a Bottle of Rum, and to take t'other Trip, because no Time should be lost: This provoked the Boat's Crew, but particularly *Low,* who takes up a loaded Musquet and fires at the Captain, but missing him, shot another poor Fellow thro' the Head, then put off the Boat, and with his twelve Companions goes to Sea: The next Day they took a small Vessel, and go in her, make a black Flag, and declare War against all the World.

    They then proceeded to the Island of the *Grand Caimanes,* intending to have fitted up their small Vessel, and prepare themselves as well as their Circumstances would permit, for their honourable Employment; but falling in Company with *George Lowther,* another Pyrate there, who paying his Compliments to *Low,* as great Folks do to one another when they meet, and offering himself as an Ally; *Low* accepted of the Terms, and so the Treaty was presently sign'd without Plenipo's or any other Formalities.

We have already given an Account of their joynt Pyracies, under *Lowther* as chief Commander, till the 28th of *May,* 1722, when they took a Brigantine of *Boston,* bound thither from St. *Christophers,* at which Time they parted, and *Edward Low* went into the Brigantine, with forty four others, who chose him their Captain: They took with them two Guns, four Swivels, six Quarter-Casks of Powder, Provisions and some Stores, and so left *Lowther* to prosecute his Adventures, with the Men he had left.

Their first Adventure in the Brigantine, was on *Sunday* the 3d Day of *June,* when they took a Vessel belonging to *Amboy, John Hance* Master, whom he rifled of his Provisions, and let go; the same Day he met with a Sloop, *James Calquhoon* Master, off of *Rhode Island,* bound into that Port, whom he first plundered, and then cut away his Boltsprit, and all his Rigging, also his Sails from the Yards, and wounded the Master, to prevent his getting in to give Intelligence, and then stood away to the South-Eastward, with all the Sail he could make, there being then but little Wind.

Low judged right in making sail from the Coast, for a longer stay had proved fatal to him, for notwithstanding the disabled Condition he had rendered the Sloop in, she made shift to get into *Block Island,* at 12 o'Clock that Night, and immediately dispatched a Whale-Boat to *Rhode Island,* which got thither by seven the next Morning, with an Account of the Pyrate, his Force, and what had happened to him: As soon as the Governor had received this Information, he ordered a Drum to beat up for Volunteers, and two of the best Sloops then in the Harbour, to be fitted out: He gave Commissions to one Captain *John Headland,* and Captain *John Brown,* jun. for ten Days; the former had eight Guns and two Swivels, and the latter six Guns, well fitted with small Arms, and in both Sloops 140 stout Fellows; all this was performed with so much Expedition, that before Sun-set, they were under Sail, turning out of the Harbour, at the same Time the Pyrate was seen from *Block Island,* which gave great Hopes that the Sloops would be Masters of her the next Day, which however did not happen, for the Sloops returned into Harbour some Days afterwards, without so much as seeing their Enemy.

After this Escape, Captain *Low,* went into Port, upon the Coast, for he had not fresh Water enough to run to the Islands, where he staid a few Days, getting Provisions and what Necessaries the Crew wanted, and then sailed for Purchase, (as they call it) steering their Course towards *Marblehead.*

About the 12th of *July,* the Brigantine sailed into the Harbour of Port *Rosemary,* and there found thirteen Ships and Vessels, but none of Force, at Anchor, they spread their black Flag, and ran in among them; *Low* telling them from the Brigantine, they should have no Quarters if they resisted; in the mean Time they mann'd and arm'd their Boat, and took Possession of every one of them, plundered them of what they thought fit, and converted one to their own Use, *viz.* a Scooner of 80 Tuns, aboard of which they put 10 Carriage Guns, and 50 Men, and *Low* himself went Captain, and nam'd her the *Fancy,* making one *Charles Harris,* (who was at first forced into their Service out of the *Greyhound* of *Boston,* by *Lowther,* of which Ship *Harris* was second Mate) Captain of the Brigantine: Out of these Vessels they took several Hands, and encreased the Company to 80 Men, who all signed the Articles, some willingly, and a few perhaps by Force, and so sailed away from *Marblehead.*

Some Time after this, they met with two Sloops bound for *Boston,* with Provisions for the Garrison, and the Scooner coming up first, attacked them, but there happening to be an Officer and some Soldiers on Board, who gave them a warm Reception, *Low* chose to stay till he should be joyned by the Brigantine; in the mean while the Sloops made the best of their Way, and the Pyrates gave them Chace two Days, and at last lost sight of them in a Fog.

They now steered for the Leeward Islands, but in their Voyage met with such a Hurricane of Wind, that the like had not been known; the Sea ran Mountains high, and seemed to threaten them every Moment with Destruction; it was no Time now to look out for Plunder, but to save themselves, if possible, from perishing. All Hands were continually employed Night, and Day, on Board the Brigantine, and all little enough, for the Waves went over her, so that they were forced to keep the pump constantly going, besides baling with Buckets; but finding themselves not able to keep her free, and seeing the utmost Danger before their Eyes, they turn'd to the Takle, and hoisted out their Provisions, and other heavy Goods, and threw them over-board, with six of their Guns, so that by lightening the Vessel, she might rise to the Top of the Sea with the Waves: They were also going to cut away their Mast; but considering how dangerous it would be, to be left in such a Condition, they resolved to delay it to the last, which was Prudence in them to do; for a Ship without Masts or Sails, lies like a Log upon the Water, and if attack'd, must fight with Disadvantage, the working of her being the most artful Part of the Engagement, because she may sometimes bring all her great Guns on one Side, to bear upon her Enemy, when the disabled Ship can do little or nothing.

But to proceed; by their throwing over-board the heavy Goods, the Vessel made considerable less Water, and they could keep it under with the Pump only, which gave them Hopes and new Life; so that instead of cutting all away, they took necessary Measures to secure the Mast, by making Preventor-Shrowds, &c. and then wore and lay too upon the other Tack, till the Storm was over. The Scooner made somewhat better Weather of it, of the two, but was pretty roughly handled notwithstanding, having split her Main-sail, sprung her Boltsprit, and cut her Anchors from her Bows. The Brigantine by running away to Leeward, when she wore upon the Larboard Tack, had lost Sight of the Scooner; but not knowing whether she might be safe or not, as soon as the Wind abated, she set her Main-Sail and Top-Sail, and made short Trips to Windward; and the next Day had the good Fortune to come in Sight of their Consort, who, upon a Signal, which the other knew, bore down to her, and the Crew were overjoy'd to meet again, after such ill Treatment from the Winds and Seas.

After the Storm, *Low* got safe to a small Island, one of the Weathermost of the *Caribbees,* and there fitted their Vessels, as well as the Place could afford; they got Provisions of the Natives, in exchange for Goods of their own; and as soon as the Brigantine was ready, 'twas judg'd necessary to take a short Cruize, and leave the Scooner in the Harbour till her Return. The Brigantine sail'd out accordingly, and had not been out many Days before they met a Ship at Sea, that had lost all her Masts; on Board of whom they went, and took from her in Money and Goods, to the Value of 1000 *l.* and so left her in the Condition they found her: This Ship was bound home from *Barbadoes,* but losing her Masts in the late Storm, was making for *Antegoa,* to refit, where she afterwards arriv'd.

The Storm just spoken of, was found to have done incredible Damage in those Parts of the World; but however, it appear'd to have been more violent at *Jamaica,* both to the Island and Shipping, there was such a prodigious Swell of the Sea, that several hundred Tuns of Stones and Rocks, were thrown over the Wall of the Town of *Port Royal,* and the Town it self was overflowed, and above half destroy'd, there being the next Morning five Foot Water from one End to the other; the Cannon of Fort *Charles* were dismounted, and some washed into the Sea, and four hundred People lost their Lives; a more melancholly Sight was scarce ever seen when the Water ebb'd away, all the Streets being covered with Ruins of Houses, Wrecks of Vessels, and a great Number of dead Bodies, for forty Sail of Ships, in the Harbour, were cast away.

The Brigantine return'd to the Island, where she had left the Scooner, who being ready to sail, it was put to the Vote of the Company, what Voyage to take next; and herein they follow'd the Advice of the Captain, who thought it not adviseable to go any farther to Leeward, because of the Men of War who were cruising in their several Stations, which they were not at all fond of meeting, and therefore it was agreed to go to the *Azores,* or Western Islands.

The latter End of *July, Low* took a *French* Ship of 34 Guns, and carried her along with him to the *Azores.* He came into St. *Michael*'s Road the 3d of *August,* and took seven Sail that were lying there, *viz.* the *Nostre Dame, Mere de Dien,* Captain *Roach* Commander; the *Dove,* Capt. *Cox;* the *Rose* Pink, formerly a Man of War, Capt. *Thompson;* another *English* Ship, Capt. *Chandler;* and three other Vessels. He threatened all with present Death who resisted, which struck such a Terror to them, that they yielded themselves up a Prey to the Villains, without firing a Gun.

The Pyrates being in great Want of Water and fresh Provisions, *Low* sent to the Governor of St. *Michael*'s for a Supply, and promised upon that Condition to release the Ships he had taken, but otherwise to burn them all; which Demand the Governor thought it not prudent to refuse, but sent the Provision he required, upon which he released six of the Ships, (after he had plundered them of what he thought fit,) and the other, *viz.* the *Rose* Pink, was made a Pyrate Ship, which *Low* himself took the Command of.

The Pyrates took several of the Guns out of the *French* Ship, and mounted them aboard the *Rose,* which proved very fit for their Turn, and condemned the former to the Flames. They took all the Crew out of her, but the Cook, who, they said, being a greazy Fellow would fry well in the Fire; so the poor Man was bound to the Main-Mast, and burnt in the Ship, to the no small Diversion of *Low* and his *Mirmidons.*

Low ordered the Scooner to lye in the Fare between St. *Michael*'s and St. *Mary*'s, where, about the 20th of *August,* Captain *Carter* in the *Wright* Galley, had the ill Fortune to come in her Way; and because at first they showed Inclinations to defend themselves, and what they had, the Pyrates cut and mangled them in a barbarous Manner; particularly some *Portuguese* Passengers, two of which being Friers, they triced up at each Arm of the Fore-Yard, but let them down again before they were quite dead, and this they repeated several Times out of Sport.

Another *Portuguese,* who was also Captain *Carter's* Passenger, putting on a sorrowful Countenance at what he saw acted, one of this vile Crew attacked him upon the Deck, saying, *he did not like his Looks,* and thereupon gave him one Blow a-cross his Belly with his Cutlash, that cut out his Bowels, and he fell down dead without speaking a Word. At the same Time another of these Rogues cutting at a Prisoner, missed his Mark, and Captain *Low* standing in his Way, very opportunely received the Stroke upon his under Jaw, which laid the Teeth bare; upon this the Surgeon was called, who immediately stitched up the Wound, but *Low* finding fault with the Operation, the Surgeon being tollerably drunk, as it was customary for every Body to be, struck *Low* such a Blow with his Fist, that broke out all the Stitches, and then bid him sew up his Chops himself and be damned, so that *Low* made a very pitiful Figure for some Time after.

When they had plundered Captain *Carter's* Ship, several of them were for burning her, as they had done the *French* Man, but it was otherwise resolved at last; for after they had cut her Cables, Rigging and Sails to Pieces, they left her to the Mercy of the Sea.

After these Depredations, they steered for the Island of *Madera,* where missing other Booty, they took up with a Fishing-Boat, with two old Men and a Boy in her, one of which they detained on Board, but sent the other ashore with a Flag of Truce, demanding a Boat of Water of the Governor, on Pain of taking away the old Man's Life, whom they threatened to hang at the Yard-Arm, upon their refusal; but the Thing being complied with, the old Man was honourably (as the Pyrates say) discharged, and all the three much handsomer cloathed than when they took them. From this Island they sailed to the *Canaries,* but meeting with no Prey there, they continued their Course for the *Cape de Verd* Islands, and at *Bonavista,* took a Ship called the *Liverpool Merchant,* Captain *Goulding,* from whom they stole a great Quantity of Provisions and dry Goods, 300 Gallons of Brandy, two Guns and Carriages, a Mast, Yard and Hawsers, besides six of his Men, and then would not let them Trade there, nor at St. *Nicholas,* but obliged Captain *Goulding* to go with his Ship, to the Isle of *May.*

The Pyrate also took among these Islands, a Ship belonging to *Liverpool, Scot* Commander; two *Portuguese* Sloops bound for *Brasil;* a small *English* Sloop trading there, *James Pease* Master, bound to *Sancta Crux,* and three Sloops from St. *Thomas* bound to *Curaso,* the Masters Names were *Lilly, Staples* and *Simpkins,* all which they plundered, and then let go about their Business, except one Sloop which they fitted up for the following Purpose.

Low had heard by one of the above mentioned Ships, that two small Gallies were expected every Day at the *Western Islands, viz.* the *Greyhound,* Captain *Glass,* and the *Joliff,* Captain *Aram;* the former of which was designed to be fitted for the piratical Trade to *Brasil,* if Things had happened to their Minds. They mann'd the Sloop, and sent her in Quest of one or both of these Ships to the *Western Islands* aforesaid, whilst they carreen'd their Ship *Rose,* at one of the

Cape de Verds: But now Fortune that had hitherto been so propitious to them, left her Minions, and baffled for the present all their Hopes, for the Sloop missing of their Prey, was reduced to great Necessities for want of Provisions and Water, so that they ventured to go ashore at St. *Michael*'s for a Supply, and pass for a Trader; but they play'd their Parts so aukwardly, that they were suspected by the Governor to be what they really were, and he was soon put out of doubt by a Visit some *Portuguese* made them, who happened unluckily to be Passengers in Captain *Carter*'s Ship, when *Low* took her, and knew the Gentlemen's Faces very well; upon which the whole Crew was conducted into the Castle, where they were provided for as long as they liv'd.

Low, in the mean Time, did not fare quite so ill, but had his intended Voyage to *Brasil* spoil'd, by the oversetting of his Ship, when she was upon the Careen, whereby she was lost, so that he was reduc'd to his old Scooner, which he called the *Fancy,* aboard of which they all went, to the Number of 100, as vile Rogues as ever ended their Lives at *Tyburn*. They proceeded now to the *West-Indies,* but before they had gotten far on their Voyage, they attack'd a rich *Portuguese* Ship, call'd the *Nostre Signiora de Victoria,* bound home from *Bahia,* and after some Resistance, took her. *Low* tortur'd several of the Men, to make them declare where the Money, (which he suppos'd they had on Board) lay, and extorted by that Means, a Confession that the Captain had, during the Chace, hung out of the Cabin Window, a Bag with 11,000 Moidores, which, assoon as he was taken, he cut the Rope off, and let it drop into the Sea.

Low, upon hearing what a Prize had escap'd him, rav'd like a Fury, swore a thousand Oaths, and ordered the Captain's Lips to be cut off, which he broil'd before his Face, and afterwards murthered him and all the Crew, being thirty two Persons.

After this bloody Action, they continued their Course, till they came to the Northward of all the Islands, and there cruiz'd for about a Month, in which Time they made Prizes of the following Vessels, *viz.* a Snow from *New-York* to *Curacoa, Robert Leonard* Master; a Sloop from the Bay, bound to *New-York, Craig* Master; a Snow from *London* and *Jamaica,* bound to *New-York;* and the *Stanhope* Pink, *Andrew Delbridge* Master, from *Jamaica* to *Boston;* which last they burnt, because of *Low*'s irreconcileable Aversion to *New-England* Men.

After this Cruize, they went into one of the Islands and clean'd, and then steered for the Bay of *Honduras,* where they arrived about the Middle of *March* 1722-3, and met a Sloop turning out of the said Bay. The Pyrates had hoisted up *Spanish* Colours, and continued them till they drew near the Sloop, then they hall'd them down, hoisted their black Flag, fired a Broadside, and boarded her. This Sloop was a *Spaniard* of six Guns, and 70 Men, that came into the Bay that Morning, and meeting there with five *English* Sloops, and a Pink, made Prizes of them all, plundered them, and brought the Masters of the Vessels away Prisoners, for the ransom of the Logwood; their Names were *Tuthill, Norton, Newbury, Sprafort, Clark* and *Parrot*. The *Spaniards* made no Resistance, so that the *English*Pyrates soon became their Masters and fell to rifling; but finding the above-mentioned People in the Hold, and several *English* Goods, they consulted *Low* the Captain thereupon, and without examining any further, the Resolution pass'd to kill all the Company; and the Pyrates, without any Ceremony, fell Pell-Mell to Execution with their Swords, Cutlashes, Poll-Axes and Pistols, cutting, slashing and shooting the poor *Spaniards* at a sad Rate. Some of the miserable Creatures jump'd down into the Hold, but could not avoid the Massacre; they met Death every where, for if they escaped it from one Hand, they were sure to perish by another; the only Prospect they had of Life, was to fly from the Rage of those merciless Men, and to trust to the more merciful Sea; and accordingly a great many leap'd over-board, and swam for the Shore; but *Low* perceiving it, ordered the Canoa to be mann'd, and sent in pursuit of them, by which Means several of the poor unhappy Men were knock'd in the Head in the Water, as they were endeavouring to get to Land; however, about 12 of them did reach the Shore, but in a miserable Condition, being very much wounded, and what became of them afterwards was not known, except one, who while the Pyrates were at their Sports and Pastimes ashore, finding himself very weak and fainting with his Wounds, and not knowing where to go for Help and Relief, in this Extremity, he came back to them, and begg'd for God sake, in the most earnest Manner possible, that they would give him Quarters;

upon which, one of the Villains took hold of him, and said, *G — d — n him, he would give him good Quarters presently,* and made the poor *Spaniard* kneel down on his Knees, then taking his Fusil, put the Muzzle of it into his Mouth, and fired down his Throat. 'Twas thought the rest did not long survive their miserable Condition, and could only prolong their Lives, to add to the Misery of them.

When the murdering Work was over, they rumaged the *Spanish*Pyrate, and brought all the Booty aboard their own Vessels: The six Masters aforementioned, found in the Hold, they restored to their respective Vessels: They forced away the Carpenter from the Pink, and then set Fire to the *Spanish* Sloop, and burnt her; which last Scene concluded the Destruction of their Enemy, Ship and Crew.

Low set the Masters of the Vessels free, but would not suffer them to steer for *Jamaica*, where they were then bound, for fear the Men of War should get Intelligence of them, but forced them all to go to *New-York*, threat'ning them with Death, when they met them again, if they refused to comply with their Demands.

In the next Cruize, which was between the Leeward Islands and the Main, they took two Snows, bound from *Jamaica* to *Liverpool*, and a Snow from *Jamaica* to *London*, *Bridds* Master; as also a Ship from *Biddford* to *Jamaica*, *John Pinkham* Commander; and two Sloops from *Jamaica* to *Virginia*.

On the 27th of *May*, *Low* and his Consort *Harris*, came off *South-Carolina*, and met with three good Ships, *viz.* the *Crown*, Captain *Lovereigne*, the *King William*, the *Carteret*, and a Brigantine, who all came out of *Carolina* together two Days before. The Pyrates were at the Trouble of chacing them, and Captain *Lovereigne* being the sternmost, she fell first a Prey into their Hands; and they spent all the Day in coming up with the rest.

Within a few Days they took a Ship called the *Amsterdam Merchant,* Captain *Willard*, from *Jamaica*, but belonging to *New-England*; as *Low* let none of that Country depart without some Marks of his Rage, he cut off this Gentleman's Ears, slit up his Nose, and cut him in several Places of his Body, and, after plundering his Ship, let him pursue his Voyage.

After this he took a Sloop bound to *Amboy*, *William Frazier*, Master, with whom Mr. *Low* happening to be displeased, he ordered lighted Matches to be ty'd between the Mens Fingers, which burnt all the Flesh off the Bones; then cut them in several Parts of their Bodies with Knives and Cutlashes; afterwards took all their Provisions away, and set some of them ashore in an uninhabited Part of the Country.

The *Kingston,* Captain *Estwick,* another Ship, one *Burrington* Master, two Brigantines from *Carolina* to *London;* a Sloop from *Virginia* to *Bermudas;* a Ship from *Glasgow* to *Virginia;* a Scooner from *New-York* to *South-Carolina;* a Pink from *Virginia* to *Dartmouth*, and a Sloop from *Philadelphia* to *Surinam*, fell a Prey to these Villains, upon this Cruize, besides those above-mentioned.

It happened that at this Time one of his Majesty's Ships was upon a Cruize, on this Station, and got Intelligence of some of the mischievous Actions of this Miscreant, by one of the Vessels that had been plundered by him, who steering as directed, came in Sight of the Pyrates by break of Day, on the 10th of *June,* of all Days in the Year. The Rovers looking out for Prey, soon saw, and gave Chace to the Man of War, which was called the *Greyhound,* a Ship of 20 Guns, and 120 Men, rather inferiour in Force to the two Pyrate Vessels: The *Greyhound* finding them so eager, was in no doubt what they should be, and therefore tack'd and stood from them, giving the Pyrates an Opportunity to chace her for two Hours, till all Things were in Readiness for an Engagement, and the Pyrates about Gun-shot off; then the *Greyhound* tack'd again, and stood towards the two Sloops, one of them called the *Fancy,* commanded by *Low* himself, and the other the *Ranger,* commanded by *Harris,* both which hoisted their piratical Colours, and fired each a Gun. When the *Greyhound* came within Musquet-shot, she halled up her Main-sail, and clapp'd close upon a Wind, to keep the Pyrates from running to Leeward, and then engaged: But when the Rogues found who they had to deal with, they edg'd away under the Man of War's Stern, and the *Greyhound* standing after them, they made a running Fight for about two

Hours; but little Wind happening, the Sloops gained from her, by the help of their Oars; upon which the *Greyhound* left off firing, and turned all Hands to her own Oars, and at three in the Afternoon came up with them. The Pyrates haul'd upon a Wind to receive the Man of War, and the Fight was immediately renewed, with a brisk Fire on both Sides, till the *Ranger*'s Main-Yard was shot down, and the *Greyhound* pressing close upon the disabled Sloop, *Low*, in the other, thought fit to bear away and leave his Consort a Sacrifice to his Enemy, who (seing the Cowardice and Treachery of his Commadore and Leader, having ten or twelve Men killed and wounded, and that there was no possibility of escaping,) called out for *Quar*ters, and surrendered themselves to Justice, which proved severe enough to them a-while afterwards.

The Conduct of *Low* was surprizing in this Adventure, because his reputed Courage and Boldness, had, hitherto, so possess'd the Minds of all People, that he became a Terror, even to his own Men; but his Behaviour throughout this whole Action, showed him to be a base cowardly Villain, for had *Low*'s Sloop fought half so briskly as *Harris*'s had done, (as they were under a solemn Oath to do,) the Man of War, in my Opinion, could never have hurted them.

The *Greyhound* carried in their Prize to *Rhode Island,* to the great Joy of the whole Province, tho' it had been more compleat, if the great *LOW* himself had grac'd the Triumph. The Prisoners were strongly secured in a Goal, till a Court of Vice-Admiralty could be held for their Tryals, which begun on the 10th of *July,* at *Newport,* and continued three Days. The Court was made up of the following Gentlemen.

William Dummer, Esq; Lieutenant Governor of the *Massachusets,* President.
Nathaniel Paine, Esq;
Addington Davonport, Esq;
Thomas Fitch, Esq;
Spencer Phipps, Esq;
John Lechmere, Esq; Surveyor-General.
John Valentine, Esq; Advocate-General.
Samuel Cranston, Governor of *Rhode-Island.*
John Menzies, Esq; Judge of the Admiralty,
Richard Ward, Esq; Register.
Mr. *Jahleel Brinton,* Provost-Marshal.
Robert Auchmuta, Esq; was assigned, by the Court, Council for the Prisoners here under mention'd.

Prisoners Names.	Ages.	Places of Birth.
*Charles Harris,*Captain	25	London.
William Blads	28	Rhode-Island.
Daniel Hide	23	Virginia.
*Thomas Powel,*jun.	21	Connecticut N. E.
Stephen Mundon	20	London.
Thomas Huggit	30	London.
William Read	35	Londonderry, Ireland.
Peter Kneeves	32	*Exeter*in*Devon.*
James Brinkly	28	*Suffolk*in*England.*
Joseph Sound	28	City of*Westminster.*
William Shutfield	40	*Lancafter*in*England.*
Edward Eaton	38	*Wrexham*in*Wales.*
John Brown	29	County of*Durham.*
Edward Lawson	20	Isle of Man.

Owen Rice	27	South-Wales.
John Tomkins	23	Gloucestershire.
John Fitzgerrald	21	*Limerick* in *Ireland*.
Abraham Lacy	21	Devonshire.
Thomas Linister	21	Lancashire.
Francis Leyton	39	New-York.
John Waters, Quart.-Mr.	35	County of *Devon*.
William Jones	28	London.
Charles Church	21	St. *Margaret*'s, *Westm.*
Thomas Hazel	50	———
John Bright	25	———

These 25 were found guilty, and executed the 19th of *July,* 1723, near *Newport* in *Rhode-Island.*

John Brown	17	Liverpoole.
Patrick Cunningham	25	———

These two were found guilty, but respited for one Year, and recommended to the King's Favour.

John Wilson	23	*New-London* County
Henry Barnes	22	Barbadoes.
Thomas Jones	17	*Flur* in *Wales.*
Joseph Switzer	24	*Boston* in *New-England.*
Thomas Mumper Indian.		*Mather's Vineyard* N. E.
John Hincher, Doctor	22	Near *Edinburgh, Scot.*
John Fletcher	17	———
Thomas Child	15	———

These eight were found Not Guilty.

The destroying this Pyrate was look'd upon by the Province, to be of such a signal Service to the Public, and particular Advantage to the Colony of *New-York,* that it was thought necessary to make some handsome Acknowledgement to Captain *Peter Solgard* for it; and therefore it was resolved, in an Assembly of the Common-Council, to compliment him with the Freedom of their Corporation. The Resolution, together with the Preamble of the Captain's Freedom, being curious in their Kind, I subjoin them for the Satisfaction of the Reader.

Resolution of the Mayor and Common-Council of the City of *New-York,* at a Common-Council held at the City Hall of the said City, on *Thursday* the 25th of *July, Anno. Dom.* 1723.

Present *Robert Walter,* Esq; Mayor.

City of New-York, *ss.*

This court having taken into their Consideration the great Service lately done to this Province in particular, as well as to all other his Majesty's good Subjects in general, by Captain Peter Solgard, *Commander of his Majesty's Ship the* Greyhound, *the Station Ship of the Province, who lately in a Cruize* upon this Coast, in due Execution and Discharge of his Duty, upon Intelligence given him, sought for, pursued and engaged two Pyrate Sloops, commanded by one Low, *(a notorious and inhumane Pyrate,)* one of which Sloops he took, after a resolute Resistance, and very much shattered the other, who by the Favour of the Night escaped. Twenty six of which Pyrates so taken, being lattly executed at Rhode Island, *not only eased this City and Province of a very great Trouble, but of a very considerable Expence,* &c. *It is therefore resolved (*Nemine Contradicente*) that this Corporation do present the said Captain* Solgard *with the Freedom of this Corporation, as a Mark of the great Esteem they have for his Person, as well as for the aforesaid great and good Services;*

and that the Seal of the said Freedom be enclosed in a Gold Box; that Mr. Recorder *and Mr.* Bickley *do draw the Draught of the said Freedom, signifying therein, the grateful Sense of this Corporation, for so signal a Service to the Public, and Benefit and Advantage of Mankind. That Alderman* Kip, *and Alderman* Cruger, *do prepare the said Box; that the Arms of the Corporation be engraved on one Side thereof, and a Representation of the Engagement on the other, with this Motto,* (viz.) (Quesitos Humani Generos Hostes Debellare superbum, 10 Junii, 1723.) *That the Town-Clerk cause the same Freedom to be handsomly engrossed on Parchment, and that the whole Corporation do wait upon him, to present the saine.*

By Order of the Common-Council.
William Sharpas, *Clerk.*

The Preamble of Captain Peter Solgard's Copy of his Freedom

Robert Walter, Esq; Mayor, and the Aldermen of the City of *New-York.*

City of *New-York, ss.*
TO all whom these Persents shall come, send Greeting.

WHEREAS, *Captain* Peter Solgard, *Commander of his Majesty's Ship the* Greyhound, *(the present Station Ship of this Province,) in his Cruize, having Intelligence of two Pyrate Sloops of considerable Force in Consortship, under the Command of one* Low, *a notorious Pyrate, that had for upward of two Years, committed many Depredations, Murders and Barbarities, upon many of his Majesty's Subjects and Allies, lately come upon this Coast, hath, with great Diligence, and utmost Application, pursued, overtaken, and after a stubborn Resistance, vanquished and overcome both of them, taking one, and driving the other from our Coast; which Action, as it is glorious in it self, so it is glorious in the public Benefits and Advantages that slow from it, (to wit) The Safety and Freedom of our own Trade and Commerce, and of all the neighbouring Provinces on this Continent, such signal Service done against the Enemies of Mankind, merits the Applause of all good Men, but more immediately from those of this Province, who are appointed his particular Care and Charge.* WE *therefore, the Mayor, Aldermen and Commonalty of the City of* New-York, *assembled in Common Council, to express our grateful Sense and Acknowledgment, to the said Captain* Peter Solgard, *for so noble and faithful a Discharge of his Duty, and as a particular Mark of the great Esteem and just Regard we bear to his kind Acceptance of the Freedom of the Corporation of this City of* New-York, *and that he will please to become a Fellow Citizen with us.* These are therefore *to certify and declare, that the said Captain* Peter Solgard *is hereby admitted, received and allowed a Freeman and Citizen of the said City of* New-York, *to have, hold, enjoy and partake of all and singular Advantages, Benefits, Liberties, Privileges, Franchises, Freedoms and Immunities whatsoever, granted or belonging to the same City:* In Testimony *thereof, the said Mayor hath hereunto subscribed his Name, and caused the Seal of the said City to be affix'd the* 25th Day of July, *in the ninth Year of the Reign of our Sovereign Lord* George, *by the Grace of God, King of* Great Britain, France *and* Ireland, *Defender of the Faith,* &c. Anno. Dom. 1723.

William Sharpas, *Clerk.*
R. Walter *Mayor.*

    This narrow Escape of *Low* and his Companions, one would have thought might have brought them to a little Consideration of their black and horrid Crimes, and to look upon this Interval as an Opportunity put into their Hands by Providence, to reconcile themselves to God, by a hearty and sincere Repentance. But alass they were dead to all Goodness, and had not so much as one Spark of Virtue to stir them up to be thankful for such an eminent Deliverance: But instead thereof, vented a Million of Oaths and Curses upon the Captain of the *Greyhound,* vowing to execute Vengeance upon all they should meet with afterwards, for the Indignity he put upon them.

    The first Prey that they met with, after their Flight, was a small Sloop belonging to *Nantucket,* a Whale-Fishing, about 80 Miles from Land; the Master of which, one *Nathan Skiff,* a brisk young Fellow, the Pyrates cruelly whipp'd naked about the Deck, making his Torture their Sport; after which they cut of his Ears, and last of all shot him through the Head, and then sunk his Vessel; putting the rest of the Hands into their Whale-Boat, with a Compass, a little Water, and a few Biskets; and it being good Weather, they providentially got safe to *Nantucket,* beyond all Expectation.

    There was another Whale-Boat belonging to this Sloop last mentioned, which happened to be at some Distance from her, and perceiving what was doing, rowed with all speed to another Sloop not far off, to acquaint her with the Misfortune, that the Men might take Care of themselves; and she happily got away in Time. Some Days after, *Low* took a Fishing-Boat off of *Block Island,* but did not perpetrate so much Cruelty to her, contenting himself with only cutting off the Master's Head: But after taking two Whale-Boats near *Rhode Island,* he caused one of the Master's Bodies to be ripp'd up, and his Intrails to be taken out; and cut off the Ears of the other, and made him eat them himself with Pepper and Salt; which hard Injunction he comply'd with, without making a Word. Several other Persons he would have murthered, but Humanity prevailing in the tender Hearts of his Companions, they refused to put his savage Orders in Execution.

    From the Coast of *New-England, Low* sailed directly for *Newfoundland,* and, near Cape *Briton,* took two or three and twenty *French* Vessels; and one of them of 22 Guns he mann'd with Pyrates, making a sort of a Man of War of her; with which he scower'd the Harbours and Banks of *Newfoundland,* and took sixteen or eighteen other Ships and Vessels, all which they plundered, and some destroyed.

    Thus these inhumane Wretches went on, who could not be contented to satisfy their Avarice only, and travel in the common Road of Wickedness; but, like their Patron, the Devil, must make Mischief their Sport, Cruelty their Delight, and damning of Souls their constant Employment. Of all the piratical Crews that were ever heard of, none of the *English* Name came up to this, in Barbarity; their Mirth and their Anger had much the same Effect, for both were usually gratified with the Cries and Groans of their Prisoners; so that they almost as often murthered a Man from the Excess of good Humour, as out of Passion and Resentment; and the Unfortunate could never be assured of Safety from them, for Danger lurked in their very Smiles. An Instance of this had liked to have happened to one Captain *Graves,* Master of a *Virginia* Ship last taken; for as soon as he came aboard of the Pyrate, *Low* takes a Bowl of Punch in his Hand, and drinks to him, saying, *Captain* Graves, *here's half this to you.* But the poor Gentleman being too sensibly touched at the Misfortune of falling into his Hands, modestly desired to be excused, for that he could not drink; whereupon *Low* draws out a Pistol, cocks it, and with the Bowl in 'tother Hand, told him, he should either take one or the other: So *Graves,* without Hesitation, made Choice of the Vehicle that contained the Punch, and guttled down about a Quart, when he had the least Inclination that ever he had in his Life to be merry.

    The latter End of *July,* (1723,) *Low* took a large Ship, called the *Merry Christmas,* and fitted her for a Pyrate, cut several Ports in her, and mounted her with 34 Guns. *Low* goes aboard of this Ship, assumes the Title of Admiral, and hoists a black Flag, with the Figure of Death in red, at the Main-topmast Head, and takes another Voyage to the *Western Islands,* where he arrived the Beginning of *September*. The first Vessel he met with there, was a Brigantine, formerly an *English* Sloop, commanded by *Elias Wild,* but lately bought by a *Portuguese* Nobleman, and altered: She was manned partly with *English,* and partly *Portuguese;* the latter *Low* caused to be hang'd, by Way of Reprisal, for some of his own Men sent thither in a Sloop from the *Cape de Verd* Islands, as has been mentioned: The *English* Men he thrust into their own Boat, to shift for themselves, and set Fire to the Vessel.

At St. *Michaels,* they sent in their Boats and cut out of the Road, a new *London* built Ship of 14 Guns, commanded by Captain *Thompson,* who was taken there the Year before, by *Low,* in the *Rose* Pink. The Boats had fewer Men than the Ship, and Captain *Thompson* would have defended himself, but his Men through Cowardize, or too great an Inclination of becoming Pyrates themselves, refused to stand by him, and he was obliged to surrender; and when he came aboard the Pyrate, had his Ears cut off close to his Head, for only proposing to resist Admiral *Low*'s black Flag; they gave him one of his own Boats, and burnt his Ship.

The next was a *Portuguese* Bark that fell into their Hands, whose Men came off somewhat better than usual, for they only cut them with their Cutlashes, out of Wantonness, turned them all into their Boat, and set their Vessel on Fire. When the Boat was going from the Side of the Ship, one of *Low*'s Men, who, we may suppose, was forced into his Gang, was drinking with a Silver Tankard at one of the Ports, and took his Opportunity to drop into the Boat among the *Portuguese,* and lye down in the Bottom, in order to escape along with them: After he had stowed himself in the Boat, so as not to be seen, it came into his Head, that the Tankard might prove of some Use to him, where he was going; so he got up again, laid hold of the Utensil, and went off, without being discover'd: In which Attempt had he failed, no doubt his Life, if not the Lives of all the People in the Boat, would have paid for it: The Name of this Man is *Richard Hains*.

Low took his old Tour to the *Canaries, Cape de Verd* Islands, and so to the Coast of *Guiney;* but nothing extraordinary happened till they arrived near *Sierraleon* in *Africa,* where they met with a Ship call'd the *Delight,* Captain *Hunt* Commander; this Ship they thought fit for their own Purpose, for she had been a small Man of War, and carried 12 Guns; however, they mounted 16 on Board her, mann'd her with 60 Men, and appointed one *Spriggs,* who was then their Quarter-Master, to be Captain of her, who, two Days after, separated from the Admiral, and went to the *West-Indies* a-pirating, upon his own, and particular Company's, Account, where for the present we shall leave him.

In *January* last, *Low* took a Ship, called the *Squirrel,* Captain *Stephenson;* but what became of him afterwards, I can't tell; we have had no News concerning him come to *England,* since this I have now mentioned; but I have heard that he talk'd of going to *Brazil;* and if so, it is likely we may too soon hear of some Exploit or other; tho' the best Information we could receive, would be, that he and all his Crew were at the Bottom of the Sea.

Chap. XV
Of Capt. *John Evans,* And his Crew

>Begins with House-breaking. Seizes a Sloop. Robs a House the same Night. Put to Sea, and take valuable Prizes. Evans spot dead by his Boatswain. His Death reveng'd. The Company breaks up.

John Evans was a *Welch* Man, had been formerly Master of a Sloop belonging to *Nevis,* but losing his Employ there, he sailed for some Time out of *Jamaica* as Mate, till happening in Company of three or four of his Comrades, and Wages not being so good as formerly, and Births scarce, because of the great Number of Seamen; they agreed to go abroad in search of Adventures. They sailed, or rather rowed out of *Port Royal* in *Jamaica,* the latter End of *September* 1722, in a Canoa; and coming on the North-Side of the Island, went ashore in the Night, broke open a House or two, and robb'd them of some Money, and every Thing else they could find that was portable, and brought the Booty on Board the Canoa.

This was very well for the first Time, but this kind of Robbery did not please so well, they wanted to get out to Sea, but having no Vessel but their Canoa, they were prevented in their laudable Design; however, they kept a good look out, and traversed the Island, in Expectation that Providence would send some unfortunate Vessel as a Sacrifice, and in a few Days their Wishes were accomplished; for at *Duns Hole,* they found a small Sloop at an Anchor, belonging to *Bermudas:* They made bold and went aboard, and *Evans* informed the Folks that belonged to her, that he was Captain of the Vessel, which was a Piece of News they knew not before. After they had put their Affairs in a proper Disposition aboard, they went ashore to a little Village for Refreshments, and lived jovially the remaining Part of the Day, at a Tavern, spending three Pistols, and then departed. The People of the House admired at the merry Guests they had got, were mightily pleased, and wished for their Company at another Time, which happened too soon for their Profit; for, in the middle of the Night, they came ashore all Hands, rifled the House, and carried what they could aboard their Sloop.

The next Day they weighed in the Sloop, aboard of which they mounted four Guns, called her the *Scowerer,* and sailed to *Hispaniola;* on the North Part of which Island they took a *Spanish* Sloop, which proved an extraordinary rich Prize, as it fell among so few Persons as this Company consisted of, for they shared upwards of 150 *l.* a Man.

In Pursuance of the Game, and beating up for the Windward Islands, the *Scowerer* met with a Ship from *New-England,* bound to *Jamaica,* 120 Tons, called the *Dove,* Captain *Diamond* Master, off *Porto Rico:* They plundered her, and strengthened their own Company, by taking out the Mate, and two or three other Men; they discharged the Prize, and run into one of the Islands for fresh Water and Necessaries, and staid there some Time.

The next Prize they made, was the *Lucretia and Catherine,* Captain *Mills,* of 200 Ton Burthen; they came up with her near the Island *Disseada, January* 11th. Upon seizing of this Ship, the Pyrates began to take upon themselves the Distribution of Justice, examining the Men concerning their Master's Usage of them, according to the Custom of other Pyrates; but the Captain over-hearing the Matter, put an End to the judicial Proceedings, and fell to rumaging the Ship, saying to them, *What have we to do to turn Reformers, 'tis Money we want?* And speaking to the Prisoners, he asked them, *Does your Captain give you Victuals enough?* And they answering in the Affirmative: *Why then,* said he, *he ought to give you Work enough.*

After the taking of this Prize, they went to the little Island of *Avis,* with a Design to clean, and carried the *Lucretia* along with them, in order to heave down the *Scowerer* by her; but meeting there with a Sloop, the Pyrate gave Chace till the Evening, when she was within Gun-Shot of her; but fearing to lose Company with the *Lucretia,* who was a heavy Sailor, they left off, and saw her no more. This Chace brought them to Leeward of their Port, so that they were obliged to look out for another Place of Retreat, and the Island of *Ruby* not being far distant, they steered for that, and anchored there accordingly; but the next Day a *Dutch* Sloop coming as it were, into their Mouths, they could not forbear dealing, and so making her their Prize, they plundered her of what came, when shared, to fifty Pounds a Man.

They found this Sloop more for their Purpose than the *Lucretia,* to clean their own Sloop by, as being much lower in the Wast, and therefore capable of heaving her Bottom farther out of the Water, so she was discharged, and the *Dutch* Man kept in her Room; but not thinking it convenient to lay up here, for fear a discovery should be made, they turned their Thoughts another Way, and steered to the Coast of *Jamaica,* where they took a Sugar Drover, and then run to the *Grand Caimanes,* about 30 Leagues to Leeward of *Jamaica,* with Intention to clean there; but an unhappy Accident put an End to their Pyracies, which hitherto had proved very successful to them.

The Boatswain of the Pyrate being a noisy surly Fellow, the Captain had at several TimesWords with him, relating to his Behaviour, who thinking himself ill treated, not only returned ill Language, but also challenged the Captain to fight him on the next Shore they came to, with Pistols and Sword, as is the Custom among these Outlaws. When the Sloop arrived, as abovementioned, the Captain proposed the Duel; but the cowardly Boatswain refused to fight, or go ashore, tho' it was his own Challenge. When Captain *Evans* saw there was nothing to be done with him, he took his Cane, and gave him a hearty drubbing; but the Boatswain not being able to bear such an Indignity, drew out a Pistol and shot *Evans* thro' the Head, so that he fell down dead; and the Boatswain immediately jumped over-board, and swam towards the Shore; but the Boat was quickly mann'd and sent after him, which took him up and brought him aboard.

The Death of the Captain in that Manner, provoked all the Crew, and they resolved the Criminal should die by the most exquisite Tortures; but while they were considering of the Punishment, the Gunner, transported with Passion, discharged a Pistol, and shot him thro' the Body; but not killing him outright, the Delinquent in very moving Words, desired a Week for Repentance only; but another stepping up to him, told him, *that he* should repent and be damned to him, and without more ado shot him dead.

I should have observed, that when the Lucretia and Katharine was suffered to go away, the Pyrates detained their Mate, who was now the only Man aboard, who understood Navigation, and him they desired to take upon him the Command of the Sloop, in the Room of Captain *Evans* deceased; but he desired to be excused that Honour, and at length positively refused it; so they agreed to break up the Company, and leave the Mate in Possession of the Vessel: Accordingly they went ashore at the *Caimanes,* carrying with them about nine thousand Pounds among thirty Persons; and it being fair Weather, the Mate and a Boy brought the Vessel into *Port Royal,* in *Jamaica.*

Chap. XVI
Of Captain *John Phillips,* And his Crew

Phillips his Original. How he became a Pyrate. His Return to England accounted for. Ships again for Newfoundland. Deserts his Ship in Peter Harbour. He and four others seize a Vessel. Sail out a pirating. Articles sworn to upon a Hatchet. A Copy of the Articles. Ill Blood amongst them, and why. Are almost starved. Take Prizes. Phillips proposes to clean at Tobago, and why. Meets an old Acquaintance. Frighten'd from the Island. A Conspyracy to run away with the Prize. A Skirmish. The Carpenter's Dexterity in cutting off Legs. Fern kill'd by Phillips, and why. The Danger of attempting an Escape among the Pyrates. Captain Mortimer's Bravery, and hard Fate. Captain Mortimer's Brother escapes, and how. Cheeseman's Steps for overthrowing the Pyrates Government. A Digression concerning Newfoundland, and its Trade. The Pyrates recruited with Men from thence. Phillips his Conscience pricks him. Dependence Ellery, a Saint, oblig'd to dance by the Pyrates. A brave Action perform'd by Cheesemen. Carries the Pyrate Ship into Boston. The dying Declarations of John Rose Archer, and William White.

John Phillips was bred a Carpenter, and sailing to *Newfoundland* in a West-Country Ship, was taken by *Anstis* in the *Good Fortune* Brigantine, the next Day after he had left his Consort and Commadore, Captain *Roberts*. *Phillips* was soon reconciled to the Life of a Pyrate, and being a brisk Fellow, was appointed Carpenter of the Vessel, for at first his Ambition reach'd no higher; there he remain'd till they broke up at *Tabago,* and was one of those who came home in a Sloop that we have mentioned to be sunk in *Bristol* Channel.

His Stay was not long in *England,* for whilst he was paying his first Visits to his Friends in *Devonshire,* he heard of the Misfortune of some of his Companions, that is, of their being taken and committed to *Bristol* Goal; and there being good Reason for his apprehending Danger from a Wind that blew from the same Quarter, he mov'd off immediately to *Topsham,* the nearest Port, and there shipp'd himself with one Captain *Wadham,* for a Voyage to *Newfoundland,* and home again; which, by the way, Mr. *Phillips* never design'd to perform, or to see *England* any more. When the Ship came to *Peter* Harbour in *Newfoundland* aforesaid, he ran away from her, and hired himself a Splitter in the Fishery, for the Season: But this was only till he could have an Opportunity of prosecuting his intended Rogueries; in order to which, he combined with several others, in the same Employ, to go off with one of the Vessels that lay in the Harbour, upon the piratical Account; accordingly the Time was fix'd, *viz.* the 29th of *August* 1723, at Night; but whether Remorse or Fear prevented their coming together, I know not, but of sixteen Men that were in the Combination, five only kept the Appointment: Notwithstanding which, *Phillips* was for pushing forward with that small Number, assuring his Companions, that they should soon encrease their Company; and they agreeing, a Vessel was seiz'd on, and out of the Harbour they sailed.

The first Thing they had now to do, was to chuse Officers, draw up Articles, and settle their little Commonwealth, to prevent Disputes and Ranglings afterwards; so *John Phillips* was made Captain, *John Nutt,* Master, (or Navigator) of the Vessel; *James Sparks,* Gunner; *Thomas Fern,* Carpenter; and *Wiliam White* was the only private Man in the whole Crew: When this was done, one of them writ out the following Articles (which we have taken *verbatim*) and all swore to 'em upon a Hatchet for want of a Bible.

The Articles on Board the Revenge.

1. *Every Man shall obey civil Command; the Captain shall have one full Share and a half in all Prizes; the Master, Carpenter, Boatswain and Gunner ſhall have one Share and quarter.*

2. *If any Man shall offer to run away, or keep any Secret from the Company, he shall be marroon'd, with one Bottle of Powder, one Bottle of Water, one small Arm, and Shot.*

3. *If any Man shall steal any Thing in the Company, or game, to the Value of a Piece of Eight, he shall be marroon'd or shot.*

4. *If at any Time we should meet another Marrooner (that is,* Pyrate,*) that Man that shall sign his Articles without the Consent of our company, shall suffer such Punishment as the Captain and Company shall think fit.*

5. *That Man that shall strike another whilst these Articles are in force, shall receive* Moses's *Law (that is,* 40 *Stripes lacking one) on the bare Back.*

6. *That Man that shall snap his Arms, or smoak Tobacco in the Hold, without a Cap to his Pipe, or carry a Candle lighted without a Lanthorn, shall suffer the same Punishment as in the former Article.*

7. *That Man that shall not keep his Arms clean, fit for an Engagement, or neglect his Business, shall be cut off from his Share, and suffer such other Punishment as the Captain and the Company shall think fit.*

8. *If any Man shall lose a Joint in time of an Engagement, shall have* 400 *Pieces of Eight; if a Limb,* 800.

9. *If at any time you meet with a prudent Woman, that Man that offers to meddle with her, without her Consent, shall suffer present Death.*

Thus prepar'd, this bold Crew set out, and before they left the Banks they made Prize of several small Fishing-Vessels, out of which they got a few Hands, some *French* and some *English,* and then sail'd for the *West-Indies;* in one of these Vessels they took out one *John Rose Archer,* who having been a Pyrate under the famous *Black-beard,* was immediately preferr'd over other People's Heads, to be Quarter-Master to the Company; which sudden Promotion so disgusted some of the older Standers, especially *Fern,* the Carpenter, that it occasioned some Mischief to follow, as we shall show by and by.

The Pyrates came off *Barbadoes* the beginning of *October,* and cruised there, and among other Islands, above three Months, without speaking with a Vessel, so that they were almost starv'd for want of Provisions, being reduc'd to a Pound of Meat a Day between ten; at length they fell in with a *Martinico* Man of 12 Guns and 35 Hands, far superior in Force, and what they would not have ventur'd on at another Time, but *Hunger will break down Stone Walls;* they were resolved to show the *French* Men their black Flag; and if that would not do, they must seek out elsewhere; accordingly, they boldly ran up a-long-side of the Sloop, with their piratical Colours flying, and told them, if they did not strike immediately, they would give them no Quarters; which so intimidated the *Frenchmen,* that they never fired a Gun. This proved a seasonable Supply; they took her Provisions, and four of her Men, and let her go. They took presently after, a Sloop belonging to *New-York,* and a *Virginia* Man, *Huffam* Master.

Having now occasion to clean their Vessel, *Phillips* propos'd *Tobago,* where the Company he formerly belong'd to, under *Anstis* and *Fenn,* broke up; to induce them to it, he told them when he left the Island, there was left behind six or eight of their Company that were not willing to go to *England,* with three Negroes: Whereupon they sail'd to the Island, and after a careful Search, found only one of the Negroes, whose Name was *Pedro,* who inform'd Captain *Phillips,* that those that were left behind were taken by a Man of War's Crew, and hang'd at *Antegoa,* among whom was *Fenn,* their Captain.

They took *Pedro* on Board, and then fell to Business, careening their Vessel; and just as they had finished their Work, a Man of War's Boat came into the Harbour, the Ship being cruising to Leeward of the Island. It was easily guess'd upon what Errant she was sent, and therefore they lost no Time, but, as soon as the Boat went away, warp'd out, and ply'd to Windward for Security, but left the four *French* Men, they took out of the *Martinico* Sloop, behind.

In a few Days they took a Snow with a few Hands, and *Fern,* the Carpenter, one *William Phillips, Wood* and *Taylor,* went aboard to take Possession of her. *Fern,* not forgetting the Affront of having *Archer* preferr'd before him, resolv'd to go off with the Prize, and brought the rest into the same Measures; however *Phillips,* the Captain, keeping a good Look-out, perceiv'd their Design, and gave them Chace, who coming up with the Vessel, a Skirmish ensu'd, wherein *Wood* was kill'd and *Taylor* wounded in his Leg; upon which the other two surrender'd. There was no Surgeon aboard, and therefore it was advis'd, upon a learned Consultation, that *Phillips*'s Leg should be cut off; but who should perform the Operation was the Dispute; at length the Carpenter was appointed, as the most proper Man: Upon which, he fetch'd up the biggest Saw, and taking the Limb under his Arm, fell to Work, and separated it from the Body of the Patient, in as little Time as he could have cut a Deal Board in two; after that he heated his Ax red hot in the Fire, and cauteriz'd the Wound, but not with so much Art as he perform'd the other Part, for he so burnt his Flesh distant from the Place of Amputation, that it had like to have mortify'd; however nature perform'd a Cure at last without any other Assistance.

From *Tobago* they stood away to the Northward and took a *Portugueze* bound for *Brazil,* and two or three Sloops from *Jamaita,* in one of which, *Fern* the Carpenter, endeavouring to go off, was kill'd by *Phillips* the Captain, pursuant to their Articles; another had the same Fate some Days after for the like Attempt. These Severities made it dangerous for any to consult or project an Escape; the Terror of which made several sign their Articles and set down quietly, waiting impatiently for Redemption, which as yet they saw no great likelyhood of, and should they have been taken before such Circumstances appear'd in their Actions or Characters, as afterwards happen'd, to denote their Innocence, they might have lost their Lives upon a Tryal at a Court of Admiralty; for pretty strong Evidence is expected in their Favour, to ballance that of being taken aboard a Vessel which is prov'd to be in actual Pyracy, and they assisting therein.

Thus was many an honest Man's Case made most desperate by the consummate Villany of a few hardned Wretches, who fear neither God or Devil, as this *Phillips* us'd often blasphemously to express himself.

On the 25th of *March* they took two Ships from *Virginia* for *London, John Phillips,* the Pyrate Captain's Namesake, was Master of one, and Captain *Robert Mortimer,* the other, a brisk young Fellow, that deserv'd a better Fate than he met with. *Phillips* the Pyrate staid on Board of Captain *Mortimer*'s Ship, while they transported the Crew to the Sloop, and the Boat returning along side, one of the Pyrates therein calls to *Phillips,* and tells him, there was a Mutiny aboard their Vessel, *Mortimer* had two Men in his Ship, and the Pyrate Captain had two, therefore thought it a good Opportunity to recover his Ship, and directly took up a Handspike and struck *Phillips* over the Head, giving him a dangerous wound, but not knocking him down, he recovered and wounded *Mortimer* with his Sword; and the two Pyrates that were aboard coming in to Captain *Phillips*'s Assistance, Captain *Mortimer* was presently cut to Pieces, while his own two Men stood by and did nothing.

This was the first Voyage that *Mortimer* had the Command of a Vessel, by whose Death is a poor disconsolate Widow made miserable, more in regard of the mutual Love and Fidelity they lived in, than the Loss of what would have been a handsome and comfortable Provision for themselves and Children, which, I think, now ought to be made up by the Public, since 'twas in the public Service he fell; for had his Attempt succeeded, in all Probability he would not only have regained his own Ship, but entirely subdued and destroy'd the Enemy, there being several, as it afterwards proved, that would have seconded such an Enterprize when ever they found a Beginning made.

This Affair ended without any other Consequence than a strict Search after a Brother of Captain *Mortimer,* who was on Board, in order to have put him likewise to death; but he had the good Fortune to meet with a Townsman among the Crew, who hid him for four and twenty

Hours in a Stay-Sail, till the Heat of their Fury was over, and by that Means happily missed of the Fate designed him.

Out of the other *Virginia* Man before spoken of, they took one *Edward Cheeseman,* a Carpenter, to supply the Place of their late Carpenter, *Fern.* He was a modest sober young Man, very averse to their unlawful Practice, and a brave gallant Fellow.

There was one *John Philmore* of *Ipswich,* formerly taken by them, ordered to row *Cheeseman* aboard of *Mortimer*'s Ship, which the Pyrates possess'd themselves of, who, seeing with what Reluctance and Uneasiness *Cheeseman* was brought away, told him, he would join with him, in some Measures, to over-throw the piratical Government, telling him withal, their present Condition, what Difficulties *Phillips* had met with to make up his Company, and how few voluntary Pyrates there were on Board, and the like. But, however specious this seemed, *Cheeseman* out of Prudence rejected his Offers of Assistance, till he saw some Proofs of his Sincerity, which after a few Days he was convinced of, and then they often consulted; but as the old Pyrates were always jealous of the new Comers, and consequently observant of their Behaviour; this was done with the utmost Caution, chiefly when they were lying down together, as tho' asleep, and, at other Times, when they were playing at Cards; both which they feigned often to do for that Purpose.

The Pyrates went on all the while, plundering and robbing several Ships and Vessels, bending their Course towards *Newfoundland,* where they designed to raise more Men, and do all the Mischief they could on the Banks, and in the Harbours.

Newfoundland is an Island on the North Continent of *America,* contained between the 46 and 538 of N. Latitude, discovered first by St. *Sebastion Cabot* A. D. 1497, but never settled till the Year 1610; when Mr. *Guy* of *Bristol* revived the Affair, and obtained a Patent, and himself to be Governor. The Island is deserted by the Natives and neglected by us, being desolate and Woody, and the Coast and Harbour only held for the Conveniency of the Cod Fishery, for which alone they were settled.

The Bays and Harbours about it, are very numerous and convenient, and being deeply indented, makes it easy for any Intelligence quickly to pass from one Harbour to another over Land; especially the principal, St. *John*'s and *Placentia,* when the Appearance of an Enemy makes them apprehend Danger.

They are able to cure and export about 100000 Quintals (100 Weight each) of Fish, annually, which returns to *England* in Money, or the necessary Commodities of *Portugal, Spain* and *Italy.* As it therefore expends abundance of Rum, Molossus and Sugar, the Product of our *West-India* Colonies, and employs a Number of Fishermen from home every Season, by whose Industry and Labour only this Fish is purchased, it may very well be reckon'd an advantagious Branch of Trade.

But the present Design of this Digression being not to give an exact Description of the Country or Fishery; but rather how it accidentally contributes to raise, or support the Pyrates already rais'd, I shall observe,

First, That our West Country Fishing-Ships, *viz.* from *Topsham, Barnstable* and *Bristol,* who chiefly attend the Fishing Seasons, transport over a considerable Number of poor Fellows every Summer, whom they engage at low Wages, and are by their Terms to pay for Passage back to *England.* When the *Newfoundland* Ships left that Country, towards Winter, in the Year 1720, these Passengers muster'd 1100, who, during the Season of Business, (the Hardness of their Labour, and Chilness of the Nights, pinching them very much) are mostly fond of drinking Black Strap, (a strong Liquor used there, and made from Rum, Molossus, and Chowder Beer;) by this the Majority of them out-run the Constable, and then are necessitated to come under hard Articles of Servitude for their Maintenance in the Winter; no ordinary Charge, indeed, when the Barrenness of the Country is consider'd, and the Stock of Provision laid in, happen to fall short, in Proportion to the Computation made of the People remaining there the Winter, which are generally about 17 or 1800. The Masters residing there think Advantages taken on their Necessities, no more than a just and lawful Gain; and either bind such for the next Summer's Service, or sell their Provisions out to them at extravagant Rates; Bread from 15s.

to 50, immediately at the departing of the Ships, and so of other sorts of Food in Proportion; wherefore not being able to subsist themselves, or in any likely Way of clearing the Reckoning to the Masters, they sometimes run away with Shallops and Boats, and begin on piratical Exploits, as *Phillips* and his Companions, whom we are now treating of, had done.

And secondly (which is more opportunely for them,) they are visited every Summer, almost, by some Set of Pyrates or other, already rais'd, who call here for the same Purpose, (if young Beginners) and to lay in a Store of Water and Provisions, which they find imported, much or little, by all the Ships that use the Trade.

Towards this Country *Phillips* was making his Way, and took on the Voyage, besides those abovementioned, one *Salter*, in a Sloop off the Isle of *Sables*, which Vessel they made use of themselves, and gave back *Mortimer*'s Ship to the Mate and Crew. The same Day, *viz.* the 4th of *April*, took a Scooner, one *Chadwell*, Master, which they scuttled, in order to sink; but Capt. *Phillips* understanding that she belong'd to Mr. *Minors* at *Newfoundland*, with whose Vessel they first went off a pirating, a Qualm of Conscience came athwart his Stomach, and he said to his Companions, *We have done him Injury enough already;* so order'd the Vessel immediately to be repair'd, and return'd her to the Master.

That Afternoon they chac'd another Vessel, and at Night came up with her, the Master of which was a Saint of *New-England,* nam'd *Dependance Ellery,* who taking *Phillips* for a Pyrate, he told him was the Reason that he gave him the Trouble of chacing so long; which being resented by these Men of Honour, they made poor *Dependance* dance about the Deck till he was weary.

Within few Days several other Vessels had the same Misfortune, the Masters Names were as follow, *Joshua Elwell, Samuel Elwell,* Mr. *Combs,* Mr. *Lansly, James Babston, Edward Freeman,* Mr. *Start, Obediah Beal, Erick Erickson* and *Benjamin Wheeler.*

The 14th of *April* they took a Sloop belonging to Cape *Ann, Andrew Harradine* Master; they look'd upon this Vessel more fit for their Purpose, and so came aboard, keeping only the Master of her Prisoner, and sending *Harradine*'s Crew away in *Salter*'s Vessel, which they, till this Time, detain'd. To this *Harradine, Cheeseman* the Carpenter, broke his Mind, and brought him into the Confederacy to destroy the Crew, which was put in Execution four Days afterwards.

Harradine and the rest were for doing the Business in the Night, as believing they might be more opportunely surpriz'd; for *Nut,* the Master, being a Fellow of great Strength, and no less Courage, it was thought dangerous to attack him without Fire-Arms; however, *Cheeseman* was resolute to have it perform'd by Day-light, as the least liable to Confusion; and as to the Master, he offer'd to lay Hands on him first: Upon this 'twas concluded on, 12 at Noon was the appointed Time; in order for the Business *Cheeseman* leaves his working Tools on the Deck, as though he had been going to use them, and walked aft; but perceiving some Signs of Timidity in *Harradine,* he comes back, fetches his Brandy Bottle and gives him and the rest a Dram, then drnak to *Burril,* the Boatswain, and the Master, *To their next merry Meeting,* and up he puts the Bottle; then he takes a Turn with *Nut,* asking what he thought of the Weather, and such like. In the mean while *Filemore* takes up the Axe, and turns it round upon the Point, as if at Play, then both he and *Harradine* wink at him, thereby letting him know they were ready; upon which Signal he seizes *Nut* by the Collar, with one Hand between his Legs, and toss'd him over the Side of the Vessel, but, he holding by *Cheeseman*'s Sleeve, said, *Lord have Mercy upon me! what are you going to do, Carpenter?* He told him it was an unnecessary Question, *For,* says he, *Master, you are a dead Man,* so strikes him over the Arm, *Nut* looses his Hold, tumbles into the Sea, and never spoke more.

By this time the Boatswain was dead; for as soon as *Filemore* saw the Master laid hold of, he raised up the Axe, and divided his Enemy's Head in two: The Noise brought the Captain upon Deck, whom *Cheeseman* saluted with the Blow of a Mallet, which broke his Jaw-Bone, but did not knock him down; *Harradine* came in then with the Carpenter's Adds, but *Sparks,* the Gunner, interposing between him and Captain *Phillips, Cheeseman* trips up his Heels, and flung him into the Arms of *Charles Jvymay,* one of his Consorts, who that Instant discharg'd him into the Sea; and at the same Time *Harradine* compassed his Business with the Captain aforesaid: *Cheeseman* lost no Time, but from the Deck jumps into the Hold, and was about to beat out the Brains of *Archer,* the Quarter-Master, having struck him two or three Blows with his blunt Weapon the Mallet, when *Harry Giles,* a young Lad, came down after him, and desir'd his Life might be spar'd, as an Evidence of their own Innocence; that he having all the Spoil and Plunder in his Custody, it may appear, that these tragick Proccedings were not undertaken with any dishonest View of seizing or appropriating the Effects to themselves; which prudent Advice prevail'd, and he and three more were made Prisoners, and secured.

The Work being done, they went about Ship, altered the Course from *Newfoundland* to *Boston,* and arrived safe the 3d of *May* following, to the great Joy of that Province.

On the 12th of *May,* 1724, a special Court of Admiralty was held for the Tryal of these Pyrates, when *John Filmore, Edward Cheeseman, John Combs, Henry Giles, Charles Ivymay, John Bootman,* and *Henry Payne,* the seven that confederated together for the Pyrates Destruction, were honourably acquitted; as also three *French* Men, *John Baptis, Peter Taffery,* and *Isaac Lassen,* and three Negroes, *Pedro, Francisco,* and *Pierro.* And *John Rose Archer,* the Quarter-Master, *William White, William Taylor,* and *William Phillips,* were condemned; the two latter were reprieved for a Year and a Day, in order to be recommended (though I don't know for what) as Objects of his Majesty's Mercy. The two former were executed on the 2d of *June,* and dy'd very penitently, making the following Declarations at the Place of Execution, with the Assistance of two grave Divines that attended them.

The dying Declarations of John Rose Archer and William White, on the Day of their Exetion at Boston, June 2, 1724, for the Crimes of Pyracy.

First, separately, of Archer.

I Greatly bewail my Profanations of the Lord's Day, and my Disobedience to my Parents.

And my Cursing and Swearing, and my blasperning the Name of the glorious God.

Unto which I have added, the Sins of Unchastity. And I have provoked the Holy One, at length, to leave me unto the Crimes of Pyracy and Robbery; wherein, at last, I have brought my self under the Guilt of Murder also.

But one Wickedness that has led me as much as any, to all the rest, has been my brutish Drunkenness. By strong Drink I have been heated and hardened into the Crimes that are now more bitter than Death unto me.

I could wish that Masters of Vessels would not use their Men with so much Severity, as many of them do, which exposes to great Temptations.

And then of White.

I am now, with Sorrow, reaping the Fruits of my Disobedience to my Parents, who used their Endeavours to have me instructed in my Bible, and my Catechism.

And the Fruits of my neglecting the public Worship of God, and prophaning the holy Sabbath.

And of my blaspheming the Name of God, my Maker.

But my Drunkenness has had a great Hand in bringing my Ruin upon me. I was drunk when I was enticed aboard the Pyrate.

And now, for all the vile Things I did aboard, I own the Justice of God and Man, in what is done unto me.

Of both together

We hope, we truly hate the Sins, whereof we have the Burthen lying so heavy upon our Consciences.

We warn all People, and particularly young People, against such Sins as these. We wish, all may take Warning by us.

We beg for Pardon, for the sake of Christ, our Saviour; and our Hope is in him alone. Oh! *that in his Blood our Scarlet and Crimson Guilt may be all washed away!*

We are sensible of an hard Heart in us, full of Wickedness. And we look upon God for his renewing Grace upon us.

We bless God for the Space of Repentance which he has given us; and that he has not cut us off in the Midst and Heighth of our Wickedness.

We are not without Hope, that God has been savingly at work upon our Souls.

We are made sensible of our absolute Need of the Righteousness of Christ; that we may stand justified before God in that. We renounce all Dependance on our own.

We are humbly thankful to the Ministers of Christ, for the great Pains they have taken for our Good. The Lord Reward their Kindness.

We don't Despair of Mercy; but hope, through Christ, that when we dye, we shall find Mercy with God, and be received into his Kingdom.

We wish others, and especially the Sea-faring, may get Good by what they see this Day befalling of us.

Declared in the Presence of J. W. D. M.

Chap. XVII
Of Captain *Spriggs,* And his Crew

>Spriggs his Beginning. How he set up for himself. Sweats his Prisoners for Diversion. The Pyrates mistake in drinking Healths. Take Hawkins a second time. Burn his Ship, and why. An odd Entertainment given him by the Pyrates. Captain Hawkins how disposed of. Spriggs barbarous Usage of his Prisoners. Takes a Ship loaden with Horses. An odd Frolic of the Pyrates. Two particular Relations of Pyracy .

Spriggs sailed with *Low* for a pretty while, and I believe came away from *Lowther,* along with him; he was Quarter-Master to the Company, and consequently had a great Share in all the Barbarities committed by that execrable Gang, till the Time they parted; which was about *Christmas* last, when *Low* took a Ship of 12 Guns on the Coast of *Guiney,* called the *Delight,* (formerly the *Squirrel* Man of War,) commanded by Captain *Hunt. Spriggs* took Possession of the Ship with eighteen Men, left *Low* in the Night, and came to the *West-Indies.* This Separation was occasioned by a Quarrel with *Low,* concerning a Piece of Justice *Spriggs* would have executed upon one of the Crew, for killing a Man in cold Blood, as they call it, one insisting that he should be hang'd, and the other that he should not.

A Day or two after they parted, *Spriggs* was chose Captain by the rest, and a black Ensign was made, which they called *Jolly Roger,* with the same Device that Captain *Low* carried, *viz.* a white Skeliton in the Middle of it, with a Dart in one Hand striking a bleeding Heart, and in the other, an Hour-Glass; when this was finished and hoisted, they fired all their Guns to salute their Captain and themselves, and then looked out for Prey.

In their Voyage to the *West-Indies,* these Pyrates took a *Portuguese* Bark, wherein they got valuable Plunder, but not contented with that alone, they said they would have a little Game with the Men, and so ordered them a Sweat, more for the Brutes Diversion, than the poor Men's Healths; which Operation is performed after this Manner; they stick up lighted Candles circularly round the Mizon-Mast, between Decks, within which the Patients one at a Time enter; without the Candles, the Pyrates post themselves, as many as can stand, forming another Circle, and armed with Pen-Knives, Tucks, Forks, Compasses, *&c.* and as he runs round and round, the Music playing at the same Time, they prick him with those Instuments; this usually lasts for 10 or 12 Minutes, which is as long as the miserable Man can support himself. When the Sweating was over, they gave the *Portuguese* their Boat with a small Quantity of Provisions, and set their Vessel on Fire.

Near the Island of St. *Lucia,* they took a Sloop belonging to *Barbadoes,* which they plundered, and then burnt, forcing some of the Men to sign their Articles, the others they beat and cut in a barbarous Manner, because they refused to take on with the Crew, and then sent them away in the Boat, who all got safe afterwards to *Barbadoes.*

The next was a *Martinico* Man, which they served as bad as they had done the others, but did not burn their Ship. Some Days afterwards in running down to Leeward, they took one Captain *Hawkins,* coming from *Jamaica,* loaden chiefly with Logwood; they took out of her, Stores, Arms, Ammunition, and several other Things, as they thought fit, and what they did not want they threw over-board or destroy'd; they cut the Cables to pieces, knocked down the Cabins, broke all the Windows, and in short took all the Pains in the World to be Mischievous. They took by Force, out of her, Mr. *Burridge* and Mr. *Stephens,* the two Mates, and some other Hands; and after detaining the Ship from the 22d of *March,* to the 29th, they let her go. On the 27th they took a *Rhode Island* Sloop, Captain *Pike,* and all his Men were obliged to go aboard the Pyrate; but the Mate being a grave sober Man, and not inclinable to stay, they told him, he should have his Discharge, and that it should be immediately writ on his Back; whereupon he was sentenced to receive ten Lashes from every Man in the Ship, which was rigorously put in Execution.

The next Day Mr. *Burridge,* Captain *Hawkins*'s Mate, sign'd their Articles, which was so agreeable to them (he being a good Artist and Sailor) that they gave three Huzza's, fir'd all the Guns in the Ship, and appointed him Master: The Day was spent in boysterous Mirth, roaring and drinking of Healths, among which was, by Mistake, that of King *George* the II. for you must know, now and then the Gentry are provok'd to sudden Fits of Loyalty, by the Expectation of an Act of Grace: It seems Captain *Pike* had heard at *Jamaica* that the King was dead, so the Pyrates immediately hoisted their Ensign Half-Mast (the Death Signal) and proclaim'd his Royal Highness, saying, *They doubted not but there would be a general Pardon in a twelve Month, which they would embrace and come in upon, but damn 'em if they should be excepted out of it, they would murder every* Englishman *that should fall into their Hands.*

The second of *April,* they spy'd a Sail, and gave her Chace till 12 o'Clock at Night, the Pyrates believed her to be a *Spaniard,* when they came close up to her, they discharged a Broadside, with small and great Shot, which was follow'd by another, but the Ship making a lamentable Cry for Quarters, they ceas'd firing, and ordered the Captain to come aboard, which he did, but how disappointed the Rogues were when they found 'twas their old Friend Captain *Hawkins,* whom they had sent away three Days before, worth not one Penny? This was such a Baulk to them, that they resolved he should suffer for falling in their Way, tho' it was so contrary to his own Inclinations: About 15 of them surrounded the poor Man with sharp Cutlashes, and fell upon him, whereby he was soon laid flat on the Deck; at that Instant *Burridge* flew amongst the thickest of the Villains, and begg'd earnestly for his Life, upon whose Request 'twas granted. They were now most of 'em drunk, as is usual at this Time of Night, so they unanimously agreed to make a Bonfire of *Hawkins*'s Ship, which was immediately done, and in half an Hour she was all of a Blaze.

After this, they wanted a little more Diversion, and so Captain *Hawkins* was sent for down to the Cabin to Supper; what should the Provision be, but a Dish of Candles, which he was forced to eat, having a naked Sword and a Pistol held to his Breast all the while; when this was over, they buffeted him about for some Time, and sent him forward amongst the other Prisoners, who had been treated with the same Delicacies.

Two Days afterwards, they anchor'd at a little uninhabited Island, call'd *Rattan,* near the Bay of *Honduras,* and put ashore Captain *Hawkins,* and several other Men, (one of them his Passenger) who dy'd there of the Hardships he underwent. They gave them Powder and Ball, and a Musquet, with which they were to shift as they could, sailing away the next Day for other Adventures.

Captain *Hawkins,* and his unfortunate Companions, staid 19 Days upon this Island, supplying themselves with both Fish and Fowl, such as they were, at which Time came two Men in a Canoe, that had been left upon another marroon Island near *Benacca,* who carry'd the Company at several Times thither, it being more convenient in having a good Well of fresh Water, and Plenty of Fish, *&c.* Twelve Days afterwards they spy'd a Sloop off at Sea, which, upon their making a great Smoke, stood in, and took them off; she was the *Merriam,* Captain *Jones,* lately escaped out of the Bay of *Honduras,* from being taken by the *Spaniards.*

At an Island to the Westward, the Pyrates clean'd their Ship, and sail'd towards the Island of St. *Christophers,* to wait for one Captain *Moor,* who commanded the *Eagle* Sloop, when she took *Lowther*'s upon the Careen, at *Blanco; Spriggs* resolved to put him to Death, whenever he took him, for falling upon his Friend and Brother, but instead of *Moor,* he found a *French* Man of War from *Martinico* upon the Coast, which *Spriggs* not thinking fit to contend with, run away with all the Sail he could make, the *French* Man crowded after him, and was very likely to speak with Mr. *Spriggs,* when unfortunately his Main-Top-Mast came by the Board, which obliged him to give over the Chace.

Spriggs then stood to the Northward, towards *Burmudas,* or the *Summer Isles,* and took a Scooner belonging to *Boston;* he took out all the Men and sunk the Vessel, and had the Impudence to tell the Master, that he designed to encrease his Company on the Banks of *Newfoundland,* and then would sail for the Coast of *New-England* in quest of Captain *Solgard,* who attack'd and took their Consort *Charles Harris, Spriggs* being then in *Low*'s Sloop, who very fairly run for it. The Pyrate ask'd the Master if he knew Captain *Solgard,* who answering No;

he ask'd another the same Question, and then a third, who said he knew him very well, upon which *Spriggs* ordered him to be sweated, which was done in the Manner before describ'd.

Instead of going to *Newfoundland* as the Pyrates threat'ned, they came back to the Islands, and to Windward of St. *Christophers,* on the 4th of *June* last, took a Sloop, *Nicholas Trot* Master, belonging to St. *Eustatia,* and wanting a little Diversion, they hoisted the Men as high as the Main and Fore Tops, and let them run down amain, enough to break all the Bones in their Skins, and after they had pretty well crippled them by this cruel Usage, and whipp'd them about the Deck, they gave *Trot* his Sloop, and let him go, keeping back only 2 of his Men, besides the Plunder of the Vessel.

Within two or three Days they took a Ship coming from *Rhode-Island* to St. *Christophers,* loaden with Provisions and some Horses; the Pyrates mounted the Horses and rid them about the Deck backwards and forwards a full Gallop, like Madmen at *New-Market,* cursing, swearing, and hallowing, at such a Rate, that made the poor Creatures wild, and at length, two or three of them throwing their Riders, they fell upon the Ship's Crew, and whipp'd, and cut, and beat them in a barbarous Manner, telling them, it was for bringing Horses without Boots and Spurs, for want of which they were not able to ride them.

This is the last Account we have had of Captain *Spriggs,* I shall only add the two following Relations, and conclude.

A Brigantine belonging to *Bristol,* one *Mr. Rowry* Master, had been trading at *Gambia,* in *Africa,* and falling as low as Cape *Mount,* to finish the slaving of the Vessel, he had, by a Misfortune usual at that Part of the Coast, his Mate, Surgeon, and two more of his Men,[1] *Panyarr'd* by the Negroes. The Remainder of his Company, which was not above 5 or 6 in Number, took this Opportunity, and seiz'd the Vessel in the Road, making the Master Prisoner.

You will think it prodigious impudent that so small a Number should undertake to proceed a pirating, especially when neither of them had sufficient Skill in Navigation: Yet this they did, leaving those People, their Ship-Mates abovemention'd, to the Mercy of the barbarous Natives, and sail'd away down the Coast, making them a black Flag, which they merrily said, would be as good as 50 Men more, *i. e.* would carry as much Terror; and that they did not doubt of soon increasing their Crew, to put them in an enterprizing Capacity; but their vain Projection was soon happily frustrated, and after this Manner.

The Master whose Life they had preserved, (perhaps only for supplying their own Unskillfulness in Navigation,) advised them, that since contrary to their Expectations, they had met with no Ship between *Cape Mount,* and the *Bite* of *Calabar,* to proceed to the Island of St. *Thomas*'s, where they might recruit with Provisions and Water, and sell off the Slaves (about 70 of them) which they perceived would be a useless Lumber, and incommodious to their Design. They arrived there in *August* 1721, and one Evening, while Part of them were on Shore, applying for this Purpose to the Governor, and the other Part carelesly from the Deck, Mr. *Rowry* stepp'd into the Boat belonging to the Vessel, and pushed off, very suddenly: They heard the Noise it made, and soon were upon Deck again, but having no other Boat to pursue, nor a Musket, ready to fire, he got safe on Shore, and ran to the Governor with his Complaint, who immediately imprisoned those already there, and sent a Launch off to take the rest out of the Ship.

The *Swallow* arrived at St. *Thomas*'s the Beginning of *October* following, where, on Mr. *Rowry*'s Remonstrance, Application was made to the *Portuguese* Governor of that Island, for a Surrendery of these five *English* Prisoners then in the Castle; but he not only peremptorily excused himself from it, as a Matter out of his Power, without particular Direction from the Court of *Portugal;* but withal insinuated, that they had only taken Refuge there from the Hardships and Severity they had met with from their Master. The manner of Denial, and the avaritious Temper of the Gentleman, which I had Occasion to be acquainted with, makes it very suspicious, that he proposed considerable Gains to himself; for if Mr. *Rowry* had not made such an Escape to him, the Slaves had been his for little or nothing, as a Bribe to silence his Suspicions, which any Man, less acute than he, must have had from the awkward and unskilful Carriage of such Merchants. But enough of this; perhaps he is not the only Governor abroad that finds an Interest in countenancing these Fellows.

Chap. XVIII
An Account of the Pyracies and Murders committed by *Philip Roche, &c.*

Philip Roche was born in *Ireland,* and from his Youth had been bred up to the Sea; he was a brisk genteel Fellow, of 30 Years of Age at the Time of his Death; one whose black and savage Nature did no ways answer the Comliness of his Person, his Life being almost one continued Scene of Villany, before he was discovered to have committed the horrid Murders we are now speaking of.

This inhumane Monster had been concerned with others, in insuring Ships to a great Value, and then destroying them; by which Means, and other Rogueries, he had got a little Money; and being Mate of a Ship, was dilligent enough in trading for himself between *Ireland* and *France,* so that he was in a Way of getting himself a comfortable Livelihood: But, as he resolved to be rich, and finding fair Dealing brought in Wealth but slowly, he contriv'd to put other Things in Execution, and certainly had murthered several innocent Persons in the Prosecution of his abominable Schemes; but as I have now forgot the particular Circumstances of those Relations, I shall confine my self at present to the Fact for which he suffer'd.

Roch getting acquainted with one *Neal,* a Fisherman at *Cork,* whom he found ready for any villainous Attempt, he imparted his Design to him, who being pleas'd with the Project, brings one *Pierce Cullen* and his Brother into the Confederacy, together with one *Wise,* who at first was very unwilling to come into their Measures, and, indeed, had the least Hand in the Perpetration of what follows.

They pitch'd upon a Vessel in the Harbour, belonging to *Peter Tartoue,* a *French* Man, to execute their cruel Intentions upon, because it was a small one, and had not a great Number of Hands on Board, and 'twas easy afterwards to exchange it for one more fit for Pyracy; and therefore they apply'd themselves to the Master of her, for a Passage to *Nantz,* whereto the Ship was bound; and accordingly, the Beginning of *November* 1721, they went aboard; and when at Sea, *Philip Roche* being an experienced Sailor, the Master of the Vessel readily trusted him with the Care of her, at times, while he and the Mate went to rest.

The 15th of *November,* at Night, was the Time designed for the Tragedy; but *Francis Wise* relented, and appear'd desirous to divert them from their bloody Purposes. *Roche* (sometimes called Captain) told him, *That as* Cullen *and he had sustained great Losses at Sea, unless every Irishman present would assist in repairing their Losses, by murthering all the* French *Rogues, and running away with the Ship, he should suffer the same Fate with the* French *Men; but if all would assist, all should have a Share in the Booty.* Upon this, they all resolved alike, and Captain *Roche* ordered three *Frenchmen* and a Boy up to hand the Topsails, the Master and Mate being then asleep in their Cabins, The two first that came down, they beat out their Brains and threw them over-board: The other two seeing what was done, ran up to the Topmast Head, but *Cullen* followed them, and taking the Boy by the Arm, tost him into the Sea; then driving down the Man, those below knocked him on the Head, and threw him over-board.

Those who were asleep, being awakened by the dismal Skrieks and Groans of dying Men, ran upon Deck in Confusion, to enquire into the Cause of such unusual Noises; but the same Cruelty was immediately acted towards them, e'er they could be sensible of the Danger that threat'ned them.

They were now (as *Roche* himself afterwards confess'd) *all over as wet with the Blood that had been spilt, as if they had been dipp'd in Water, or stood in a Shower of Rain, nor did they regard it any more. Roche* said, Captain *Tartoue* used many Words for Mercy, and asked them, if he had not used them with Civility and Kindness? If they were not of the same Christian Religion, and owned the same blessed *Jesus,* and the like? But they, not regarding what he said, took Cords and bound the poor Master and his Mate Back to Back, and while that was doing, both of them begged with the utmost Earnestness, and used the most solemn Intreaties, that they would at least allow them a few Minutes to say their Prayers, and beg Mercy of God for the various Sins and Offences of their Lives: But it did not move them, (though all the rest were dead, and no

Danger could be apprehended from them two alone) for the bound Persons were hurry'd up and thrown into the Sea.

The Massacre being finished, they washed themselves a little from the Blood, and searched the Chests and Lockers, and all Places about the Ship, and then set down in the Captain's Cabin, and refreshed themselves with some Rum they found there, and (as *Roche* confessed) were never merrier in their Lives. They invested *Roche* with the Command of the Ship, and calling him Captain, talked over their Liquor, what rare Actions they would perform about Cape *Briton, Sable Isle,* and the Banks of *Newfoundland,* whither they designed to go as soon as they had recruited their Company, and got a better Ship, which they proposed speedily to do.

Roche taking upon himself the Command of the Vessel, *Andrew Cullen* was to pass for a Merchant or Super-cargo; but when they bethought themselves, that they were in Danger of being discovered by the Papers of the Ship, relating to the Cargo, as Bills of Lading, *&c.* therefore they erase and take out the Name of the *French* Master, and instead thereof, inserted the Name of *Roche,* so that it stood in the Ship's Papers, *Peter Roche* Master; that then having so few Hands on Board, they contrived if they met any Ships, to give out, that they had lost some Hands by their being washed overboard in a Storm, and by that Means screen themselves from being suspected of having committed some such wicked Act, by Reason of the Fewness of their Hands on Board; and also might prevail with some Ship to spare them some, on Consideration of their pretended Disaster.

In going to *Cales* they were in Distress by the Weather, and being near *Lisbon,* they made Complaint to a Ship, but obtained no Assistance. They were then obliged to sail back for *England,* and put into the Port of *Dartmouth;* but then they were in fear least they might be discovered, therefore to prevent that, they resolve to alter the Ship, and getting Workmen, they take down the Mizzen-Mast, and build a Spar Deck, and made Rails, (on pretence that the Sailors had been wash'd overboard) to secure the Men. Then they took down the Image of St. *Peter* at the Head of the Ship, and put up a Lion in its Place, and painted over the Stern of the Ship with Red, and new nam'd her the *Mary* Snow. The Ship being thus alter'd that they thought it could not be known, they fancy'd themselves pretty secure; but wanting Money to defray the Charge of these Alterations, *Roche,* as Master of the Vessel, and *Andrew Cullen,* as Merchant, apply themselves to the Officers of the Customs for Liberty to dispose of some of the Cargo, in order to pay the Workmen; which they having obtained, they sold fifty eight Barrels of Beef, and having hired three more Hands, they set Sail for *Ostend,* and there having sold more Barrels of Beef, they steer their Course to *Rotterdam,* dispose of the rest of the Cargo, and took in one Mr. *Annesly,* who freighted the Ship for *England;* but in their Passage, in a stormy Night, it being very dark, they took up Mr. *Annesly* their Passenger, and threw him into the Sea, who swam about the Ship a pretty while, calling out for Life, and telling them they should have all his Goods, if they would receive him again into the Vessel: But in vain were his Cries!

After this, they were obliged to put into several Ports, and by contrary Winds, came to the Coast of *France,* and hearing there was an Enquiry made after the Ship, *Roche* quits her at *Havre de Grace,* and leaves the Management to *Cullen* and the rest; who having shipp'd other Men, sail'd away to *Scotland,* and there quitted the Vessel, which was afterwards seized and brought into the River of *Thames.*

Some Time after this, *Philip Roche* came to *London,* and making some Claim for Money, he had made Insurance of, in the Name of *John Eustace,* the Officer was apprized of the Fraud, and he arrested and flung into the Compter; from whence directing a Letter to his Wife, she shewed it to a Friend, who discovered by it, that he was the principal Villain concerned in the Destruction of *Peter Tartoue,* and the Crew. Upon this, an Information was given to my Lord *Carteret,* that the Person who went by the Name of *John Eustace,* was *Philip Roche,* as aforesaid; and being brought down by his Lordships Warrant, he stifly deny'd it for some Time, notwithstanding a Letter was found in his Pocket, directed to him by the Name of *Roche;* but being confronted by a Captain of a Ship, who knew him well, he confessed it, but prevaricated in several Particulars; whereupon he was committed to *Newgate* upon violent Suspicion, and the next Day was brought down again at his own Request, confessed the whole, desired to be made an Evidence, and promised to convict three Men worse than himself. Two were discovered by him, who died miserably in the *Marshalsea,* and *Roche* himself was afterwards try'd, (no more being taken,) found Guilty of the Pyracy, and executed.

Chap. XIX
An Abstract of the Civil Law and Statute Law now in Force, in Relation to Pyracy

A Pyrate is Hostis humanis generis, *a common Enemy, with whom neither Faith nor Oath is to be kept, according to* Tully. *And by the Laws of Nature, Princes and States are responsible for their Neglect, if they do not provide Remedies for restraining these sort of Robberies. Though Pyrates are called common Enemies, yet they are properly not to be term'd so. He is only to be honour'd with that Name, says* Cicero, *who hath a Commonwealth, a Court, a Treasury, Consent and Concord of Citizens, and some Way, if Occasion be, of Peace and League: But when they have reduced themselves into a Government or State, as those of* Algier, Sally, Tripoly, Tunis, *and the like, they then are allowed the Solemnities of War, and the Rights of Legation.*

If Letters of Marque *be granted to a Merchant, and he furnishes out a Ship, with a Captain and Mariners, and they, instead of taking the Goods, cr Ships of that Nation against whom their Commission is awarded, take the Ship and Goods of a Friend, this is Pyracy; and if the Ship arrive in any Part of his Majesty's Dominions, it will be seized, and for ever lost to the Owners; but they are no way liable to make Satisfaction.*

If a Ship is assaulted and taken by the Pyrates, for Redemption of which, the Master becomes a Slave to the Captors, by the Law Marine, *the Ship and Lading are tacitly obliged for his Redemption, by a general Contribution; but if it happen through his own Folly, then no Contribution is to be made.*

If Subjects in Enmity with the Crown of England, *are abord an* English *Pyrate, in Company with* English, *and a Robbery is committed, and they are taken; it is Felony in the* English, *but not in the Stranger; for it was no Pyracy in them, but the Depredation of an Enemy, and they will be tried by a Martial Law.*

If Pyracy is committed by Subjects in Enmity with England, *upon the* British *Seas, it is properly only punishable by the Crown of* England, *who have* istud regimen & Dominnm *exclusive of all other Power.*

If Pyracy be committed on the Ocean, and the Pyrates in the Attempt be overcome, the Captors may, without any Solemnity of Condemnation, hang them up at the Main-Yard; if they are brought to the next Port, and the Judge rejects the Trial, or the Captors cannot wait for the Judge, without Peril or Loss, Justice may be done upon them by the Captors.

If Merchandize be delivered to a Master, to carry to one Port, and he carries it to another, and sells and disposes of it, this is not Felony; but if, after unlading it at the first Port, he retakes it, it is Pyracy.

If a Pyrate attack a Ship, and the Master for Redemption, gives his Oath to pay a Sum of Money, tho' there be nothing taken, yet it is Pyracy by the Law Marine.

If a Ship is riding at Anchor, and the Mariners all ashore, and a Pyrate attack her, and rob her, this is Pyracy.

If a Man commit Pyracy upon the Subjects of any Prince, or Republic, (though in Amity with us,) and brings the Goods into England, *and sells them in a Market* Overt, *the same shall bind, and the Owners are for ever excluded.*

If a Pyrate enters a Port of this Kingdom, and robs a Ship at Anchor there, it is not Pyracy, because not done, super altum Mare; *but is Robbery at common Law, because* infra Corpus Comitatus. *A Pardon of all Felonies does not extend to Pyracy, but the same ought to be especially named.*

By 28 H. 8. Murthers and Robberies committed upon the Sea, or in other Places, where the Admiral pretends Jurisdiction, shall be enquired into, try'd, heard, and determined, in such Places and Counties within the Realm, as shall be limited by the King's Commission, in like Manner as if such Offences were done at Land. And such Commissions (being under the Great Seal) shall be directed to the Lord Admiral, his Lieutenant or Deputy, and to three or four such others as the Lord Chancellor shall name

The said Commissioners, or three of them, have Power to enquire of such Offences by twelve lawful Men of the Country, so limited in their Commission, as if such Offences were done at Land, within the same County; and every Indictment so found and presented, shall be good in Law; and such Order, Progress, Judgment, and Execution shall be used, had, done, and made thereupon, as against Offenders for Murder and Felony done at Land. Also the Trial of such Offences (if they be denied) shall be had by twelve Men of the County, limited in the said Commission, (as aforesaid,) and no Challenge shall be had for the Hundred: And such as shall be convict of such Offences, shall suffer Death without Benefit of Clergy, and forfeit Land and Goods, as in Case of Felonies and Murders done at Land.

This Act shall not prejudice any Person, or Persons, (urged by Necessity) for taking Victuals, Cables, Ropes, Anchors or Sails, out of another Ship that may spare them, so as they either pay ready Money, or Money worth for them, or give a Bill for the Payment thereof; if on this Side the Straits of Gibraltar, *within four Months; if beyond, within twelve Months.*

When any such Commission shall be sent to any Place within the Jurisdiction of the Cinque-Ports, *it shall be directed to the Warden of the said Ports, or his Deputy with three or four other Persons, as the Lord Chancellor shall Name; and the Inquisition or Trial of such Offences, there, shall be made and had, by the Inhabitants of the said Ports, and Members of the same.*

By 11 and 12 W. 3. c. 7. If any natural born Subjects or Denizons of England, *commit Pyracy, or any Act of Hostility, against his Majesty's Subjects at Sea, under Colour of a Commission or Authority, from any foreign Prince or State, or Person whatsoever, such Offenders shall be adjudged Pyrates.*

If any Commander or Master of a Ship, or Seaman or Mariner, give up his Ship, &c. to Pyrates, or combine to yield up, or run away with any Ship, or lay violent Hand on his Commander, or endeavour to make a Revolt in the Ship, he shall be adjudged a Pyrate.

All Persons who after the 29th of September 1720, *shall set forth any Pyrate (or be aiding and assisting to any such Pyrate,) committing Pyracy on Land or Sea, or shall conceal such Pyrates, or receive any Vessel or Goods piratically taken, shall be adjudged accessary to such Pyracy, and suffer as Principals.*

By 4 G. c. 11. Sect. 7. All Persons who have committed, or shall commit any Offences, for which they ought to be adjudged Pyrates, by the Act 11 and 12 W. 3. c. 7. may be tried for every such Offence, in such Manner as by the Act 28 H. 8. c. 15. is directed for the Trial of Pyrates; and shall not have the Benefit of Clergy.

Sect. 8. *This Act shall not extend to Persons convicted or attainted in* Scotland.

Sect. 9. *This Act shall extend to his Majesty's Dominions in* America, *and be taken as a public Act.*

Chap. XX
Of Captain Misson

We can be somewhat particular in the Life of this Gentleman, because, by very great Accident, we have got into our Hands a *French* Manuscript, in which he himself gives a Detail of his Actions. He was born in *Provence,* of an ancient Family; his Father, whose true Name he conceals, was Master of a plentiful Fortune; but having a great Number of Children, our Rover had but little Hopes of other Fortune than what he could carve out for himself with his Sword. His Parents took Care to give him an Education equal to his Birth. After he had passed his Humanity and Logic, and was a tolerable Mathematician, at the Age of Fifteen he was sent to *Angiers,* where he was a Year learning his Exercises. His Father, at his Return home, would have put him into the Musketeers; but as he was of a roving Temper, and much affected with the Accounts he had read in Books of Travels, he chose the Sea as a Life which abounds with more Variety, and would afford him an Opportunity to gratify his Curiosity, by the Change of Countries. having made this Choice, his Father, with Letters of Recommendation, and every Thing fitting for him, sent him Volunteer on board the *Victoire,* commanded by Monsieur *Fourbin,* his Relation. He was received on Board with all possible Regard by the Captain, whose Ship was at *Marseilles,* and was order'd to cruize soon after *Misson*'s Arrival. Nothing could be more agreeable to the Inclinations of our Volunteer than this Cruize, which made him acquainted with the most noted Ports of the *Mediterranean,* and gave him a great Insight into the practical Part of Navigation. He grew fond of this Life, and was resolved to be a complete Sailor, which made him always one of the first on a Yard Arm, either to Hand or Reef, and very inquisitive in the different Methods of working a Ship: His Discourse was turn'd on no other Subject, and he would often get the Boatswain and Carpenter to teach him in their Cabbins the constituent Parts of a Ship's Hull, and how to rig her, which he generously paid 'em for; and tho' he spent a great Part of his Time with these two Officers, yet he behaved himself with such Prudence that they never attempted at a Familiarity, and always paid the Respect due to his Family. The Ship being at *Naples,* he obtained Leave of his Captain to go to *Rome,* which he had a great Desire to visit. Hence we may date his Misfortunes; for, remarking the licentious Lives of the Clergy (so different from the Regularity observ'd among the *French* Ecclesiastics,) the Luxury of the Papal Court, and that nothing but Hulls of Religion was to be found in the Metropolis of the Christian Church, he began to figure to himself that all Religion was no more than a Curb upon the Minds of the Weaker, which the wiser Sort yielded to, in Appearance only. These Sentiments, so disadvantageous to Religion and himself, were strongly riveted by accidentally becoming acquainted with a lewd Priest, who was, at his Arrival (by meer Chance) his Confessor, and after that his Procurer and Companion, for he kept him Company to his Death. One Day, having an Opportunity, he told *Misson,* a Religious was a very good Life, where a Man had a subtle enterprising Genius, and some Friends; for such a one wou'd, in a short Time, rise to such Dignities in the Church, the Hopes of which was the Motive of all the wiser Sort, who voluntarily took upon them the sacerdotal Habit. That the ecclesiastical State was govern'd with the same Policy as were secular Principalities and Kingdoms; that what was beneficial, not what was meritorious and virtuous, would be alone regarded. That there were no more Hopes for a Man of Piety and Learning in the Patrimony of St. *Peter,* than in any other Monarchy, nay, rather less; for this being known to be real, that Man's rejected as a Visionary, no way fit for Employment; as one whose Scruples might prove prejudicial; for its a Maxim, that Religion and Politics can never set up in one House. As to our Statesmen, don't imagine that the Purple makes 'em less Courtiers than are those of other Nations; they know and pursue the *Reggione del Stato* (a Term of Art which means Self-Interest) with as much Cunning and as little Conscience as any Secular; and are as artful where Art is required, and as barefaced and impudent when their Power is great enough to support 'em, in the oppressing the People, and aggrandizing their Families. What their Morals are, you may read in the Practice of their Lives, and their Sentiments of Religion from this Saying of a certain Cardinal, *Quantum Lucrum ex ista fabula*

Christi! which many of 'em may say, tho' they are not so foolish. For my Part, I am quite tir'd of the Farce, and will lay hold on the first Opportunity to throw off this masquerading Habit; for, by Reason of my Age, I must act an under Part many Years; and before I can rise to share the Spoils of the People, I shall, I fear, be too old to enjoy the Sweets of Luxury; and, as I am an Enemy to Restraint, I am apprehensive I shall never act up to my Character, and carry thro' the Hypocrite with Art enough to rise to any considerable Post in the Church. My Parents did not consult my Genius, or they would have given me a Sword instead of a Pair of Beads.

Misson advised him to go with him Volunteer, and offer'd him Money to cloath him; the Priest leap'd at the Proposal, and a Letter coming to *Misson* from his Captain, that he was going to *Leghorn,* and left to him either to come to *Naples,* or go by Land; he chose the latter, and the *Dominican,* whom he furnish'd with Money, clothing himself very Cavalierly, threw off his Habit, and preceded him two Days, staying at *Pisa* for *Misson;* from whence they went together to *Leghorn,* where they found the *Victoire,* and Signor *Caraccioli,* recommended by his Friend, was received on Board. Two Days after they weigh'd from hence, and after a Week's Cruize fell in with two *Sally* Men, the one of twenty, the other of twenty four Guns; the *Victoire* had but thirty mounted, though she had Ports for forty. The Engagement was long and bloody, for the *Sally* Man hop'd to carry the *Victoire;* and, on the contrary, Captain *Fourbin,* so far from having any Thoughts of being taken, he was resolutely bent to make Prize of his Enemies, or sink his Ship. One of the *Sally* Men was commanded by a *Spanish* Renegade, (though he had only the Title of a Lieutenant) for the Captain was a young Man who knew little of Marine Affairs.

This Ship was called the *Lyon;* and he attempted, more than once, to board the *Victoire;* but by a Shot betwixt Wind and Water, he was obliged to sheer off, and running his Guns, *&c.* on one Side, bring her on the careen to stop his Leak; this being done with too much Precipitation, she overset, and every Soul was lost: His Comrade seeing this Disaster, threw out all his small Sails, and endeavour'd to get off, but the *Victoire* wrong'd her, and oblig'd her to renew the Fight, which she did with great Obstinacy, and made Monsieur *Fourbin* despair of carrying her if he did not board; he made Preparations accordingly. Signior *Caraccioli* and *Misson* were the two first on board when the Command was given; but they and their Followers were beat back by the Despair of the *Sally* Men; the former received a Shot in his Thigh, and was carried down to the Surgeon. The *Victoire* laid her on board the second time, and the *Sally* Men defended their Decks with such Resolution, that they were cover'd with their own, and the dead Bodies of their Enemies. *Misson* seeing one of 'em jump down the Main-Hatch with a lighted Match, suspecting his Design, resolutely leap'd after him, and reaching him with his Sabre, laid him dead the Moment he was going to set Fire to the Powder. The *Victoire* pouring in more Men, the *Mahometans* quitted the Decks, finding Resistance vain, and fled for Shelter to the Cook Room, Steerage and Cabbins, and some run between Decks. The *French* gave 'em Quarters, and put the Prisoners on board the *Victoire,* the Prize yielding nothing worth mention, except Liberty to about fifteen Christian Slaves; she was carried into and sold with the Prisoners at *Leghorn.* The *Turks* lost a great many Men, the *French* not less than 35 in boarding, for they lost very few by the great Shot, the *Sally* Men firing mostly at the Masts and Rigging, hoping by disabling to carry her. The limited Time of their Cruize being out, the *Victoire* returned to *Marseilles,* from whence *Misson,* taking his Companion, went to visit his Parents, to whom the Captain sent a very advantageous Character, both of his Courage and Conduct. He was about a Month at home when his Captain wrote to him, that his Ship was order'd to *Rochelle,* from whence he was to sail for the *West-Indies* with some Merchant Men. This was very agreeable to *Misson* and Signior *Caraccioli,* who immediately set out for *Marseilles.* This Town is well fortified, has four Parish Churches, and the Number of Inhabitants is computed to be about 120,000; the Harbour is esteemed the safest in the *Mediterranean,* and is the common Station for the *French* Gallies.

Leaving this Place, they steer'd for *Rochelle,* where the *Victoire* was dock'd, the Merchant Ships not being near ready. *Misson,* who did not Care to pa's so long a Time in Idleness, proposed to his Comrade the taking a Cruize on board the *Triumph,* who was going into the *English* Channel; the *Italian* readily consented to it.

Between the Isle of *Guernsey* and the *Start Point,* they met with the *Mayflower,* Captain *Balladine* Commanded, a Merchant Ship of 18 Guns, richly laden, and coming from *Jamaica.* The Captain of the *English* made a gallant Resistance, and fought his Ship so long, that the *French* could not carry her into Harbour, wherefore they took the Money, and what was most valuable, out of her; and finding she made more Water than the Pumps could free, quitted, and saw her go down in less than four Hours after. Monsieur *le Blanc,* the *French* Captain, received Captain *Balladine* very civilly, and would not suffer either him or his Men to be stripp'd, saying, *None but Cowards ought to be treated after that Manner; that brave Men ought to treat such, though their Enemies, as Brothers; and that to use a gallant Man (who does his Duty) ill, speaks a Revenge which cannot proceed but from a Coward Soul.* He order'd that the Prisoners should have their Chests; and when some of his Men seem'd to mutter, he bid 'em remember the Grandeur of the Monarch they serv'd; that they were neither pyrates nor Privateers; and, as brave Men, they ought to show their Enemies an Example they would willingly have follow'd, and use their Prisoners as they wish'd to be us'd.

They running up the *English* Channel as high as *Beachy Head,* and, in returning, fell in with three fifty Gun Ships, which gave Chace to the *Triumph;* but as she was an excellent Sailor, she run 'em out of Sight in seven Glasses, and made the best of her Way for the *Lands-End;* they here cruized eight Days, then doubling Cape *Cornwall,* ran up the *Bristol* Channel, near as far as *Nash Point,* and intercepted a small Ship from *Barbadoes,* and stretching away to the Northward, gave Chase to a Ship they saw in the Evening, but lost her in the Night. The *Triumph* stood then towards *Milford,* and spying a Sail, endeavour'd to cut her off the Land, but found it impossible; for she got into the Haven, though they came up with her very fast, and she had surely been taken, had the Chase had been any thing longer.

Captain *Balladine,* who took the Glass, said it was the *Port Royal,* a *Bristol* Ship which left *Jamaica* in Company with him and the *Charles.* They now return'd to their own Coast, and sold their Prize at *Brest,* where, at his Desire, they left Captain *Balladine,* and Monsieur *le Blanc* made him a Present of Purse with 40 *Louis*'s for his Support; his Crew were also left here.

At the Entrance into this Harbour the *Triumph* struck upon a Rock, but received no Damage: This Entrance, called *Gonlet,* is very dangerous on Account of the Number of Rocks which lie on each Side under Water, though the Harbour is certainly the best in *France.* The Mouth of the Harbour is defended by a strong Castle; the Town is well fortified, and has a Citadel for its farther Defence, which is of considerable Strength. In 1694 the *English* attempted a Descent, but did not find their Market, for they were beat off with the Loss of their General, and a great many Men. From hence the *Triumph* return'd to *Rochel,* and in a Month after our Volunteers, who went on board the *Victoire,* took their Departure for *Martineco* and *Guadalupa;* they met with nothing in their Voyage thither worth noting.

I shall only observe, that Signior *Caraccioli,* who was as ambitious as he was irreligious, had, by this Time, made a perfect Delft of *Misson,* and thereby convinc'd him, that all Religion was no other than human Policy, and shew'd him that the Law of *Moses* was no more than what were necessary, as well for the Preservation as the Governing of the People; for Instance, said he, the *African* Negroes never heard of the Institution of Circumcision, which is said to be the Sign of the Covenant made between God and this People, and yet they circumcise their Children; doubtless for the same Reason the *Jews* and other Nations do, who inhabit the Southern Climes, the Prepuce consolidating the perspired Matter, which is of a fatal Consequence. In short, he ran through all the Ceremonies of the *Jewish,* Christian and *Mahometan* Religion, and convinced him these were, as might be observed by the Absurdity of many, far from being Institutions of Men inspired; and that *Moses,* in his Account of the Creation, was guilty of known Blunders; and the Miracles, both in the New and Old Testament, inconsistent with Reason. That God had given us this Blessing, to make Use of for our present and future Happiness, and whatever was contrary to it, notwithstanding their School Distinctions of *contrary* and *above* Reason, must be false. This Reason teaches us, that there is a first Cause of all Things, an *Ens Entium,* which we call God, and our Reason will also suggest, that he must be eternal, and, as the Author of every Thing perfect, he must be infinitely perfect.

If so, he can be subject to no Passions, and neither loves nor hates; he must be ever the same, and cannot rashly do to Day what he shall repent to Morrow. He must be perfectly happy, consequently nothing can add to an eternal State of Tranquillity, and though it becomes us to adore him, yet can our Adorations neither augment, nor our Sins take from this Happiness.

But his Arguments on this Head are too long, and too dangerous to translate; and as they are work'd up with great Subtlety, they may be pernicious to weak Men, who cannot discover their Fallacy; or, who finding 'em agreeable to their Inclinations, and would be glad to shake off the Yoke of the Christian Religion, which galls and curbs their Passions, would not give themselves the Trouble to examine them to the Bottom, but give into what pleases, glad of finding some Excuse to their Consciences. Though as his Opinion of a future State has nothing in it which impugns the Christian Religion, I shall set it down in few Words.

'That reasoning Faculty, says he, which we perceive within us, we call the Soul, but what that Soul is, is unknown to us. It may die with the Body, or it may survive. I am of Opinion its immortal; but to say that this Opinion is the Dictate of Reason, or only the Prejudice of Education, would, I own, puzzle me. If it is immortal, it must be an Emanation from the Divine Being, and consequently at its being separated from the Body, will return to its first Principle, if not contaminated. Now, my Reason tells me, if it is estranged from its first Principle, which is the Deity, all the Hells of Man's Invention can never yield Tortures adequate to such a Banishment.

As he had privately held these Discourses among the Crew, he had gained a Number of Proselytes, who look'd upon him as a new Prophet risen up to reform the Abuses in Religion; and a great Number being *Rochellers,* and, as yet, tainted with *Calvanism,* his Doctrine was the more readily embrac'd. When he had experienced the Effects of his religious Arguments, he fell upon Government, and shew'd, that every Man was born free, and had as much Right to what would support him, as to the Air he respired. A contrary Way of arguing would be accusing the Deity with Cruelty and Injustice, for he brought into the World no Man to pass a Life of Penury, and to miserably want a necessary Support; that the vast Difference between Man and Man, the one wallowing in Luxury, and the other in the most pinching Necessity, was owing only to Avarice and Ambition on the one Hand, and a pusilanimous Subjection on the other; that at first no other than a Natural was known, a paternal Government, every Father was the Head, the Prince and Monarch of his Family, and Obedience to such was both just and easy, for a Father had a compassionate Tenderness for his Children; but Ambition creeping in by Degrees, the stronger Family set upon and enslaved the Weaker; and this additional Strength over-run a third, by every Conquest gathering Force to make others, and this was the first Foundation of Monarchy. Pride encreasing with Power, Man usurped the Prerogative of God, over his Creatures, that of depriving them of Life, which was a Privilege no one had over his own; for as he did not come into the World by his own Election, he ought to stay the determined Time of his Creator: That indeed, Death given in War, was by the Law of Nature allowable, because it is for the Preservation of our own Lives; but no Crime ought to be thus punished, nor indeed any War undertaken, but in Defence of our natural Right, which is such a Share of Earth as is necessary for our Support.

These Topics he often declaimed on, and very often advised with *Misson* about the setting up for themselves; he was as ambitious as the other, and as resolute. *Caraccioli* and *Misson* were by this expert Mariners, and very capable of managing a Ship: *Caraccioli* had sounded a great many of the Men on this Subject, and found them very inclineable to listen to him. An Accident happen'd which gave *Caraccioli* a fair Opportunity to put his Designs in Execution, and he laid Hold of it; they went off *Martinico* on a Cruize, and met with the *Winchelsea,* an *English* Man of War of 40 Guns, commanded by Captain *Jones;* they made for each other, and a very smart Engagement followed, the first Broadside killed the Captain, second Captain, and the three Lieutenants, on Board the *Victoire,* and left only the Master, who would have struck, but *Misson* took up the Sword, order'd *Caraccioli* to act as Lieutenant, and encouraging the Men fought the Ship six Glasses, when by some Accident, the *Winchelsea* blew up, and not a Man was saved but Lieutenant *Franklin,* whom the *French* Boats took up, and he died in two Days. None ever knew before this Manuscript fell into my Hands how the *Winchelsea* was lost; for her Head being driven ashore at *Antegoa,* and a great Storm having happen'd a few Days before her Head was found, it was concluded, that she founder'd in that Storm. After this Engagement, *Caraccioli* came to *Misson* and saluted him Captain, and desired to know if he would chuse a momentary or a lasting Command, that he must now determine, for at his Return to *Martinico* it would be too late; and he might depend upon the Ship he fought and saved being given to another, and they would think him well rewarded if made a Lieutenant, which Piece of Justice he doubted: That he had his Fortune in his Hands, which he might either keep or let go; if he made Choice of the latter, he must never again expect she would court him to accept her Favours: That he ought to set before his Eyes his Circumstances, as a younger Brother of a good Family, but nothing to support his Character; and the many Years he must serve at the Expence of his Blood before he could make any Figure in the World; and consider the wide Difference between the commanding and being commanded: That he might with the Ship he had under Foot, and the brave Fellows under Command, bid Defiance to the Power of *Europe,* enjoy every Thing he wish'd, reign Sovereign of the Southern Seas, and lawfully make War on all the World, since it wou'd deprive him of that Liberty to which he had a Right by the Laws of Nature: That he might in Time, become as great as *Alexander* was to the *Persians;* and by encreasing his Forces by his Captures, he would every Day strengthen the Justice of his Cause, for who has Power is always in the Right. That *Harry* the Fourth and *Harry* the Seventh, attempted and succeeded in their Enterprizes on the Crown of *England,* yet their Forces did not equal his. *Mahomet* with a few Camel Drivers, founded the *Ottoman* Empire; and *Darius,* with no more than six or seven Companions got Possession of that of *Persia.*

In a Word he said so much that *Misson* resolved to follow his Advice, and calling up all Hands, he told them, 'That a great Number of them had resolved with him upon a Life of Liberty, and and had done him the Honour to create him Chief: That he designed to force no Man, and be guilty of that Injustice he blamed in others; therefore, if any were averse to the following his Fortune, which he promised should be the same to all, he desired they would declare themselves, and he would set them ashore, whence they might return with Conveniency;' having made an End, they one and all cryed, *Vive le Capitain* Misson *et son Lieutenant le Scavant* Caraccioli, God bless Capt. *Misson* and his learned Lieutenant *Caraccioli. Misson* thanked them for the Honour they conferr'd upon him, and promised he would use the Power they gave for the public Good only, and hoped, as they had the Bravery to assert their Liberty, they would be as unanimous in the preserving it, and stand by him in what should be found expedient for the Good of all; that he was their Friend and Companion, and should never exert his Power, or think himself other than their Comrade, but when the Necessity of Affairs should oblige him.

They shouted a second Time, *vive le Capitain;* he, after this, desired they would chuse their subaltern Officers, and give them Power to consult and conclude upon what might be for the common Interest, and bind themselves down by an Oath to agree to what such Officers and he should determine: This they readily gave into. The School-Master they chose for second Lieutenant, *Jean Besace* they nominated for third, and the Boatswain, and a Quarter-Master, named *Matthieu le Tondu,* with the Gunner, they desired might be their Representatives in Council.

The Choice was approved, and that every Thing might pass methodically, and with general Approbation, they were called into the great Cabbin, and the Question put, what Course they should steer? The Captain proposed the *Spanish* Coast as the most probable to afford them rich Prizes: This was agreed upon by all. The Boatswain then asked what Colours they should fight under, and advised Black as most terrifying; but *Caraccioli* objected, that they were no pyrates, but Men who were resolved to assert that Liberty which God and Nature gave them, and own no Subjection to any, farther than was for the common Good of all: That indeed, Obedience to Governors was necessary, when they knew and acted up to the Duty of their Function; were vigilant Guardians of the Peoples Rights and Liberties; saw that Justice was equally distributed; were Barriers against the Rich and Powerful, when they attempted to oppress the Weaker; when they suffered none of the one Hand to grow immensely rich, either by his own or his Ancestors Encroachments; nor on the other, any to be wretchedly miserable, either by falling into the Hands of Villains, unmerciful Creditors, or other Misfortunes. While he had Eyes impartial, and allowed nothing but Merit to distinguish between Man and Man; and instead of being a Burthen to the People by his luxurious Life, he was by his Care for, and Protection of them, a real Father, and in every Thing acted with the equal and impartial Justice of a Parent: But when a Governor, who is the Minister of the People, thinks himself rais'd to this Dignity, that he may spend his Days in Pomp and Luxury, looking upon his Subjects as so many Slaves, created for his Use and Pleasure, and therefore leaves them and their Affairs to the immeasurable Avarice and Tyranny of some one whom he has chosen for his Favourite, when nothing but Oppression, Poverty, and all the Miseries of Life flow from such an Administration; that he lavishes away the Lives and Fortunes of the People, either to gratify his Ambition, or to support the Cause of some neighbouring Prince, that he may in Return, strengthen his Hands should his People exert themselves in Defence of their native Rights; or should he run into unnecessary Wars, by the rash and thoughtless Councils of his Favourite, and not able to make Head against the Enemy he has rashly or wantonly brought upon his Hands, and buy a Peace (which is the present Case of *France,* as every one knows, by supporting King *James,* and afterwards proclaiming his Son) and drain the Subject; should the Peoples Trade be wilfully neglected, for private Interests, and while their Ships of War lie idle in their Harbours, suffer their Vessels to be taken; and the Enemy not only intercepts all Commerce, but insults their Coasts: It speaks a generous and great Soul to shake off the Yoak; and if we cannot redress our Wrongs, withdraw from sharing the Miseries which meaner Spirits submit to, and scorn to yield to the Tyranny. Such Men are we, and, if the World, as Experience may convince us it will, makes War upon us, the Law of Nature empowers us not only to be on the defensive, but also on the offensive Part. As we then do not proceed upon the same Ground with pyrates, who are Men of dissolute Lives and no Principles, let us scorn to take their Colours: Ours is a brave, a just, an innocent, and a noble Cause; the Cause of Liberty. I therefore advise a Thomas White Ensign, with Liberty painted in the Fly, and if you like the Motto, *a Deo a Libertate,* for God and Liberty, as an Emblem of our Uprightness and Resolution.

The Cabbin Door was left open, and the Bulk Head which was of Canvas rowled up, the Steerage being full of Men, who lent an attentive Ear, they cried, *Liberty, Liberty; we are free Men:* Vive *the brave Captain* Misson *and the noble Lieutenant* Caraccioli. This short Council breaking up, every Thing belonging to the deceas'd Captain, and the other Officers, and Men lost in the Engagement, was brought upon Deck and over-hawled; the Money ordered to be put into a Chest, and the Carpenter to clap on a Padlock for, and give a Key to, every one of the Council: *Misson* telling them, all should be in common, and the particular Avarice of no one should defraud the Public.

When the Plate Monsieur *Fourbin* had, was going to the Chest, the Men unanimously cried out avast, keep that out for the Captain's Use, as a Present from his Officers and Fore-mast Men. *Misson* thanked them, the Plate was returned to the great Cabbin, and the Chest secured according to Orders: *Misson* then ordered his Lieutenants and other Officers to examine who among the Men, were in most Want of Cloaths, and to distribute those of the dead Men impartially, which was done with a general Consent and Applause of the whole Crew: All but the wounded being upon Deck. *Misson* from the Baracade, spoke to the following Purpose, 'That since they had unanimously resolved to seize upon and defend their Liberty, which ambitious Men had usurped, and that this could not be esteemed by impartial Judges other than a just and brave Resolution, he was under an Obligation to recommend to them a brotherly Love to each other; the Banishment of all private Piques and Grudges, and a strict Agreement and Harmony among themselves: That in throwing off the Yoak of Tyranny of which the Action spoke an Abhorrence, he hoped none would follow the Example of Tyrants, and turn his Back upon Justice; for when

Equity was trodden under Foot, Misery, Confusion, and mutual Distrust naturally followed. — He also advised them to remember there was a Supream, the Adoration of which, Reason and Gratitude prompted us, and our own Interests would engage us (as it is best to be of the surest Side, and after-Life was allowed possible) to conciliate. — That he was satisfied Men who were born and bred in Slavery, by which their Spirits were broke, and were incapable of so generous a Way of thinking, who, ignorant of their Birth-Right, and the Sweets of Liberty, dance to the Music of their Chains, which was, indeed, the greater Part of the Inhabitants of the Globe, would brand this generous Crew with the invidious Name of pyrates, and think it meritorious, to be instrumental in their Destruction. — Self-Preservation therefore, and not a cruel Disposition, obliged him to declare War against all such as should refuse him the Entry of their Ports, and against all, who should not immediately surrender and give up what their Necessities required; but in a more particular Manner against all *European* Ships and Vessels, as concluded implacable Enemies. *And I do now,* said he, *declare such War, and, at the same time, recommend to you my Comrades a humane and generous Behaviour towards your Prisoners; which will appear by so much more the Effects of a noble Soul, as we are satisfied we should not meet the same Treatment should our ill Fortune, or more properly our Disunion, or want of Courage, give us up to their Mercy.*

After this, he required a Muster should be made, and there were able Hands two Hundred, and thirty five sick and wounded; as they were muster'd they were sworn. After Affairs were thus settled, they shaped their Course for the *Spanish West-Indies,* but resolved, in the Way, to take a Week or ten Days Cruize in the Windward Passage from *Jamaica,* because most Merchant Men, which were good Sailors and did not stay for Convoy, took this as the shorter Cut for *England.*

Off St. *Christophers* they took an *English* Sloop becalmed, with their Boats; they took out of her a couple of Puncheons of Rum, and half a dozen Hogsheads of Sugar (she was a *New England* Sloop, bound for *Boston*) and without offering the least Violence to the Men, or stripping them, they let her go. The Master of the Sloop was *Thomas Butler,* who owned, he never met with so candid an Enemy as the *French* Man of War, which took him the Day he left St. *Christophers;* they met with no other Booty in their Way, till they came upon their Station, when after three Days, they saw a Sloop which had the Impudence to give them Chace; Captain *Misson* asked what could be the Meaning that the Sloop stood for them? One of the Men, who was acquainted with the *West-Indies,* told him, it was a *Jamaica* Privateer, and he should not wonder, if he clapp'd him aboard. I am, said he, no Stranger to their Way of working, and this despicable Fellow, as those who don't know a *Jamaica* Privateer may think him, it is ten to one will give you some Trouble. It now grows towards Evening, and you'll find as soon as he has discovered your Force, he'll keep out of the Reach of your Guns till the 12 a-Clock Watch is changed at Night, and he'll then attempt to clap you aboard, with Hopes to carry you in the Hurry: Wherefore Captain, if you will give me Leave to advise you, let every Man have his small Arms; and at twelve, let the Bell ring as usual, and rather more Noise than ordinary be made, as if the one Watch was turning in, and the other out, in a Confusion and Hurry, and I'll engage he will venture to enter his Men. The Fellow's Advice was approved and resolved upon, and the Sloop work'd, as he said she would, for upon coming near enough to make distinctly the Force of the *Victoire,* on her throwing out *French* Colours, she, the Sloop, clapp'd upon a Wind, the *Victoire* gave Chace, but without Hopes of gaining upon her; she went so well to Windward, that she cou'd spare the Ship some Points in her Sheet, and yet wrong her: At Dusk of the Even, the *French* had lost Sight of her, but about Eleven at Night, they saw her hankering up their Windward Bow, which confirmed the Sailors Opinion, that she would attempt to board them, as she did at the pretended Change of the Watch; there being little or no Wind, she lashed to the Bow-Sprit of the *Victoire,* and enter'd her Men, who were very quietly taken, as they enter'd and tumbled down the Forehatch, where they were received by others, and bound without Noise, not one of the Privateers killed, few hurt, and only one *Frenchman* wounded. The *Victoire* seeing the better Part of the Sloop's Men secured, they boarded in their Turn, when the Privateer's suspecting some Stratagem, were endeavouring to cut their Lashing and get off:

Thus the *Englishman* caught a Tartar. The Prisoners being all secured, the Captain charged his Men not to discover, thro' a Desire of augmenting their Number, the Account they were upon.

The next Morning Monsieur *Misson* called for the Captain of the Privateer, he told him, he could not but allow him a brave Fellow, to venture upon a Ship of his Countenance, and for that Reason he should meet Treatment which Men of his Profession seldom afforded the Prisoners they made. He asked him how long he had been out, what was his Name, and what he had on Board? He answered he was but just come out, that he was the first Sail he had met with, and shou'd have thought himself altogether as lucky not to have spoke with him; that his Name was *Harry Ramsey,* and what he had on Board were Rags, Powder, Ball, and some few half Anchors of Rum. *Ramsey* was ordered into the Gun-Room, and a Council being held in the public Manner aforesaid, the Bulk Head of the great Cabbin rowled up. On their Conclusion, the Captain of the Privateer was called in again, when Captain *Misson* told him, he would return him his Sloop, and restore him and his Men to their Liberty, without stripping or plundering of any Thing, but what Prudence obliged him to, their Ammunition and Small-Arms, if he would give him his Word and Honour, and his Men to take an Oath, not to go out on the Privateer Account in six Months after they left him: That he did not design to continue that Station above a Week longer, at the Expiration of which Time he would let them go.

Ramsey, who had a new Sloop, did not expect this Favour, which he thanked him for, and promised punctually to comply with the Injunction, which his Men as readily swore to, tho' they had no Design to keep the Oath. The Time being expired, he and his Men were put on Board their own Sloop. At going over the Ship's Side *Ramsey* begg'd Monsieur *Misson* would allow him Powder for a salute, by way of Thanks; but he answered him, the Ceremony was needless, and he expected no other Return than that of keeping his Word, which indeed *Ramsey* did. Some of his Men had found it more to their Advantage to have been as religious.

At parting *Ramsey* gave the Ship three Chears, and *Misson* had the Complaisance to return one, which *Ramsey* answering with three more, made the best of his Way for *Jamaica,* and at the East End of the Island met with the *Diana,* who, upon Advice, turn'd back.

The *Victoire* steer'd for *Carthagene,* off which Port they cruised some Days, but meeting with nothing in the Seas, they made for *Porto Bello;* in their Way they met with two *Dutch* Traders, who had Letters of Mart, and were just come upon the Coast, the one had 20, the other 24 Guns; *Misson* engaged them, and they defended themselves with a great Deal of Resolution and Gallantry; and as they were mann'd a Peak, he durst not venture to board either of them, for fear of being at the same Time boarded by the other. His Weight of Mettal gave him a great Advantage over the *Dutch,* though they were two to one; besides, their Business, as they had Cargoes, was to get off, if possible, wherefore they made a running Fight, though they took Care to stick close to one another.

They maintained the Fight for above six Hours, when *Misson,* enraged at this Obstinacy, and fearing, if by Accident they should bring a Mast, or Top-Mast, by the board, they would get from him. He was resolved to sink the larger Ship of the two, and accordingly ordered his Men to bring all their Guns to bear a Midship, then running close along Side of him, to raise their Mettal; his Orders being punctually obey'd, he pour'd in a Broad Side, which open'd such a Gap in the *Dutch* Ship, that she went directly to the Bottom, and every Man perish'd

He then mann'd his Bowsprit, brought his Sprit-sail Yard fore and aft, and resolved to board the other, which the *Dutch* perceiving, and terrified with the unhappy Fate of their Comrade, thought a farther resistance vain, and immediately struck. *Misson* gave them good Quarters, though he was enraged at the Loss of 13 Men killed outright, beside 9 wounded, of which 6 died. They found on board a great Quantity of Gold and Silver Lace, brocade Silks, Silk Stockings Bails of Broad-Cloath, Bazes of all Colours, and *Osnabrughs.*

A Consultation being held, it was resolved Captain *Misson* should take the Name of *Fourbin,* and returning to *Carthagene,* dispose of his Prize, and set his Prisoners ashoar. Accordingly they ply'd to the Eastward, and came to an Anchor between *Boca Chieca* Fort, and the Town, for they did not think it expedient to enter the Harbour. The Barge was manned, and *Caraccioli,* with the Name of *D'Aubigny,* the first Lieutenant, who was killed in the Engagement with the *Winchelsea,* and his Commission in his Pocket, went ashore with a Letter to the Governor, sign'd *Fourbin,* whose Character, for fear of the worst, was exactly counterfeited. The Purport of his Letter was, that having discretionary Orders to cruize for three Months, and hearing the *English* infested his Coast, he was come in search of 'em, and had met two *Dutch* Men, one of which he had sunk, the other he made Prize of. That his limited Time being near expired, he should be obliged to his Excellency, if he would send on board him such Merchants as were willing to take the Ship and Cargoe off his Hands, of which he had sent the *Dutch* Invoice. Don *Joseph de la Zerda,* the then Governor, received the Lieutenant (who sent back the Barge at landing) very civilly, and agreed to take the Prisoners ashoar, and do every Thing was required of him; and ordering fresh Provisions and Sallading to be got ready as a Present for the Captain, he sent for some Merchants who were very ready to go on board, and agree for the Ship and Goods; which they did, for two and fifty thousand Pieces of Eight. The next Day the Prisoners were set ashoar; a rich Piece of Brocade which was reserv'd, sent to the Governor for a Present, a Quantity of fresh Provision bought and brought on board, the Money paid by the Merchants, the Ship and Goods deliver'd, and the *Victoire,* at the Dawn of the following Day, got under Sail. It may be wonder'd how such Dispatch could be made, but the Reader must take Notice, these Goods were sold by the *Dutch* Invoice, which the Merchant of the Prize affirmed was genuine. I shall observe, by the by, that the *Victoire* was the *French* Man of War which Admiral *Wager* sent the *Kingston* in search of, and being afterwards falsly inform'd, that she was join'd by another of seventy Guns; and that they cruiz'd together between the Capes, order'd the *Severn* up to Windward, to assist the *Kingston,* which had like to have prov'd very fatal; for these two *English* Men of War, commanded by Captain *Trevor* and Captain *Pudnor,* meeting in the Night, had prepared to engage, each taking the other for the Enemy. The *Kingston*'s Men not having a good Look-out, which must be attributed to the Negligence of the Officer of the Watch, did not see the *Severn* till she was just upon them; but, by good Luck, to Leeward, and plying up, with all the Sail she could crowd, and a clear Ship. This put the *Kingston* in such Confusion, that when the *Severn* hal'd, no Answer was return'd, for none heard her. She was got under the *Kingston*'s Stern, and Captain *Pudnor* ordered to hale for the third and last Time, and if no Answer was return'd, to give her a Broadside. The Noise on Board the *Kingston* was now a little ceas'd, and Captain *Trevor,* who was on the Poop with a speaking Trumpet to hale the *Severn,* by good Luck heard her hale him, and answering the *Kingston,* and asking the Name of the other Ship, prevented the Damage.

They cruised together some Time, and meeting nothing which answer'd their Information, return'd to *Jamaica,* as I shall to my Subject, begging Pardon for this, as I thought, necessary Digression.

Don *Juan de la Zerda* told the Captain in a Letter, that the St. *Joseph,* a Gallion of seventy Guns, was then lying at *Port a Bello,* and should be glad he could keep her Company till she was off the Coast. That she would sail in eight or ten Days for the *Havanna;* and that, if his Time would permit him, he would send an Advice-Boat. That she had on Board the Value of 800,000 Pieces of Eight in Silver and Bar Gold. *Misson* return'd Answer, that he believ'd he should be excus'd if he stretched his Orders, for a few Days; and that he would cruize off the Isle of *Pearls,* and Cape *Gratias a Dios,* and give for Signal to the Gallion, his spreading a white Ensign in his Fore-Top-Mast Shrouds, the cluing up his Fore-Sail, and the firing one Gun to Windward, and two to Leeward, which he should answer by letting run and hoisting his Fore-Top-Sail three times, and the firing as many Guns to Leeward. Don *Joseph,* extreamly pleased with this Complaisance, sent a Boat express to advise the St. *Joseph,* but she was already sailed two Days, contrary to the Governor of *Carthagene*'s Expectation, and this Advice Captain *Misson* had from the Boat, which returning with an Answer, saw the *Victoire* in the Offin, and spoke to her. It was then resolved to follow the St. *Joseph,* and accordingly they steer'd for the *Havanna,* but by what Accident they did not overtake her is unknown.

I forgot to tell my Reader, on Board the *Dutch* Ship were fourteen *French* Hugonots, whom *Misson* thought fit to detain, when they were at Sea. *Misson* called 'em up, and proposed to 'em their taking on; telling them at the same Time, he left it to their Choice, for he would have no forc'd Men; and that if they all, or any of them, disapproved the Proposal, he would either give 'em the first Vessel he met that was fit for 'em, or set 'em ashoar on some inhabited Coast; and therefore bid 'em take two Days for Consideration before they returned an Answer; and, to encourage 'em, he called all Hands up, and declar'd, that if any Man repented him of the Course of Life he had chosen, his just Dividend should be counted to him, and he would set him on Shoar, either near the *Havanna,* or some other convenient Place; but not one accepted the Offer, and the fourteen Prisoners unanimously resolved to join in with 'em; to which Resolution, no doubt, the Hopes of a good Booty from the St. *Joseph,* and this Offer of Liberty greatly contributed.

At the Entrance of the Gulph they spied and came with a large Merchant Ship bound for *London* from *Jamaica;* she had 20 Guns, but no more than 32 Hands, that its not to be wonder'd at she made no Resistance, besides, she was deep laden with Sugars. Monsieur *Misson* took out of her what Ammunition she had, about four thousand Pieces of Eight, some Puncheons of Rum, and ten Hogsheads of Sugar; and, without doing her any further Damage, let her proceed her Voyage. What he valued most in this Prize was the Men he got, for she was carrying to *Europe* twelve *French* Prisoners, two of which were necessary Hands, being a Carpenter and his Mate. They were of *Bourdeaux,* from whence they came with the *Pomechatraine,* which was taken by the *Maremaid* off *Petit Guavers,* after an obstinate Resistance, in which they lost forty Men; but they were of Opinion the *Maremaid* could not have taken 'em, having but four Guns less than she had, which was made amends for, by their having about thirty Hands. On the contrary, had not the *Guernsey* come up, they thought of boarding and carrying the *Maremaid.* These Men very willingly came into Captain *Misson*'s Measures.

These Men, who had been stripp'd to the Skin, begg'd Leave to make Reprisals, but the Captain would not suffer them, though he told the Master of the Prize, as he protected him and his Men, he thought it reasonable these *French* should be cloathed: Upon this the Master contributed of his own, and every Man bringing up his Chest, thought themselves very well off in sharing with them one half.

Though *Misson*'s Ship pass'd for a *French* Man of War, yet his Generosity in letting the Prize go, gave the *English* Grounds to suspect the Truth, neither the Ship nor Cargoe being of Use to such as were upon the grand Account.

When they had lost all Hopes of the St. *Joseph,* they coasted along the North-Side of *Cuba,* and the *Victoire* growing now foul, they ran into a Landlock'd Bay on the East North-East Point, where they hove her down by Boats and Guns, though they could not pretend to heave her Keel out; however, they scraped and tallowed as far as they could go; they, for this Reason, many of them repented they had let the last Prize go, by which they might have careened.

When they had righted the Ship, and put every Thing on Board, they consulted upon the Course they should steer. Upon this the Council divided. The Captain and *Caraccioli* were for stretching over to the *African,* and the others for the *New-England* Coast, alledging, that the Ship had a foul Bottom, and was not fit for the Voyage; and that if they met with contrary Winds, and bad Weather, their Stock of Provision might fall short; and that as they were not far from the *English* Settlement of *Carolina,* they might either on that or the Coast of *Virginia, Maryland, Pensylvania, New-York,* or *New-England,* intercept Ships which traded to the Islands with Provisions, and by that Means provide themselves with Bread, Flower, and other Necessaries. An Account of the Provisions were taken, and finding they had Provisions for four Months. Captain *Misson* called all Hands upon Deck, and told them, as the Council differed in the Course they should steer, he thought it reasonable to have it put to the Vote of the whole Company. That for his Part, he was for going to the Coasts of *Guiney,* where they might reasonably expect to meet with valuable Prizes; but should they fail in their Expectation one Way, they would be sure of having it answered another; for they could then throw themselves in that of the *East-India* Ships, and he need not tell them, that the outward bound dreined *Europe* of what Money they drew from *America*. He then gave the Sentiments of those who were against him, and their Reasons, and begg'd that every one would give his Opinion and Vote according as he thought most conducive to the Good of all. That he should be far from taking it ill if they should reject what he had proposed, since he had no private Views to serve. The Majority of Votes fell on the Captain's Side, and they accordingly shaped their Course for the Coast of *Guiney,* in which Voyage nothing remarkable happened. On their Arrival on the Gold-Coast, they fell in with the *Nieuwstadt* of *Amsterdam,* a Ship of 18 Guns, commanded by Capt. *Blaes,* who made a running Fight of five Glasses: This Ship they kept with them, putting on Board 40 Hands, and bringing all the Prisoners on Board the *Victoire,* they were Forty three in Number; they left *Amsterdam* with Fifty six, seven were killed in the Engagement, and they had lost six by Sickness and Accidents, one falling overboard, and one being taken by a Shark going overboard in a Calm.

The *Nieuwstadt* had some Gold-Dust on Board, to the Value of about 2000 l. Sterling, and a few Slaves to the Number of Seventeen, for she had but begun to Trade; the Slaves were a strengthening of their Hands, for the Captain order'd them to be cloathed out of *Dutch* Mariners Chests, and told his Men, 'That the Trading for those of our own Species, cou'd never be agreeable to the Eyes of divine Justice: That no Man had Power of the Liberty of another; and while those who profess'd a more enlightened Knowledge of the Deity, sold Men like Beasts; they prov'd that their Religion was no more than Grimace, and that they differ'd from the *Barbarians* in Name only, since their Practice was in nothing more humane: For his Part, and he hop'd, he spoke the Sentiments of all his brave Companions, he had not exempted his Neck from the galling Yoak of Slavery, and asserted his own Liberty, to enslave others. That however, these Men were distinguish'd from the *Europeans* by their Colour, Customs, or religious Rites, they were the Work of the same omnipotent Being, and endued with equal Reason: Wherefore, he desired they might be treated like Freemen (for he wou'd banish even the Name of Slavery from among them)' and divided into Messes among them, to the End they might the sooner learn their Language, be sensible of the Obligation they had to them, and more capable and zealous to defend that Liberty they owed to their Justice and Humanity.

This Speech of *Misson*'s was received with general Applause, and the Ship rang with *vive le Capitain* Misson. Long live Capt. *Misson*. — The Negroes were divided among the *French,* one to a Mess, who, by their Gesticulations, shew'd they were gratefully sensible of their being delivered from their Chains. Their Ship growing very foul, and going heavily through the Water, they run into the River of *Lagoa,* where they hove her down, taking out such Planks as had suffer'd most by the Worms, and substituting new in their Room.

After this they careened the Prize, and so put out to Sea, steering to the Southward, and keeping along the Coast, but met with Nothing. All this while, the greatest Decorum and Regularity was observed on Board the *Victoire;* but the *Dutch* Prisoners Example began to lead 'em into Swearing and Drunkenness, which the Captain remarking, thought it was best to nip these Vices in the Bud; and calling both the *French* and *Dutch* upon Deck, he address'd himself to the former, desiring their Captain, who spoke *French* excellently well, to interpret what he said to those who did not understand him. He told them, 'before he had the the Misfortune of having them on Board, his Ears were never grated with hearing the Name of the great Creator prophaned, tho' he, to his Sorrow, had often since heard his own Men guilty of that Sin, which administer'd neither Profit nor Pleasure, and might draw upon them a severe Punishment: That if they had a just Idea of that great Being, they wou'd never mention him, but they wou'd immediately reflect on his Purity and their own Vileness. That we so easily took Impression from our Company, that the *Spanish* Proverb says, *let a Hermit and a Thief live together, the Thief wou'd become Hermit, or the Hermit Thief:* That he saw this verified in his Ship, for he cou'd attribute the Oaths and Curses he had heard among his brave Companions, to nothing but the odious Example of the *Dutch:* That this was not the only Vice they had introduced, for before they were on Board, his Men were Men, but he found by their beastly Pattern they were degenerated into Brutes, by drowning that only Faculty, which distinguishes between Man and Beast, *Reason*. That as he had the Honour to command them, he could not see them run into these odious Vices without a sincere Concern, as he had a paternal Affection for them; and he should reproach himself as neglectful of the common Good, if he did not admonish them; and as by the Post which they had honour'd him, he was obliged to have a watchful Eye over their general Interest; he was obliged to tell them his Sentiments were, that the *Dutch* allured them to a dissolute Way of Life, that they might take some Advantage over them: Wherefore, as his brave Companions, he was assured, wou'd be guided by Reason, he gave the *Dutch* Notice, that the first whom he catch'd either with an Oath in his Mouth or Liquor in his Head, should be brought to the Geers, whipped and pickled, for an Example to the rest of his Nation: As to his Friends, his Companions, his Children, those gallant, those generous, noble, and heroic Souls he had the Honour to command, he entreated them to allow a small Time for Reflection, and to consider how little Pleasure, and how much Danger, might flow from imitating the Vices of their Enemies; and that they would among themselves, make a Law for the Suppression of what would otherwise estrange them from the Source of Life, and consequently leave them destitute of his Protection.'

It is not to be imagined what Efficacy this Speech had on both Nations: The *Dutch* grew continent in Fear of Punishment, and the *French* in Fear of being reproach'd by their good Captain, for they never mentioned him without this Epithet. Upon the Coast of *Angola,* they met with a second *Dutch* Ship, the Cargo of which consisted of Silk and Woolen Stuffs, Cloath, Lace, Wine, Brandy, Oyl, Spice, and hard Ware; the Prize gave Chase and engaged her, but upon the coming up of the *Victoire* she struck. This Ship opportunely came in their Way, and gave full Employ to the Taylors, who were on Board, for the whole Crew began to be out at Elbows: They plundered her of what was of Use to their own Ship, and then sunk her.

The Captain having about ninety Prisoners on Board, proposed the giving them the Prize, with what was necessary for their Voyage, and sending them away; which being agreed to, they shifted her Ammunition on Board the *Victoire,* and giving them Provision to carry them to the Settlements the *Dutch* have on the Coast, *Misson* called them up, told them what was his Design, and ask'd if any of them was willing to share his Fortune: Eleven *Dutch* came into him, two of which were Sail-makers, one an Armourer, and one a Carpenter, necessary Hands; the rest he let go, not a little surprised at the Regularity, Tranquillity, and Humanity, which they found among these new-fashioned pyrates.

They had now run the Length of *Soldinia* Bay, about ten Leagues to the Northward of *Table* Bay. As here is good Water, safe Riding, plenty of Fish and fresh Provision, to be got of the Natives for the Merchandize they had on Board, it was resolved to stay here some little Time for Refreshments. When they had the Bay open, they spied a tall Ship, which instantly got under sail, and hove out *English* Colours. The *Victoire* made a clear Ship, and hove out her *French* Ensign, and a smart Engagement began. The *English* was a new Ship built for 40 Guns, though she had but 32 mounted, and 90 Hands. *Misson* gave Orders for boarding, and his Number of fresh Men he constantly poured in, after an obstinate Dispute obliged the *English* to fly the Decks, and leave the *French* Masters of their Ship, who promised, and gave them, good Quarters, and stripp'd not a Man.

They found on Board the Prize some Bales of *English* Broad-Cloath, and about 60000 l. in *English* Crown Pieces, and *Spanish* Pieces of Eight. The *English* Captain was killed in the Engagement, and 14 of his Men: The *French* lost 12, which was no small Mortification, but did not however provoke them to use their Prisoners harshly. Captain *Misson* was sorry for the Death of the Commander, whom he buried on the Shoar, and one of his Men being a Stone-Cutter, he raised a Stone over his Grave with these Words, *Icy gist un brave Anglois,* Here lies a gallant *English* Man; when he was buried he made a tripple Discharge of 50 small Arms, and fired Minute Guns.

The *English,* knowing whose Hands they were fallen into, charm'd with *Misson*'s Humanity, 30 of them, in 3 Days Space, desired to take on with him. He accepted 'em, but at the same

Time gave 'em to understand, that in taking on with him they were not to expect they should be indulged in a dissolute and immoral Life. He now divided his Company between the two Ships, and made *Caraccioli* Captain of the Prize, giving him Officers chosen by the public Suffrage. The 17 Negroes began to understand a little *French,* and to be useful Hands, and in less than a Month all the *English* Prisoners came over to him, except their Officers.

He had two Ships well mann'd with resolute Fellows; they now doubled the Cape, and made the South End of *Madagascar,* and one of the *English* Men telling Captain *Misson,* that the *European* Ships bound for *Surat* commonly touch'd at the Island of *Johanna,* he sent for Captain *Caraccioli* on Board, and it was agreed to cruize off that Island. They accordingly sailed on the West-Side of *Madagascar* and off the Bay *de Diego.* About half Seas over between that Bay and the Island of *Johanna,* they came up with an *English East-India* Man, which made Signals of Distress as soon as she spy'd *Misson* and his Prize; they found her sinking by an unexpected Leak, and took all her Men on Board, though they could get little out of her before she went down. The *English,* who were thus miraculously saved from perishing, desired to be set on Shoar at *Johanna,* where they hop'd to meet with either a *Dutch* or *English* Ship in a little Time, and the mean while they were sure of Relief.

They arrived at *Johanna,* and were kindly received by the Queen-Regent and her Brother, on account of the *English* on the one Hand, and of their Strength on the other, which the Queen's Brother, who had the Administration of Affairs, was not able to make Head against, and hoped they might assist him against the King of *Mohila,* who threaten'd him with a Visit.

This is an Island which is contiguous, in a manner, to *Johanna,* and lies about N. W. and by N. from it. *Caraccioli* told *Misson* he might make his Advantage in widening the Breach between these two little Monarchies, and, by offering his Assistance to that of *Johanna,* in a manner rule both, for these would court him as their Protector, and those come to any Terms to buy his Friendship, by which Means he would hold the Ballance of Power between them. He followed this Advice, and offered his Friendship and Assistance to the Queen, who very readily embraced it.

I must advise the Reader, that many of this Island speak *English,* and that the *English* Men who were of *Misson's* Crew, and his Interpreters, told them, their Captain, though not an *Englishman,* was their Friend and Ally, and a Friend and Brother to the *Johanna* Men, for they esteem the *English* beyond all other Nations.

They were supplied by the Queen with all Necessaries of Life, and *Misson* married her Sister, as *Caraccioli* did the Daughter of her Brother, whose Armory, which consisted before of no more than two rusty Fire-Locks, and three Pistols, he furnish'd with thirty Fuzils, as many Pair of Pistols, and gave him two Barrels of Powder, and four of Ball.

Several of his Men took Wives, and some required their Share of the Prizes, which was justly given them, they designing to settle in this Island, but the Number of these did not exceed ten, which Loss was repaired by thirty of the Crew (they had saved from perishing) coming in to him.

While they past their Time in all manner of Diversions the Place would afford them, as hunting, feasting, and visiting the Island, the King of *Mohila* made a Descent, and alarm'd the whole Country. *Misson* advised the Queen's Brother not to give him any Impediment, but let him get into the Heart of the Island, and he would take Care to intercept their Return; but the Prince answered, should he follow his Advice the Enemy would do him and the Subjects an irreparable Damage, in destroying the Cocoa Walks, and for that Reason he must endeavour to stop his Progress. Upon this Answer he asked the *English* who were not under his Command, if they were willing to join him in repelling the Enemies of their common Host, and one and all consenting, he gave them Arms, and mixed them with his own Men, and about the same Number of *Johannians,* under the Command of *Caraccioli* and the Queen's Brother, and arming out all his Boats, he went himself to the Westward of the Island, where they made their Descent. The Party which went by Land, fell in with, and beat the *Mohilians* with great Ease, who were in the greatest Consternation, to find their Retreat cut off by *Misson's* Boats. The *Johannians,* whom they had often molested, were so enraged, that they gave Quarter to none, and out of 300 who made the Descent, if *Misson* and *Caraccioli* had not interposed, not a Soul had escaped; 113 were taken Prisoners by his Men, and carried on Board his Ships. These he sent safe to *Mohila,* with a Message to the King, to desire he would make Peace with his Friend and Ally the King of *Johanna;* but that Prince, little affected with the Service done him in the Preservation of his Subjects, sent him Word he took Laws from none, and knew when to make War and Peace without his Advice, which he neither asked nor wanted. *Misson,* irritated by this rude Answer, resolved to transfer the War into his own Country, and accordingly set sail for *Mohila,* with about 100 *Johanna* Men. The Shoar, on Sight of the Ships, was filled with Men to hinder a Descent if intended, but the great Guns soon dispersed this Rabble, and under their Cover he landed the *Johannians,* and an equal Number of *French* and *English.* They were met by about 700 *Mohilians,* who pretended to stop their Passage, but their Darts and Arrows were of little avail against *Misson*'s Fuzils; the first Discharge made a great Slaughter, and about 20 Shells which were thrown among them, put them to a confus'd Flight. The Party of *Europeans* and *Johannians* then marched to their Metropolis, without Resistance, which they reduced to ashes and the *Johannians* cut down all the Cocoa Walks that they could for the Time, for towards Evening they returned to their Ships, and stood off to Sea.

At their Return to *Johanna* the Queen made a Festival, and magnified the Bravery and Service of her Guests, Friends, and Allies. This Feast lasted four Days, at the Expiration of which Time the Queen's Brother proposed to Captain *Misson* the making another Descent, in which he would go in Person, and did not doubt subjecting the *Mohilians;* but this was not the Design of *Misson,* who had Thoughts of fixing a Retreat on the North West Side of *Madagascar,* and look'd upon the Feuds between these two Islands advantageous to his Views, and therefore no way his Interest to suffer the one to overcome the other; for while the Variance was kept up, and their Forces pretty much upon a Level, it was evident their Interest would make both Sides caress him; he therefore answer'd, that they ought to deliberate on the Consequences, for they might be deceived in their Hopes, and find the Conquest less easy than they imagined. That the King of *Mohila* would be more upon his Guard, and not only intrench himself, but gall them with frequent Ambuscades, by which they must inevitably lose a Number of Men; and, if they were forced to retire with Loss, raise the

Courage of the *Mohilians,* and make them irreconcilable Enemies to the *Johannians,* and intirely deprive him of the Advantages with which he might now make a Peace, having twice defeated them: That he could not be always with them, and at his leaving *Johanna* he might expect the King of *Mohila* would endeavour to take a bloody Revenge for the late Damages. The Queen gave intirely into *Misson*'s Sentiments.

While this was in Agitation four *Mohilians* arrived as Ambassadors to propose a Peace. They finding the *Johannians* upon high Terms, one of them spoke to this Purpose; *O ye* Johannians, *do not conclude from your late Success, that Fortune will be always favourable; she will not always give you the Protection of the* Europeans, *and without their Help its possible you might now sue for a Peace, which you seem averse to. Remember the Sun rises, comes to its Meridian Height, and stays not there, but declines in a Moment. Let this admonish you to reflect on the constant Revolution of all sublunary Affairs, and the greater is your Glory, the nearer you are to your Declension. We are taught by every Thing we see, that there is no Stability in the World, but Nature is in continual Movement. The Sea which o'er flows the Sands has its Bounds set, which it cannot pass, which the Moment it has reached, without abiding, returns back to the Bosom of the Deep. Every Herb, every Shrub and Tree, and even our own Bodies, teach us this Lesson, that nothing is durable, or can be counted upon. Time passes away insensibly, one Sun follows another, and brings its Changes with it. To Day's Globe of Light sees you strengthened by these* Europeans *elate with Victory, and we, who have been used to conquer you, come to ask a Peace. To Morrow's Sun may see you deprived of your present Succours, and the* Johannians *petitioning us; as therefore we cannot say what to Morrow may bring forth, it would be unwise on uncertain Hopes to forego a certain Advantage, as surely Peace ought to be esteem'd by every wise Man.*

Having said this, the Ambassadors withdrew, and were treated by the Queen's Orders. After the Council had concluded, they were again call'd upon, and the Queen told them, that by the Advice of her good Friends, the *Europeans,* and those of her Council, she agreed to make a Peace, which she wish'd might banish all Memory of former Injuries. That they must own the War was begun by them, and that she was far from being the Agressor; she only defended her self in her own Kingdom, which they had often invaded, though, till within few Days, she had never molested their Coasts. If then they really desired to live amicably with her, they must resolve to send two of the King's Children, and ten of the first Nobility, as Hostages, that they might, when they pleased, return, for that was the only Terms on which she would desist prosecuting the Advantages she now had, with the utmost Vigour.

The Ambassadors return'd with this Answer, and, about ten Days after, the two Ships appearing upon their Coasts, they sent off to give Notice, that their King comply'd with the Terms proposed, would send the Hostages, and desired a Cessation of all Hostility, and, at the same Time, invited the Commanders on Shoar. The *Johanna* Men on Board disswaded their accepting the Invitation; but *Misson* and *Caraccioli,* fearing nothing, went, but arm'd their Boat's Crew. They were rceived by the King with Demonstrations of Friendship, and they dined with him under a Tamerane Tree; but when they parted from him, and were returning to their Boats, they were inclosed by, at least, 100 of the *Mohilians,* who set upon them with the utmost Fury, and, in the first Flight of Arrows, wounded both the Captains, and killed four of their Boat's Crew of eight, who were with them; they, in return, discharged their Pistols with some Execution, and fell in with their Cutlasses; but all their Bravery would have stood them in little Stead, had not the Report of their Pistols alarm'd and brought the rest of their Friends to their Assistance, who took their Fuzils, and coming up while they were engaged, discharged a Volley on the Back of the Assailants, which laid twelve of them dead on the Spot. The Ships hearing this Fire, sent immediately the Yawls and Long-Boats well mann'd. Though the Islanders were a little damp'd in their Courage by this Fire of the Boats Crew, yet they did not give over the Fight, and one of them desperately threw himself upon *Caraccioli,* and gave him a deep Wound in his Side, with a long Knife, but he paid for the Rashness of the Attempt with his Life, one of the Crew cleaving his Skull. The Yawls and Long-Boats now arrived, and being guided by the Noise, reinforced their Companions, put the Traytors to Flight, and brought off their dead and wounded. The *Europeans* lost by this Treachery seven slain outright, and eight wounded, six of which recovered.

The Crew were resolved to revenge the Blood of their Officers and Comrades the next Day, and were accordingly on the Point of Landing, when two Canoes came off with two Men bound, the pretended Authors of this Treason, without the King's Knowledge, who had sent 'em that they might receive the Punishment due to their Villany. The *Johanna* Men on Board were call'd for Interpreters, who having given this Account, added, that the King only sacrificed these Men, but that they should not believe him, for he certainly had given Orders for assassinating the *Europeans;* and the better Way was to kill all the *Mohilians* that came in the Canoes as well as the two Prisoners; go back to *Johanna,* take more of their Countrymen, and give no Peace to Traytors; but *Misson* was for no such violent Measures, he was averse to every Thing that bore the Face of Cruelty and thought a bloody Revenge, if Necessity did not enforce it, spoke a groveling and timid Soul; he, therefore, sent those of the Canoes back, and bid them tell their King, if before the Evening he sent the Hostages agreed upon, he should give Credit to his Excuse, but if he did not, he should believe him the Author of the late vile Attempt on his Life.

The Canoes went off but returned not with an Answer, wherefore, he bid the *Johanna* Men tell the two Prisoners that they should be set on Shore the next Morning, and order'd them to acquaint their King, he was no Executioner to put those to Death whom he had condemn'd, but that he should find, he knew how to revenge himself of his Treason. The Prisoners being unbound, threw themselves at his Feet, and begg'd that he would not send them ashore, for they should be surely put to Death, for the Crime they had committed, was, the dissuading the barbarous Action of which they were accused as Authors.

Next Day the two Ships landed 200 Men, under the Cover of their Canon; but that Precaution of bringing their Ships close to the Shore they found needless; not a Soul appearing, they march'd two Leagues up the Country, when they saw a Body of Men appear behind some Shrubs; *Caraccioli*'s Lieutenant, who commanded the right Wing, with fifty Men made up to them, but found he had got among Pit Falls artificially cover'd, several of his Men falling into them, which made him halt, and not pursue those *Mobilians* who made a feint Retreat to ensnare him, thinking it dangerous to proceed farther; and seeing no Enemy would face them, they retired the same Way they came, and getting into their Boats, went on Board the Ships, resolving to return with a strong Reinforcement, and make Descents at one and the same Time in different Parts of the Island. They ask'd the two Prisoners how the Country lay, and what the Soil was on the North Side the Island; and they answer'd it was morass, and the most dangerous Part to attempt, it being a Place where they shelter on any imminent Danger.

The Ships return'd to *Johanna,* where the greatest Tenderness and Care was shown for the Recovery and Cure of the two Captains and of their Men; they lay six Weeks before they were able to walk the Decks, for neither of them would quit his Ship. Their *Johanna* Wives expressed a Concern they did not think them capable of, nay, a Wife of one of the wounded Men who died, stood some Time looking upon the Corpse as motionless as a Statue, then embracing it, without shedding a Tear, desired she might take it ashore to wash and bury it; and at the same Time, by an Interpreter, and with a little Mixture of *European* Language, she had, begg'd her late Husband's Friends would take their Leave of him the next Day.

Accordingly a Number went ashore, and carried with them the Dividend, which fell to his Share, which the Captain order'd to be given his Widow; when she saw the Money, she smil'd, and ask'd if all, all that was for her? Being answered in the affirmative, and what Good will all that shining Dirt do me, if I could with it purchase the Life of my Husband, and call him back from the Grave, I would accept it with Pleasure, but as it is not sufficient to allure him back to this World, I have no Use for it; do with it what you please. Then she desired they would go with her and perform the last Ceremonies to her Husband's dead Body, after their Country Fashion, least he should be displeased, that she could not stay with them, to be a Witness, because she was in haste to go and be married again. She startled the *Europeans* who heard this latter Part of her Speech so dissonant from the Beginning; however, they followed her, and she led them into a Plantane Walk, where they found a great many *Johanna* Men and Women, sitting under the Shade of Plantanes, round the Corpse, which lay (as they all sate) on the Ground, covered with Flowers. She embraced them round, and then the *Europeans,* one by one, and after these Ceremonies, she poured out a Number of bitter Imprecations against the *Mobila* Men, whose Treachery had darken'd her Husband's Eyes, and made him insensible of her Caresses, who was her first Love, to whom she had given her Heart, with her Virginity. She then proceeded in his Praises, calling him the Joy of Infants, the Love of Virgins, the Delight of the old, and the Wonder of the young, adding, he was strong and beautiful as the Cedar, brave as the Bull, tender as the Kid, and loving as the Ground Turtle; having finished this Oration, not unlike those of the *Romans,* which the nearest Relation of the deceas'd used to pronounce from the Rostrum, she laid her down by the Side of her Husband, embracing him, and sitting up again, gave herself a deep Wound under the left Breast with a Bayonet, and fell dead on her Husband's Corpse.

The *Europeans* were astonished at the Tenderness and Resolution of the Girl, for she was not, by what her Mien spoke her, past seventeen; and they now admired, as much as they had secretly detested, her, for saying she was in haste to be married again, the Meaning of which they did not understand.

After the Husband and Wife were buried, the Crew return'd on Board, and gave an Account of what had pass'd; the Captains Wives (for *Misson* and his were on Board the *Bijoux,* the Name they had given their Prize from her Make and Gilding) seem'd not in the least surprized, and *Caraccioli*'s Lady only said, she must be of noble Descent, for none but the Families of the Nobility had the Privilege allowed them of following their Husbands, on pain, if they transgressed, of being thrown into the Sea, to be eat by Fish; and they knew, that their Souls could not rest as long as any of the Fish, who fed upon them, lived. *Misson* asked, if they intended to have done the same Thing had they died? We should not, answer'd his Wife, have disgraced our Families; nor is our Tenderness for our Husbands inferior to hers whom you seem to admire.

After their Recovery, *Misson* proposed a Cruize, on the Coast of *Zangueber,* which being agreed to, he and *Caraccioli* took Leave of the Queen and her Brother, and would have left their Wives on the Island, but they could by no Means be induced to the Separation; it was in vain to urge the Shortness of the Time they were to Cruize; they answer'd it was farther than *Mohila* they intended to go, and if they were miserable in that short Absence, they could never support a longer; and if they would not allow them to keep them Company the Voyage, they must not expect to see them at their Return, if they intended one.

In a Word they were obliged to yield to them, but told them, if the Wives of their Men should insist as strongly on following their Example, their Tenderness, would be their Ruin, and make them a Prey to their Enemies; they answer'd the Queen should prevent that, by ordering no Woman should go on Board, and if any were in the Ships, they should return on Shore: This Order was accordingly made, and they set Sail for the River of *Mozembique*. In about ten Days Cruize after they had left *Johanna,* and about 15 Leagues to the Eastward of this River, they fell in with a stout *Portuguese* Ship of 60 Guns, which engaged them from Break of Day till Two in the Afternoon, when the Captain being killed, and a great Number of Men lost, she struck: This proved a very rich Prize, for she had the Value of 250000 l. Sterling on Board, in Gold-Dust. The two Women never quitted the Decks all the Time of the Engagement, neither gave they the least Mark of Fear, except for their Husbands: This Engagement cost them thirty Men, and *Caraccioli* lost his right Leg; the Slaughter fell mostly on the *English,* for of the above Number, twenty were of that Nation: The *Portuguese* lost double the Number. *Caraccioli*'s Wound made them resolve to make the best of their Way for *Johanna,* where the greatest Care was taken of their wounded, not one of whom died, tho' their Number amounted to Twenty seven.

Caraccioli kept his Bed two Months, but *Misson* seeing him in a fair way of Recovery, took what Hands could be spar'd from the *Bijoux,* leaving her sufficient for Defence, and went out, having mounted ten of the *Portuguese* Guns, for he had hitherto carried but thirty, though he had Ports for forty. He stretched over to *Madagascar,* and coasted along this Island to the Northward, as far as the most northerly Point, when turning back, he enter'd a Bay to the northward of *Diego Suares.* He run ten Leagues up this Bay, and on the larboard Side found it afforded a large, and safe, Harbour, with plenty of fresh Water. He came here to an

Anchor, went ashore and examined into the Nature of the Soil, which he found rich, the Air wholesome, and the Country level. He told his Men, that this was an excellent Place for an Asylum, and that he determined here to fortify and raise a small Town, and make Docks for Shipping, that they might have some Place to call their own; and a Receptacle, when Age or Wounds had render'd them incapable of Hardship, where they might enjoy the Fruits of their Labour, and go to their Graves in Peace. That he would not, however, set about this, till he had the Approbation of the whole Company; and were he sure they would all approve this Design, which he hoped, it being evidently for the general Good, he should not think it adviseable to begin any Works, lest the Natives should, in his Absence, destroy them; but however, as they had nothing upon their Hands, if they were of his Opinion, they might begin to fall and square Timber, ready for the raising a wooden Fort, when they return'd with their Companions.

The Captain's Motion was universally applauded, and in ten Days they fell'd and rough hew'd a hundred and fifty large Trees, without any Interruption from, or seeing any of, the Inhabitants. They fell'd their Timber at the Waters Edge, so that they had not the Trouble of hawling them any way, which would have employ'd a great deal more Time: They returned again, and acquainted their Companions with what they had seen and done, and with the Captain's Resolution, which they one and all came into.

Captain *Misson* then told the Queen, as he had been serviceable to her in her War with the Island of *Mohila,* and might continue to be of farther Use, he did not question her lending him Assistance in the settling himself on the Coast of *Madagascar,* and to that end, furnish him with 300 Men, to help in his Buildings; the Queen answered, she could do nothing without Consent of Council, and that she would assemble her Nobility, and did not question their agreeing to any Thing he could reasonably desire, for they were sensible of the Obligations the *Johanians* had to him. The Council was accordingly called, and *Misson*'s Demand being told, one of the eldest said, he did not think it expedient to comply with it, nor safe to refuse; that they should in agreeing to give him that Assistance, help to raise a Power, which might prove formidable to themselves, by the being so near a Neighbour; and these Men who had lately protected, might, when they found it for their Interest, enslave them. On the other hand, if they did not comply, they had the Power to do them great Damage. That they were to make choice of the least of two possible Evils, for he could prognosticate no Good to *Johanna,* by their settling near it. Another answered, that many of them had *Johanna* Wives, that it was not likely they would make Enemies of the *Johanna* Men at first settling, because their Friendship might be of Use to them; and from their Children there was nothing to be apprehended in the next Generation, for they would be half their own Blood; that in the mean while, if they comply'd with the Request, they might be sure of an Ally, and Protector, against the King of *Mohila;* wherefore, he was for agreeing to the Demand.

After a long Debate, in which every Inconvenience, and Advantage, was maturely considered, it was agreed to send with him the Number of Men he required, on Condition he should send them back in four Moons, make an Alliance with them, and War against *Mohila;* this being agreed to, they staid till *Caraccioli* was thoroughly recovered, then putting the *Johannians* on board the *Portuguese* Ship with 40 *French* and *English* and 15 *Portuguese* to work her, and setting Sail, they arrived at the Place where *Misson* designed his Settlement, which he called *Libertalia,* and gave the Name of *Liberi* to his People, desiring in that might be drown'd the distinguish'd Names of *French, English, Dutch, Africans,* &c.

The first Thing they sat about was, the raising a Fort on each Side the Harbour, which they made of an octogon Figure, and having finished and mounted them with 40 Guns taken out of the *Portuguese,* they raised a Battery on an Angle of ten Guns, and began to raise Houses and Magazines under the Protection of their Forts and Ships; the *Portuguese* was unrigg'd, and all her Sails and Cordage carefully laid up. While they were very busily employed in the raising a Town, a Party which had often hunted and rambled four or five Leagues off their Settlement, resolved to venture farther into the Country. They made themselves some Huts, at about 4 Leagues distance from their Companions, and travell'd East South East, about 5 Leagues farther into the Country, when they came up with a Black, who was arm'd with a Bow, Arrows, and a Javelin; they with a friendly Appearance engaged the Fellow to lay by his Fear and go with them. They carried him to their Companions, and there entertained him three Days with a great Deal of Humanity, and then returned with him near the Place they found him, made him a Present of a Piece of scarlet Baze, and an Ax; he appeared overjoy'd at the Present, and left them with seeming Satisfaction.

The Hunters imagined that there might be some Village not far off, and observing that he look'd at the Sun, and then took his Way direct South, they travell'd on the same Point of the Compass, and from the Top of a Hill they spied a pretty large Village, and went down to it; the Men came out with their Arms, such as before described, Bows, Arrows, and Javelins, but upon two only of the Whites advancing, with Presents of Axes, and Baze in their Hands, they sent only four to meet them. The Misfortune was, that they could not understand one another, but by their pointing to the Sun, and holding up one Finger, and making one of them go forward, and return again with showing their Circumcision, and pointing up to Heaven with one Finger, they apprehended, they gave them to understand, there was but one God, who had sent one Prophet, and concluded from thence, and their Circumcision they were *Mahometans;* the Presents were carried to their Chief, and he seem'd to receive them kindly, and by Signs invited the Whites into their Village; but they, remembring the late Treachery of the *Mobilians,* made Signs for Victuals to be brought them where they were.

More of the History of these Adventurers in another Place.

Chap. XXI
Of Capt. JOHN Bowen

The exact Time of this Person's setting out I am not certain of; I find him cruising on the *Mallabar* Coast in the Year 1700, commanding a Ship called the *Speaker,* whose Crew consisted of Men of all Nations, and their Pyracies were committed upon Ships of all Nations likewise. The pyrates here met with no Manner of Inconveniencies in carrying on their Designs, for it was made so much a Trade, that the Merchants of one Town never scrupled the buying Commodities taken from another, though but ten Miles distant, in a public Sale, furnishing the Robbers at the same Time with all Necessaries, even of Vessels, when they had Occasion to go on any Expedition, which they themselves would often advise them of.

Among the rest an *English East-India* Man, Captain *Coneway* from *Bengal,* fell into the Hands of this Crew, which they made Prize of, near *Callequilon;* they carried her in, and put her up to sale, dividing the Ship and Cargoe into three Shares; one Third was sold to a Merchant, Native of *Callequilon* aforesaid, another Third to a Merchant of *Porca,* and the other to one *Malpa,* à *Dutch* Factor.

Loaded with the Spoil of this and several Country Ships, they left the Coast, and steer'd for *Madagascar;* but in their Voyage thither, meeting with adverse Winds, and, being negligent in their Steerage, they ran upon St. *Thomas*'s Reef, at the the Island of *Mauritius,* where the Ship was lost; but *Bowen* and the greatest Part of the Crew got safe ashore.

They met here with all the Civility and good Treatment imaginable; *Bowen* was complimented in a particular Manner by the Governor, and splendidly entertained in his House; the sick Men were got, with great Care, into the Fort, and cured by their Doctor, and no Supplies of any sort wanting for the rest. They spent here three Months, but yet resolving to set down at *Madagascar,* they bought a Sloop, which they converted into a Brigantine, and, about the middle of *March* 1701, departed, having first taken formal Leave of the Governor, by making a Present of 2500 Pieces of Eight, leaving him, besides, the Wreck of their Ship, with the Guns, Stores, and every Thing else that was saved. The Governor, on his Part, supply'd them with Necessaries for their Voyage, which was but short, and gave them a kind Invitation to make that Island a Place of Refreshment in the Course of their future Adventures, promising that nothing should be wanting to them that his Government afforded.

Upon their Arrival at *Madagascar,* they put in at a Place on the East-Side, called *Maritan,* quitted their Vessel, and settled themselves ashore in a fruitful Plain on the Side of a River. They built themselves a Fort on the River's Mouth towards the Sea, and another small one on the other Side towards the Country; the first to prevent a Surprize from Shipping, and the other as a Security from the Natives, many of whom they employed in the Building. They built also a little Town for their Habitation, which took up the Remainder of the Year 1701.

When this was done, they soon became dissatisfied with their new Situation, having a hankering Mind after their old Employment, and accordingly resolved to fit up the Brigantine they had from the *Dutch* at *Mauritius,* which was laid in a Cove near their Settlement, but an Accident, that they improved, provided for them in a better Manner, and saved them a great deal of Trouble.

It happened that about the beginning of the Year 1702, a Ship called the *Speedy Return,* belonging to the *Scotch-African* and *East-India* Company, Captain *Drummond* Commander, came into the Port of *Maritan* in *Madagascar,* with a Brigantine that belonged to her; they had before taken in Negroes at St. *Mary*'s, a little Island adjoining to the main Island of *Madagascar,* and carried them to Don *Mascarenhas,* from whence they sailed to this Port on the same Trade.

On the Ship's Arrival, Captain *Drummond,* with *Andrew Wilky,* his Surgeon, and several others of the Crew, went on Shore; in the mean while *John Bowen,* with four others of his Consorts, goes off in a little Boat, on Pretence of buying some of their Merchandize brought from *Europe,* and finding a fair Opportunity, the chief Mate, Boatswain, and a Hand or two more only upon the Deck, and the rest at Work in the Hold, they threw off their Mask; each drew out a Pistol and Hanger, and told them, they were all dead Men if they did not retire that Moment to the Cabin. The Surprize was sudden, and they thought it necessary to obey; one of the pyrates placed himself Centry at the Door, with his Arms in his Hands, and the rest immediately laid the Hatches, and then made a Signal to their Fellows on Shore, as agreed on; upon which, about forty or fifty came on Board, and took quiet Possession of the Ship, and afterwards the Brigantine, without Bloodshed, or striking a Stroke.

Bowen was made, or rather made himself, of Course, Captain; he detained the old Crew, or the greatest Part thereof, burnt the Brigantine as being of no Use to them, cleaned and fitted the Ship, took Water, Provisions, and what Necessaries were wanting, and made ready for new Adventures.

I shall leave them a while, to relate an unfortunate Story of a worthy honest Gentleman, who suffered through the Rashness and Folly of a headstrong People, for piratically taking and murdering the Captain and Crew of this very Ship *Bowen* and his Gang now seized.

An *English-India* Man, commanded by Captain *Thomas Green*, called the *Worcester*, in her Voyage home to *England*, was drove by southerly Winds into *Scotland*, in the Month of *July* 1704, and anchored in *Leith* Road; the Captain, and several of the Ship's Company, going ashore for Refreshments, the People of the Town, who had Acquaintance and Friends in Captain *Drummond*'s Ship, understanding the *Worcester* came from the *East-Indies*, were very importunate in their Enquiries after this Ship, and being told that they had heard of no such Ship in *India*, the Enquirers pretended to be very much surprized; so that, in short, it grew into a Suspicion that the *Worcester* had not dealt fairly by the *Scotch* Ship, which they had not heard of themselves since her Departure. In short, the Magistrates were inform'd that some of the Crew had dropt Words that plainly indicated the supposed Robbery and Murders of their Countrymen. Upon this several Men were privately examined; sometimes they were threaten'd to be hanged, and then again large Promises were made to encourage 'em to discover the pretended Fact; till at length an *Indian* Boy was prevailed on to confess the whole Matter upon Oath, as they might think. Then the Captain, chief Mate and Crew, were seized and sent to Prison, the Ship was unloaded, and almost ripp'd to Pieces, to search for Goods, Writings, &c. to confirm the *Indian*'s Deposition, but nothing could be found; therefore they were obliged to try them, and try them they did, upon this Evidence, and some small Circumstances sworn to by *Charles May*, the Surgeon, which carried great Improbabilities along with it. The Depositions were as follow; the *Indian*, whose Name was *Antonio Ferdinando* swore, 'That on the Coast of *Mallabar* he came aboard the Sloop that attended the *Worcester*, and thereafter saw an Engagement between the said Sloop, the *Worcester* and another Ship, sailed by White Men, speaking *English*, and bearing *English* Colours. That they did engage the said Ship for three Days, and on the third Day the said Ship was boarded by those in the Sloop, who took up the Crew of the said Ship from under Deck, killed them with Hatchets, and threw them overboard.

Charles May only deposed, 'That being ashore at *Callequillon* he heard Guns firing at Sea, and asking some Body he met at the Landing Place, what meant this shooting? He was answered, the *Worcester* was gone out, and was fighting at Sea with another Ship. That the next Morning he saw the *Worcester* riding at her Birth, where she had rid the Day before, and another Ship riding at her Stern. That the *Worcester*'s Long-Boat coming ashore, and he asking the Men what brought them ashore? They answered, they were sent for Water, they having spilt and staved all their Water; and that they had been busking all Night. That *this Evidence* going aboard five or six Days after, saw the Ship lumber'd with Goods, and that he was inform'd that the Ship that was riding at the *Worcester*'s Stern, was sold to *Cogo Comodo*, Merchant at *Quilon*. That *Antonio Ferdinando* was wounded, and some others; and when he ask'd the Patients how they came by their Wounds, they were forbid to answer by Mr. *Madder*, the chief Mate. That all this fell out between the Months of *January* and *February* 1703.

As to *Antonio*'s Deposition, it appear'd to be all Invention, and nothing true in it; and *Charles May*'s a Heap of sly Insinuations, drawn from a known Fact, which was this; the *Worcester* departing from *Callequillon* to *Carnipole*, was drove by Stress of Weather from near the Road of *Quillon* to *Anjango,* where coming near the *Aureng Zeb, India* Man, she saluted her with five Guns, which were the Guns the Surgeon heard; and the *Aureng Zeb* came in along with the *Worcester,* and anchor'd at her Stern, which was the Ship taken Notice of by him. By busking all Night is meant only beating to Windward, which she did in order to fetch *Quillon,* the Wind being contrary. The *Worcester* spar'd her Water to the *Aureng Zeb,* which occasioned their sending for more, and the wounded Men, which were proved to be no more than three in the Voyage; one was from a Fall in the Hold, another by fighting with Knives, between two *Dutch* Men, and the other by cutting of Wood.

'Tis observable likewise, that *May*'s Evidence, which is brought to support *Antonio*'s, contradicted it in several Parts; for *Antonio* swore the Fact to be done between *Callicut* and *Tallecherry,* (where, by the Way, the Ship never was, as was own'd by the Surgeon, and prov'd by the Captain's and other Journals) and *May* heard the Guns at *Callequillon,* which could not be less then 140 Miles asunder. *Antonio* makes the supposed Engagement hold three Days; according to *May,* the *Worcester* was busking only one Night; all the rest of his Evidence is, *As he was inform'd, As he was told,* &c. And what's remarkable of this *May,* is, he was eighteen Months after this in the said Ship, and own'd on the Trial, that he never heard in all that Time one Word spoken of a Fight with any other Ship, or a Prize taken, or any Thing relating to such an Action, which must be very strange, if the Matter had been true.

In short, Captain *Green* and the rest of the Crew were convicted, and received Sentence for the supposed Crimes, as follows, *Green, Madder, Sympson, Keigle* and *Haines* to be hanged on *Wednesday, April* 4th. *Taylor, Glenn, Kitchen* and *Robertson,* on *Wednesday, April* 11th, and *Brown, Bruckley, Wilcocks, Ballantyne* and *Linsey,* on *Wednesday, April* 18th.

I cannot but here take Notice (though with much Concern) that upon the Condemnation of these unhappy Men, there seemed a universal Joy in and about the City; it was the only Discourse for some Days, and every Man thought himself nearly concerned in it; and some could not forbear in Words openly to express their brutal Joy: *Now,* said they, *we'll* Darien *'em: By this they shall see we'll do our selves Justice,* &c.

After Sentence, the Prisoners desired not to be disturb'd in their dying Moments, that they might improve 'em to the best Advantage; but now they were not only insulted with the most opprobrious Language, by such as could get to 'em, but continually worried by the religious Kirk Teachers. The most dismal Threatnings were denounc'd against 'em, and nothing but God's Wrath and eternal Torments in all its Horrors, were to be their Portion, if they died obdurate (as they call'd it) that is, without owning themselves guilty; and all this delivered with that Passion peculiar to that bitter Sett of Men. Nay, so restless were they, that even now, after Condemnation, they singled out some they found more terrified by their Cant, and assur'd 'em of Life if they would ingenuously acknowledge the Crimes they were condemned for; and, at last, worked so far upon *Haines* and *Linsey,* that they brought them to own almost what they pleased. The former of these, upon their Pardons being granted, gave a frightful Account of the whole Pyracy and Murther upon *Drummond*'s Ship, and took Care, as near as he could, to keep close with *Ferdinando*'s Evidence, only here and there he was out in very material Points, as Men always are that don't relate Matters of Fact. There was a great many bloody Circumstances added to colour the whole, as their Manner of Swearing when they commenced pyrates (much like the ridiculous Ceremonies at making of Witches) which, he said, was thus; Every one of 'em was let Blood, which they mixed together, and after every Man had drank part, they all swore to Secrecy, *&c.* with abundance of such Stuff. *Linsey,* a Man of better Sense, contented himself with saying as little as possible, which was excusable, he being on shoar in the pretended Engagement, so that most of what he said, consisted in Hearsays of the *Indians, &c.* Thus these poor Wretches screen'd themselves from this fatal Blow, at the Expence of Faith and a good Conscience, and to enjoy a troublesome Life, perhaps a few Years.

As soon as their Confessions were made public, the Gentry, as well as the Mob, was transported with Rage, and the poor Wretches were blackened and reviled in a shameful Manner;

and so violent was the Torrent of their Fury, that it reached even their Council for their Tryals, and they were obliged, for their own Safety, to withdraw into the Country.

In the midst of this Confusion two Men, who were known to be of *Drummond*'s Crew, came home in the *Raper* Galley, and made Affidavits of the Loss of the said Ship to the pyrates, as has been mentioned; upon which her Majesty and Council first reprieved them for eight Days, and afterwards desired Execution might be farther respited till they heard from above.

The common People, who for some Time past, with raised Expectations, had waited for the Execution, began to grow very impatient, bitterly inveighing against the Reprieve; and the Council met on the 11th of *April* in the Morning, to consider what was to be done; which the Mob perceiving, imagined 'twas in order to a further Reprieve or Pardon; immediately all Shops were shut up, and the Streets filled with incredible Numbers of Men, Women and Children, calling for Justice upon those *English* Murtherers. The Lord Chancellour *Seafield*'s Coach happening to pass by, they stopp'd it, broke the Sashes, haul'd him out, and oblig'd him to promise Execution should speedily be done before he could get from 'em.

According to the Chancellor's Promise, soon after, on the same Day, being *Wednesday,* Captain *Green, Madder,* and *Sympson* were brought out, and convey'd to Execution, which was at *Leith Road* upon the Sands, and all the Way were huzza'd in Triumph as it were, and insulted with the sharpest and most bitter Invectives.

Thus fell these unhappy Men a well-pleasing Sacrifice to the Malice of wicked Men.

As for Captain *Green*'s Speech; after he had taken Notice of the Crimes he was to dye for, and appealed to all present to charge him, or the Crew, with any Injustice, since he had lived there; he goes on in giving an Account of his Faith, his living and dying in the *Church of England,* of their Manner of Life abroad, their Observance of religious Duties, and the Sense he had of the Impossibility of Salvation, if he dy'd with a Falshood in his Mouth. Then follows, — 'Pursuant to which, I in the Presence of Almighty God, declare to you his People, that I am innocent in Design or Deed, and free from the Crimes for which I am condemned. That to my Knowledge, I never all my Life-time wrong'd Man in his Person or Goods, or had Accession thereto. What the Custom of pyrates is, I thank God I know not: But I understand my Accusers and Persecuters will have you to believe, that I think it unnecessary to confess before Men. Take what I say as good Christians ought to do; if you have no Charity, you wrong your selves, and cannot hurt me.

'I am told some of my Crew have confess'd the Crimes, and load us with Guilt; this is done since Sentence, and in hopes of saving themselves, which I wish they may do by lawful Means, and not have Accession to the shedding innocent Blood. I am a dying, these are still in hopes to live, chuse you which of us to believe, *&c.*

To return to Captain *Bowen,* who piratically possessed himself of Captain *Drummond*'s Ship and Brigantine, as aforesaid, he, being inform'd by the Crew, that when they left Don *Mascarenhas,* a Ship called the *Rook* Galley, Captain *Honeycomb* Commander, was lying in that Bay, resolved, with the other pyrates, to sail thither, but it taking up seven or eight Days in watering their Vessels, and settling their private Affairs, they arrived not at the Island till after the Departure of the said Galley, who thereby happily escaped the villainous Snare of their unprovok'd Enemies.

The Night after the pyrates left *Maritan,* the Brigantine ran on a Ledge of Rocks off the West Side of the Island *Madagascar,* which not being perceived by the Ship, *Bowen* came into *Mascarenhas* without her, not knowing what was become of his Consort.

Here Captain *Bowen* staid eight or ten Days, in which Time he supplied the Ship with Provisions, and judging, that the *Rook* Galley was gone to some other Island, the Ship sail'd to *Mauritius,* in search of her; but the pyrates seeing four or five Ships in the N. W. Harbour, they thought themselves too weak to attempt any thing there, so they stood immediately for *Madagascar* again, and arrived safe, first to *Port Dauphin,* and then to *Augustin Bay.* In a few Days the *Content* Brigantine, which they supposed either to have been lost, or revolted that honourable Service, came into the same Bay, and informed their Brethren of the Misfortune that happened to them: The Rogues were glad, no doubt, of seeing one another again, and calling a Council together, they found the Brigantine in no Condition for Business, being then very leaky, therefore she was condemned, and forthwith halled ashore and burnt, and the Crew united, and all went aboard the *Speedy Return.*

At this Place the pyrates were made acquainted, by the Negroes, of the Adventures of another Gang that had settled for some Time near that Harbour, and had one *Howard* for their Captain. It was the Misfortune of an *India* Ship called the *Prosperous,* to come into the Bay at a Time that these Rogues were looking out for Employment; who, under the Pretence of trading (almost in the same Manner that *Bowen* and his Gang had seized the *Speedy Return*) made themselves Masters of her, and sailed with her to *New Mathelage.* *Bowen* and his Gang consulting together on this Intelligence, concluded 'twas more for their Interest to join in Alliance with this new Company, than to act single, they being too weak of themselves to undertake any considerable Enterprize, remembring how they were obliged to bear away from the Island of *Mauritius,* when they were in search of the *Rook* Gally, which they might have taken, with several others, had they had at that Time a Confort of equal Force to their own Ship.

They accordingly set sail from the Bay, and came into *New Mathelage,* but found no Ship there, tho' upon Enquiry they understood that the Pyrate they look'd for, had been at the Place, but was gone; so after some Stay they proceeded to *Johanna,* but the *Prosperous* not being there neither, they sailed to *Mayotta,* where they found her lying at Anchor; this was about *Christmas* 1702.

Here these two Powers struck up an Alliance, *Howard* liking the Proposals, came readily into it, and the Treaty was ratified by both Companies. They staid above two Months at this Island, thinking it, perhaps, as likely a Place to meet with Prey as cruising out for it, and so indeed it happened; for about the beginning of *March,* the Ship *Pembroke* belonging to our *East-India* Company, coming in for Water, was boarded by their Boats, and taken, with the Loss of the chief Mate and another Man that were killed in the Skirmish.

The two Pyrate Ships weighed, and went out to Sea along with their Prize, and that Day and the next plundered her of the best Part of her Cargo, Provisions and Stores, and then taking the Captain and Carpenter away, they let the *Pembroke* go where the Remainder of her Crew pleased, and came with their Ships into *New Methelage.* Here the two Captains consulted, and laid a Plan for a

Cruize to *India,* for which Purpose they detained Captain *Woolley* of the *Pembroke* lately taken, in order to be their Pilot in those Seas; but a very hot Dispute arose between the two Companies, which Ship he should go aboard of, insomuch that they had gone together by the Ears, if an Expedient had not been found to satisfy each Party, that one might not have the Advantage of the other by the Captain's Skill and Knowledge of the *Indian* Coast, and this was to knock the poor Man on the Head; and murder him; but at last, by the Authority of *Bowen,* Captain *Woolley* escaped the threaten'd Danger, by bringing his Company to consent to his remaining on board the *Prosperous,* where he then was.

The *Speedy Return* being foul, and wanting a little Repair, it was judged proper for her to go back to *Augustin* Bay to clean; in the mean while the *Prosperous* was to have a Pair of Boot-Tops where she lay, and likewise to take in Water and Provision, and then to join their Confort again at *Mayotta,* the Island appointed for the Rendezvous.

The *Prosperous* put into *Mayotta* as agreed on, and waiting there some Time for *Bowen's* Ship, without seeing or hearing any News of her, went to *Johanna,* but not meeting with her there, they apprehended some Accident had befel her, and therefore left the Place, and sailed on the Expedition themselves. As to the *Speedy Return,* she arrived safe at St. *Augustin's* Bay at *Madagascar,* and there cleaned and victualled; but tarrying there somewhat too long, the Winds hung contrary, and they could not for their Lives beat up to *Mayotta,* and therefore went to *Johanna,* where, hearing that their Friends had lately left that Island, they steered for the *Red Sea,* but the Wind not proving fair for their Design, they bore away for the High Land of St. *John's,* near *Surat,* where they once more fell in Company with their Brethren of the *Prosperous.*

They cruiz'd together, as was first agreed on, and after some Time they had Sight of four Ships, to whom they gave Chace; but these separating, two standing to Northward, and two to the Southward, the pyrates separated likewise, *Bowen* standing after those that steered Southerly, and *Howard* crowded after the others. *Bowen* came up with the heaviest of the two, which proved to be a *Moorish* Ship of 700 Tun, bound from the Gulph of *Mocha* to *Surat*. The pyrates brought the Prize into *Rajapora*, on the Coast of *India*, where they plundered her; the Merchandize they sold to the Natives, but a small Sum of current Gold they found aboard, amounting to 22,000 *l*. *English* Money, they put into their Pockets. Two Days after the *Prosperous* came in, but without any Prize; however, they soon made their Friends acquainted that they had not succeeded worse than themselves, for at *Surat* River's Mouth, where all the four Ships were bound, they came up with their Chace; and with a Broadside, one of them struck, but the other got into the Bay. They stood down the Coast with the Prize till they had plundered her of the best of her Cargoe, the most valuable of which was 84,000 *Chequins*, a Piece of about ten Shillings each, and then they left her adrift, without either Anchor or Cable, off *Daman*.

While they were lying at *Rajapora* they past a Survey on their Shipping, and judging their own to be less serviceable than their Prize, they voted them to the Flames, and straightway fitted up the *Surat* Ship; they transported both Companies aboard of her, and then set Fire to the *Prosperous* and *Speedy Return*. They mustered at this Place 164 fighting Men, 43 only were *English*, the greater

Number *French*, the rest *Danes, Swedes* and *Dutch;* they took aboard 70 *Indians* to do the Drudgery of the Ship, and mounted 56 Guns, calling her the *Defiance*, and sailed from *Rajapora* the latter End of *October*, in the Year 1703, to cruize on the Coast of *Mallabar:*

But not meeting with Prey in this first Cruise, they came to an Anchor about three Leagues to the Northward of *Cochen*, expecting some Boats to come off with Supplies of Refreshments, for which Purpose they fired several Guns, by way of Signal, but none appearing, the Quarter-Master was sent in the Pinnace to confer with the People, which he did with some Caution, keeping the Boat upon their Oars at the Shore-Side: In short, they agreed very well, the pyrates were promised whatever Necessaries they wanted, and the Boat returned aboard.

The next Day a Boat came off from the Town with Hogs, Goats, Wine, *&c.* with a private Intimation from *Malpa*, the *Dutch* Broker, an old Friend of the pyrates, that a Ship of that Country called the *Rimæ*, lay then in *Mudbay*, not many Leagues off, and if they would go out and take her, he would purchase the Cargo of them, and likewise promised that they should be further supplied with Pitch, Tar, and all other Necessaries, which was made good to them; for People from the Factory flocked aboard every Hour, and dealt with them as in open Market, for all Sorts of Merchandize, Refreshments, Jewels and Plate, returning with Coffers of Money, *&c.* to a great Value.

The Advice of the Ship was taken very kindly, but the pyrates judging their own Ship too large to go close into the Bay, consulted their Friend upon Means for taking the said Ship, who readily treated with them for the Sale of one of less Burthen that lay then in the Harbour; but *Malpa* speaking to one *Punt* of the Factory to carry her out, he not only refused to be concerned in such a Piece of Villainy, but reproved *Malpa* for corresponding with the pyrates, and told him, if he should be guilty of so base an Action, he must never see the Face of any of his Countrymen more; which made the honest Broker change both his Countenance and his Purpose.

At this Place Captain *Woolley*, whom they had taken for their Pilot on the *India* Coast, being in a very sick and weak Condition, was, at his earnest Intreaty, discharged from his severe Confinement among them, and set ashore, and the next Day the pyrates sailed, and ranged along the *Mallabar* Coast, in quest of more Booty. In their Way they met a second time with the *Pembroke*, and plundered her of some Sugar, and other small Things, and let her go again. From the Coast they sail'd back for the Island of *Mauritius*, where they lay some Time, and lived after their usual extravagant Manner.

At *Mauritius* two of the Crew, *viz. Israel Phipeny* and *Peter Freeland*, left the pyrates and concealed themselves in the Island till the Ship sailed. These two Men were part of *Drum-*

mond's Crew, who found an Opportunity of coming to *England* soon after on board the *Raper* Galley, and arrived at *Portsmouth* in *March* 1725. When this came to be known, Mr. *John Green,* Brother to Capt. *Green,* then under Sentence, went thither and got the Affidavits of the said *Phipeny* and *Freeland,* made before the Mayor of *Portsmouth,* containing several Matters herein mentioned, which Affidavits were immediately brought to *London,* and by the Secretary of State sent away Express to *Scotland,* which arrived there some Hours before Capt. *Green* was executed.

Chap. XXII
Of Capt. WILLIAM KID

We are now going to give an Account of one whose Name is better known in *England,* than most of those whose Histories we have already related; the Person we mean is Captain *Kid,* whose public Trial and Execution here, rendered him the Subject of all Conversation, so that his Actions have been chanted about in Ballads; however, it is now a considerable Time since these Things passed, and though the People knew in general that Captain *Kid* was hanged, and that his Crime was Pyracy, yet there were scarce any, even at that Time, who were acquainted with his Life or Actions, or could account for his turning Pyrate.

In the Beginning of King *William's* War, Captain *Kid* commanded a Privateer in the *West-Indies,* and by several adventurous Actions acquired the Reputation of a brave Man, as well as an experienced Seaman. About this Time the pyrates were very troublesome in those Parts, wherefore Captain *Kid* was recommended by the Lord *Bellamont,* then Governor of *Barbadoes,* as well as by several other Persons, to the Government here, as a Person very fit to be entrusted with the Command of a Government Ship, and to be employed in cruising upon the pyrates, as knowing those Seas perfectly well, and being acquainted with all their lurking Places; but what Reasons governed the Politics of those Times, I cannot tell, but this Proposal met with no Encouragement here, though it is certain it would have been of great Consequence to the Subject, our Merchants suffering incredible Damages by those Robbers.

Upon this Neglect the Lord *Bellamont* and some others, who knew what great Captures had been made by the pyrates, and what a prodigious Wealth must be in their Possession, were tempted to fit out a Ship at their own private Charge, and to give the Command of it to Captain *Kid;* and, to give the Thing a greater Reputation, as well as to keep their Seamen under the better Command, they procured the King's Commission for the said Captain *Kid,* of which the following is an exact Copy.

William Rex,

> *William* the Third, by the Grace of God, King of *England, Scotland, France* and *Ireland,* Defender of the Faith, *&c.* To our trusty and well beloved Captain *William Kid,* Commander of the Ship the *Adventure* Gally, or to any other the Commander of the same for the Time being, GREETING; Whereas we are informed, that Captain *Thomas Too, John Ireland,* Captain *Thomas Wake,* and Captain *William Maze,* or *Mace,* and other Subjects, Natives or Inhabitants of *New-York,* and elsewhere, in our Plantations in *America,* have associated themselves, with divers others, wicked and ill disposed Persons, and do, against the Law of Nations, commit many and great Pyracies, Robberies and Depredations on the Seas upon the Parts of *America,* and in other Parts, to the great Hinderance and Discouragement of Trade and Navigation, and to the great Danger and Hurt of our loving Subjects, our Allies, and all others, navigating the Seas upon their lawful Occasions. Now KNOW YE, that we being desirous to prevent the aforesaid Mischiefs, and, as much as in us lies, to bring the said pyrates, Free Booters and Sea Rovers to Justice, have thought fit, and do hereby give and grant to the said *William Kid* (to whom our Commissioners for exercising the Office of Lord High Admiral of *England,* have granted a Commission as a private Man of War, bearing Date the 11th Day of *December* 1695, and unto the Commander of the said Ship for the Time being, and unto the Officers, Mariners, and others, which shall be under your Command, full Power and Authority to apprehend, sieze, and take into your Custody as well the said Captain *Thomas Too, John Ireland,* Captain *Thomas Wake,* and Captain *William Maze,* or *Mace,* as all such pyrates, Free Booters and Sea Rovers, being either our Subjects, or of other Nations associated with them, which you shall meet with upon the Seas, or Coasts of *America,* or upon any other Seas or Coasts, with all their Ships and Vessels; and all such Merchandizes, Money, Goods

and Wares as shall be found on Board, or with them, in Case they shall willingly yield themselves; but if they will not yield without fighting, then you are by Force to compel them to yield. And we do also require you to bring, or cause to be brought, such pyrates, Free Booters, or Sea Rovers, as you shall seize, to a legal Tryal, to the End they may be proceeded against according to the Law in such Cases. And we do hereby command all our Officers, Ministers, and other our loving Subjects whatsover, to be aiding and assisting to you in the Premisses. And we do hereby enjoin you to keep an exact Journal of your Proceedings in the Execution of the Premisses, and set down the Names of such pyrates, and of their Officers and Company, and the Names of such Ships and Vessels as you shall by Vertue of these Presents take and seize, and the Quantities of Arms, Ammunition, Provision and Lading of such Ships, and the true Value of the same, as near as you judge. And we do hereby strictly charge and command you as you will answer the contrary at your Peril, that you do not, in any Manner, offend or molest our Friends or Allies, their Ships, or Subjects, by Colour or Pretence of these Presents, or the Authority thereby granted. In Witness whereof we have caused our Great Seal of *England* to be affix'd to these Presents. Given at our Court of *Kensington,* the 26th Day of *January* 1695,in the seventh Year of our Reign.

Captain *Kid* had also another Commission, which was called a Commission of Reprisals; for it being then War Time, this Commission was to justify him in the taking of *French* Merchant Ships, in Case he should meet with any; but as this Commission is nothing to our present Purpose, we shall not burthen the Readers with it.

With these two Commissions he sail'd out of *Plymouth* in *May* 1696, in the *Adventure* Gally of thirty Guns, and eighty Men; the Place he first design'd for was *New-York;* in his Voyage thither he took a *French* Banker, but this was no Act of Pyracy, he having a Commission for that Purpose, as we have just observ'd.

When he arrived at *New York* he put up Articles for engaging more Hands, it being necessary to his Ships Crew, since he proposed to deal with a desperate Enemy: The Terms he offered were, that every Man should have a Share of what was taken, reserving for himself and Owners forty

Shares. Upon which Encouragement he soon increas'd his Company to a hundred and fifty five Men.

With this Company he sail'd first for *Maderas,* where he took in Wine and some other Necessaries; from thence he proceeded to *Bonavist,* one of the *Cape de Verd Islands,* to furnish the Ship with Salt, and from thence went immediately to St. *Jago,* another of the *Cape de Verd Islands,* in order to stock himself with Provisions. When all this was done, he bent his Course to *Madagascar,* the known Rendezvouz of pyrates; in his Way he fell in with Captain *Warren,* Commadore of three Men of War; he acquainted them with his Design, kept them Company two or three Days, and then leaving them, made the best Way for *Madagascar,* where he arrived in *February* 1696, just nine Months from his Departure from *Plymouth.*

It happen'd that at this Time the Pyrate Ships were most of them out in search of Prey; so that according to the best Intelligence Captain *Kid* could get, there was not one of them at that Time about the Island, wherefore having spent some Time in watering his Ship, and taking in more Provisions, he thought of trying his Fortune on the Coast of *Malabar,* where he arrived in the Month of *June* following, four Months from his reaching *Madagascar.* Hereabouts he made an unsuccessful Cruize, touching sometimes at the Island of *Mahala,* sometimes at that of *Joanna,* betwixt *Malabar* and *Madagascar:* His Provisions were every Day wasting, and his Ship began to want Repair; wherefore, when he was at *Joanna,* he found Means of borrowing a Sum of Money from some *French* Men who had lost their Ship, but saved their Effects, and with this he purchas'd Materials for putting his Ship in good Repair.

It does not appear all this while that he had the least Design of turning Pyrate; for near *Mahala* and *Joanna* both, he met with several *Indian* Ships richly laden, to which he did not offer the least Violence, tho' he was strong enough to have done what he pleas'd with them; and the first Outrage or Depredation I find he committed upon Mankind, was after his repairing his Ship, and leaving *Joanna;* he touch'd at a Place call'd *Mabbee,* upon the *Red Sea,* where he took some *Guinea* Corn from the Natives, by Force.

After this he sail'd to *Bab's Key,* a Place upon a little Island at the Entrance of the *Red Sea;* here it was that he first began to open himself to his Ship's Company, and let them understand that he intended to change his Measures; for, happening to talk of the *Moca* Fleet which was to sail that Way, he said, *We have been unsuccessful hitherto, but Courage, my Boys, we'll make our Fortunes out of this Fleet:* And finding that none of them appear'd averse to it, he order'd a Boat out, well mann'd, to go upon the Coast to make Discoveries, commanding them to take a Prisoner and bring to him, or get Intelligence any Way they could. The Boat return'd in a few Days, bringing him Word, that they saw fourteen or fifteen Ships ready to sail, some with *English,* some with *Dutch,* and some with *Moorish* Colours.

We cannot account for this sudden Change in his Conduct, otherwise than by supposing that he first meant well, while he had Hopes of making his Fortune by taking of pyrates; but now, weary of ill Success, and fearing least his Owners, out of Humour at their great Expences, should dismiss him, and he should want Employment, and be mark'd out for an unlucky Man; rather, I say, than run the Hazard of Poverty, he resolved to do his Business one Way, since he could not do it another.

He therefore order'd a Man continually to watch at the Mast Head, least this Fleet should go by them; and about four Days after, towards Evening, it appear'd in Sight, being convoy'd by one *English* and one *Dutch* Man of War. *Kid* soon fell in with them, and getting into the midst of them, fir'd at a *Moorish* Ship which was next him; but the Men of War taking the Alarm, bore down upon *Kid,* and firing upon him, obliged him to sheer off, he not being strong enough to contend with them. Now he had begun Hostilities, he resolv'd to go on, and therefore he went and cruis'd along the Coast of *Malabar;* the first Prize he met was a small Vessel belonging to *Aden,* the Vessel was *Moorish,* and the Owners were *Moorish* Merchants, but the Master was an *English* Man, his Name was *Parker. Kid* forc'd him and a *Portugueze* that was call'd *Don Antonio,* which were all the *Europeans* on Board, to take on with them; the first he design'd as a Pilot, and the last as an Interpreter. He also used the Men very cruelly, causing them to be hoisted up by the Arms, and drubb'd with a naked Cutlash, to force them to discover whether they had Money on Board, and where it lay; but as they had neither Gold nor Silver on Board, he got nothing by his Cruelty; however, he took from them a Bale of Pepper, and a Bale of Coffee, and so let them go.

A little Time after he touch'd at *Carawar,* a Place upon the same Coast, where, before he arrived, the News of what he had done to the *Moorish* Ship had reach'd them; for some of the *English* Merchants there had received an Account of it from the Owners, who corresponded with them; wherefore, as soon as *Kid* came in, he was suspected to be the Person who committed this Pyracy; and one Mr. *Harvey* and Mr. *Mason,* two of the *English* Factory, came on Board and ask'd for *Parker,* and *Antonio* the *Portuguese;* but *Kid* deny'd that he knew any such Persons, having secur'd them both in a private Place in the Hold, where they were kept for seven or eight Days, that is, till *Kid* sail'd from thence.

However, the Coast was alarm'd, and a *Portuguese* Man of War was sent out to cruize: *Kid* met with her, and fought her about six Hours, gallantly enough; but finding her too strong to be taken, he quitted her; for he was able to run away from her when he would: Then he went to a Place call'd *Porco,* where he water'd the Ship, and bought a Number of Hogs of the Natives to victual his Company.

Soon after this, he came up with a *Moorish* Ship, the Master whereof was a *Dutch* Man, call'd *Schipper Mitchel,* and chased her under *French* Colours, which they observing, hoisted *French* Colours too: When he came up with her, he hail'd her in *French,* and they having a *French* Man on Board, answer'd him in the same Language; upon which he order'd them to send their Boat on Board; they were oblig'd to do so, and having examin'd who they were, and from whence they came; he ask'd the *French* Man, who was a Passenger, if he had a *French* Pass for himself? The *French* Man gave him to understand that he had. Then he told the *French* Man he must pass for Captain, and by G — d, says he, you are the Captain: The *French* Man durst not refuse doing as he would have him: The Meaning of this was, that he would seize the Ship as fair Prize, and as if she had belong'd to *French* Subjects, according to a Commission he had for that Purpose; tho', one would think, after what he had already done, that he need not have Recourse to a Quibble to give his Actions a Colour.

In short, he took the Cargoe and sold it some Time after; yet still he seem'd to have some Fears upon him least these Proceedings should have a bad End; for, coming up with a *Dutch* Ship some Time, when his Men thought of nothing but attacking her, *Kid* oppos'd it; upon which a Mutiny arose, and the Majority being for taking the said Ship, and arming themselves to Man the Boat to go and seize her, he told them, such as did, never should come on Board him again; which put an End to the Design, so that he kept Company with the said Ship some Time, without offering her any Violence: However, this Dispute was the Occasion of an Accident, upon which an Indictment was afterwards grounded against *Kid;* for *Moor,* the Gunner, being one Day upon Deck, and talking with *Kid* about the said *Dutch* Ship, some Words arose betwixt them, and *Moor* told *Kid,* that he had ruin'd them all; upon which, *Kid,* calling him Dog, took up a Bucket and struck him with it, which breaking his Skull, he died the next Day.

But *Kid*'s penitential Fit did not last long, for coasting along *Malabar,* he met with a great Number of Boats, all which he plunder'd. Upon the same Coast he also light upon a *Portuguese* Ship, which he kept Possession of a Week, and then having taken out of her some Chests of *India* Goods, thirty Jars of Butter, with some Wax, Iron, and a hundred Bags of Rice, he let her go.

Much about the same Time he went to one of the *Malabar* Islands for Wood and Water, and his Cooper being ashore, was murder'd by the Natives; upon which *Kid* himself landed, and burnt and pillaged several of their Houses, the People running away; but having taken one, he caused him to be tied to a Tree, and commanded one of his Men to shoot him; then putting to Sea again he took the greatest Prize, which fell into his Hands, while he followed this Trade; this was a *Moorish* Ship of 400 Tons richly laden, named the *Queda* Merchant, the Master whereof was an *English* Man, he was call'd *Wright,* for the *Indians* often make Use of *English* or *Dutch* Men to command their Ships, their own Mariners not being so good Artists in Navigation. — *Kid* chased her under *French* Colours, and having come up with her, he ordered her to hoist out her Boat, and to send on Board of him, which being done, he told *Wright* he was his Prisoner; and informing himself concerning the said Ship, he understood there were no *Europeans* on Board, except two *Dutch,* and one *Frenchman,* all the Rest being *Indians* or *Armenians,* and that the *Armenians* were Part Owners of the Cargoe. *Kid* gave the *Armenians* to understand, that if they would offer any Thing that was worth his taking for their Ransome, he would hearken to it: Upon which, they proposed to pay him twenty thousand Rupees, not quite three thousand Pounds Sterling; but *Kid* judged this would be making a bad Bargain, wherefore he rejected it, and setting the Crew on Shore, at different Places on the Coast, he soon sold as much of the Cargoe as came to near ten thousand Pounds. With Part of it he also trafficked, receiving in Exchange Provisions, or such other Goods as he wanted; by Degrees he disposed of the whole Cargoe, and when the Division was made, it came to about two hundred Pounds a Man, and having reserved forty Shares to himself, his Dividend amounted to about eight thousand Pounds Sterling.

The *Indians* along the Coast came on Board and traffick'd with all Freedom, and he punctually performed his Bargains, till about the Time he was ready to sail; and then thinking he should have no further Occasion for them, he made no Scruple of taking their Goods, and setting them on Shore without any Payment in Money or Goods, which they little expected; for as they had been used to deal with pyrates, they always found them Men of Honour in the Way of Trade: A People, Enemies to Deceit, and that scorn'd to rob but in their own Way.

Kid put some of his Men on Board the *Queda* Merchant, and with this Ship and his own sail'd for *Madagascar;* as soon as he was arrived and had cast Anchor, there came on Board of him a Canoe, in which were several *Englishmen,* who had formerly been well acquainted with *Kid;* as soon as they saw him they saluted him, and told him, they were informed he was come to take them, and hang them, which would be a little unkind in such an old Acquaintance; *Kid* soon dissipated their Doubts, by swearing he had no such Design, and that he was now in every Respect their Brother, and just as bad as they; and calling for a Cup of Bomboo, drank their Captain's Health.

These Men belong'd to a Pyrate Ship, call'd the *Resolution,* formerly the *Mocco* Merchant, whereof one Captain *Culliford* was Commander, and which lay at an Anchor not far from them; *Kid* went on Board with them, promising them his Friendship and Assistance, and *Culliford* in his Turn came on Board of *Kid;* and *Kid* to testify his Sincerity in Iniquity, finding *Culliford* in want of some Necessaries, made him a Present of an Anchor and some Guns, to fit him out for the Sea again.

The *Adventure* Galley was now so old and leaky, that they were forced to keep two Pumps continually going, wherefore *Kid* shifted all the Guns and Tackle out of her into the *Queda* Merchant, intending her for his Man of War; and as he had divided the Money before, he now made a Division of the Remainder of the Cargo: Soon after which, the greatest Part of the Company left him, some going on Board Captain *Culliford,* and others absconding in the Country, so that he had not above forty Men left.

He put to Sea and happened to touch at *Amboyna,* one of the *Dutch* Spice Islands, where he was told, that the News of his Actions had reach'd *England,* and that he was there declared a Pyrate.

The Truth on't is, his Pyracies so alarmed our Merchants, that some Motions were made in Parliament, to enquire into the Commission that was given him, and the Persons who fitted him out: These Proceedings seem'd to lean a little hard upon the Lord *Bellamont,* who thought himself so much touch'd thereby, that he published a Justification of himself in a Pamphlet after *Kid*'s Execution. In the mean Time, it was thought adviseable, in order to stop the Course of these Pyracies, to publish a Proclamation, offering the King's free Pardon to all such pyrates as should voluntarily surrender themselves, whatever Pyracies they had been guilty of at any Time, before the last Day of *April,* 1699. — That is to say, for all Pyracies committed Eastward of the *Cape* of *Good Hope,* to the Longitude and Meridian of *Socatora,* and *Cape Camorin.* In which Proclamation, *Avery* and *Kid* were excepted by Name.

When *Kid* left *Amboyna* he knew nothing of this Proclamation, for certainly had he had Notice of his being excepted in it, he would not have been so infatuated, to run himself into the very Jaws of Danger; but relying upon his Interest with the Lord *Bellamont,* and fancying, that a *French* Pass or two he found on Board some of the Ships he took, would serve to countenance the Matter, and that Part of the Booty he got would gain him new Friends. — I say, all these Things made him flatter himself that all would be hushed, and that

Justice would but wink at him. — Wherefore he sail'd directly for *New-York,* where he was no sooner arrived, but by the Lord *Bellamont*'s Orders, he was secured with all his Papers and Effects. Many of his Fellow-Adventurers who had forsook him at *Madagascar,* came over from thence Passengers, some to *New England* and some to *Jersey;* where hearing of the King's Proclamation for pardoning of pyrates, they surrendered themselves to the Governor of those Places: At first they were admitted to Bail, but soon after were laid in strict Confinement where they were kept for some time, till an Opportunity happened of sending them with their Captain over to *England* to be tried.

Accordingly a Sessions of Admiralty being held at the *Old Baily,* in *May* 1701, Captain *Kid, Nicholas Churchill, James How, Robert Lumley, William Jenkins, Gabriel Loff, Hugh Parrot, Richard Barlicorn, Abel Owens,* and *Darby Mullins,* were arraign'd for Pyracy and Robbery on the High Seas, and all found guilty, except three; these were *Robert Lumley, William Jenkins,* and *Richard Barlicorne,* who proving themselves to be Apprentices to some of the Officers of the Ship, and producing their Indentures in Court, were acquitted.

The three above-mentioned, tho' they were proved to be concern'd in taking and sharing the Ship and Goods mentioned in the Indictment, yet, as the Gentlemen of the long Robe rightly distinguished, there was a great Difference between their Circumstances and the rest; for there must go an Intention of the Mind and a Freedom of the Will to the committing an Act of Felony or Pyracy. A Pyrate is not to be understood to be under Constraint, but a free Agent; for in this Case, the bare Act will not make a Man guilty, unless the Will make it so.

Now a Servant, it is true, if he go voluntarily and have his Proportion, he must be accounted a Pyrate, for then he acts upon his own Account, and not by Compulsion; and these Persons, according to the Evidence, received their Part, but whether they accounted to their Masters for their Shares afterwards, is the Matter in Question, and what distinguishes them as free Agents or Men, that did go under the Compulsion of their Masters, which being left to the Consideration of the Jury, they found them Not Guilty.

Kid was tryed upon an Indictment of Murder also, *viz.* for killing *Moor* the Gunner, and found guilty of the same. *Nicholas Churchill* and *James How* pleaded the King's Pardon, as having surrendered themselves within the Time limited in the Proclamation, and Colonel *Bass,* Governor of *West Jersey,* to whom they surrendered, being in Court, and called upon, proved the same; however, this Plea was over-ruled by the Court, because there being four Commissioners named in the Proclamation, *viz.* Captain *Thomas Warren, Israel Hayes, Peter Delannoye,* and *Christopher Pollard,* Esqrs; who were appointed Commissioners, and sent over on Purpose to receive the Submissions of such pyrates as should surrender, it was adjudged no other Person was qualified to receive their Surrender, and that they could not be intitled to the Benefit of the said Proclamation, because they had not in all Circumstances complied with the Conditions of it.

Darby Mullins urg'd in his Defence, that he serv'd under the King's Commission, and therefore could not disobey his Commander without incurring great Punishments; that whenever a Ship or Ships went out upon any Expedition under the King's Commissioners, the Men were never allowed to call their Officers to an Account, why they did this, or, why they did that, because such a Liberty would destroy all Discipline; that if any Thing was done which was unlawful, the Officers were to answer it, for the Men did no more than their Duty in obeying Orders. He was told by the Court, that acting under the Commission justified in what was lawful, but not in what was unlawful; he answered, he stood in Need of nothing to justify him in what was lawful, but that the Case of Seamen must be very hard, if they must be brought into such Danger for obeying the Commands of their Officers, and punished for not obeying them; and if they were allowed to dispute the Orders, there could be no such Thing as Command kept up at Sea.

This seem'd to be the best Defence the Thing could bear; but his taking a Share of the Plunder, the Seamens mutinying on Board several Times, and taking upon them to controul the Captain, showed there was no Obedience paid to the Commission; and that they acted in all Things according to the Custom of pyrates and Free-booters, which weighing with the Jury, they brought him in guilty with the rest.

As to Capt. *Kid*'s Defence, he insisted much upon his own Innocence, and the Villany of his Men; he said, he went out in a laudable Employment, and had no Occasion, being then in good Circumstances, to go a Pirating; that the Men often mutinied against him, and did as they pleas'd; that he was threatened to be shot in his Cabin, and that Ninety five left him at one Time, and set Fire to his Boat, so that he was disabled from bringing his Ship home, or the Prizes he took, to have them regularly condemn'd, which he said were taken by Virtue of a Commission under the Broad Seal, they having *French* Passes. — The Captain called one Col. *Hewson* to his Reputation, who gave him an extraordinary Character, and declared to the Court, that he had served under his Command, and been in two Engagements with him against the *French,* in which he fought as well as any Man he ever saw; that there were only *Kid*'s Ship and his own against Monsieur *du Cass,* who commanded a Squadron of six Sail, and they got the better of him. — But this being several Years before the Facts mentioned in the Indictment were committed, prov'd of no manner of Service to the Prisoner on his Tryal.

As to the Friendship shown to *Culliford,* a notorious Pyrate, *Kid* deny'd, and said, he intended to have taken him, but his Men being a Parcel of Rogues and Villains refused to stand by him, and several of them ran away from his Ship to the said Pyrate. — But the Evidence being full and particular against him, he was found guilty as before mentioned.

When *Kid* was asked what he had to say why Sentence should not pass against him, he answered, That *he had nothing to say, but that he had been sworn against by perjured wicked People.* And when Sentence was pronounced, he said, *My Lord, it is a very hard Sentence. For my Part, I am the innocentest Person of them all, only I have been sworn against by perjured Persons.*

Wherefore about a Week after, Capt. *Kid, Nicholas Churchill, James How, Gabriel Loff, Hugh Parrot, Abel Owen,* and *Darby Mullins,* were executed at *Execution Dock,* and afterwards hung up in Chains, at some Distance from each other, down the River, where their Bodies hung exposed for many Years.

Chap. XXIII
Of Captain Tew, And his Crew

Before I enter on the Adventures of this Pyrate, I must take Notice to the Reader of the Reasons which made me not continue the Life of *Misson*.

In reading the Notes, which I have by me, relating to Captain *Tew,* I found him join'd with *Misson;* and that I must either be guilty of Repetition, or give an Account of *Tew* in *Misson*'s Life, which is contrary to the Method I propos'd, that of giving a distinct Relation of every Pyrate who has made any Figure: And surely *Tew,* in Point of Gallantry, was inferior to none, and may justly claim a particular Account of his Actions.

However, before I enter on the Life of this Pyrate, I shall continue that of *Misson* to the Time that these two Commanders met.

The Blacks seeing them so much upon their Guard, brought out boiled Rice and Fowls, and after they had satisfied their Hunger, the Chief made Signs that they were the same who had carried a Negroe to their Ships, and sent for the Ax and Piece of Baze they had given him: While this pass'd, the very Negroe came from hunting, who seem'd overjoy'd to see them. The Chief made Signs that they might return, and ten Negroes coming to them laden with Fowls and Kids; he gave them to understand, they should accompany them to their Ships with these Presents.

They parted very amicably, and in hopes of settling a good Correspondence with these Natives; all the Houses were neatly framed and jointed, not built from any Foundation, but so made, that half a dozen Men could lift and transport them from Place to Place; and sometimes a whole Village shall be in Motion, which would be an odd Sight in *Europe,* and surprizing to see Houses moving. The Hunters returning to their Ships, with these Presents and Negroes, were joyfully received; and the Negroes not only caressed, but laden with Baze, Iron Kettles, and Rum, besides the Present of a Cutlash for the Chief.

While the Negroes stay'd, which was the Space of three Days, they examined and admired the Forts and growing Town, in which all Hands were busied, and not even the Prisoners excused.

As Monsieur *Misson* apprehended no Danger from the Land, his Fort (tho' of Wood) being, he thought, a sufficient Defence to his infant Colony; he took a hundred and sixty Hands, and went a second Time on the Coast of *Zanguebor,* and off *Quiloa* he gave Chase to a large Ship, which lay by for him: She prov'd an over-match for the *Victoire,* which engag'd her, with great Loss of Men, near eight Glasses; but finding he was more likely to be took, than to make a Prize, by the Advice of his Officers and Men, endeavour'd to leave the *Portuguese,* which was a 50 Gun Ship, and had 300 Men on Board; but he found this Attempt vain, for the *Portuguese* went as well as the *Victoire,* and the Commander was a resolute and brave Man, who, seeing him endeavour to shake him off, clapp'd him on Board, but lost most of the Men he enter'd. *Misson*'s Crew not used to be attack'd, and expecting no Quarter, fought so desperately, that they not thoroly clear'd their Decks, but some of them follow'd the *Portuguese,* who leap'd into their own Ship; which *Misson* seeing, hop'd to make an Advantage of their Despair, and crying out, *Elle est a nous, a l'abordage.* She's our own, board, board her, so many of his Men followed the few, that hardly were there enough left to work the Ship; *Misson* observing this Resolution in his Men, grappled the *Portuguese* Ship, and leap'd himself on Board, crying out, *la Mort, ou la Victoire,* Death or Victory. The *Portuguese,* who thought themselves in a manner Conquerors, seeing the Enemy not only drive off those who enter'd them, but board with that Resolution, began to quit the Decks in Spight of their Officers: The Captain and *Misson* met, as he was endeavouring to hinder the Flight of his Men; they engaged with equal Bravery with their Cutlashes; but *Misson* striking him on the Neck, he fell down the main Hatch, which put an End to the Fight, for the *Portuguese* seeing their Captain fall, threw down their Arms, and call'd for Quarters, which was granted; and all the Prisoners without Distinction being order'd between Decks, and the Powder-Room secured, he put 35 Men on Board the Prize, and made the best of his Way for *Libertatia.* This was the dearest Prize he ever made, for he lost fifty six Men: She was vastly rich in Gold, having near 200,000 l. Sterling on Board, being her own and the Cargo of her Companion, which was lost upon the Coast, of whose Crew she had saved 100 Men out of 120, the rest being lost, by endeavouring to swim ashore; whereas had their Fear suffer'd them to have staid, there had not been a Soul lost, the Tide of Ebb leaving their Ship dry: This was the Reason that the Prize was so well mann'd, and proved so considerable.

Being within Sight of *Madagascar,* they spied a Sloop which stood for them, and when in Gun-Shot, threw out black Colours, and fired a Gun to Windward; *Misson* brought to, fired another to Leeward, and hoisted out his Boat, which the Sloop perceiving, lay by for. *Misson's* Lieutenant went on Board, and was received very civilly by Captain *Tew,* who was the Commander, to whom the Lieutenant gave a short Account of their Adventures and new Settlement, inviting him very kindly on Board Captain *Misson. Tew* told him, he could not consent to go with him till he had the Opinion of his Men; in the mean while *Misson,* coming along-side, hal'd the Sloop, and invited the Captain on Board, desiring his Lieutenant would stay as an Hostage, if they were in the least jealous of him; which they had no Reason to be, since he was of Force so much superior, that he need not employ Stratagem. This determined the Company on Board the Sloop, who advised their Captain to go with the Lieutenant, whom they would not suffer to stay behind, to show the greater Confidence in their new Friends.

My Reader may be surpriz'd that a single Sloop should venture to give Chase to two Ships of such Countenance as were the *Victoire* and her Prize: But this Wonder will cease, when he is acquainted with the Sequel.

Captain *Tew* after being handsomely regal'd on Board the *Victoire,* and thoroughly satisfied, returned on Board his Sloop, gave an Account of what he had learned, and his Men consenting, he gave Orders to steer the same Course with *Misson,* whose Settlement it was agreed to visit.

I shall here leave them to give an Account of Captain *Tew.*

Mr. *Richier,* Governor of *Bermudas,* fitted out two Sloops on the Privateer Account, commanded by Captain *George Drew,* and Captain *Thomas Tew,* with Instructions to make the best of their Way to the River *Gambia* in *Africa,* and there, with the Advice and Assistance of the Agent for the Royal *African* Company, to attempt the taking the *French* Factory of *Goorie* on that Coast.

The above Commanders having their Commissions and Instructions from the Governor, took their Departure from *Bermudas,* and kept Company some Time; but *Drew* springing his Mast, and a violent Storm coming upon them, they lost each other.

Tew being separated from his Consort, thought of providing for his future case, by making one bold Push; and accordingly, calling all Hands on Deck, he spoke to them to this Purpose.

'That they were not ignorant of the Design with which the Governor fitted them out; the taking and destroying the *French* Factory; that he, indeed, readily agreed to take a Commission to this end, tho' contrary to his Judgment, because it was being employ'd; but that he thought it a very injudicious Expedition, which did they succeed in, would be of no Use to the Public, and only advantage a private Company of Men, from whom they could expect no Reward of their Bravery; that he could see nothing but Danger in the Undertaking, without the least Prospect of a Booty; that he could not suppose any Man fond of fighting, for fighting-sake; and few ventured their Lives, but with some View either of particular Interest or public Good; but here was not the least Appearance of either. Wherefore, he was of Opinion, that they should turn their Thoughts on what might better their Circumstances; and if they were so inclined, he would undertake to shape a Course which should lead them to Ease and Plenty, in which they might pass the rest of their Days. That one bold Push would do their Business, and they might return home, not only without Danger, but even with Reputation.' The Crew finding he expected their Resolution, cry'd out, one and all, *A gold Chain, or a wooden Leg,* we'll stand by you.

Hearing this, he desired they would chuse a Quarter Master, who might consult with him for the Common Good; which was accordingly done.

I must acquaint the Reader, that on Board the *West-India* Privateers and Free-booters, the Quarter Master's Opinion is like the Mufti's among the *Turk's;* the Captain can undertake nothing which the Quarter Master does not approve. We may say, the Quarter Master is an humble Imitation of the *Roman* Tribune of the People; he speaks for, and looks after the Interest of the Crew.

Tew now, instead of his proceeding on his Voyage to *Gambia,* shaped his Course for the Cape of *Good Hope,* which doubling, he steered for the Streights of *Babel Mandel,* entring into the *Red Sea,* where they came up with a tall Ship bound from the *Indies* to *Arabia;* she was richly laden, and as she was to clear the Coasts of Rovers, five more, extreamly rich (one especially in Gold) being to follow her, she had 300 Soldiers on Board, beside her Seamen.

Tew, on making this Ship, told his Men she carried their Fortunes, which they would find no Difficulty to take Possession of; for though he was satisfied she was full of Men, and was mounted with a great Number of Guns, they wanted the two Things necessary, Skill and Courage; and, indeed, so it proved, for he boarded and carried her without Loss, every one taking more Care to run from the Danger, than to exert himself in the Defence of his Goods.

In rummaging this Prize, the pyrates threw over a great many rich Bales, to search for Gold, Silver, and Jewels; and, having taken what they thought proper, together with the Powder, part of which (as being more than they could handsomely stow) they threw into the Sea; they left her, sharing 3000 l. Sterling a Man.

Encouraged by this Success, Captain *Tew* proposed the going in quest of the other five Ships, of which he had Intelligence from the Prize; but the Quarter-Master opposing him, he was obliged to drop the Design, and steer for *Madagascar.*

Here the Quarter Master finding this Island productive of all the Necessaries of Life; that the Air was wholesome, the Soil fruitful, and the Sea abounding with Fish, proposed settling; but only three and twenty of the Crew came into the Proposal: The rest staid with Captain *Tew,* who having given the new Settlers their Share of Plunder, designed to return to *America,* as they afterwards did; but spying the *Victoire* and her Prize, he thought he might, by their Means, return somewhat richer, and resolved to speak with them, as I have already said.

Tew and his Company having taken the above Resolution of visiting Mons. *Misson*'s Colony, arrived with him, and was not a little surprized to see his Fortifications.

When they came under the first Fort, they saluted it with nine Guns, and they were answered with an equal Number; all the Prisoners, at their coming to an Anchor, were suffer'd to come up, a Privilege they had never before granted them, on account of the few Hands left them, except two or three at a time.

The Joy those ashore expressed at the Sight of so considerable a Prize as they judged her at first Sight, was vastly allay'd, when they heard how dear a Purchase she had prov'd to them; however, the Reinforcement of the Sloop made some amends; Captain *Tew* was received by *Caraccioli* and the rest, with great Civility and Respect, who did not a little admire his Courage, both in attacking the Prize he made, and afterwards in giving Chase to *Misson;* he was called to the Council of Officers, which was immediately held, to consider what Methods should be taken with the Prisoners, who were, by 190 brought in by this new Prize, near as numerous as those of his own Party, though *Tew* join them with 70 Men; it was therefore resolved to keep them separate from the *Portuguese* and *English,* who were before taken, to make them believe they were in Amity with a Prince of the Natives, who was very powerful, and to propose to them, at their Choice, the assisting the new Colony in their Works, or the being sent Prisoners up the Country, if they rejected the entering with them. Seventy three took on, and the rest desired they might be any way employ'd, rather than be sent up the Country; 117 then were set to Work upon a Dock, which was laid out about half a Mile above the Mouth of the Harbour, and the other Prisoners were forbid to pass such Bounds as were prescribed them on Pain of Death; lest they, knowing their own Strength, should revolt; for I must acquaint the Reader, that on the Arrival of the *Victoire,* both their Loss and the Number of *Portuguese* they brought in, was known to none but themselves, and the Number of those who came over, magnified; besides, the *Johanna* Men were all arm'd and disciplin'd, and the *Bijoux* laid a Guardship, where the last Prisoners were set to Work; but while they provided for their Security, both within and without, they did not neglect providing also for their Support, for they dug and sow'd a large Plat of Ground with *Indian* and *European* Corn, and other Seeds which they had found on Board their Prizes. In the mean while *Caraccioli,* who had the Art of Perswasion, wrought on many of the *Portuguese,* who saw no Hopes of returning home, to join them. *Misson,* who could not be easy in an inactive Life, would have taken another Cruize; but fearing the Revolt of the Prisoners, durst not weaken his Colony by the Hands he must necessarily take with him: Wherefore, he propos'd giving the last Prize to, and sending away the Prisoners. *Carracioli* and Captain *Tew* were against it, saying, that it would discover their Retreat, and cause their being attacked by the *Europeans,* who had Settlements along the Continent, before they were able to defend themselves. *Misson* reply'd, he could not bear to be always diffident of those about him; that it was better die once, than live in continual Apprehensions of Death. That the Time was come for the sending away the *Johanna* Men, and that they could not go without a Ship, neither durst he trust a Ship out, not well mann'd, nor man her while so many Prisoners were with him. Wherefore there was a Necessity of sending them off, or of putting them all to the Sword. A Barbarity by which he would not purchase his Security. A Council was called, and what Captain *Misson* had proposed, agreed to. The Prisoners were then summon'd and he told them, in few Words, that he knew the Consequence of giving them Liberty; that he expected to be attacked as soon as the Place of his Retreat was known, and had it in his Hands, by putting them to Death to avoid the doubtful Fate of War; but his Humanity would not suffer him to entertain a Thought so cruel, and his Alliances with the Natives, he hoped, would enable him to repel his Assailants; but he required an Oath of every one, that he should not serve against him: He then enquired into the Circumstances of every particular Man, and what they had lost, all which he return'd, telling the Company it should be reckoned as Part of his Share, and the Prisoners, that he did not make War with the Oppressed, but the Oppressors. The Prisoners were charm'd with this Mark of Generosity and Humanity, and wished he might never meet a Treatment unworthy of that he gave them. The Ship being victualled for a Voyage to the Coast of *Zanguebar,* all her Guns and Ammunitions taken out, with the spare Sails, and spare Rigging, all were ordered to be gone, and 137 departed, highly applauding the Behaviour of their Enemies. All this while they had heard nothing from the Natives, nor had the hunting Parties met with any of them, which made *Misson* suspect they were afraid of his being their Neighbour, and had shifted their Quarters; but as the *Johanna* Men were upon going away, there came about 50 Negroes to them, driving about 100 Head of black Cattle, 20 Negroe Men bound, and 25 Women, for which Cattle and Prisoners they barter'd Rum, Hatchets, Baze and Beads; some Hogsheads of which last Commodity they had taken on the Coast of *Angola*. Here the Negroes belonging to *Misson* were provided with Wives: The Natives were caress'd, and to the Slaves Signs made that their Liberty was given them, they were immediately cloathed and put under the Care of as many Whites, who, by all possible Demonstrations, endeavoured to make them understand that they were Enemies to Slavery. The

Natives staid ten Days, which retarded the Departure of the *Johanna* Men; but, upon their retiring, the *Bijoux* sailed with 100 of them on Board, under the command of *Caraccioli*'s Lieutenant, who excused the keeping them a Month longer than was promised, and not bringing them at once, having no more than two Ships. The *Portuguese* Ship, which was unrigg'd, being made a Hulk, the ten Men of *Misson*'s Company who had settled at *Johanna,* being desirous to return, were brought to *Libertatia* with their Wives (of which they had two and three a piece) and their Children, the *Bijoux,* at two more Voyages, carried over the rest of the *Johannians.*

Misson hove down the *Bijoux,* and resolving on a Cruise on the Coast of *Guiney,* to strengthen his Colony by the Capture of some slaving Ship, he gave the Command of her to Captain *Tew,* and he and *Caraccioli* press'd the Work of the Dock; he gave him also 200 Hands, of which 40 were *Portuguese,* 37 *Negroes,* 17 of them expert Sailors, 30 *English,* and the rest *French. Tew* met with nothing in his Way till he came to the Northward of the Cape of *Good Hope,* when he fell in with a *Dutch East-India* Galley of 18 Guns, which he took after a small Resistance, and with the Loss of one Man only; on the Coast of *Angola* he took an *English* Man with 240

Slaves, Men, Women, and Boys. The Negroes, who had before been taken on this Coast, found among these a great many of their Acquaintance, and several of their Relations, to whom they reported their happy and unexpected change of Fortune, the great Captain (for so they now called *Misson*) humanly having knocked off their Chains, and of Slaves made them free Men, and Sharers in his Fortunes. That the same good Fortune had attended them in their falling into his Hands, for he abhorr'd even the Name of Slavery. *Tew* following the Orders, and acquainted with the Policy of *Misson,* order'd their Fetters and Handcuffs to be taken off, upon his Negroe Sailors, assuring him they would not revolt, and were sensible of their Happiness in falling into his Hands. Content with these Prizes, he made the best of his Way home to *Libertatia,* where he arrived without any sinister Accident; but I forgot to tell my Reader, that he set his *Dutch* Prisoners (nine excepted, who took on with him) ashore, about 30 Miles to the Northward of the Cape, in *Soldinia* Bay, where had been buried, by Captain *Misson,* the *English* Commander; he found a great Quantity of *English* Crowns on Board his *Dutch* Prize, which were carried into the common Treasury, Money being of no Use where every Thing was in common, and no Hedge bounded any particular Man's Property. The Slaves he had released in this last Cruize were employ'd in the perfecting the Dock, and treated on the Foot of free People. They were not ignorant of the Change of their Condition, and were therefore extreamly diligent and faithful. A White Man, or one of the old standing Negroes, wrought with every four, and made them understand the *French* Words (by often Repetition, and the Help of their Country Mens interpreting) used in their Works. *Misson* ordered a couple of Sloops to be built in a Creek, of 80 Tun each, which he mounted with 8 Guns a piece, out of the *Dutch* Prize. These were perfected in a little Time, and proved not only shapely Vessels, but excellent Sailors. The Officers of these Sloops were chosen by ballotting, and as their first Design was only to discover and lay down a Chart of the Coast, Sands, Shoals, and Depths of Water round the Island of *Madagascar;*

The School Master being sent for that Reason with the Command of one, *Tew* desired, and had the other. They were mann'd, each Sloop with 50 Whites and 50 black Men. Which Voyage round the Island was of vast Advantage in giving the new released *Angola* Negroes a Notion of the working a Vessel; and they were very industrious both in endeavouring to learn the *French* Language, and to be useful. These Sloops, the one of which was called the *Childhood,* and the other the *Liberty,* were near four Months on this Expedition; in the mean while a few of the Natives had come often to the Settlement, and they began to speak a little broken *French,* mix'd with the other *European* Languages, which they heard among *Misson*'s People, and six of the native Families fixed among them, which was of vast Use to the Planters of this new Colony; for they made a very advantageous Report to their Country Men of the Regularity and Harmony they observed in them. The Sloops being return'd, and an exact Chart taken of the Coast, *Carraccioli* had a mind for a Cruize; he proposed the visiting all the neighbouring Islands, accordingly he went out to *Mascarenas,* and the other Islands near it, taking one half of his Crew of Negroes, and return'd with a *Dutch* Prize, which he took off the abovementioned Island, where they were about fixing a Colony. This Prize, as it had on Board all Sorts of *European* Goods, and Necessaries for settling, was more valuable than if it had been vastly richer. The Negroes growing useful Hands, *Misson* resolved on a Cruize to the Northward, encouraged by *Tew*'s Success; and, with all the Blacks, which he divided between the two Ships, one of which Captain *Tew* commanded, set out with 500 Men: Off the Coast of *Arabia Fælix,* they fell in with a Ship belonging to the *Great Mogul,* bound for *Zidon,* with Pilgrims to *Mecca,* who, with *Moor* Mariners, made up the Number of 1600 Souls. This Ship carried 110 Guns, but made a very poor Defence, being encumber'd with the Goods and Number of Passengers they carried. The two Adventurers did not think it their Business to cannonade, they therefore boarded as soon as they came up with her, and the *Moors* no sooner saw them enter'd, but they discharged one Volley of small Arms at Randon, we may suppose, because no Execution was done, and fled the Decks. Being Masters of this Ship, which did not cost them a single Man, they consulted what they should do with her, and the Prisoners, and it was resolved to set them ashore between

Ain and *Aden;* but as they wanted Women, to keep all the unmarried, and to navigate the Ship to *Libertatia;* as the Guns might be of Use to them; and, by letting her go, or sinking, they might lose, perhaps, a considerable Booty, which the *Moors,* might have hid in her Cielings or Ballast.

This Resolution was put in Execution, and they brought off 100 Girls, from 12 to 18 Years old, who designed to make the Pilgrimage with their Parents. The Lamentations this Separation caused among the Prisoners, had such Effect on *Misson,* that he was for letting them go, but every one of his Men were against him. They now made the best of their Way for *Madagascar,* putting 200 Hands on board the Prize, which proved a very heavy Sailer, and retarded them very much. Off the Cape *Guarde Fin* they were overtaken with a cruel Storm, which was very near wrecking them on the Island called *Irmanos;* but the Wind coming about due North, they had the good Luck to escape this Danger. Though the Fury of the Wind abated, yet it blew so hard for 12 Days together, that they could only carry their Courses reef'd. They spy'd a Sail in their Passage, but the Weather would not permit their endeavouring to speak with her. In a Word, they return'd to *Libertatia* with their Prize, without any other Accident, but the Captors could make no Estimate of her Value, she having on Board a vast Quantity of Diamonds, besides rich Silks, raw Silks, Spices, Carpets, and wrought and bar Gold. The Prize was taken to pieces, as she was of no Use; her Cordage and knee Timber preserv'd, with all the Bolts, Eyes, Chains, and other Iron Work, and her Guns planted on two Points of the Harbour, where they raised Batteries, so that they were now so strongly fortified they apprehended no Danger from any Number of Shipping which could be brought into those Seas to attack them. They had, by this Time, clear'd, sown, and enclosed a good Parcel of Ground, and taken in a Quantity of Pasturage, where they had above 300 Head of black Cattle, bought of the Natives. The Dock was now finish'd, and the *Victoire* growing old and unfit for a long Voyage, and the last Storm having shook and loosened her very much, she was pull'd to pieces and rebuilt, keeping the same Name. She was rigg'd, victuall'd, and fit to go to Sea, and was to sail to the Coast of *Guinea* for more Negroes, when one of the Sloops came in, which had been sent out rather to exercise the Negroes, than with any View of making a Prize, and brought Word five tall Ships chac'd her into the Bay, and stood for their Harbour; that she judg'd them to be *Portuguese* by their Built, and 50 Gun Ships, full of Men. This prov'd the real Truth. The Alarm was given, the Forts and Batteries mann'd, and every Man stood to his Arms. *Misson* took upon him the Command of 100 Negroes, who were well disciplin'd, (for every Morning they had been used to perform their Exercise, which was taught them by a *French* Serjeant, one of their Company, who belong'd to the *Victoire*) to be ready where his Assistance should be requir'd. *Tew* commanded all the *English.* They had hardly order'd their Affairs when these Ships hove in Sight, and stood directly for the Harbour with *Portuguese* Colours. They were warmly received by the two Forts, which did not stop them, though it brought one of them on the Careen; they enter'd the Harbour, and thought they had done their Business, but were saluted to warmly from the Forts and Batteries, Sloops and Ships, that two of them sunk downright, and a great many Men were drowned, though some got on Board the other Ships. The *Portuguese,* who did not imagine they had been so well fortified, and thought in passing the two Forts they should, without Difficulty, land their Men, and easily root out this Nest of pyrates, found now their Mistake, for they durst not venture to hoist out a Boat. They had wisely, however, contriv'd to enter just before the Turn of the Tide. Finding the Attempt vain, and that they lost a great many Men, they clapp'd upon a Wind, and with the Help of the Tide of Ebb, made more Haste out than they did to get in, leaving two of their Ships sunk in the Harbour; but they did not get off so cheaply, for no sooner were they clear of the Forts, but *Misson* manning, with the utmost Expedition, both the Ships and the Sloops, he gave them Chase, and engag'd them at the Mouth of the Bay. The *Portuguese* defended themselves with a great deal of Gallantry, and one of them put off the *Libertatians* twice, who boarded them from the two Sloops; two of them, finding themselves hard press'd, made a running Fight, and got off, and left the third to shift as well as he could. The *Bijoux* and *Victoire* finding the *Portuguese* endeavour'd to clear themselves, and knowing there was little to be got by the Captures, gave over the Chase, and fell upon the third, who defended himself till his Decks swam with Blood, and the greater Number of his Men killed; but finding all Resistance vain, and that he was left to an unequal Fight by his Companions, he called for Quarter, and good Quarter was given, both to himself and Men. This Prize yielded them a great Quantity of Powder and Shot, and, indeed, they expected nothing of Value out of her. None of the Prisoners were stripp'd, and the Officers, *Misson, Caraccioli* and *Tew,* invited to their Tables, treating them very civilly, and extolling the Courage they had shown in their Defence. Unhappily two Prisoners were found on Board, who had been released, and had sworn never to serve against them; these were clapp'd in Irons, and publicly tried for their Perjury. The *Portuguese* Officers being present, the Witnesses proved them the very discharged Men, and they were condemned to be hanged at the Point of each Fort; which Execution was performed the next Morning after their Condemnation, with the Assistance of the *Portuguese* Chaplain, who attended, confess'd and absolv'd them. This was the Engagement with the pyrates, which made so much Noise in the *Lisbon* Gazette, and these the Men whom the *English* ignorantly took for *Avery;* who, we had a Notion here in *London,* had 32 Sail of Men of War, and had taken upon him the State and Title of King, a Mistake we have already spoken to in the first Volume.

    This Execution seeming to impugn the Maxims of the Chiefs, *Caraccioli* made an Harangue, in which he told them, that there was no Rule could be laid down which did not allow Exceptions: That they were all sensible how tender the Commadore, Monsieur *Misson,* was in shedding of Blood; and that it was a Tenet of his Faith, that none had Power over the Life of another, but God alone, who gave it; but notwithstanding, Self-Preservation sometimes made it absolutely necessary to take away the Life of another, especially an avow'd and an obliged Enemy, even in cool Blood. As to the Blood shed in a lawful War, in Defence of that Liberty they had generously asserted, it was needless to say any Thing, but thought it proper to lay before them Reasons for the Execution of the Criminals, and the Heinousness of their Crimes. They had not only received their Lives from the Bounty of the *Libertatians,* but their Liberty, and had every Thing restored them which they laid claim to, consequently their Ingratitude rose in Proportion to the generous Treatment they had met with. That, indeed, both he and Captain *Misson* would have passed by the Perjury and Ingratitude they had been guilty of, with a corporal Punishment, which had not extended to the Deprivation of Life, but their gallant Friend and Companion the *English* Commander, Captain *Tew* used such cogent Reasons for an exemplary Punissment, to deter others from the like Crimes, that they must have been Enemies to their own Preservation in not following his Advice. That the Lives of their whole Body ought to be preferr'd to those of declared and perjured Enemies, who would not cease to endeavour their Ruin; and, as they were well acquainted with their Settlement, might be fatal Instruments of it, if they were again restored to that Liberty which they had already abused. That he was obliged to do Captain *Tew* the Justice, to acknowledge he was inclined to the Side of Mercy, till he was thoroughly informed of the Blackness of their Ingratitude, and then he thought it would be Cruelty to themselves to let those Miscreants experience a second Time their Clemency; thus an absolute Necessity had obliged them to act contrary to their declar'd Principles; tho', to state the Case rightly, these Men, not the *Libertatians,* were the Authors of their own Deaths: Here the Assembly crying out, *their Blood is on their own Heads, they sought their Deaths, and hanging was too good for them; Caraccioli* gave over, and every one returned satisfied to his private or the public Affairs.

    Some Differences arising between *Misson*'s and *Tew*'s Men, on a national Quarrel, which the latter began; Captain *Tew* proposed their deciding the Quarrel by the Sword, but *Caraccioli* was entirely against it, alledging, that such a Decision must necessarily be a Damage to the Public, since the brave Men who fell, would be a weakening of their Colony; he therefore desired Captain *Tew* to interpose the Authority he had over his Crew, as he and *Misson* would endeavour to bring their Men to an amicable Agreement; and for the future, as this Accident proved the Necessity, wholesome Laws should be made, and a Form of Government entered upon, both Parties were call'd, and *Caraccioli* shew'd them the Necessity of their living in Unity among themselves, who had the whole World for Enemies; and as he had a perswasive and insinuating Way of Argument, with the Assistance of Captain *Tew,* this Affair was ended to the Satisfaction of both Parties.

The next Day the whole Colony was assembled, and the three Commanders propos'd a Form of Government, being taken up, as necessary to their Conservation; for where there were no coercive Laws, the weakest would always be the Sufferers, and every Thing must tend to Confusion: That Mens Passions blinding them to Justice, and making them ever partial to themselves, they ought to submit the Differences which might arise to calm and disinterested Persons, who could examine with Temper, and determine according to Reason and Equity: That they look'd upon a Democratical Form, where the People were themselves the Makers and Judges of their own Laws, the most agreeable; and therefore, desired they would divide themselves into Companies of ten Men, and every such Company chuse one to assist in the settling a Form of Government, and in making wholesome Laws for the Good of the whole: That the Treasure and Cattle they were Masters of should be equally divided, and such Lands as any particular Man would enclose, should, for the future, be deem'd his Property, which no other should lay any Claim to, if not alienated by a Sale.

The Proposal was received with Applause, and they decimated themselves that very Day, but put off the meeting of the States till a House was built, which they set about very chearfully, and finish'd in about a Fortnight; it being of framed Timber, and they having among them a great many who understood the handling an Ax.

When this Body of Politicians met, *Caraccioli* open'd the Sessions with a handsome Speech, showing the Advantage flowing from Order; and then spoke to the Necessity of lodging a supream Power in the Hands of one, who should have that of rewarding brave and vertuous Actions, and of punishing the vicious, according to the Laws which the State should make; by which, he was to be guided. That such a Power however should not be for Life, nor hereditary, but determinate at the end of three Years, when a new Choice should be made by the State, or the Old confirm'd for three Years longer; by which means, the ablest Men would always be at the Head of Affairs, and their Power being of short Duration, none would dare to abuse it: That such a Chief should have the Title of Lord Conservator, and all the Ensigns of Royalty to attend him.

This was approv'd *Nemine contradicente,* and *Misson* was chose Conservator, with Power to create great Officers, *&c.* and with the Title of Supream Excellence.

Then a Law was made for the meeting of the State once every Year at least, but oftner, if the Conservator and his Council thought it necessary for the common Good to convene them; and that nothing of Moment should be undertaken without the Approbation of the State.

In a Word, their first Sessions lasted ten Days; and a great many wholesome Laws were enacted, register'd in the State-Book, printed and dispers'd (for they had some Printers and Letter Founders among them) and then the Conservator dissolved them.

Captain *Tew,* the Conservator, honoured with the Title of Admiral, and *Caraccioli* made Secretary of State; he chose a Council of the ablest among them, without Distinction of Nation or Colour; and the different Languages began to be incorporated, and one made out of the many: An equal Division was made of their Treasure and Cattle, and every one began either to inclose Land for himself or his Neighbour, who would hire his Assistance.

Admiral *Tew* propos'd the building an Arsenal, and augmenting their Naval Force; the first was agreed to be propos'd to the State at the next Convention, but the latter was thought unnecessary, till the Number of Inhabitants was augmented; for should they all be employed in the Sea Service, the Husbandry would be neglected, which would be of fatal Consequence to the growing Colony.

The Admiral then proposed the fetching in those *Englishmen* who had followed the Quarter Master; but the Council rejected this, alledging, that as they deserted their Captain, it was a Mark of a mutinous Temper, and they might infect others with a Spirit of Disorder; that however, they might have Notice given them of the Settlement, and if they made it their earnest

Intreaty to be admitted, and would desert the Quarter-Master, it should be granted as a particular Favour done them, at the instance of the Admiral, and upon his engaging his Parole of Honour for their quiet Behaviour.

The Admiral then desired he might take a Cruize; that he hop'd to meet with some *East-India* Ships, and bring in some Volunties, for the Number of Subjects being the Riches of a Nation, he thought the Colony stood more in need of Men, than of any Thing else; that he would lie in the Way of the Cape, and did not question doing good Service; and as he went to the Northward, would call upon his own Men.

The *Victoire* was according to the Admiral's Desire fitted out, and in few Days he sail'd with 300 Men on board; he came to an Anchor at the Settlement his Men had made, and hoisted an *English* Ensign in his Fore Shrouds, and fir'd a Gun; but after he had waited some Time, perceiving no Signal from the Shore, he landed and sent back his Boat; soon after the Boat was returned towards the Ship, two of his Men came up to him, to whom he gave an Account of *Misson*'s Settlement: They invited him into the Wood to see that of theirs, and to advise with their Companions, about the propos'd Migration. The Governor, *aliàs* Quarter-Master, received him mighty civilly, but told him, that he could see no Advantage to themselves in changing their present Situation, tho' they might prove a great One to the new Colony, by adding to their Force so many brave Fellows: That they there enjoy'd all the Necessaries of Life; were free and independent of all the World; and it would be Madness again to subject themselves to any Government, which, however mild, still exerted some Power. That he was Governor for three Months, by the Choice of his Companions; but his Power extended no farther than to the judging in Matters of small Difference which might arise, which he hop'd to do impartially while his Authority continued; that they had agreed among themselves, and confirm'd that Agreement by Oath, to support the Decrees of the Governor for the Time, that their Tranquillity might not be disturb'd by the capricious Humour of any one Man; and that this Power of determining, was to devolve at the Expiration of three Months, to him on whom the Lot should fall by balloting, provided he had not before enjoyed the Honour, for such a one was not to draw; by which Agreement, every one would be raised, in Time, to the supream Command, which prevented all canvassing and making Interest for Votes, as when it determined by Suffrage; left no Open for making Divisions and Parties, and was a Means to continue to them that Repose inseparable from a Unity among themselves. However, continu'd he, if you will go to *America* or *Europe,* and show the Advantages which may accrue to the *English,* by fixing a Colony here, out of that Love we bear our Country, and to wipe away the odious Appellation of pyrates, with Pleasure we'll submit to any who shall come with a Commission from a lawful Government; but 'tis ridiculous to think we will become Subjects to greater Rogues than our selves; and that you may know what to say on this Head, if you think it expedient to follow my Advice, take with you some few Thoughts, which I have couch'd in Writing, and which I'll fetch you; he went into his Cabbin, for, tho' the Governor's, it did not deserve the Name of a House, brought out some written Papers, and gave them him.

Captain *Tew* finding the Quarter-Master spoke the Sentiments of his Companions, took Leave, and returned to his Ship.

When the Captain was in his Cabbin, he read the Quarter-Master's Papers, which, as the Contents of them may oblige the curious, I shall set down.

This Island of *Madagascar* affords all the Necessaries of Life, and yields to none either in the Wholesomeness of the Air, or Fruitfulness of the Soil: The Seas around it are well stor'd with Fish, the Woods with Fowl, and the Intrails of the Earth are enrich'd with Mines of excellent Iron, as I have learn'd from some Natives, by their having Arms of that Metal; and, doubtless there are here both Gold and Silver Mines in the Mountains.

The Soil will produce Sugar, Cotton, Indigo, and other Growths of our *American* Colonies, at a far inferior Expence, as I will make plain, by comparing the Charge of erecting a Mill, *&c.* in *Barbadoes,* with what it would be here.

A Windmill in *Barbadoes* will cost 100 l. all Materials and Labour being very dear; but here Wood and Stone may be had for Labour only; so that with Artificers, and the needful Iron and Copper Work brought from *Europe*, a Sugar Work may be set up for very little Money.

Negroes in *Barbadoes* are at 30, 40, 50 l. *per* Head; and I dare answer 10 s. in *European* Goods, will purchase a Negroe Slave at *Madagascar*, since we have purchas'd for an old Coat, a lusty Fellow.

Food is very dear at *Barbadoes*, and here you may feed a Slave, as well as your self without Expence; consequently he will do more Work than a *Barbadoes* Slave, who is, by the Dearness of Provision, half-starved.

Tho' a Cattle Mill is of less Expence in *Barbadoes*, yet the feeding of Horses and Oxen at *Barbadoes* is very dear.

But, to proceed to other Advantages, all Sorts of medicinal and dying Woods may be carried from hence to *Europe;* and your Woods for fine Works, as Iron, Wood, Cedar, Mahogony, *&c.* are here in great Abundance.

If a Colony, with a lawful Power, were settled here, no doubt, but many of the Commodities which we fetch from the *Indies* might be made here, as Silk, Cotton, *&c.* the Soil being proper for their Production.

The Natives are, or seem to be, very human; and they have such Plenty of black Cattle, that we have bought an Ox of 800 lb. Weight, for a Pair of Breeches.

Besides, a Settlement here would be a Curb on pyrates, and a Protection, as well as a great Conveniency to our *East India* Ships, who might here be stored with fresh or salt Provisions, and consequently not be obliged to carry with them so great a Quantity as they now do, and save a great Deal of Money to the Company in their Victualling.

Captain *Tew* went on Shore again in the Evening, the Wind not serving to weigh, it blowing due *West;* he asked the Governor, how he got acquainted with the Natives? and he answered, by meeting them a Hunting, and using them well; that he wheedled one of them down to their Huts, the Fellow being alone, and they three in Company, he suppos'd, thought it best to go with seeming Willingness. After him several came, and they liv'd very friendly with them: The Captain had brought ashore with him some Rum and Brandy, and they were drinking a Bowl of Punch, when, on a sudden, a violent Storm arose; Captain *Tew* ran to the Shore, and made a Signal for his Boat to carry him off, but the Sea ran too high to venture out of the Ship: The Storm all the while increas'd, and the *Victoire,* in less than two Hours, parted her Cables, was drove ashore where it was steep to, and perished, with all her Men, in Captain *Tew*'s Sight.

The Captain staid with his old Companions, without knowing which Way to return to his Friends he had left with *Misson,* not one of whom was (luckily for them,) on board the Ship. At the End of three Months, as far as they could discover a Hutt, they saw a large Ship, which *Tew* believed was the *Bijoux;* but she took no Notice of the Fires they made: As he expected she would return after a short Cruize, he, and his Companions, made large Fires every Night on the Shore, and visited the Coast very often. About a Month after this, as they came early to the Sea-Side, they were surpriz'd at the Sight of two Sloops which lay at an Anchor, about a Canon Shot from the Shore; they had not been long looking upon them, when a Canoe was hoisted out of One, and made to them, with six Men who row'd, and one Sitter.

Tew soon knew him to be Captain *Misson;* he came ashore, and embracing the former, told him, all their propos'd Happiness was vanished; for without the least Provocation given, in the Dead of the Night, the Natives came down upon them in two great Bodies, and made a great Slaughter, without Distinction of Age or Sex, before they could put themselves in a Posture of Defence; that *Caraccioli* (who died in the Action) and he got what Men together they could, to make a Stand; but finding all Resistance vain against such Numbers, he made a Shift to secure a considerable Quantity of rough Diamonds and Bar Gold, and to get on board the two Sloops with 45 Men: That the *Bijoux* being gone to cruize, and the Number of Men he had carried with him in the *Victoire,* weaken'd the Colony, and given the Natives the Boldness to attack them as they did, but for what Reason he could not imagine.

Tew gave him an Account of the Disaster which had happen'd; and after having mutually condol'd their Misfortunes, *Tew* propos'd their going to *America,* where *Misson* might, with the Riches he had, pass his Life unknown, and in a comfortable Manner.

Misson answer'd he could not yet take any Resolution, tho' he had Thoughts of returning to *Europe,* and privately visiting his Family, if any where alive, and then to retire from the World.

They dined with the Quaster-Master, who press'd their Return to *America,* to procure a Commission for the settling a Colony.

Misson told *Tew,* he should have one of the Sloops, and what Volunteers would keep him Company, for his Misfortunes had erased all Thoughts of future Settlements; that what Riches they had saved, he would distribute equally, nay, he would be content, if he had only a bare Support left him.

On this Answer, four of the Quarter-Master's Company offer'd to join Captain *Tew.*

In the Afternoon they visited both Sloops, and *Misson* putting the Question to the Men, thirty went on board of one Sloop, tho' they parted with great Reluctance from their old Commander; and fifteen staid with *Misson.* The four Men who join'd *Tew* made the Number of his Crew 34; they staid about a Week, in hopes of the *Bijoux*'s Return upon the Coast; but she not appearing, they set sail, Captain *Misson* having first shared the Treasure, with *Tew* and his other Friends and Companions, hoping to meet the *Bijoux* on the *Guiney* Coast, for which they shaped their Course.

Off Cape *Infantes,* they were over-taken with a Storm, in which the unhappy *Misson*'s Sloop went down, within a Musket Shot of Captain *Tew,* who could give him no Assistance.

Tew continued his Course for *America,* and arrived at *Rhode Island* without any Accident; his Men dispersed themselves, as they thought fit, and *Tew* sent to *Bermudas* for his Owners Account fourteen Times the Value of their Sloop, and not being questioned by any, liv'd in great Tranquillity; the *French* belonging to *Misson,* took different Routs, one of whom dying at *Rochelle,* the *French* Manuscript of *Misson*'s Life was found among his Papers, and transmitted to me by a Friend and Correspondent.

Captain *Tew* lived unquestion'd, *&c.* he had an easy Fortune, and designed to live quietly at home; but those of his Men, who lived near him, having squandered their Shares, were continually solliciting him to take another Trip: He withstood their Request a considerable Time; but they having got together (by the Report they made of the vast Riches to be acquired) a Number of resolute Fellows, they, in a Body, begg'd him to head them but for one Voyage. They were so earnest in their Desire, that he could not refuse complying. They prepared a small

Sloop, and made the best of their Way to the *Streights,* entering the *Red Sea,* where they met with, and attack'd a Ship belonging to the Great *Mogul;* in the Engagement, a Shot carried away the Rim of *Tew*'s Belly, who held his Bowels with his Hands some small Space; when he dropp'd, it struck such a Terror in his Men, that they suffered themselves to be taken, without making Resistance.

Chap. XXIV
Of Capt. Halsey, And his Crew

John Halsey was a *Boston* Man, of *New England,* commanded the *Charles* Brigantine, and went out with a Commission from the Governor, to cruize on the Banks of *Newfoundland,* where he took a *French* Banker, which he appointed to meet him at *Fyal;* but missing his Prize here, he went among the *Canary* Islands, where he took a *Spanish Barcalonga,* which he plundered and sunk; from thence he went to the Island of *Bravo,* one of the *Cape de Verd,* where he wooded and watered, turn'd ashore his Lieutenant, and several of his Men here running away from him, the Governor sent them on board again, his Commission being as yet in Force; from hence he stood away then to the Southward, and doubling the *Cape* of *Good Hope,* made for *Madagascar* and the Bay of *Augustine,* where he took in Wood and Water, with some straggling Seamen, who were cast away in the *Degrave India* Man, Capt. *Young,* Commander. After this, he shap'd his Course for the *Red Sea,* and met with a *Dutchman* of 60 Guns, coming from *Mocha,* whom he kept Company with a Week. Tho' he was resolved upon turning Pyrate, he intended to rob only the *Moor* Ships, which occasioned a Dispute between him and his Men; they insisting on the Ship's being a *Moor,* he as strenuously asserting she was *Dutch,* was positive in his Resolve of meddling with no *European* Ships. The Men were for boarding, but his Obstinacy not being to be conquered, they broke *Halsey* and his Gunner, confining both, and were ready to board the *Dutchman,* when one of the Crew perceiving he was about to run out his lower Tire, knock'd down the Quarter-Master (whose Business it is to be at the Helm in Time of Chase or Engagement, according to the Rules of pyrates) clapp'd the Helm hard a Weather, and wore the *Brigantine:* The *Dutchman* staid, and fired a Shot, which taking a Swivel Gun carried it aft, narrowly miss'd the Man at Helm, and shatter'd the Tafrel; the Men perceiving they had catch'd a *Tartar,* made the best of their Way to shake her off, and some were running down between Decks, whom the Surgeon prick'd up again with his Sword, tho' he no Way was consenting to their design'd Pyracy. The Captain and a Gunner were again reinstated after they had seen their Mistake, and then they steer'd for the *Nicobar* Islands, where they met with a Country Ship, called the *Buffalo,* commanded by Captain *Buckley,* an *Englishman,* coming from *Bengal,* which they took after a short Engagement, there being only three *Europeans* aboard, the Captain and two Mates, the rest were *Moors.* This Ship fell seasonably in their Way, she being bound for *Achen,* with Butter, Rice, and Cloath, and the pyrates, at that Time, being in great Streights both for Provision and Cloathing. They took the two Mates to Sea with them, but left the Captain and the *Moors* at *Cara Nicobar,* at an Anchor, and then took a Cruize. Captain *Buckley,* who was sick, died before their Return; in the Cruize they met with Captain *Collins* in a Country Sloop, bound also to *Achen:* He had also two *English* Mates with him, but the rest of his Company consisted of *Moors;* him they carried to the same Harbour where they left the *Buffalo.*

Here a Dispute arose among the pyrates, some were for returning to the *West Indies,* others were against it, for they had got no Money, and that was what engaged their Search; they parted upon this; one Part went on board the *Buffalo,* made one *Rowe* Captain, and *Myers,* a *Frenchman,* Master, whom they had pick'd up at *Madagascar.* The Sloop's Deck they ripp'd up, and mended with it the Bottom of the *Brigantine,* which *Halsey* still commanded; the Ship shaped her Course for *Madagascar,* and the *Brigantine* made for the Streights of *Malacca,* to lie in the Tract of the *Manila* Ships. I must observe, that Capt. *Buckley's* two Mates, whom they intended to force with them, were by Strength of Intreaty, permitted to go away with a Canoe. In these Streights, they met an *Europe* built Ship, of 26 Guns, which they had not the Courage to attack, being sour'd by the *Dutchman.* They afterwards stood in Shore, and came to an Anchor; few Days after they made a Vessel, which they supposed a *China* Jonque, and gave Chase, but when they came pretty nigh, notwithstanding the Pilot assured them, she was what they supposed, they swore it was a *Dutchman,* and would not venture upon him; so leaving off their Chase stood in Shore, and came again to an Anchor under the *Peninsula;* they lay here some Days, and then spied a tall Vessel, which they chased, and proved the *Albemarle East India Man*, Captain *Bews*, Commander, come from *China;* they came up with him, but thinking it too warm a Ship, after exchanging a few Shot, the *Brigantine* made off, and the *Albemarle* chased in her Turn: They however got clear, having a better Share of Heels, and came again to an Anchor, having not above 40 Hands, their Water growing scarce, and not daring to venture ashore for Fear of the *Dutch*, a Council was called, and it was resolved to make the best of their Way to *Madagascar,* to pick up more Hands, refresh, and set out on new Adventures; pursuant to this Resolution, they steer'd for that Island, but fell in their Way on *Mascarenas* where, making a small Present to the Governor, they were supplied with what they wanted; from hence they went to a Place on *Madagascar,* call'd by the pyrates *Hopeful Point;* by the Natives, *Harangby,* near the Island of St. *Mary*'s, on the Lat. of 17. 40 S. where they met with the *Buffalo,* and the *Dorothy,* a Prize, made by Captain *Thomas White* and his Company, being about 90 or 100 Men, settled near the same Place, in petty Governments of their own, having some of them 500 or 600, some 1000 Negroe Subjects, who acknowledged their Sovereignty. Here they again repaired their Brigantine, took in Provisions and all Necessaries, augmented their Company to about 100 Men, and set out for the *Red Sea;* they touch'd at *Johanna,* and there took in a Quantity of Goats and Cocoa Nuts for fresh Provisions, and thence in eleven Days reach'd the Streights of *Babel Mandel:* They had not cruised here many Days, when they spied the *Moors* Fleet from *Mocha* and *Jufa,* consisting of 25 Sail, which they fell in with, and had been taken, if their Oars had not help'd them off, it falling a dead Calm. They had not apprehended the Danger so great, if they had not judged these Ships convoy'd by some *Portuguese* Men of War: Some Days after this, they met a one Mast Vessel, called a Grab, coming from *Mocha,* which they spied within Gun-Shot, in a thick Fog; they fired a Shot which out her Halliards, and then they took Possession of her with their Boats; she was laden with Drugs, but they took only some Necessaries and 2000 Dollars, and having learned that 4 *English* Vessels lay at *Mocoa,* of which one was from *Jufa,* they let her go.

Three Days after they spied the 4 Ships, which they at first took for the Trees of *Babel Mandel;* at Night they fell in with, and kept them Company till Morning, the Trumpets sounding on both Sides all the Time, for the Pyrate had two on board as well as the *English*. When it was clear Day the four Ships drew into a Line, for they had haled the Pyrate, who made no Ceremony of owning who he was, by answering according to their Manner *From the Seas*. The *Brigantine* bore up till she had slung her Garf. One of the Ships perceiving this, advised Captain *Jago,* who led the Van, in a Ship of 24 Guns and 70 Men, to give Chace, for the Pyrate was on the Run; but a Mate, who was acquainted with the Way of working among pyrates, answered he would find his Mistake, and said he had seen many a warm Day, but feared this would be the hottest. The *Brigantine* turn'd up again, and coming a Stern, clapp'd the *Rising Eagle* aboard, a Ship of 16 Guns and the Sternmost; tho' they entered their Men, the *Rising Eagle* held them a warm Dispute for 3 Quarters of an Hour, in which Captain *Chamberlain*'s chief Mate and several others were killed, the Purser was wounded, jumped over-board, and drowned: In the mean while the other Ships call'd to Captain *Jago* to board the Pyrate; who bearing away, to clap him aboard, the Pyrate gave him a Shot, which raked him fore and aft, and determined Captain *Jago* to get out of Danger; for he run away with all the Sail he could pack, tho' he was fitted out to protect the Coast against pyrates. His Example was followed by the rest, every one steering a different Course: Thus they became Masters of the *Rising Eagle*. I can't but take Notice, that the second Mate of the *Rising Eagle,* after Quarters were called for, fired from out of the Forecastle, and killed two of the pyrates, one of whom was the Gunner's Confort, who would have revenged his Death by shooting the Mate, but several *Irish* and *Scots,* together with one Captain *Thomas White,* once a Commander among the pyrates, but then a private Man, interposed and saved him, in regard that he was an *Irishman.* They examined the Prisoners to know which was the Ship came from *Juffa,* for that had Money on board; and having learn'd it was the *Essex,* they gave Chace, came up with her, hoisted the bloody Flag at the Mainmast-head, fired one single Gun, and she struck; tho' the *Essex* was fitted for close

Quarters, there were not on board the *Brigantine* above 20 Hands, and the Prize was a Stern so far, that her Top-mast scarce appeared out of the Water; in chacing this Ship, they pass'd the other two, who held the Fly of their Ensigns in their Hands ready to strike. When the Ship had struck, the Captain of her asked who commanded that *Brigantine*, he was answered, Captain *Halsey*; asking again who was Quarter-Master? He was told, *Nathaniel North*, to whom he called, as he knew him very well. *North* learning his Name was *Punt*, said Captain *Thomas Punt, I am sorry you are fallen into our Hands;* he was civilly treated, and nothing belonging to himself or the *English* Gentlemen, who were Passengers, touch'd, tho' they made bold to lay Hands on 40000 l. in Money belonging to the Ship. They had about 10000 l. in Money out of the *Rising Eagle*. They discharged the *Essex*, and with the other Prize and the Brigantine, steer'd for *Madagascar*, where they arrived and shared their Booty. Some of the Passengers, who had been so well treated, came afterwards with a small Ship from *India* (with License from the Governor of *Maderas*) called the *Greyhound*, laden with Necessaries, in Hopes to barter with the pyrates for the dry Goods they had taken, and recover them at an easy Rate: They were received very kindly, an Invoice of their Goods was asked, the Goods agreed for, shared and paid in Money and Bale Goods. In the mean while came in a Ship from *Scotland*, called the *Neptune*, 26 Guns, 54 Men, commanded by Captain *James Miller*, with a Design to slave, and to go thence to *Batavia* to dispose of her Negroes (having a Supercargo on board, brought up among the *Dutch*) and thence to *Malacco*, to take on board the Cargo of a Ship, call'd the *Speedwell*, lost on her Return from *China;* but finding here another Ship trading with the pyrates, and having many Necessaries, *French* Brandy, *Madera* Wine, and *English* Stout on board, Captain *Miller* thought it better to trade for Money than Slaves. The Merchants of the *Greyhound* nettled to see any but themselves take Money, for the pyrates never haggled about a Price, told 'em, *They could not do the Governor of* Maderas *a more grateful Piece of Service, than to make Prize of the* Neptune, *which was a Ship fit for their Purpose.* To which some of the *Scotch* and *Irish* answered, *they had not best put such a Design on Foot, for if the Company once got it into their Heads to take one, they'd go nigh to take both Ships.* In a short Time after came on a Hurricane, which obliged the *Neptune* to cut away all her Masts, and lost the three Ships belonging to the pyrates, which was their whole Fleet. They having now no Ship, and several of them no Money, having been stripp'd at Play, their Thoughts were bent on the *Neptune*. The Chief Mate of her *Daniel Burgis*, who had a Spleen to the Captain, joining privately with the pyrates (among whom he died) got all the small Masts and Yards ashore; and the pyrates being requested to find him proper Trees for Masting, told Captain *Miller*, they had found such as would serve his Turn, desiring he would take a Number of Hands ashore to get them down to the Water, which he (suspecting no harm) accordingly did, and he and his Men were seized, and the Long Boat detained ashore. The Captain was forced to send for the second Mate, and afterwards for the Gunner; the Mate, who was the Captain's Brother, went, but the Gunner suspecting foul Play refused: In the Evening *Burgess* came on board, and advised the Surrender of the Ship, which, tho' but sixteen were left on board, they scrupled, and proposed going under the Cover of their own Guns to fetch their Top-masts and Yards, and with them to put to Sea; but the Chief Mate *Burgess*, whose Villany was not then known, persuaded them to give up a Ship they could neither defend nor sail; which was no small Satisfaction to the Merchants in the *Greyhound*, little thinking how soon they would meet with the same Treatment; for two Days after the pyrates mann'd the *Neptune*'s Pinnace, seized the *Greyhound*, took away all the Money they had paid, and shifting out of the *Neptune* ten Pipes of *Madera*, with two Hogsheads of Brandy, into the *Greyhound*, and putting on board the Captain, second Mate, Boatswain and Gunner of the *Neptune*, and about 14 of her Hands, ordered her to Sea; the rest of the *Neptune*'s Company being young Men fit for their Purpose, they detained, most of which, by hard drinking, fell into Distempers and died. As to Captain *Halsey*, while the *Scotch* Ship was fitting, he fell ill of a Fever, died and was buried with great Solemnity and Ceremony; the Prayers of the *Church of England* were read over him, Colours were flying, and his Sword and Pistol laid on his Coffin, which was covered with a Ship's Jack; as many Minute Guns fired as he was Years old, *viz.* 46, and three

English Vollies, and one *French* Volley of small Arms. He was brave in his Person, courteous to all his Prisoners, lived beloved, and died regretted by his own People. His Grave was made in a Garden of Water Melons, and fenced in with Pallisades to prevent his being rooted up by wild Hogs, of which there are Plenty in those Parts.

P. S. The *Neptune* seized as above, was the Year after Captain *Halsey*'s Death, ready to go to Sea; but a Hurricane happening she was lost, and prov'd the last Ship that Gang of pyrates ever got Possession of.

Chap. XXV
Of Captain Thomas White, And his Crew

He was born at *Plymouth,* where his Mother kept a Public House; she took great Care of his Education and when he was grown up, as he had an Inclination to the Sea, procur'd him the King's Letter. After he had served some Years on board a Man of War, he went to *Barbadoes,* where he married, got into the Merchants Service, and designed to settle in the Island: He had the Command of the *Marygold Brigantine* given him, in which he made two successful Voyages to *Guiney* and back to *Barbadoes;* in his third, he had the Misfortune to be taken by a *French*Pyrate, as were several other *English* Ships, the Masters and inferior Officers of which they detained, being in Want of good Artists.

The Brigantine belonging to *White* they kept for their own Use, and sunk the Vessel they before sailed in; but meeting with a Ship on the *Guiney* Coast more fit for their Purpose, they went on board her, and burnt the Brigantine.

It is not my Business here to give an Acount of this *French*Pyrate, any farther than Captain *White*'s Story obliges me, tho' I beg Leave to take Notice of their Barbarity to the *English* Prisoners, for they would set them up as a Butt or Mark to shoot at; several of whom were thus murdered in cool Blood, by Way of Diversion.

White was marked out for a Sacrifice by one of these Villains, who, for I know not what Reason, had sworn his Death, which he escaped thus. One of the Crew, who had a Friendship for *White,* knew this Fellow's Design, to kill him in the Night, and therefore advised him to lye between him and the Ship's Side, with Intention to save him; which indeed he did, but was himself shot dead by the murderous Villain, who mistook him for *White;* but this by the Bye.

After some Time cruizing along the Coast, the pyrates doubled the *Cape* of *Good Hope,* and shaped their Course for *Madagascar,* where, being drunk and mad, they knock'd their Ship on the Head, at the *South* End of the Island, at a Place called by the Natives *Elexa;* the Country thereabouts was governed by a King, named *Mafaly.*

When the Ship struck, Captain *White,* Captain *Boreman,* (born in the Isle of *White,* formerly a lieutenant of a Man of War, but in the Merchants Service when he fell into the Hands of the pyrates) Captain *Bowen* and some other Prisoners got to the Long-Boat, and with broken Oars and Barrel Staves, which they found in the Bottom of the Boat, paddled to *Augustine* Bay; that is about 14 or 15 Leagues from the Wreck where they landed, and were kindly received by the King of *Bavaw* (the Name of that Part of the Island) who spoke good *English.*

They staid here a Year and a half at the King's Expence, who gave them a plentiful Allowance of Provision, as was his Custom to all White Men, who met with any Misfortune on his Coast; his Humanity not only provided for all such, but the first *European* Vessel that came in, he always obliged them to take in the unfortunate People, let the Vessel be what it would; for he had no Notion of any Difference between pyrates and Merchants.

At the Expiration of the above Term, a Pyrate Brigantine came in, aboard which the King obliged them to enter, or travel by Land to some other Place, which they durst not do; and of two Evils chose the least, that of going on board the Pyrate Vessel, which was commanded by one *William Read,* who received them very civilly.

This Commander went along the Coast, and pick'd up what *Europeans* he could meet with; his Crew however did not exceed forty Men, he would have been glad of taking on board some of the wreck'd *Frenchmen,* but for the Barbarity they had used towards the *English* Prisoners; however, it was impracticable, for the *French* pretending to lord it over the Natives, whom they began to treat inhumanly, were set upon by them, one half of their Number cut off, and the other half made Slaves.

Read, with this Gang, and a Brigantine of 60 Tons, steer'd his Course for the Gulf of *Persia,* where they met a Grabb (a one masted Vessel) of about 200 Tons, which was made Prize.

They found nothing on board but Bale Goods, most of which they threw over-board to search for Gold, and to make Room in the Vessel; but as they learned afterwards, they threw over in their Search, what they so greedily hunted after, for there was a considerable Quantity of Gold concealed in one of the Bales they toss'd into the Sea.

In this Cruise Captain *Read* fell ill and died; he was succeeded by one *James*. The Brigantine being small, crazy, and worm eaten, they shaped their Course for the Island of *Magotta,* where they took out the Masts of the Brigantine, sitted up the Grabb, and made a Ship of her: Here they took in a Quantity of fresh Provision, which is in this Island very plentiful, and very cheap; and found a twelve oar'd Boat, which formerly belonged to the *Ruby East India* Man, which had been lost there.

They staid here all the Mousson Time, which is about six Months; after which they resolved for *Madagascar.* As they came in with the Land, they spied a Sail coming round from the *East* Side of the Island; they gave Chase on both Sides, so that they soon met: They haled each other, and receiving the same Answer from each Vessel, *viz. from the Seas,* they joined Company.

This Vessel was a small *French* Ship, laden with Liquors from *Martinico,* first commanded by one *Fourgette,* to trade with the pyrates for Slaves, at *Ambonawoula,* on the *East* Side the Island, in the Lat. of 17. 30. and was by them taken after the following Manner.

The pyrates, who were headed by *George Booth,* Commander of the Ship, went on board (as they had often done) to the Number of ten, and carried Money with them under Pretence of purchasing what they wanted. (This *Booth* had formerly been Gunner of a Pyrate Ship, called the *Dolphin*) Captain *Fourgette* was pretty much upon his Guard, and searched every Man as he came over the Side, and a Pair of Pocket Pistols were found upon a *Dutchman,* who was the first enter'd; the Captain told him, *he was a Rogue, and had a*

Design upon his Ship, and the Pprates pretended to be so angry with this Fellow's offering to come on board with Arms, that they threatned to knock on the Head, and tossing him roughly into the Boat, ordered him ashore, tho' they had before taken an Oath on the Bible, either to carry the Ship or die in the Undertaking.

They were all searched, but they however contrived to get on board 4 Pistols, which were all the Arms they had for the Enterprize, tho' *Fourgette* had 20 Hands on board, and his small Arms on the Arning to be in Readiness.

The Captain invited them into the Cabbin to Dinner, but *Booth* chose to dine with the petty Officers, tho' one *Johnson, Isaac,* and another, went down.

Booth was to give the Watch Word, which was *Hurrah;* he pretending to make Water over the Side of the Gunnel, laid his Hand on the Arning, and being a nimble Fellow, at one Spring threw himself upon it, drew the Arms to him, fired his Pistol forward among the Men, one of whom he wounded, (who jumping over-board was lost) and gave the Signal.

Three I said were in the Cabbin, and seven upon Deck, who with Handspikes and the Arms seized, secured the Ship's Crew. The Captain and his two Mates, who were at Dinner in the Cabbin, hearing the Pistol, fell upon *Johnson,* and stabb'd him in several Places with their Forks, but they being Silver, did him no great Damage. *Fourgette* snatch'd his Piece which he snapp'd at *Isaac*'s Breast several Times, but it would not go off; at last, finding his Resistance vain, he submitted, and the pyrates set him, and those of his Men who would not join them, on Shore, allowing him to take his Books, Papers, and whatever else he claimed as belonging to himself; and besides treating him very humanly gave him several Casks of Liquor, with Arms and Powder, to purchase Provisions in the Country.

I hope this Digression, as it was in a Manner needful, will be excused; I shall now proceed.

After they had taken in the *Dolphin*'s Company, which were on the Island, and encreased by that Means their Crew to the Number of 80 Hands, they sail'd to St. *Mary*'s, where Captain *Mosson*'s Ship lay at Anchor, between the Island and the Main: This Gentleman and his whole Ship's Company had been cut off, at the Instigation of *Ort Vantyle,* a *Dutchman* of *New-York.*

Out of her they took Water Casks and other Necessaries, which having done, they designed for the River *Methelage,* on the West Side *Madagascar,* in the Lat. of 16 or thereabouts, to salt up Provisions and to proceed to the *East Indies,* cruize off the Islands of St. *John,* and lie in Wait for the *Moors* Ships from *Mocha.*

In their Way to *Methelage* they fell in (as I have said) with the Pyrate, on board of which was Captain *White;* they join'd Company, came to an Anchor together in the above-nam'd River, where they had cleaned, salted up, taken in their Provisions, and were ready to go to Sea, when a large Ship appeared in Sight, and stood into the same River.

The pyrates knew not whether she was a Merchant Man or Man of War; she had been the latter, belonging to the *French* King, and could mount 50 Guns; but being taken by the *English,* she was bought by some *London* Merchants, and fitted out from that Port, to slave at *Madagascar,* and go to *Jamaica*. The Captain was a young unexperienced Man, who was put in with a Nurse.

The pyrates sent their Boats to speak with him, but the Ship firing at them, they concluded it a Man of War, and rowed to Shore, the two pyrates slipp'd and run ashore; the Grabb standing in, and not keeping her Wind so well as the *French* built Ship, run among a Parcel of Mangroves, and a Stump piercing her Bottom, she sunk; the other run aground, let go her Anchor, and came to no Damage, for the Tide of Flood fetch'd her off.

The Captain of the *Speaker,* for that was the Name of the Ship which frighten'd the pyrates, was not a little vain of having forced these two Vessels ashore, tho' he did not know whether they were pyrates or Merchant Men, and could not help expressing himself in these Words; *How will my Name ring on the* Exchange, *when it is known I have run two pyrates aground,* which gave Handle to a satyrical Return from one of his Men after he was taken, who said, Lord, *How our Captain's Name will ring on the* Exchange, *when it is heard, he frighten'd two Pyrate Ships ashore, and was taken by their two Boats afterwards.*

When the *Speaker* came within Shot, she fired several at the two Vessels; and when she came to an Anchor, several more into the Country, which alarm'd the Negroes, who, acquainting their King, he would allow him no Trade, till the pyrates living ashore, and who had a Design on his Ship, interceded for 'em, telling the King, they were their Countrymen, and what had happened was thro' a Mistake, it being a Custom among them to fire their Guns by Way of Respect, and it was owing to the Gunner of the Ship's Negligence, that they fir'd Shot.

The Captain of the *Speaker* sent his Purser ashore, to go up the Country to the King, who lived about 24 Miles from the Coast, to carry a couple of small Arms inlaid with Gold, a couple of Brass Blunderbusses, and a Pair of Pistols, as Presents, and to require Trade.

As soon as the Purser was ashore, he was taken Prisoner, by one *Tom Collins,* a *Welchman,* born in *Pembroke,* who lived on Shore, and had belong'd to the *Charming Mary* of *Barbadoes,* which went out with a Commission, but was converted to a Pyrate; he told the Purser, he was his Prisoner, and must answer the Damage done two Merchants, who were slaving.

The Purser answer'd, that he was not Commander, that the Captain was a hot rash Youth, put into a Business by his Friends, which he did not understand; but however, Satisfaction should be made.

He was carried by *Collins* on board *Booth*'s Ship, where, at first, he was talked to in pretty strong Terms; but after a while very civilly us'd, and the next Morning sent up to the King with a Guide, and Peace made for him, as already said.

The King allowed them Trade, and sent down the usual Presents, a couple of Oxen, between 20 and 30 People laden with Rice, and as many more with the Country Liquor, called *Toke.*

The Captain then settled the Factory on the Shore Side, and began to buy Slaves and Provisions; the pyrates were among them, and had Opportunities of sounding the Men, and knowing in what Posture the Ship lay. They found by one *Hugh Man,* belonging to the *Speaker,* that there were not above 40 Men on board, and that they had lost the second Mate and 20 Hands in the Long Boat, on the Coast, before they came into this Harbour, but that they kept a good Look-out, and had their Guns ready primed; however, he, for a hundred Pounds, undertook to wet all the Priming, and assist in the taking the Ship.

After some Days the Captain of the *Speaker* came on Shore, and was received with a great Deal of Civility by the Heads of the pyrates, having agreed before to make Satisfaction; in a Day or two after, he was invited by them to eat a Barbacute Shoot, which Invitation he accepted.

After Dinner, Captain *Bowen,* who was, I have already said, a Prisoner on board the *French*Pyrate, but now become one of the Fraternity, and Master of the *Grab,* went out, and returned with a Case of Pistols in his Hand, and told the Captain of the *Speaker,* whose Name I won't mention, that he was his Prisoner; he asked, upon what Account? *Bowen* answered, they wanted a Ship, his was a good One, and they were resolved to have her, to make amends for the Damage he had done them.

In the mean while his Boats Crew, and the rest of his Men ashore, were told by other of the pyrates, who were drinking with them, that they were also Prisoners; some of them answer'd, *Z — ds, we don't trouble our Heads what we are, let's have t'other Bowl of Punch.*

A Watch Word was given, and no Boat to be admitted on board the Ship; this Word, which was for that Night, *Coventry,* was known to them: At Eight a-Clock they mann'd the twelve-oar'd Boat, and that they found at *Mayotta,* with 24 Men, and set out for the Ship.

When they were put off, the Captain of the *Speaker* desired them to come back, he wanted to speak with them; Captain *Booth* asked, what he wanted? He said, they could never take his Ship, then said *Booth,* we'll die in or along Side of her; but replied the Captain, if you will go with Safety, don't board on the Lar-board Side, for there is a Gun out of the Steerage loaded with Patridge, will clear the Decks; they thank'd him, and proceeded.

When they were near the Ship they were haled, and the Answer was, *the Coventry;* all well, said the Mate, get the Lights over the Side, but spying the second Boat, he asked what Boat that was? one answered, it was a Raft of Water, another, that it was a Boat of Beef; this Disagreement in the Answers made the Mate suspicious, who cried out *pyrates, take to your Arms my Lads,* and immediately clapp'd a Match to a Gun, which, as the Priming was before wet by the Treachery of *Hugh Man,* only fizz'd; they boarded in the Instant, and made themselves Masters of her, without the Loss of a Man on either Side.

The next Day they put necessary Provisions on board the *French* built Ship, and gave her to the Captain of the *Speaker,* and those Men who would go off with him, among whom was *Man,* who had betray'd his Ship; for the pyrates had both paid him the 100 l. agreed, and kept his Secret. The Captain having thus lost his Ship, sail'd in that the pyrates gave him, for *Johanna,* where he fell ill and died with Grief.

The pyrates having here victualled, they sail'd for the Bay of St. *Augustine,* where they took in between 70 and 80 Men, who had belonged to the Ship *Alexander,* commanded by Captain *James,* a Pyrate; they also took up her Guns, and mounted the *Speaker* with 54, which made up their Number 240 Men besides Slaves, of which they had about 20.

From hence they sailed for the *East Indies,* but stopp'd at *Zanguebar* for fresh Provisions, where the *Portuguese* had once a Settlement, but now inhabited by *Arabians;* some of them went ashore with the Captain to buy Provisions, the Captain was sent for by the Governor, who went with about 14 in Company: They past thro' the Guard, and when they were entered the Governor's House, they were all cut off; and, at the same Time, others who were in different Houses of the Town were set upon, which made them fly to the Shore; the Long-Boat, which lay off at a Grapling, was immediately put in by those who look'd after her: There were not above half a dozen of the pyrates who brought their Arms ashore, but they played them so well, for they were in the Boat, that most of the Men got into her, the Quarter-Master ran down Sword in Hand, and tho' he was attack'd by many, he behaved himself so well, that he got into a little Canoe, put her off and reached the Long-Boat.

In the Interim, the little Fort the *Arabians* had, play'd upon the Ship, which returned the Salute very warmly. Thus they got on board, with the Loss of Captain *Booth* and twenty Men, and set Sail for the *East-Indies.*

When they were under Sail, they went to Voting for a new Captain, and the Quarter-Master, who had behaved so well in the last Affair with the *Arabians,* was chosen; but he declining all Command, the Crew made Choice of *Bowen* for Captain, *Pickering* to succeed him as Master, *Samuel Herault,* a *Frenchman,* for Quarter-Master, and *Nathaniel North,* for Captain Quarter-Master.

Things being thus settled, they came to the Mouth of the *Red Sea,* and fell in with 13 Sail of *Moors* Ships, which they kept Company with the greater Part of the Day, but were afraid to venture on them as they took them for *Portuguese* Men of War; at length part were for boarding, and advised it, the Captain, tho' he said little, did not seem inclin'd, for he was but a young Pyrate, tho' an old Commander of a Merchant Man.

Those who push'd for boarding then, desired Captain *Boreman,* already mentioned, to take the Command; but he said, he would not usurp on any, that no Body was more fit for it than he who had it, that for his Part, he would stand by his Fufil and went forward to the Forecastle with such as would have had him taken the Command, to be ready to board; on which, the Captain's Quarter-Master said, if they were resolved to engage their Captain, (whose Representative he was) did not want Resolution, therefore, he ordered them to get their Tacks on board (for they had already made a clear Ship) and get ready for boarding; which they accordingly did, and coming up with the sternmost Ship, they fired a Broadside into her, which killed two *Moors,* clapp'd her on board and carried her; but Night coming on, they made only this Prize, which yielded them 500 l. *per* Man.

From hence they sailed to the Coast of *Mallabar;* the Adventures of these pyrates on this Coast are already set down in Captain *Bowen*'s Life, to which I refer the Reader, and shall only observe, Captain *White* was all this while asore the Mast, being a forced Man from the Beginning.

Bowen's Crew dispersing, Captain *White* went to *Methelage,* where he lived ashore with the King, not having any Opportunity of getting off the Island, till another Pyrate Ship, called the *Prosperous,* commanded by one *Thomas Howard,* who had been bred a Lighterman on the River of *Thames,* came in: This Ship was taken at *Augustine,* by some pyrates from Shore, and the Crew of their own Long-Boat, which join'd them, at the Instigation of one *Ranten,* Boatswain's Mate, who was sent for Water. They came on board in the Night and surprized her, tho' not without Resistance, in which the Captain and chief Mate was killed, and several others wounded, the Particulars of which will be found in *Hore*'s Life. Those who were ashore with Captain *White,* resolving to enter in this Ship, determined him to go also, rather than be left alone with the Natives, hoping, by some Accident or other, to have an Opportunity of returning home. He continu'd on board this Ship, in which he was made Quarter-Master, till they met with, and all went on board of *Bowen,* as is set down in his Life, in which Ship he continued after *Bowen* left them, as shall be mentioned in the Appendix. At *Port Dolphin* he went off in the Boat to fetch some of the Crew left ashoar, the Ship being blown to Sea the Night before. The Ship not being able to get in, and he supposing her gone to the West-Side of the Island, as they had formerly proposed, he steered that Course in his Boat with 26 Men. They touch'd at *Augustine* expecting the Ship, but she not appearing in a Week, the Time they waited, the King order'd 'em to be gone, telling 'em they impos'd on him with Lies, for he did not believe they had any Ship; however, he gave 'em fresh Provision. They took in Water, and made for *Methelage.* Here, as Captain *White* was known to the King, they were kindly received, and staid about a Fortnight in Expectation of their Ship, but she not appearing, they raised their Boat a-streak, salted up the Provisions the King gave 'em, put Water aboard, and stood for the North-End of the Island, designing to go round, believing their Ship might be at the Island of St. *Mary.* When they came to the North-End, the Current, which sets to the North-West for eight Months in the Year, was so strong they found it impossible to get round. Wherefore they got into a Harbour, of which there are many for small Vessels. Here they staid about three Weeks or a Month, when part of the Crew were for burning the Boat, and for travelling over Land to a black King of their Acquaintance, whose Name was *Reberimbo,* who lived at a Place called *Manangaromasigh,* in the Latitude of 15, or thereabouts. As this King had been several times assisted by the Whites in his Wars, he was a great Friend to them. Captain *White* disswaded them from this Undertaking, and, with much ado, saved the Boat; but one half of the Men being resolved to go by Land, they took what Provisions they thought necessary, and set out, Captain *White,* and those who staid with him, convoy'd 'em a Day's Journey, and then returning, he got into the Boat with his Companions, and went back to *Methelage,* fearing these Men might return, prevail with the rest, and burn the Boat.

Here he built a Deck on his Boat, and lay by three Months, in which Time there came in three pyrates with a Boat, who had formerly been trepann'd on board the *Severn* and *Scarborough* Men of War, which had been looking sixteen pyrates on the East-Side; from which Ships they made their escape at *Mohila,* in a small Canoe to *Johanna,* and from *Johanna* to *Mayotta,* where the King built 'em the Boat which brought 'em to *Methelage.* The Time of the Current's setting with Violence to the North-West being over, they proceeded together in *White*'s Boat (burning that of *Mayotta*) to the North-End, where the Current running yet too strong to get round, they went into a Harbour and staid there a Month, maintaining themselves with Fish and wild Hog, of which there was great Plenty. At length, having a Slatch of fine Weather, and the Strength of the Current abating, they got round; and after sailing about 40 Mile on the East-Side, they went into a Harbour, where they found a Piece of a Jacket, which they knew belong'd to one of those Men who had left 'em to go over Land; he had been a forced Man, and a Ship Carpenter; this they supposed he had torn to wrap round his Feet, that Part of the Country being barren and rocky. As they sailed along this Coast, they came to an Anchor in convenient Harbours every Night, till they got as far as *Manangaromasigh* where King *Reberimbo* resided, where they went in to enquire for their Men, who left 'em at the North-End, and to recruit with Provisions. The latter was given 'em, but they could have no Information of their Companions.

From hence they went to the Island of St. *Mary,* where a Canoe came off to 'em with a Letter directed to any White Man. They knew it to be the Hand of one of their former Ship-Mates. The Contents of this Letter was to advise 'em to be on their Guard, and not trust too much to the Blacks of this Place, they having been formerly treacherous. They enquired after their Ship, and was inform'd, that the Company had given her to the *Moors,* who were gone away with her, and that they themselves were settled at *Ambonavoula,* about 20 Leagues to the Southward of St. *Mary,* where they lived among the Negroes as so many sovereign Princes.

One of the Blacks, who brought off the Letter, went on board their Boat, carried them to the Place called *Olumbah,* a Point of Land made by a River on one Side, and the Sea on the other, where twelve of 'em lived together in a large House they had built, and fortified with about 20 Pieces of Canon.

The rest of them were settled in small Companies of about 12 or 14 together, more or less, up the said River, and along the Coast, every Nation by it self, as the *English, French, Dutch, &c.* They made Enquiry of their Consorts after the Shares of Prizes which belong'd to them, and they found all very justly laid by to be given them, if ever they return'd, as were what belong'd to the Men who went over Land. Captain *White* hankering after home, proposed going out again in the Boat; for he was averse to settling with them; and many others agreed to go under his Command; and if they could not meet with a Ship to carry them to *Europe,* to follow their old Vocation. But the others did not think it reasonable he should have the Boat, but that it should be set to Sale for the Benefit of the Company. Accordingly it was set up, and Captain *White* bought it for 400 Pieces of Eight, and with some of his old Consorts, whose Number was increas'd by others of the Ship's Crew, he went back the Way he had come, to Methelage Here he met with a *French* Ship of about 50 Tuns and 6 Guns; she had been taken by some pyrates who lived at *Maratan,* on the East-Side of the Island, and some of the *Degrave East-India* Man's Crew, to whom the Master of her refused a Passage to *Europe;* for as he had himself been a Pyrate and Quarter-Master to *Bowen* in the *Speaker,* he apprehended their taking away his Ship, War being then between *England* and *France,* he thought they might do it without being called in question as pyrates. The pyrates who had been concerned in taking *Herault*'s Ship, for that was his Name, had gone up the Country, and left her to the Men belonging to the *Degrave,* who had fitted her up, clean'd and taffow'd her, and got in some Provision, with a Design to go to the *East-Indies,* that they might light on some Ship to return to their own Country.

Captain *White* finding these Men proposed their joining him, and going round to *Ambonavoula,* to make up a Company, which they agreed to, and unanimously chose him

Commander. They accordingly put to Sea, and stood away round the South End of the Island, and touch'd at *Don Mascarena,* where he took in a Surgeon, and stretching over again to *Madagascar,* fell in with *Ambonavoula,* and made up his Complement 60 Men. From hence he shaped his Course for the Island of *Mayotta,* where he cleaned his Ship, and staid for the Season to go into the *Red Seas:* His Provisions being taken in, the Time proper, and the Ship well fitted, he steer'd for *Babelmandel,* and running into a Harbour waited for the *Mocha* Ships.

He here took two Grabs laden with Provision, and having some small Money and Drugs aboard; these he plunder'd of what was for his Turn, kept 'em a Fortnight by him, and then let them go. Soon after they spied a tall Ship, upon which they put to Sea; but finding her *Europe* built, and too strong to attempt, for it was a *Dutch* Man, they gave over the Chace, and were glad to shake him off, and return to their Station. Fancying they were here discover'd, from the Coast of *Arabia,* or that the Grabs had given Information of them, they stood over for the *Ethiopian* Shore, keeping a good look out for the *Mocha* Ships.

Few Days after they met with a large Ship of about 1000 Tuns and 600 Men, called the *Malabar,* which they chased, kept Company with all Night, and took in the Morning, with the Loss only of their Boatswain, and two or three Men wounded. In the taking this Ship they damaged their own so much, by springing their Foremast, carrying away their Bowsprit, and beating in part of their upper Works, that they did not think her longer fit for their Use, therefore filled her with Prisoners, gave 'em Provision, and sent them away.

Some Days after this they spied a *Portuguese* Man of War of 44 Guns, which they chased, but gave it over, by carrying away their Main-Top-Mast, so that they did not speak with her, for the *Portuguese* took no Notice of them.

Four Days after they had left this Man of War, they fell in with a *Portuguese* Merchant-Man, which they chased with the *English* Colours flying, the Chace taking *White* for an *English* Man of War or *East-India* Man, made no Sail to get from him, but on his coming up brought to, and sent his Boat on board with a Present of Sweet-Meats for the *English* Captain; his Boat's Crew was detain'd, and the pyrates getting into his Boat with their Arms, went on board, and fir'd on the *Portueguese,* who being surpriz'd, asked if War was broke out between *England* and *Portugal?* They answer'd in the Affirmative, but the Captain could not believe 'em. However, they took what they liked, and kept him with them.

After two Days they met with the *Dorothy,* an *English* Ship, Captain *Penruddock* Commander, coming from *Mocha.* They exchanged several Shot in the Chace, but when they came a Long-side her, they entered their Men, and found no Resistance, she being navigated by *Moors,* no *Europeans* except the Officers being on board. On a Vote they gave Captain *Penruddock* (from whom they took a considerable Quantity of Money) the *Portuguese* Ship and Cargoe, with what Bales he pleased to take out of his own, bid him go about his Business, and make what he could of her. As to the *English* Ship, they kept her for their own Use.

Soon after they plunder'd the *Mallabar* Ship, out of which they took as much Money as came to 200 l. Sterling a man, but miss'd 50000 Chequins which were hid in a Jar under a Cow's-Stall, kept for the giving Milk to the *Moor* Supercargoe, an ancient Man. They then put the *Portuguese* and *Moor* Prisoners on board the *Mallabar,* and sent them about their Business. The Day after they had sent them away, one Captain *Benjamin Stacy,* in a Ketch of six Guns fell into their Hands; they took what Money he had, and what Goods and Provisions they wanted. Among the Money were 500 Dollars, a Silver Mug and two Spoons belonging to a Couple of Children on board, and under the Care of *Stacy.* The Children took on for their Loss, and the Captain asking the Reason of their Tears, was answer'd by *Stacy,* that the above Sum and Plate was all the Children had to bring them up.

Captain *White* made a Speech to his Men, and told 'em, it was cruel to rob the innocent Children; upon which, by unanimous Consent, all was restor'd them again; besides, they made a Gathering among themselves, and made a Present to *Stacy*'s Mate, and other his inferior Officers, and about 120 Dollars to the Children; they then discharged *Stacy* and his Crew, and made the best of their Way out of the *Red Sea.*

They came into the Bay of *Defarr,* where they found a Ketch at an Anchor, which the People had made Prize of, by seizing the Master and Boat's Crew ashoar. They found a *French* Gentleman, one Monsieur *Berger,* on board, whom they carried with 'em, took out about 2000 Dollars, and sold the Ketch to the Chief ashoar for Provisions.

Hence they sailed for *Madagascar,* but touch'd at *Mascarena,* where several of 'em went ashoar with their Booty, about 1200 l. a Man. Here taking in fresh Provision, *White* steer'd for *Madagascar,* and fell in with *Hopeful Point,* where they shar'd their Goods, and took up Settlements ashoar, where *White* built a House, bought Cattle, took off the upper Deck of his Ship, and was fitting her up for the next Season. When she was near ready for Sea, Captain *John Halsey,* who had made a broken Voyage, came in with a Brigantine, which being a properer Vessel for their Turn, they desisted from working on the Ship, and who had a Mind for fresh Adventures, went on board *Halsey,* among whom Captain *White* enter'd afore the Mast.

At his return to *Madagascar, White* was taken ill of a Flux, which in about 5 or 6 Months ended his Days: finding his Time was drawing nigh, he made his Will, left several Legacies, and nam'd three Men of different Nations, Guardian to a Son he had by a Woman of the Country, requiring he might be sent to *England* with the Money he left him, by the first *English* Ship, to be brought up in the Christian Religion in hopes he might live a better Man than his Father. He was buried with the same Ceremony they use at the Funerals of their Companions, which is mention'd in the Account of *Halsey.* Some Years after an *English* Ship touching there, the Guardians faithfully discharged their Trust, and put him on board with the Captain, who brought up the Boy with Care, acting by him as became a Man of Probity and Honour.

Chap. XXVI
Of Captain Condent, And his Crew

Captain *Condent* was a *Plymouth* Man born, but we are as yet ignorant of the Motives, and Time of his first turning Pyrate; he was one of those who thought fit to retire from *Providence* (on Governor *Roger's* Arrival at that Island) in a Sloop belonging to Mr. *Simpson,* of *New York,* a *Jew* Merchant, of which Sloop he was then Quarter-Master. Soon after they left the Island, an Accident happened on board, which put the whole Crew into Consternation; they had among them an *Indian* Man, whom some of them had beat; in revenge, he got most of the Arms forward into the Hold, and designed to blow up the Sloop. Upon which, some advised scuttling the Deck and throwing Grenade Shells down, but *Condent* said, that was too tedious and dangerous, since the Fellow might fire thro' the Decks and kill several of them; he, therefore, taking a Pistol in one Hand, and his Cutlash in the other, leaped into the Hold; the *Indian* discharged a Piece at him, which broke his Arm, but, however, he ran up to and shot the *Indian.* When he was dead the Crew hack'd him to Pieces, and the Gunner ripping up his Belly, tore out his Heart, broiled and eat it.

After this, they took a Merchant Man, called, the *Duke of York;* and some Disputes arising among the pyrates, the Captain, and one half of the Company, went on board the Prize; the other half, who continued in the Sloop, chose *Condent* Captain; he shaped his Course for the *Cape de Verd* Islands, and in his Way, took a Merchant Ship from *Maderas,* laden with Wine, bound for the *West Indies,* which he plundered and let go; then coming to the Isle of *May,* one of the said Islands, he took the whole Salt Fleet, consisting of about 20 Sail; he wanting a Boom, took out the Mainmost of one of these Ships, to supply the Want: Here he took upon him the Administration of Justice, enquiring into the Manner of the Commander's Behaviour to their Men, and those, against whom Complaint was made, he whipp'd and pickled. He took what Provisions and other Necessaries he wanted, and having augmented his Company, by Volunteers and forced Men, he left the Ships and sailed to St. *Jago,* where he took a *Dutch* Ship, which had formerly been a Privateer; this prov'd also an easy Prize, for he fired but one Broadside, and clapping her on board, carried her without Resistance, for the Captain and several Men were killed, beside some wounded by his great Shot.

This Ship proving for his Purpose, he gave her the Name of the *Flying Dragon,* went on board with his Crew, and made a Present of his Sloop to a Mate of an *English* Prize, whom he had forced with him; from hence he stood away for the Coast of *Brazil,* and in his Cruize, took several *Portuguese* Ships, which he plundered and let go.

After these, he fell in with the *Wright* Galley, Captain *John Spelt,* Commander, hired by the *South-Sea* Company, to go to the Coast of *Angela* for
Slaves, and thence to *Buenos Ayres.* This Ship he detained a considerable Time, and the Captain being his Townsman, treated him very civilly; few Days after he took *Spelt,* he made Prize of a *Portuguese,* laden with Bale Goods and Stores; he new rigg'd the *Wright* Galley, and put on board her several Goods.

Soon after he had discharged the *Portuguese,* he met with a *Dutch East-India* Man of 26 Guns, whose Captain was kill'd the first Broadside, and took her with little Resistance, for he had hoisted the pyrates Colours on board *Spelt's* Ship.

He now, with three Sail, steer'd for the Island of *Ferdinando,* where he hove down and clean'd the *Flying Dragon;* having careen'd, he put 11 *Dutchmen* on board Captain *Spelt,* to make Amends for the Hands he had forced from him, and sent him away, making him a Present of the Goods he took from the *Portuguese* Ship. When he sail'd himself, he ordered the *Dutch* to stay at *Ferdinando* 24 Hours after his Departure; threatning, if he did not comply, to sink his Ship; if he fell a second Time into his Hands, and to put all the Company to the Sword. He then stood for the Coast of *Brazil,* where he met a *Portuguese* Man of War of 70 Guns, which he came up with; the *Portuguese* hal'd him, and he answer'd, *from London,* bound for *Buenos Ayres:* The *Portuguese* mann'd his Shrouds and chear'd him, when *Condent* fired a Broadside and a Volley of small Arms, which began a smart Engagement for the Space of 3 Glasses; but *Condent* finding himself over-match'd, made the best of his Way, and, being the better Sailor, got off.

Few Days after he took a Vessel of the same Nation, who gave an Account, that he had killed above 40 Men in the *Guarda del Costa,* beside a Number wounded; he kept along the Coast to the Southward, and took a *French* Ship of 18 Guns, laden with Wine and Brandy, bound for the *South-Sea,* which he carried with him into the River of *Plate.* He sent some of his Men ashore to kill some wild Cattle, but they were taken by the Crew of a *Spanish* Man of War; on their Examination before the Captain, they said they were two *Guiney* Ships, with Slaves belonging to the *South-Sea* Company, and on this Story were allowed to return to their Boats: Here five of his forced Men ran away with his Canoe, he plundered the *French* Ship, cut her adrift, and she was stranded. He proceeded along the *Brazil* Coast, and hearing a Pyrate Ship was lost upon it, and the pyrates imprisoned, he used all the *Portuguese,* who fell into his Hands, who were many, very barbarously, cutting off their Ears and Noses; and as his Master was a Papist, when they took a Priest, they made him say Mass at the Main-mast, and would afterwards get on his Back and ride him about the Decks, or else load and drive him like a Beast. He from this went to the *Guiney* Coast, and took Captain *Hill* in the *Indian Queen.*

In *Luengo* Bay he saw two Ships at Anchor, one a *Dutchman* of 44 Guns, the other an *English* Ship, called the *Fame,* Captain *Bowen,* Commander; they both cut and ran ashore, the *Fame* was lost, but the *Dutch* Ship, the Pyrate, got off and took with him. When he was at Sea again he discharged Captain *Hill,* and stood away for the *East-Indies.* Near the Cape he took an *Ostend East-India* Man, of which Mr. *Nash,* a noted Merchant in *London,* was Supercargo. Soon after he took a *Dutch East-India* Man, discharged the *Ostender,* and made for *Madagascar;* at the Isle of St. *Mary,* he met with some of Captain *Halsey's* Crew, whom he took on board with other Stragglers, and shaped his Course for the *East-Indies,* and in the Way, at the Island of *Johanna,* took, in Company of two other pyrates he met at St *Mary's,* the *Cassandra East-India* Man, commanded by Captain *James Macragh;* he continued his Course for the *East-Indies,* where he made a very great Booty, and returning, touch'd at the Isle of *Mascarenas,* where he met with a *Portuguese* Ship of 70 Guns, with the Vice-Roy of *Goa,* on board. This Ship he made Prize of, and hearing she had Money on board, they would allow of no Ransom, but carried her to the Coast of *Zanguebar,* where was a *Dutch* Fortification, which they took and plunder'd, razed the Fort, and carried off several Men who enter'd voluntarily. From hence they stood for St. *Mary's,* where they shared their Booty, broke up their Company, and settled among the Natives: Here a *Snow* came from *Bristol,* which they obliged to carry a Petition to the Governor of *Mascarenas* for a Pardon, tho' they paid the Master very generously. The Governor returned Answer, he would take them into Protection if they would destroy their Ships, which they agreed to, and accordingly sunk the *Flying Dragon,* &c. *Condent* and some others went to *Mascarenas,* where *Condent* married the Governor's Sister-in-Law, and stay'd some Time; but as I have been credibly inform'd, he is since come to *France,* settled at St. *Maloes,* and drives a considerable Trade as a Merchant.

Chap. XXVII
A Description of Magadoxa

Taken partly from the Journal of Captain Beavis, and also from an original Manuscript of a Molotto, who was taken by the Natives, and lived amongst them sixteen Years

In the Year 1700, Capt. *William Beavis,* Commander of the Ship, called the *Albemarle,* then in the Service of the *East-India* Company, sail'd from *England,* bound for *Surrat,* in the *East-Indies,* but after having been some Months at Sea, having the Misfortune to meet with contrary Masorns, he lost his Passage, so that he was forced on the Coast of *Zanguebar,* in the higher *Ethiopia,* or the Continent of *Africa,* where he endeavoured to find out some Place of Safety, that the Ship might ride secure, and where he might meet with some Necessaries for refreshing his Company, while he waited for the Change of Winds, which he could not expect in less than three or four Months.

They came in with the Land, and cast Anchor on the ninth of *November,* the Year before-mentioned; the Tenth it blew hard, but on the Eleventh the Weather being pretty fair, the Captain sent the Yawl on Shore, in two different Places, at considerable Distance from each other, they found the Land every where sandy, and all over green with Shrubs, but saw no Houses, nor could they discover the least Track of any human Creature; however, they saw Deer, but could not come near enough to have a Shot at them; they also found the Dung of Wolves, Hares, and some other Animals, but saw none; and near the Water-side they found the Shells of a great Number of Craw-Fish, but met with none alive; wherefore, they guessed that they were left here by some Creatures, who fished them up and usually fed upon them.

Finding this Place altogether inhospitable, they weigh'd Anchor and sail'd along the Shore, till the 17th of the same Month, when the Captain looking thro' his Spying-glass, saw three or four Men walking along the Sea-Side, and sometimes sitting down, but could not discern any House, Fire, or Smoak, but when they had sail'd about a League farther, they perceived an Inlet or Bay, where the Captain fancied there might be a River; he could also perceive several tall Trees, which were the first they had seen since they came upon the Coast, which made the Captain conjecture, that there must be some Inhabitants.

Upon this, they came to an Anchor, and manning out the Boat, the Captain sent Mr. Baldwin the third Mate in her, to go into the Bay, in order to discover whether there was any River which discharged itself into it; when they were in with the Shore, they perceived about fifty or sixty People standing upon a Bank near the Water-side, and one separating himself from the Rest, approached nearer to them, and held up a white Piece of Linnen at the End of a Stick, and waved it at them, which they understood to be a Flag of Friendship, and which the Boat answered by the like Signal; then the Person on Shore beckon'd to them with his Hand, which they took to be an Invitation to come on Shore, and accordingly they ventured; there were two of the Boat's Men who spoke a little *Portuguese,* who saluted this Man in that Language; as soon as they came near him, his Gesture appeared very civil, but they could not understand a Syllable of what he said in Answer, but by his Signs, they fancied he invited them to come to their Huts, in order to eat and drink.

However, they did not think fit to stay longer at this Time, but returned on Board, to give the Captain an Account of what had pass'd, and to let him know, that they could discover no River in the Bay; they described the People to be pretty tall and well made, their Colour jet black, their Heads and Beards close shaved, wearing upon their Heads Turbants made of a Kind of Linnen, and a Sort of Sash made of Dungeree Linnen about their Wastes, the Rest of their Bodies being quite naked; whereupon, consulting with a Molotto, one of the Ship's Company, who understood the *Turkish* and *Arabian* Languages, what he thought the Language of these People might be, he judg'd it to be a Kind of corrupted *Arabic,* because their Dress was not unlike that of the *Arabians* of the Desert, and that it was not unlikely, but that they might be some Way descended from them; wherefore, the Captain resolved to mann the Boat again, and to send the Molotto ashore with them, to try if he could so far understand their Language, as to learn from them, where there was fresh Water, or any other Refreshments to be had; and also to enquire for some Port or Bay, where the Ship might be with Safety till the breaking up of those Easterly Winds.

The Wind blew so fresh all that Day, which was the 19th, that they could not send the Boat on Shore. At Night they watched to see if they could discover any Appearance of Fire any where upon Land, but they could discern nothing like it; wherefore, it seemed strange to them, that in a Country inhabited, there should be neither Smoak by Day, nor Fire by Night, which made them suppose, the Huts of the Natives were far up the Country.

However, the next Day the Boat was sent on Shore with the Molotto Interpreter, and Mr. *Courser* the fourth Mate; and for Fear of any Surprize, the Captain ordered them to carry Arms in the Boat. When they approach'd near the Shore, several of the Natives made towards the Waterside, but seeing the Boat's Men take their Arms in their Hands at their Landing, they fled affrighted up the Country, nor would they ever come near them after; the Men went a little Way up the Land and met with some Huts, which were covered with the Shells of Turtles, which Creatures it is supposed the Natives catch in their proper Season for Food, and then making a Covering of their Shells for their Houses; they also saw several Cows, at some Distance, which are very swift at running, and not larger than our Deer; they saw some other Animals, but took none, and so returned on Board without gaining any Intelligence.

The Mistake here was, that they did not lye off with their Boat, and make a Signal as they did at first, which would have disposed the Natives to have staid for them, as they did before, but going ashore abruptly with Arms in their Hands, frighten'd the Natives, as if they had come to kill them; wherefore, there was no Expectation of making any Discovery here, which induced the Captain to weigh Anchor, and steer a little farther Westward.

The next Morning, which was the twenty second, they came to an Anchor, and sent their Boat on Shore again, with Mr. *Baldwin* the third Mate, and the Gunner; there being some high Hills not far from the Place where they landed, the Mate and Gunner resolved to walk to the Top of one of the highest of those Hills, in order to take a View of the Country beneath. About four in the Afternoon they returned again to the Ship, bringing Word, that there was a pleasant Valley on the other Side, about five Miles in Length, and near as far in Breadth, but that they could see no Houses or other Signs of Inhabitants, but that the Valley seemed to abound with Deer, and several other Creatures; they brought on Board three Antilopes, and two large Guiney Hens, which they shot, and saw great Numbers of both these Creatures about the Bushes on the Sides of those Hills; the Antilopes were small, but extreamly beautiful, their Bodies no bigger than that of a Hare, but their Legs much longer, their Colour was a Mixture of black and white, very smooth, and very bright, with Horns about three Inches long.

They weigh'd and crept along ashore to the Westward, and next Day, which was the Twenty third, the Captain with his Spying-glass saw seven or eight Men near the Shore; wherefore, he sent the Boat to endeavour to speak with them. As soon as they saw the Boat approach them, they went off; the Men however went on Shore, and at some Distance saw two Camels and two Asses loaden, pass along with Men attending them; they did what they could to speak with these too, but when they perceived the Boat's Men to make towards them, they drove so fast there was no coming near them.

The next Morning the Weather being clearer than ordinary, the Captain looking thro' his Glass, fancied he saw several tall Spires to the Westward; he weigh'd Anchor, and stood away for them; by four in the Afternoon, he plainly perceived a large Town, and by six came to an Anchor right over against it; however, he did not send the Boat on Shore that Night, but next Morning he ordered Mr. *Baldwin* the third Mate, Mr. *Sale* the Purser, with the Molotto before-mentioned, who spoke the *Turkish* and *Arabian* Languages, to take the Yawl with four Hands, and to carry with them a white Flag, that they might appear to come in a friendly and peaceable Manner, charging them at the same Time to say or do nothing which might appear harsh or offensive. The Boat was no sooner in with the Shore, but the Natives flock'd as it were to meet them, and appeared very courteous: The Molotto spoke to them in *Arabian* Tongue, giving them to understand, that they were driven upon their Coasts by the Misfortune of having lost their Voyage, that they were in Want of Water, and begg'd they would show them where they might be supplied, and that if they would think fit to furnish them with fresh Provision they would pay them in Money, or any Goods or Curiosities of *Europe.*

It happened the Language they spoke was a Kind of *Arabic,* so that the Molotto could discourse with them perfectly well; they answered him, that the King was absent from the City, and that they could do nothing till his Return, but that he would be there as that Night, for they had sent him Word of the coming of a Ship, as soon as it appeared in Sight. That however, they might assure themselves, that all they requested should be granted, and showed them where there were several fine Springs of Water: These Springs being a pretty Way from the Water-side, and the Ground near them craggy and uneven; the Molotto told them it would be difficult to rowl their Casks so long a Way, and over such bad Ground, and ask'd them if there were not any Spring nearer the Sea. They answered them no, but that the King would give them Oxen to draw their Casks to the Boat; and so they returned on Board with a Present from the King's Son of a Sarne of mash'd Dates, a matted Jar of Sweet-Meats, and four Sheep.

Betimes the next Morning, being the 26th, the Captain sent the Yawl on Shore again with the same Officers, to know if the King was come, and to beg Leave to bring on Board some fresh Water, ordering them to make a Signal for the Long-Boat to be sent on Shore, in Case they obtained the Permission to water; the Yawl had not been long gone before the appointed Signal was made, and the Long-Boat was accordingly sent immediately; after which, the Captain perceived the Yawl was returning back again to the Ship: She came with four Hands in her to advise the Captain, that the Long-Boat would immediately return with a Cow as a Present to him, and to put him in Mind, that it would be proper to send something back for a Present to the *Shubander,* (the Name by which they call the King's Son) with whom they, *viz.* the third Mate Mr. *Baldwin,* the Gunner, and the Molotto Interpreter, who served in the Ship as a Quartier, were gone to dine.

The Captain was surprized at their Indiscretion, and the more because he had ordered them, to be upon their Guard for Fear of Treachery, having furnished them with Arms for that Purpose, and charged them not to stir far from their Boat; however, there was no Remedy now, so that he sent the Yawl back again with a Present of a small Looking-glass (a great Curiosity there) for the Prince, ordering one Man to carry it, and to tell the Mate, Gunner, and Molotto to come off as soon as they could, the rest to lye a little off with the Yawl, their Arms ready, but out of Sight.

The Captain observing the Yawl with his Glass, perceived the Men contrary to his Orders were gone on Shore, and looking again a little after, saw the Boat without a Mast, or so much as one Hand in her, drag'd towards the Town quite on Shore, and in a little Time after she was hawl'd out of Sight.

This Rashness of his Men gave him a great Deal of Uneasiness, he apprehended some fatal Consequence from it, (and indeed he had Reason) for he knew the Natives of some Part of the Coast were Cannibals; therefore, for Fear of venturing too much at once, he resolved not to trust the Long-Boat on Shore, till he had some Tideings from the Yawl.

All that Day he pass'd with the utmost Uneasiness, keeping a Man continually on the Watch, looking towards the Shore with a Spying-glass, to try if any Thing could be discovered of his Men on the Shore, but all to no Purpose; for nothing could be discerned either of them or the Boat the whole Day. That Night was spent in many doubtful Reflections, and Tears for the Condition of those who were on Shore. Next Morning the Captain resolved to send the Long-Boat towards the Land, with Mr. *Nyn* his first Mate, and some other of his Officers in her, ordering them to show a white Flag, as soon as they should discover any People to come near them; but not to venture to go ashore, but to talk and make Signs to the Natives out of the Boat, and to try to discover the Reason of our Mens being detained; and in Case they found they kept them Prisoners, or intended them for Slaves, to try by Means of the Molotto Interpreter to treat with them for their Ransom.

Mr. *Nyn* obey'd his Orders punctually, and when he came near the Land he lay by, with a white Flag display'd at the End of a Mast, at which Time he observed a great Body of People coming from the Town towards the Sea-Side; the Captain could also discern them from the Ship with his Spying-glass, and judg'd them to be betwixt four and five Thousand, but instead of coming to parley, they marched in a Body behind a Bank, which stood opposite the Boat, where they lay in a Kind of Ambuscade, without returning any Signal, or showing any Inclination to speak with the Boat.

This look'd plainly, as if they intended to surprize the Men, in Case they should venture to land; wherefore Mr. *Nyn* resolved to return on Board, and plying along Shore, in order to find the Passage thro' the Ridge of Rocks of Coral, which runs along ashore, the Natives let fly a Shower of Arrows at the Boat, which however did no Harm, because they fell short; upon which Mr. *Nyn* commanded his Men to fire their Arms towards the Banks, in order to frighten them, for being so intrench'd, he knew he could do them no Harm; after which he returned on Board.

The Captain now began to despair of ever seeing his Men more; the best he could think which could befal them, was, to be made Slaves, for still he did not apprehend that they had met with so melancholy and cruel a Fate, as their Confidence in the Natives had really brought upon them; he therefore resolved to make one Attempt more, in order to learn some News of what had befallen them: In order to which, he thought of a Stratagem, by which he should run no Hazard of losing any more of his Men, and by which it seemed probable he must hear of them if they were alive. He writ a Letter, which Letter he caused to be fix'd to the Top of a long Pole, which he ordered to be carried on Shore in the Silence of the Night; the Men were to fix the Pole in the Ground, and to make it the more conspicuous, there was a Flag also fastened to the Pole.

He did not doubt, but that if any of his Men had the Liberty of walking about, they would come for the Letter which they must see, and if they had not that Liberty, the Natives not being able to read it themselves, would carry it to them.

In this Letter he advised Mr. *Baldwin,* and Mr. *Sale,* the third Mate and Purser, to treat about their own Ransom themselves, and that of the five Men with them (including the Molotto) and since there was no other Way of procuring their Liberty, he would comply with the Terms, let them be what they would; he directed them to fix their Answer upon the same Pole, and least they should want Pen and Ink, he inclosed a Pencil, and also a Sheet of Paper. And in Hopes an Answer should be left, he commanded the Pole to be fix'd just at the Waters Edge, where there was no Bank near, that it might be taken off without the Danger of an Ambuscade.

This was the best Expedient he could think of, for relieving his unhappy Countrymen, who now, alas! were past all Relief. Accordingly the Boat was sent with the said Letter, and two of the Men went on Shore and fixed it, and having returned into the Boat, the Boat put off, and came to an Anchor at some Distance from the Shore, in order to observe what should become of the Letter; they waited till Noon to no Purpose, then taking up their Anchor, in order to come on Board for some Refreshment, they were but a little while under Sail, when they saw a Man come and carry off the Pole; a little while after which, as they ply'd along the Shore, and were opposite to the Bank before described, they were saluted with a Volley of Musquet-Shot, one Ball falling into the Boat, and several others come very near it; wherefore, they made all the Sail they could to give the Captain an Account of what had pass'd.

The Fire Arms they made use of were these they found in the Boat, where they also met with six Cartouch Boxes full of Charges, and their making use of them in this Manner, convinced the Captain that they had no Mind to come to any Parley with them, or to listen to any Terms about the Release of their unhappy Ship Mates; however they were continually upon the Watch, looking out with wishing Eyes, in Expectation of seeing the appointed Signal made for the Answer of the Letter; long they expected to no Purpose, which made the Captain think something very fatal had happened to them, and that he should never see them more; but in the midst of his Despair, a Thought came into his Head, which administered to him a little

Comfort, he fancied that perhaps they might be carried up the Country, to the Place where the King at that Time was gone, and that the Natives might send the Letter after them, which might be the Reason there was no Answer yet left. Upon this little Glimmering of Hope, he resolved to wait some Days longer, for he was willing to lay Hold of any Hope, rather than bear the Thoughts of going away without them.

Thus Day after Day they waited in Expectation of some Answer, sending the Boat to lye off near the Shore, to be ready in Case any Signal should be made. — One Day they perceived a great Number of People to come out of the Town, and make towards the Shore, which gave them an Expectation that the Delivery of their Friends was at Hand; they watched their Motions with earnest Eyes, hoping every Minute to see a Flag of Truce, instead of which, they observed them to march directly behind the Bank, where they seem'd to place themselves in a Kind of Ambuscade.

Now there seem'd to be an End of all their Hopes, the Boat return'd on Board, and made a Report to the Captain of what they saw, who calling a Consultation of all his Officers to hear if any Thing could be offered for the Relief of their Companions; it was proposed by one to send the Boat on Shore, to burn some Junks which were hawl'd up about a Musquet-Shot from the Waterside, but the Captain considered, that tho' this might gratifie their Revenge, it would bring no Relief to their poor captive Friends: On the contrary, the Natives might be provoked to destroy them for it, if they had not done it already, besides as these Junks lay not far from the Bank, their Men might be exposed to the Arrows of the Natives (who now lay in continual Ambuscade) and so they might run the Hazard of losing more Men without the least Advantage to themselves, or unhappy Companions.

Wherefore, this Project was laid aside, and the Winds often blowing hard, and the Captain not judging it safe to lye any longer in that open Road, he weighed Anchor on the fourth of *December,* steering along ashore, in Search of some Bay or Inlet, where they might ride shelter'd from the Wind and Weather; and still with a View that if either their Companions might have an Opportunity of making their Escape, or the Natives should relent and think of letting them go for a Ransom, they might be near enough to receive them. After about three or four Hours gentle Sail he dropp'd an Anchor, the Town of *Magadoxa* then bearing N E b'E of them, they perceived it was all along a flat smooth Shore, without any Bay or other Shelter, for Ships to ride; wherefore, the next Day, which was the fifth of *December,* they stood off to Sea, and then came to a Consultation what Measures to take in their present Condition; and having considered that they had met with no Place where they could ride with any Safety, and if they should meet with a convenient Bay much farther down the Coast, it would be of no Service to their unhappy Companions, who would never hear of them; and besides they could not venture to traffic with the Natives for Refreshments, for Fear of Surprize and Treachery; and their Men beginning to grow weak and distempered for want of fresh Provisions, they resolved to make for the Island of *Joanna,* being forced to leave their Companions to Providence, in great Trouble and Anxiety for their unhappy Fate.

We shall leave them to pursue their Voyage, which was happy enough, bating this Accident, and relate what had passd on Shore, as we had it from a Munuscript, written by the Molotto Interpreter, who was the only Person who escaped, and return'd to *England,* after he had lived sixteen Years amongst the Barbarians.

It has been already taken Notice that Mr. *Baldwin* the third Mate, and Mr. *Sale* the Purser (unhappily for them) not observing the Cautions the Captain gave them to be upon their Guard, were so indiscreet, to be tempted to accept of an Invitation to dine with the King's Son; so that having sent the Yawl on Board again, for a Present as has been related, they with the Molotto Interpreter went towards the Town, accompanied by several of the Natives, who made them the Invitation in the Name of the King's Son. They were no sooner arrived at the first Gate of the City, but they were surrounded by a great Multitude of People, and violently dragg'd into a little Door under the Gateway, and shut up in a dark Hole. When they had remained here about the Space of two Hours, they heard a very great Noise without; soon after which, the Doors leading to their Dungeon were all opened, and they were dragg'd out again; when they were out, they found that what occasioned that great Noise, was the Return of their Men, whom they had sent on Board for a Present for the King's Son, who were seized in the same Manner they had been, and being encompassed by such a Number of People, they lost them in a Minute; they were also separated from one another, and the Molotto desiring to know of them the Meaning of all this, and in what they had offended them, they only answered him, that they must go before the *Accabo,* (the Name by which they call the King, who had not been out of Town as they gave out before) accordingly he was conducted with a sufficient Guard, expecting there to meet his Companions again.

When he arrived at the King's House (which shall be hereafter described) he was led thro' several Rooms to that where the King was present, whom he found sitting upon the Ground, the Floor being matted; he was dress'd in a long Pair of Drawers of blewish purple Silk, which reach'd down to his Toes, having neither Shoes nor Stockings on, a large Mantle of the same Silk, and a white Turbant on his Head; there were eight others who sat about him, whose Dress was the same with his, as to Form and Fashion, but their Drawers and Mantles were made of a blew and white strip'd Dungeree Stuff, instead of Silk; these were his Councellors and Favourites. The King spoke to him in a Kind of *Arabic,* asking of what Country he was? he answered of *Canton* in *China.* Then he ask'd him, how he came to associate himself with those horrid white Men? The poor Molotto began to tremble at this Question, but excus'd himself by speaking in their Favour, highly extolling them for their Civility of Behaviour, as well as Generosity, and praising them in all Things to the King, telling him, he was sure the Captain would ransom them, if it was his Pleasure to consent to it; to which he returned no Answer, but ask'd what the Ship had in her, the Molotto gave him an Account of her Lading; then he desired to know whether the rest of the Men would come on Shore, he answered, he could not tell, but in Case they were suffered to return again on Board, he was sure they would come on Shore, and that the Captain himself designed to come and see the King, as soon as they should return; but the King made no Offer of suffering that, but commanded him to be carried back to Prison.

The Prison which they call *Haulaub,* is a square Stone-Building, about twenty Foot high, and flat at Top, fronting one of their broadest Streets; there are no Windows or Iron Bars, as we see in our Prisons, but there are several little Holes about eight or nine Inches square, quite thro' the Wall, thro' which, the Place within receives both Light and Air. Here the poor Molotto was put, very anxious about the Fate of his poor Companions, whom he had not seen since their being separated at their first coming out of the Dungeon; wherefore, seeing an old Man looking thro' one of the Holes before described, he enquired of him what was become of them, who gave him this melancholy Account; that those who came last out of the Boat, which were the four Sailors sent on Board the Ship for the Present for the King's Son, were kill'd in the Streets by the Multitude, and that making some Resistance, they were torn to Pieces, every Man thinking himself happy that could procure a Piece of their Flesh, showing a Bit of about two Ounces, which he begg'd of one who had got a great Piece, which many of them eat; that they were all from their Childhood taught to have an Aversion to white Men, and that these were the first that had been seen in the Memory of Man, that as to the tall Man and the little Man which had been in the Dungeon with him (which were Mr. *Baldwin* and Mr. *Sale,* the Mate and Purser) they were by the King's Order carried to the *Boderzau* (a Place where Tygers and other fierce Beasts are kept for the King's Pleasure) and delivered up to be torn to Pieces by those Animals.

This was in Effect, the true Account of the most bloody Massacre that was committed upon these unhappy Men; the Story of which, it may be imagined, must throw the poor Molotto into the utmost Consternation and Fear, as imagining himself to be near suffering some cruel Death; sometimes he flattered himself that they would spare him, because of his being a Molotto, but on the other Side, when he reflected on his having given the white Men a good Character, he look'd upon himself to be a dead Man, thinking that alone was sufficient to destroy him.

Betwixt these Doubts and Fears he pass'd the Night, in a Place all covered with Nastiness, where there was not the least Conveniency for easing Nature, and where, had his Mind been at rest, it would have been hard for him to have slept. In the Morning a Man look'd thro' one of the Holes, and with great Joy in his Countenance, told him, there were more white Men coming on Shore; the Fellow did not relate it as good News to him, but told it for the Pleasure they should have in destroying more of them. The Molotto wish'd within himself, that he could have given Notice of what had pass'd, and some Advice to beware of themselves, but it was safest for him to keep his Wishes to himself; therefore he said nothing. Some Hours after he was sent to go again before the King; now he thought his Execution was at Hand, but when he was brought into the King's Presence, they put a Letter into his Hand, commanding him to tell what it meant, for that those who had come on Shore had stuck it upon a Pole, and went off before they could be spoke to. He saw at one Cast of an Eye, that it was from the Captain, who talk'd of Ransom, and a sudden Thought came into his Head, that if he had explained it to the King, they would make him some Way instrumental, in decoying more of the Men on Shore, in order to murder them; and knowing his Companions to be past all Ransom, he said he did not know the Ways of the white Men, and could not understand what that meant. The King then ask'd him if he could persuade the white Men, who were at that Time lying at an Anchor, in their Boat some Distance from the Land, to come on Shore, he answered he would endeavour to do it, if it was his Pleasure; upon which the King whisper'd with some others, who were near him, but said no more of it, as being unwilling to trust him. And the Truth on't is, he designed to tell them what had pass'd, and if the Natives did not hold him fast, to throw himself into the Sea, and venture to swim to them, not doubting, but those in the Boat might with their Fire Arms, secure him from being pursued, but they gave no Opportunity of making the Attempt.

The King then call'd for one of the Fire-Arms, which had been taken in the Boat, and commanded him to show them how they were to be used, which he was forced to do; and they made use of them soon after, by firing at the Boat as has been related. He was then carried back to Prison, and talking with the Jaylor (whom in their Language they call *Kasboo*) he ask'd him what he thought the King intended to do with him? The Jaylor answered, he was sure he did not intend to have him kill'd, as the white Men had been, because he had ordered him to give him Food; this News a little revived his drooping Spirits, accordingly he brought him some Plantanes and Bonanas, which was the first Nourishment he had taken since he came on Shore; and having refreshed himself therewith, and with an *Alabo* of Water, that is, a Vessel not unlike a Pitcher, he begg'd for something to clean the Place, the Jaylor brought him a Parcel of green Sticks tied together, which they call a *Tosee*, and serves for the Use of a Broom; with this and a Thing like a Shovel, he made a Shift to sweeten the Place pretty well; when it was done, he observed an old Man looking thro' one of the Holes at him, with whom he fell into Discourse, and enquired of him whether the Ship was gone, the old Man told him no, but that there was another Boat with white Men lying off the Land, and that there were great Numbers of People from the Town lying in Wait for their coming on Shore. He begg'd this old Man to get him a few Palmatu Leaves to lay on the Floor under him, which the old Man did, so that that Night he rested very comfortably to what he had done before.

The next Morning he was again sent for before the King, who ask'd him, if he could kill a *Coway* with one of those Musquets? he answered he could, and glad he was to be so employed, thinking by these Means he might please the King, at least gain his Favour so far, as to induce him to spare his Life. He was led out to the River-side, the King himself being in Company, and one of the Musquets was put into his Hand, he took the Ball and beat it into a great Length, and then divided it into small Bits about the Size of Swan Shot, for he would not venture to shoot with a single Ball, not knowing but his Life might depend upon the Success of his Shoot, by these Means he kill'd one the first Shot. The King seemed very well pleased, and made him charge the Piece again in the same Manner, and taking it into his own Hands discharged it at another *Coway* which he also kill'd.

A *Coway* is a fine beautiful Bird larger than a Swan, and not much unlike it in Shape, the Body is as white as Milk, but the Tuft it wears on its Head, as also its Tail, are adorned with Variety of Colours, the Bill is a little crooked, and uneven, its Legs of a fine Yellow, but its Form is best expressed by the Figure. They are in great Plenty always living near the Water, hatching fourteen or fifteen young Ones at a Time, and set four Times a Year; they are excellent to eat, nor do they taste at all fishy.

After this, he was ordered back to his Prison, as he went along he ask'd the Jaylor (with whom he was now grown more familiar) what he thought the King intended to do with him. The *Kasboo* or Jaylor told him, he believed he intended to keep him there till the Ship (which they call a *Schabew*) and the white Men were gone, and that then he would order him to be releas'd from his Confinement, and employ him in some Service. The Jaylor seem'd to talk to him, and use him in a much kinder Manner than before; and when he arrived at the Prison, he brought him a *Patue* (in their Language a *Dith*) of boiled Rice with Oyl, which is look'd upon to be very good Food; he left him two large *Alaboes* or Pitchers of Water, sufficient to drink and to clean his Kennel, after which, he took a comfortable Nights Rest.

The poor Fellow now began to wish that the Ship was gone, since he had no Prospect of making his Escape, and that their Departure would procure him greater Liberty. Next Morning seeing the old Man who had furnish'd him with the Palmatu Leaves, looking thro' one of the Holes at him, he enquired of him, whether the Ship was still in Sight? He told him it was, that there were still great Numbers of People lying behind the Bank, having with them those Things which were taken in the Boats, describing the Musquets, and great Numbers of Arrows, ready to shoot if they should either Land, or come near enough with their Ship; he begg'd of him to let him know what should happen, and particularly to inform him when the Ship should go off: The old Man whose Name was *Morasab,* seem'd obliging and kind, and promised him to do so, and that he would return towards Night (which in their Language they call *Raham.*)

A little after the *Kasboo* or Jaylor came in, bringing some Plantanes and Bonana's to him for his Breakfast, and opened a Door which went into a little back Yard, where there was a Spring of fine fresh Water, bidding him draw what Water he pleased in his *Alaboes,* and clean his Prison, leaving the Place open to him for that Purpose, there being no Way for him to get out; towards Evening he came to him again, bringing him some boyl'd Rice and Oyl, and then he shut up the Door before described, and leaving him Water enough, left him for that Night.

Morasab appeared at one of the Holes according to his Promise, acquainting him, that the Ship remained still in the same Station, and that the Boat had not been seen near the Land that Day. Next Morning *Morasab* came again, and with great Joy told him, the Ship was then going off, being under Sail; a little after the *Kasboo* or Jaylor came in as usual, bringing some boyl'd Rice, and gave him the same Account of the Ship.

Tho' he despaired now of ever getting off, yet he expected to be enlarged from his Prison, and enjoy Liberty, the sweetest Thing to Man. In the Evening *Morazab* came again to let him know, that the Ship was almost out of Sight, and that the King had sent a Party of Men to the East, and another to the West, to watch the Coast, and lye in Wait for the white Men, in Case they should Land any where else for Water or to get Provisions. The next Day he came again and gave him Notice, that Word had been brought to the King that the Ship had been seen again a great Way off to the Westward, but that the Men had not come on Shore; and the Day following he visited him again, with an Account, that News was brought to the King that the Ship was gone off again, and sail'd out of Sight.

Upon this, he expected to be immediately releas'd from his Confinement, yet he was kept close to his Prison ten Days longer; the Reason as he afterwards found, was, least the Ship might be hovering somewhere upon the Coast, and having his Liberty he might find an Opportunity of escaping to her; but when they seem'd pretty well assured that the Ship was quite gone off, the King sent for him, and ask'd him, if he should give him his Liberty, whether he would attempt to escape? He promised he would not, and indeed any Attempt now would have been in Vain, for to escape would have been a Thing impossible; upon which, the King appointed him to attend upon his Person, and to live with his other Servants, giving him Orders at the same Time not to go out of the City.

There was nothing at all uncomfortable in the Life he led here, for the Service was easy, having very little to do; his chief Business was carrying up the Pataes or Dishes for the King's Dinner, who eat upon the Ground, the Floor being sometimes covered with a Mat instead of a Cloth, and sometimes bare without any Thing; the Diet was generally boiled Rice, with broiled Meat, sometimes Venison, sometimes wild Goat; as also Fowl of all Sorts, which are smaller than those of *Europe,* but of an excellent Taste; they have also several Fowl not known to us; their Beef and Mutton are both excellent, but small; they also had Variety of Fish which they dress, either by boiling or broiling, as for Sawce, the King himself had none, except *Kajan,* Pepper, for they eat most of their Things very hot, and boiled Rice is what serves them instead of Bread.

Thus he lived in Plenty, eating as much as he would of what was left, when the King had done Dinner, so that few People as to Eating and Drinking tasted so great a Variety as he did; the Diet of the common Sort of People, consists generally of Plantanes, Bonana's, boiled Rice (which they call *Pasida*) and Oil, and a Dish they call *Kaja,* which is Plantanes and Rice boiled together, sometimes indeed they have Venison and wild Goat, which they kill themselves, but whatever it is, they eat it out of the Crock it is boiled in, for none but those of great Condition have the Use of *Pataes* or Dishes; if it be broiled, whether it be Fish or Flesh, they eat it off the Coals, and to avoid burning their Fingers, they take a Bit of green Stick which they break half through, and so bending it together, it serves the Use of a Pair of Tongues as well as a Fork, in turning the Meat upon the Coals as well as taking it off when it is ready. As for Knives and Forks the King himself is not acquainted with the Use of them; so that he pulls his Meat to Pieces with his Fingers, which is generally so well done that it requires no great Labour.

It was about two Months before he ventured to stir abroad beyond the Palace; but one Day one of the Servants who had Business about the City, ask'd him to go along with him, and in Discourse told him, the King would not be displeas'd, if he should go out often; upon this Encouragement he used to walk about the City almost every Day, chusing the Time when the King went to sleep, which was constantly his Practice every Afternoon. He took this Liberty three or four Months together, sometimes being absent several Hours without receiving the least Reprimand; he made an Acquaintance with several in the City, and had Leisure to satisfie his Curiosity, in observing every Thing that appeared new and strange, to one who had lived so long amongst the *Europeans.*

The City of *Magadoxa* lies (as has been observ'd) in the Latitude of one Degree and fifty one Minutes: It is built betwixt two Hills or rather on the Sides of two Hills, the greatest Part of it standing on the Declivity of that Hill next the Sea, so that there is scarce any of it to be seen by any Ship in the Road, or that passes by, which indeed are but few; for scarce any ever touch there, except driven by 'stress of Weather, as was the Case of the *Albemarle.* They have no Vessels of their own, except a few employ'd in Fishing, which they call Juncks, and not above ten or twelve of those; and tho' some of them are large enough to carry thirteen or fourteen Ton, they never venture far from the Land.

The City contains betwixt three and four thousand Houses, some built of rough Stone, others of Marble, of which they have many Quaries, extreamly fine, and of various Colours, but they want the Art of polishing it; but the most esteemed and most expensive Houses, are those of rough Stone covered over with a Kind of Plaister, which is peculiar to this Country; after it is laid on, it is not above three Days in drying, and grows as hard and durable as the Stone itself; but the greatest Curiosity of it is, that they can make it of what Colour they please; and as the Houses of all Persons of Condition are covered with it, It has a mighty pretty Effect to the Eye, for some have their Houses white, others red, some yellow, and some blue, that of the King was green, while the Inside is floor'd with the same Plaister, the Rooms all differing in Colour from each other, which Variety makes the City appear very beautiful, tho' the Streets are very narrow and very nasty.

Notwithstanding the Houses look so bright without Side, their Furniture within consists of very little more than Cobwebs, for they have neither Tables, Chairs, nor Glasses, they have indeed Matts which serve them instead of Table-Cloths by Day, and Beds by Night, upon which they lie without either Pillow or Bolster, with a Covering of Mokaz or thick Dungeree over them, which is so call'd from a Tree of that Name, of the Bark of which it is made, which being beaten, is drawn into long Threads, and wove or rather work'd with fine Needles made of Wood, either thick or thin, according to which it is intended; and to such a Perfection are they arrived in this Sort of Manufacture, that they can make it as smooth, and as soft, as a Piece of *English* Broad-Cloth, and much stronger.

We should have observed that they have no such Things as Glass-Windows to their Houses, however there are either large round or square Vacancies in every Room to receive both Air and Light; these Sort of Windows are covered generally all Day with Shutters of thick Plank, in which many Holes are bored, in order to keep out the Heat of the Sun. As for Chimneys they have no such Thing: In all great Houses there is a Room appropriated for the Dressing the Victuals, where the Fire is made in a Corner upon the Ground, and those that are employ'd in that Service must be well smoaked. The common People frequently make their Fires without Doors, for Rice and Fish they never eat without some Sort of Dressing, but Flesh, to save Trouble and Fire, they frequently eat raw.

The King maintains nothing which has the State or Air of a Court, having no Guards about his Person, so that he frequently walks abroad in the Streets in the Dress before described, without either Shoes or Stockings: All those that meet him pass him by, and go on upon their Business without showing him any external Mark of Respect; nay so little a Notion have they of Ceremony, that it is common for Persons of both Sexes to ease Nature in the Streets, perhaps when the King is passing by, and yet he is as well obey'd as any Prince in the World.

The Nobility walk about in as careless a Manner as the King, and are known by their Turbants; the better Sort of the common People wear Caps of various Colours, the Rest go intirely naked.

The Queen also walks about the Streets without either Guards or Attendants, and would pass as unregarded as the King, were it not that the Gaiety of her Dress must draw the Eyes of the Spectators; she commonly wears a Garment of either purple or green Silk, which being tied about her Waste reaches down to her Heels, with Variety of white, red, and green Feathers artfully disposed in her Hair, however she is bare-footed like the Rest, whilst all the poorer Sort of the Sex go quite naked, without thinking they carry any Thing about them they ought to be ashamed of.

The Wives of the Men of Condition indeed all wear Clothes, and are dress'd in the same Fashion with the Queen, tho' not all so gay or so rich; but whatever their Habits may be, they take Care always to show their naked Breasts, which hang down to their Bellies, if they have had any Children; and which we suppose is look'd upon as a Beauty, by their taking Care to expose them to View; they also paint the Nipples red, which is the only Art they use in setting off their Persons; they bring their Children into the World with little or no Pain, and without an Hour's Confinement from the common Occupations of Life.

The only Occasion when the King appears with any Thing that looks like Pomp or Magnificence is, when he rides abroad to take the Air, then he is mounted upon one of his Elephants, with his Favourites and Companions about him; they have a Way of fixing upon the Back of the Elephant, a Frame of Boards about eight or ten Foot Square, on which, he, with such as he carries with him to bear him Company, sit as commodiously as if in a Room, whilst two of his Servants on Foot conduct the Beast; yet even here, tho' he goes thro' any Crowd of People, no Man stops to do him Homage, or to pay him any Sort of Obedience, nor does he seem to expect it, having no Notion, that the Subjects are to be kept in Awe by the Show of Grandeur which surrounds their Prince: A Mark of good Sense, beyond what is to be met with in the Courts of *European* Princes.

His Way of maintaining an inward Respect in the Hearts of the People which they have Sense enough to know, is preferable to that External which consist only in Show and Appearance, and sometimes conceals Contempt and Hatred at Bottom, is by doing Justice in his Person, according to the best of his Judgment and Capacity; he is himself both King and Judge, and decides all Disputes betwixt Man and Man (which indeed are very few) by a personal Hearing of the Cause of Complaint. He is assisted by seven or eight Persons, who always sit about him for that Purpose, and may be called his Councellors; nor was it ever so much as suspected that any of these, either for Bribe, or Reward, or Promise, endeavoured to influence the King in his Judgment.

It rarely happens that any Persons is condemn'd to die; for as every Thing they feed on, except Rice, Plantanes, Oil, *&c.* is acquired by hunting and fishing, there are few Occasions for Theft amongst them; however, when any Person has merited that Punishment, the common Way of executing is, by throwing the Criminal, into the Den (which they call *Bodyzaw*) amongst the wild Beasts, such as Tygers, Leopards, and Crocodiles which are kept hungry before-hand for that Purpose.

There are many other Creatures kept in that *Bodizaw* or Den which are peculiar to this Country, such as the *Augazet,* which is the largest of all their Beasts, except the Elephant; it is of a white or rather yellowish Colour, with Streaks of Black running like Veins all over it, and also black Spots, the Face is not unlike that of a Cat, it has long sharp Claws; when it is wild, it is extreamly fierce, but may be rendered as gentle and tractable as a Household Dog.

A *Bozee* is an amphibious Creature, which always lives by the Sides of Rivers, and feeds principally upon Fish; it has a long Bill, and in all Respects the Shape and Form of a Bird, but wants Wings to fly, and instead of Feathers, is covered all over with a hard Scale resembling the Bark of a Tree, and so tough that an Arrow will not enter it; their Legs are very thick and scaled in the same Manner with their Bodies, having sharp Claws to their Feet; the Natives are more afraid of this Creature than of any other in the whole Country, especially, if they are obliged to travel any where by Night, near the Sides of Rivers, for they say it is so fierce and voracious, that it will seize either Man or Beast.

The *Massau* is another amphibious Creature, very large, whose Body is scaly like that of the *Bozee,* but it is of a different Colour, being reddish; the Bill also differs from that of the *Bozee,* for it is short and shaped like that of a Pidgeon; It is a timorous Creature, that upon hearing the least Noise immediately rushes for the Water; its Food is chiefly Weeds.

A *Sachew* is a Beast about the Size of a large Lion, of a dark brown Colour, with Shades of black all over the Body, and a Scale down his Back as hard as Horn, the Eyes are extreamly fierce, and in all Respects a terrible Creature to look at, but yet a Child would frighten it. — At the Sight of any human Creature it flies with great Swiftness to the Woods.

One of the King's Diversions is, to go to this *Bodizaw* or Den of wild Beasts to see them play; they are perfectly under the Command of their Keepers, and are taught to play Tricks like Dogs; nay, it is almost his only Diversion, unless sleeping half the Day can be called a Diversion. As for riding out upon his Elephants, as we took Notice before, he does it so seldom, it can scarce be reckon'd amongst his Pleasures.

Ease, Plenty, and the Heat of the Climate have render'd the People in general inclined to be slothful, they have no Trade with the Neighbouring Nations, nor do they desire to have any; it is true, they have a little Sort of Traffic amongst themselves, as those that hunt and shoot Goats, Venison, *&c.* give them often in Exchange for Dungeree Stuffs; they have also Gold and Silver amongst themselves, but very base; — they don't seem inclined to Cruelty, unless against white Men, whom they are taught to hate, tho' they scarce ever see any; but there is a Kind of historical Tradition amongst them (for they have no Books) that their Country was once invaded by white Men, who committed many Cruelties upon them, and indeed it is likely that the *Portuguese* might formerly have landed amongst them, while they were making their *India* Discoveries, and perhaps might have treated them like Slaves, from whence comes this Tradition, and which is the Case of their inbred Hatred to white Men to this Day.

Thus the Molotto had Leisure to divert himself with observing the Customs and Manners of these strange People, who have no Commerce or

Communication with the Rest of the World. One Day as he was walking in the City, he was extreamly surpriz'd and terrified at the Sight of a Bird of a monstruous Size, which stalk'd close by him in the Street: It was what they call a *Pyone,* but he had never seen one of them before, so that tho' it is tame and inoffensive, it is no Wonder he should be frighten'd at it.

A *Pyone,* as to Shape, differs from all Birds amongst us; their Colour is a whitish brown, and in the Pinion of each Wing they have five black, and five scarlet Feathers, very broad, and above a Foot long; their Legs are of a bright red, something small for so large a Body, and above three Foot in Length; their Necks are also extreamly long, so that from the Foot to the Top of their Heads they are generally ten Foot in Heighth; they breed in the Mountains, never sit on more than two Eggs at a Time, which always produce a Male and Female: The People catch them when they are young, and let them loose in the Streets, taking Pleasure in the Sight of them, for they do no Mischief, and feed on any Thing they can pick up.

He was so encouraged by this Indulgence which was shew'd him, that he thought he might go where he pleased, and that the Restriction which was laid upon him, was as good as taken off; wherefore, he was tempted by his Curiosity one Day to walk out of the City, and was seen by a great many People. The Day following the *Accabo* or King, with a stern Countenance, ask'd him if he had been out of the City? He was so terrified at his Looks, knowing also, that he had been commanded not to take that Liberty, that he was not able to answer: The King's Son who was present, smilingly ask'd him, why he did not speak? This recovered him a little from his Astonishment, so that he had the Courage to own he had; then the King with a more pleasing Aspect, desired to know of him, whether he had been to see his *Moorzacks,* or Tombs, he answered no; tho' he had a great Desire of seeing them, because he had heard much Talk of them. So the Thing pass'd over without any farther Reprimand for this Time.

The next Day in the Afternoon, the King rid out on an Elephant in the Manner before described, ordering the Molotto to attend him, and went to visit the *Moorzacks,* or Monuments of his Ancestors, which are situated about three or four Miles from the City: The Magnificence and Beauty of these Tombs, are almost incredible, considering that it is in a Country of *Barbarians* that they are made; the Molotto was greatly surprized at their extraordinary Grandeur; the King took Notice of his Astonishment, and was not displeased at it, and enquiring of him how he liked them, the Molotto answered, he had never seen any Thing equal to them, in all his Life, and that he believed Strangers would travel from all Parts of the World to see them, did they but know such Things were there. The King then enquired of him concerning the Tombs of the white Men, and ask'd several Questions about the Ceremonies used in Funerals in all the Countries he had been in; the Molotto gave him the best Account he could, still extolling the Beauty of these Monuments above those of all the World. The King then enquired of him whether he knew how Gunpowder was made, he answered no; that it was made by the white Men, and that he was but little acquainted with their Ways. He answer'd in this Manner, knowing that if he should speak with Respect of white Men, it might do him some Prejudice, because of the Aversion he found they had towards them. Upon the whole, the King appeared pleased with the Conversation of this Day, and the Molotto fancied he should grow into Favour.

But two or three Days after, an Accident happened which put him again into a Fright, going out to walk as usual, he ventured as far as the *Moorzacks,* or Tombs, for he took a singular Pleasure in the Sight of them. It happened in the mean Time that they wanted him, he was not to be found in the King's House, or about the City; upon which, there were several Persons sent in Search of him different Ways, one of them found him among the *Moorzacks,* or Tombs, and brought him home, he was dismally frightened, when he understood the King's Displeasure; wherefore, as soon as he came into his Presence, he fell down upon his Face, as is practiced by those with whom he is displeased. The King ask'd him in an angry Tone where he had been? he answered at the *Moorzacks,* or Tombs; then the King enquired of those that had been sent in Search of him, whether it was true, they assured him they had found him there; upon hearing of which, he seemed to be immediately pacified, and said to him (*Korah*) which signifies properly to rise, but is never said, except when he forgives. Then the King ask'd him, if he would not attempt to run away, provided he should appoint him to live constantly among the Guards, who were maintained for watching those Monuments? he answered no; and that he should be pleased to pass the Remainder of his Days in so delightful a Place, without ever having a Wish for seeing his own Country again.

For this Time he was dismiss'd, but next Day being call'd up before the King, he was told that he must go to the *Moorzacks,* or Tombs, there to wait and do Duty as one of the Guards; there was a *Bamzau* or Priest sent along with him, who was to instruct him in his Duty there. On the Way as he went, the *Bamzau* or Priest told him, that he must live constantly among the Monuments, and that he would have Meat, Drink, and Lodging provided for him without any Trouble, that he must not take the Liberty of coming to the City, or going beyond the Bounds prescribed, which the Rest of the Guards whom they call *Passaus* would show him; that he must be obliged to watch every second Night, to take Care that the Lamps which burnt in the Tombs were supplied with Oil, and never went out, and to keep the Tombs from any Filth or Nastiness.

When they arrived at the Place, the *Bamzau* or Priest commanded all the *Passaus* or Guards to be called together, acquainting them that the King had sent this Molotto amongst them to do the same Duty, and ordered one whom he called out from amongst the Rest, to return to the King with him, it being the King's Pleasure that the Molotto should supply his Place. This was readily obeyed, and they departed together.

The *Passaus* or Guards received him civilly enough, they immediately began Acquaintance with him, explaining to him all the Particulars of their Duty, and showed him the Bounds with in which he was to confine himself; telling him if he pass'd those Limits, they must be obliged to kill him. This Order seemed a little too severe, but he fancied it was only said to terrify him, least he should take it into his Head to attempt an Escape; he flattered himself so for two Reasons, First, because of the Indulgence which had been shown him when he ventured to exceed his Orders in going out of the City; and secondly he took Notice that the *Bamzau* or Priest spoke to the *Passaus* or Guards apart, which he fancied was instructing them to keep him in Ignorance as to the Truth of their Orders; they brought some boiled Rice and Oil cold, and told him he must watch that Night, because it was the Turn of the Person in whose Place he was come; in order to which, they brought him a Watch-Coat made of Hair, which they work very curiously with Needles, so that the whole Coat is of one entire Piece without a Seam; it hangs from the Shoulders down to the Ground, but has no Sleeves, so that it is more like a Cloak than a Coat.

The Sun being set, which is the Time they enter upon the Watch, every two Men began to fix their *Pohalick,* over against the Door of the *Moorzack* they were to watch; but to understand this Matter, it will be necessary to explain what a *Pohalick* is — A *Pohalick* is a Kind of a Tent, contrived to shelter them from the Inclemencies of the Weather, for the Nights are sometimes very cold there, especially if it rains; wherefore, they take four Poles of about eight Foot long, which, instead of fixing in the Ground, are plac'd in four Stone-Sockets, placed on Purpose, opposite to each *Moorzack,* for that Use, with Cross-Poles reaching from one to the other; but instead of Canvass they hang over it a Covering of Palmatu Leaves sewen together; the two oldest Standers have their Post opposite to the King's *Moorzack,* the Rest are posted according to their Seniority, for they are exact Observers of the Rules of Precedence; the youngest also in each Pohalick, fetches Wood for Fire, which is also absolutely necessary, as well to keep off the Musketoos which would be, otherwise, very troublesome, as to correct the Damps. As soon as the Sun rises, he also takes down the Pohalick, sweeps up the Ashes very clean, which remain of the Fire, and carries them away, that the Place may appear perfectly neat. It is his Duty also to go to the *Bankoos* (so they call the Steward of the *Moorzacks*) for the Provision of the Day, which he is afterwards to dress both for himself and his Comrade.

This Part of the Duty was not disagreeable to the Molotto, for having no Books to read, he would have grown melancholly for Want of something to divert his Time, had he been entirely idle; their Allowance of Provision was sufficient, and very good in its Kind. On *Sundays* and *Tuesdays* it was Flesh, either Beef, Mutton, or Goat, and Rice for Bread. On *Wednesdays,* Kaja (we have already told what that is) *Mondays* and *Fridays,* Fish and Plantanes. *Thursdays* and *Saturdays* Plantanes, Rice, and Oil. Their Fish was excellent in its Kind, but they usually dress'd it without taking out the Guts, and which they eat with it instead of Sauce, but the Molotto corrected this Part of their Cookery, and having gutted the Fish before he broiled it, he found his Comrades very well pleas'd, and they always managed it so after.

While he pass'd his Life here pleasantly enough, one Day the *Accabo,* or King, sent a Guard to fetch him to the City; he was extreamly frightened at this unexpected Turn, and enquired of those that conducted him, into the Meaning of it, but they could give him no Account of it, but hurried him along very quick; when they arriv'd at the City, they did not carry him before the *Accabo,* or King, as he expected, but conducted him strait to the *Haulob,* or Prison, where he had been before confined. He had not been there above two Hours when his old Friend *Morasab* came to make him a Visit, whose Opinion he ask'd concerning his Confinement, *Morasab* told him, he judged it to be for no other Reason, than because there had been a *Schabew,* or Ship, seen that Morning at a great Distance off the Coast, that there were Men on the Hills then watching of her, and others lying in Wait to surprize any that should attempt to come on Shore. While they were in Discourse, the *Kasboo* or Jaylor came in with some boiled Rice and Fish, and confirmed what *Morasab* had told him, and cheared him up by assuring him, that no Harm was intended him, that he was only confined to prevent his making his Escape. The Molotto knowing that every Thing he should say, would be told again the King, because any Person may speak to him with the utmost Freedom at any Time, except when he is sitting in Judgment, told the *Kasboo,* that he had given over all Thoughts of visiting his native Country more, having neither Wife nor Children; nor was he desirous of seeing any other Part of that Country, having taken a firm Resolution to obey the Orders very punctually of never going beyond the Limits of the *Moorzacks;* the *Kasboo* told him, that if he had any Value for his Life, it would be best for him to do so, for if he should at any Time be catch'd attempting any Escape, he would be served just as the white Men had been, the Molotto answered he should deserve it, since the King had been so gracious to him, not only to give him his Life, but to appoint him to live in a Place which he liked above any Thing he had ever seen.

All this Discourse was reported that Night to the King, the Consequence of which was, that he was sent for the next Morning; the first Question the King ask'd him was, whether that *shabew* or Ship which had appear'd in Sight, was the same in which he came? He answered, he could not tell, unless he was to see it, (but that could not be done now, for she was gone off without coming to an Anchor, or sending her Boat on Shore.) The King then ask'd him, whether he had a Desire to return back to the *Moorzacks?* He answered, it was what he longed for of all Things, and repeated the same Things concerning the Pleasure he took in that Place, which he had done before to the *Kasboo;* he found this tickled the King's Vanity, and put him into good Humour, wherefore, he commanded him to be conducted back, whither he arrived with a much lighter Heart than he left it, having the Satisfaction also of seeing his Comrades mighty well pleas'd at his safe Return amongst them.

Here he pass'd his Time without any Care, having every Thing provided for him, being at Leisure all the Day long to divert himself as he would, for except taking his Watch in his Turn, he had nothing to do, but to clean the *Moorzacks* every new Moon, both within and without, and to take Care that the Lamps around them should be supplied with Oil, and never go out.

He observ'd his Companions employed their Leisure Time all in some Work, most of them in making some little Curiosities, which the Towns-People used to walk out, and buy of them, and which enabled them to purchase Liquor and other Things they had an Inclination for; his Comrade in particular used to amuse himself with making Fishing-Nets, but these Nets are very different from those used in *Europe,* they are made of Sea-Grass, wove out into a certain Length, and the Fisherman before he uses them, fastens to them a certain Number of Hooks (for they are ignorant of the Art of contriving Nets to catch Fish without Hooks) his Comrade with a great Deal of Ease used to make one of these a Week, and he observing how he work'd them, did not doubt but he could do the same; therefore he begg'd of his Comrade to give him a little of his Sea-Grass, with which he began to make Trial, and succeeded so well, that in a few Days he finished a Net, which he truck'd away for a Quantity of Sea Grass.

He was now set up for a new Trade, and was so industrious in it, that he work'd his Nets with much more Curiosity than any of his Partners, and of Consequence had better Business; so that in a little Time he was able to purchase a Piece of Dungeree Linnen with his own Earnings, of which he made himself a Wastecoat after the *English* Fashion, and a Pair of long Drawers; but he had not worn them above a Day or two when the *Bankoo,* or Steward of the *Moorzacks,* commanded him to leave off the Wastecoat, that he might appear like the rest, who wore nothing but a Piece of any Stuff they could get, about their Wastes, to cover their Nakedness.

Upon the whole, he found he should have no great Occasion to provide for his Back, which occasioned his being less diligent in his Work; however, he purchased a *Mohaz* Covering to keep him warm in the Night, with the *Bankoo*'s Permission, and happening to talk sometimes with his Comrades about Nets, and describing how they were made in *Europe,* the *Bankoo* asked him if he could make one in the same Manner? But finding he was not to lay out his Earnings to please himself, he answered, he could not; however, an Accident fell out soon after which brought him into great Favour.

As it was Part of his Duty to go to the *Bankoo*'s generally in the Morning, for the Allowance of Provision for the Day for himself and Comrade, he observed, that tho' their Allowance was sufficient in all other Respects, it was very short as to Salt. One Day, when they had Plantanes, Rice and Oil, he begg'd hard for a little more Salt, but the *Bankoo* told him it could not be done without defrauding some of the rest, for Salt is exceeding scarce amongst them, having no Way of making it, nor any Way of providing it but by searching among the Rocks, near the Sea Side, where they pick it up in Bits about the Bigness of a Nut, and sometimes larger; here Nature makes it by the continual beating of the Sea in one Place; but the Quantities they are able to procure this Way are very small; wherefore, finding himself disappointed, he happened to say, that if he was at Liberty he could make Salt as plenty in *Magadoxa* as it was in *Europe.* The *Bankoo* the same Day acquainted the *Accabo* with what he had said, so that the next Day he was sent for: He was no sooner arrived in the Presence of the *Accabo* but he immediately asked him if he could make Salt? He answered, he believed he could, (and the Truth on't was he had often seen it made.) At the same Time he described the Manner of making it. The *Accabo* immediately order'd him to go to Work, and to have what Assistance he requir'd; he did so, and was so industrious and successful in it, that in six Months Salt was as plenty amongst them as any where else.

The *Accabo* sent for him again, and inquired of him concerning Fishing-Nets, as they were used in *Europe:* He described them to him; upon which he asked him if he could make one of them? He had been asked the same Question before by the *Bankoo,* and denied that he had any Skill that Way; but considering with himself now that since he was likely to pass his whole Life amongst these People, it was his Business to gain their Favour all the Ways he could, he answered, he never had made any; however, if he (the *Accabo*) thought fit, he would try and do the best he could.

The *Accabo* seemed mightily pleased with his Willingness, and asked him if he should want any to assist him? He answered he should, and desired eight Persons to be employed in Spinning, and six in Knitting. These People were to follow his Directions, accordingly they fell to Work, and, in the Space of two Months, finished a Net eighty Fathom long.

When it was finished the *Accabo* himself had a Mind to see what Effect it would have beyond their own Nets; accordingly he went on board one of their Junks, attended by his Favourites, having with him also several of their most experienced Fishermen: They had the good Luck to take a good Number of Fish the first Hawl, among which were several Sorts they had never before seen, being such Fish as will not take the Hook, and such as always keep deep in the Water. The *Accabo* appeared highly contented with this Success, and ordered several more of them to be made, which could be done without him now that he had shown them a Way, so that Fish soon became infinitely more plenty than ever it had been before.

The Molotto expected no less than to be rewarded with some extraordinary Recompence for the public Services; the least Favour he thought could be granted him would be to give him the Liberty of a Freeman, and to let him live as an Inhabitant of the City, and to get his living amongst them, by any Sort of Industry he could; but he found himself greatly mistaken, for all his Reward consisted in being sent back to the *Moorzacks,* upon the same Foot he had been before.

It is true, he passed his Time here with a great deal of Tranquility, and began to reconcile himself to the Thoughts of remaining there his whole Life, he was convinced that nothing he could do to ingratiate himself, would procure him any Favour or Liberty; and an Accident fell out which gave him a terrible Notion of their Severity: One of the *Passaus* or Guards, on a Night when it was not his Turn to be upon the Watch, went privately into the City, contrary to Orders, and returned again before it was Day, but not so privately but he was seen by some Person, who went and discovered it to the *Accabo;* the Consequence of which was, that he was sent for under a Guard the next Morning, and, being brought into the King's Presence, was, without any more Ceremony, executed in the following Manner: He was obliged to kneel down, leaning his Head forwards, whilst the Executioner, with a heavy Bar of Timber, struck him on the lower part of his Head, and beat out his Brains.

This Example so terrified the poor Molotto, that in fifteen Years he was in that Place he never ventured beyond the Limits, except when he was sent for by the *Accabo,* or to attend a Burial, which he was obliged to do when any of the *Passaus* or Guards died, for they were not buried among the *Moorzacks,* no more than any of the other of the common People.

But it is Time that we describe this Place, which is not only the greatest Curiosity of this Country, but would pass for a Piece of Magnificence in those Nations where Arts and Sciences are known, and it is fit to be the more particular in it, as it may appear strange, that those People who are Barbarians in all other Respects, should observe so much Pomp and Decoration in their funeral Ceremonies.

This burying Place, which they call *Hoynatz,* is pleasantly situated in a beautiful Valley between two Hills, about two *English* Miles from the City of *Magadoxa;* there are in it twenty nine *Moorzacks* or Tombs, all which were first built by the Kings, at whose Expence the *Passaus* or Guards are kept, their being four to each *Moorzack,* who watch two and two by Turns, who take Care of the Lamps, which continually burn within, and keep every Thing clean to the greatest Nicety.

Tho' these *Moorzacks* may be said properly all to belong to the King, yet several other Persons of the first Rank are buried in them, by the King's special Favour, for he sometimes gives a *Moorzack* to some Favourite, as a burying Place for his Family; notwithstanding which Gift, when any of the said Family dies, the King's Permission must be asked anew for burying him in the *Moorzack,* the Reason is, that it frequently happens that when a Person who has this Kind of Right to be buried in a *Moorzack* disobliges the King, he takes no Notice of it as long as the Party lives; but when he dies, he forbids him to be buried in the *Moorzack,* by way of Punishment.

This may show what a Veneration they have for these Places, when they seem to think that all Happiness, as well as Honour, consisted in laying the Body after Death in one of these *Moorzacks;* and, indeed, it is one of the chief Pleasures of the King, as well as of the common People to visit these Places often, which they do with a Kind of religious Respect.

The largest *Moorzack* or Tomb of all is the King's own, no other Person being ever buried therein; it is eighty Foot square, built of black and white Marble mix'd, with a Kind of Cupola at Top, and over it a long Spire, the Inside, both Floor and Sides, is white Marble curiously polished, and the Cieling or Cupola painted green: There are in it forty five *Boozes* of Gold, standing on as many Pedestals of black Marble, of about four Foot high.

A *Booze* is a kind of round Pot with a Cover, about eight Inches deep, and five Diameter, in which are placed the Ashes of the Dead of those that are deposited there; I say the Ashes, because the Bodies are first burned.

There are also sixteen large Lamps of Gold, with nine Lights to each, four in a Corner, and one large one in the Middle, with two Lights; the large ones are never lighted but at Funerals, when they make a fine Show, but that in the Middle burns constantly.

By the forty five *Boozes,* wherein are deposited the Ashes, it may be conjectured that as many of their Kings lie there, and so the Molotto was informed.

The second for Largeness belongs to the *Coffues* or Queens, (for, it must be observed, that the Males and Females are never buried in the same *Moorzack:*) It is built all of white Marble, and is fifty nine Foot square, the inside Wall exactly the same with the outside, but the Floor is of black and white Marble laid in Squares, much like what may be seen in Noblemens Houses in *Europe.* There are fifty six *Boozes* of Gold, standing on black Marble Pedestals; there are twelve large Lamps, each with seven Lights, three in each Corner, and one of Silver in the Middle, which burns constantly, as in the King's.

The third belongs to the *Acobibs,* or Princes; it is also built of white Marble; its Form is exactly round, being seventy nine Foot in Circumference; there are in it fifty three *Boozes* standing on black Marble Pedestals, with thirteen Lamps of Silver with seven Lights each; twelve of them are plac'd in a circular Form, and the thirteenth in the Middle, which burns constantly, the Cieling is painted green.

The fourth belongs to the *Matotzes* or Princesses; It is built of a greenish Marble, vein'd with black, being of a circular Form like that of the *Acobibs* or Princes, and much about the same in Circumference; the inside Wall is of white Marble; the Floor of various Colours, as black, white, and green; and the Cieling which is made in the Form of a Cupola, is yellow: It hath sixty four *Boozes,* standing on Pedestals of black and white Marble, and eight large Silver Lamps with seven Lights to each, placed in a circular Form, besides one in the middle which burns constantly.

The fifth belongs to the *Poramzeps* or Male Children of the Prince; it is built of a white Marble, with large black Veins in it, both the inside Wall and Floor being of a light grey Marble; it is thirty Foot square, having nineteen *Boozes* of Gold, and sixty of Silver, standing on Pedestals of the same Sort of Marble, with the outside Wall; there are in it eight large Silver Lamps, hanging two in each Corner, besides one in the middle which burns continually.

The sixth *Moorzack* belongs to the *Squeenzibs* or Female Children of the Prince; it is built of a curious red Marble, with Veins of white running thro' it, and is twenty eight Foot square, the inside Wall and Floor being of white Marble; it has a hundred and nineteen *Boozes* of Silver standing on Pedestals of a blewish grey Marble; it has eight Silver Lamps disposed two in a Corner, besides one in the middle that burns continually.

All these here taken Notice of, belong to those of the King's own Blood, but as it may seem a little too tedious to be particular in the Description of them all, we shall only observe who the great Persons are, who are distinguished by having *Moorzacks* assigned to them alone, or to their Families.

First, There is one appointed for the burying Place of the *Baamzan* or chief Priest; one to the *Baulumzu* or Treasurer; one to the *Jocybauthaux* or chief Councellor; one to the *Moorenzep* or Head General; — one to the *Caffa* or Secretary; — one to the *Paremzebs,* which are a few People so called by Way of Title, and are their chief Nobility; — one to their Wives, whom they call *Tepshoyes;* — one to the *Morepzus* or Generals of the Elephants; — one to the *Hammons* or Governors of Towns; — one to the *Hoyzepa* or Head Teacher of the Elephants; — one to the *Sancof* or Head Doctor.

There is also one particularly kept for such as not being otherwise intitled to this Honour, shall perform some brave Action in the War — there is one belonging to the *Zanshaw* or Master of the King's Music — One to the *Divatzabowes* or Concubines of the King — One to the *Panpuzams* or Male Children of the King's Concubines — One to the *Parrasquas* or Male

Children of the High Priest — One to the *Gauzets* or Wives of the chief General — One to the *Matotzas* or Wives of the Governors of Towns — One to the *Hoydenebs* or Wives of the Treasurer — One to the *Okenzegs* or Wives of the chief Councellor.

But when I mention a *Moorzack* to belong to the Treasurer, or to the General, it must not be understood to be for the Use of him and his Heirs, but the next Person who succeeds in his Post is to be buried there, and his Heirs are no Ways intitled, unless they happen to succeed him in his Post.

These are all built of Marble of different Colours, some larger, and some less, some square, others quite round, some having a small Spire at Top, and others without; yet the Ornaments within are as rich in many of them, as in those belonging to the King or Prince — As for Example, in the *Moorzack* of the *Baamzan* or high Priest, of the *Baumlozn* or Treasurer, of the *Morewzep* or General, and of the *Caffa* or Secretary, the *Boozes* are all Gold; in others there are some of Gold and some of Silver, and considering what a great Number there are of them, these Monuments contain a vast Wealth.

When the King, Prince, or any other Person who is intitled to a Place in one of these Monuments dies, the Corps is immediately stripp'd naked, (let it be Man or Woman) after which, it is laid upon a Bier, and a thin Piece of Purple Silk being thrown over it, it is carried to be lain in State for some Days to a certain House, or Hall, built for that Purpose, a little Way without the City. — This Building consists of one large Room, sixty Foot in Length, and twenty six broad, being thirty Foot high, and flat at Top; the Stone is a curious white Marble, it is illuminated within with a great Number of Silver Lamps; in the middle stands a white Marble Table, supported by six Marble Pedestals about three Foot high, on which is laid the Body.

When they intend to remove it to the *Hoynabs* or burying Place, they exactly observe the Setting of the Sun; at which Time comes the chief Priest, attended by all those who have a Right to be buried in these Places (for no others must assist upon these Occasions) and drawing out a sharp Instrument, which they call a *Mockdoo,* and which serves the Use of a Knife, he opens the Body of the deceas'd, takes out the Heart, and delivers it into the Hands of the nearest Relation, who stands ready for that Purpose, at the Priest's right Hand; when this is done, the Body is carried to the lower End of the Hall, where a Fire is prepared in a Hole, five Foot deep in the Ground, and about as many broad; the Body is put into the said Fire, where it is consumed; then the Heart is again delivered into the Hands of the Priest, who places it in a little Stone-Pot, and puts it into the Fire, where it remains till it is dried to a Powder; then the Ashes of the Body being dried up, are put into the *Booze,* as is also the Heart; after which, they proceed to the *Hoynatz,* the nearest Relation carrying the *Booze.* When they arrive at the *Moorzack,* which upon this Occasion is all illuminated, the *Booze* is again delivered into the Hands of the Priest, who going into the *Moorzack* alone, shuts the Door after him, he remains a Quarter of an Hour, places the *Booze* upon the Pedestal prepared for it, and then returns, which makes an End of the whole Ceremony.

All this is done without a Word; nor is there any Sign of Sorrow or Lamentation amongst the Kindred, of the deceas'd, nor is it the Custom ever to speak of him, or name him at all after he is dead.

Thus we have given an Account of the Order and Ceremonies of their Funerals, and of the Magnificence of their Monuments, which make a most glorious Show at a Distance, nor are they less beautiful when near, the Materials of which they are built being very fine, and their Scituation delightful.

But as to their Religion we can give but imperfect Accounts, for they scarce know what it is themselves; they never ask'd the Molotto one Word concerning his Religion, and when he enquired of theirs, they had very little to say about it, but told such an incoherent Story, that he could make neither Head nor Tail of it. There is a Mosque or Temple about half a Mile out of the City, of which they give a fabulous Account, as that it was built in one Night, but no Man could tell how, or by whom; but their general Opinion was, that it was built by *Hios* God of the Sea, and at certain Times they used to flock, and pay a Kind of Devotion there, but they could not tell why or wherefore. However by the best Observations our Molotto could make, it appear'd to him as if they had several Worships amongst them, for he took Notice that some paid their Devotions to a little Image, not unlike a Wolf, which they kept in their Houses, and which are so common, that the poorer Sort of People make them of Bits of Wood, of about four or five Inches long, and sell them about the Streets.

They bear no Sort of Hatred or Antipathy to Christians, as Christians, as we see the *Turks* and most of the Sects of *Mahomet* do; but the Truth on't is, they do not know what a Christian is, yet (as we observed before) they are bred up in a Notion that white Men are all a Kind of Monsters, and they hate and detest them, as we do Toads or other poisonous Creatures, not for their Religion, but their Colour. In Respect to one another they observe the Laws of Society very well, and perhaps there is less Fraud and fewer Acts of Injustice committed amongst them, than in any Christian Country we can name. So that our Molotto who was now in a Manner naturaliz'd amongst them, and whose Complexion was black enough not to appear odious and terrible to them, was as well used as the rest of the *Passaus* or Guards, or any other Person of equal Rank with him.

It is certain he once flattered himself with the Hopes of being placed in a better Condition of Life amongst them, or being set at full Liberty, by Way of Recompence, for his instructing them in some useful Things, which proved of public Advantage to them, but he had long laid aside those vain Thoughts, for he found the *Accabo* had no Notion of Generosity, or Gratitude: He, therefore, with a Kind of Philosophy, seem'd to confine his Wishes to that melancholy quiet Life he was obliged to lead within the Limits of the *Moorzacks,* till an Accident fell out, which quite changed his Sentiments in this Respect, and which proves how natural the Love of Liberty is to Man.

It happened that the *Hamman* or Governor of the Town of *Saeni,* a Place about twenty Leagues to the Eastward of *Magadoxa,* in the same Kingdom of *Zanguebar,* having committed some Violences, by which he got the ill Will of the People, they rose against him, and kill'd him. This News was no sooner brought to *Magadoxa,* than the *Accabo,* tho' he keeps no Army or Guards, except the *Passaus* to watch the *Moorzacks,* immediately rais'd a Body of two thousand Men, arm'd with Bows and Arrows, and march'd in Person at the Head of them, to suppress the Rebels. The second Days March, Advice was brought him that the *Schabew* or Ship had been seen near a little Town call'd *Bandan,* ten Leagues Eastward of *Saeni,* and thirty of *Magadoxa*: Upon which Intelligence, he forthwith commanded six Men to march back to the *Moorzacks* as expeditiously as they could, in order to fetch our Molotto, and with him to join the Army as soon as they could. They found him upon his Duty, and commanded him to march away immediately, with his Bow and Arrows, which were the Arms that belonged to him, as a *Passau* or Guard of the Moorzacks, so that he seem'd to march as a Soldier more than a Prisoner.

After two Days hard March they came up with the Army which had made a Halt, at some Distance from the Town of *Saeni,* and the *Accabo* having sent out a Detachment to lie in Ambuscade near the Town, they took some Prisoners, who being brought in, declared that all the Inhabitants had abandoned the Town upon the News of the King's Approach, and were fled away for Fear. At the same Time they gave such Instances of the Tyranny of the late *Hamman* or Governor, and of the Necessity they were under of doing as they did, that the King appeared satisfied with their Behaviour; and to lay aside all Resentment, ordered several of them to go and find out the Rest, and give them Notice, that they might return to their Habitations, for that all was pardon'd, and that he would send them a better Governor. And, as if all had been over, the next Day he began to move with his Army back towards *Magadoxa,* but marched extreamly slow; towards Night, they came near a great Wood, into which he commanded his whole Army to enter, in order to lie that Night; the next Morning he gave Orders that no Man upon Pain of Death should go out of the Wood.

In the mean Time the scattered Inhabitants of *Saeni* having heard the good News, were returning to their Habitations; but no sooner was it dark that Night, but the *Accabo* gave Orders for a March, and making all the Expedition they could, they silently enter'd the Town of

Saeni before Morning, while the Inhabitants newly return'd were all asleep; however, they were alarm'd, and running into the Streets, the *Accabo* commanded his Men to fall upon them, who killed a great Number of them, whilst a great many favoured by the Darkness of the Night, had the good Luck to make their Escape; but of those that could not escape by Flight, there were only forty three made Prisoners, all the Rest being kill'd.

Our Molotto happen'd to fall into Discourse with one of these Prisoners, who lamenting the hard Fate, of his poor Townsmen, and giving him an Account of their Flight from the City, and their Return back, told him, that as they went near the Sea-side, about ten Leagues from thence, and a League or two from *Bandon,* they saw a *Schabew* or Ship, and so described him the Way to the Place where she lay; the Molotto perceiv'd it was directly East of the Place they were then at, *viz. Saeni,* he ask'd several Questions concerning the Size of the Ship, the Prisoner answer'd him to the best of his Understanding; and in his Manner of describing her, gave the Molotto to understand, that her Yards and Topmasts were down, which was a Sign she designed to lye there some Time; he then desired to know of him when he had seen her last, he answered him two Days before.

It immediately came into his Head that Providence had now given him the Means of making his Escape, and that in all Probability if he miss'd this, he never would have an Opportunity more; he knew that nothing could hinder him from making off by Night, and that in all Probability, he would be gone several Hours before he should be miss'd; so that he flattered himself, that those who should be sent in Pursuit of him would never overtake him, tho' they should hit the right Way, and he thought it might very well happen they should be out there too.

All that Day he pass'd betwixt Hope and Fear, sometimes he was terrified at the dismal Apprehensions of losing his Way himself, or of the Ship's being sail'd off, in either of which Cases there was nothing for him but certain Destruction, for he could have no Chance of concealing himself in the Country as a Native might do. — On the other Side, he spirited himself up with an Assurance that the Ship could not be yet sail'd, having her Yards and Topmasts down but two Days before; and again, that he knew so well how the Place bore, that there could be no Danger of his losing his Way; so that that Day he did nothing but mark out the Way with his Eye, that he intended to go, at his first setting out.

As soon as all was silent that Night, and his Comrades (who were a Kind of Guards upon him) were all asleep, he ventured to set out, nor did he meet with any Frights or Interruptions at the Beginning, getting clear of the Army without being questioned, or so much as seen or heard of any; for as they knew nothing of military Discipline, they have no Centinels in the Night. He marched all Night with all his Might, for indeed it was for Life; in the Morning when the Day was clear, he saw a little Town about two Miles from him, he judg'd this to be the Town of *Bandon,* by the Description which the Prisoner gave him of it; he guessed now that he was near the Sea, and that it was nothing but the high Land before him, which hindered him from the Sight of it; he therefore set his best Foot forwards, to gain the Top of one of the Hills before him; when he reached the Top, he had a fair View of the Ocean, and looking stedfastly every Way, he fancied he saw something like a Ship Eastward, but it was so far off, it was scarce discernable, however, it revived his Heart, and he now thought himself safe; he also perceived a pretty large River, at some Distance below him, in the Valleys, which he must of Necessity pass, because it lay directly in his Way, but as he was expert at Swimming, this gave him no great Dread, therefore he made the best of his Way towards the said River; when he arrived at the Banks, he perceived it was so rapid, that he apprehended (he being a little weakened with the Fatigue of his Journey) the Current would be too strong for him, and carry him into the Sea; he thought therefore, there was no Way for him to get over, but to walk up further in the Country, to find a Place where the Course of the River was crooked, which always breaks the Rapidity of the Stream, and where he might cross with less Danger.

While he was considering on this Matter, he chanced to look about, and turning his Eyes upwards towards the Hill from whence he was newly descended, and which was now betwixt two and three Miles Distance from him, he saw six Men on the Top thereof; they seemed to stand still and look about them for a while, but suddenly they started forwards, and with great Precipitation made directly towards him; he could think no less than that they were some sent in Pursuit of him, and that their standing still at first, was to no other Purpose, than to try if they could see him, and that their discovering him, was the Occasion of their running so suddenly down the Hill afterwards. The Fear of the cruel Death he should suffer, in Case he should be taken, hinder'd all further Consideration, so that without any more examining them, he plunged himself into the River, the Current was very strong, however, he made Shift to stem it better than he expected; and when he got over near the other Side, Providence so order'd it, that he was forced into a Part of the River, where there was an eddy Water, which drove him upon the Bank, so that in about the Space of half an Hour or a little more, he landed safely on the other Side.

He was a little spent with his Swimming, when sitting down to take a little Breath, he saw a Sight which terrified him as much as an Army of Enemies at his Heels could have done; it was a monstruous Aligator lying near the Bank-side, it appeared like some prodigious Oak in the Water, and he has declared and given it under his Hand, that it seemed to him large enough to swallow an Ox. At the same Time he beheld his Pursuers, who were now arrived pretty near the opposite Bank, he started up, and wing'd with Fear, flew rather than run, and there being some shrubby low Wood near the River, he had Presence of Mind enough to make his Way through them, knowing that if the Monster should follow him, it could not pass that Way, because the Thickness of the Wood would hinder it, besides it must presently lose Sight of him, and indeed it is likely, that he owed his Escape to this lucky Thought; he run on with greater Swiftness than at his first setting out, (for his Fear had supplied him with new Spirits,) but not without often looking back, which gave him the Comfort of knowing that the Monster and his Pursuers were both out of Sight: When he had continued this Pace about two Hours, he came to a Valley betwixt two rising Grounds, which lay open to the Sea, where he was joyfully surprized with a full View of the Ship lying at an Anchor, not above a Mile from the Shore, he hastened immediately towards the Edge of the Water, and made a Signal to them, by waving his Cap over his Head, for he thought it to no Purpose to hollow r call because they were at too great a Distance to hear him. He continued this Action a considerable Time, and began to grow impatient and uneasy to the last Degree, because he saw them return no Signal in Answer to him, whereby he might understand that they saw him, or intended to succour him; but he was soon relieved from this Fright also, by the sudden Appearance of the Boat which was coming round the Point of Land very near him, she being employed for some Time in rowing along Shore, in order to discover if the Country was inhabited.

So great was his Joy at this Sight, and such was his Eagerness of speaking with them, knowing by their Dress they were *Europeans,* that he had not Patience to wait for their coming to him, but he ran hastily into the Water to meet them; when he waded up to the Neck, he set himself afloat and swam to the Boat, they proved to be *Dutchmen;* however, they took him in, and observing the extream Satisfaction and Joy which appeared in his Countenance, they were very desirous of knowing who he was, and whence he came, they spoke to him in *Dutch,* and tho' he knew but little of that Language, yet he made a Shift to let them understand that he spoke *English;* there were two or three amongst them that understood our Language, and one of them spoke it very well; when he knew this, he gave them to understand in few Words that he was a Christian, that he had been a Prisoner or Slave in that Country for sixteen Years, that he had now made his Escape, and was pursued by six Barbarians who were once come in Sight of him.

As they had Arms in their Boat, they had a Mind to stay a-while and see whether these Barbarians would appear, for they had not beheld a human Creature since they had lain there, and were of Opinion that the Country was not inhabited, (tho' the Ship had been seen from the Hills by the Natives) so they lay upon their Oars.

In about half an Hour five Men appear'd arm'd with Bows and Arrows, and running a great Pace, they came to the Water-side, and beheld the Boat, which was but a little Distance from them; the *Dutchmen* fired two Musquets, upon which they dispersed and fled hastily away, but a little while after two of them came back again, and throwing down their Bows and Arrows, upon the Shoreside, plung'd into the Sea, and seem'd to direct their Way towards the Boat; the *Dutchmen* were surpriz'd what they could mean, but however, as nothing was to be fear'd from two naked Men, they lay still to see what it would come to: In fine, the two Barbarians swam to the Boat, and speaking to the Molotto, begg'd to be taken in, and to go along with them, for that they should certainly be put to some cruel Death if they went back, for not having taken him and brought him back with them.

The *Dutchmen* were willing to receive them, knowing they would be worth Money to be sold for Slaves. When they got into the Boat, they gave an Account of losing one of their Company in swimming over the River, where they first had Sight of the Molotto, who was devoured by an Alligator, in all Probability the same the Molotto had seen, and that the other three would travel as far as they could from their own Country, in order to save their Lives; but for their Parts, they chose rather to put themselves on the Mercy of the white Men, than run the Hazard of being taken, or starved in passing thro' Countries they did not know.

When he came on Board the Ship, he related to the Captain the whole Story of his Adventures, who finding he had been a Sea-faring Man, and that he understood Navigation pretty well, put him upon the Foot of an able Seaman.

They remain'd here about three Weeks, the Winds continuing contrary till then, in which Time they laid in Water and Wood, and diverted themselves with Fishing; after this they sail'd for *Batavia* in the *East-Indies,* where having unladed and taken in a Cargoe of *India* Goods, they sail'd home for *Holland;* the Molotto made two or three Voyages with them, but in the Year 1724, he being in *Holland,* and having a great Desire to see his old Captain, he embark'd on the 28th of *March* in *Holland,* and pass'd into *England,* he found out his Captain who was alive, and who being overjoy'd to see him, prov'd very generous to him, and prevail'd with him to give in Writing the Particulars of all his Adventures, from whose Copy the foregoing Narrative is faithfully taken.

As to the Molotto he return'd back to *Holland,* and sails still in the Service of the *Dutch East-India* Company, unless he is lately dead.

Chap. XXVIII
Of Capt. Bellamy

As we cannot, with any Certainty, deduce this Man from his Origin, we shall begin where we find him first a declared Enemy to Mankind. Capt. *Bellamy* and *Paul Williams,* in two Sloops, had been upon a *Spanish* Wreck, and not finding their Expectation answered, as has been mentioned in former Parts of this History, they resolved not to lose their Labour, and agreed to go upon the Account, a Term among the pyrates, which speaks their Profession. The first, who had the Misfortune to fall in their Way, was Captain *Prince,* bound from *Jamaica* to *London,* in a Galley built at that Port, whose Cargo consisted of Elephants Teeth, Gold Dust, and other rich Merchandize. This Prize not only enrich'd, but strengthened them; they immediately mounted this Galley with 28 Guns, and put aboard 150 Hands of different Nations; *Bellamy* was declared Captain, and the Vessel had her old Name continued, which was *Whidaw*: This happen'd about the latter End of *February,* 1717. They, now thus fitted for the continuing of their desperate Resolution, shaped their Course for *Virginia,* which Coast they very much infested, taking several Vessels: They were upon shifting this Station, when they were very near, as the Psalmist expresses it, *going quick down into Hell,* for the Heaven's beginning to lowre, prognosticated a Storm; at the first Appearance of the Sky being likely to be overcast, *Bellamy* took in all his small Sails, and *Williams* double reefed his main Sail, which was hardly done when a Thunder Shower overtook them with such Violence, that the *Whidaw* was very near over-setting; they immediately put before the Wind, for they had no other Way of working, having only the Goose Wings of the Fore-Sail to scud with; happy for them the Wind was at *West* and by *North,* for had it been Easterly, they must have infallibly perish'd upon the Coast. The Storm encreased towards Night, and not only put them by all Sail, but obliged the *Whidaw* to bring her Yards aportland, and all they could do with Tackles to the Goose Neck of the Tiller, four Men in the Gun Room, and two at the Wheel, was to keep her Head to the Sea, for had she once broach'd to, they must infallibly have founder'd. The Heavens, in the mean while, were cover'd with Sheets of Lightning, which the Sea by the Agitation of the saline Particles seem'd to imitate; the Darkness of the Night was such, as the Scripture says, as might be felt; the terrible hollow roaring of the Winds, cou'd be only equalled by the repeated, I may say, incessant Claps of Thunder, sufficient to strike a Dread of the supream Being, who commands the Sea and the Winds, one would imagine in every Heart; but among these Wretches, the Effect was different, for they endeavoured by their Blasphemies, Oaths, and horrid Imprecations, to drown the Uproar of jarring Elements. *Bellamy* swore he was sorry he could not run out his Guns to return the Salute, meaning the Thunder, that he fancied the Gods had got drunk over their Tipple, and were gone together by the Ears:

They continued scudding all that Night under their bare Poles, the next Morning the Main-Mast being sprung in the Step, they were forced to cut it away, and, at the same time, the Mizzen came by the Board. These Misfortunes made the Ship ring with Blasphemy, which was encreased, when, by trying the Pumps, they found the Ship made a great Deal of Water; tho' by continually plying them, it kept it from gaining upon them: The Sloop as well as the Ship, was left to the Mercy of the Winds, tho' the former, not having a Tant-Mast, did not lose it. The Wind shifting round the Compass, made so outrageous and short a Sea, that they had little Hopes of Safety; it broke upon the Poop, drove in the Taveril, and wash'd the two Men away from the Wheel, who were saved in the Netting. The Wind after four Days and three Nights abated of its Fury, and fixed in the North, North East Point, hourly decreasing, and the Weather clearing up, so that they spoke to the Sloop, and resolv'd for the Coast of *Carolina;* they continued this Course but a Day and a Night, when the Wind coming about to the Southward, they changed their Resolution to that of going to *Rhode Island.* All this while the *Whidaw*'s Leak continued, and it was as much as the Lee-Pump could do to keep the Water from gaining, tho' it was kept continually going. Jury-Masts were set up, and the Carpenter finding the Leak to be in the Bows, occasioned by the Oakam spewing out of a

Seam, the Crew became very jovial again; the Sloop received no other Damage than the Loss of the Main-Sail, which the first Flurry tore away from the Boom. In their Cruise off *Rhode Island,* the Beginning of *April,* they took a Sloop commanded by Capt. *Beer,* belonging to *Boston,* in the Lat. of *South Carolina,* 40 Leagues from Land; they put the said Captain on Board the *Whidaw* Commodore, while they rifled and plundered his Vessel, which *Williams* and *Bellamy* proposed returning to him, but the Crews being averse to it, they sunk her, and put the Captain ashore upon *Block Island.*

I can't pass by in Silence, Capt. *Bellamy*'s Speech to Capt. *Beer.* D — n my Bl — d, *says he, I am sorry they won't let you have your Sloop again, for I scorn to do any one a Mischief, when it is not for my Advantage; damn the Sloop, we must sink her, and she might be of Use to you. Tho', damn ye, you are a sneaking Puppy, and so are all those who will submit to be governed by Laws which rich Men have made for their own Security, for the cowardly Whelps have not the Courage otherwise to defend what they get by their Knavery; but damn ye altogether: Damn them for a Pack of crafty Rascals, and you, who serve them, for a Parcel of hen-hearted Numskuls. They villify us, the Scoundrels do, when there is only this Difference, they rob the Poor under the Cover of Law, forsooth, and we plunder the Rich under the Protection of our own Courage; had you not better make One of us, than sneak after the A — s of these Villains for Employment?* Capt. *Beer* told him, that his Conscience would not allow him to break thro' the Laws of God and Man. *You are a devilish Conscience Rascal, d — n ye,* replied *Bellamy, I am a free Prince, and I have as much Authority to make War on the whole World, as he who has a hundred Sail of Ships at Sea, and an Army of* 100,000 *Men in the Field; and this my Conscience tells me; but there is no arguing with such sniveling Puppies, who allow Superiors to kick them about Deck at Pleasure; and pin their Faith upon a Pimp of a Parson; a Squab, who neither practices nor believes what he puts upon the chuckle-headed Fools he preaches to.* — The pyrates wanting neither Provision nor Water, and the *Whidaw*'s Damage being repaired, they past their Time very jovially. One of the Crew had been a Stroler, a Fellow who had pass'd thro' a great many real as well as fictitious Scenes of Life, the stroling Business not answering the Greatness of his Soul (as he expressed it) he thought it more profitable, and less fatiguing, to turn Collector. Accordingly in *Yorkshire* he borrowed an excellent Gelding, (I make Use of his own Terms) with a hunting Saddle and Bridle, and with a Case of Pocket Pistols, which he before had, he set out to seek Adventures, without taking Leave of his Company; he met, he said, with several Knights Errant, whom as they declined the Combat, he spoiled and sent to offer themselves at the Feet of his *Dulcinea,* but being under the Influence of some malicious Enchanter, who envied his glorious Fears of Arms, and fear'd they would eclipse by the Brightness of their Lustre, those of some favourite Knight whom he protected; or otherwise, knowing by his Skill, that he should one Day succumb under the Weight of his irresistable Arm, by his magical Power, threw him into a loathsome Dungeon loaded with Irons, whence the wise Man, who had Care of his Affairs, and was destined to write the History of his heroick Deeds delivered, and putting him on board a Ship, transported him to the famous Island of *Jamaica;* and after various Turns of Fortune, link'd him in Society with these Marine Heroes, the Scourge of Tyrants and Avarice, and the brave Asserters of Liberty.

This whimsical Fellow made a Play whilst he was on Board, which he called the *Royal Pyrate;* and this (which to see once would make a a Cynick laugh) was acted on the Quarter-Deck with great Applause, both of the Actors and Poet; but an Accident which turn'd the Farce into Tragedy, occasioned an Order of Council to forbid its being play'd a second Time. The Case was thus; *Alexander* the Great, environ'd by his Guards, was examining a Pyrate who was brought before him: The Gunner, who was drunk, took this to be in earnest, and that his Mess-Mate was in Danger, and hearing *Alexander* say,

Know'st thou that Death attends thy mighty Crimes, And thou shall'st hang to Morrow Morn betimes.

Swore by G — d he'd try that, and running into the Gun Room where he left three Companions over a Bowl of Rum Punch as drunk as himself, told them, they were going to hang honest *Jack Spinckes;* and if they suffered it, they should be all hang'd one after another, but by G—d, they should not hang him, for he'd clear the Decks; and taking a Grenade with a lighted Match, followed by his Comrades with their Cutlash, he set Fire to the Fuze and threw it among the Actors. The Audience was on the Gang Ways and Poop, and falling in with their Cutlash, poor *Alexander* had his left Arm cut off, and *Jack Spinckes* his Leg broke with the bursting of the Shell: The Ship was immediately in an Uproar, and the Aggressors seiz'd, who else would have made Havock with the Guards, or have been cut to Pieces by them, for they had all Cutlashes. *Alexander* the Great revenged the Loss of his Arm by the Death of him who deprived him of his Limb. The Gunner and two surviving Comrades were that Night clapp'd into Irons, and the next Day at a Court-Marshal, not only acquitted but applauded for their Zeal. *Alexander* and his Enemies were reconciled, and the Play forbad any more to be acted.

A Fortnight after the setting Capt. *Beer* ashore, *Williams* boarded and took a Vessel off *Cape Cod*, laden with Wine; the Crew of which encreased the Number of their Prisoners: They put seven Men on Board the Prize, with Orders to keep Company with the Ship and Sloop, commanded by

Bellamy and *Williams*, and left aboard her the Master.

As the Ship and Sloop had been long off the *Carreen*, they stretch'd away to the Northward, and made the best of their Way to *Penobscott* River, which lies between *Nova Scotia* and the Province of *Main*, where they designed to heave down. This Tract of Land is along the Coast about 190 Miles from West to East, reckoning from the Province of *Main* to St. *Croix;* and about 200 Miles over from North to South, counting from the River *Quebeck* to the Sea. King *Charles* the Second made a Grant of it in 1663, to his Royal Highness *James* Duke of *York*, who made a Settlement at *Pemaquid;* it abounds in all Sorts of Timber, and would bear excellent Hemp and Flax, and all Sorts of Naval Stores; is rich in Copper, Lead, and Iron Ore; and the Seas are stock'd with Whales, Cod, Sturgeon, Herrings, Mackrel, Salmon, Oysters, Cockles, *&c.* the Soil produces all Sort of *European* Grain and Fruits; and the Woods shelter a great Number of Deer, as Elks, Red and Fallow Deer, *&c.* and this Country, if settled, would certainly be of great Advantage to *England*. I hope the Reader will pardon this small Digression which the Interest I take in every Thing, which may tend to the enriching or extending the Dominions of our glorious *Britain,* my dearly loved Country, forced me into: But to return, when they were at the Mouth of this River, it was thought more eligible to careen in the River *Mechisses;* they entered it as agreed, and run up about two Miles and a half, when they came to an Anchor, with their Prizes. The next Morning all the Prisoners were set ashore with Drivers, and Orders to assist in the building Huts; the Guns were also set ashore, and a Breast Work raised, with Embrazures, for the Canon on each Side the River, this took up four Days: A Magazine was dug deep in the Earth, and a Roof rais'd over it by the poor Slaves the Prisoners, whom they treated after the same Manner as the Negroes are used by the *West-India* Planters. The Powder being secured, and every Thing out, they hove down the Sloop, cleaned her, and when she had all in again, they careened the *Whidaw*, by the largest Prize. Here the Stroler told the two Commanders, that they might lay the Foundation of a new Kingdom, which, in time, might subject the World, and extend its Conquests beyond those of the *Roman* Empire. *I am, it is true,* said he, *by Birth, the Son of a Miller, but I have Ambition, Avarice, and Learning enough, to be a Secretary of State, for I was a Servitor at* Oxford *before I turn'd Stroler; and if you think fit to erect this Tract of Land into an Empire, and your joint Imperial Majesties will employ my Abilities, don't question but I will prove a true Patriot; that is, by the Figure I will make, I will be a Credit to your Court, and by the squeezing your Subjects (whom under the specious Pretence of Liberty, I will keep in abject Slavery) drain such Sums as shall ever keep them poor, and your and my Treasury full.* Rome, *the Mistress of the World, was founded by a couple of Sheep-Stealers, and peopled by run-away Slaves and insolvent Debtors; how much more advantageously might you two undertake the erecting of a new Monarchy, whose Subjects are no Strangers to the Art of War, who are not environ'd as they were with invidious Neighbours, and who may encrease your Power, and propagate the Species, by taking into your Protection the* Indians *of these Parts, and the discontented and desperate People of the neighbouring* English *and* French *Colonies? To strengthen your selves, raise every useful Man to some*

Dignity in the State, and share the Prisoners (*I mean such as won't swear Allegiance*) *as so many Slaves unworthy of Liberty among your great Men; build more Vessels, keep them constantly on the Cruize, and force all the Prisoners either by fair or*

foul to acknowledge your Sovereignty; it was thus the greatest Empires of the World were founded; superior Force was always acknowledged a just Title; and the Ancients ever esteem'd the Prisoners they made, whose Lives were in their Power by the Law of Arms, lawful Slaves; and the employing their Lives in the Service of the Conqueror, but a grateful Retribution for preserving of them. I leave it to the mature Deliberation of your great Wisdom, whether it is not more eligible to found here an Empire, and make War by a lawful Authority derived from your Royal selves, than lie under the opprobrious Appellations of Robbers, Thieves, profligate Rogues and pyrates; for begging Pardon of your Majesties, for that Freedom of Speech, which my Zeal for your Royal Service, and the public Good oblige me to; the World treats you and your loyal Subjects with no softer Terms. But, when you have once declared your selves lawful Monarchs, and that you have Strength enough to defend your Title, all the Universities in the World will declare you have a Right Jure Divino; *and the Kings and Princes of the Earth, will send their Ambassadors to court your Alliance.*

Bellamy and *Williams* told him, *They would consider on his Proposal, and they would let him know what they should in their great Wisdom conclude upon. In the mean while, they thank'd him for his Advice, promis'd when they began to found their Monarchy,* (should they find it expedient,) *to make him Prime Minister, or Quarter-Master ashore; and when he had enriched himself and Family, by the fleecing their Subjects, they assured him they would pass an Act of Indemnity for his Security;* and concluded with ordering a Bowl of Punch for every Mess.

The *Whidaw* being clean'd, they thought of cruizing again, and accordingly steer'd for *Fortunes Bay* in *New foundland;* they made some Prizes on the Banks, forced all the Men, and sunk the Vessels.

They had not been long on this Coast before they were separated by a Storm, which held some Days. Off the Island of St. *Paul* the *Whidaw* spied a Sail, which she immediately gave Chase to; the Ship brought to and lay by for her, she prov'd a *French* Man of 36 Guns, carrying Soldiers to *Quebeck*. The *Whidaw* engag'd with great Resolution, and the *French* did not show less, for he boarded the *Whidaw,* and was twice put off, with the Loss of Men on both Sides. *Bellamy* after two Hours Engagement thought the *Frenchman* too hard a Match, and was for shaking him off; but his Enemy was not as willing to part with him, for he gave Chase, and as he sail'd altogether as well as *Bellamy,* the latter had certainly been taken and had received the due Punishment of his Crimes, had not the Night coming on favour'd his Escape: He lost in this Engagement 36 Hands, beside several wounded, the poor Minister of State, our before-mentioned Stroller, was in the Number of the slain.

The *Widaw* returned to the Coast of *Newfoundland,* and off *Placentia* Bay met with his Consort and the Prize.

They resolved to visit again the Coast of *New England,* the *Whidaw* being much shatter'd in the late Engagement, having receiv'd a great many Shot in her Hull; they ran down this Coast, and between St. *George*'s Banks and *Nantuket*'s Shoals, took the *Mary Anne*.

The Master of the Vessel, taken formerly off *Cape Cod,* was left on board her, and as he was very well acquainted with the Coast, they order'd him to carry the Light and go a-head; and the pyrates commonly kept him at Helm: He upon a Night of public Rejoicing, seeing all the pyrates drunk, laid hold on the Opportunity, and run his Vessel ashore about Midnight, near the Land of *Eastham,* out of which he alone escap'd with Life. The *Whidaw* steering after the Light, met with the same Fate; the small Vessel ran into a sandy Bay, and the Men got ashore without Difficulty.

When the *Whidaw* struck, the pyrates murder'd all their Prisoners, that is, all their forced Men; as it is concluded, from the mangled Carcasses which were wash'd ashore; but not a Soul escaped out of her or *William*'s, who was also lost.

The pyrates, to the Number of seven who escaped, were seiz'd by the Inhabitants, and on the Information of the Master who escap'd, and on their own Confession, were imprison'd, condemn'd, and executed. They were all Foreigners, very ignorant and obstinate; but by the indefatigable Pains of a pious and learned Divine, who constantly attended them, they were, at length, by the special Grace of God, made sensible of, and truly penitent, for the enormous Crimes they had been guilty of. As the Trial of these pyrates, and their Behaviour while under Sentence, and at the Place of Execution, was printed at *Boston,* and is to be had in Town, I shall refer the curious Reader to that small Tract.

Chap. XXIX
Of Captain William Fly, And his Crew

As to the Birth of this Pyrate, we can discover nothing by the Enquiries we have hitherto made; and, indeed, had we succeeded in our Search, could it have been of any great Consequence? For, its certain, by the Behaviour of the Man, he must have been of very obscure Parents; and, by his Education, (as he was no Artist) very unfit, in all Respects, except that of Cruelty, for the villainous Business he was in. We have been inform'd, that he had been a Pyrate in a private Capacity, and having escaped Justice, had an Opportunity of repenting his former Crimes, and, as a foremast Man, or petty Officer, of getting his Bread in a warrantable Way: But no; ignorant as he was of Letters, he was ambitious of Power, and capable of the most barbarous Actions to acquire it.

Captain *Green* of *Bristol*, in *April* 1726, shipp'd this *Fly* as Boatswain, at *Jamaica*, being bound, in the *Elizabeth* Snow of *Bristol*, for the Coast of *Guinea. Fly*, who had insinuated himself with some of the Men, whom he found ripe for any Villainy, resolved to seize the said Snow, and murder the Captain and Mate, and, taking the Command on himself, turn Pyrate. He proposed this his Design to his Brothers in Iniquity, who approving it, he, having the Watch at one o' Clock in the Morning, on the 27th Day of *May*, went up to one *Morrice Cundon*, then at the Helm, accompanied by *Alexander Mitchel, Henry Hill, Samuel Cole, Thomas Winthrop*, and other Conspirators, and swore damn him, if he spoke one Word, or stirr'd either Hand or Foot, he would blow his Brains out; and, tucking up his Shirt above his Elbow, with a Cutlass in his Hand, he, with *Mitchel*, went into the Captain's Cabbin, and told him, he must turn out. The Captain asking what was the Matter, was answered, by *Mitchel*, they had no Time to answer impertinent Questions; that if he would turn out, and go upon Deck quietly, it would save 'em the Trouble of scraping the Cabbin; if he would not, a few Buckets of Water and a Scraper would take his Blood out of the Decks. That they had chosen Captain *Fly* for Commander, and damn his Blood, they would allow of no other, and would not waste their Provisions to feed useless Men.

The Captain reply'd, that since they had so resolved he should make no Resistance; but begged they would not murder him, since his living could be no Obstacle to their Designs; that he had never been harsh to either of them, and therefore they could not kill him out of revenge; and if it was only for their Security, he desired, if they would not take his Word to do nothing to obstruct the Measures they had resolved on, they would secure him in Irons till he might be put somewhere on Shore. Ay, G — d d — mn ye, says *Fly*, to live and hang us, if we are ever taken: No, no, walk up and be damn'd, that Bite won't take, it has hanged many an honest Fellow already. *Mitchel* and *Fly* then laying hold of him, pulled him out of his Bed. The poor Captain intreating to spare his Life, for his Soul's sake, told 'em he would bind himself down by the most solemn Oaths, never to appear against them; that he was unfit to appear before the Judgment-Seat of a just and pure God; that he was loaded with Sins, and to take him off before he had washed those Stains which sullied his Soul by the Tears of Repentance, would be a Cruelty beyond Comparison greater than that of depriving him of Life, were he prepared for Death, since it would be, without any Offence committed against them, dooming him to eternal Misery; however, if they would not be perswaded that his Life was consistent with their Safety, he begg'd they would allow him some Time to prepare himself for the great Change. That he begg'd no other Mercy than what the Justice and Compassion of the Laws would allow them, should they hereafter be taken. *D — n your Blood,* said Mitchel, *no Preaching. Be damn'd an you will, what's that to us? Let him look out who has the Watch. Upon Deck, you Dog, for me shall lose no more Time about you.*

They hawl'd him into the Steerage, and forc'd him upon Deck, where one of the Hell-Hounds asked if he had rather take a Leap like a brave Fellow, or be to toss'd over like a sneaking Rascal. The Captain, addressing himself to *Fly*, said, *Boatswain, for God's sake don't throw me overboard, if you do, I am for ever lost; Hell's the Portion of my Crimes.* — Damn him answer'd

Fly, since he's so devilish godly, we'll give him Time to say his Prayers, and I'll be Parson. Say after me. *Lord, have Mercy on me.* Short Prayers are best, so no more Words, and over with him, my Lads.

The Captain still cry'd for Mercy, and begg'd an Hour's respite only, but all in vain; he was seized by the Villains, and thrown over Board; catch'd however, and hung by the Main-Sheet, which *Winthorp* seeing, fetch'd the Cooper's broad Ax, and chopping off the unhappy Master's Hand, he was swallowed up by the Sea.

The Captain being thus dispatched, *Thomas Jenkins,* the Mate, was secured and brought upon Deck, to share the same cruel Fate. His Intreaties were as useless as the Captain's; the Sentence they had passed upon him was not to be reversed; they were deaf to his Prayers and Remonstrances, Strangers to Humanity and Compassion. He was of the Captain's Mess, they said, and they should e'en drink together; it was Pity to part good Company.

Thus they jested with his Agonies; he, however, made some Struggle, which irritating his Murderers, one of them snatched up the Ax, with which *Winthorp* had lopped off the Captain's Hand, and gave him a great Cut on the Shoulder, by missing his Head, where the Blow was aimed, and he was thrown into the Sea. He swam notwithstanding, and called out to the Doctor to throw him a Rope, who, poor Man, could not hear him, being secured, and laid in Irons in his own Cabin; and had he heard, and been able to have thrown the Rope required, could it be expected that these harden'd Wretches would have relented, and shown him Mercy? But the sinking Man will catch at a Straw, and Hope, they say, is the last that deserts us. While we have Life we are apt to flatter our selves, some lucky Accident may favour us.

It was next debated what should be done with the Doctor. Some were for sending him to look after the Captain and Mate, but the Majority, as he was a useful Man, thought it better to keep him. All obstacles being removed, *Mitchel* saluted *Fly* Captain, and, with the rest of the Crew who had been in the Conspyracy, with some Ceremony, gave him Possession of the great Cabin.

Here a Bowl of Punch being made, *Morice Cundon* was called down, and one *John Fitzherbert* set to the Helm in his Place. At the same Time the Carpenter and *Thomas Streaton* were brought before the Captain, who told them they were three Rascals, and richly deserved to be sent after the Captain and Mate, but that they were willing to to show them Mercy, and not put them to Death in cold Blood, and he would therefore only put them in Irons, for the Security of the Ship's Crew; they were accordingly ordered out, and iron'd. *Fly* then told his Comrades it was convenient to resolve on some Course, when Word was brought them, that a Ship was very near them. The Council broke up, and made a clear Ship, when, in a very little while after, they found it was the *Pompey,* which had left *Jamaica* in Company with the Snow; the *Pompey* standing for the Snow, which did not make from her, soon haled, and asked how Captain *Green* did, and was answered by *Fly,* that he was very well. They did not think fit to attack this Ship, but returning to hold their Consultation, it was resolved to steer for *North Carolina.*

Upon their Arrival on that Coast they spied a Sloop at Anchor within the *Bar;* she was call'd the *John* and *Hannah,* and commanded by Captain *Fulker,* who thinking the Snow might want a Pilot stepp'd into his Boat with his Mate, Mr. *Atkinson,* and Mr. *Roan,* two Passengers, and a young

Lad, in order to bring her in. When they came on board, they were told, that the Snow was come with a Cargoe from *Jamaica;* Captain *Fulker* and Mr. *Roan* were desired to walk down to the Captain, who was in the Cabbin; *Fly* received them very civilly, ordered a Bowl of Punch, and hearing Captain *Fulker* had brought another Passenger on Board, Mr. *Atkinson* was also invited down.

The Punch being brought in, Captain *Fly* told his Guest, *that he was no Man to mince Matters; that he and his Comrades were Gentlemen of Fortune, and should make bold to try if Captain* Fulker's *Sloop was a better Sailor than the* Snow, *if she was, she would prove much fitter for their Business, and they must have her:* The *Snow* came to an Anchor about a League off the Sloop, and *Fly* ordered *Fulker,* with six of his own Hands, into the Boat, to bring her alongside of the *Snow;* but the

Wind proving contrary, their Endeavours proved also vain, and they returned again in the Boat, bringing Captain *Fulker* back with them.

As soon as they came on board the *Snow*, *Fly* fell into a violent Passion, cursing and damning *Fulker* for not bringing off the Sloop; he gave him his Reason, and said, it was impossible. *Damn ye,* replied the Pyrate, *you lie you Dog, but d — n my B — d, your Hide shall pay for your Roguery, and if I can't bring her off I'll burn her her where she lies.* He then order'd Captain *Fulker* to the Geers; no Reason, no Arguments, could prevail; he was stripp'd and lash'd after a very inhuman Manner: And the Boat's Crew being sent again, with much ado carried her off as far as the Barr, where she bilged and sunk. The pyrates then endeavoured to set what remained of her out of Water on Fire, but they could not burn her.

The *Snow* getting under Sail to look out for some Booty, *Fulker* and the others desired they might be set at Liberty, but it was denied them for the present, tho' not without a Promise that they should be released the first Vessel they took.

The fifth of *June* they left *Carolina,* and the next Day they spied a Sail, which prov'd the *John* and *Betty,* commanded by Capt. *Gale,* bound from *Barbadoes* to *Guiney*. *Fly* gave Chase, but finding the Ship wronged him, he made a Signal of Distress, hoisting his Jack at the main Top-Mast Head; but this Decoy did not hinder the Ship making the best of her Way. *Fly* continued the Chace all Night, and the Wind slackening, he came within Shot of the Ship, and fir'd several Guns at her under his black Ensign; the Ship being of no Force, and the pyrates ready to board, the Captain struck; and *Fly* manning his Long-Boat, which carried a Pateraro in the Bow, the Crew being well armed with Pistols and Cutlashes went on Board the Prize, and sent Capt. *Gale,* after having secured his Men, Prisoner on board the *Snow.*

This Prize was of little Value to the pyrates, who took nothing but some 'Sail-Cloaths and small Arms, and after two Days let her go, but took away six of his Men,' setting on board Capt. *Fulker* and a Passenger (Mr. *Atkinson* was detained) and Capt. *Green*'s Surgeon; they kept this Gentleman, Mr. *Atkinson,* knowing he was a good Artist, and lately Master of the *Boneta* Brigantine, as a Pilot for the Coast of *New England,* which they were satisfied he was well acquainted with.

Upon Mr. *Atkinson*'s desiring to have his Liberty with the others, Captain *Fly* made him the following Speech: *Look ye, Captain* Atkinson, *it is*
not that we care a T — d for your Company, G — d d — n ye; G — d d — n my Soul, not a T — d by G — d, and that's fair; but G — d d — n ye, and G — d's B — d and W — ds, if you don't act like an honest Man G — d d — n ye, and offer to play us any Rogues Tricks by G — d, and G — d sink me, but I'll blow your Brains out; G — d d — n me, if I don't. Now, Capt. Atkinson, *you may do as you please, you may be a Son of a Whore and pilot us wrong, which, G — d d — n ye, would be a rascally Trick by G — d, because you would betray Men who trust in you; but, by the eternal J — s, you shan't live to see us hang'd. I don't love many Words, G — d d — n ye, if you have a Mind to be well used you shall, G — d's B — d; but if you will be a Villain and betray your Trust, may G — d strike me dead, and may I drink a Bowl of Brimstone and Fire with the D — l, if I don't send you head-long to H — ll, G — d d — n me; and so there needs no more Arguments by G — d, for I've told you my Mind, and here's all the Ships Crew for Witnesses, that if I do blow your Brains out, you may blame no Body but your self, G — d d — n ye.*

Mr. *Atkinson* answered, it was very hard he should be forced to take upon him the Pilotage, when he did not pretend to know the Coast, and that his Life should answer for any Mistake his Ignorance of the Coast might make him guilty of, and therefore begg'd he might be set on board Capt. *Gale;* and that they would trust to their own Knowledge, since he did not doubt there being better Artists on Board. *No, No,* replied *Fly, that won't do by G — d, your palavring won't save your Bacon.* Muchas palabras no valen nada, *as the* Spaniards *say; so either discharge your Trust like an honest Man, for go you shan't by G — d, or I'll send you with my Service to the D — l; so no more Words, G — d d — n ye.*

There was no Reply made, and they stood for the Coast of *New England;* off *Delaware*'s Bay they made a Sloop, commanded by one *Harris,* bound from *New York* to *Pensilvania:* She had on Board about fifty Passengers; *Fly* gave Chase, and coming up with her, hoisted his black Ensign, and ordered her to strike, which she immediately did; and *Fly* sent Capt. *Atkinson* on Board with three of his Hands, to sail her, tho' he would not allow him, (*Atkinson*) any Arms: They, the pyrates, ransack'd this Prize, but not finding her of any Use to them, after a Detention of 24 Hours, they let her go, with her Men, excepting only a well made young Fellow, whose Name was *James Benbrooke,* whom they kept.

Fly, after having releas'd the Prize, ordered Captain *Atkinson* to carry the *Snow* into *Martha's* Vineyard, but, he willfully miss'd this Place. *Fly* finding himself beyond *Nantuckets,* and that his Design was baulk'd, called to *Atkinson,* and told him, *he was a rascally Son of an envenom'd Bitch, and d — n his Blood it was a Piece of Cruelty to let such a Son of a Whore live, who design'd the Death of so many honest Fellows. Atkinson,* in his Defence said, he never pretended to know the Coast, and that it was very hard he should die for being thought an abler Man than he really was; had he pretended to be their Pilot, and did not know his Business, he deserved Punishment; but when he was forc'd upon a Business which he before declared he did not understand, it would be certainly cruel to make him suffer for their Mistake. — G — d d — n ye, replied *Fly, you are an obstinate Villain, and your Design is to hang us; but, B — d and W — ds you Dog, you shan't live to see it,* and saying this, he ran into his Cabbin and fetch'd a Pistol with Design to shoot *Atkinson;* but by the Interposition of *Mitchell,* who thought him innocent of any Design, he escaped.

Atkinson, who perceived his Life every Minute in Danger, began to ingratiate himself with the pyrates, and gave them Hopes, that with good and gentle Usage, he might be brought to join them; this he did not say in express Terms, but by Words he now and then let drop, as by Accident: They were not a little rejoiced at the View of having so good an Artist to join them; nay, some of them hinted to him, that if he would take upon him the Command, they were ready to dispossess Capt. *Fly,* who carried his Command too high, and was known to all the Crew to be no Artist, and to understand nothing beyond the Business of a Boatswain. *Atkinson* thought it his Interest to keep them in the Opinion that he would join; but always declined hearing any Thing as to the Command.

This made him less severely us'd, and protected him from the Insults of *Fly,* who imagined he would betray them the first Opportunity, and therefore more than once proposed his being thrown over Board, which was never approved by the *Snow's* Company.

From *Nantuket* they stood to the Eastward, and off *Brown's Bank* made a Fishing Schooner. *Fly* coming up with her fired a Gun, and hoisting his black Ensign, swore, *d — n his Blood, if they did not instantly bring to, and send their Boat on Board, he would sink her:* The Schooner obeyed, and sent away her Boat on Board the *Snow;* he examined the Captain what Vessels were to be met with, and promised, if he could put him in the Way of meeting with a good Sailor, to let him go, and give him his Vessel, or he should otherwise keep her: The poor Man told him, he had a Companion which would soon be in Sight, and was a much better Vessel; accordingly about 12 at Noon the same Day, which was the 23d of *June,* the other Schooner hove in Sight; upon which, *Fly* mann'd this Prize with six pyrates, and a Prisoner nam'd *George Tasker,* and sent her in Chase, having himself on Board the *Snow,* no more than three pyrates, Captain *Atkinson,* (who had work'd himself into some Favour with him) and fifteen forced Men; but he took Care to have his Arms upon Deck by him.

The Men who had not taken on with *Fly,* were, *Atkinson,* Capt. *Fulker's* Mate, and two Youths belonging to him; the Carpenter and Gunner belonging formerly to Captain *Green;* six of Captain *Gate's* Men, and the aforesaid *Benbrooke,* who belonged to Captain *Harris,* with three of the Men out of the Schooner. *Atkinson* seeing the Prisoners and forced Men were five to one of the pyrates, thought of delivering himself from the Bondage he was in; and, as by good Luck, several other Fishing Vessels hove in Sight, right a-head of the *Snow,* he call'd to Captain *Fly,* and told him, he spied several other Vessels a-head, desiring, he would come forward and bring his Glass; *Fly* did so, and leaving his Arms on the Quarter-Deck, sat him on the Windlass to see if he could make what they were. *Atkinson,* who had concerted his Measures, with one *Walker* and the above-mention'd *Benbrook,* secured the Arms on the Quarter-Deck, and gave them a Signal to seize *Fly,* which they did, with very little Trouble, and after made themselves Masters of the other three pyrates and the *Snow;* the rest of the Prisoners, not knowing any Thing of, or what the Design might be, remaining altogether inactive, and brought the *Snow* and pyrates to *Great Brewster,* where a Guard was put on Board *June* 28, 1726.

Soon after, the said pyrates were brought to their Trial, that is, on the fourth of *July* following, before the Honourable *William Dummer,* Esq; Lieutenant Governor and Commander in chief, of the Province of *Massachuset*'s Bay, President of the special Court of *Admiralty,* held at the Court-house of *Boston,* assisted by 18 Gentlemen of the Council, before whom they were found guilty of Murder and Pyracy, condemn'd to be executed, and accordingly were executed the 12th of *July; Fly* was order'd to be hang'd in Chains at the Entrance of the Harbour of *Boston.* Thus ended the short Reign of an obdurate Wretch, who only wanted Skill and Power to be as infamous as any who had scoured the Seas; the Names of the three pyrates, executed with him, were *Samuel Cole, George Condick* and *Henry Greenvill.*

Chap. XXX
Of Capt. Thomas Howard, And his Crew

We have said in another Life, *viz. White's*, that he was a Lighterman on the River *Thames,* his Father was of the Business, and had the Character of a very honest Man. After his Father's Decease, he grew very extravagant, and squander'd away not only what he had left his Son, but what he had allotted for his Widow Mother to our Adventurer, whose Indulgence putting every Thing into her Son's Hands, was follow'd by being her self turn'd out of Doors, for he sold the House over her Head. After having ruin'd himself and Mother, his Friends fearing the Wickedness of his Inclinations would bring a Scandal upon them, persuaded him to go to Sea, and procur'd him a Voyage to *Jamaica,* on board a Merchant Ship. At this Island he ran away from his Ship, and associating himself with some desperate Fellows, they stole a Canoe, and went away to the grand *Camanas* to join some others of their own Stamp, who lurked thereabouts, with Design to go on the *Account,* the Term for Pirating: They met those they look'd for, made up a Company of 20 Men, surprized and made themselves Masters of a Turtling Sloop, and set out in Search of Booty.

The first Prizes they made were only Turtlers, which, however, encreas'd the Number of their Crew, some being willing to join them, others being forced, with Threats of being set ashore on some desolate Key.

They after some Time cruizing met with an *Irish* Brigantine, who had Provisions and Servants on board. They made an Exchange with the Master, gave him Provision to carry him to *Jamaica,* and allow'd five Hands to go with him; the rest (except the Servants, who readily took on with the pyrates) were all forced.

Not long after, they surprized a Sloop which had been trading on the *Spanish* Coast; as she had 6 Guns, and was a fit Vessel for their Turn, they chang'd her against the Brigantine; several Hands belonging to this Sloop enter'd Volunteers, and several more were obliged to join them by Compulsion.

After this Capture, they steer'd for the Coast of *Virginia,* and, in their Way, met with a large *New England* Brigantine, laden with Provisions, bound for *Barbadoes.* This they made Prize of; and shifting their own Guns on board her, sent the Master away in the Sloop; after forcing some of his Men with them. They had now a Vessel of 10 Guns, and a Crew of 80 Men, of whom one *James* was Captain, and *Howard* Quarter-Master.

While they lay on the Coast of *Virginia,* they made Prize of several Ships from *England,* out of which they took Men, Liquors, Provisions, Cloaths, and whatever else they either liked or thought necessary. As these Ships had several Felons on board, who were Transports, they had out of them a Number of Volunteers, beside forced Men; so that they had a large Complement. Among other *Virginia* Ships which fell into their Hands, they made Prize, with little Trouble, of a fine Galley, mounted with 24 Guns, which afforded them a great many Volunteers, as she had a Number of transported Malefactors and Servants on board. They changed their Brigantine for this Ship, and soon after, the Man of War, which waited on this Coast, heaving in Sight, they thought proper to take their Departure.

From the Coast of *Virginia,* they shap'd their Course for that of *Guiney,* where they took a great many Ships of different Nations, all which they rifled of what they thought fit: Out of these Ships they forced on board a Number of Men, equal to the Number of those formerly compell'd, who desired, and whom they permitted, to be discharged, after much Entreaty.

After they had been some Months on the Coast, they spied a large three deck'd *Portuguese* Ship from *Brazil,* mounted with 36 Guns; they gave Chase and came up with her: The Captain would make no Resistance, but his Mate, who was an *Englishman,* named *Rutland,* thinking it Shame to give up such a Ship, resolved to defend her; which the *Portuguese* Captain consented to, but went himself out of Harm's Way. *Rutland,* who had been Master of an *English* Brigantine, taken from him on the same Coast by another Gang of pyrates, fought them the better Part of a Forenoon; but the *Portuguese* flying the Decks, and only thirty Men, who were

English, Dutch, and *French,* standing by him, he was obliged to ask Quarters, which were given. When the pyrates came on board, they asked *Rutland,* if he was Commander? he answer'd, No. They enquired after him, and being told, he was somewhere in the Hold, they search'd, and found him hid in the Powder-Room; whence they hawled him up, and whipp'd him round the Deck for his

Cowardice. *Rutland,* and those who fought the Ship, they forced on board, and their Complement being now 180 Men, they exchanged their Galley for the *Portuguese* Ship, carried her in Shore, and ripping off her upper Deck, made her deep wasted, and much snugger, by cutting down some of her Gunnel. This Prize they named the *Alexander.*

They went down the Coast in this Ship, and made several Prizes, some of which they discharged, and put on board such of their forced Men as begg'd their Discharge; others, they sunk, and burnt others; but forced on board all Carpenters, Cawlkers, Armorers, Surgeons, and Musicians. In their Way to *Cape Lopez,* where they designed, and afterwards did clean, they found a large *Bristol* Ship at an Anchor, which had lost a great many Men by Sickness, and had then but few healthy on board, who got into the Boat, and endeavoured to get to Shore, but were prevented by the pyrates: Here they changed some more of their forced Men, and did intend to change their Ship; but on a Survey, found the *Bristol* Man too old for their Purpose, and therefore left her at an Anchor, after they had taken what they thought of Use to them; this Ship belong'd to one Mr. *Godly* of *Bristol.*

They met with nothing else in their Way to *Cape Lopez,* where they clean'd their Ship, took in Wood and Water, and then stood away to Sea again.

At their leaving *Cape Lopez,* they spied an *English* Ship, which they came up with and engaged; the Merchant Man made an obstinate Defence, and finding the Design to board, made to close Quarters. *Howard* and seven or eight more entered, but the Pyrate's Boatswain not having secured his lashing, they fell a-stern, and left these Men on board the Merchant-Ship, who seeing themselves in Danger, hawl'd up the Boat, which the Chace had a-stern, and, cutting the Rope, got on board the *Alexander,* which being considerably the larger Ship, and drawing a great deal more Water, stuck on an unknown Bank, which the Merchant Man went over, and by this lucky Accident escaped.

This obliged the pyrates to start their Water, and throw over the Wood to get the Ship off, which put 'em under a Necessity of going back to *Cape Lopez* to take in those Necessaries. After having a second time wooded and water'd, they put again to Sea, fell in with and took two *Portuguese* Brigantines, which they burnt, and setting the Men on Shoar, they made for, and doubled the Cape of *Good Hope,* and shap'd their Course for *Madagascar,* where to the Northward of, and forty Mile from, the Bay of *Augustine,* and near a small Island, they run the Ship on a Reef, where she stuck fast. The Captain being then sick in his Bed, the Men went ashoar on the small adjacent Island, and carried off a great deal of Provision and Water to lighten the Ship, on board of which none but the Captain, the Quarter-Master, and about eleven more were left.

The Quarter-Master, who was *Howard,* with the others, took all the Treasure, and put it on board the Boats, made off for the Main of *Madagascar;* the Captain, hearing no Body stir upon Deck, made shift to crawl out of his Cabbin, and seeing 'em put off, fir'd the two fore chace Guns at 'em, which alarm'd (to no Purpose) the Men ashoar; as the Sea ebb'd, the Ship lay dry, and they could walk to her from the Island. She might have been saved had they had the Boats to carry out an Anchor; but for want of them they brought every Thing ashoar, at Tide of Flood, upon Rafts.

As the Ship lay in a quiet Place, they had Opportunity to rip her up, and build a Vessel out of her Wreck. The major Part of the Crew being *English* and *Dutch,* who sided together, they forced about 36 *Portuguese* and *French* (thinking the Crew too numerous for their Provisions in their present Circumstances) to get upon a Raft, and take their Chance with the Sea-Breeze to get to the Island of *Madagascar,* about 3 Leagues from them. They finish'd a Vessel of 60

Tuns, but the Day they design'd to have launch'd her, a Pyrate Brigantine hove in Sight, who took 'em on board.

Howard and his Consorts stood along the West-Side of the Island, with Design to round the North End, and to go to St. *Mary*'s, but finding the Current too strong to stem, they lay there about a Fortnight; in the Interim they spied three Sail of tall Ships, which were Men of War under Commadore *Littleton,* (viz. the *Anglesea, Hastings* and *Lizard,*) who had carried a Pardon to the Island of St. *Mary,* accepted of by many of the pyrates. Thinking these might be also pyrates, they made a Smoak, which brought the Boats ashoar; but finding they were Men of Wars Boats, the pyrates thought fit to abscond wherefore finding nothing, nor any Body, the said Men of War's Boats return'd, and the Ships kept their Cruise.

They had here plenty of Fish and wild Hogs, which they found in the Wood. One Day, when *Howard* was Hunting, his Comrades took the Opportunity, went off, rounded the North End, and left Mr. *Howard* to provide for himself.

About four or five and twenty Leagues from the Cape, they went into a fine Harbour on the East Side, not frequented nay, hardly known to the *European* Ships. They were here received handsomely, treated and provided with fresh Meat, and what Necessaries they wanted, by the King of this District, whose Name was *Mushmango,* who had formerly been driven from *Augustine* by War, and travelling thro' the Heart of the Country, had here fixed his Settlement. When the Boats were victualled, and while >*Johnson,* who took on him the Command after they had deserted *Howard,* was ashoar with three more, the rest went off with the Boars and Booty, and stood away to the Southward, along the Coast, designing for St. *Mary*'s, going every Night into some Harbour, or coming to an Anchor under some Point when the Winds proved contrary.

Johnson addressed himself to the King, and told him the Boat and Goods were his Property; upon which he went along Shore with a Number of Men, and found the Boat at an Anchor, and all asleep, except one to look out, at whom the King fired his Blunderbuss, and kill'd him; the Report of the Piece awaken'd the others, who cut and stood off the Coast. The King return'd, gave *Johnson* an Account of his Expedition, and furnish'd him a Canoe, some Calabashes of fresh Water, Provisions and Launces, that he might pursue after his People.

Johnson kept the Shoar on Board till he came to the Island of St. *Mary*'s, where he heard his Comrade Fugitives were gone to, and settled at *Ambonavoula,* in a Village belonging to the Natives on the River of *Manansallang;* leaving his Canoe, he went into one belonging to an Inhabitant, who carried him to his Companions.

After he had been here some few Months *Fourgette,* already mention'd in *White*'s Life, came in with his Ship from *Martinico*: With this Vessel they fail'd to the West-Side, and came to an Anchor at an Island called *Anquawla,* 30 Leagues from the Place where they left *Howard.*

Some of the Subjects of the King of *Anquawla* had before met with, and brought hither, Captain *Howard,* who seeing the Ship at an Anchor near Shore, haled her, and desired the Boat might be sent to fetch him off, which was accordingly done, and he joined the rest of the Crew.

Here two Boys ran away from them, whom they demanded of the King; but he not delivering them, they went ashore by Day-Break, surpriz'd his Town, and brought off 12 of his Concubines, whom they detain'd on board, till their Boys, who were Blacks, were returned, and then delivered them back. From this Ship he went on board the *Speaker,* where he continued till she was lost on *Mauritius,* when he came back to *Madagascar,* and settled at *Augustine,* here he staid till the *Prosperous,* a Ship of 36 Guns, commanded by Captain *Hilliard,* came in; which *Howard* and some other pyrates, (with the Assistance of the Boatswain and some of the Crew belonging to the Ship) seized. In the taking this Ship, the Captain and his chief Mate were killed, and several others wounded. *Howard* was by the Company declared Captain.

Several of the Ship's Crew took on with them, and they went round the South End to the East Side, till they came the Length of *Maritan,* where they found some of the *Speaker*'s Company, whom they took on board, and made up their Complement about 70 Men.

From hence they steer'd for the Island of St. *Mary,* where they heel'd their Ship, water'd, wooded, and shipp'd some more Hands: Here they had an Invitation from one *Ort Van Tyle,*

282

who liv'd on the Main of *Madagascar,* to come to the Ceremony of christening two of his Children; they were kindly received and treated by him, but it having been reported, that this *Ort Van Tyle* had murdered some pyrates, they in Revenge, tho' they had no Certainty of the Fact, took him Prisoner, plunder'd his House, and what Goods they could not take off in a great Canoe belonging to him, they threw into the River or burnt. *Ort Van Tyle* they design'd to carry on board, and hang at a Yard Arm, but one of the pyrates help'd him to escape, and he took into the Woods, where meeting some of his Blacks, he way-laid his Canoa, and *Howard*'s Pinnace by the River Side; besides what Goods they had on board of this *Dutchman*'s, they had several Women and Children belonging to him, and some white Men, who had left them under his Care. The pyrates set the Women to the Paddles, and the Canoa was over-set on the Bar; *Ort Van Tyle* fired on the Men, and shot one thro' the Arm and thro' the Thigh, whom with his Comrade, he took Prisoner, and kept with him: The rest of the Men got ashore on the South-Side the River and escaped him; the Women on the North-Side, and returned home. When the *Pinnace* came down, he fir'd and shot the Captain thro' the Arm, but he got on board, where his Arm was set. After this, the *Prosperous* sail'd for *Methelage,* where they victualled, with a Design to go to the *East-Indies;* while he lay here, came in a large *Dutch* Ship, well mann'd, and of 40 Guns; the *Prosperous* was not strong enough to attack her, and the *Dutch* fearing he should spoil his Trade, would not meddle with Captain *Howard,* tho' hard Words pass'd, and the *Dutchmen* threatned to fall foul on him if he did not leave the Place, which *Howard* thought fit to do, and sail'd to *Mayotta.*

Few Days after the Departure of the *Prosperous,* Captain *Bowen,* in the *Scotch* Ship, came in, anchored within small Arm-Shot, and right a-head of the *Dutchman,* whom he saluted with 11 Guns Shot and all, which the other returned, with 15 after the same Manner; Drums beating, and Trumpets sounding, on both Sides. The *Dutchman,* however, was surpized, and under Apprehensions; he hal'd the Pyrate, and answer was return'd, *From the Seas;* he then bid 'em send their Boat on Board, which accordingly went with the Quarter-Master, who told the Captain, that they had no Design on him, but were going against the *Moors,* and came in for Provision; he replied, they could get none there, and the best Way was to be gone; however the Quarter-Master went ashore (where the *Dutch* had made his Factory, and had some Goods) and shot down three Oxen, which he ordered the Natives to help to cut in Pieces; the *Dutchman* perceiving a Friendship between the Natives and pyrates, seeing *Bowen* full of Men, and hearing two more pyrates were expected, thought fit to go off in the Night, and leave the Goods he had put on shore.

Few Days after *Bowen* seizing the Goods left, went for *Mayotta,* where he join'd the *Prosperous,* and lay for the Season to go to the *East-Indies.* After some Stay here, their Salt Provisions perishing, they return'd to *Madagascar* to revictual, *Bowen* to St. *Augustin*'s, and *Howard* (on board of whose Ship was Captain *Whaley,* taken as is said in *Bowen*'s Life) to *Methelage,* agreeing to meet at the Island of St. *John*'s, to lie for the *Moors* Fleet; where, after some Disappoints, they met, and got Sight of the *Moors* Fleet, one of which sell a Prize to *Bowen;* but the *Prosperous* being a heavy Sailor, did not come up with them till they were at an Anchor at the Bar of *Surat,* where they waited to lighten. The *Moors,* seeing few Hands on board, for *Howard* concealed his Men; and not imagining a Pyrate would venture up, they concluded him an *English East-India* Man: *Howard* clapp'd the largest on board, which stood him a smart Engagement, and killed him about 30 Men. At length the pyrates forced Captain *Whaley,* who spoke the *Moors* Language, to go on board and offer Quarter, which they accepted: There was on board this Prize a Nobleman belonging to the Great *Mogul,* who had been at *Juffa* to buy Horses for his Master; the Prize yielded them a great Booty, tho' they found but Part of the Money which was on board. They intended to carry her to *Madagascar,* but her Bowsprit being wounded in the boarding, she lost all her Masts, wherefore, they set her a-drift, and she ran ashore at *Deman,* belonging to the *Portuguese.*

From hence he steer'd to the *Malabar* Coast, where he met *Bowen* in his Prize, which mounted 56 Guns; here a Dispute arose, as shall be mention'd in the Appendix of *Bowen*'s

Life, both Crews went on board *Bowen,* sunk the *Prosperous,* and burnt the *Scotch* Ship, called the *Speedy Return:* Hence they stood along the Coast of *India,* and *Howard,* with about 20 more, landed with what they had, and retired among the Natives, where *Howard* married a Woman of the Country, and being a morose ill natur'd Fellow, and using her ill, he was murder'd by her Relations.

Chap. XXXI
Of Captain Lewis. And his Crew

This worthy Gentleman was an early Pyrate; we first find him a Boy on Board the Pyrate *Banister*, who was hang'd at the Yard Arm of a Man of War in sight of *Port-Royal* in *Jamaica*. This *Lewis* and another Boy were taken with him, and brought into the Island hanging by the Middle at the Mizzen-Peak. He had a great Aptitude for Languages, and spoke perfectly well that of the *Mosquill Indians,* the *French, Spanish* and *English*. I mention our own, because it is doubted whether he was *French* or *English,* for we cannot trace him back to his Original.

He sailed out of *Jamaica* till he was a lusty Lad, and was then taken by the *Spaniards* at the *Havana,* where he staid some Time; but at length he and six more ran away with a small Canoe, and surprized a *Spanish* Periagua, out of which two Men joined them, so that they were now nine in Company: With this Pariagua they suprized a Turtleing Sloop, and forced some of the Hands to take on with them, the others they sent away in the Periagua.

He play'd at this small Game, surprising and taking Coasters and Turtlers, till with forced Men and Volunties he made up a Complement of 40 Men.

With these he took a large Pink built Ship, bound from *Jamaica* to the Bay of *Campeachy,* and after her several others bound to the said Bay; and having Intelligence that there lay in the Bay a fine *Bermudas* built Brigantine of 10 Guns, commanded by Captain *Tucker;* he sent the Captain of the Pink to him with a Letter, the Purport of which was, that he wanted such a Brigantine, and if he would part with her, he would pay him honestly 10000 Pieces of Eight; if he refused this, he would take Care to lie in his Way, for he was resolved, either by fair or foul Means, to have the Vessel. Captain *Tucker* having read the Letter, sent for the Masters of Vessels then lying in the Bay, and told them, after he had shown the Letter, that if they would made him up 54 Men (for there were about 10 *Bermudas* Sloops) he would go out and fight the pyrates. They said, No, they would not hazard their Men, they depended on their Sailing, and every one must take Care of himself as well as he could.

However, they all put to Sea together, and spied a Sail under the Land, which had a Breeze while they lay becalmed; some said he was a Turtler, others, the Pyrate, and so it proved; for it was honest Captain *Lewis,* who putting out his Oars, got in among them. Some of the Sloops had four Guns, some two, some none. *Joseph Dill* had two, which he brought on one Side, and fired smartly at the Pyrate, but unfortunately one of them split, and killed him three Men. *Tucker* called to all the Sloops to send him Men, and he would fight *Lewis,* but to no Purpose; no Body came on board him. In the mean while a Breeze sprung up, and *Tucker* trimming his Sails left them, who all fell a Prey to the Pyrate; into whom however he fired a Broadside at going off. One Sloop, whose Master I won't Name, was a very good Sailer, and was going off; but *Lewis* firing a Shot at him, brought her to, and he lay by till all the Sloops were visited and secured. Then *Lewis* sent on board him, and ordered the Master into his Sloop. As soon as he was aboard, he asked the Reason of his lying by, and betraying the Trust his Owners had reposed in him, which was doing like a Knave and Coward, and he would punish him accordingly; for, he said, you might have got off, being so much a better Sailer than my Vessel. After this Speech he fell upon him with a Rope's End, and then snatching up his Cane, drove him about the Decks without Mercy. The Master, thinking to pacify him, told him he had been out trading in that Sloop several Months, and had on board a good Quantity of Money, which was hid, and which, if he would send on board a Black belonging to the Owners, he would discover it to him.

This had not the desired Effect, but one quite contrary; for *Lewis* told him he was a Rascal and Villain for this Discovery, and, by G — d, he would pay him for betraying his Owners, and redoubled his Strokes. However, he sent and took the Money and Negroe, who was an able Sailor. He took out of his Prizes what he had occasion for, 40 able Negroe Sailors, and a white Carpenter; the largest Sloop, which was about 90 Tuns, he took for his own Use, and mounted her with 12 Guns; his Crew was now about 80 Men, whites and Blacks.

After these Captures he cruised in the Gulf of *Florida,* lying in wait for the *West-India* homeward bound Ships which took the Leeward Passage, several of which falling into his Hands were plundered by him, and released; from hence he went to the Coast of *Carolina,* where he cleaned his Sloop, and a great many Men, whom he had forced, ran away from him; however, the Natives traded with him for Rum and Sugar, and brought him all he wanted, without the Government's having any Knowledge of him, for he had got into a very private Creek; tho' he was very much on his Guard, that he might not be surprized from the Shoar.

From *Carolina* he cruized on the Coast of *Virginia,* where he took and plunder'd several Merchant Men, and forced several Men, and then return'd to the Coast of *Carolina,* where he did abundance of Mischief.

As he had now abundance of *French* on board who had entered with him, and *Lewis* hearing the *English* had a Design to Maroon them, he secured the Men he suspected, and put them in a Boat, with all the other *English,* 10 Leagues from Shoar, with only 10 Pieces of Beef, and sent them away, keeping none but *French* and *Negroes*; these Men, it is supposed, all perished in the Sea.

From the Coast of *Carolina* he shaped his Course for the Banks of *Newfoundland,* where he overhawled several Fishing Vessels, and then went into a commodious Harbour, where he cleaned his Sloop, and went into *Trinity Harbour* in *Conception Bay,* where there lay several Merchants, and siezed a 24 Gun Galley, called the *Herman:* The Commander, Captain *Beal,* told *Lewis,* if he would send his Quarter-Master ashoar he would furnish him with Necessaries. He being sent ashoar, a Council was held among the Masters, the Consequence of which was, the seizing the Quarter-Master, whom they carried to Captain *Woodes Rogers;* he chained him to a Sheet Anchor which was ashoar, and planted Guns at the Point, to prevent the Pyrate getting out, but to little Purpose; for the People from one of these Points firing too soon, *Lewis* quitted the Ship, and, by the Help of Oars and the Favour of the Night, got out in his Sloop, though she received many Shot in her Hull. The last Shot that was fired at the Pyrate did him considerable Damage.

He lay off and on the Harbour, swearing he would have his Quarter-Master, and intercepted two fishing Shallops, on board of one was the Captain of the Galley's Brother; he detained them, and sent Word, if his Quarter-Master did not immediately come off, he would put all his Prisoners to Death; he was sent on board him without Hesitation. *Lewis* and the Crew enquired, how he had been used? and he answered, very civilly. Its well, said the Pyrate; for had you been ill treated, I would have put all these Rascals to the Sword. They were dismiss'd, and the Captain's Brother going over the Side, the Quarter-Master stopp'd him, saying, he must drink the Gentlemens Health ashoar, in particular Captain *Roger*'s, and, whispering him in the Ear, told him, if the Crew had known of his being chain'd all Night, he would have been cut in Pieces, with all his Men. After this poor Man and his Shallop's Company were gone, the Quarter-Master told the Usage he had met with, which enraged *Lewis,* and made him reproach his Quarter-Master, whose Answer was, that he did not think it just the Innocent should suffer for the Guilty.

The Masters of the Merchant Men sent to Captain *Tudor Trevor,* who lay at St. *John*'s in the *Sheerness* Man of War; he immediately got under Sail, and miss'd the Pyrate but four Hours.

She kept along the Coast, and made several Prizes, *French* and *English,* and put into a Harbour where a *French* Ship lay making Fish: She was built at the latter End of the War for a Privateer, was an excellent Sailer, and mounted 24 Guns. The Commander haled him; the Pyrate answered, from *Jamaica* with Rum and Sugar. The *French* Man bid him go about his Business; that a Pyrate Sloop was on the Coast, and he might be the Rogue; if he did not immediately sheer off he would fire a Broadside into him. He went off and lay a Fortnight out at Sea, so far as not to be descry'd from Shoar, with Resolution to have the Ship. The *French* Man being on his Guard, in the mean while raised a Battery on the Shoar, which commanded the Harbour. After a Fortnight, when he was thought to be gone off, he return'd, and took two of the fishing Shallops belonging to the *French* Man, and manning them with pyrates, they went in; one Shallop attack'd the Battery, the other surpriz'd, boarded, and carry'd the Ship, just as the Morning Star appear'd, for which Reason he gave her that Name. In the Engagement the Owner's Son was kill'd, who made the Voyage out of Curiosity only. The Ship being taken, 7 Guns were fired, which was the Signal, and the Sloop came down and lay a Long-side the Ship. The Captain told him, he suppos'd he only wanted his Liquor; but *Lewis* made Answer, he wanted his Ship, and accordingly hoisted all his Ammunition and Provision into her. When the *French* Man saw they would take away his Ship, he told her Trim, and *Lewis* gave him the Sloop; and, excepting what he took for Provision, all the Fish he had made. Several of the *French* took on with him, who, with others, *English* and *French*, had by Force or voluntarily, made him up 200 Men.

From *Newfoundland* he steer'd for the Coast of *Guiney*, where he took a great many Ships, *English*, *Dutch*, and *Portuguese;* among these Ships was one belonging to *Carolina*, commanded by Captain *Smith*.

While he was in Chace of this Vessel an Accident happen'd, which made his Men believe he dealt with the Devil; for he carried away his Fore and Main-Top Mast; and he, *Lewis*, running up the Shrouds to the Main-Top, tore off a Handful of Hair, and throwing it into the Air, used this Expression, *Good Devil take this till I come:* And, it was observed, that he came afterwards faster up with the Chace than before the Loss of his Top-Masts.

Smith being taken, *Lewis* used him very civilly, and gave him as much, or more in Value, than he took from him, and let him go, saying, he would come to *Carolina* when he had made Money on the Coast, and would rely on his Friendship.

They kept some Time on the Coast, when they quarrell'd among themselves, the *French* and *English*, of which the former was more numerous, and they resolved to part: The *French* therefore chose a large Sloop newly taken, thinking the Ship's Bottom, which was not Sheath'd, damaged by the Worms.

According to this Agreement they took on board what Ammunition and Provision they thought fit out of the Ship, and put off, chusing one *le Barre* Captain. As it blew hard, and the Decks were encumbered, they came to an Anchor under the Coast, to stow away their Ammunition, Goods, *&c. Lewis* told his Men, they were a Parcel of Rogues, and he would make 'em refund; accordingly run a Long-side his Guns, being all loaded and new primed, and ordered him to cut away his Mast, or he would sink him. *le Barre* was obliged to obey. Then he ordered them all ashoar; they begged to have Liberty of carrying their Arms, Goods, *&c.* with 'em, but he allow'd 'em only their small Arms, and Cartridge Boxes. Then he brought the Sloop a Long-side, put every Thing on board the Ship, and sunk the Sloop.

le Barre and the rest begg'd to be taken on board; however, though he denied 'em, he suffered *le Barre* and some few to come, with whom he and his Men drank plentifully. The Negroes on board *Lewis* told him, the *French* had a Plot against him. He answer'd, he could not withstand his Destiny; for the Devil told him in the great Cabin, he should be murdered that Night.

In the dead of Night came the rest of the *French* on board in Canoes, got into the Cabbin and killed *Lewis;* they fell on the Crew, but, after an Hour and Half's Dispute, the *French* were beat off, and the Quarter-Master, *John Cornelius*, an *Irish* Man, succeeded *Lewis*.

Chap. XXXII
Of Captain Cornelius, And his Crew

Having now the Command of the *Morning Star, Cornelius* kept on the Coast, and made several Prizes both *English* and *Portuguese;* the former he always discharged, after he had taken what he thought fitting, but the latter he commonly burnt.

While he was thus ravaging the Coast, two *English* Ships which had slaved at *Whydah,* one of 36 Guns, and the other of 12, which fought close, were ready to sail; and having Notice of a Pyrate, who had done great Mischief, resolved to keep Company together for their Defence. The Captain of the small Ship lay sick in his Cabbin, and she was left to the Care of the Mates. When they had got under Sail, 200 Negroes jump'd over board from the larger Ships, which obliged her to bring to and get out her Boats; the Mate of the other went into the Cabbin, told the Accident, and advised lying by, and sending their Boats to assist their Consort; but the Captain being ill, and willing to get off the Coast, bid him keep on his Way, for it would be dangerous, having 400 Slaves on board, and being but weakly mann'd, when the Boats were gone they might rise upon him. The Mate urged the Danger of the pyrates, should they leave their Consort. The Captain answered, the Seas were wide, and he would not bring to; accordingly they kept on their Way with a fresh Gale.

Two Days after, the Mate about Eight in the Morning, ordered a Man to the Mast-head, who spied a Sail, which made them prepare for an Engagement. There was on board one *Joseph Williams,* who had served the *African* Company three Years on the *Guiney* Coast, who spoke the Negroe Tongue very well; he told the Slaves he had pick'd out to the Number of 50, that the Ship in Sight he believed would fight them, and if they got the better, would certainly, as they were Cannibals, kill and eat them all, and therefore it behoved them to fight for their Lives; they had Lances and small Arms given them.

About Ten *Cornelius* came up with them, and being haled, answered, he was a Man of War, in Search of pyrates, and bid them send their Boat on board; but they refusing to trust him, tho' he had *English* Colours and Pendent aboard, the Pyrate fired a Broadside, and they began a running Fight of about 10 Hours, in which Time the Negroes discharged their Arms so smartly, that *Cornelius* never durst attempt to board. About 8 at Night the Ship blew up abast, they immediately cut the Lashings of the Long-Boat, but the Ship going down they had not Time to get her out, and barely enough to launch the Yawl, which lay on the Forecastle. The Ship went down on one Side, and *Joseph Williams* running on the other was hook'd by the Mizzen-Truss, and was carried down with her; but having his Knife in his Hand, and a great Presence of Mind, he cut the Wastband of his Trowzers where he was catch'd, got clear, and swam after the Boat, into which about 16 had gotten, and either knock'd those on the Head, or cut off their Hands, who laid hold on it; however, with much Entreaty, he was permitted to lay one Hand on to ease him: They made to the Pyrate, who refused to receive them, without they would enter with him, which, to save their Lives, they all agreed to, and was then civilly received, and dry Cloaths given them; these and one Negroe were all the Souls saved.

In a little Time after this he took two *Portuguese* Ships, which he plundered and kept with him; and one foggy Morning hearing the firing of Guns, which, by the distance of Time, he judg'd to be Minute Guns, as they really were, for the Death of an *English* Commander; he called his Men on board from the Prizes, sent them about their Business, and directed his Course by the Report of the Canon he had heard.

In about two Hours he spied the Ship that had fired, came up with her very soon, and took her without Resistance. The Officers of the Ship which blew up, finding this Prize *English,* and that the Pyrate did not intend to detain it, begg'd to be discharged, as they had all large Families, which must perish without their Support.

Cornelius taking them into Consideration, discharged Mr. *Powis* of *Limehouse,* who has since been a Commander, and raised a Fortune; the then chief Mate, Mr. *George Forelong,* the Boatswain, Carpenter, and other married Men, set them on board the Prize, and was very generous to them out of the Plunder of the *Portuguese* Ships, because they had made a broken Voyage; but *Joseph Williams* and the Batchelors he detained, and forced some out of the Prize, which he let go.

After this he took three *Portuguese* Ships at an Anchor, which he plundered and burnt, after he had hove down by one of them; he continued some Time longer on the Coast, did a great Deal of Mischief to the Trade, and forced a great many Men: These he put to do all the Slavery of the Ship, and they were beat about the Decks, without daring to strike again. I shall take Notice of an Instance of this Kind, to show how far Revenge will carry a Man. One *Robert Bland* was at Helm, and called *Joseph Williams* to take the Whipstaff, till he went to play, *Williams* refused it; upon which *Bland* drubb'd him with the Lanyard of the Whipstaff very severely, *Williams* that he might revenge himself, and have Liberty to fight *Bland,* went that Instant and entered himself a Volunteer in the Ships Books, and ask'd Leave to fight *Bland,* which was allowed him, but with no other Weapons than his Fists; he, however, challenged his Antagonist, who was too hard for him; so that he turned Pyrate to be heartily thresh'd.

Cornelius thinking they had been long enough on the *Guiney* Coast, doubled the Cape, off which he spide the *Lizard* and two more Men of War, under the Command of Commadore *Littleton; Cornelius* was for giving Chase, but finding his Men unwilling, there being, as they gave for Reason, 70 forc'd Men on board, and these Ships being, as they suspected, Men of War, he made the best of his Way for *Madagascar,* went up the River *Methelage,* on the West Side, and anchored against *Pombotoque,* a small Village of Blacks.

The Quarter-Master went ashore, and the black Governor examined him, for several of these Blacks speak *English;* he told the Governor they were come for Provision and to trade: Upon which he sent a Couple of Oxen on board, and then ordered some of the Inhabitants to go up with the Quarter-Master to the King. The Boat's Crew seeing a Number of Blacks come upon the Strand without the Quarter-Master, apprehended some Mischief had befallen him; but were eas'd of their Fears, when they saw two Oxen given them, and were told, the white Man, who was gone to the King, would be back next Day, it not being above 20 Miles from the Shore.

When the Quarter-Master, who carried up a Blunderbuss, a fine Gun, and a Pair of Pistols, for a Present to the King, told him they wanted Provisions, he asked where they were bound? To which he answered, to seek their Fortunes, for, at present, they were very poor. Look ye, replied the King, I require nothing of you, all white Men I look upon as my Children; they help'd me to conquer this Country, and all the Cattle in it is at their Service. I will send you down Provisions enough, and when that is spent you shall have more; he accordingly sent 1000 Head of Cattle, out of which he bid them chuse what they would, and they salted up a 100 fat Oxen.

It may be an Amusement to the Reader to have a short History of this King, who was called *Andian Chimenatto,* that is, King *Chimenatto:* He was 2d Son of *Andian Lifouchy,* whose Country lay between *Methelage* and St. *Augustine,* his elder Brother was *Timanangarivo.*

At the Death of *Andian Lyfouchy, Chimenatto,* assisted by a younger Brother, and a great Number of the People, endeavour'd to wrest the Kingdom from his elder Brother *Timanangarivo;* but he was defeated, and with his Party obliged to retire, however, he still made War upon his Brother, till he was, by repeated Losses, very much weaken'd, and apprehensive of being attack'd by him; he retir'd farther Northward, where he made War on *Andian Methelage,* but without great success so that he settled on a Point of Land by the Sea-Coast, where the *Tyloutes,* that is, Inhabitants of the Sea, who are descended from the *Arabs,* and the *Vaujimbos,* who are esteem'd the meanest Cast on the whole Island, were very vexatious and troublesome to him, and kept him in continual Alarms.

In the mean while a couple of Ships arrived at *Yungowl* (the Country of *Timanangarivo*) belonging to *Frederick Phillips,* of *New York,* to slave; but hearing the old King was dead, who had a great Respect for the whites, and that *Timanangarivo* had cut off the Crew of a Brigantine, on Pretence that they had poison'd his Father *Andian Lyfouchy,* for he drunk on board her so much Brandy that he died of it; they would not stay here, but went farther on the Coast to look for Trade

Andian Chimenatto spying them, caused a Smoak to be made, which brought one of their Boats on Shoar; *Chimenatto* received the Crew very civilly, and invited the Ships in, promising Trade.

The Commanders ask'd if he had Slaves? He said he had but few; however, if they would allow some of their Men to go with him to War, he would slave both Ships: They answered, that *Timanangarivo* his Brother, had murder'd some of their Countrymen, and they could put no Confidence in him; upon which he gave them the History of his Wars, said his Brother was a wicked Man for what he had done; but if they would send some Men with him, he would give his Wives and nearest Relations for Hostages, to be kept on board.

This was agreed to, and *Chimenatto* furnished them with as much fresh Provision as they could dispose of; twenty whites went with him to War, and they took a Town and a great Number of Slaves, out of whom he ordered the Captain to pick and cull what they pleas'd; they asked the

Price, he said, he required nothing, if they would let their Men go out once more. They went on a second Expedition, took several Towns, and brought down some thousand Slaves, beside great Droves of Cattle.

The two Ships took their Choice of about 6000 Slaves, which with fresh Provision, and Provision for their Voyage, cost them only 2 or 3 Barrels of Powder, and a few Arms.

The King told them, if they would leave those Men and come again, he would again slave them for nothing; the Men being willing to stay, the Ships sail'd, came again the next Season, were slaved according to Promise, and relieved those whites, such of them as would return, and left others, who were willing, in their Steads. With this Assistance *Chimenatto* soon conquered the *Antylouts* and *Vaujimbos,* and afterwards made himself Master of the whole Country of *Methelage,* of such Reputation are the *Europeans* among these People, for they who have a white Man on their Side go on as to certain Victory; and the Sight of a white Man against them is such a Damp to their Spirits, that despairing of Success, they are preparing for Flight before they engage.

But to return, besides the Present of Oxen, the King sent 100 Blacks laden with Rice. *Cornelius* sent him a Present of 2 Barrels of Powder, and would have given him more, with small Arms in Return, but he sent them Word he would have no more, nor any of their Arms, not being in Want of either; on the contrary, if they wanted he would send them ten Barrels of Powder, as they were his Children; bid them proceed on their Voyage, and if they were richer when they came back, and would send him any Present, he would accept it, but not now that they were poor.

Here *Cornelius* lost 70 Men by their Excesses, having been long without fresh Provision, the eating immoderately, drinking Toke (a Liquor made of Honey) to Excess, and being too free with the Women, they fell into violent Fevers, which carried them off.

The Blacks having given *Cornelius* an Account of the *Speaker*'s being sail'd from *Methelage* about three Months before for the *East-Indies,* he, having taken in his Provsions, steer'd the same Course, in Hopes to join in Consort with her; but the *Speaker* lying off the *Red Sea,* and the *Morning Star* going into the Gulf of *Persia* they never met: They run up a pretty Way in the Gulf, and lay under *Antelope* Island, where they kept a Look-out, and whence they made their Excursions, and took a Number of Prizes.

Here they designed to heave down and clean, and they had got a good Part of their Goods and Water Casks ashore, when the Look-out discovered two tall Ships, one of them wearing a Flag at the Foretop-Mast Head; this put them into a great Confusion, they got what Casks and Necessaries they could on board, and lay till the Ships came a-breast of them; then they got under Sail at once, their Sails being furl'd with Rope Yarns, and came close along-side the larger Ship, which was a *Portuguese* of 70 Guns, as the other was of 26; they exchanged a Broadside with her, and the smaller Ship engaged her so close, that they threw Hand Grenades into each other; but *Cornelius*'s Business was to run, and the great Ship put a Stays twice to follow him, but missing, was obliged to Ware, which gave the Pyrate a great Advantage; the small Ship in staying, tail'd aground, she, however, gave Chase till she had run a good Way a-head of her Consort, which the Pyrate seeing, brought to, and stay'd for her, as did the

Portuguese for her Consort, not caring to engage him singly. When it was quite dark *Cornelius* ran up the other Shore, pass'd the *Portuguese* Ships (which kept down the Gulf) and came again to Anchor at his old Station, where he found his Enemies had been ashore in their Boats and staved his Casks; he here cleaned, and finding no Money to be got out of any Prizes made, and Bale Goods being of little Value to them, they from hence went away to the Island of *Johanna*, where it was designed to moroon the Blacks, who were the greater Number, and all bred among the *English*; *Joseph Williams*, fearing they would next moroon the *English*, who were not above a third of the whites, gave the Negroes Notice of the Design, who secured all the Arms of the Ship, and gave *Williams* the Command till they should get to *Madagascar*, keeping a good Guard on the *French* and *Dutch*. When they came to *Methelage* they gave the Ship to the King, her Bottom being eaten so much with the Worms, that she was no longer fit for Service; and they all went and lived with the new King *Chimave*, Son to *Andian Chimenatto*, who died before their Return: About five Months after they broke up, *Cornelius* died, and was buried with the usual Ceremony.

Chap. XXXIII
Of Capt. David Williams, And his Crew

This Man was born in *Wales,* of very poor Parents, who bred him up to the Plough and the following of Sheep, the only Things he had any Notion of till he went to Sea. He was never esteem'd among the pyrates as a Man of good natural Parts, perhaps, on account of his Ignorance of Letters, for, as he had no Education, he knew as little of the sailing a Ship, set aside the Business of a foremast Man, as he did of History, in which, and natural Philosophy, he was equally vers'd: He was of a morose, sour, unsociable Temper, very choleric, and easily resented as an Affront what as brave and a more knowing Man would not think worth Notice; but he was not cruel, neither did he turn Pyrate from a wicked or avaritious Inclination, but by Necessity, and we may say, tho' he was no forced Man, he could not well avoid that Life he fell into.

When he was grown a lusty Lad he would see the World, and go seek his Fortune, as the Term is among the Country Youths, who think fit to withdraw themselves from the Subjection of their

Parents; with this Whim in his Head he got to *Chester,* where he was received, and sailed on board a Coaster, till he had made himself acquainted with the Rigging, learned to knot, splice, and do the other Parts of a common Sailor's Duty; then coming to *London,* he shipp'd himself on board the *Mary India* Man, bound for *Bengal* and *Maderas,* which Voyage he performed outward, and it was not his Fault that he did not come home in the same Ship; for, in her Return, falling short of Water, they steer'd for the Island of *Madagascar,* and fell in with the East Side, in the Lat. of 20, or thereabouts. The Captain mann'd and sent ashore the Long-Boat to seek for Water, but a large Surf running, she came to an Anchor, at some little Distance from Shore, and *David Williams* with another, being both good Swimmers, stripp'd and swam off in Search of Water: While they were ashore, the Wind which blew full upon the Island and freshning, the Surf ran too high for them to get off; and the Long-Boat, after waiting some time, seeing no Possibility of getting these Men on board, weigh'd and stood for the Ship, which filled her Sails and stood for St. *Augustine*'s Bay, where she watered and proceeded on her Voyage.

Thus our poor *Welshman* and his Companion were left destitute on an Island altogether unknown to them, without Cloaths or Subsistance, but what the Fruits of the Trees offer'd. They rambled some little Time along the Coast, and were met with by the Natives, and by them carried up into the Country, where they were humanly treated, and provided with all the Necessaries of Life, tho' this was not sufficient to expel his Consort's Melancholy, who took his being left behind so much to Heart, that he sicken'd and died in a very little Time.

Some time after, the Prince of the Country, who entertained *Williams,* had a Quarrel with a neighbouring King, which broke into a War. *Williams* took the Field with his Patron, but the Enemy being superior in Number, got the Victory, and took a great many Prisoners, among whom was the unfortunate *Welshman:* The King, whose Prisoner he was, treated him very kindly; and being Master of an old Musket, gave it him, saying, 'such Arms were better in the Hands of a white Man than in those of any of his Subjects, who were not so much used to them; that he should be his Friend and Companion, and should fare as well as himself, if he would assist him in his Wars.

It will not be amiss here to take Notice, that this Island, on the East Side, is divided into a great Number of Principalities or Kingdoms, which are almost in continual War one with another; the Grounds of which are very trivial, for they will pick a Quarrel with a Neighbour, especially, if he has a Number of Cattle (in which, and Slaves, consist their Riches) on the slightest Occasion, that they may have an Opportunity of Plunder; and when a Battle or two is lost, the conquer'd makes his Peace, by delivering up such a certain Number of Bullocks and Slaves as shall be demanded by the victorious Prince. On the West Side the Island, the Principalities are mostly reduced under one Prince, who resides near *Methelage,* and who is, as we have said in the Lives of other pyrates, a great Friend to white Men; for his Father, who founded his Empire by the Assistance of the *Europeans,* left it in Charge with his Son, to assist them with what Necessaries they should require, and do them all friendly Offices; but if he disobeyed this Command, and should ever fall out with the white Men, or spill any of their Blood, he threaten'd to come again, turn him out of his Kingdom, and give it to his younger Brother. These Menaces had a very great Effect upon him, for he firmly believed his Father would, on his Disobedience, put them in Execution; for there is not on Earth, a Race of Men equally superstitious.

But to return to *Williams,* he lived with this Prince in great Tranquility, and was very much esteem'd by him (for Necessity taught him Complaisance) after some time, his new Patron was informed, that his vanquish'd Enemy had form'd a grand Alliance, in order to make War upon him; wherefore, he resolved to begin, and march into the Countries of the Allies, and ravage the nearest before they could join their Forces. He rais'd an Army, and accordingly march'd Southward; at the News of his Approach, the Inhabitants abandoned all the small Towns, and sending Messengers to their Friends, rais'd a considerable Body to oppose him, suffering him to over-run a great Deal of Ground without Molestation. At length being reinforced, they took their Opportunity, and setting upon him when his Men were fatigued, and his Army incumber'd with Booty, they gained a signal Victory; the King had the good Luck to get off, but *Williams* was a second Time taken Prisoner.

He was carried before the Conqueror, who, (having been an Eye-witness of his Bravery, for *Williams* kill'd a Number of his Enemies with his Shot, and behav'd very well, defending himself with the Butt End of his Musket for some Time, when he was surrounded) reach'd him his Hand, and told him, he made War with his Enemies only, that he did not esteem the white Men such, but should be glad of their Friendship.

Here *Williams* was used with more Respect than he had been even by his last Patron, and lived with this Prince some Years; but a War breaking out, he was routed in a set Battle, in which *Williams* was his Companion; in the Pursuit the poor *Welshman* finding he could not get off, clappd his Musket at the Foot of a Tree, and climbing up, he capitulated: He was now terribly afraid of being cut to Pieces, for he had shot and wounded a great Number of the Enemy; they, however, promis'd him good Quarter, and kept their Word.

The King of *Maratan,* who took him, used him as well as any of the former had done; and carried him always with him to the Wars, in which Fortune was more propitious, for the Parties *Williams* commanded had constantly the better of their Enemies, and never returned but with great Booties of Cattle and Slaves, for all the Prisoners they take are so, till redeem'd; tho' these Prisoners are, for the most part, Women and Children, they seldom giving Quarter to any other.

The Fame of his Bravery and Success, spread it self round the Country; and his Name alone was so terrible, that the giving out he was at the Head of any Party, was giving the Enemies an Overthrow without a Battle.

This reaching the Ears of *Dempaino,* a mighty Prince who lived 200 Miles from him, and who had several Petty Princes Tributaries, he sent an Embassador to demand the white Man; but his Patron, who had no Mind to part with him, denied that he had any white Man with him, that he who was called so was a Native of the Country. For the Readers better understanding this Passage, I must inform him, that there is a Race of what they call white Men, who have been settled on *Madagascar,* Time out of Mind, and are descended from the *Arabs;* but mixing with the Negroes, have propagated a Race of Molattoes, who differ in nothing from the Manner of living of the Black Natives.

To proceed, the Embassador desired to see this Man, and *Williams* coming to him, being extremely tann'd, he had pass'd for what he was reported, had he been before apprized of what had been said, to have answered accordingly, for he spoke the Language perfectly; or had the Embassador not examined him; who, after he had some Time viewed him, ask'd of what Country he was, and whether it was true that he was one of *Madagascar? Williams* answered, he was an *Englishman,* and was left in the Country, relating the Particulars, as I have already set them down, adding, he had been five Years in the Island.

The Embassador then told the King, that he must send the white Man with him, for such were the Orders of his Master the great *Dempaino,* who was Lord over most of the Kings on the Side the Country where he resided; and that it would be dangerous for him to disobey the Commands of so great a Monarch.

The King answered, those who were subject to *Dempaino* ought to obey his Commands, but for him, he knew no Man greater than himself, therefore should receive Laws from none; and with this Answer dismiss'd the Ambassador; who, at his Return, reported to his Master the very Words, adding, they were delivered in a haughty Strain. *Dempaino,* who was not used to have his Commands disputed, order'd one of his Generals to march with 6000 Men, and demand the white Man, and in Case of Refusal, to denounce War, that he should send him back an Express of it, and he would follow in Person with an Army to enforce a Compliance.

These Orders were put in Execution with the greatest Dispatch and Secrecy; so that the Town was invested, before any Advice was given of the Approach of an Enemy. The General told the King, it was in his Choice to have Peace or War with his Master, since it depended on the Delivery of the white Man.

The King thus surpriz'd, was obliged, however contrary to his Inclinations, to give *Williams* up to the General, who return'd with him to *Dempaino,* without committing any Hostilities; tho' he threatned to besiege the Town, and put all but the Women and Children to the Sword, if the King of *Maratan* did not pay the Expence of his Master's sending for the white Man, which he rated at 100 Slaves, and 500 Head of Cattle, the King objected to this as a hard Condition and an unjust Imposition, but was obliged to acquiesce in it.

One Thing, remarkable enough, had like to have slipp'd me; which is, the King of *Maratan* sent *Williams* to the General without any Attendance, which made him ask, if the white Man was a Slave? The King answered, he had not used him like one. I may very well, said the General, be of a contrary Opinion, since you have sent no Body to wait upon him: Upon which Reprimand, the King sent *Williams* a Present of a Slave.

He was received by *Dempaino* with a great many Caresses, was handsomely cloathed according to the Country Manner, had Slaves allotted to wait on him, and every Thing that was necessary and convenient; so that King *Dempaino* was at the Trouble of sending 6000 Men, one would think, for no other End than to show the great Value and Esteem he had for the *Europeans.* He continued with this Prince till the Arrival of a Ship, which was some Years after his leaving *Maratan;* when the *Bedford* Galley, a Pyrate, commanded by *Achen Jones,* a *Welshman,* came on the Coast, on board of which Ship *Williams* was permitted to enter; they went to *Augustine,* where, laying the Ship on Shore, by Carelesness they broke her Back, and lost her. The Crew lived here till the Arrival of the *Pelican,* another Pyrate, mentioned in *North*'s Life; some of them went on board this Ship, and steer'd for the *East-Indies.* *Williams* shifted out of this on board the *Mocha* Frigate, a Pyrate, commanded by Captain *Culliford,* and made a Voyage; then, returning to St. *Mary*'s, they shared the Booty they had got in the Red Seas. I shall not here mention the Particulars of this last Expedition, designing to write Captain *Culliford*'s Life, which it more properly belongs to.

Some of the Crew, being *West Indians,* having an Opportunity, returned home; but *Williams* remain'd here till the Arrival and taking of Capt. *Forgette,* which has been already mentioned: He was one of those who took the *Speaker,* (the Manner has been told before, in another Life) went a Voyage in her, and returned to *Maratan,* as is said in *North*'s Life. Here the King seeing him, ask'd what Present he intended to make him for former Kindness? *Williams* answered, he had been over paid by the Prince whom he took him from and by his Services, which Answer so irritated his *Maratanian* Majesty, that he ordered him to quit his Country; and he could hardly after that see him with Patience.

From hence he went on board the *Prosperous,* Captain *Howard,* Commander, who went to St. *Mary*'s, and thence to the Main, as is said in that Pyrate's Life, and was one of the Men left behind when they had a Design to carry off *Ort Van Tyle.* This *Dutchman* kept him to hard Labour, as planting Potatoes, *&c.* in revenge for the Destruction and Havock made in his Plantations by the Crew of the *Prosperous;* he was here in the Condition of a Slave six Months, at the Expiration of which Time, he had an Opportunity (and embraced it) to run away, leaving his Consort, *Tho. Collins,* behind him, who had his Arm broke when he was taken by the *Dutchman.*

Having made his Escape from a rigid, revengeful Master, he got to a Black Prince, named *Rebaiharang,* with whom he lived half a Year; he from hence went and kept Company with one *John Pro,* another *Dutchman,* who had a small Settlement on Shore, till the Arrival of the Men of War, commanded by Commodore *Richards,* who took both *Pro* and his Guest *Williams,* put them in Irons (on board the *Severn*) till they came to *Johanna,* where the Captain of the *Severn* undertook for 2000 Dollars to go against the *Mohilians,* in which Expedition several of the Man of War's Crew were killed, and the two pyrates made their Escape in a small Canoe to *Mohila,* where they shelter'd themselves a while in the Woods, out of which they got Provisions, and made over for *Johanna;* here they recruited themselves and went away for Mayotta an Island 18 Leagues in Length. The King of this Island built them a Boat, and giving them Provisions and what Necessaries they required, they made for and arrived at *Madagascar;* where, at *Methelage,* in the Lat. of 16, 40, or thereabouts, they join'd, as has been said, Captain *White.*

Here they lay about 3 Months, then setting Fire to their Boat, they went into *White*'s, and rounding the North End came to *Ambonavoula;* here *Williams* staid till Captain *White* brought the Ship *Hopewell,* on board of which he entered before the Mast, made a Voyage to the Red Seas, towards the End of which he was chosen Quarter-Master. At their Return they touch'd at *Mascarenas* for Provisions, where almost half the Company went ashore and took up their Habitations.

From *Mascarenas* they steer'd for *Hopewell* (by some call'd *Hopefull*) Point, on *Madagascar,* where dividing their Plunder, they settled themselves.

Twelve Months after, the *Charles* Brigantine, Captain *Halsey,* came in, as is mentioned in his Life. *Williams* went on board him and made a Voyage; at their Return they came to *Maratan,* lived ashore, and assisted the King in his War against his Brother, which being ended in the Destruction of the latter, and a Pyrate lying at *Ambonavoula,* sending his Long-Boat to *Manangcaro,* within ten Leagues of *Maratan, Williams* and the rest went on board, and in three Months after he had been at *Ambonavoula* he was chosen Captain of the *Scotch* Ship, mentioned in *Halsey*'s Life.

This Ship he work'd upon with great Earnestness, and made the *Scots* Prisoners labour hard at the fitting her up for a Voyage; and she was near ready for the Seas when a Hurricane forced her ashore, and she was wreck'd.

Some Time after this he set up and finished a Sloop, in which he and ten of his Men, design'd for *Mascarenas,* but missing the Island they went round *Madagascar,* to a Place called *Methelage,* where he laid his Vessel ashore and staid a Year; but the King being tired with his morose Temper, and he disagreeing with every Body, he was order'd to be gone, and accordingly fitting up his Vessel he put to Sea, intending to go round the North End of the Island; but the Wind being at E. S. E. and the Current setting to N. W. he put back to a Port, called the *Boyne,* within 10 Leagues of *Methelage,* in the same King's Dominions whom he had left. The Governor of this Place was descended from the *Arabs,* and it was here that the *Arabians* traded.

When he came to an Anchor, he and three of his Men (he had but 5 with him) went on Shore, paddled by two Negroes. *David Eaton* and *William Damson* two of the Men, required a Guide, to show them the Way to the King's Town; the Governor order'd them one, and, at the same time, laid an Ambush for them in the Road, and caused them to be murdered. When they had left the *Boyn, Williams* and *Meyeurs,* a *Frenchman,* who also came ashore in the Canoe, went to buy some *Samsams,* which are agate Beads; as they were looking over these Goods, a Number of the Governor's Men came about them, seiz'd them both, and immediately dispatch'd *Meyeurs, Williams* they bound, and tortur'd almost a whole Day, by throwing hot Ashes on his Head and in his Face, and putting little Boys to beat him with Sticks; he offer'd the Governor 2000

Dollars for his Life, but he answer'd, he'd have both that and the Money too; and accordingly when he was near expiring, they made an End of him with their Lances.

After this barbarous Murder, the Governor thought of seizing the Sloop, on board of which were no more than two white Men, six Negroe Boys, and some Women Slaves of the same Colour; however, he thought it best to proceed by Stratagem, and therefore putting a Goat and some Calabashes of Toke on board *William*'s Canoe, with twelve Negroes arm'd, and the Sloop Negroes to paddle, he sent to surprize her. When the Canoe came pretty near the Vessel, they hal'd, and ask'd if they would let them come aboard? One of the Men ask'd *William*'s Negroes where the Captain was? He answered, drinking Toke with the Governor, and sent them Provision and Toke. A Negroe Wench advised the white Man, whose Name was *William Noakes,* not to let them come on board, for as four white Men went ashore, and none of them appear'd, she suspected some Treachery; however, on the Answer made him from the Canoe, he resolved to admit them, and giving the Wench a Kick, cryed, *D — m ye, must we have no fresh Provisions for your Whimsies;* he called them on board, and no sooner were they on Deck but one of them snatching *Noakes* his Pistol, shot him thro' the Head, and seizing the other white Man, threw him over-board and drown'd him; after which, being Masters of the Vessel, they carried her in and rifled her.

The King was at this Time a hunting, as is his Custom to hunt Boars three Months in the Year; but the Account of these Murders soon reach'd him, however, he staid the accustom'd Time of his Diversion; but when he returned home, and the whites, who were about him, demanded Justice, he bid them be quiet, they might depend upon his doing it: He sent to the Governor of *Boyn,* and told him, he was glad that he had cut off *Williams* and his Crew, an Example he was resolved to follow and clear the Country of them all. That he had some Affairs to communicate to him, and desired he would come to Court as soon as possible, but take Care he was not seen by any of the whites, for fear by his, they shou'd revenge the Death of their Companions.

The Governor on these Orders came away immediately, and stopp'd two Miles short, at a little Town two Miles distant from the King's, and sent Word he there waited for his Commands.

The King ordered him to be with him early next Morning, before the white Men were out of their Beds: he set forward accordingly the next Day betimes, but was seiz'd on the Road by Negroes placed for that Purpose, and brought bound to the King, who, after having reproach'd him with the Barbarity of his Action, sent him to the white Men, bidding them put him to what Death they pleased; but they sent Word back, he might dispose of his Subjects Lives as he thought fit, but for their Part they would never draw a Drop of Blood of any who belonged to him. Upon which Answer the King's Uncle ordered him to be speared, and he was accordingly thrust thro' the Body with Lances. The King, after this Execution, sent to *Boyn,* and had every Thing brought which had belonged to *Williams* and his Men, and divided it among the whites, saying, *He was sorry the Villain had but one Life to make Attonement for the Barbarity he had been guilty of.*

Chap. XXXIV
Of Capt. Samuel Burgess, And his Crew

Capt. *Samuel Burgess* was born in *New-York,* and had a good Education; he was what they call a well-set Man, and bandy legg'd; he sail'd some Time as a Privateer in the *West-Indies,* and very often, the Gang, he was with, when the Time of their cruizing was expir'd, would make no Ceremony of prolonging the Commission by their own Authority.

By his Privateering he got together some little Money, and returned home, where the Government having no Notice, or, at least, taking none, of his piratical Practice, in staying beyond the Date of his Commission: He went out Mate of a Ship, in the Service of *Frederick Phillips,* bound to the Island of *Madagascar,* to trade with the pyrates, where they had the Misfortune to lose their Ship, and lived eighteen Months at *Augustine,* when an *English*Pyrate coming in, the King of the Country obliged him to go on board her, tho' much against his Inclination, for he was tired of a roving Life; but their Choice was to go or starve, for the King would keep them no longer.

He went with this free Booter to the *East Indies,* where they made several rich Prizes; returned to St. *Mary*'s, where they took in Provisions, Wood, and Water. Several of their Gang knock'd off here; but the Captain, *Burgess,* and the Remainder, went away for the *West Indies,* disposed of their Plunder on the *Spanish* Coast, and then returning to *New York,* purposely knocked the Ship on the Head at *Sandy Hook,* after they had secur'd their Money ashore.

The Government not being inform'd of their Pyracy, they lived here without Molestation, and, in a short Time, *Burgess* married a Relation of Mr. *Phillip*'s, who built a Ship, called the *Pembroke,* and sent him a second Time to *Madagascar.* In his Way to this Island, he went into the River of *Dilagou* on the *African* Coast, where he took in a Quantity of Elephants Teeth; and thence to *Augustine,* where he met with several of his old Ship Mates, with whom he traded for Money and Slaves. Leaving this Place he went to *Methelage,* where he also took some Money and Negroes; and from thence he shaped his Course for St. *Mary*'s, on the East Side, where he also drove a considerable Trade with his old Comrades, took several of them Passengers, who paid very generously for their Passage; and taking with him an Account of what was proper to bring in another Trip, he return'd to *New York,* without any sinister Accident: This Voyage clear'd 5,000 l. Ship and Charges paid.

His Owner encouraged by this Success, bid him chuse what Cargoe he pleas'd, and set out again; accordingly he laded with Wine, Beer, *&c.* and returning to *Madagascar* arrived at *Maratan* on the East Side, where he disposed of a great Part of his Cargoe at his own Rates. At *Methelage* he disposed of the rest, and return'd, clearing for himself and Owner 10,000 l. besides 300 Slaves he brought to *New York.*

After a short Stay at home, he set out again on the old Voyage, fell in first with *Methelage,* where he victualled and traded; from thence he went round the South End, touch'd and sold Part of his Cargoe at a large Profit, to his old Acquaintance. He made a trading Voyage round the Island, and at St. *Mary*'s met another Ship belonging to his Owner, which had Order to follow his Directions; he stay'd at this Port till he had disposed of the Cargoe of both Ships; he then shaped his Course homewards, with about 20 pyrates Passengers, who had accepted the Pardon brought by Commadore *Littleton.*

In his Way he touch'd at the *Cape* of *Good Hope,* for Wood, Water, and fresh Provision: While he was here, the *Loyal Cook,* an *East India* Man came in, who made Prize of *Burgess,* and carried him to the *East Indies;* he there would have delivered *Burgess*'s Ship to the Governor of *Maderass,* but the Governor would have no Hand in the Affair, and told the Captain, he must answer to the *East-India* Company and *Burgess*'s Owner for what he had done.

Most of the Pyrate's Passengers thought themselves clear'd by the Act of Grace; but some of them, not willing to trust to it, got off with what Gold they could, in a *Dutch* Boat; they who trusted to the Pardon were clapp'd in Goal, and died in their Irons. I cannot omit the Simplicity of one of them, who had, however, the Wit to get off: When he designed to go away, he look'd for his Comrade for the Key of his Chest, to take his Gold with him, which amounted to Seventeen hundred Pounds; but this Comrade being ashore, he would not break open Chest, for it was Pity, he said, to spoil a good new Lock, so left his Money for the Captain of the *East-India* Man.

The News of this Capture came to the Owner before the Ship return'd, and he sued the Company; but, at their Request, staid for the Arrival of the *Loyal Cook,* which brought *Burgess* Prisoner to *England* soon after. The Captain finding himself in an Error, and that what he had done could not be justified, absconded; the Company made good the Ship and Cargo to the Owner. *Burgess* was set at Liberty, continued some Time in *London,* was impeach'd, and Pyracy sworn against him by *Culliford* (mentioned in *Williams*'s Life) who notwithstanding, he came home on the Act of Grace, was clapp'd into *Newgate,* tried and acquitted, tho' he was beggar'd.

Burgess's Owner stickled very hard for him, and expended great Sums of Money to save him; however, tho' he pleaded the Necessity of his going on board the Pyrate, (as his Life shows it) he was tried and condemn'd; but by the Intercession of the Bishops of *London* and *Canterbury,* was pardon'd by the Queen.

After this, he made a broken Voyage to the *South Sea,* Lieutenant to a Privateer, and returning to *London,* was out of Business a whole Year.

He then shipp'd himself Mate on board the *Hannah,* afterwards called the *Neptune,* and went to *Scotland* to take in her Cargo, the Owner being of that Nation; but before she got thither he the Owner broke, and the Ship was stopp'd, and lay 18 Months before she was dispos'd of: But being set to Sale, and six *Scotch* Gentlemen buying her, the old Officers were continued, and she proceeded on her first designed Voyage to *Madagascar,* in which the Captain and *Burgess* quarrelling, was the Loss of the Ship; for the latter, who was acquainted with the pyrates, when they arrived at *Madagascar,* spirited them up to surprize her: The Manner how, being already set down in *Halsey*'s Life, I need not repeat.

I shall only take Notice, that Captain *Miller* being decoy'd ashore, under Pretence of being shew'd some Trees, fit for Masting, *Halsey* invited him to a Surloin of Beef, and a Bowl of Arrack Punch; he accepted the Invitation, with about 20 of the pyrates. One *Emmy,* who had been a Waterman on the *Thames,* did not come to Table, but sat by, mustled up in a great Coat, pretending he was attack'd by the Ague, tho' he had put it on to conceal his Pistols only. After Dinner, when *Halsey* went out, as for something to entertain his Guests, (*Miller* and his Supercargo,) *Emmy* clapp'd a Pistol to the Captain's Breast, and told him, he was his Prisoner; at the same Instant, two other pyrates enter'd the Room, with each a Blunderbuss in his Hand, and told the Captain and his Supercargoe, that no Harm should come to either, if they did not bring it upon themselves by an useless Resistance. While this past within Doors, the Wood being lined with pyrates, all *Miller*'s Men, whom he had brought ashore to fell Timber, were secur'd, but none hurt, and all civilly treated. When they had afterwards got Possession of the Ship, in the Manner mention'd before, they set all their Prisoners at Liberty.

Miller, with eleven of his Men, was sent off, as is said in *Halsey*'s Life: The Company chose *Burgess* Quarter-Master, and shar'd the Booty they had made out of the *Scotch* Ship, and the *Greyhound.*

Soon after happen'd *Halsey*'s Death, who left *Burgess* Executor in Trust for his Widow and Children, with a considerable Legacy for himself, and the other pyrates grumbling at a new Comer's being preferr'd to all of them, took from *Burgess* 3,000 l. of *Halsey*'s Money, and 1200 l. of his own, which was his Share of the two Prizes. Tho' he had been treated in this Manner, they were idle enough to give him the Command of the *Scots* Ship, and order'd him to fit her out with all Expedition, and to take on board some Men and Goods left in the Brigantine: He set to work on the Ship, with full Design to run away with her; but some pyrates, who were in another Part of the Island, being informed of these Proceedings, thought it not prudent to trust him, so he left the Ship, and getting among his old Comrades, by their Interposition, had all his Money return'd.

After this he lived five Months on the Island of St. *Mary*'s, where his House was, by Accident, burnt down, out of which he saved nothing but his Money; he then went on board *David Williams,* when he miss'd the Island of *Mascarenas,* and returned to *Methelage,* where he staid with the King, and was one of the Men among whom he divided *William*'s Effects.

From *Methelage* he went with a Parcel of Samsams to *Augustine,* with which he bought fifty Slaves, whom he sold to the *Arabians.* In his Return to *Methelage,* he met Captain *North* in a Sloop, with thirty of *Miller*'s Men on board; these Men propos'd the taking *Burgess,* who had, they said, betrayed, ruined, and banished them their Country, by forcing them to turn pyrates; but *North* would not consent: Upon which, they confined him, took *North* and stripp'd him of all the

Money, and then releasing their Captain, gave him 300 l. as his Share, which he returned to *Burgess* on his Arrival at *Methelage.*

Burgess lived here two or three Years, till he was carried off by some *Dutchmen;* they belonged to an *East-India* Man, and were taken by two *French* Ships, which being bound for *Mocha,* and scarce of Provisions, came into *Methelage* to victual, where they set 80 of their Prisoners ashore. When they parted from this Port they sail'd for *Johanna,* where they left the *Dutch* Officers, who built a Ship, and came back for their Men. *Burgess* being of great Use to them, they took him on board, and steer'd for a Port, where some *Dutch,* taken in another Ship, were maroon'd; but they were wreck'd at *Youngoul,* where *Burgess* continued eighteen Months. After this Time was expir'd, he was desirous of leaving the Place, and addressing himself to the King, who was Uncle to the King of *Methelage,* he requested his black Majesty to send him back to that Port, which he readily complied with, where *Burgess* continued almost five Years, afflicted with Sickness, in which he lost one Eye. While he was here, the *Drake* Pink, of *London,* came in for Slaves, he took *Burgess,* with Design to carry him home; but Captain *Harvey* in the *Henry,* which belong'd to the same Owners, arriving, and being a Stranger to the Trade, at the Request of Captain *Maggot,* Commander of the *Drake,* and on Promise of a Ship when in the *West Indies,* he enter'd as third Mate, and continued with him. Captain *Harvey* carrying it pretty high, and disagreeing with the King, lay here 9 Months before he could slave. *Burgess* was sent up to tell the King he had not fulfil'd his Agreement with Captain *Harvey;* the King resented the being reproach'd by a Man whom he had entertained so many Years, and reviled him; he was, however, carried to Dinner with some of the principal Blacks, and drank very plentifully with them of Honey Toke, in which it is supposed he was poison'd, for he fell ill and died soon after, leaving what he had to the Care of the chief Mate, for the Use of his Wife and Children.

Appendix

I. Of Capt. Nathaniel North, And his Crew

We have placed this Life in the Appendix, which will not perhaps be thought a proper Place; but we could not gather the Particulars, which were collected out of several different Journals, Time enough to insert it in the Body of the Book, and therefore, thought of reserving this Life for Part of another Volume; but when we had compiled it, and found it was a Sort of Recapitulation of the Adventures of the *Madagascar* pyrates which went before, we judged it more proper to give it in the Appendix than to separate this Gentleman from his Companions; and we were the rather induc'd to this, as the Reader will here find an Account of *Bowen*'s Death, which we had not learn'd at the Time we wrote his Life; the Papers which we got after a long Search, and which has furnish'd us with some other Particulars of that Rover's Life, not being at that Time to be found.

Captain *North* was born at *Bermudas,* and was the Son of a Sawyer, which Business he himself was bred up to, but took, at last, to the Seas, at the Age of 17 or 18, shipping himself Cook on board a Sloop, built at *Bermudas,* for some Gentlemen of *Barbadoes,* with Design to fit her out for a Privateer. She was bound to her Owners, but the Master took *Santa Udas* in the Way, and loaded with Salt. When they came to *Barbadoes* all the Crew was press'd, and *North* with his Companions were put on board the *Reserve.*

The Master applied himself to the Governor, and got all his Men clear'd, *North* excepted, who, as he was a Lad, was neglected, and left on board the Man of War, which soon after sail'd for *Jamaica;* some Time before the *Reserve* was relieved from this Station, he laid Hold of an Opportunity to run away, and shipp'd himself on board a Sugar Drover, in which Way of Life he continued about two Years, and being an able Sailor, tho' no Artist, he was offer'd to go Master of one of these Coasters, which he refus'd, and went on board a Privateer.

The first Voyage he made, as a Privateer, they took a couple of good Prizes, which made every Man's Share very considerable; but *North,* as he had got his Money lightly, so he spent it, making the Companions of his Dangers the Companions of his Diversions, or rather joining himself with them, and following their Example; which all (who are acquainted with the Way of Life of a successful *Jamaica* Privateer) know is not an Example of the greatest Sobriety and Oeconomy.

His Money being all spent, he took the same Method for a Recruit, that is, he went a second Time a Privateering, and met with such Success, that he engag'd very heartily in this Course of Life, and made several lucky Cruizes.

Some Time after he grew tir'd, thought of trading, and shipp'd himself on board a Brigantine, bound for the *Spanish* Coast, commanded by one Captain *Reesby:* This Vessel went both on the Trading and Privateer Account, so that the Men shipp'd for half Wages, and equal Shares of what Prizes they should make, in the same Manner, as to the Shares, as on board a Privateer; their trading answer'd very poorly, and their privateering Business still worse, for they return'd without making any Prize.

They were forced to leave the *Spanish* Coast, on Account of a *Spanish Guarda la Costa,* of 40 Guns and Three hundred and fifty *Frenchmen,* commanded by a Captain of the same Nation. When they made the Island of *Jamaica,* they fell in with *Bluefields,* off which Place two *French* Privateer Sloops were cruizing, one of which was formerly a Privateer of *Jamaica,* called the *Paradox;* they immediately clapp'd Capt. *Reesby* on board, taking him for a Trader, come from the *Spanish* Coast, and weakly mann'd; however, they were soon made sensible of the Mistake, for they came to fetch Wool, and one of them went away shorn; I mean *Reesby* took one of them, and the other was obliged to a good Pair of Heels for his Safety. *Reesby* lost ten Men, killed outright in the Engagement, and had seven wounded; the latter, tho' he had made but a broken Voyage, he put ashore at *Bluefields,* and ordered great Care to be taken of them, at the Owners Expence: Here he took in fresh Provision, and then beat up to *Port Royal,* where *Reesby* paid them very honourably, gave them a handsome Entertainment, and begg'd they would not leave him, as he had a very great Value for them all; but for *North* particularly, who was a good Swimmer, manag'd a Canoe, with great Dexterity, and fear'd nothing.

Upon this Desire of the Captain's, *North* and the greater Part staid ashore till Captain *Reesby* was refitted, and went a second Voyage with him to the Coast, at seventeen Dollars a Month, and no Share; they carried 300 Negroes, beside Bale Goods; they staid four Months on the Coast, and dispos'd of all the Slaves and Goods to great Advantage. Upon their Return to *Jamaica,* after some Stay on the Island, Captain *Reesby* not going out again, *North* went once more a Privateering, and made a considerable Booty. While *North* was ashore after a Cruize, he was press'd on board the *Mary* Man of War: He made a Cruize in her to the *Spanish* Coast, and return'd to *Jamaica;* but hearing the *Mary* was soon to go to *England,* he, and three more, resolv'd to swim ashore from the Keys, where the Men of War lie, but he was taken as he was going off the Head, and whipp'd; he, however, found Means to make his Escape, before the Ship left the Island, and went on board the *Neptune* Sloop, a Privateer, commanded by Captain *Lycence,* then Lieutenant of the *Reserve,* who, while the Ship was in the Carpenter's Hands, got a Commission of the Governor to take a Cruize. Captain *Moses,* who commanded the *Reserve,* went on board their Sloop, under the Command of his Lieutenant, for Diversion only: They cruized off *Hispaniola,* where they met with a *French* Letter of Mart Merchant Man, of 18 Guns, and 118 Men, who had the Day before engaged the *Swan* Man of War, and shook her off.

The *Neptune* attack'd her, and Captain *Moses* was wounded one of the first, and carried down; *Lycense* order'd to board, but the Quarter-Master, who steer'd, mistook the Helm, the Sloop fell off, and the *French* pouring in a Volley of small Shot, Captain *Lycence* was kill'd, which being told to *Moses,* as the Surgeon dress'd him, he order'd *North* to the Helm, bid them not be discouraged, and he would be upon Deck immediately. Accordingly he came up as soon as dress'd, laid the Ship on board, where they made a very obstinate

Resistance; but the *French* Captain being kill'd, who received eleven Shot before he dropp'd, they, at length, became Masters.

The Privateer lost ten Men, and twenty were wounded: The *French* had fifty Men killed and wounded, among whom was the Captain, who had received two Shot, as he was going down to the Surgeon to get his Blood staunch'd, and came upon Deck just as he was boarded, where, encouraging his Men, he was distinguished and aimed at.

When they had brought the Prize into *Jamaica,* as she was an *English* Bottom, built at *Bristol,* and called the *Crown,* the former Owners sued to have half the Ship and Cargo, and recovered one third.

North went again a Privateering, Captain *Moses* his Ship being not fitted, he would take a second Cruize, and *North* with him. Some Time after their Return, Captain *Moses* being a cruizing in the *Reserve, North,* who was ashore, was press'd on board the *Assistance* Man of War; and on the *Reserve*'s coming, being recommended by Captain *Moses* to his own Captain, he was handsomely treated, and made one of the Barge's Crew: He was very easy till the *Assistance* was order'd to *England,* and then, as he was apprehensive of going into a cold Climate, he took his Leave of the Man of War, and said nothing. He then went on board a Privateer again, and made several Prizes, two of which were *English* Bottoms, and sued for by former Owners; *North* thinking it hard to venture his Life, and have Part of his Prize Money taken away, and the Press being hot in *Jamaica,* he resolved to sail no more with the *English;* but went to *Curasoe* into the *Dutch* Service, and sail'd with a *Spanish* Trader to the Coast of *New Spain* several Voyages. In the last he made, they were chased ashore by a couple of *French* Sloops, one of which was commanded by a *Dutchman,* named *Lawrence,* who, with his Comrade, took Possession of their Vessel, and rifled her; the Crew of the Prize called to them, and asked, if they would give them good Quarters? which they promis'd; took them all on board, and used 'em very handsomely.

The *French* gave the Prisoners a small Sloop they took a while after, and they returned to *Curaso.*

He having now forgot his Resentment, he return'd to *Jamaica,* and went on board and cruiz'd in a *Spanish Barca Longa,* of 10 Guns, commanded by Captain *Lovering,* born at *Jamaica;* they cruiz'd three Months in the *West Indies,* and making but a small Hand of it, they put for *Newfoundland,* to try their Fortune on the Banks: Here they met a Man of War, who renew'd their Commission for six Months longer. The first Prize they made was a *French* Ketch, with a *Spanish* Pass, and would have pass'd for a *Spaniard,* but by strict Search, and threatning of the Men, they discovered her to be what she really was, tho' she had, as a *Spaniard,* slipp'd thro' the Fingers of a Man of War before.

They carried their Prize into Harbour, went again upon the Cruize, met with a *French* Letter of Mart Merchant Man, a *Bristol* built Ship, called the *Pelican,* of 18 Guns, and Seventy five Men, half laden with Fish: This Ship stood them a long Argument; they clapp'd her on board, and two of their Men enter'd, but missing lashing, the *Barca Longa* fell a-stern, and the two Men were made Prisoners; however, they came up with her again, clapp'd her on board a second Time, and carried her into the same Port where they had left the Ketch.

They after this put to Sea again, and being discovered by the *French* Settlement ashore, they went into St. *Mary's* Bay, where they fell in with a large *French* Fly-Boat, of 800 Tons, eighty Men, and 18 Guns, and laden with Fish: They chased and came up with her, under *French* Colours; when they were pretty near the *Frenchman* they haled, and ask'd, whence they came? a *Guernsey* Man, at the Bowsprit End, answer'd, from *Petit Guavers;* that they had been cruizing on the Banks, and were going into the Bay for Refreshment. The *Frenchman* bid them come no nearer, but send their Boat on board; they keeping on the Chase he fired at them, they did not mind this, but run up a long Side and boarded him; the *French* ran to their close Quarters, and disputed the Ship three Quarters of an Hour, when they all call'd for Quarters except one Man, who wou'd take none, but ran like a Madman into the Thick of the *English,* and wounded several, tho' he was soon dispatch'd by their Pistols.

They carried this Prize to join the others, and turning all the Prisoners ashore, except what were necessary to condemn their Prizes; they stood, with a Fleet of four Sail, for *Rhode Island.*

Here they condemn'd the Fly-Boat and Ketch, but found a great Difficulty in getting the *Pelican* condemn'd, the *English* Owners putting in their Claim; but, at length, a *Scotch* Lawyer did their Business, upon leaving 300 l. in his Hands to bear the Charge of any future Suit. Captain *Lovering* dying here, the Ship's Company bought the *Pelican,* broke up the *Barca Longa,* sent her Owners their Shares, and got a Commission for the Master to cruize Southward as far as the Line, and to be valid for eighteen Months certain, two Years allowing for Accidents.

They fitted this Ship for a long Voyage, out of the Joint Stock of the Company; but Iron Hoops being scarce in *New England,* they were obliged to take Casks hoop'd with Wood, which I mention, because it proved the Ruin of their Voyage to the *East Indies* for a whole Year.

They being fitted for the Sea, they set Sail and steer'd for the *Cape* of *Good Hope,* which they doubled in the Month of *June,* made the best of their Way to *Madagascar,* and went into *Augustine* Bay, where they victualled and watered, but before this was done it was *August,* which was too late to go to the *East-Indies;* which they propos'd to do with Design, to cruize on the *Moors,* not intending to Pyrate among the *Europeans,* but honestly and quietly to rob what *Moors* fell in their Way, and return home with clean Consciences, and clean, but full Hands, within the limited Time of their Commission.

From *Augustine* they went to *Johanna,* and the Provisions they had salted up at *Madagascar* not being well done, it began to spoil; this and their Cloaths wanting Repair, made them desperately resolve to take the King of *Johanna* and make him ransome himself, but the Master wou'd not take Charge of the Ship, being unacquainted with the Coast: They cruiz'd among the Islands, landed at *Comaro,* and took the Town, but found no Booty, excepting some Silver Chains, and check'd Linnen. From hence they went to *Mayotta,* where they took in a *Frenchman* who had been morooned there, and maintain'd by the King; they consulted with him about the surprizing and taking his Town. The *Frenchman* was averse to it, as he owed him the Obligation of being preserved; however, he was in their Hands, and must do as they would have him: They surrounded the King's House after they had been three Days in his Town, and took him and all the Inhabitants; but the King's Son made his Way thro' the thickest of them with his Cutlash, tho' he was shot afterward. The Pretence they made use of for this inhospitable Manner, was, that the King had poison'd the Crew of a Ship, which was their Consort; he denied it, as well he might, for they themselves never heard of a Ship of the Name they gave this fictitious one. The King they carried on board, the other Prisoners they put into a Sort of a Temple, with a Guard over them of 36 Men.

The Alarm being given in the Country, the Natives came down in a Body of some Thousands, and attack'd the Guard; but the Ship hearing the Fire, and seeing the Hills covered with Blacks, discharged several great Guns, loaded with Patridge, which making a very great Slaughter, obliged them to retire.

The King ransom'd himself for some Silver Chains to the Value of a thousand Dollars, and for what Provision they demanded; and at the setting him ashore, swore Allegiance to them as Masters of the Country, and took an Oath besides, never to poison any more white Men.

After this notable Expedition, they staid here a Fortnight, tho' always on their Guard, and then went back for *Augustine* with about 20 Slaves, they carried away with them for Servants.

Here a Sickness coming among them, they built Huts ashore; they lost, notwithstanding all their Care and Precaution, their Captain and thirty Men, by the Distemper which they contracted; but it abating, they thought of going to Sea again, but on examining their Water Casks, they found the Hoops all worm eaten and rotten, so that there was no Proceeding, but this Defect was repaired by their Cooper, who was an ingenious Fellow; he went into the Woods with the *Mayotta* Slaves, and with Withies and other Stuff he gathered, fitted them up, and made them tight, in acknowledging of which Service, they chose him Captain, and *North* was made Quarter-Master.

At *Augustine* they pick'd up some Straglers, among whom was *David Williams,* and on a Muster, they found they had a hundred and five Men. They then made their Vessel a free Ship, that is, they agreed every Man should have an equal Share in all Prizes; and proceeded for the Mouth of the *Red Seas.*

In the Night, after they had reach'd their Station, they made two Ships, one was the *Mocha* Frigate, of 40 Guns, commanded by *Culliford:* she had been an *East India* Man, and under the Command of one Captain *Stout;* the other Ship was called the *Soldada,* a Ship of 16 Guns, the Captain's Name *Shivers;* they haled one another, and on both Sides gave the same Answers, *from the Seas,* and upon Agreement, they all lay by that Night: In the Morning they consorted, and agreed to make an equal Division of all Prizes, which any of the three should take from that Time for two Months to come.

The *Pelican* spared Wood, Water, and some of her Hands to Captain *Culliford,* and here *Williams* shifted on board him. About ten Days after, these three had join'd Company a large *Moor's* Ship, on which they afterwards mounted 70 Guns, hove in Sight.

They all gave Chase, but the small Ship came first up with the *Moor,* who exchang'd several Shot with the *Soldada* and *Pelican;* but the *Soldada* clapp'd her on board, and before the *Pelican* could enter a Man, the *Moors* call'd for Quarters: In boarding the *Moor,* she fired a Broadside upon the *Soldada,* but only two Shot hull'd her, and kill'd two Men, which was the only Loss they had in taking a thousand Prisoners, Passengers, and Sailors.

All the Money was carried on board the *Mocha* Frigate, and divided between her Crew and the *Soldada,* excluding without other Reason than *sic volumus,* the *Pelican* from any Share.

The Crew of the *Pelican* expostulated with them, and bid them remember they had spared both Wood and Water, or the *Mocha* could not have kept the Station; instead of any Answer, they receiv'd a Command to be gone, or they would sink them; they answering, they could not go by themselves, wanting the Water and Wood they had spared. The two Consorts gave them a thousand Dollars, and some Water out of the *Moor,* bidding them buy Wood, where they could purchase it, and so left the *Pelican* to her self, going away for the Coast of *Malabar,* where they put the Prisoners and Horses they had taken ashore, sunk the *Soldada,* and thence went to the Isle of St. *Mary's* on *Madagascar,* where the *Moor's* Ship now lies sunk. They shared out of this Prize a thousand Pounds a Man in Silver and Gold besides other Goods; and the two pyrates amounted to the Number of 350 Men.

The *Pelican* kept the same Station for some Days, when a large *Moor* Ship hove in Sight, they gave Chase, and the *Moor,* not suspecting her for an Enemy, did not endeavour to get away; when the *Pelican* came up, she fired for the *Moor* to bring to, which made him set his small Sails, tho' with the Loss of several Men; for the *Pelican* being close up, brought them down with the small Arms. When the *Moor* had, at length, hove out his small Sails, the *Pelican* could not gain upon him enough to board, tho' she was not a Pistol Shot a-stern; whenever she came upon his Lee Quarter, the *Moor* being a tall Ship, took away the Wind from the *Pelican,* and she could never get to Windward of him. She ply'd her fore Chase all this while, and drove the *Moors* from their stern Chase, but could not, as they endeavour'd to do, strike the *Moors* Rudder, or any other Way disable him. At length, by the Fear and bad Steerage of the *Moor,* the *Pelican* ran up along Side of them, but as she miss'd lashing, she was obliged to shoot a head; in the mean while the *Moor* Wore round, the *Pelican* put to Stays after him but not Staying, and they being all in Confusion, they Wore also; but in this Time the *Moor* had got the Start, and setting all the Canvas he could pack on his Ship's Back, wrong'd the *Pelican,* and got off.

The Loss of this Ship made the Crew almost distracted, and made, for some Time, a great Division among them, some cursing the Ship for a heavy Sailor, and proposing to return home, others cursing themselves, and the ill Management by which they miss'd lashing, and propos'd going to *Madagascar,* and the breaking her up, since as she was a single Bottom, she must be worm-eaten; but Time, which mollifies the greatest Rage, abated these Contentions, and put an End to the Animosities which sprung from their Disappointment.

They being cool, resolved for the *Malabar* Coast, on which they took three *Moor* Ships in a little Time; the first they discharged, after taking out 6000 Dollars; the second they took for their own Use, mounted her with 26 Guns, and called her the *Dolphin;* the third they sold on the same Coast for 18000 Dollars. Their own Ship they set adrift. From this Coast they made for *Madagascar,* and near the Island *Mascarenas* lost all their Masts in a Hurricane. They put up Jury-Masts, came to

St. *Mary*'s and new masted. Here they found Captain *Culliford,* Captain *Shivers,* and their Prize, with three Merchant Men from *America,* which were come to trade with them, one of which was the *Pembrook,* commanded by *Samuel Burges,* belonging to *Frederick Phillips,* Merchant at *New-York.* The Captain of the *Dolphin,* and some of the Men being weary of this Life, went home in these Merchant Ships, and the Crew chose one *Samuel Inless,* who lived on the Island, for their Captain; they fitted out for the *Streights* of *Malacca,* where they made several Prizes of *Moor* Ships, but of little value to them.

North on board one of the Prizes, was separated from the rest by bad Weather, and drove to great Straights for Water. The *Moor* Merchant, who was on board with him, and whom he had treated very humanely, showed him a Draught, by which he came to a small Island not far from the *Dutch* Settlement, and watered. The *Moor* told him, that he ran the Risque of his Life should it be known that he had given him a Sight of this Draught. In return for this Service, when he met with his Companions, he got the *Moor*'s Ship discharged.

They, after this, made for *Nicobar,* near *Achen,* and, in the Way, met a large *Dane* Ship, which they plunder'd, and hove down by, clean'd, and return'd to *Madagascar,* where they shar'd their Booty, which was, besides Goods, between 3 and 400 l. a Man. A Month after their Arrival three *English* Men of War appear'd in Sight, the *Anglesea,* Captain *Littleton,* the *Hastings,* Captain *White,* and the *Lizard,* Captain *Ramsey.* These Ships occasioned their hawling up the *Dolphin,* which, as they could not get her as high as they design'd, they set Fire to.

Commadore *Littleton* brought a Pardon for such of the pyrates as would accept it, and many of them, among whom were *Culliford* and *Shivers* did, and went home with Merchant Men. *North* accepted it also, but would not trust to it, finding the Time fixed for their Surrender was elapsed before the Men of War arrived.

Most of the pyrates having left the Isle of St. *Mary*'s, where the King's Ships lay, *North* thought it not safe for him to stay, and therefore putting all he had into the *Dolphin*'s Boat, he design'd to join his Comrades on the Main of *Madagascar;* but being overset by a Squawl, all the People were lost except himself, who swam four Leagues, and a Negroe Woman, whom he put on the Bottom of the Boat.

Being now on the Main, and quite naked, he frighted the Negroes he met with, as he got out of the Water, for they took him for a Sea-Devil; but one Woman, who had been used to sell Fowls at the white Mens Houses, had the Courage not to run away, and, when he came near, knew him; she gave him half her Petticoat to cover his Nakedness, and calling a Negroe Man who carried her Things, and was run into the Woods; they help'd him to perform his Journey to the Dwelling of some white Men, which was sixteen Miles from the Place where he come on Shore; a great Journey for a Man so feeble with swimming. He was kindly received and cloathed by his Comrades, whom he staid with, till he had recovered his Strength, and then he went to a black Prince of his Acquaintance, with whom he staid till the Arrival of Captain *Fourgette,* which was a full Year.

In this Vessel (which I have already said in *White*'s Life was taken) he went round the North-End to the West-Side, and came into *Methelage,* where they surprized the *Speaker;* the Manner of which Surprize is also mentioned in the same Life; and, after the Death of Captain *Booth,* was chosen Captain's Quarter-Master, by *Bowen,* who succeeded in the Voyage, and the Consequences of it are already set down, for he was in the *Speaker* till she was lost.

The next Voyage he made was in the *Speedy Return* (taken from Captain *Drummond,*) in the Capacity of Company's Quarter-Master, with Design to cruise in the *Red Seas;* but touching at the Island of *Mayotta,* they consorted with Captain *Howard,* whom they met with at the Island, as is already said. From thence they went and victualled at *Augustine,* having promised Captain *Bowen* to meet him in two Months; accordingly returning thither, and missing him, they went to *Mayotta* to enquire after him; but hearing there that he was gone a Voyage, and as the Place of Rendezvous was off the Highlands of St. *John*'s, they steered their Course thither, to join him, and lie for the *Moor*'s Fleet from *Mocoa.*

In their Passage they met with a violent Storm, in which they were near foundering, it beat in their Stern, and obliged them to throw over all their Guns (two excepted, which lay in the Hold) and forced them into the Gulf of *Persia,* where they took several small Vessels, which they ripp'd up to mend their Ship.

Being very much in want of Water, having staved all their Casks, to save themselves in the Storm, and meeting with little in the Vessels taken, they hoisted out the Canoe to chase a Fishing Vessel, that they might be inform'd where they should find Water. This Boat made from them with all their Force, but the Ship firing, the People all leap'd into the Water, some of whom were drowned, and the rest got ashoar, except one Man, whom they came up with; but as soon as they thought to lay hold on him, he dived, and kept them in play near an Hour and a half: They would not shoot him, because it did not answer their Ends; but, at length, *North,* who was in the Boat, took the Sprit, and struck at him as he rose, hoping to disable him, but he broke his Jaw. They took him by this Means, brought him on board, sent him to the Surgeon, and when they despair'd of his being able to speak, he asked for a Pipe of Tobacco, which he smoak'd, and drunk a Dram; after which he seem'd very hearty. As the pyrates had on board several black Slaves, who spoke the *East-India* Tongue, one of them was ordered to enquire of him where they might find Water, promising him his Liberty if he would direct them. On this Promise he carried them to a convenient landing Place, where he showed a Well full of Dirt, out of which, after a great deal of Trouble to come at it, they drew but three Buckets of Water, which sufficed those only who went on Shoar, to the Number of 30. Enraged with this Disappointment after so much Labour, they threaten'd their Prisoner with Death, who told them, if they would have Patience till the Sun was set, they would have Plenty, for the Spring would rise, and flow all Night; which they found to be Fact, and filled twenty Tun of Water, and return'd on board, carrying the Man with them, for whom they made a gathering of some

Goods, and about thirty Dollars; these they gave him, and exacted a Promise, that whenever he saw any Ship on that Coast, which made the same Signals they had made, he would go on board and render them what Service he could, assuring him he would always meet with civil Treatment, and be well rewarded.

After this they cruised on the Gulf of *Persia* some Days, in hopes of meeting their Consort, not doubting but she had some Share in the Storm.

The Time of their Consortship being now over, and she not appearing, they steered for the Highlands of St. *John* near *Surat,* the Place of Rendezvous. When they made the Land they spied a tall Ship, and immediately making all clear for an Engagement, they gave chase. The other Ship doing the like, they soon met, and, to the great Joy of both Parties, she proved their Consort. Upon Enquiry they found the *Prosperous* had been ten Days on this Station, and had not met with the Storm which had so roughly handled the *Speedy Return,* on giving an Account of their Misfortune, *viz.* their being obliged to throw over their Guns, and a Quantity of Provisions, Captain *Howard* spared them some fresh Provisions, and expressing great Concern for the Accident, renewed his Consortship for two Months longer; that is, they agreed whatever Prizes were taken should be equally divided between the Crews of both Ships. After they had cruised here fourteen Days, they spied seven Sail of tall Ships, which proved to be the *Moors* from *Mocoa;* they both gave Chace, but the *Speedy Return* being the better Sailor first came up with one of them, laid her on board, and carried her in a very little Time, with little more Damage than the Loss of her Bowsprit. The *Prosperous* kept on the Chace, and having Captain *Whaley* on board as a Pilot, took another at an Anchor, as is said (so need not be repeated) in Captain *Howard*'s Life.

The *Speedy Return* steered with her Prize for the Coast of *Malabar,* where, by Agreement, she was to wait ten Days for her Consort. In six Days the *Prosperous* joined them, but without any Prize, having rifled her, as is before said in another Life.

Here they made an equal Dividend of their Prizes, burnt the *Speedy Return,* sunk the *Prosperous,* went all on board the *Moor*'s Ship, put to Sea, and cruised on this Coast, where they made several Prizes. When they came over against *Cachine,* some black Merchants, Goldsmiths, and several *Dutch* Men, came on board to trade with them, bringing a great many Sequins, and other Gold Coin, to change for *Spanish* Dollars; as many of the pyrates designed to knock off and return home, they gave 500 Dollars for 200 Sequins, for the Conveniency of close Stowage about them. The Goldsmiths set up their Forges on board the Ship, and were fully employed in making them Buttons, Buckles, and what else they fancied, so that they had a fair Opportunity of putting what Alloy they thought proper. They here also furnished themselves with a good Quantity of Arrack, Provisions, and Stores, and then leaving the Coast, shaped their Course for *Madagascar,* but, in the Way, fell in with the Island of *Mauritius,* and put into a Port called the *North-West Harbour.* Here they wooded and watered. This Port affords great abundance of a poisonous Fish called the *Red-Snapper,* the Nature of which was well known to Captain *Bowen,* who perswaded his Men not to eat of them, but they were in Port, and then are all Commanders, so that this wholesome Advice was thrown away upon them. The Captain seeing their Obstinacy, and that they could not be disswaded, eat with them, chusing rather to share the same Fate than be left alone to the Mercy of the *Dutch,* as he was conscious of what he merited.

They supp'd plentifully on the Fish, and drank very heartily after it. Soon after they began to swell in a frightful Manner. The next Morning some Planters came on board with Fowls, Goats, *&c* and seeing the pyrates in a miserable Condition, and some of these Fish lying on the Decks, asked if they had not eat of them? Being answer'd they had, advised their drinking plentifully of strong Liquors, which was the only way to expel the Poyson, which had dispatch'd them all in less Time, had they not done it after their unfortunate Meal. They readily followed this Advice, as the Prescription was agreeable, and by this Means, with the Care of the Surgeons, of whom they had several expert in their Business, and stock'd with good Medicines, they all recovered, four excepted, who paid their Obstinacy with their Lives.

They here heel'd their Ship, scrubb'd, tallow'd, and took in what they wanted. When they had staid three Months in this Port, the Governor sent and desired them to put to Sea, for he expected the Arrival of the *Dutch East-India* Men; they accordingly got every Thing ready, and went out, but left several of their Men behind them, as we have said in *Bowen*'s Life.

From hence they steered for *Madagascar,* and in their Passage stopped at *Don Mascarenas,* where they took in a Quantity of Hogs, Goat, Sheep, Fowls of all Sorts, and Green Turtle. Captain *Bowen* here went ashoar with 40 of his Men, having obtained the Governor's Protection by the Force of Presents. These Men design'd to give over their Pyracy, and return home the first Opportunities offer'd them. In six Months after they had staid here, Captain *Bowen* was taken ill of the dry Belly Ach, a Distemper as rise here as in the *West-India* Islands, and was buried in the Highway, for the Priests would not allow him holy Ground, as he was a Heretic.

But to return; when *Bowen* went ashoar *North* was chosen Captain. The Ceremony of this Installation is, the Crew having made choice of him to Command, either by an unanimous Consent, or by a Majority of Suffrages, they carry him a Sword in a very solemn Manner, make him some Complements, and desire he will take upon him the Command, as he is the most capable among them. That he will take Possession of the great Cabin; and, on his accepting the Office, he is led into the Cabin in State, and placed at a Table, where only one Chair is set at the upper End, and one at the lower End of the Table for the Company's Quarter-Master. The Captain and he being placed, the latter succinctly tells him, that the Company having Experience of his Conduct and Courage, do him the Honour to elect him for their Head, not doubting his behaving himself with his usual Bravery, and doing every Thing which may conduce to the public Good; in Confidence of which, he, in the Name of the Company, promised to obey all his lawful Commands, and declared him Captain. Then the Quarter-Master takes up the Sword, which he had before presented him, and he had returned, puts it into his Hand, and says, *This is the Commission under which you are to act, may you prove fortunate to your self and us.* The Guns are then fired round, Shot and all; he is saluted with three Chears; the Ceremony is ended with an Invitation from the Captain to such as he thinks fit to have dine with him, and a large Bowl of Punch is ordered to every Mess.

Captain *North* leaving this Island steered for *Madagascar,* and came to Cape *Dolphin* at the South End, as is said in *White*'s Life, where he came to an Anchor, and took on board some Refreshments, but it blowing hard, he was obliged to put to Sea, and leave his Boat with 30 Men behind him. He ran along the East-Side of the Island, and came to a Place called *Ambonavoula,* in the Latitude of 17. 38. where they put on Shore some of their Goods, and settled themselves among the Negroes, several living in a House; here they lived as Sovereign Princes among the Inhabitants.

The *Moor* Prisoners they kept on board, and allowed them sufficient fresh Provisions. *North* privately bid the Boatswain of the *Moors* take the Advantage of the Land Breeze in the Night Time, and go off with the Ship, and what Goods were left on board; or the pyrates would soon hawl up the Ship, take every Thing on Shore, and they (marooned there) would never see their own Country again.

Accordingly the Boatswain following this Advice, laid hold of the Opportunity of a dark Night, and communicating his Design to the other *Moors,* whom he did not acquaint with this Advice, as *North* charg'd him not, till he was on the Point of executing his Design, they weigh'd with great Silence and stood to Sea.

The next Morning some of the pyrates propos'd to go on Board and fetch off some Iron and other Things to trade with in the Country; but they were strangely surpriz'd when they miss'd the Ship; they alarm'd the rest of their Comrades, and went in a Body to Captain *North* to tell him what had happen'd. He answer'd, if the *Moors* were gone off with the Ship, it was their own Fault; they ought to have left a sufficient Number of Hands on Board to have secur'd her; that there was now no Remedy but Patience, for they had no Vessel to pursue with, except they thought the Canoe proper.

Some of the pyrates thought as she lay in foul Ground the Cable might be cut by some Rock, and the Ship blown off to Sea by that Accident; on starting this, some of them ran up to an Eminence, and from thence spy'd the Ship as far as they could well see, with all Sails set, which was a cruel and convincing Proof that their Loss was irreparable.

They endeavoured to make themselves easy, since there was no Help; and transporting their Goods to different Abodes, at small Distances, they settled themselves, buying Cattle and Slaves, and lived in a neighbourly Manner one among another five Years; clear'd a great deal of Ground, and planted Provisions as Yamms, Potatoes, *&c.* The Natives among whom they fix'd, had frequent Broils and Wars among themselves, but the pyrates interposed, and endeavoured to reconcile all differences; *North* deciding their Disputes not seldom, with that Impartiality and strict Regard to distributive Justice (for he was allowed, by all, a Man of admirable good natural Parts) that he ever sent away, even the Party who was cast, satisfied with the Reason, and content with the Equity of his Decisions.

These Inclinations which the pyrates showed to Peace, and the Example they set of an amicable Way of Life; for they carefully avoided all Jars, and agreed to refer all Cause of Complaint among themselves which might arise, to a cool Hearing before *North,* and twelve of their Companions, gave them a great Character among the Natives, who were before very much prejudiced against the white Men. Nay, in this Point of keeping up a Harmony among themselves, they were so exact, that whosoever spoke but in an angry or peevish Tone, was rebuked by all the Company, especially if before any of the Country, tho' even but a Slave, of their own; for they thought, and very justly, that Unity and Concord were the only Means to warrant their Safety; for the People being ready to make War on one another upon the slightest Occasion, they did not doubt but they would take the Advantage of any Division which they might observe among the whites, and cut them off whenever a fair Opportunity offered.

North often set this before them, and as often made them remark the Effects of their Unanimity, which were, the being treated with great Respect and Deference, and having a Homage paid them as to sovereign Princes. Nature, we see, teaches the most Illiterate the necessary Prudence for their Preservation, and Fear works Changes which Religion has lost the Power of doing, since it has been looked upon as a Trade, and debased by the scandalous Lives of those who think it their Business to teach it only, and, satisfied with the Theory, leave the practical Part to the Laity: For these Men whom we term, and not without Reason, the Scandal of humane Nature, who were abandoned to all Vice, and lived by Rapine; when they judged it for their Interest, not only (politically) were strictly just, both among themselves, and in composing the Differences of the neighbouring Natives, but grew continent and sober, as no doubt they esteemed their Security to depend on showing the Blacks they could govern those Passions to which they themselves were Slaves. Its true, they were all Polygamists, but that was no Scandal among a People who thought the cohabiting with a pregnant Woman a Sin against Nature in acting contrary to her Design, which is by Generation to propagate the animal Race; and who should be guilty of this Crime among them, they esteemed worse than Beasts, which following Nature, obey her Orders exactly, and set Men a Lesson of Prudence. When then, I say, they were continent, I mean they never invaded the Rights either of their Compations, or of the Natives.

The Reader may, perhaps, be well enough pleased to hear how on the smallest Difference they proceeded to a Reconciliation; for, as I have said, it was a Maxim with them, that the least Discord among a few Particulars would be the Ruin of a whole Body; as from a small neglected Spark, a general Conflagration may arise and lay the noblest City waste.

On any Mistake from which a Dispute arose, or on any ill-manner'd Expression let fall in Company, they all broke up, and one of the Company poured what Liquor was before them on the Ground, saying, no Contention could creep in among them without Loss; and therefore he sacrificed that Liquor to the evil Fiend, to prevent a greater Damage. Then both the contending Parties, on Pain of being banished the Society, and sent to another Part of the Island, were summon'd to appear at Captain *North*'s, the next Morning, and, in the mean while, they were commanded to keep their respective Houses.

The next Morning both the Parties being met, and all the whites summon'd to attend, the Captain set the Plaintiff and Defendant on one Side, and told them, that till the Aggressor had consented to do Justice, and till the Person injured had forgot his Resentment, they must esteem them both Enemies to the Public, and not look upon them as their Friends and Companions. He then wrote down the Names of all the Assembly, roll'd them up, and put them into a Hat, out of which, each Party shaking the Hat, chose six Tickets; and these twelve Rowls or Tickets contained the Names of the assistant Judges, who, with the Captain, heard and determined in the Cause, calling and examining the Witnesses. When the Matter was fully debated, the Court was adjourned to the next Day, and the Litigators commanded to appear again, and, in the Interim, not to stir out their Houses, to which they were respectively conducted by two or three each, lest the Slaves, or the neighbouring Blacks, should, by a greater Number, have any Suspicion of their Disagreement.

The second Day the Examination began afresh, and the Witnesses were sifted, as if they had not before been examined, and this to try if they were consistent with their former Evidence, which was noted down. Then the Court was again adjourned, and the disagreeing Parties remanded home till next Morning, when Judgment was given, which was a Fine in Proportion to the Affront.

The Reason of confining those who had Dissension was to deter them, by this small Punishment, from all future Quarrels, and to prevent any ill Accident which might happen by their being at full Liberty.

The Example they set, and the Care they took to accommodate Differences among their Neighbours, had calmed all the Country round them. After they had staid here near three Years, Captain *North,* and some of his Companions, had a Mind to visit the Country Southward, and trade for more Slaves and Cattle; to which End taking a considerable Quantity of Powder and Arms, beside what they might use, with 50 whites and 300 Natives, he set forward on his Journey. When they had travelled about fourscore Miles Southward, they came to a Nation rich in Slaves and Cattle, who inhabited the Banks of the largest River on the East-Side the Island, called *Mangora*. With these People he trafficked for a great Number of Slaves and Cattle, which he purchased for Guns and Powder: They being at War when Captain *North* came among them, with a neighbouring Prince, he was intreated to give his Assistance, for which they, the *Mangorians,* promised him a hundred Slaves with 500 Head of Cattle, and all the Prisoners they should take. On these Conditions he joined them, and marched to a very large Town of the Enemy's, which was naturally very strong, and esteemed by the Natives impregnable, being situated on a high and craggy Rock, which could be ascended by the Way only leading to the Gate, where was kept a strong Guard. The Blacks in *North*'s Army were for leaving this Town unattempted, and marching farther into the Country, in search of Booty; but *North* told 'em it was not safe to leave a Garrison of Enemies at their Backs, which would continually infest them, by falling on their Rear, and which would be an Obstacle to their carrying off what Plunder they might get together; beside, it would be an Azyle for all the Country, which would fly thither till they had gather'd a Body considerable enough to come down and face them in the Field, which the Enemy might do with reasonable Hopes of Success, as their Men would be all fresh, while those of his Party would be fatigued with Marches, may be encumbered by Plunder, and worn down with the Inconveniencies of lying exposed in the Fields.

The chief of his Allies allowed his Reasons good, were an Attempt on the Town practicable, which Experience told him was not; for, tho' several times besieged, it never could be taken, it would be the Loss of a great deal of Time, and many Mens Lives to offer at it.

North desired he would leave the Management of this Siege to him.

The Chief answered, he should do as he pleased, but it was against his Judgment to attack a Town which Nature her self had fortified, which God Almighty would never suffer to be taken, and which had, to no Purpose, cost the Lives of a

Number scarce to be told, of his Countrymen, in the several Attempts they had made to be Masters of it.

North disposed his Army, and invested the Rock on every Side, then sent Word to the Town, if they did not surrender he would give no Quarter to either Sex or Age. The Inhabitants laugh'd at his Message, told him, they did not believe he had learnt the Art of flying, and till he had, they thought themselves very secure from his putting such Menaces in Execution.

Out of the White Men, *North* chose 30, whom he set at the Head of 3 Companies, consisting of 100 Blacks each; and as he had some Grenade-Shells with 'em, soon dispersed the Guard at the Foot of the Rock, and made a Lodgment; tho' the Blacks were acquainted with Fire-Arms, the Shells were entirely new to them, and as they saw their terrible Effect, threw down their Arms, and gained the Middle of the Rock, where they had another *Corps de Guarde,* tho' not without some Loss. Those who were at the Bottom of the Rock being put to flight, *North* sent 10 whites and 500 Blacks to take that Post, and Orders to the other whites to mount the Rock, and having beat that Guard, if possible, to enter the Town with them. They accordingly ascended in this Order, as the Road was so narrow, only three could pass on a-breast, and the Enemy, when within Cast of a Dart, threw down a Shower upon them, three unarmed Blacks with their Shields march'd before three small Shot Men, and shelter'd them from the Enemies Weapons; these were followed by others, with the same Precaution, the white Men being mix'd with those who thus went up, that is to say, one White Musketeer to two Blacks.

The Enemy seem'd resolute to defend the Pass, but when they had, to no Purpose, spent a Number or Darts, and had lost some Men by the Shot, they swiftly took to the Top of the Rock, where, joined with fresh Men from the Town, they made a Stand and Show of Resistance; *North*'s Men followed, and pouring in a Volley, put them into Confusion, which gave the Assailants an Opportuty to come near enough to throw in their Shells, half a dozen of which bursting with considerable Damage, and the Slaughter of several Men, they thought to shelter themselves in the Town, but the Inhabitants fearing the Enemy's entering with them, shut the Gates against both, so that the Blacks of *North*'s Army, notwithstanding all the Whites could do to the contrary, made a great Slaughter; however, they saved some, whom they sent Prisoners to the Camp, desiring, at the same Time, a Supply of Powder to make a Petarde.

In the mean while the Enemy from the Town threw a prodigious Quantity of Darts, which the Besiegers received upon their Shields, at least, the greater Part.

The Town was again summon'd, but they refus'd to surrender, wherefore, they were obliged to shelter themselves as well as they could, and expect the Powder from the Camp; tho' in the mean while, the small Shot from without being warmly plied, made the throwing Darts from the Town less frequent, for none could show his Head but with the greatest Danger.

When the Powder came, they cut down and hollowed a Tree, which they filled with Powder, and plugg'd up very tight, and under the Protection of their Shields and Muskets got it to the Gate, under which they dug a Hole large enough to receive it, then setting Fire to the Fuze, it burst with a terrible Crack, tore their Gate to

Shatters, and left an open Passage, which the Besiegers, who had been join'd with 500 more Blacks, who came up with the Powder, enter'd, and began a very great Slaughter; the Whites protected all they could who submitted, but notwithstanding their Diligence, the Town was strew'd with dead and dying Men. At length what with being tir'd, and what with Persuasion, the Slaughter ceas'd, the Town was reduced to Ashes, and the Conquerors return'd to the Camp with 3000 Prisoners, whom his Allies led to their own Quarters, where calling out, the old Women, Children, and useless Slaves, they sent them to *North,* as if by these, they thought themselves releas'd from the Promise made to induce his Assistance.

When *North* saw the Dishonesty of these People, he sent for their Prince, and told him, 'According to Agreement all the Slaves belong'd to him; nay, according to Justice he alone had a Right to them, since he despair'd of taking the Town, so far as to dissuade his besieging it; and that he not only owed to him their Success, but even the Safety of his Army, and all the Plunder they should make in the Prosecution of the War, for Reasons already given, and by himself allow'd to be good. That he thought he had allied himself with a People of Integrity, but he was sorry to say, he found himself quite mistaken in his Opinion, since they were so far from making good their Treaty; that they sent him out of the Slaves taken, instead of all, those only whom they knew not what to do with; that they must not imagine him so blind as not to perceive how disingenuously he was dealt with; or that he wanted either Strength or Resolution to resent the Usage.'

He then ask'd what was become of a Number of young and handsome Women he had seen among the Captives?

The Prince answer'd, 'That those he enquired after were his and his Countrymens Relations, and as such they could not consent to, nor could he require their being made Slaves.

This Answer made, the Chief left him; as it was delivered in a pretty haughty Tone, it did not a little nettle both *North* and his Comrades; the latter were for immediately doing themselves Justice, but the former begg'd they would have Patience and rely on him; they followed his Advice, and he sent an Interpreter, who privately enquired among the Women what Relation they had to the People of the River; the Prisoners answered, that some of their Forefathers had inter-married with that Nation.

I must here take Notice, that notwithstanding the Inhabitants of *Madagascar* have but one Language which is common to the whole Island, the Difference of the Dialect in different Nations makes it very difficult for any but the Natives, or those who have been a great many Years (more than *North* and his Companions had been) among them to understand them perfectly, which is the Reason he made use of an Interpreter, as well between him and the Chief, as between the Slaves and him.

When he had received this Answer from the Prisoners, he went to the Prince, and told him, It was very odd he should make War on his Relations, however, he should keep them since he declared them such, till he could prove his Right better than the Prince could his Nearness of Blood; that as he had once taken them, he would try if he could not support the Justice of his Claim, and bid him therefore be upon his Guard, for he openly declared, he was no longer the Ally, but the profess'd Enemy of faithless People.

Saying this, he and his Blacks separated themselves from the *Mangorians,* and *North* divided them into Companies, with his White Men at the Head of each, and order'd them to fire Ball over the Heads of their late Allies; the first Volley was a prodigious Astonishment to the *Mangorians,* several of whom ran away, but *North* firing two more immediately, and marching up to them, brought the Prince and the Head Officers of his Army to him, crawling on all four; they (as the Custom of showing the greatest Submission is among them) kiss'd the Feet of the Whites, and begg'd they would continue their Friendship, and dispose of every Thing as they thought proper.

North told him, 'Deceit was the Sign of a mean and coward Soul; that had he, the Prince, thought too considerable, what, however, was justly his Due, because not only promised to, but taken by him, he ought to have expostulated with him, *North,* and have told him his Sentiments, which might have, it was possible, made no Division, for neither he nor his Men were greedy or unreasonable; but as the Prince had not the Courage publicly to claim the Slaves, he would have basely stolen them by false Pretences of Kindred, it was a Sign he did not think such Claim justifiable, as certainly it was not, for all his Captains could witness their Prince had agreed the Prisoners taken should be given to the Whites, and his Companions, a sufficient Title, to mention no other. That he had resolved to show them, by a severe Chastisement, the Abhorrence those of his Colour have to Ingratitude and Deceit, and what Difference there was in fighting on the Ground of Justice, and the supporting Wrong and Injury; but as they acknowledg'd their Error, he should not only forgive but forget what was past, provided no new Treachery, in his Return, which he resolved upon, refresh'd his Memory. He then order'd them to bring all the Slaves, and they punctually complied without Reply.

North chose out the finest and ablest among them, and dividing the whole Number of Prisoners into two equal Bands, he kept that in which he had placed the chosen Slaves, and sent the other to the Prince, telling him, 'tho' neither Fraud nor Compulsion could wring a Slave from him, yet Justice, as some of his Troops had shared the Danger, and a generous Temper, had sent him that Present, which was half the Spoil; tho' he could not think of going any farther on with the War, that he ought to content himself with the taking a Town they thought impregnable, and blame his own Conduct, if he should continue in the Field, and hereafter find the Want of his Assistance.

The Prince and his People admired the Penetration, Bravery, and Generosity of the Whites, and sent them Word, 'He was more obliged to them for the Lesson they had taught him by their Practice, than for the Slaves they had presented him, tho' he esteem'd the Present as he ought. That for the future he should have an Abhorrence from every mean Action, since he had learned from them the Beauty of a candid open Procedure. At the same Time he thank'd him for the Present, and the not suffering his Resentment to go farther than the frightning him into his Duty; for he was sensible his Balls were not fir'd over their Heads, but by Orders proceeding from the Humanity of the Whites, who, he observed, tender over the Lives of of their Enemies, contrary to the Custom of his Countrymen, who give Quarter to none, the Females and Infants excepted, that there may hereafter be none to take Revenge; he begg'd, that he would suffer their Submission to get the better of his Design to depart. This could not prevail, the Whites and their Friends, who came with them, turn'd their Faces towards home, taking their Slaves and Cattle with them; tho' the *Mangorians* were sensibly touch'd at the Obstinacy of *North*'s Resolution, yet they parted very amicably.

As the Whites were returning home with their Company, they fell in with another Nation, the *Timouses,* whose Prince join'd *North,* with 500 Men, and swore a strict Amity with him and his Crew.

The Ceremony used among the Natives, as it is uncommon, so an Account of it may, perhaps, be agreeable to my Readers. The Parties, who swear to each other, interweave their Toes and Fingers, so that they must necessarily sit very close to each other. When they have thus knit their Hands and Feet, they reciprocally swear to do each other all friendly Offices, to be a Friend or Enemy to the Friend or Enemy of the Party to whom they swear; and if they falsify the Oath they make, they imprecate several Curses on themselves, as may they fall by the Lance, be devoured by the Alligator, or struck dead by the Hand of God; then an Assistant scarifies each of the contracting Parties on the Chest, and wiping up the Blood with a Piece of Bread, gives this bloody Bread to each of them to eat, that is, each eats the Blood of the other; and this Oath whether it be with equal Parties, or with a Prince and his Subject, where the one promises Protection, and the other Obedience (which was the Nature of that taken between *North* and this Prince) is look'd upon inviolable, and they have few Examples of its being broken; but where any has been wicked enough to violate this solemn Oath, they say, they have been ever punish'd according to their Imprecations.

As this Prince had War with powerful Neighbours, he left his Country, taking with him all his great Men, Wives, and Relations, and with a Company of about 500 fighting Men, followed *North,* and settled by him, where he staid two Years, the Time *North* staid; during this Space, being supplied with Arms, Powder, and several Natives by Captain *North,* he made several Inroads into his Enemies Countries, and made all he conquer'd, swear Allegiance to Capt. *North.*

At the Expiration of two Years, Captain *Halsey* came in with a Brigantine, as is said in the Life of Captain *White.*

This Crew having made a broken Voyage were discontented with their Captain, and desired *North* to take the Command upon him; but he declined it, saying, *Halsey* was every Way as capable, and that they ought not to depose a Man, whom they could not tax with either Want of Courage or Conduct; and for his Part, he would never take the Command from any who did not justly merit to be turn'd out, which was not *Halsey*'s Case.

The Crew were not, however, satisfied, and they made the same Offer to *White,* but by *North*'s Industry, they were, at last, prevail'd on to continue their old Commander; and as *North* and his Companions had expended their Money in the settling their Plantations, and wanted Cloaths, the former, therefore, accepted of the Quarter-Master's Post under *Halsey,* and the others went in the Capacity of private Gentlemen Adventurers, I mean plain foremast Men, as may be gathered in the

Life of that Pyrate, to which I refer for an Account of the Expedition they made in the *Red Seas,* beginning at Page 113. Captain *Halsey* on board a Prize left *North* to command the Brigantine they set out in.

The two Commanders were separated by a Storm, but both made for *Madagascar; Halsey* got to *Ambonavoula,* but *North* fell in with *Maratan,* where, finding the Brigantine was very much worm eaten, and made a great Deal of Water, with one Consent they took ashore all their Goods, and laid up their Vessel.

They were all very well received; the King being then at War with his Brother, *North* prevail'd on his Majesty's Sister to pass her solitary Hours with him; at the King's Return, having defeated his Brother, he was very much incens'd against *North,* for being so free with the Royal Family, and resolved to fine him 200 Sequins for the Affront done to his illustrious House; but *North* having some Inkling of his Design, pacified him, by making a Present of one hundred.

The pyrates continued here a whole Year, when being desirous to go to *Ambonavoula,* they ask'd the King's Assistance to build a Boat, and he for 1000 Dollars, set Negroes to work, under the Directions of Captain *North,* and a Vessel of 15 Tons was set up and launch'd with great Dispatch.

In this Boat they went to a River, called *Manangaro,* thirty Leagues to the Northward of *Maratan:* Here some of their Comrades came to them in a Boat belonging to the *Scotch* Ship *Neptune,* and help'd to transport their Goods to *Ambonavoula,* where he had before settled, and had a Woman and three Children.

He had not been long return'd before his neighbouring Natives reported, that the *Timouses,* who had followed him from the Southward, had a Design to rebel against, and murder him and the other Whites, which giving too easy Credit to, he made War upon, and drove these poor People out of the Country.

Some Time after he built a Sloop, and went to *Antonguil,* where he purchas'd 90 Slaves, and took in the *Scots* Supercargo, Mr. *George Crookshank,* with a Design to carry him to *Mascarenas;* but all his Comrades were against it, saying, when he got to *Europe* he would prove their Destruction. *North* answered, nothing could be more cruel, after they had taken the greater Part of what the poor Gentleman had, than to keep him from his Country, Family, and Friends; for his Part were he his Prisoner, he should not ask their Consents in doing an Act of Humanity, and the only one they were able towards making him some Reparation, since they could not return his Goods, which were parcel'd out into so many Shares.

On *North*'s saying thus much, they put the Affair in Question to the Vote, and there being many who had Obligations to *North,* and whom he influenced in Favour of the Supercargo, 48 out of 54 voted for the discharging him. *North* having gained this Point, the pyrates ask'd if he also designed to take with him one *J. B.* a great Favourite of his, who had been Midship Man on board the *Neptune* (a young *Scotch* Man, who was a good Artist, a thorough Seaman, and very capable of taking on him the Command in any Voyage) he answered there was a Necessity of taking him, since he should want his Assistance in the Voyage; as he depended on his Knowledge, his Companions said *J. B.* would certainly give him the Slip, which would be a Loss to them all, as he was an Artist, and a clean hail young Fellow, and therefore his being detained was necessary to their common Good. To this *North* answered, his own Security would oblige his taking Care that he should not get from him, since no other on board was capable to find the Way back to *Ambonavoula.*

He went to *Mascarenas,* where the Supercargo and his Negroe were put on Shore with all the Money he had, which was about 1600 Dollars; for when the pyrates made Prize of the *Neptune,* in the Manner already said, they took none of the Money, they themselves had before paid for Liquors, *&c.* either from the Captain, Supercargo, or any other on board; for that, they look'd upon it a base, as well as dishonest Action, but for the Ship and remaining Part of the

Cargo, they had a fair Title to, *viz.* they wanted both. It is true, they made the Merchants of the *Greyhound* refund what Money they had taken; but before the Reader taxes them with Injustice, and acting against the above Maxim, let him consider Circumstances, and call to Mind the whole Story.

They did not take that Ship, on the contrary, they sent her away well victualled, and provided with Necessaries for her Voyage; and, I hope, it will be allow'd, they had a lawful Claim to her, as she belong'd to an Enemy, and came into a Port of theirs, without a Pass: Again, they did not rob these Merchants of the Money they had before laid out with them, but took it in Payment for the Liquors they had put on board the *Greyhound,* out of the *Neptune,* which the Merchants themselves, if they had any Honesty, could not expect for nothing: But let us suppose they had taken this Money by Force, and not traded for it on the fair Foot, as its evident they did; yet, was it no more than an Act of Justice, such as might reasonably be expected from the Probity of these Gentlemen, who never suffer an ill Action to go unpunished: And no Body can justify the Proceedings of those Merchants who advised the seizing the *Scots* Ship. But to return.

North would not suffer *J. B.* to go ashore; however, to make him amends for his Confinement, he gave him four Negroes, whom he sold for 300 Dollars, and took Care that he should live plentifully and well on board. *North*'s Business, at this Island, was to get Leave to carry his Children there to be educated in the Christian Faith, which after some rich Presents made the Governor, he obtained, and return'd to *Madagascar.* In the Voyage, as *J. B.* was very greatly in his Favour, and his Confident, he told him, his Design was to leave his Children at *Mascarenas,* and place Fortunes for them in the Hands of some honest Priest, who would give them a Christian Education (for he thought it better to have them Papists, than not Christians) and would then go back to *Maratan,* and endeavour, by his Penitence, to make Attonement for his former Life, and never more go off the Island on any Account; that he would give his Sloop to *J. B.* with two hundred Dollars, that he might find some Means to return home, since he very wisely refus'd to join with the pyrates.

When he came on the *Madagascar* Coast, he heard a *French* Ship had touch'd there, and left some Men behind her; upon which Account, *North* ran to the Southward 100 Leagues out of his Way, to enquire after and assist these People: A Piece of Humanity which ought not to be pass'd by in Silence, for it may shame not a few among us who carry a Face of Religion, and act with greater Barbarity than those whom we hunt and destroy as a Nusance to the World, and a Scandal to the Name of Man. If any thinks this Reflection severe, let him examine into the Number of Thousands who are perishing in Goals, by the Cruelty of Creditors, sensible of their Inability to pay: Let him take a View of the Miseries which reign in those Tombs of the Living, let him enquire into the Number of those who are yearly starved to Death, to gratify an implacable Spirit, and then, if he can, clear the *English* Laws, which allow a Creditor to punish an unfortunate Man, for his being so, with the most cruel of all invented Deaths, that of Famine; let him, I say, clear them from the Imputation of Barbarity. I beg Pardon for this Digression, which my Concern for the *English* Character, for this only Reason sunk among Foreigners forced me into.

North found but one Man, whom he took home with him, cloathed and maintained him. When he came back to *Ambonavoula,* he found the Country all in an Uproar, and the Rest of his Companions preparing for a War with the Natives, but his Arrival restor'd their former Quiet. After four Months Stay at home, he fitted his Sloop to go out and purchase Slaves at *Antonguil;* but finding few there to his Mind, for in two Months he bought but forty, he return'd to his Settlement. He design'd now to carry his Children to *Mascarenas,* but dissuaded on Account of the Season, by *J. B.* he went to *Methelage* on the West Side of the Island, to trade for Samsams.

Having purchas'd a considerable Quantity of Samsams he went to *Johanna,* and thence to *Mayotta,* return'd again to *Madagascar,* but not being able to get round the North End, on Account of the Current, he put for *Mayotta* again; on the West Side of this Island put into a Port, called *Sorez,* where, some Time before, came a Ship from *England* to trade, commanded by one *Price,* who going ashore with his Doctor was detained (as was also his Boat's Crew) till he redeem'd himself and Surgeon, with 200 Barrels of Powder and 1000 Small Arms; but was forced to leave his Boat's Crew, not having wherewithal to ransom them, tho' the Demand was only two Small Arms for each Man. These poor Creatures were afterwards sold to the *Arabians;* in Revenge *North* and his Crew landed, burnt a large Town, and did all the Damage they could. From *Mayotta* he went again to *Madagascar,* where a King of his Acquaintance told him, the Whites and Natives were at War at *Ambonavoula;* he bought thirty Slaves, refreshed his Crew, and went home. On the News of his Arrival the Natives sent to conclude a Peace, but he would not listen to them; on the contrary, rais'd an Army, burnt a Number of Towns, and took a great many Prisoners.

This Success brought the Natives to sue in a very humble Manner for a Cessation of Arms, that a general Peace might follow: This he agreed to about four Months after his Arrival.

His Enemies, having now the Opportunity, corrupted some of his neighbouring Natives, and in the Night surprized and murder'd him in his Bed. His Comrades, however, being alarmed, took to their Arms, drove the treacherous Multitude before them with great Slaughter; and to revenge *North*'s Death continued the War seven Years, in which Time they became Masters of all the Country round, and drove out all who did not swear Allegiance to them.

North had his Will lying by him, which directed *J. B.* to carry his Children to *Mascarenas,* in his Sloop which he left to the said *J. B.* who was at the Charge to fit her up, and laid out the greater Part of the Money *North* bequeathed him; but the pyrates would not suffer him to stir while the Wars lasted, fearing he would not return, having never join'd them in any Pyracies; and therefore, by one Consent, setting Fire to the Sloop, they detained him several Years, if he is not still there.

FINIS.

II. Of Captain Teach

We shall add here a few Particulars (not mentioned in our first Volume) of the famous *Blackbeard,* relating to his taking the South *Carolina* Ships, and insulting that Colony. This was at the Time that the pyrates had obtained such an Acquisition of Strength, that they were in no Concern about preserving themselves from the the Justice of Laws, but of advancing their Power, and maintaining their Sovereignty, not over the Seas only, but to stretch their Dominions to the Plantations themselves, and the Governors thereof, insomuch that when their Prisoners came aboard their Captors Ships, the pyrates freely own'd their Acquaintance with them, and never endeavour'd to conceal their Names, or Habitations, as if they had been Inhabitants of a legal Commonwealth, and were resolved to treat with all the World on the Foot of a free State; and all judicial Acts went in the Name of *Teach,* under the Title of Commodore.

All the *Carolina* Prisoners were lodg'd aboard the Commodore's Ship, after being strictly examin'd concerning the Lading of their Vessels, and the Number and Condition of other Traders in the Harbour; when they thought they would sail, and whither bound: And the Enquiry was so solemnly carried on, that the pyrates swore, that it should be Death for that Man that told a Lye, or otherwise shifted or evaded in his Answers. At the same Time all their Papers were perused with the same Diligence as though it had been at the Secretary's Office here in *England.* When this Business was gone through, Word was given, that all the Prisoners should be immediately turn'd aboard their own Ship, out of which they had already taken their Provisions and Stores. This was done with that Hurry and Precipitation, that it struck a great Terror in the unfortunate People, verily believing they were then going to their Destruction; and what seem'd to confirm them in this Notion was, that no Regard was had to the Qualities of the Prisoners, but Merchants, Gentlemen of Rank, and even a Child of Mr. *Wragg*'s, were thrust aboard in a tumultuous and confus'd Manner, and lock'd all under the Hatches, where not so much as one Pyrate stay'd amongst them.

In this melancholly Situation were these innocent People left, bewailing their Condition for several Hours, expecting every Moment that pass'd either that a Match would be laid to a Train to blow them up, or that the Ship was to be set on Fire, or sunk; no Body could tell which, but every one supposed they were, one Way or other, destin'd for a Sacrifice to their brutal Humours.

But, at length, a Gleam of Light shot in upon them, that recover'd their drooping Souls; the Hatches were unlaid, and they were immediately order'd back on board the Commodore: They began then to think the pyrates had changed their savage Resolution; and that God had inspired them with Sentiments less shocking to Nature and Humanity, and they went aboard, as it were, with new Life. The Chief of them were brought before *Blackbeard,* the pyrates General, who acquainted them with the Occasion of that extraordinary Procedure; and that they were only put out of the Way while a general Council was held, at which Time they suffer'd no Prisoner to be present. He told them, the Company was in want of Medicines, and must be supply'd from the Province; that their first Surgeon had drawn up a Catalogue, which he would send to the Governor and Council, by two of his own Officers, for whose safe Return, as well as for the Chest it self, they had come to a Resolution of keeping all the Prisoners as Hostages, who would all be put to Death, if such their Demands were not comply'd with punctually.

Mr. *Wragg* answer'd, that, perhaps, it might not be in their Power to comply with every Part of it; and, he fear'd, that some certain Drugs in the Surgeon's List, were not to be had in the Province; and, if it should prove so, he hop'd they would be contented to have that Want made up by substituting something else in the Place. He likewise proposed, that one of them might go with the two Gentlemen that were to be sent on the Embassy, who might truly represent the Danger they were in, and induce them more readily to submit, in order to save the Lives of so many of the King's Subjects; and further, to prevent any Insult from the common People, (for whose Conduct, on such an Occasion, they could not answer) on the Persons of his Envoys.

His Excellency *Blackbeard* thought this Advice reasonable, and therefore call'd another Council, who likewise approv'd of the Amendment; thereupon Mr. *Wragg*, who was the first in Authority, and known to be a Man of good Understanding among the *Carolinians,* was offer'd, and the Gentleman, himself, was willing to leave a young Son in the Hands of the pyrates, till he should return, which he promis'd to do, though the Government should refuse the Terms of their Releasement:

But *Blackbeard* positively deny'd this Request, saying, he knew too well of what consequence he was in the *Provence,* and he would be equally so to them, and therefore he should be the last Man they would part with.

After some Debate, Mr. *Mark* was agreed upon to accompany the Ambassadors, and accordingly they went off from the Fleet in a Canoe, and two Days were appointed for their Return; in the mean while the Commadore lay too at five or six Leagues Distance from the Land, expecting the Conditions of Peace; but the Time expiring, and nothing appearing from the Harbour, Mr. *Wragg* was sent for up before *Teach,* who putting on a terrible Countenance, told him, they were not to be trifled with, that he imagined some foul Treachery was play'd them, and that nothing but immediate Death to them all should be the Consequence of it. Mr. *Wragg* begg'd to respite the dreadful Execution one Day longer, for, that he was sure, the Province regarded their Lives so much, that they would be sollicitous to the last Degree to redeem them; that, perhaps, some Misfortune might have befallen the Canoe in going in, or it might be their own Men that occasioned the Delay, for either of which it would be hard for them to suffer.

Teach was pacified for the present, and allow'd a Day more for their coming back; but at the End of that Time, how was he enraged to find himself disappointed, calling them Villains a thousand Times, and swearing, they should not live two Hours. Mr. *Wragg,* humour'd him all he could, and desired a good Look-out should be kept. Matters seem'd now to be coming to Extremities, and no Body thought their Lives worth a Day's Purchase; the innocent People were under great Agonies of Mind, expecting that nothing but a Miracle could preserve them from being crush'd by the Weight of the Enemy's Power, when Word was given from the Forecastle, that a small Boat appear'd in Sight. This raised their drooping Spirits, and reviv'd their Hopes; *Blackbeard* went forward himself with his Spying-Glass, and declared he could perceive his own Scarlet Cloak he lent Mr. *Mark* to go ashore in; this was thought to be a sure Reprieve, till the Boat came aboard, and then their Fears returned, seeing neither the pyrates, Mr. *Mark,* nor the Chest of Medicines in the Boat.

This Boat, it seems, was sent off by Mr. *Mark* very discreetly, lest a Misconstruction should be put upon the Stay, that an unfortunate Accident had occasioned, and which the Men that belong'd to her acquainted the Commodore of, *viz.* That the Boat they had sent ashore was cast away, being overset by a sudden Squall of Wind, and the Men with great Trouble had got ashore at the uninhabited Island of three or four Leagues from the Main, that having staid there some time till reduced to Extremity, there being no Provision of any Kind, and fearing what Disaster might befal the Prisoners aboard; the Persons belonging to their Company, set Mr. *Mark* upon a Hatch, and floated it upon the Sea, after which, they stripp'd and flung themselves in, and swimming after it, and thrust the Float forward, endeavouring, by that means, to get to Town. This prov'd a very tedious Voiture, and in all Likelihood they had perished, had not this Fishing Boat sail'd by in the Morning, and perceiving something in the Water, made to it, and took them in, when they were near spent with their Labour.

When they were thus providentially preserv'd, Mr. *Mark* went into and there hired a Boat which carried them to *Charles Town;* in the mean time he had sent this Boat to give them an Account of the Accident. Mr. *Teach* was pacified with this Relation, and consented to stay two Days longer, since there appeared no Fault of theirs in causing this Delay. At the End of two Days, they lost all Patience, and the Commodore could not be prevail'd on to give them any longer Time than the next Morning to live, if the Boat did not return by that Time. Still expecting and still disappointed, the Gentlemen knew not what to say, nor how to excuse their Friends at Land; some of them told the pyrates, that they had equal Reason with them to blame their Conduct; that they doubted not, by what had already happen'd, of Mr. *Mark*'s doing his Duty faithfully; and since they had received Notice of the Boat's going safe into *Charles Town,* they could not conceive what should hinder the Execution of the Business, unless they put a greater Value on the Chest of Medicines, than on the Lives of fourscore Men now on the Verge of Destruction. *Teach,* for his Part, believed they had imprisoned his Men, and refused the Condition of the Prisoner's Enlargement, and swore a thousand Times, that they should not only die, but every *Carolina* Man that hereafter should fall into his Hands. The Prisoners, at last, petitioned to have this one Favour granted, *viz.* That the Fleet should weigh and stand off the Harbour, and if they should not then see the Boat coming out, that they the Prisoners would pilot them in before the Town, which, if they pleased to batter down, they would stand by them to the last Man.

This Proposal of taking Revenge for the supposed Treachery (as the Commodore was pleased to term it) suited well enough the Savage Temper of the General and his Brutes, and he acquiesc'd at once. The Project was likewise approv'd on by the Myrmidons, and accordingly they weigh'd Anchor, being in all eight Sail of Ships, which were the Prizes they had in Custody, and rang'd along the Town; the Inhabitants then had their Share of the Fright, expecting nothing less than a general Attack; the Men were brought all under Arms, but not in so regular a manner as might have been done, had the Surprize been less; but the Women and Children ran about the Street like mad Things. However, before Matters came to Extremities, the Boat was seen coming out, which brought Redemption to the poor Captives, and Peace to all.

The Chest was brought aboard, and accepted of, and it further appear'd, that Mr. *Mark* had done his Duty, and the Blame of the Delay was deservedly thrown on the two pyrates that were sent on the Embassy; for while the Gentlemen attended the Governor and Council upon the Business, the other fine Gentlemen were visiting and drinking with their *quondam* Friends and Acquaintance, and going from House to House, so that they were not to be found when the Medicines were ready to go aboard; and Mr. *Mark* knew it were Death to them all to go without them, for the Commodore would not easily have believ'd, had they not returned, that there had been no foul Play acted by them. But now none but smiling Countenances were seen aboard; the Storm that threatned the Prisoners so heavily, blew over, and a Day of Sun-shine succeeded; in short, *Blackbeard* released them as he had promised, and sent them away in the Ships after he had done with them, and then sail'd off the Coast, as has been mentioned in *Vol.* I. *page* 73.

What follows, contains Reflections on a Gentleman now deceas'd, who was Governor of *North Carolina,* namely, *Charles Eden,* Esq; which, we apprehend, by Accounts since receiv'd, to be without just Grounds, therefore, it will be necessary to say something in this Place, to take off the Calumny thrown on his Character, by Persons who have misjudged of his Conduct by the Height Things appeared in at that time.

Upon a Review of this Part of *Blackbeard*'s Story, it does not seem, by any Matters of Fact candidly considered, that the said Governour held any private or criminal Correspondence with this Pyrate; and I have been inform'd since, by very good Hands, that Mr. *Eden* always behaved, as far as he had Power, in a manner suitable to his Post, and bore the Character of a good Governor, and an honest Man.

But his Misfortune was, the Weakness of the Colony he commanded, wanting Strength to punish the Disorders of *Teach,* who lorded it at Pleasure, not only in the Plantation, but in the Governor's own Habitation, threatening to destroy the Town with Fire and Sword, if any Injury was offer'd to him or his Companions, insomuch, that he sometimes drew up his Vessel against the Town, and once, when he suspected that there was a Design of seizing him, he went ashore to the Governor well armed, and left Orders with his Men on board, that in Case he should not return in an Hour's Time (as he determined, if at Liberty) to batter down the House about their Ears, without any more to do, notwithstanding he himself were to be in it. Such were the outragious Insolencies of this Villain, who was so big with Mischief, that he resolved to be revenged upon his Enemies at all Events, even tho' he should give up his own Life, as a Sacrifice, to obtain those wicked Ends.

It is to be observed, that *Blackbeard,* nevertheless, as to his Pyracies, had comply'd with the Proclamation, and thereby satisfied the Law, and having a Certificate thereof from under the Hand of his Excellency, he could not be prosecuted for any of those Crimes committed heretofore, because they were wiped off by the said Proclamation of Pardon: And as to condemning the *French Martinico* Man that *Blackbeard* brought in to *North Carolina* afterwards, the Governor proceeded judicially upon her. He called a Court of Vice Admiralty, by virtue of his Commission; at which four of the Crew swore they found the Ship at Sea with no Person on board her, so the Court condemn'd her, as any other Court must have done, and the Cargo was disposed of according to Law.

As to the secret Expedition from *Virginia,* undertaken by the Governor and the two Captains of Men of War, they had their secret Views in it: The Men of War had lain up these ten Months whilst the pyrates infested the Coast, and did great Mischief, for which, 'tis likely, they might have been called to an Account; but the Success of the Enterprize againsh *Teach,* alias *Blackbeard,* perhaps prevented such Enquiry, tho' I am at a Loss to know what Acts of Pyracy he had committed after this Surrender to the Proclamation; the *French* Ship was lawfully condemned, as has been said before, and if he had committed any Depredations amongst the Planters, as they seem'd to complain of, they were not upon the high Sea, but either in the River, or on Shore, and could not come within the Jurisdiction of the Admiralty, nor under any Laws of Pyracy. The Governor of *Virginia* found his Interest in the Affair; for he sent, at the same time, a Force by Land, and seiz'd considerable Effects of *Blackbeard*'s in *Eden*'s Province, which was certainly a new Thing for the Governor of one Province, whose Commission was limited to that Jurisdiction, to exercise Authority in another Government, and the Governour himself upon the Spot. Thus was poor Mr. *Eden* insulted and abused on all Sides, without having the Power of doing himself Justice, and asserting his lawful Rights.

In fine, to do Justice to Governor *Eden*'s Character, who is since dead, there did not appear from any Writings or Letters found in *Blackbeard*'s Sloop, or from any other Evidence whatsoever, that the said Governor was concerned at all in any Male Practice; but on the contrary, that during his Continuance in that Post, he was honour'd and beloved by his Colony, for his Uprightness, Probity, and prudent Conduct in his Administration; what Affairs were carried on privately by his then Secretary I know not; he died a few Days after *Blackbeard*'s Destruction, and no Enquiry was made; perhaps there might be no Occasion for it.

III. Of Major Bonnet

I have but few Words to add to Major *Bonnet*'s Life and Actions; when his Dissolution drew nigh, all his Resolution fail'd him, and his Fears and Agonies so wrought upon him, that he was scarce sensible when he came to the Place of Execution. His piteous Behaviour under Sentence, very much affected the People of the Province, particularly the Women, and great Application was made to the Governor for saving his Life, but in vain; not that his Excellency Colonel *Johnson* pleased himself in Acts of severe Justice, but he knew his Duty too well to be misled by the Tears and Prayers of weak and inconsiderate People, when the public Good, as well as his own Honour, stood in Question. Had not *Bonnet* escap'd out of his Keeper's Hand, after he was taken, and occasioned the Death of his Fellow-Prisoner *Harriot*, by resisting the Governor's Authority, and therein given a new Specimen of his disloyal Intentions, something might have been done in his Favour; but he was become too notorious, and too dangerous a Criminal, to give Life to. However, the Governor who conducted himself in his Post as well as in his private Capacity, with great Probity, Honour, and Candour, hearkened to a Proposal of *Bonnet*'s Friends, which was to send him Prisoner to *England,* that his Case might be referr'd to his Majesty. Col. *Rhet* offer'd to go with him, and sufficient Security was to be given for yielding him up there, to be dealt with according to his Majesty's Pleasure; but the Major's Friends considered, at last, that it would be a great Expence and Trouble to no manner of purpose, except the lengthening out a wretched Life some small Time longer; for they conceived as little Hope of obtaining a Pardon in *England* as in *South Carolina;* so they even submitted to the Execution of that Sentence upon the Major, that had with so much Justice pass'd upon him. I shall subjoin here a Copy of a Letter, writ to the Governor from the Prisoner sometime before he died.

Honoured Sir,

'I Have presumed, on the Confidence of your eminent Goodness, to throw my self, after this manner, at your Feet, to implore you'll graciously be pleased to look upon me with tender Bowels of Pity and Compassion; and believe me to be the most miserable Man this Day breathing: That the Tears proceeding from my most sorrowful Soul may soften your Heart, and incline you to consider my dismal State, wholly, I must confess, unprepared to receive so soon the dreadful Execution you have been pleas'd to appoint me; and therefore beseech you to think me an Object of your Mercy.

'For God Sake, good Sir, let the Oaths of three Christian Men weigh something with you, who are ready to depose, when you please to allow them the Liberty, the Compulsions I lay under in committing those Acts, for which I am doom'd to die.

'I intreat you not to let me fall a Sacrifice to the Envy and ungodly Rage of some few Men, who, not being yet satisfied with Blood, feign to believe, that if I had the Happiness of a longer Life in this World, I should still employ it in a wicked Manner; which, to remove that and all other Doubts with your Honour, I heartily beseech you'll permit me to live, and I'll voluntarily put it ever out of my Power, by separating all my Limbs from my Body, only reserving the Use of my Tongue, to call continually on, and pray to the Lord, my God, and mourn all my Days in Sack-cloth and Ashes to work out confident Hopes of my Salvation, at that great and dreadful Day, when all righteous Souls shall receive their just Rewards: And to render your Honour a further Assurance of being incapable to prejudice any of my Fellow-Christians, if I was so wickedly bent; I humbly beg you will (as a Punishment of my Sins for my poor Soul's Sake) indent me a menial Servant to your Honour and this Government, during my Life, and send me up to the farthest Inland Garrison or Settlement in the Country, or any otherways you'll be pleased to dispose of me; and likewise that you'll receive the Willingness of my Friends to be bound for my good Behaviour, and constant Attendance to your Commands.

'I once more beg for the Lord's Sake, dear Sir, that as you are a Christian, you will be so charitable to have Mercy and Compassion on my miserable Soul, but too newly awaked from an Habit of Sin, to entertain so confident Hopes and Assurance of its being received into the Arms of my blessed Jesus, as is necessary to reconcile me to so speedy a Death; wherefore, as my Life, Blood, Reputation of my Family, and future happy State lies entirely at your Disposal; I implore you to consider me with a christian and charitable Heart, and determine mercifully of me, that I may ever acknowledge and esteem you next to God my Saviour; and oblige me ever to pray, that our heavenly Father will also forgive your Trespasses.

'Now the God of Peace, that brought again from the Dead our Lord Jesus, that great Shepherd of the Sheep, thro' the Blood of the everlasting Covenant, make you perfect in every good Work to do his Will, working in you that which is well pleasing in his Sight, through Jesus Christ, to whom be Glory for ever and ever, is the hearty Prayer of

Your Honour's
Most miserable, and
Afflicted Servant,
STEDE Bonnet.

IV. Of Captain Worley

The history of the pyrates being an Undertaking of great Length and Variety, the Author readily owns, that in some Parts, he may not be so exact, as they who have been occasionally upon the Spot when these particular Incidents have happen'd. But in any Circumstances he has omitted or misrepresented, he applies to such Persons for better Information; which Correction or Addition (as several others have been) shall be inserted as a Supplement to the whole.

And he hereby acknowledges himself much obliged to the worthy Gentleman who sent the following Letter, for his kind Assistance, in promoting his chief Design, which is to render as complete as possible, a Work of so difficult a Nature.

To Mr. Johnson, *Author of the Lives of the pyrates.*

SIR,

IN perusing your Book, Entitled, *A General History of the Robberies and Murders of the most notorious pyrates,* &c. I find there an Account of the taking Captain *Worley* and his Crew, in many Particulars of which you have been very much misinformed, and consequently the Public is so; that Pyrate having been taken off the Bar of *Charles Town* in *South Carolina* by Col. *Robert Johnson,* the then Governor, in Person; to whom to do Justice, I have sent you the following Account of the taking him; for, as to his Beginning and Rise, I cannot say but your Account may be right, as you have set it forth in your aforesaid Book.

In *October,* 1718, Governor *Johnson* was informed, that there was a Pyrate Ship off the Bar of *Charles Town,* commanded by one *Moody,* carrying 50 Guns, and near 200 Men, that he had taken two Ships bound to that Port from *New England,* and was come to an Anchor with them to the Southward of the Bar; whereupon, he called his Council and the principal Gentlemen of the Place, and proposed to them, to fit out a proper Force to go out and attack him, fearing he might lie there some Time, as *Thatch* and *Vane* had done before, and annoy the Trade; which they unanimously agreeing, and there being, at that Time, 14 or 15 Ships in the Harbour, he impress'd the *Mediterranean* Gally, *Arthur Loan,* and the King *William, John Watkinson,* Commanders; and two Sloops, one of which was the *Revenge,* taken from *Stede Bonnet,* the Pyrate, and another from *Philadelphia;* the former, Captain *John Masters* commanded, and the latter, Captain *Fayrer Hall;* which two Captains had lately commanded the same Sloops that took *Bonnet* at *Cape Fear,* about a Month before. On board the *Mediterranean* was put 24 Guns, and 30 on Board the King *William;* the *Revenge* Sloop had 8, and the other Sloop 6 Guns; and being thus equipp'd, the Governor issued a Proclamation, to encourage Volunteers to go on Board, promising 'em all the Booty to be shar'd among them, and that he himself would go in Person with 'em; but the Ships and Sloops before-mentioned being impress'd, it was natural for the Commanders to desire some Assurance of Satisfaction to be made the Owners, in Case of a Misfortune; so that the Governor found it necessary to call the General Assembly of the Province, without whom it was impossible for him to give them the Satisfaction they desired, and who, without any Hesitation, pass'd a Vote, that they would pay for the said Vessels, in Case they were lost, according to an Appraisement then made of them, and what other Expences accrued to carry on this necessary Expedition. This Way of Proceeding took up a Week's Time, during which, the Governor ordered Scout Boats to ply up and down the River, as well to guard the Port from any Attempts the pyrates might make to Land, as to hinder them from having Advice of what was doing, and also laid an Embargo on the Shipping.

About three Days before the Governor sail'd, there appear'd off the Barr a Ship, and a Sloop, who came to an Anchor, and made a Signal for a Pilot; but they being suppos'd to be *Moody,* and a Sloop that had join'd him (as it was said he expected) no Pilot was permitted to go near them, and thus they rid for four Days, once or twice attempting to send their Boat on Shore, to an Island, call'd, *Suilivants* Island (as they afterwards confess'd) to fetch Water, of which they were in great Want; but they were prevented by the Scout Boats before-mentioned: And, for Want of which, they were obliged to continue in the same Station, in hopes some Ship would be coming in or going out, to relieve their Necessities, they being very short also of Provisions.

And now all Things being ready, and about Three hundred Men on Board the four Vessels, the Governor thought himself a Match for *Moody* in his 50 Gun Ship, although he should be, as they thought he was, join'd by a Sloop: And therefore, he sail'd with his Fleet below *Johnson*'s Fort over Night, and the next Morning by Break of Day, weigh'd Anchor, and by Eight in the Morning, they were over the Bar.

The Pyrate Sloop immediately slipt her Cable, hoisted a black Flag, and stood to get between the Bar and the Governor's Ships, to prevent their going in again, as they expected they would have done; and in a small Time after, the Pyrate Ship also hoisted a black Flag, and made Sail after the Sloop; during all this Time, the Men on Board the Governor's Vessels did not appear, nor was there any Shew of Guns, until they came within half Gun-shot; when the Governor hoisted a Flag at the Main-top-mast Head of the *Mediterranean,* they all flung out their Guns, and giving them their Broad-sides, the pyrates immediately run, whereupon, the Governor ordered the two Sloops after the Pyrate Sloop, who stood in towards the Shore, while himself and the King *William* followed the Ship who stood the contrary Way to Sea. She seemed to have many Ports, and very full of Men, tho' she had fir'd but from two Guns, which occasion'd no small Wonder on Board the Governor, why she had not flung open her Ports, and made Use of more Guns, she being imagined all this while to be *Moody.*

The Sloop, which proved to be *Worley,* was attacked by the two Sloops so warmly, that the Men run into the Hold, all except *Worley* himself and some few others, who were killed on the Deck; and being boarded, they took her within Sight of *Charles Town:* The People seeing the Action from the Tops of their Houses, and the Masts of the Ships in the Harbour, where they had placed themselves for that Purpose; but it was Three in the Afternoon before the Governor and the King *William* came up with the Ship, who, during the Chase, had taken down her Flagg, and wrapping the small Arms in it, had thrown them over-board; and also flung over her Boat and what other Things they thought would lighten her, but all would not do: The King *William* came first up with her, and firing his Chase Guns, killed several of the People on board, and they immediately struck; when, to the no small Surprize of the Governor and his Company, there appeared near as many Women on board as Men, who were not a few neither. The Ship proving to be the *Eagle,* bound from *London* to *Virginia,* with Convicts; but had been taken by *Worley* off the *Cape* of *Virginia,* and had upwards of 100 Men and 30 Women on board. Many of the Men had taken on with the pyrates, and as such, found in *Carolina* the Fate they had deserved at home, being hang'd at *Charles Town;* the virtuous Ladies were designed to have been landed on one of the uninhabited *Bahama* Islands, where there was a proper Port for these Rovers to put in, at any Time, to refresh themselves, after the Fatigue of the Sea. And thus a most hopeful Colony would have commenced, if they had had but Provisions and Water sufficient to have carried them to Sea; but their Fate kept them so long before the Port of *Charles Town,* until they were destroyed, and an End put to their wicked Lives, in the Manner before-mentioned.

Notwithstanding all the Governor's Care, that no Advice should be given *Moody* of the Preparations making for him, some People from the Shore were so wicked, as to go off in the Night and give him a particular Account of the Ships, Sloops, and Men, that were preparing to go out against him; whereupon, he having taken (about three Days before the Governor went) the *Minerva,* Captain *Smyter,* from the *Maderas,* laden with Wine, he immediately weighed Anchor and took his Prize with him, and stood out above one hundred Leagues to

Sea, where he plundered her, and named to the Master not only the Vessels, but some of the very Persons were coming out to attack him, by which Advice he escaped, and *Worley* coming just as the other was gone, met the Fate designed for *Moody;* who having taken out most of the Wine from on board the *Minerva,* and plundered her, he discharged, and sail'd for *Providence,* and soon after took the Benefit of his Majesty's Royal Proclamation.

The Governor kept the Ships and Vessels in sailing Order some Time, in Hopes *Moody* might have come off the Bar again; but being informed by the *Minerva* he was sailed for *Providence,* he discharged them, giving the small Booty taken to the Men who were the Captors, as he had promised them.

Your Account of the taking of *Bonnet* is pretty just, which was done by Governor *Johnson*'s Direction and Commission also.

V. Of Captain Martel

To Captain Johnson.

SIR,

Though I can contribute nothing to your Second Volume of pyrates you have (as I hear) in Hand, yet, by your Character of Veracity, I perswade my self I shall oblige you, in rectifying a Mistake you made in your first. In the Life of Captain *Martel* you say, the *Greyhound* Galley of *London,* which I then commanded, fell into the Hands of that Pyrate, who plunder'd her of some Gold Dust, Elephants Teeth, and 40 Slaves. The latter Part of this is just, except the Elephants Teeth, of which I lost, I think, none; but you are misled in the former, for *Martel's* Company had deposed him, on Account, as they themselves told me, of his Cruelty; had given him, and those who were willing to follow his Fortunes, a Sloop, and, sending him away, chose a more righteous in his Place, whose Name was *Kennedy,* by Descent an *Irishman,* by Birth a *Spaniard* of *Cuba,* and a Hunter. On my coming on Board the Pyrate, Captain *Saunders* of the *Weymouth,* who was taken the Day before, was the first Man who spoke to me, telling me, he was sorry for my Misfortune. I took him for the Commander of the Pyrate; but I soon found my Mistake, by his carrying me aft to the Captain, who bid me welcome, and drank to me in a Can of Wine; and some of the Crew told me, that it was happy for me I did not fall into the Hands of their late Captain; for a Ship with *Madera* Wine thought fit to give them the Trouble to lose some Time, and fire a couple of Chase-Guns before she shorten'd Sail, which Captain *Martel* took for so great an Affront, that all the Company was cut off. But I shall now give you the Particulars of my being taken. As I have said, I commanded the *Greyhound* Galley, on board of which I had 250 Slaves, bound from the Coast of *Guiney* to *Jamaica,* and consign'd to Messieurs *Feak* and *Aldcroft,* on Account of Mr. *Bignell* and others. On the 16th of *October* 1716, about 10 Leagues S. S. W. from the Island of *Monna,* in the grey of the Morning, my second Mate came down and acquainted me, that a Ship was almost on board us. We then steer'd about W. half South, and the Pyrate stood to the S. E. His coming very near us made us edge away from him, and call out to desire he would keep his Luff, or he would be on board us. No Answer was given, and not a Soul appear'd on his Decks, but the Man at the Helm, and about two more; however the *Greyhound* got clear, and crowded, as usual, for a Market. As soon as the Pyrate got into our Wake, she wore, and made all the Sail she could, by which Means she soon came up with us (for she was clean, and we foul) and clewing up her Sprit-Sail, fir'd a Gun with Shot, and at the same Time let fly her Jack, Ensign and Pendant, in which was the Figure of a Man, with a Sword in his Hand, and an Hour-Glass before him, with a Death's Head and Bones. In the Jack and Pendant were only the Head and Cross Bones. I did not think fit to shorten Sail, which occasioned a second Shot from the Pyrate, which went through our Main Top-Sail. Upon this I consulted my Officers, and they advised the shortening sail, as we were no Way in a Capacity to make any Defence. I followed their Advice, and was order'd on board the Pyrate, who ask'd me, pretty civilly, the usual Questions, Whence I came? Whether bound? *&c.* My second Mate, and some of my Men, were soon shifted into the Pyrate, with 40 of the best Men Slaves; the Women Slaves they diverted themselves with, and took off the Irons from all the Negroes I had on board. The Captain asked me if I had no Gold? I assured him I had not; and, indeed, I had no more than 100 Ounces, which, before I went on board the Pyrate, my Carpenter had let into the Ceiling of the great Cabbin. He answer'd only, it was very strange that I should take no Gold on the Coast. I answer'd, I had taken a considerable Quantity, but as I took it in one Place, I parted with it in another; which, if he would inspect my Books, he would find exactly as I said. We had no more Discourse then on the Subject, but a while after, I and my Mate were sent for into the great Cabbin, where the Council sat. Immediately cock'd Pistols were clapp'd to our Breasts, and we were threaten'd with Death, in Case we did not confess what Gold we had on board, and where it was hid. I deny'd that we had any, and desir'd he would satisfy himself of the Truth, by examining my Books. The Mate answer'd, he knew nothing of my Dealings on the Coasts, and therefore could give no

Answer. He knew, indeed, I had received Gold on the Coast, as he had seen it brought on board; but he had seen a considerable Quantity carry'd out of the Ship. Upon this, we were order'd to withdraw, and nothing more was said; but I hearing their Design was to torture me with lighted Matches between my Fingers, I thought the Loss of the Use of my Hands would be but poorly compensated with the saving 100 Ounces of Gold, and therefore desired to speak to the

Captain himself; to him I discover'd what I had, and where it was concealed. He immediately sent his Boat on board the *Greyhound,* with my Carpenter and half a dozen of his own Crew, who were so impatient to be at the Gold, they made a meer Pincushion of the Fellow's Breech, continually pricking his Backside with their Swords, to hasten him. My Lodging was in the Hold, where one *Taffier,* the Gunner, came down to me, and snapp'd a Pistol at my Breast, which he fired afterwards upon Deck; and the same Man one Day, as I was on the Quarter-Deck, struck me, in the Presence of his Captain, with his Cutlass, after having reproach'd me with my private Consession, and asking, if every Man there had not as good and just Pretension to the Gold as the Captain. Whether it was by Accident or Design that he struck with the Flat of his Cutlass, I know not, but the Blow knock'd me down, and depriv'd me of my Senses for some Time.

Captain *Kennedy,* who seem'd to have more Humanity than is commonly found in Men of his Profession, resented this Treatment of me so far, that he got into his Yawl, and put off from the Ship, swearing he would not sail with Men who so barbarously abused their Prisoners. He, however, returned on board at their Perswasions, and on their Promise, that nothing like it should happen for the future. The Night of the Day in which we were taken, the Pyrate came to an Anchor under the Island of *Savona,* where he kept us till the 20th, and then let us go in Company with Captain *Saunders,* of the Ship *Weymouth,* from *Boston,* laden with Fish and Lumber for *Jamaica,* at which Island we arrived and anchor'd at *Port Royal* the 25th in the Morning.

The Pyrate, a little before I was taken, had met with two interloping *Dutch* Men, supposed to be bound for the Main, who gave him a rough Entertainment, and made him glad to sheer off.

The *Weymouth* had two Women Passengers on board; how they pass'd their Time I need not say; though, I fancy, as they had formerly made a Trip or two to the Bay, there was no Rape committed.

Notwithstanding the melancholy Situation I was in, I could not refrain laughing when I saw the Fellows who went on board the *Greyhound,* return to their own Ship; for they had, in rummaging my Cabbin, met with a Leather Powder Bag and Puff, with which they had powder'd themselves from Head to Foot, walk'd the Decks with their Hats under their Arms, minced their Oaths, and affected all the Airs of a Beau, with an Aukwardness would have forced a Smile from a Cynick.

When I was permitted to return on board the *Greyhound,* and prosecute my Voyage, I found all my Papers torn, and every Thing turn'd topsy-turvy; but this was nothing to their leaving all my Negroes out of Irons, of whom I was more in fear than I had been of the pyrates; for, among them, the Captain's Humanity protected us; but we could expect no Quarter from the Negroes should they rebel; and, in such Case, we had no Prospect of quelling them, for the pyrates had taken away all our Arms, and by opening a Cask of Knives, which they had scatter'd about the Ship, they had armed the Negroes, one of whom had the Insolence to collar and shake one of my Men. I therefore called my People aft, and told them, our Security depended altogether on our Resolution; wherefore arming selves with Handspikes, we drove the Negroes into the Hold, and afterwards calling them up one by one, we put on their Irons, which the pyrates had not taken with them, took away their Knives, and, by these Means, arrived safely at our Port. If this Detail is of any Service to you, I have my Ends. I hope, if you intend a third Volume, it may induce others who have had the same Misfortune of falling into the Hands of pyrates, to assist you with their Minutes.

I am, SIR, Your very humble Servant,
J. EVANS.

Feb. 2.
1727-8.

P.S. Four of my Men took on with the pyrates, though I remember the Names of two only, *Bryant Ryley, John Hammond.*

VI. The Trial of the Pyrates at Providence

To Captain Johnson.

SIR,

As I am credibly informed you intend to oblige the Public with a Second Volume of *The Lives and Actions of the pyrates,* and are now actually collecting Matter; I was of Opinion, that the sending you some Minutes I have by me, which are authentic, would be no unacceptable Office; and I hope, the Gentleman who was then Governor of the *Bahama Islands,* will not take the Publication of the following Tryals in ill Part, for I am informed he is in Town. Before I would send them to you, I examined very thoroughly whether he could have any Ground to be offended; but, as I find them Mark of his Prudence and Resolution, and that in the Condemnation and Execution of the pyrates, he had a just Regard to the public Good, and was not to be deterr'd from vigorously pursuing it, in Circumstances which would have intimidated many brave Men: I think the Publication will do him both Honour and Justice, and therefore shall make no Apology, but come to the Point.

Trial and Condemnation of the pyrates, who were executed at *Providence,* His Excellency *Woodes Rogers,* Esq; being then Captain General, Governor, and Vice-Admiral of the *Bahama Islands.*

At a private Consultation, held on *Friday* the 28th of *November,* 1718, at the *Secretary's* Office in the City of *Nassau.*

New Providence *ss.*

THE Governor *acquainting us, That Captain* Cockrem *and Captain* Hornigold *have, by Virtue of a Commission, issued and directed to them for the apprehending of certain pyrates, had the Success to bring ten of them Prisoners to this Part, who were now confined by an especial* Mittimus *on board the Ship* Delicia; *therefore, desired we might agree to join in one Opinion concerning the said Prisoners which being maturely debated and considered, and that as the necessary Guards set on the Prisoners for Want of a Goal, very much fatigued both the Soldiers and Seamen, who equally guarded the Fort and Ship; and as many as could be spar'd, daily work'd on the Fortifications, and did the Duty of Centinels at Night, thereby harrassing our small Numbers of Men, and hindering the public Work. And there being suspected Persons still remaining in these Islands, who may give frequent Intelligence of our Condition; should any Fear be shown on our Part, it might animate several now here, to invite the pyrates without, to attempt the Rescue of these in Custody: Therefore, we do believe it most for the public Good, when the Fort is in a better State of Defence, and Captain* Beauchamps *and* Burgis, *with about* 60 *Soldiers and Seamen, at this time gone to prevent the Designs of* Vane the Pyrate, *are returned to strengthen us: The Governor ought then as soon as possible (notwithstanding he has made known to us, that he has no direct Commission for Trial of pyrates; yet according to the Intent and Meaning of the sixth Article of the Governor's Instructions, which, in this Case, refers to the fourth Article in those given to the Governor of* Jamaica, *a Copy of whose Instructions he has for his Directions to govern himself by, as near as the Circumstances of the Place will admit. This corroborated with the Power in the Governor's Commission of Governor, Captain General, and Vice-Admiral of the* Bahama Islands, *show the Intention of his Majesty, for such Authority here; and having an Account that the Proprietory Government of* Carolina *had executed 22 pyrates, lately carried in there, which together with the provoking ill Example and Behaviour of these Prisoners, who have all accepted his Majesty's Act of Grace, and afterwards turned pyrates again, and considering it would be a great Risque and Trouble to send so many to Great Britain, and much greater to keep them Prisoners here; we are entirely of Opinion, his Majesty will approve of the Necessity for the Governor's judicial Proceeding with these pyrates, by a Trial in the best Manner we can according to Law; and do verily believe the speediest Execution for those who shall be found guilty, will conduce most to the Welfare of this Government.*

N. B. Thus this stands in the Council-Book, the Governor's Secretary is answerable for Want of Connexion, or the Secretary of the Islands; for I cannot find what these Words can refer to, *the Governor ought then as soon as possible,* what ought he? But may be, it is an Error in my Friend, who himself brought over this Copy, written in his own Hand, which with the following, I found among his Papers after his Decease.

His Excellency *Woodes Rogers,* Esq; Captain-General, Governor, and Vice-Admiral of the *Bahama Islands.*

To *William Fairfax,* Esq; Captain *Robert Beauchamps, Tho. Walker,* Esq; Capt. *Wingate Gale, Nathaniel Taylor,* Esq; Capt. *Josias Burgiss,* and Capt. *Peter Courant.*

Providence, ss.

'BY Virtue of a Commission from his most sacred Majesty King *George,* King of *Great-Britain,* &c. to be Governor, *&c.* of these Islands, thereby empowering me to authorize, commissionate, and constitute all Judges, Justices and Magistrates in these Islands, *&c.* as also by Virtue of my Commission, to be Vice-Admiral of these Islands, have Power and Authority to authorize and empower, constitute and commissionate, proper Judges and Commissioners, for the trying, determining, adjudging, and condemning, of all or any Pyrate or pyrates taken, apprehended, and brought into this Government; and in Confidence of the Loyalty, Prudence, and Integrity of you the aforesaid *William Fairfax,* Esq; Captain *Robert Beauchamps, Thomas Walker,* Esq; Captain *Wingate Gale, Nathaniel Taylor,* Esq; Captain *Josias Burgiss,* and Captain *Peter Courant,* I do by Virtue of these Presents, authorize, commissionate, and appoint you Deputy, Judges, and Commissioners of the said Especial Court, by these Presents erected and appointed to be, and set in the City of *Nassau,* on *Tuesday* the 9th of this Instant, to examine, hear, try, judge, determine, and condemn, all such Pyrate or pyrates who are now in Custody, and to be brought before the said Court, to be tryed for the Offences of Pyracy by them lately committed in and about these Islands, and to proceed as my Assistants, and as Commissioners aforesaid, according to the Laws of *England,* and Rules of the said Court in such Cases; and for your so doing, this shall be your sufficient Commission and Authority.

Given under my Hand and Seal at Nassau, *this fifth Day of* December, Anno Regni quinto *Georgii* Regis *Magnæ Britanniæ,* &c. Annoq; Domini, 1718.

WOODES Rogers.

New Providence, ss. Chief of the *Bahama Islands.*

AT an especial Admiralty Sessions, held in his Majesty's Guard-Room in the City of *Nassau,* on *Tuesday* the 9th, and *Wednesday* the 10th of *December,* 1718.

Before his Excellency *Woodes Rogers,* Esq; Governor, and Vice-Admiral, *&c.*

Will. Fairfax, Esq; Judge of the *Admiralty.*

Robert Beauchamp, Esq;

Thomas Walker, Esq;

Captain *Wingate Gale.*

Nathaniel Taylor, Esq;

Captain *Josias Burgiss.*

Captain *Peter Courant.*

Proclamation being made as usual, the Register opened and read the Governor's especial Commission, for erecting this Court according to the Intent and Meaning of a late Act of Parliament, Entitled, *An Act for the more effectual Suppression of Pyracy,* by Virtue of which said Commission, the seven afore-named Commissioners are appointed Assistant Judges, for the hearing, trying, judging, and condemning the several Persons now in Custody, who stand committed for Mutiny, Felony, and Pyracy.

Proclamation being again made, that all Persons concern'd or summon'd, and required to appear at this Court, do give their due Attendance.

Ordered, That the Prisoners be brought to the Bar, which being done, they were called by their respective Names, viz. *John Augur, Will. Cunningham, John Hipps, Dennis Mackarthy, George Rounsivel, Will. Dowling, Will. Lewis, Thomas Morris, George Bendall,* and *Will Ling.*

Ordered, That the afore-named Prisoners, now at the Bar, do all hold up their Hands.

Ordered, That the Accusation against the Prisoners be read, which was as follows.

New Providence, ss.

THE Articles and Accusations against *John Augur*, late Master of the Sloop *Mary*, of *Providence*; *William Cunningham*, Gunner and Mariner, on board the Schooner, called the *Batchelors Adventure*; *Henry White*, Master, *John Hipps*, Boatswain and Mariner, on board the Sloop *Lancaster*; *William Greenaway*, Master, *Dennis Mackarthy*, Mariner, on board the *Scooner*, *William Dowling*, Mariner, on board the said *Scooner*; *William Lewis*, Mariner, on board the Sloop *Mary*; *Tho. Morris*, Mariner, on board the said *Scooner*; *George Bendall*, Mariner, on board the said Sloop *Lancaster*, and *William Ling*, Mariner, on board the said *Scooner*.

You the said *John Augur, Will. Cunningham, John Hipps, Dennis Mackarthy, George Rounsivel, William Dowling, William Lewis, Thomas Morris, George Bendall*, and *William Ling*, having all of you lately received the Benefit of his Majesty's most gracious Pardon, for your former Offences and Acts of Robbery and Pyracy, and having since taken the Oaths of Allegiance to his most sacred Majesty King *George*, and thereupon Trust has been reposed in you the said *John Augur*, and in the others of you, lawful Employments been bestow'd to divert you all from your former and unlawful Courses of Life, and to enable and support you all in just and lawful Ways of Living; and you not having the Fear of God before your Eyes, nor any Regard to your Oaths of Allegiance taken to your Sovereign, nor to the Performance of Loyalty, Truth, and Justice: But, being instigated and deluded by the Devil, to return to your former unlawful evil Courses, of Robbery and Pyracy, and that you *John Augur, Will. Cunningham, John Hipps, Dennis Mackarthy, George Rounsivel, Will. Dowling, Will. Lewis, Tho. Morris, Geo. Bendall*, and *Will. Ling*, late Master and Mariners aforesaid, did on the 6th Day of *October* last, about Seven in that Evening, in the 5th Year of the Reign of our Sovereign Lord *George*, by the Grace of God, King of *Great Britain*, &c. plot and combine together, at a desolate Island, called *Green Key*, within the Jurisdiction of this Vice-Admiralty, to mutiny and feloniously and piratically steal, take, and carry away, from the Commanders and Owners of the afore-named Vessels, the said Sloops and Cargoes, Tackle, Apparel, and Furniture, to the Value of above 900 l. current Money of these Islands, and by Force cause to be put ashore on the said desolate Island, one Mr. *James Kerr*, Merchant, and sundry others with him; and the said *John Augur*, as then Commander of one of the said Sloops, did proceed as Commander of the said pyrates from the said Island of *Green Key* to *Exuma*, whereby, by Virtue of a Commission, directed to Captain *John Cockrem* and Captain *Benjamin Hornigold*, you the said *John Augur*, and the rest of your piratical Company, were there taken and apprehended as pyrates, and thereupon brought into this Port, to be proceeded against according to Law.

The Prisoners holding up their Hands, and the Accusation being read, all the said Prisoners were asked by the Register, Whether Guilty, or, Not Guilty; and they pleaded Not Guilty.

Ordered, That the Evidence for the King be severally sworn and examined.

James Kerr.

The Examination of *James Kerr*, Gent. upon Oath saith, That he being Supercargo in Trust, and outward bound from *Providence*, a trading Voyage in the Sloop *Mary*, and in about two Days Sail from the said Island, did arrive at *Green Key* with two other Vessels in Company, bound also on the said trading Account, where, on the 6th of *October* last, one *Phineas Bunce*, one of the said Vessel's Company, and the head Mutineer of the pyrates now at the Bar, but since deceas'd, did then and there come on board the said Sloop *Mary*, and very vilely treat this Deponent, and in the Evening did turn the Deponent ashore upon the said *Green Key*, a desolate Island; and this Deponent farther saith, that *Dennis Mackarthy*, one of the Prisoners now at the Bar, was the only Person of all the said pyrates and Mutineers who shew'd this Deponent any civil Treatment, and that the said *Mackarthy* did not reflect on the King and Government as others of them now at the Bar did, in this Deponent's Hearing.

Wm. Greenaway.

The Examination of Captain *William Greenaway* upon Oath saith, That on the 6th of *October* last *John Hipps*, one of the Prisoners now at the Bar, with some others of them, came on board the Vessel under this Deponent's Command, and then riding at *Green Key*, with Pretensions of getting Tobacco, and told this Deponent, that Mr. *Kerr* had a Mind to sail that Night; and this Deponent having order'd his Boat to go on board the Scooner, then belonging to the said Company, to give them Notice of the said *Kerr*'s Design; in which Interim came on board *John Augur* and *George Rounsivel,* both Prisoners now at the Bar, *James Matthews* and *John Johnson,* who wanted this Deponent to go on board the Scooner, which he did, where *Phineas Bunce,* since dead, met this Deponent at the Side; upon which, this Deponent demanded of the said *Bunce,* the Reason he did not prepare for sailing, as the rest did. Whereupon *Bunce,* the head Mutineer, asked this Deponent to walk down into the Cabbin, and, when there, *Bunce* asked him to fit down by him; whereupon the said *Bunce* told this Deponent, he was his Prisoner; upon which, *Dennis Macarthey,* now Prisoner at the Bar, presented a Pistol at this Deponent's Breast, and told him, if he spoke a Word, he, this Deponent, was a dead Man; and the said *Phineas Bunce* told this Deponent, he had best be easy, for that the better Part of the People belonging to the Sloop *Mary* was on his Side, as were some of the People he had with him. And then the said *Phineas Bunce,* with others, the Mutineers, went on board the Sloop *Mary,* and took her. But this Deponent cannot particularize the Names of the Men who were with *Bunce,* being Night-time. Afterwards the said *Bunce,* and the Prisoners now at the Bar, except *John Hipps,* put Mr. *James Kerr, Richard Turnly, Thomas Rich, John Taylor,* and *John Cox,* all ashore at *Green Key,* a desolate Island, and had the Boat ready prepared to carry this Deponent ashore also; but *Bunce* hereupon declared, that this Deponent, being a *Bermudian,* would swim aboard again, and therefore confin'd this Deponent a Prisoner, and plundered his Vessel, leaving him not wherewithal to proceed any where, but a small Quantity of Flower and Beef, obliging this Deponent not to sail from *Green Key* in 24 Hours after his Departure; but this Deponent did sail the next Morning for *Providence,* and, in his Way, fell in Sight of the said Mutineers and pyrates, of whom the Prisoners at the Bar were some, who gave Chase. Whereupon this Deponent went back to *Green Key,* and took to the Shore, where he saw the pyrates and said Mutineers cut away the Mast of this Deponent's Vessel, and then were coming on Shore, as this Deponent apprehended, to take his Person. Whereupon this Deponent made his Escape to hide himself from them upon the said *Key.* Then the People who were left on board this Deponent's Vessel, coming ashore, told this Deponent, that the pyrates had scuttled her, turn'd the Yawl adrift, and from *Green Key* the said pyrates proceeded to *Stocking* Island, where meeting the *Spaniards,* the pyrates were themselves taken, and put ashore.

John Taylor.

The Examination of *John Taylor* upon Oath saith, That all the Prisoners at the Bar, except *John Hipps,* did join with *Bunce,* the Mutineer; and that *Bunce* and two more, whom the Deponent knew not, being Night, took the Vessel he belong'd to; and further saith, That *John Hipps* was at first confined with the said *Greenaway* by *Bunce.*

Richard Turnly.

The Examination of *Richard Turnly* upon Oath saith, That on the 6th of *October* last, *Bunce* the head Mutineer and two others, naming *William Dowling* and *Thomas Morris,* Prisoners at the Bar, did come on board the Sloop *Mary* at *Green Key,* and ask'd Mr. *Kerr* and this Deponent for a Bottle of Beer, which was given them, and afterwards a Second, and they commanded a third; and then with the Men, belonging to the said Sloop *Mary,* took up Arms, and took Mr. *Kerr, Thomas Cox,* and this Deponent Prisoners, and forced them to go on Shore at *Green Key,* a desolate Island, about 25 Leagues distant from *Providence.*

John Cox.

The Examination of *John Cox* upon Oath saith, That he being on board the Sloop *Mary,* of which *John Augur* went out of *Providence* Master: The said *John Augur* came on board his said Sloop in the Evening of the 6th Day of *October* last, and lay down as if he designed to sleep. Soon after, Capt. *Greenaway,* Master of the Sloop *Lancaster,* came on board, and ask'd the said *Augur,* if he intended to set Sail? He answer'd, he could not tell; thereupon Captain *Greenaway* went on board the Scooner, call'd the *Batchelor*'s *Adventure, Henry White,* Master, and in about half an Hour afterwards, came on board another Boat with *John Hipps, Greenaway*'s Boatswain, to enquire for Captain *Greenaway;* and in a little Time after, *Phineas Bunce* came on board the Sloop *Mary* from the *Scooner* with 2 or 3 Men more. *Bunce* ask'd for Captain *Augur*, and whether they had any Thing to drink, and coming to Mr. *Kerr*, ask'd him for a Bottle of Beer, which Mr. *Kerr* gave him; then the said *Bunce* went into the Cabbin, and brought up a Cutlash, and stood at the Cabbin-Door to drink, and swore that he was Captain of that Vessel, and would be so, which made Captain *Augur* ask him his Meaning; but presently the said *Bunce* and *Augur* seem'd to be good Friends, and *Bunce* ask'd for another Bottle of Beer, then struck Mr. *Kerr* with a Cutlash on his Back, and turn'd him and others ashore; and this Deponent well knew all the several Prisoners at the Bar, except *Hipps* the Boatswain, and that all the rest were Aiders, Assistants, and Abettors to the Mutiny, Felony, and Pyracy, committed upon the Vessels and Cargoes at *Green Key*.

Thomas Rich.

The Examination of *Thomas Rich* upon Oath saith, That he knows the several Prisoners at the Bar; and that they all, except *Hipps*, were the Actors of the Mutiny and Pyracy, committed upon the Vessels and Cargoes at *Green Key*; and this Deponent was taken by them in the *Mary* Sloop, and put ashore with Mr. *Kerr* and the other Evidences for the King.

Thomas Petty.

The Examination of *Thomas Petty* upon Oath saith, That he saw *Hipps* beat by *Bunce*, and believes he was forced to go with him; and that *Bunce* would have forc'd this Deponent also; but *Dennis Mackarthy*, Prisoner at the Bar, said if *Bunce* forc'd the Doponent, he the said Prisoner would leave *Bunce* and his Company.

And then the Court adjourn'd till 3 a-Clock in the Afternoon.

The Court being met according to Adjournment, and all the Evidences for the King being called and examined, then the Prisoners at the Bar were severally called, to know what Defence each had to make, *viz*.

John Augur.

John Augur being first called to make Defence for himself, saith no other than that he was in Liquor, and knew not of *Phineas Bunce* his Design, when the said *Bunce* enter'd on board the Sloop *Mary*, whereof the Prisoner was Master; but could call no Evidence to prove himself not guilty.

Wm. Cunningham.

William Cunningham being next called and examined said, That he was asleep when *Bunce* went on board the *Scooner* (to which the Prisoner belong'd) at *Green Key*, and that *Bunce* brought the said Prisoner Punch, and told him, that he the Prisoner must either join him the said *Bunce*, or be put upon a *Moroon Key*, alias a desolate Key.

John Hipps.

John Hipps, Prisoner, said in his Defence, that he did not in any wise enter with *Bunce* and his Company; but went on board the aforesaid *Scooner*, to enquire for *William Greenaway* his Captain, where he was immediately confined by *Bunce*, together with *Greenaway*, and afterwards put on Shore with Mr. *Kerr* and others, where *Bunce* beat the said Prisoner, and compell'd him at length to join *Bunce*, but nevertheless declared his Intention to leave the said *Bunce* and Company on the first Opportunity, and desired Mr. *Kerr*, Captain *Greenaway*, *Richard Turnly*, *Thomas Terrell*, *Benjamin Hutchins*, *John Taylor*, *John Janson*, *Thomas Petty* and *David Meredith*, might be examin'd for him.

Mr. *James Kerr* being sworn as Evidence for the Prisoner declared, That *Bunce* used much threatning Language against *John Hipps*, Prisoner, that if he did not join him the said *Bunce* and piratical Company, and go with them into a Boat, provided on Purpose to carry the pyrates to their Rendezvous, *Hipps* should repent the Refusal; and farther says, that he saw or knew of no Blows given to compel the Prisoner to assist or join the said pyrates, but that the Prisoner afterwards accepted the Office and Command of Boatswain to the said piratical Company.

Captain *Greenaway* being sworn for the Prisoner says, that the Prisoner went with him on board the *Scooner*, and was in the Cabbin with him, and made Prisoner with him on board the said *Scooner*, where the Prisoner made Proposal to the Deponent to surprize *Dennis Mackarthy*,

Prisoner at the Bar, then a Centinel upon Deck, and throw the said *Mackarthy* over-board; but the Deponent seeing no Probability of escaping the Rest, advised the Prisoner to keep his Mind to himself, till he could have a better Opportunity; and farther saith, that the Prisoner was put ashore with Mr. *Kerr,* &c.

Richard Turnly being sworn for the Prisoner deposed, That to the best of his Knowledge and Remembrance, the Prisoner was forc'd to accept of any Duty the said *Bunce* and Company put upon him, if the Command of Words be allowed by the Court sufficient to excuse him; but he never saw *Bunce,* or any of the rest of the pyrates, use Blows to force him to join them.

Thomas Terrell, Inhabitant, being sworn, gave the Prisoner the Character of being an honest Man, who was recommended to him by *Thomas Bowling,* Master of the Sloop *Sarah,* belonging to the said *Thomas Terrell,* that during a late Voyage perform'd to *Cuba,* about two Months ago, there was a Mutiny suspected by *Thomas Bowling,* of which the said *Bowling* declared, that *John Hipps* Prisoner, was not only innocent, but believed a Suppressor of the said Mutiny; and farther declares, that *Thomas Bowling* had acknowledged the Safety of the Vessel to be much owing to *John Hipps,* Prisoner at the Bar.

Benjamin Hutchins being sworn for the Prisoner, and examined, declared, that the Prisoner after having been matriculated and seduced by *Bunce* and his Accomplices, often complain'd to him the Deponent, that he would desert them the first Opportunity, and shew'd his Intentions by many Tears shed, as Tokens of Sorrow for his late Misfortune.

John Taylor being examined upon Oath declared, that the Prisoner was confined as a Person not trusted by *Bunce* and his piratical Company.

John Jansen being examined upon Oath, had nothing to declare for or against the Prisoner worth Notice.

Thomas Petty being sworn for the Prisoner declared, that *Bunce* threatned the Prisoner, that if he would not consent to be of his piratical Company, he should be frequently beat; and also be put on the first *Moroon Key,* where he might not find Provision, Water, or any other Sustenance, which the Deponent thinks compell'd the Prisoner to proceed with *Bunce* for his Safety.

David Meredith being also examined upon Oath declared, That when *Phineas Bunce* first made Seizure of the Vessel, he particularly spoke to *Hipps* the Prisoner, that if he would not take on in their Way, he the said *Bunce* would moroon him, upon some desolate Key or Island; and the more to compel him, gave him several Blows with his Cutlash, and thinks the Prisoner was forced to join with *Bunce,* &c.

Dennis Mackarthy.

Dennis Mackarthy Prisoner being next called, and desiring that Mr. *Kerr,* Captain *Greenaway, John Taylor, Thomas Rich,* and *Thomas Petty,* might be admitted to give Evidence for him.

Mr. *Kerr* being examined upon Oath declared, That *Mackarthy,* Prisoner, was as active as any other of the Prisoners in their piratical Designs, and has nothing more to speak in his Favour, than that the Prisoner treated him and all others that were of the Deponent's Company, with more Civility than any others of the piratical Crew did.

Captain *Greenaway* being sworn for the Prisoner declared, That when *Bunce* beat the said Deponent, the Prisoner said, that he would see who ought to be Strikers amongst them for the future.

John Taylor being examined upon Oath declares, that the Prisoner should say, that he would leave *Bunce* and his Accomplices.

Thomas Rich being sworn declares, that he heard the Prisoner say, that since he had begun, he thought himself obliged to go on with them, meaning *Bunce* and his piratical Company.

Thomas Petty being also sworn declares, That after *Mackarthy* had been an Accomplice of *Bunce*'s Pyracy, he heard the Prisoner say, he was sorry for his Unadvisedness, which might bring great Troubles on his poor Wife, having a small Child.

George Rounsivel.

George Rounsivel, Prisoner, being next called, desired *Turnly* to be Evidence for him; who being sworn, declared, That *Geo. Rounsivel,* after having consented to be of *Bunce*'s piratical Company, shew'd some Token of Sorrow, but withal said, that as he had begun, could not without Danger of Life, desert the pyrates he had combined with.

Wm. Dowling.

William Dowling, Prisoner, being next called, and desiring *Thomas Petty* to be Evidence for him, he was sworn, and said, that he had very little to say for him, because he had seen the Prisoner as consenting to their piratical Designs as any of the said Prisoners.

William Lewis.

William Lewis, Prisoner, being next called, had very little to say for himself, otherwise than that one *David Meredith* had heard him say, he wished to be at *John Cullemore*'s House to drink a Bottle of Beer, which *David Meredith,* being sworn as Evidence for the Prisoner, only confirmed.

Thomas Morris.

Thomas Morris, Prisoner, being next called, had very little else to say, than that he had the Fever and Ague when he was first commanded by *Bunce* to join them, and desiring *Thomas Rich* as Evidence, he was sworn, and declared, that the Prisoner, as much as he took Notice of him, appeared as active as the most capable, and could not say, that the Prisoner ever relented.

George Bendall.

George Bendall, Prisoner, being next called, and desiring *Richard Turnly* for Evidence, he was sworn, and declared, that the Prisoner was desired to make his Escape, but was resolved to continue with the pyrates.

William Ling.

William Ling, Prisoner, being next called, who having nothing to say farther, than a Request that *Richard Turnly* might give in Evidence for him; he was sworn, and declared, that the Prisoner bore Arms, and was as resolved as any of the pyrates.

Then the Court adjourned till Ten a-Clock next Morning, being the 10th Instant.

December 10, 1718.

The Court having met according to the Adjournment, and Proclamation made, the Prisoners were again brought to the Bar, and severally ask'd, if they had considered of any farther Evidence or Defence they could propose.

First, *John Augur* had no more to offer, in his Justification than before.

The second, *William Cunningham,* the same as before.

The Third, *John Hipps* having the same Question put, answer'd, that if *John Raddon* and *Henry White* had not been absent, they could have declared many Things in his Favour.

Then the Court proposed to every Person, who was an Auditor of the Trial, that any might have Leave to declare upon Oath, any Thing they had heard *John Raddon* or *Henry White* say in Behalf of *John Hipps,* Prisoner: Upon which, *Samuel Lawford,* Constable, appear'd, and being sworn, declared, That he heard *George Raddon* say, that he should have been glad to have done the old Boatswain any Service, meaning *Hipps,* the Prisoner at the Bar; for the said *Raddon* had seen him cry for his having consented, tho' by Force, to join *Bunce,* &c. the Prisoner having also declared to *Raddon,* that he would fight each of the pyrates singly, if he could by that Means get clear of them. This Deponent farther said, that *Raddon* told him, he firmly believed the Prisoner at the Bar would have escaped from the other pyrates, as soon as he could have got an Opportunity.

The Fourth, *Dennis Mackarthy,* Prisoner, made some faint Excuse, and at length desired Captain *Benjamin Hornigold,* as farther Evidence for him; who being sworn, declared, That when he the said *Hornigold* went to apprehend the Prisoners, who were on one of the *Exuma*

336

Keys, he the said Prisoner was one of the first taken, and seem'd to the said *Hornigold* to throw himself, and to have Dependance, on the Mercy of the Governor.

The Fifth, *George Rounsivel,* Prisoner, had no farther Plea to make.

The Sixth, *William Dowling,* Prisoner, only desired *Thomas Petty* to be again call'd, who being sworn, only declared, That he the Prisoner had Offers made by the *Spaniards* to go in their Service, but the Prisoner refused them.

The Seventh, *William Lewis* desired *Richard Turnley* might be again called, who being sworn, declared, That he the Deponent did not see the said Prisoner when the Sloop *Mary* was first taken, but the Day after he saw the Prisoner under Arms, as active as any one of the pyrates.

The Eighth, *Thomas Morris,* Prisoner, had little more to say than pretending that several Persons who were absent, would say something in his Justification; but no one present declared any Thing in his Favour.

The Ninth, *George Bendall,* Prisoner, had nothing to plead for himself; but desiring Mr. *Kerr* for Evidence, he was sworn, and declared, That he heard the Prisoner say, that he wish'd he had begun the Life sooner, for he thought it a pleasant One, meaning that of a Pyrate; and farther deposed, that the Prisoner reported, that he had once a strong Inclination to have smother'd *John Graves,* Esq; his Majesty's Collector for the Islands, as he lay feeble in his Bed, whose Servant the Prisoner was, but a short Time before he shipp'd himself for the intended Voyage, when he join'd the other Prisoners at the Bar in their Mutiny and Pyracy.

David Meredith being also sworn, declared, That *Bunce* did once beat the Prisoner, who told him, that if *Bunce,* &c. beat him once more, he would desert them the first Opportunity.

The Tenth, *William Ling* had nothing farther to say for himself.

Then the Prisoners were remanded to the Fort; after which, all Manner of Persons were comm nded by Proclamation to withdraw.

Then the Court summ'd up the Evidences for the King and the Prisoners, which being debated and considered, all the Prisoners, except *John Hipps,* were unanimously voted guilty of their Indictment, and the Register was ordered to draw up their Sentence. It was thought convenient to respite the Judgment on *John Hipps,* Prisoner, till *Monday* next; and the Court adjourn'd till Four this Afternoon, at which Time being met according to Adjournment, and Proclamation made, the Prisoners were brought to the Bar. Then *John Hipps* was remanded to the Guardship in Irons, and all the rest asked, if they knew any Cause why Sentence of Death should not be pronounced against them? They had nothing more to say, but to desire some Length of Time for Repentance.

Then the Sentence was read, as follows.

The Court having duly considered of the Evidence which hath been given both for and against you the said John Augur, William Cunningham, Dennis Mackarthy, Geo. Rounsivel, Wm Dowling, Wm Lewis, Tho. Morris, Geo. Bendall *and* Wm Ling; *and having also debated the several Circumstances of the Cases, it is adjudged, that you the said* John Augur, Wm Cunningham, Dennis Mackarthy, Geo. Rounsivel, Wm Dowling, Wm Lewis, Tho. Morris, Geo. Bendall *and* Wm Ling, *are guilty of the Mutiny, Felony, and Pyracy, wherewith you and every of you stand accused. And the Court doth accordingly pass Sentence, that you the said* John Augur, Wm. Cunningham, Dennis Mackarthy, Geo. Rounsivel, Wm. Dowling, Wm. Lewis, Tho. Morris, Geo. Bendall *and* Wm. Ling, *be carried to Prison from whence you came, and from thence to the Place of Execution, where you are to be hanged by the Neck till you shall be dead, dead, dead; and God have Mercy on your Souls.* Given under our Hands this 10th Day of *October, Annoq; Dom.* 1718, sign'd

Woodes Rogers,
Wm Fairfax,
Robert Beauchamp,
Thomas Walker,
Wingate Gale,
Nathaniel Taylor,
Josias Burgiss,

Peter Courant.

After Sentence of Death pass'd upon the Prisoners, the Governor, as President of the Court, appointed their Execution to be at Ten a Clock on *Friday* next in the Morning being the 12th Instant.

Whereupon the Prisoners pray'd for longer Time to repent and prepare for Death; but the Governor told them, that from the Time of their being apprehended, which was on the 15th of *November,* they ought to have accounted themselves as condemn'd by the Laws of all Nations, which was only sealed now; and that the securing them hitherto, and the Favour that the Court had allowed them in making as long a Defence as they could, wholly took up that Time, which the Affairs of the Settlement required in working at the Fortifications; besides the Fatigue thereby occasion'd to the whole Garrison in the necessary Guards, set over them by the Want of a Goal, and the Garrison having been very much lessened by Death and Sickness since his Arrival; also that he was obliged to employ all his People to assist in mounting the great Guns, and in finishing the present Works, with all possible Dispatch, because of the expected War with *Spain;* and there being many more pyrates amongst these Islands, and this Place left destitute of all Relief from any Man of War or Station Ship, much wanted, join'd to other Reasons he had, too long to enumerate in Court, he thought himself indispensably obliged, for the Welfare of the Settlement, to give them no longer Time.

Then the Prisoners were ordered to the Place of their Imprisonment in the Fort, where Leave was given them to send for any Persons to read and pray with them

On *Friday* Morning each of the Prisoners were call'd in private, to know if they had any Load upon their Spirits, for Actions committed as yet unknown to the World, the declaring of which was absolutely required, to prepare themselves for a fit Repentance; but they each refused to declare any Thing, as well as making known to the Governor, if they knew of any Conspyracy against the Government.

Wherefore, about Ten a-Clock, the Prisoners were releas'd of their Irons, and committed to the Charge and Care of *Thomas Robinson,* Esq; commissioned Provost Marshal for the Day, who, according to custom in such Cases, pinion'd them, *&c.* and order'd the Guards appointed to assist him, to lead them to the Top of the Rampart, fronting the Sea, which was well guarded by the Governor's Soldiers and People, to the Number of about 100. At the Prisoners Request, several select Prayers and Psalms were read, in which all present join'd; when the Service was ended, Orders was given to the Marshal, and he conducted the Prisoners down a Ladder, provided on Purpose, to the Foot of the Wall, were was a Gallows erected, and a black Flag hoisted thereon, and under it a Stage, supported by three Butts, on which they ascended by another Ladder, where the Hangman fasten'd the Cords. They had three Quarters of an Hour allowed under the Gallows, which was spent by them in singing of Psalms, and some Exhortations to their old Consorts, and the other Spectators, who got as near to the Foot of the Gallows as the Marshal's Guard would suffer them. When the Governor ordered the Marshal to make ready, and all the Prisoners expecting the Launch, the Governor thought fit to order *George Rounsivel* to be untied, and when brought off the Stage, the Buts having Ropes about them, were hawl'd away; upon which, the Stage fell, and the Prisoners were suspended.

A short Account of the Prisoners executed.

First, *John Augur,* being about 40 Years of Age, had been a noted Master of Vessels at *Jamaica,* and since among the pyrates; but on his accepting of his Majesty's Act of Grace, and Recommendations to the Governor, he was, notwithstanding, entrusted with a good Vessel and Cargo, in which betraying his Trust, and knowing himself guilty of the Indictment, he all along appeared very penitent, and neither wash'd, shav'd, or shifted his old Cloaths, when carried to be executed; and when he had a small Glass of Wine given him on the Rampart, drank it with Wishes for the good Success of the *Bahama* Islands and the Governor.

The Second, *William Cunningham,* aged 45, had been Gunner with *Thatch* the Pyrate, who being also conscious of his own Guilt, was seemingly penitent, and behaved himself as such.

The Third, *Dennis Mackarthy,* aged 28, who had also been formerly a Pyrate, but accepted of the King's Act of Grace; and the Governor had made him an Ensign of the Militia, being recommended as a sober civiliz'd Person, which Commission he had at the Time of his joining the pyrates, which very much aggravated his other Crimes. During his Imprisonment, he behaved himself tolerably well; but when he thought he was to die, and the Morning came, without his expected

Reprieve, he shifted his Cloaths, and wore long blue Ribbons at his Neck, Wrists, Knees, and Cap; and when on the Rampart, look'd cheerfully round him, saying, *He knew the Time when there were many brave Fellows on the Island, who would not have suffered him to die like a Dog;* and at the same Time pull'd off his Shooes, kicking them over the Parapet of the Fort, saying, *He had promis'd not to die with his Shooes on;* so descended the Fort Wall, and ascended the Stage, with as much Agility and in a Dress of a Prize-Fighter; when mounted, he exhorted the People, who were at the Foot of the Walls, to have Compassion on him, but, however willing, they saw too much Power over their Heads to attempt any Thing in his Favour.

The Fourth, *William Dowling,* of about 24 Years of Age, had been a considerable Time amongst the pyrates, of a wicked Life, which his Majesty's Act of Grace did not reform; his Behaviour was very loose on the Stage, and after his Death, some of his Acquaintance declared, he had confess'd to them, that he had murder'd his Mother before he left *Ireland.*

The Fifth, *William Lewis,* aged about 34 Years, as he had been a hardy Pyrate and Prize Fighter, affected an Unconcern at Death; but heartily desired Liquors to drink with his Sufferers on the Stage, and with the Standers by.

The Sixth, *Thomas Morris,* aged about 22, had been a very incorrigible Youth and Pyrate, and seem'd to have very little Anxiety of Mind by his frequent Smiles when at the Bar, being dress'd with red Ribbons as *Mackarthy* was with blue, he said, going over the Ramparts, *We have a new Governor, but a harsh One;* and a little before he was turn'd off, said aloud, *that he might have been a greater Plague to these Islands, and now wish'd he had been so.*

The Sixth, *George Bendall,* aged about 18, tho' he said, *he had never been a Pyrate before, yet he had all the villainous Inclinations that the most profligate Youth could be infected with;* his Behaviour was sullen.

The Eighth, *William Ling,* aged about 30, not taken Notice of before the last Attempt, behaved himself as becoming a true Penitent, and was not heard to say any other than by Reply to *Lewis,* when he demanded Wine to drink, *that Water was more suitable to them at that Time.*

It was observed that there were but few (beside the Governor's Adherents) among the Spectators, who had not deserved the same Fate, but pardon'd by his Majesty's Act of Grace.

VII. Of Captain Vane

We have given what Account came to our Hands of *Charles Vane* in the first Volume, beginning at the Time he left *Providence* on the Governor's Arrival; but we have since had some Particulars sent us, which relate to Pyracies, both before and after that Date.

In the latter End of *March* 1718, he, with about 12 more lewd Fellows, who had squander'd all their Money got by former Villanies, took a Canoe, and went out on the old Account. Soon after their setting out they made Prize of a Sloop belonging to *Jamaica*, brought her into *Potters Key*, where they came to an Anchor, and put all the Hands on Shore, except the Master, to whom they promis'd to return his Sloop as soon as they met with another more fit for their Purpose; which soon after happen'd, for cruizing off *Harbour Island* in the beginning of *April*, they took the *Lark* Sloop, which had been taken from the pyrates by Captain *Pierce*, in the *Phœnix* Man of War, who fitted her out with a Cargo to trade at St. *Augustin*'s. He brought his Prize into *Providence* Harbour, with his black Ensign hoisted, in Defiance of the above named Man of War, which he loudly threaten'd to burn. *Vane*, at *Providence*, augmented his Number of Men to 75, sailed in search of Booty, and on the 4th of *July* return'd with a *French* Ship of 20 Guns, a *French* Brigantine laden with Sugar, Indigo, Brandy, Claret, white Wine, and other Merchandize; the *Drake* Sloop, *John Draper*, Master, which he took in his Passage from *Providence* to *Harbour Island*, and plunder'd of a considerable Sum of Money, shifting into her some Sugars out of the *French* Brigantine; the *Ulster* Sloop, *John Fredd*, Master, laden with Timber from *Andros* Island, into this Vessel he put 70 Casks of Sugar; and the *Eagle* Sloop, *Robert Brown*, Master, bound to *South-Carolina*, which he took with a two-masted Boat, commanded by *Edward England*, his Quarter Master; he put on board this last 20 Terses of Sugar, 6 of Bread, and some other Things. In the Harbour he seized on the *Lancaster* Sloop, *Neal Walker*, Master, and the *Dove* Sloop, *William Harris*, Master, designed for *Jamaica*, which he plunder'd of what he thought proper, and shifted 22 Hogsheads of Sugar, some *Spanish* Hides and old Rigging.

He had the Impudence to come ashore with his Sword in Hand, threaten to burn the principal Houses of the Town, and to make Examples of many of the People; and though he committed no Murders, his Behaviour was extreamly insolent to all who were not as great Villains as himself. He reign'd here as Governor 20 Days, stopp'd all Vessels which came in, and would suffer none to go out, being inform'd of a Governor being sent from *England*, he swore, while he was in the Harbour, he would suffer no other Governor than himself. He clean'd and fitted the *French* Ship, with Intent to visit the Coast of *Brazil*, and design'd to sail in 3 or 4 Days; but the Governor appearing on the 24th, made him change his Resolution, and think of accepting a Pardon, if it might be granted on his own Terms, as will appear by the Letter which he sent off by a Boat to the Governor, and of which the following is an exact Copy.

July the 24th, 1718.

'YOUR Excellency may please to understand that we are willing to accept his Majesty's most gracious Pardon on the following Terms, *viz.*

'That you will suffer us to dispose of all our Goods now in our Possession. Likewise, to act as we think fit with every Thing belonging to us, as his Majesty's Act of Grace specifies.

'If your Excellency shall please to comply with this, we shall, with all Readiness, accept of his Majesty's Act of Grace. If not, we are obliged to stand on our Defence. So conclude

Your humble Servants, *Charles Vane*, and Company.

The Susperscription was —

To his Excellency the Governor of New Providence. And at the Bottom of it. — *We wait a speedy Answer.*

The Governor could not get in that Night, but was forced to keep at Sea, so that Mr. *Vane* could not so speedily have an Answer as his Excellency design'd, which he intended to carry himself. About Four that Afternoon the *Rose* Man of War and *Shark* Sloop got in, and were saluted with four Shot from *Vane,* which, however, did no other Damage than the cutting the *Rose*'s Rigging. In the Evening Captain *Whitney* sent his Lieutenant on Board *Vane,* who was higher up the Harbour in the *French* Ship. They detained this Gentleman two Hours, and the Crew, most of which was drunk, treated him, some with Threats, showing the black Flag, and some with Contempt and Ridicule, and order'd him back to tell his Captain their Resolution was to fight it out to the last.

When Captain *Whitney* fired the eight a Clock Gun, *Vane* did the like with Shot, directed at the *Rose*. At Ten he pointed all the Guns of the *French* Ship (double loaded) at the Man of War, and, after setting Fire to her, went with 40 Hands into a Sloop belonging to one *Yates.* As the *French* Man burnt, the Guns fired, and cut some more of the *Rose*'s Rigging. Captain *Whitney* apprehending Danger from the fir'd Ship, together with the *Shark* Sloop, cut and put out to Sea, which gave *Vane* an Opportunity he laid hold on, to take what he thought fit off Shore, and to force the best Carpenter and Pilot in the Island on Board him. When he had done, he went to, and lay at *Potters Key* all Night, and the next Morning got under Sail.

His Excellency dispatch'd after him the *Buck* Sloop and another small one, both well mann'd and fitted, which gain'd while he was upon a Wind, and came, before he clear'd the East End of the Island, within Gun-Shot; but he easing out his Main-Sheet, and setting his Flying-Jibb, left them soon after; wherefore, Night coming on, and their Pursuit being fruitless, they return'd.

Soon after *Vane* sent the Governor of *Providence* Word, he would make him a Visit, and burn his Guardship, for sending two Sloops to chase him instead of answering his Letter.

The 30th of *August* he took the *Neptune* of 400 Tuns, and the *Emperor* of 200 Tuns, the Particulars of which are in the subjoin'd Protest.

The 9th of *September* he arrived at *Allens Key* in a *Spanish* Brigantine; he had before taken a *Spanish* Ship of the *Havanna;* here he forced on Board a Pilot, took a Sloop and went to *Green Turtle Key.*

I have only to add: This Pyrate, whose Death is set down in the first Volume, betray'd the Coward when at the Gallows, and died in Agonies equal to his Villainies, which he gave no Ground to believe proceeded from the Apprehensions of a future State, but the Fear of Death. He shew'd not the least Remorse for the Crimes of his past Life, which was taken Notice of by the Spectators of his deserved Punishment, and told me by a worthy Gentleman who saw Justice done on him at *Gallows Point* on *Port Royal.*

The Protest of Captain *King,* Commander of the *Neptune* Hagboat.

'BY this public Instrument of Protest be it made known and manifest, that on the 30th Day of *August* 1718, *John King,* lately Commander of the *Neptune* Hagboat of *London,* but now in the Island of *Providence,* one of his Majesty's *Bahama* Islands, came before me *Woodes Rogers,* Esq; Governor, *&c.* and declared to me, that on the Day and Date above-written, he sailed with the said Ship *Neptune* Hagboat over the Bar of *Carolina,* in Company with three more Ships bound for *London, viz.* the *Emperor,* Captain *Arnold Powers,* Commander, and the Pink *Antamasia,* Captain *Dumford,* Commander, and the Pink, Captain *Evers,* Commander, and about two Hours after he was over the Bar of *South-Carolina,* he saw four Sail of Vessels standing some one Way, some another; but one of them being a Brigantine, gave Chase, and, in about two Hours time, came up with his Ship with a black Flag flying, and after having fir'd several Guns, demanded him to strike, and to come on Board the Brigantine, commanded by one *Charles Vane,* a Pyrate, who detained him and four of his Men on board the said Brigantine, and sent several of his Men on board the *Neptune;* and when they came on board they commanded him to make Sail, and began to rob and rifle as they thought fit, *&c.* taking only the *Neptune* and *Emperor* with them; for by the Information of the Captain of the *Neptune* and *Emperor,* the other two were loaded with Pitch and Tar, which was not for their Turn, so they would not give Chace to them; but in a small Time after they had held a Consultation together, they concluded to carry the Ship *Neptune* and *Emperor,* with their Crew, to *Green Turtle Key,* on *Abbaco,* so steered their Course accordingly for the said Place. About four Days after *John King,* Commander of the *Neptune* declares, he fell sick of a violent Fever on board the said *Vane*'s Brigantine, and *Vane* asked him, if he would go on board his own Ship? he readily answered, Yes, if he pleased; so hoisted out his Boat, and sent him on board. And about four Days afterwards the pyrates held a Consultation on board their own Vessel. The Captain, and most of the Officers, were for taking what they wanted out of the Ship *Neptune* and *Emperor,* and so let them go about their Business; but the rest of the Company was not willing for it, because, they said, What should they clean their Vessel by? And what Defence should they have whilst they were cleaning? So concluded to proceed on to *Green Turtle Key,* which they did, and arrived there on or about the 12th of *September* 1718, and began to make Preparations for careening their Vessels, which held about three Weeks, and at the latter End of this Time they had taken from both Ships such Things as they wanted, and then took their Leaves of the said Ships and Captains, wishing them a good Voyage home, so set Sail; but in a little Time after made a Sloop coming into the Harbour of *Green Turtle Key,* perceiving her to come towards them without any Fear, came to an Anchor again, and sent away the two Mast Boat after them with about twelve Men in her, expecting it was a Sloop from *Providence* with fifty Men, according to Promise, when they left *Providence,* but in three Hours, or thereabouts, they spoke with her, which gave them Account that they came from *Providence;* and also laying down the State and Condition of that Island, it being the expected Sloop aforesaid, out of which some of the Men entered with *Vane,* but know not how many. And likewise the said *King* farther declares, that he heard some of the pyrates say, that Sloop had brought Ammunition and Provisions, *&c.* and the Commander's Name was one *Nicholas Woodall.* The said *King* asked what was the best News at *Providence?* They replied, None good: But bid him ask not many Questions, but sit up his Ship, in order to go for *England* or *Providence;* if the latter, they would take Care to see us to *Providence,* and did believe they should go in and surrender themselves up to the King's Pardon. The next Morning, being very much disturb'd with the News that the Sloop brought from *Providence* by the said *Woodall,* they voted to Maroon Captain *Walker,* but that did not take Place, so put it to Vote again to maroon and destroy the *Neptune,* which they did with cutting away the Masts, Rigging, Sails, Beams, and firing a Gun, double loaded with Shot down her Hold, and totally disabled her from ever proceeding her Voyage home to *England.* And the said *King* does verily believe, that the said *Woodall*'s Sloop coming there, was the Occasion of all the aforesaid Mischief, believing what was done was to pay him for his great Favour done them. And farther, the said Captain *King* says, that some of the pyrates, who were his Friends, told him, that if that Sloop had not come, this Damage would not have been; and that they were very sorry for it; so by the said *Vane*'s Order they went to work to load this *Woodall*'s Sloop with Rice, Pitch, Tar, Deer Skins, Sails, Rigging, *&c.* After she was loaded, being the next Day, they all sailed together as pyrates, taking with them one of Captain *Walker*'s Sons, with his Sloop, to tend on them, and as Pilot; but before they got out of the Channel, arrived to the Ships *Neptune* and *Emperor,* a Sloop from *Providence,* sent by the Governor to hear what was the best News there, hearing that *Vane* was there. The Captains of the said Sloop, *Hornigold* and *Cockram* told the Captains *Powers* and *King,* that they were come by the Governor's Order to assist them in what they could, who accordingly did, with making Dispatch to *Providence,* to acquaint his Excellency the Governor what sad Condition they were in by the pyrates hard Usage, leaving them without Provisions, *&c.* So the said Captains *Hornigold* and *Cockram* set Sail that Night, and in three or four Days after took the Sloop *Woolfe, Nicholas Woodall,* Master, that had traded with *Charles Vane,* the Pyrate, and carried him to his Excellency the Governor of *Providence,* who seized his Vessel, and consined him Prisoner. By that Time *Vane* came in a second time to *Green Turtle Key,* and began a second Plunder, taking from the Ships Rice, Rigging, Masts, Sails, *&c.* from both Ships, and told the said *King,* that if he offered to touch his Prize he would burn her, and him in her, if ever he catched him again; so sailed away the second time: And about three Weeks after arrived the said Captains *Hornigold* and *Cockram,* with five Sloops from *Providence,* sent down by the Governor, to save what Goods they could out of the *Neptune,* that was in so much Danger. The next Day they began to load the Sloops, and got them loaded in two Days, so sailed away. The said *King* came to *Providence* to consult and agree with the Governor what to do in such a Case. After some Time spent it was concluded to fit out the *Willing Mind* with Guns and Men, enough to stand an Engagement with *Vane,* and fell the *Neptune;* and, in a few Days after, did accordingly put her up public to Sale, and it was thus fold to one Mr. *George Hooper,* for seventy one Pounds current Money of *Jamaica,* he being the Person that bid the most Money for her. The *Willing Mind* being sitted, sailed from *Providence* the 15th of *November* 1718, and arrived at *Green Turtle Key* the 19th, and took the Goods out of the *Neptune,* being in a very bad Condition; and after they had taken out all her Cargo, finding the *Neptune* to be better than they did expect; and, having a fair Wind, brought both Ships up to *Providence,* the *Neptune* got in safe, but the *Willing Mind* struck on the Bar, and sprung a Leak, insomuch that she was forced to unload and careen, and, when down, found her to be very bad, a Piece of her main Keel being gone, so was forced to hawl her ashore; and when the Carpenters had done what could be done to her, she could not be got up again by all the Strength that could be made, and tried for several Days, breaking and tearing all to pieces, but all to no Purpose; so the Governor order'd a Warrant of Survey on her, and was found by the Surveyors not sufficient to proceed any further, being very much damaged in her Wood-Work and Iron-Work, *&c.* Whereupon the said *King* desired a second Survey of his Ship and Goods, they lying in a very bad Condition. Now in the Harbour of *Providence* there being no Vessels to carry them to *England,* he therefore is now going to *Carolina* to consult with Mr. *Richard Splat,* who shipp'd the Goods on board, and to know of him what further may be done with the said Goods, and that he may rightly apprize all they concern'd, of the present Condition of the Ship and Goods; he has further taken the Opinion of Captain *Thomas Walker,* Captain *Richard Thompson,* and Captain *Edward Holmes,* Persons who are well acquainted what sad Condition the Ship and Goods are now in; whereupon the said *King,* and one of the Mariners belonging to the Ship *Neptune,* did, and doth hereby protest against the said *Charles Vane,* and the rest of the Mariners, pyrates and Robbers, belonging to the Brigantine aforesaid, and for the feloniously and piratically taking, boarding, entering and plundering, and for sinking and disabling within the Harbour of *Green Turtle Key,* the said Ship *Neptune,* and for all Damages and Losses accruing thereby to the Owners, Freighters, or any other Persons concern'd therein. In Testimony whereof we have hereunto set our Hand and Seals this 5th Day of *February, Anno Dom.* 1718-9.

Jurat Coram me hoc die Decem Februaris, Woodes Rogers. John King, X *The Mark of* John Morrison.

VIII. Of Captain Bowen

Could the Reader conceive the Pains we have been at, to collect Matters for the composing a genuine History of the Lives of the pyrates, and the great Care we have taken to deliver nothing but the Truth, he would readily forgive, nay, would be apt to commend our placing those Particulars in the Appendix of the same Book, which we could not possibly obtain (notwithstanding our diligent Enquiries) before the Lives were printed, and the Book in a manner ready for Publication.

What we have said in the foregoing Part of this Volume, of Captain *Bowen*, may be depended on as Truth; but as we had not that Certainty of his Original we now have, we rather chose to be silent than impose on our Readers with Fables of our own Invention: We have since learn'd (and it is with Reason we can depend on our Account, having it from one who personally knew, and often convers'd with him) that he was born of creditable Parents, in the Island of *Bermudas*, who took Care to give him a good Education answerable to the Vocation he was design'd for, which was the Sea.

The first Voyage he made was to *Carolina*, where some Merchants finding him every Way capable, and that he was a sober intelligent Man, gave him the Command of a Ship, and sent him to the *West-Indies*. He continued in this Employ for several Years, but one Voyage, in his Return, he had the Misfortune to fall in with, and be taken, by a *French*Pyrate, who having no Artist on board, detain'd Captain *Bowen* to navigate their Vessel; and after cruizing some Time in the *West-Indies*, shap'd their Course for the *Guiney* Coast, where they made several Prizes, and took several good Artists; but having Experience of Captain *Bowen*, he could by no Means prevail on them for a Discharge; tho' notwithstanding the Service he was to them, they treated him as roughly as they did their other Prisoners, of which I have already taken Notice in Captain *White*'s Life.

They (the pyrates) doubled the *Cape* of *Good Hope*, steer'd for, refresh'd at *Johanna*, and having made their Voyage to the *East-Indies*, lost their Ship, as is already shown in the above Life, (and need not be here repeated) on *Madagascar:* The other Particularities which are not set down in *Bowen*'s own Life, will be found in those of his Companions; as his going with Captain *Read;* the taking the *Grabb;* the coming to *Mayotta*, and from thence in the *Grabb* to *Madagascar;* the joining of that Vessel and *Fourgette*'s; the taking the *Speaker;* his succeeding *Booth* in the Command, and his Death at *Mascarenas*.

Footnotes

1. Term for stealing of Men used all over the Coast.

Printed in Great Britain
by Amazon